Red Hat® Certified Technician & Engineer

Exams
RH202 and RH302
Red Hat Enterprise Linux 5

Training Guide and Administrator's Reference

August 2009

Asghar Ghori

1246 Heil Quaker Blvd., La Vergne, TN USA 37086
Chapter House, Pitfield, Kiln Farm, Milton Keynes, UK MK11-3LW
www.lightningsource.com

Technical Reviewers: Syed Ali, Kurt Glasgow, Oleg Waisberg and Aasim Ajaz
Cover Design: Endeavor Technologies Inc.
Printers and Distributors: Lightning Source Inc.

Printed in the United States of America and the United Kingdom.

ISBN: 978-1-61584-430-2
Library of Congress Control Number: 2009906909

Printed and Distributed by: Lightning Source Inc.

To order in bulk, please contact the author.
asghar_ghori2002@yahoo.com

Preface

Red Hat's RH202 and RH302 exams are performance-based and touch a wide array of topics. The exams present configuration, maintenance and troubleshooting scenarios to be accomplished on live systems within a limited time period. This book provides a single, comprehensive resource that equips readers with enough knowledge to pass the exams with flying colors. At the same time, the book furnishes procedures and troubleshooting scenarios to help setup, administer and troubleshoot a Red Hat Enterprise Linux (RHEL) 5 based computing environment effectively and efficiently.

Throughout the book, step-by-step implementation procedures are provided, along with several troubleshooting scenarios in the last chapter. My suggestion to you is to perform sample exam exercises presented in appendices after you have finished studying the entire book, performed all installation, configuration and administration tasks offered, and resolved troubleshooting scenarios. While you go through the book, have at least two systems (physical or virtual) available with RHEL 5 loaded for practice. Prefer to obtain a licensed copy and subscription of RHEL 5 for at least one system so you have access to the software repository and benefits offered by Red Hat Network. For those of you who do not wish to spend money, obtain a copy of Fedora or CentOS Linux, which are free, non-commercial versions of RHEL. You may also want to register a domain name for some real life exercises, or use www.example.com, www.example.net and/or www.example.org to practice on the local network. While performing exercises, if a command does not produce desired results, see what message it generates and try to resolve it. Minor issues such as wrong path, prevent commands from being executed. Sometimes, there are syntax errors in the command construct. RHEL manual pages prove helpful and useful in comprehending commands and their syntax. There is a whole slew of commands, options and configuration files in the operating system, discussing all of them is not possible within the scope of this book.

There are four areas where you should be focusing to gain expertise with RHEL, as well as prepare yourselves for the exams – grasping concepts, mastering step-by-step implementation procedures, learning commands, configuration files and service daemons, and be able to troubleshoot and resolve problems. An excellent understanding of which command involves and updates which files, which daemon provides what services, etc. should also be developed. This way you would have a better overall understanding developed of what exactly happens in the background when a command is executed. This book provides all that knowledge. Troubleshooting becomes easier when concepts are clear and working knowledge is solid.

I am maintaining *www.getitcertify.com* website where errors encountered in the book, additional exam information and links to useful resources are made available. I encourage you to visit it.

At the end, I would like to ask you to forward your constructive feedback to my personal email address *asghar_ghori2002@yahoo.com* about the content, structure, layout, consistency, clarity and flow of the book. Please also let me know if you come across any errors or mistakes. Improvement is a continuous process and I am sure your feedback will help me publish a better and improved next edition.

Good luck in your endeavors.

Asghar Ghori
August 2009
Toronto, Canada

Acknowledgments

I am grateful to God who enabled me to write this book successfully.

I would like to thank my friends, colleagues, students and peers who supported and encouraged me to write this book. I am grateful to all for their invariable support, constant encouragement, constructive feedback and valuable assistance.

Finally, I would like to pay my special thanks to my wife, two daughters and son, who endured me through the lifecycle of this project and extended their full assistance, support and love. I would not be able to complete this project without their cooperation and support.

Asghar Ghori

About the Author

Currently working as a technical consultant, Asghar Ghori has been in the IT industry for 20 years. He started his career as a UNIX support engineer working with SCO UNIX and SCO XENIX visiting customers and providing UNIX technical support services. He has worked with several flavors of the UNIX operating system including HP-UX, SUN Solaris, IBM AIX, Microsoft XENIX, AT&T UNIX, SGI's IRIS, ISC UNIX, DYNIX/ptx, Stratus UNIX as well as Red Hat Enterprise Linux and a few other Linux distributions. He has worked in different capacities such as UNIX support engineer, UNIX/Linux administrator, UNIX/Linux specialist, technical lead, solution design lead and technology consultant serving business and government customers. In addition, he has architected and deployed solutions that involved enterprise-class servers, large storage subsystems, Storage Area Networks, clustering technologies, systems management software and so on.

Asghar has been involved in planning, developing and executing IT infrastructure disaster recovery procedures for multiple large corporations.

Asghar holds a BS in Engineering, and has delivered and attended numerous training programs. He has been delivering courses on UNIX for the past eight years at local colleges in Toronto, Canada. He is Red Hat Certified Technician (RHCT), HP Certified Systems Administrator (HP0-A01, HP0-095, HP0-091, HP0-002), HP Certified Systems Engineer (lab – HP-UX operations), SUN Certified System Administrator (SCSA) for various Solaris versions, IBM Certified Specialist for AIX, Certified Novell Engineer (CNE) and holds Project Management Professional (PMP) certification designation.

Conventions Used in this Book

The following typographic and other conventions are used throughout this book:

Book Antiqua Italic is used in text paragraphs for special words or phrases that are emphasized. For example:

> "Linux, like UNIX operating systems, is a *multi-user, multi-tasking, multi-processing* and *multi-threading* operating system. This means that ....."

Times Roman Italic is used in text paragraphs to highlight file and directory names, commands, daemons, hostnames, usernames, printer names and URLs. For example:

> "Install a new disk and use *fdisk* or *parted* to create */dev/sdc1* on it with the same size as it was before. Now run the ....."

Times Roman Bold is used to highlight commands and command line arguments that the user is expected to type at the command prompt. For example:

> **$ ls –lt**

All headings and sub-headings are in California FB font, and are bold.

Ctrl+x key sequence means that you hold down the Ctrl key on the keyboard and then press the other key. Courier New font is used for them.

Courier New is used to highlight keyboard keys such as Enter, Esc and so on.

Light grey background is used to segregate output generated by commands and shell scripts from surrounding text.

. . . . Dotted lines show the continuation in command outputs.

 Indicates additional information.

Indicates a task performed using a RHEL graphical tool.

About RHCT™ and RHCE™ Exams

The Red Hat Certified Technician (RHCT™) and the Red Hat Certified Engineer (RHCE™) certification exams are designed for Linux/UNIX professionals. The official exam objectives are listed at *https://www.redhat.com/certification/rhct* and *https://www.redhat.com/certification/rhce*, and are also given below. Visit the URLs for an up-to-date and more in-depth information. The exam objectives are covered in sufficient detail in chapters throughout the book.

Common Skills Required for Both Exams:

1. Use standard command line tools (e.g., ls, cp, mv, rm, tail, cat, etc.) to create, remove, view, and investigate files and directories
2. Use grep, sed, and awk to process text streams and files
3. Use a terminal-based text editor such as vim or nano, to modify text files
4. Use input/output redirection
5. Understand basic principles of TCP/IP networking, including IP addresses, netmasks, and gateways for IPv4 and IPv6
6. Use su to switch user accounts
7. Use passwd to set passwords
8. Use tar, gzip, and bzip2
9. Configure an email client on Red Hat Enterprise Linux
10. Use text and/or graphical browser to access HTTP/HTTPS URLs
11. Use lftp to access FTP URLs

RHCT™ Installation and Configuration Skills:

1. Perform network OS installation
2. Implement a custom partitioning scheme
3. Configure printing
4. Configure the scheduling of tasks using cron and at
5. Attach system to a network directory service such as NIS or LDAP
6. Configure autofs
7. Add and manage users, groups, quotas, and File Access Control Lists
8. Configure filesystem permissions for collaboration
9. Install and update packages using rpm
10. Properly update the kernel package
11. Configure the system to update/install packages from remote repositories using yum or pup
12. Modify the system bootloader
13. Implement software RAID at install-time and run-time
14. Use /proc/sys and sysctl to modify and set kernel run-time parameters
15. Use scripting to automate system maintenance tasks
16. Configure NTP for time synchronization with a higher-stratum server

RHCT™ Troubleshooting and System Maintenance Skills:

1. Boot systems into different run levels for troubleshooting and system maintenance
2. Diagnose and correct misconfigured networking
3. Diagnose and correct hostname resolution problems
4. Configure the X Window System and a desktop environment
5. Add new partitions, filesystems, and swap to existing systems

6. Use standard command-line tools to analyze problems and configure system

RHCE™ Installation and Configuration Skills:

Must be capable of configuring HTTP/HTTPS, SMB, NFS, FTP, Web proxy, SMTP, IMAP/IMAPS/POP3, SSH, DNS (caching and slave servers) and NTP network services. For each of these services, RHCEs must be able to:

- Install the packages needed to provide the service
- Configure SELinux to support the service
- Configure the service to start when the system is booted
- Configure the service for basic operation
- Configure host-based and user-based security for the service

RHCEs must also be able to:

- Configure hands-free installation using Kickstart
- Implement logical volumes at install-time
- Use iptables to implement packet filtering and/or NAT
- Use PAM to implement user-level restrictions

RHCE™ Troubleshooting and System Maintenance Skills:

1. Use the rescue environment provided by first installation CD
2. Diagnose and correct boot failures arising from bootloader, module, and filesystem errors
3. Diagnose and correct problems with HTTP/HTTPS, SMB, NFS, FTP, Web proxy, SMTP, IMAP/IMAPS/POP3, SSH, DNS and NTP network services
4. Add, remove and resize logical volumes
5. Diagnose and correct problems with HTTP/HTTPS, SMB, NFS, FTP, Web proxy, SMTP, IMAP/IMAPS/POP3, SSH, DNS and NTP network services where SELinux contexts are interfering with proper operation.

Suggestions and Points to Note When Taking the Exam

1. Save time wherever possible as time is of the essence. Perform tasks using either text or graphical tools whichever you feel more comfortable with. Install a graphical tool if you need it and is not already loaded. Prefer using text mode installation method if performing installation part of the exam.
2. Make certain that any changes you make are available across system reboots.
3. Use any text editor to modify files that you feel comfortable with.
4. Check installation requirements, if installation is part of the exam, and select only those components that are listed. Try to accomplish as much as possible during installation.
5. Inform exam proctor if you identify a hardware problem with your system.
6. The exams are administered with books closed and no access to the Internet and electronic devices.

Exam Fees and How to Register

The fee for the RHCT exam is US$399 and that for the RHCE US$799 (RHCE includes RHCT). To register for an exam, visit *www.redhat.com/training* and enroll online, or call the numbers provided. Note that the exams are administered on Fridays only and typically begin at 9am.

About this Book

This book covers three main objectives – to provide a resource to individuals, including novice, IT/Non-Red Hat Enterprise Linux (RHEL) administrators and Linux/UNIX administrators who intend to take the new Red Hat Certified Technician (RH202) and/or Red Hat Certified Engineer (RH302) exams and pass them; to provide a quick and valuable on-the-job resource to RHEL administrators, administrators of UNIX and other Linux operating systems, IT managers, programmers and DBAs working in the RHEL environment; and to provide an easy-to-understand guide to novice and IT/non-RHEL administrators who intend to learn RHEL from the beginning.

The book has 31 chapters and is structured to facilitate readers to grasp concepts, understand implementation procedures, learn command syntax, configuration files and daemons involved, and comprehend troubleshooting. The chapters are divided into four key areas: Linux Essentials, RHEL System Administration, RHEL Network and Security Administration, and RHEL Troubleshooting.

1. **RHEL 5 Essentials** (chapters 1 to 7) covers the basics of Linux. Information provided includes general Linux concepts, basic commands, file manipulation and file security techniques, text file editors, shell features, basic shell and awk programming and other essential topics.

2. **RHEL 5 System Administration** (chapters 8 to 19) covers RHEL-specific system administration concepts and topics including hardware management, local installation, X Window and desktop managers, software and user/group account administration, disk partitioning using standard, RAID and LVM, file system and swap management, system shutdown and boot procedures, kernel management, backup, restore and compression functions, print services administration, and automation and system logging.

3. **RHEL 5 Network and Security Administration** (chapters 20 to 30) covers RHEL network and security administration concepts and topics such as OSI and TCP/IP reference models, subnetting and IP aliasing, network interface administration, routing, basic network testing and troubleshooting tools, naming services (DNS, NIS, LDAP) and DHCP; Internet services and electronic mail management, time synchronization with NTP, resource sharing with NFS, AutoFS and Samba, network-based and hands-free automated installation, Apache web server and Squid caching/proxy server, secure shell, PAM, TCP Wrappers, IPTables firewall, NATting, SELinux and common system hardening recommendations.

4. **RHEL 5 Troubleshooting** (chapter 31) covers a number of sample system, network and security troubleshooting scenarios from an exam perspective.

Each chapter in the book begins with a list of major topics covered in the chapter and ends with a summary. Throughout the book, tables, figures, screen shots and examples are furnished for explanation. The book includes several appendices, the first two of which contain sample exercises, and you are expected to perform them using the knowledge and skills gained from reading the book and practicing the procedures. Tables of commands, important files and service daemons follow in subsequent appendices.

TABLE OF CONTENTS

List of Figures

List of Tables

Overview of Linux

This chapter covers the following major topics:

- ✓ A brief history of Linux and Open Source
- ✓ A brief introduction of Linux distributions from Red Hat
- ✓ Structure and features of Linux
- ✓ How to log in and out
- ✓ Command line components and how to build a command
- ✓ General Linux commands and how to execute them
- ✓ Linux online help

Linux is a free computer operating system and is similar to the UNIX operating system in terms of concepts, features and functionality, and, therefore, it is referred to as UNIX-like operating system.

In 1984, an initiative was undertaken by Richard Stallman whose primary goal was to create a completely free, UNIX-compatible, open source operating system with global collaboration from software developers. The initiative was called the GNU (*GNU's Not Unix*) Project and by 1991 significant software had been developed. The only critical piece missing was a kernel to drive the operating system. This gap was filled by the kernel created by Linus Torvalds in 1991 during his computer science studies at the University of Helsinki in Finland. The name "Linux" was given to the new operating system kernel that Linus developed which was very UNIX-like. Linux operating system was released under the GNU *General Public License* (GPL) and initially written to run on Intel x86 architecture computers. The first version (0.01) of the operating system was released in September 1991 with little more than 10,000 lines of code. In March 1994, the first major release (1.0.0) debuted followed by version 2.0.0 in June 1996, 2.2.0 in January 1999, 2.4.0 in January 2001 and 2.6.0 in December 2003. Presently, version 2.6.27.7 with several million lines of code is in circulation. The Linux kernel, and the operating system in general, has been enhanced with contributions from thousands of software programmers around the world under the GNU GPL, which provides general public access to the Linux source code free of charge with full consent for amendments and redistribution.

Today, Linux runs on a variety of computer hardware platforms, from laptop and desktop computers to massive mainframe systems. Linux also runs as the base operating system on a range of other electronic devices such as routers, switches, RAID arrays, tape libraries, video games and mobile phones. Numerous vendors including Red Hat, HP, IBM, Sun, Novell and Dell offer support to Linux users worldwide.

The functionality, adaptability, portability and cost-effectiveness that Linux offers has made this operating system the main alternative to proprietary UNIX and Windows operating systems. At present, more than hundred different flavors of Linux are available from various vendors, organizations and individuals; only a few of them are popular and have wide acceptance.

Linux is generally used by government agencies, corporate businesses, academic institutions, scientific organizations and home users. Linux usage in home computers is rapidly rising.

Linux Distributions from Red Hat

Red Hat, Inc., a company founded in 1993, assembled an operating system under GNU GPL called *Red Hat Linux* (RHL) and released the first version as Red Hat Linux 1.0 in November 1994. Several versions followed until the last version in the series called Red Hat Linux 9 (later also referred to as RHEL 3) was released in March 2003 based on 2.4.20 kernel. In 2003, Red Hat renamed the Red Hat Linux operating system series to *Red Hat Enterprise Linux* (RHEL).

RHL was originally assembled and enhanced within the Red Hat company. In 2003, Red Hat began sponsoring a project called *fedora* inviting user community to participate in enhancing the source code. This enabled the company to include the improved code in successive versions of RHEL. The fedora distribution is completely free, whereas RHEL is commercially available. RHEL 4 (February 2005) and the latest RHEL 5 (based on 2.6.18 kernel and released March 2007) are based on Fedora distributions 3 and 6, respectively. The following are RHEL 5 editions available for commercial purposes:

- ✓ Desktop (targeted for desktop and laptop computers and includes OpenOffice suite and Evolution mail client programs)
- ✓ Desktop with Multi-OS Option (targeted for running several operating system instances in a virtualized environment)
- ✓ Desktop with Workstation Option (targeted for high-end desktop application usages)
- ✓ Desktop with both Multi-OS and Workstation Options
- ✓ Server (targeted for small deployments with support for running up to four operating system instances in a virtualized environment)
- ✓ Server Advanced Platform (targeted for enterprise deployments and includes support for storage virtualization, clustering and running an unlimited number of operating system instances in a virtualized environment
- ✓ For Mainframe Computing
- ✓ For High Performance and Grid Computing

A 100% rebuild of Red Hat Enterprise Linux called CentOS (*Community Enterprise Operating System*) is also available for Linux users as a free of charge distribution. This rebuild is not sponsored or supported by Red Hat. CentOS may be downloaded from its official website at *www.centos.org*.

System Structure

The structure of the Linux system comprises of three main components: the *kernel*, the *shell* and the *hierarchical directory structure*. These components are illustrated in Figure 1-1 and explained below.

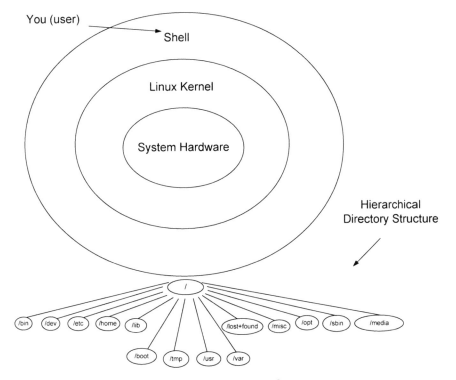

Figure 1-1 Linux System Structure

The Kernel

The kernel controls everything inside-out on a system that runs the Linux operating system. It controls system hardware including memory, processors, disks and I/O (Input/Output) devices, schedules processes, enforces security and so on. The kernel receives instructions from the shell, engages appropriate hardware resources and acts as instructed.

The Shell

The shell is the interface between a user and the kernel. User provides instructions (commands) to the shell, which are interpreted and passed to the kernel for processing. The shell handles input and output, keeps track of data stored on disks and communicates with peripheral devices such as monitors, hard disk drives, tape devices, CD/DVD drives, USB drives, printers, modems and terminals. Chapter 05 "The Shells" discusses shells in detail.

The Hierarchical Directory Structure

Linux uses the conventional hierarchical directory structure where directories may contain both files and sub-directories. Sub-directories may further hold more files and sub-directories. A sub-directory, also referred to as *child* directory, is a directory located under a *parent* directory. That parent directory is a sub-directory of some other higher-level directory. In other words, the Linux directory structure is similar to an inverted tree where the top is the root of the directory, and branches and leaves are sub-directories and files, respectively. The root of the directory is represented by the forward slash (/) character, which is also used as a directory separator in a path as shown below:

   /home/user1/dir1/subdir1

In this example, *home* sub-directory (child) is located under *root* (/), which is parent directory for *home*. *user1* (child) is located under *home* (parent), *dir1* (child) is located under *user1* (parent) and at the very bottom *subdir1* (child) is located under *dir1* (parent).

Each directory has a parent directory and a child directory with the exception of the root (/) and the lowest level directories. The root (/) directory has no parent and the lowest level sub-directory has no child.

 The term sub-directory is used for a directory that has a parent directory.

The hierarchical directory structure keeps related information together in a logical fashion. Compare the concept with a file cabinet that has several drawers with each storing multiple file folders.

Features

Linux, like UNIX operating systems, is a *multi-user, multi-tasking, multi-processing* and *multi-threading* operating system. This means that several users can access a Linux system simultaneously and share available resources. The system allows each logged in user to run any number of programs concurrently. The kernel is capable of handling multiple processors (CPU) installed in the system and breaking large running programs into smaller, more manageable pieces called *threads*, for improved performance.

 A resource may be a hardware device or a software program or service.

The kernel allows *time-sharing* among running programs, and runs them in a round-robin fashion to satisfy their processing requirements.

Logging In and Out

A user must log in to a Linux system to use it. The login process identifies a user to the system. There are two common ways of logging in – over the network using commands such as *telnet*, *rlogin* or *ssh*, and at the graphical screen. The following sub-sections show how to log in via *telnet* and *ssh* commands and using the graphical interface. Logging in using *rlogin* is covered later in the book. Also *ssh* is covered in more detail.

Logging In and Out via Commands

The two common methods of logging on are by using the *telnet* and the *ssh* commands from a Windows, UNIX or another Linux system on the network. Both commands require either an IP address of the Linux system or its hostname to connect. Login prompts similar to the following are displayed when you attempt to access a system called *rhel01* via the commands:

> **$ telnet rhel01**
> Red Hat Enterprise Linux Server release 5.2 (Tikanga)
> Kernel 2.6.18-128.1.6.el5 on an i686
> login:
> **$ ssh rhel01**
> login as:

Enter a valid username and password to access the system. Both username and password are case sensitive.

Use the *exit* command or press Ctrl+d to log out.

When you log in using one of the methods mentioned above, you are placed into a directory, referred to as your *home* directory. Each user on the system is assigned a home directory where the user normally keeps private files.

Logging In and Out via Graphical Interface

The default graphical login interface is called *GNOME* and it is shown in Figure 1-2. For details, refer to Chapter 10 "X Window System and Desktop Managers".

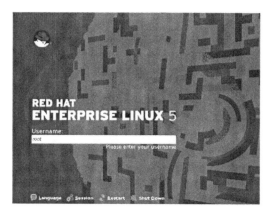

Figure 1-2 Graphical Login Interface

Enter a username (*root* for example) and press the Enter key. On the next screen, enter the user's password and again press the Enter key. On successful login, you will see a window similar to the one displayed in Figure 1-3.

Figure 1-3 Main Window

After you are done, click System at the top and choose "Log Out root" to log off.

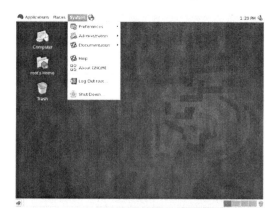

Figure 1-4 Log Out Window

Common Linux Commands

There are hundreds of commands available in Linux. This section provides an understanding on how commands are formed and describes some of them that are commonly used in routine system administration.

What is the Command Line?

The *command line* refers to the Linux command prompt where you enter commands for execution. Commands may or may not have arguments supplied with them. Arguments are used with commands for better, restricted or enhanced output, or a combination. The basic syntax of a command is:

> **$ command argument1 argument2 argument3 ....**

where:

Command:	specifies what to do
Argument:	is a file or directory name, some text or an option

Not every command requires an argument. In fact, many commands run without an argument specified. Some commands do require that you specify one, more than one or a fixed number of arguments.

The following examples use arguments. The text on the right tells if and how many arguments are supplied with the command.

$ cal 2009	(one argument)
$ cal 01 2009	(two arguments)
$ ls	(no arguments)
$ ls –l	(an argument, which is an option)
$ ls directory_name	(one argument)
$ ls –l directory_name	(two arguments of which the first one is an option)

The ls Command and its Variations

The *ls* (list) command displays a list of files and directories. It supports several options some of which are listed in Table 1-1 along with a short description of each.

Option	Description
–a	Lists hidden files also. If the name of a file starts with a period (.), it is referred to as a hidden file. For the *root* user, hidden files are also displayed without using this option.
–F	Displays file types. Shows (/) for directories, (*) for executable files, (@) for symbolic links and nothing for text files.
–lh	Displays long listing with file sizes in human readable format.
–l	Displays long listing with detailed file information including file type, permissions, link count, owner, group, size, date and time of last modification, and name of the file.
–ld	Displays long listing of the specified directory, but hides its contents.
–R	Lists contents of the specified directory and all its sub-directories (recursive listing).

Option	Description
–t	Lists all files sorted by date and time with the newest file first.
–tr	Lists all files sorted by date and time with the oldest file first.

Table 1-1 ls Command Options

Following examples help you understand impact of options used with the *ls* command:

To list files in the current directory with an assumption that you are in the / directory:

```
$ ls
bin   dev home lost+found misc  net  proc sbin    srv tftpboot usr
boot  etc lib    media       mnt  opt  root selinux sys tmp          var
```

To list files in the current directory with detailed information, use any of the following:

```
$ ll
$ ls –l
total 152
drwxr-xr-x    2 root root  4096 Feb 19 14:28 bin
drwxr-xr-x    4 root root  4096 Feb 19 13:59 boot
drwxr-xr-x   10 root root  3600 Feb 19 14:45 dev
drwxr-xr-x 101 root root 12288 Feb 19 14:46 etc
drwxr-xr-x    3 root root  4096 Oct 10 2006 home
drwxr-xr-x   14 root root  4096 Feb 19 14:05 lib
drwx------    2 root root 16384 Feb 19 13:51 lost+found
. . . . . . . .
```

To display all files in the current directory with their file types:

```
$ ls –F
bin/   etc/    lost+found/ mnt/   proc/   selinux/   tftpboot/   var/
boot/  home/   media/      net/   root/   srv/       tmp/
dev/   lib/    misc/       opt/   sbin/   sys/       usr/
```

To list all files in the current directory with detailed information and sorted by date and time with the newest file first:

```
$ ls –lt
total 152
drwxr-x---    2 root root  4096 Feb 19 14:51 root
drwxr-xr-x 101 root root 12288 Feb 19 14:46 etc
drwxr-xr-x   10 root root  3600 Feb 19 14:45 dev
drwxrwxrwt  5 root root   4096 Feb 19 14:44 tmp
drwxr-xr-x   2 root root      0 Feb 19 14:44 net
drwxr-xr-x   2 root root      0 Feb 19 14:44 misc
drwxr-xr-x   4 root root      0 Feb 19 14:43 selinux
drwxr-xr-x 11 root root      0 Feb 19 14:43 sys
. . . . . . . .
```

Red Hat Certified Technician & Engineer

To display all files in the current directory with their sizes in human readable format:

```
$ ls –lh
total 217K
drwxr-xr-x    2 root root 4.0K Jun  1 07:01 bin
drwxr-xr-x    6 root root 1.0K Jun  1 10:26 boot
drwxr-xr-x   10 root root 3.8K Jun 24 11:28 dev
drwxr-xr-x  102 root root  12K Jun 24 11:28 etc
drwxr-xr-x    7 root root 4.0K Apr 12 08:53 home
drwxr-xr-x   14 root root 4.0K Jun  1 06:59 lib
drwx------    2 root root  16K Apr  6 10:32 lost+found
drwxr-xr-x    2 root root 4.0K Jun 24 11:28 media
drwxr-xr-x    2 root root 4.0K Apr  3  2008 misc
drwxr-xr-x    2 root root 4.0K Oct 10  2006 mnt
dr-xr-xr-x    2 root root 4.0K Apr 13 09:24 net
drwxr-xr-x    2 root root 4.0K Oct 10  2006 opt
dr-xr-xr-x  105 root root    0 Jun 24 07:24 proc
drwxr-x---   27 root root 4.0K Jun 13 05:25 root
drwxr-xr-x    2 root root  12K Jun  1 07:01 sbin
. . . . . . . .
```

To list all files, including the hidden files, in the current directory with detailed information:

```
$ ls –la
total 172
drwxr-xr-x  24 root root  4096 Feb 19 14:44 .
drwxr-xr-x  24 root root  4096 Feb 19 14:44 ..
-rw-r--r--   1 root root     0 Feb 19 14:44 .autofsck
drwxr-xr-x   2 root root  4096 Feb 19 14:28 bin
drwxr-xr-x   4 root root  4096 Feb 19 13:59 boot
drwxr-xr-x  10 root root  3600 Feb 19 14:45 dev
drwxr-xr-x 101 root root 12288 Feb 19 14:46 etc
drwxr-xr-x   3 root root  4096 Oct 10  2006 home
drwxr-xr-x  14 root root  4096 Feb 19 14:05 lib
drwx------   2 root root 16384 Feb 19 13:51 lost+found
. . . . . . . .
```

To list contents of the */etc* directory recursively:

```
$ ls –R /etc
        < a very long output will be generated >
```

The pwd Command

The *pwd* (present working directory) command displays a user's current location in the directory tree. The following example shows that *user1* is in the */home/user1* directory:

```
$ pwd
/home/user1
```

The cd Command

The *cd* (change directory) command is used to navigate the directory tree. Perform the following examples as *user1*.

To change directory to */usr/bin*:

$ cd /usr/bin

To go back to the home directory, do either of the two:

$ cd
$ cd ~

To go directly from */etc* into a sub-directory *dir1* under *user1's* home directory:

$ cd ~/dir1

tilde (~) is used as an abbreviation for absolute pathname to a user's home directory. Refer to Chapter 02 "Files and Directories" to understand what an absolute path is.

To go to the home directory of *user2* from anywhere in the directory structure, use the ~ character and specify the login name. Note that there is no space between ~ and *user2*.

$ cd ~user2

Usage of the ~ character as demonstrated, is called *tilde substitution*. Refer to Chapter 05 "The Shells" for more information.

To go to the root directory, use the forward slash character:

$ cd /

To go one directory up to the parent directory, use period twice:

$ cd ..

To switch between current and previous directories, repeat the *cd* command with the dash (–) character.

$ cd –

The tty Command

This command displays the pseudo terminal where you are currently logged in:

$ tty
/dev/pts/1

The who Command

The *who* command displays information about all currently logged in users:

```
$ who
user1   pts/1     2008-11-25 18:05 (192.168.0.203)
root    pts/2     2008-11-25 18:09 (192.168.0.202)
```

where:

user1	name of the real user
pts/1	the first pseudo terminal session
2008-11-25 18:05	date and time the user logged in
192.168.0.203	IP address the user is connected from

The *who* command shows information only about the user that runs it if executed with "am i" arguments:

```
$ who am i
user1   pts/1     2008-11-25 18:05 (192.168.0.203)
```

The w Command

The *w* (what) command displays information similar to what the *who* command does, but in more detail. It also tells how long the user has been idle for, his CPU utilization and current activity. It shows on the first line the current system time, how long the system has been up for, how many users are currently logged in and what the current average load on the system is over the past 1, 5 and 15 minutes.

```
$ w
18:13:05 up 20 days, 9 min,  2 users,  load average: 0.00, 0.00, 0.00
USER      TTY     FROM           LOGIN@    IDLE   JCPU   PCPU   WHAT
user1     pts/1   192.168.0.203  18:05     0.00s  0.03s  0.00s  w
root      pts/2   192.168.0.202  18:09     7.00s  0.02s  0.02s  -bash
```

The whoami Command

The *whoami* (who am i) command displays the username of the user who executes this command. The output may either be the current or the effective username. The current username is the name of the user who logs in and runs this command. When this user uses the command *su* to switch identity, he becomes the effective user.

```
$ whoami
user1
```

The logname Command

The *logname* (login name) command shows the name of the real user who logs in initially. If that user uses the *su* command to switch identity, the *logname* command, unlike the *whoami* command, will still show the real username.

$ logname
user1

The id Command

The *id* (identification) command displays a user's UID (*user identification*), username, GID (*group identification*), group name and all secondary groups that the user is a member:

$ id
uid=503(user1) gid=503(user1) groups=503(user1)

Each user and group has a corresponding number (called UID and GID) for identification purposes. See Chapter 12 "Users and Groups" for more information".

The groups Command

The *groups* command lists all groups that a user is a member of:

$ groups
user1

The first group listed is the primary group for the user, all others are secondary (or supplementary) groups. Consult Chapter 12 "Users and Groups" for further details.

The uname Command

The *uname* command produces basic information about the system. Without any options, this command displays the operating system name only. You can use –a to get more information.

$ uname
Linux
$ uname –a
Linux rhel01 2.6.18-92.el5 #1 SMP Tue Apr 29 13:16:15 EDT 2008 x86_64 x86_64 x86_64 GNU/Linux

where:

Linux	kernel name
rhel01	hostname
2.6.18-92.el5 #1 SMP	kernel version and release
Tue Apr 29 13:16:15 EDT 2008	date and time
x86_64	machine hardware name
x86_64	processor type
x86_64	hardware platform

Try running *uname* with –s, –n, –r, –v, –m, –p, –i and –o options to view specific information.

The hostname Command

The *hostname* command displays the system name:

$ **hostname**
rhel01

The clear Command

The *clear* command clears the terminal screen and places the cursor at the beginning of the screen:

$ **clear**

 You must have proper terminal type set in order for this command to produce desired results.

The date Command

The *date* command displays current system date and time. This command can also be used to modify system date and time.

$ **date**
Wed Nov 26 08:24:16 EST 2008

The hwclock Command

The *hwclock* command displays date and time based on the hardware clock. This command can also be used to alter hardware clock.

$ **/sbin/hwclock**
Wed 26 Nov 2008 08:24:00 AM EST -0.998760 seconds

The cal Command

The *cal* (calendar) command displays calendar for the current month:

$ **cal**

```
              November 2008
    Su    Mo    Tu    We    Th    Fr    Sa
                                         1
     2     3     4     5     6     7     8
     9    10    11    12    13    14    15
    16    17    18    19    20    21    22
    23    24    25    26    27    28    29
    30
```

The uptime Command

The *uptime* command shows the system's current time, how long it has been up for, number of users currently logged in and average number of processes over the past 1, 5 and 15 minutes. For example, the output below shows that the current system time is 8:30 am, system has been up for 20 days, 14 hours and 28 minutes, there is currently one user logged in and the system load averages over the past 1, 5 and 15 minutes are 0.04, 0.23 and 0.15, respectively.

```
$ uptime
08:30:49 up 20 days, 14:28,  3 user,  load average: 0.04, 0.23, 0.15
```

The which Command

The *which* command shows the absolute path of the command that will be executed if run without using the absolute path:

```
$ which cat
/bin/cat
```

The output means that the *cat* command will be executed from */bin* directory if you run it without specifying its full path.

The whereis Command

The *whereis* command displays the binary name and the full pathname of the command along with the location of its manual pages:

```
$ whereis cat
cat: /bin/cat /usr/share/man/man1p/cat.1p.gz /usr/share/man/man1/cat.1.gz
```

The wc Command

The *wc* (word count) command displays number of lines, words and characters (or bytes) contained in a text file or input supplied. For example, when you run this command on the */etc/profile* file, you will see output similar to the following:

```
$ wc /etc/profile
54  146  937  /etc/profile
```

where:

> the 1st column indicates the number of lines (54)
> the 2nd column indicates the number of words (146)
> the 3rd column indicates the number of characters (or bytes) (937)
> the 4th column indicates the file name (*/etc/profile*)

You can use the options listed in Table 1-2 to obtain desired output.

Option	Action
–l	Prints line count.
–w	Prints word count.
–c	Prints byte count.
–m	Prints character count.

Table 1-2 wc Command Options

The following example displays only the number of lines in */etc/profile*:

$ wc –l /etc/profile
54 /etc/profile

Try running *wc* with the other options and view the results.

The wall Command

The *wall* command is used to broadcast a message to all logged in users on the system.

Type the *wall* command and hit the Enter key. Start typing a message and press Ctrl+d when finished to broadcast it.

 # wall

Online Help

While working on the system you require help to obtain information about a command, its usage and options available. RHEL offers online help via *man* (manual) pages. man pages are installed as part of RHEL installation, and provide detailed information on commands and configuration files including short and long description, usage, options, bugs, additional references and author.

Use the *man* command to view help on a command. The following example shows how to check man pages of the *passwd* command:

$ man passwd
PASSWD(1)   User utilities   PASSWD(1)

NAME
        passwd - update a userâs authentication tokens(s)

SYNOPSIS
        passwd [-k] [-l] [-u [-f]] [-d] [-n mindays] [-x maxdays] [-w warndays]
        [-i inactivedays] [-S] [--stdin] [username]

DESCRIPTION
        Passwd is used to update a userâs authentication token(s).

. . . .
        # a proposed password before updating it.
:

While you are in man pages, some common keys listed in Table 1-3 help you navigate efficiently.

Key	Action
Enter / Down arrow	Moves forward one line.
Up arrow	Moves backward one line.
f / Spacebar / Page down	Moves forward one page.
b / Page up	Moves backward one page.
d / u	Moves down / up half a page.
g / G	Moves to the beginning / end of the man pages.
:f	Displays line number and bytes being viewed.
q	Quits the man pages.
/pattern	Searches forward for the specified pattern.
?pattern	Searches backward for the specified pattern.
n / N	Finds the next / previous occurrence of a pattern.
h	Gives help on navigational keys.

Table 1-3 Navigating within man Pages

man Sections

There are several sections within man pages. For example, section 1 refers to user commands, section 4 contains special files, section 5 describes system configuration files, section 8 includes system administration commands, and so on.

To look for information on a configuration file */etc/passwd*, do the following:

$ man 5 passwd
PASSWD(5)   Linux Programmerâs Manual   PASSWD(5)

NAME
    passwd - password file

DESCRIPTION
    Passwd is a text file, that contains a list of the systemâs accounts, giving for each account some
. . . .
    Regardless of whether shadow passwords are used, many sysadmins use an
:

Searching by Keyword

Sometimes you need to use a command but do not know it name. Linux allows you to perform a keyword search on all available man pages using the *man* command with *–k* option or the *apropos* command. The search is performed in the *whatis* database that contains details about commands and files, and lists names of all man pages that include the specified keyword. The whatis database is updated once a day by the */etc/cron.daily/makewhatis.cron* script. You can manually update it as well using the *makewhatis* command.

```
$ man –k password
$ apropos password
    1 chage                (1) - change user password expiry information
    2 chpasswd             (8) - update passwords in batch mode
    3 cracklib             (rpm) - A password-checking library.
    4 crypt                (3) - password and data encryption
    5 endpwent [getpwent]  (3) - get password file entry
. . . . . . . .
```

Another way of quickly determine options available with a command and a short description of each is to supply the --help or -? option with the command. For example, to get quick help on the *passwd* command, do either of the following:

```
# passwd --help
# passwd -?
Usage: passwd [OPTION...]    <accountName>
  -k, --keep-tokens    keep non-expired authentication tokens
  -d, --delete         delete the password for the named account (root only)
  -l, --lock           lock the named account (root only)
  -u, --unlock         unlock the named account (root only)
  -f, --force          force operation

  -x, --maximum=DAYS   maximum password lifetime (root only)
  -n, --minimum=DAYS   minimum password lifetime (root only)
  -w, --warning=DAYS   number of days warning users receives before password expiration (root
only)
  -i, --inactive=DAYS  number of days after password expiration when an account becomes
disabled (root only)
  -S, --status         report password status on the named account (root only)
  --stdin              read new tokens from stdin (root only)

Help options:
  -?, --help           Show this help message
  --usage              Display brief usage message
```

Displaying Short Description

The *whatis* command provies a quick method of searching the specified command or file in the whatis database for a short description. For example, the following shows outputs of the command when run on *yum.conf* and *passwd* files:

```
# whatis yum.conf
yum.conf [yum]     (5) - Configuration file for yum(8)
# whatis passwd
Passwd             (1) - update a user's authentication tokens(s)
Passwd             (5) - password file
Passwd             (rpm) - The passwd utility for setting/changing passwords using PAM
passwd [sslpasswd] (1ssl) - compute password hashes
```

The first output indicates that the specified file is a configuration file associated with the *yum* command and the second output points to four entries for the *passwd* file.

Alternative to the *whatis* command, you can use the *man* command with –f option to produce identical results:

> **# man –f yum.conf**
> **# man –f passwd**

Summary

In this chapter basics of Linux was covered. You were provided with an overview of the structure and components that make up the core of the Linux system. You looked at some of the common features associated with Linux, and learned how to log in to a system using various methods.

You saw how to construct a command; and then executed a number of basic Linux commands to display information such as directory path, directory and file listing, directory navigation, user login names, logged in user information, user identity, and basic system and hardware data.

Finally, you learned how to access online help on commands and configuration files. You performed a keyword search on all available man pages that listed commands and configuration files with the keyword included. You looked at the command that performed a search operation on the specified command or file.

## 02

Files and Directories

This chapter covers the following major topics:

- ✓ Red Hat Enterprise Linux directory structure
- ✓ Nautilus file manager
- ✓ Static and dynamic directories
- ✓ Access files using absolute and relative pathnames
- ✓ Types of files
- ✓ Naming convention for files and directories
- ✓ Manage and manipulate files and directories including creating, listing, displaying, copying, moving, renaming and removing them
- ✓ Search for text within files
- ✓ Search for files in the directory system
- ✓ Sort contents of text files
- ✓ Create file and directory links

Linux files are organized in a logical fashion for ease of administration. This logical division of files is maintained in hundreds of directories that are located in larger containers called *file systems*. Red Hat Enterprise Linux follows the *File system Hierarchy Standard* (FHS) for file organization. There are two types of file systems – *disk-based* and *memory-based*. Disk-based file systems are created on physical media such as a hard disk and memory-based file systems, also called *virtual file systems*, are created at system boot up and destroyed at shut down.

File System Tree

The Linux file system structure is like an inverted tree with the root of the tree at the top and branches and leaves at the bottom. The top-level is referred to as *root* and represented by the forward slash (/) character. This is the point where the entire file system structure is ultimately connected to.

Two file systems – / and */boot* – are created, by default, when RHEL is installed. The custom installation procedure provided later in this book also creates */var*, */usr*, */tmp*, */opt* and */home* file systems in addition to / and */boot*. The main directories under the / and other file systems are shown in Figure 2-1. Some of these directories hold *static* data while others contain *dynamic* (or *variable*) information. The static data refers to file contents that are not usually modified. The dynamic or variable data refers to file contents that are modified as required. Static directories normally contain commands, library routines, kernel files, device files, etc. and dynamic directories hold log files, status files, configuration files, temporary files, etc.

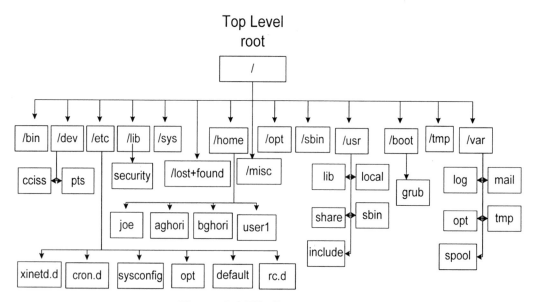

Figure 2-1 File System Tree

RHEL provides a graphical file manager called *Nautilus* that can be used to view and navigate within the directory structure. This tool can be invoked by issuing the *nautilus* command. By default, it opens up the home directory of the user who initiates it. Figure 2-2 shows the interface started by *root*. There are many choices available under the menu options for file and directory management.

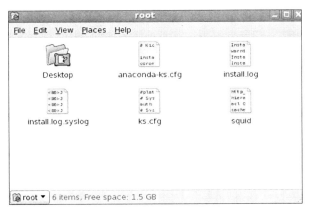

Figure 2-2 Nautilus File Manager

A brief description of disk-based and virtual file systems is provided in the following sub-sections.

The Root File System (/) – Disk-Based

The *root* file system is the top-level file system in the FHS and contains many higher-level directories holding specific information. Some of the key directories are given below:

The Binary Directory (/bin)

The *binary* directory contains crucial user executable commands. This directory holds static data files.

The Library Directory (/lib)

The *library* directory contains shared library files required by programs. It contains sub-directories that hold library routines.

In Figure 2-1, *security* under */lib* refers to library files used by security system.

The */lib* directory holds static data files.

The System Binary Directory (/sbin)

Most commands required at system boot up are located in the *system binary* directory. In addition, most commands requiring root privileges to run are also located here. In other words, this directory contains crucial system administration commands that are not intended for regular users (albeit they still can run a few of them). This directory is not included in normal users' default search path because of the nature of commands it contains.

The */sbin* directory holds static data files.

The Etcetera Directory (/etc)

The *etcetera* directory holds most system configuration files. Some of the more common sub-directories under */etc* are: *sysconfig, default, opt, cups, lvm, xinetd.d, mail, rc.d, skel, kde* and *gnome*. These sub-directories contain, in that sequence, configuration files for various system services, user account defaults, additional software installed on the system, printers, Logical

Volume Manager, internet services, mail subsystem, system startup and shutdown scripts, user profile templates and the last two hold KDE and GNOME desktop configuration files.

The */etc* directory contains dynamic data files.

The lost+found Directory (/lost+found)

This directory is used to hold files that become orphan after a system crash. An *orphan* file is a file that has lost its name. A detailed discussion on this is covered in Chapter 14 "File Systems and Swap".

If the *lost+found* directory is deleted, it should be re-created with the *mklost+found* command:

> **# mklost+found**
> mklost+found 1.39 (29-May-2006)

This directory is automatically created in a file system when the file system is created, and holds dynamic information.

The /root Directory

This is the default home directory location for the *root* user.

The /srv Directory

This directory holds server data associated with databases, web sites, etc.

The Boot File System (/boot) – Disk-Based

The */boot* file system contains Linux kernel(s), boot loader(s) and boot configuration file(s) in addition to other files required to boot RHEL. The default size of this file system is 100MB, and is altered only when an update to the kernel is performed. More information is provided in Chapter 17 "Linux Kernel".

The */boot* file system contains static data files.

The Variable File System (/var) – Disk-Based

/var contains data that frequently change while the system is up and running. Files holding log, status, spool and other dynamic data are typically located in this file system.

Some common sub-directories under */var* are briefly discussed below:

The /var/log Directory

Most system log files are located here. This directory contains system logs, boot logs, failed user logs, user logs, installation logs, cron logs, mail logs, etc.

The /var/spool/mail Directory

This is the location for user mailboxes.

The /var/opt Directory

For additional software installed in */opt*, this directory contains log, status and other variable data files for that software.

The /var/spool Directory

Directories that hold print jobs, cron jobs, email messages and other queued items before being sent out, are located here.

The /var/tmp Directory

Large temporary files or temporary files that need to exist for extended periods of time than what is allowed in */tmp*, are stored here. These files survive system reboots and are not automatically deleted.

The UNIX System Resources File System (/usr) – Disk-Based

This file system contains general files related to the system.

Some of the more important sub-directories under */usr* are briefly discussed below:

The /usr/bin Directory

Contains additional user executable commands.

The /usr/sbin Directory

Contains additional system administration commands.

The /usr/local Directory

System administrator repository to keep commands and tools that they download from the web, develop in-house or obtain elsewhere. These commands and tools are not generally included with original Linux software distribution. In particular, */usr/local/bin* holds executable files, */usr/local/etc* contains their configuration files and */usr/local/man* holds associated man pages.

The /usr/include Directory

Contains header files for the *C* language.

The /usr/share Directory

Directory location for man pages, documentation, sample templates, configuration files, etc. that may be shared on multi-vendor Linux/UNIX platforms with heterogeneous hardware architectures.

The /usr/lib Directory

Contains library files pertaining to programming sub-routines.

The Temporary File System (/tmp) – Disk-Based

This file system is a repository for temporary files. Many programs create temporary files as they run or being installed. Some programs delete the temporary files that they create after they are finished, while others do not.

The Optional File System (/opt) – Disk-Based

This file system holds additional software packages installed on the system. A sub-directory is created for each installed software.

The Home File System (/home) – Disk-Based

The /home file system is designed to hold user *home* directories. Each user account is assigned a home directory for storing personal files. Each home directory is owned by the user the directory is assigned to. No other user usually has access to other users' home directories.

In Figure 2-1, users *joe, aghori, bghori* and *user1* have their home directories located under */home*.

The directories discussed thus far are RHEL system related. It is highly recommended that you create separate file systems for data and applications. A detailed discussion on file systems and how to create and access them is covered in Chapter 14 "File Systems and Swap".

The Devices File System (/dev) – Virtual

The /dev (devices) file system contains device files for hardware and virtual devices. Linux kernel communicates with system hardware and virtual devices through corresponding device files located in here.

There are two types of device files: *character* special device files (a.k.a. *raw* device files) and *block* special device files. The kernel accesses devices using one or both types of device files.

Character devices are accessed in a serial manner where streams of bits are transferred during kernel and device communication. Examples of such devices are serial printers, mouse, keyboard, terminals, floppy disks, hard disk devices, tape drives, etc.

Block devices are accessed in a parallel fashion meaning that data is transferred between the kernel and the device in blocks (parallel) when communication between the two takes place. Examples of block devices are hard disk devices, CD/DVD drives, floppy disks, parallel printers, etc.

 Some utilities access hard disk devices as block devices while others access them as character special devices.

Some key sub-directories under /dev are *disk*, *pts* and *VolGroup00*, and contain device files for hard disks (*disk*), pseudo terminals (*pts*) and root volume group (*VolGroup00*).

The /dev file system holds static data files.

The /net File System (/net) – Virtual

If AutoFS is used to mount NFS file systems using a special map, all available NFS file systems on the network get mounted under their corresponding hostnames beneath /net. AutoFS and the special map are explained in detail in Chapter 26 "NFS and AutoFS".

The Media File System (/media) – Virtual

This virtual file system is used to automatically mount removable media such as floppy, CD, DVD, USB and Zip disks.

The Miscellaneous File System (/misc) – Virtual

This location is used by AutoFS to mount local resources. A detailed discussion on AutoFS is covered in Chapter 26 "NFS and AutoFS".

The Process File System (/proc) – Virtual

Information about the current state of the running kernel is maintained in this file system. This information includes details on CPU, memory, partitioning, interrupts, I/O addresses, DMA channels and running processes, and is represented by various files. These files do not actually store the information, rather, they point to the information in the memory. This file system is automatically maintained by the system.

The */proc* file system contains dynamic data files.

The System File System (/sys) – Virtual

Information about the currently configured hardware is stored and maintained in this file system. This file system is automatically maintained by the system.

The SELinux File System (/selinux) – Virtual

If SELinux packages are installed, this file system stores all current settings for SELinux. A detailed discussion on SELinux is covered in Chapter 30 "System and Network Security".

Absolute and Relative Paths

A *path* is like a road map which shows how to get from one place in the directory tree to another. It uniquely identifies a particular file or directory by its absolute or relative location in the directory structure.

At any given time, you are located in one directory within the directory tree, which is referred to as your *present* (or *current*) working directory. When you log in to the system, the current directory is set to your home directory by default. Use the *pwd* command to verify after you are in.

Absolute Path

An *absolute path* (a.k.a. *full path* or *fully qualified path*) points to a file or directory in relation to root (/). An absolute path must always start with a forward slash (/) character. The *pwd* command displays your current location in the tree.

```
$ pwd
/home/user1/dir1/scripts
```

This example shows that you are in */home/user1/dir1/scripts* directory, which represents the full path with respect to root (/).

Relative Path

A *relative path* points to a file or directory in relation to your current location in the directory tree. A relative path never begins with a forward slash (/) character; it always begins with one of the following three ways:

<u>With a period:</u> A period represents the current working directory. For example, if you are located in */home/user1/dir1/scripts* directory and wish to run a script *file1* from there, you would type:

./file1

<u>With a pair of periods:</u> A pair of period characters represents the parent directory in relation to your current working directory. A parent directory is one level higher than the current working directory. For example, to go back one level up to parent directory, type:

$ cd ..

<u>With a sub-directory name:</u> Say you are currently in */home/user1* directory and want to go to the *scripts* sub-directory under *dir1*, you will need to do the following:

$ cd dir1/scripts

File Types

RHEL supports several different types of files. Some of the common file types are regular files, directory files, executable files, symbolic link files, device files, named pipe files and socket files, and are described in the following sub-sections.

Regular Files

Regular files may contain text or binary data. These files can be shell scripts or commands. When you do an *ll* on a directory, all line entries for files in the output that begin with " – " represent regular files:

$ ll /bin
```
. . . . . . . .
-rwxr-xr-x  1 root root    21496 Sep  5 09:13 alsaunmute
-rwxr-xr-x  1 root root     7288 Oct 12 16:20 arch
-rwxr-xr-x  1 root root   118592 Jun 15 2004 ash
-rwxr-xr-x  1 root root   627232 Jun 15 2004 ash.static

. . . . . . . .
```

You can use the *file* command to determine the file type. For example, the following shows that *.bash_profile* contains ascii text:

$ file .bash_profile
.bash_profile: ASCII English text

Directory Files

Directories are logical containers that hold files and sub-directories. Do an *ll* on the root (/) directory and output similar to the following will be displayed:

```
$ ll /
total 152
drwxr-xr-x    2 root root   4096 Feb 19 14:34 bin
drwxr-xr-x    4 root root   4096 Feb 19 13:51 boot
drwxr-xr-x   10 root root   3640 Feb 19 14:51 dev
drwxr-xr-x  100 root root  12288 Feb 19 15:34 etc
drwxr-xr-x    6 root root   4096 Feb 19 15:34 home
drwxr-xr-x   14 root root   4096 Feb 19 14:07 lib

. . . . . . . .
```

The letter "d" at the beginning of each line entry indicates a directory. Use the *file* command to determine the type. For example:

```
$ file /root
/root:    directory
```

Executable Files

Executable files could be commands or shell scripts. In other words, any file that can be run is an executable file. A file that has an "x" in the 4th, 7th or the 10th field in the output of the *ll* command is executable.

```
$ ll /usr/sbin
. . . . . . . .
-rwxr-xr-x  1 root root       15808 Oct 12 16:20 vipw
-rwxr-xr-x  1 root root       68872 Jul 21  2005 visudo
-rwxr-xr-x  1 root root       73136 Nov 1  2006 warnquota
-rwxr-xr-x  1 root root     2614648 Oct 31 15:18 winbindd
-rwxr-xr-x  1 root root      164008 Jun 23  2005 xinetd
-r-xr-xr-x  1 root root       16208 Sep 10 2004 yppoll
-r-xr-xr-x  1 root root       13648 Sep 10 2004 ypset

. . . . . . . .
```

Use the *file* command to identify the type. For example:

```
$ file /usr/bin/who
/usr/bin/who: ELF 32-bit LSB executable, Intel 80386, version 1 (SYSV), for GNU/Linux 2.6.9,
dynamically linked (uses shared libs), for GNU/Linux 2.6.9, stripped
```

Symbolic Link Files

A *symbolic link* (a.k.a. *soft link* or *symlink*) may be considered as a shortcut to another file or directory. When you do an *ll* on a symbolically linked file or directory, you will notice two things.

One, the line entry begins with the letter "l" and two, there is an arrow pointing to the linked file or directory. For example:

$ ll /usr/sbin/sendmail
lrwxrwxrwx 1 root root 21 Oct 9 13:10 /usr/sbin/sendmail -> /etc/alternatives/mta

The *file* command tells if the specified file or directory is linked:

$ file /usr/sbin/sendmail
/usr/sbin/sendmail: symbolic link to `/etc/alternatives/mta'

Device Files

Each piece of hardware in the system has an associated file used by the kernel to communicate with it. This type of file is called *device file*. There are two types of device files: a *character* (or *raw*) device file and a *block* device file. The following example outputs from the *ll* command display them:

$ ll /dev/sd*
brw-r----- 1 root disk 8, 0 Nov 5 18:03 sda
brw-r----- 1 root disk 8, 1 Nov 5 18:03 sda1
brw-r----- 1 root disk 8, 2 Nov 5 18:03 sda2
$ ll /dev/tty*
crw-rw-rw- 1 root tty 5, 0 Nov 5 18:03 tty
crw-rw---- 1 root root 4, 0 Nov 5 18:03 tty0
crw------- 1 root root 4, 1 Nov 5 18:04 tty1
. . . .

The first character in each line entry tells if the file is block or character special. A "b" denotes a block and a "c" stands for character device file. The *file* command shows their type:

$ file /dev/sda
/dev/sda: block special (8/0)
$ file /dev/tty0
/dev/tty0: character special (4/0)

Named Pipe Files

A *named pipe* allows two unrelated processes running on the same system or on two different systems to communicate with each other and exchange data. Named pipes are uni-directional. They are also referred to as FIFO because they use *First In First Out* mechanism. Named pipes make *Inter Process Communication* (IPC) possible. The output of the *ll* command shows a "p" as the first character in the line entry to represent a named pipe file:

 # ll /dev/initctl
prw-------   1   root   root   0   Jan 26 11:39   /dev/initctl

IPC allows processes to communicate directly with each other by sharing parts of their virtual memory address space, and then reading and writing data stored in that shared virtual memory.

The *file* command shows the type of a named pipe file as fifo. See the following example:

$ file /dev/initctl
/dev/initctl: fifo (named pipe)

Socket Files

A *socket* is a named pipe that works in both directions. In other words, a socket is a two-way named pipe. It is also a type of IPC. Sockets are used by client/server programs. Notice an "s" as the first character in the output of the *ll* command below that points to a socket file:

$ ll /dev/log
srw-rw-rw- 1   root   root   0   Jan 26 11:39   /dev/log

The *file* command shows the type of socket file as follows:

$ file /dev/log
/dev/log: socket

File and Directory Operations

This section discusses file and directory naming rules and describes various operations on files and directories that users can perform. These operations include creating, listing, displaying contents of, copying, moving, renaming, deleting and displaying statistics of files and directories.

File and Directory Naming Convention

Files and directories are assigned names when they are created. There are certain rules, listed below, that you should remember and follow while assigning names. A file or directory name:

✓ Can contain a maximum of 255 alphanumeric characters (letters and numbers).
✓ Can contain non-alphanumeric characters such as underscore (_), hyphen (–), space and period (.).
✓ Should not include special characters such as asterisk (*), question mark (?), tilde (~), ampersand (&), pipe (|), double quotes ("), single back quote (` ), single forward quote ( `), semi-colon (;), redirection symbols (< >) and dollar sign ($). These characters hold special meaning to the shell.
✓ May or may not have an extension. Some users prefer using extensions, others do not.

Creating Files and Directories

Files can be created in multiple ways; however, there is only one command to create directories.

Creating Files Using the touch Command

The *touch* command creates an empty file. If the file already exists, the time stamp on it is updated with the current system date and time. Do the following as *user1* to create *file1*:

```
$ cd
$ touch file1
$ ll file1
-rw-rw-r-- 1 user1 user1 0 Nov 26 12:11 file1
```

As indicated in the output, the fifth field is 0 "zero" meaning that *file1* is created with zero bytes. Now, if you run the command again on *file1* you will notice that the time stamp is updated.

```
$ touch file1
$ ll file1
-rw-rw-r-- 1 user1 user1 0 Nov 26 12:13 file1
```

Creating Files Using the cat Command

The *cat* command allows you to create short text files:

```
$ cat > newfile
```

Nothing will be displayed when you execute this command. The system expects you to input something. Press Ctrl+d when done to save what you have typed to a file called *newfile*.

Creating Files Using the vi, vim, or nano Command

These are Linux text editing tools of which the most common is the vi editor, but any of these may be used to create and modify text files.

Refer to Chapter 04 "Text Editors and Processors" for a detailed understanding of the *vi* editor. Chapter 04 also touched *vim* and *nano*.

Creating Directories Using the mkdir Command

The *mkdir* command is used to create directories. The following example shows how to create a new directory by the name *scripts1* in *user1*'s home directory (*/home/user1*):

```
$ cd
$ pwd
/home/user1
$ mkdir scripts1
```

You must have appropriate permissions to create a directory; otherwise, you will get an error message complaining lack of permissions.

You can create a hierarchy of sub-directories using the *mkdir* command with the –p option. In the following example, *mkdir* creates a directory *scripts2* in *user1*'s home directory. At the same time, it creates a directory *perl* as a sub-directory of *scripts2* and a sub-directory *perl5* under *perl*.

```
$ mkdir –p scripts2/perl/perl5
```

Listing Files and Directories

To list files and directories, use the *ls* or *ll* command. The following example runs *ll* as *user1* in *user1's* home directory:

```
$ ll
total 12
-rw-rw-r--  1 user1 user1    0 Nov 26 12:14 file1
-rw-rw-r--  1 user1 user1    6 Nov 26 12:24 newfile
drwxrwxr-x 2 user1 user1 4096 Nov 26 12:23 scripts1
drwxrwxr-x 2 user1 user1 4096 Nov 26 12:24 scripts2
```

Notice that there are nine columns in the output, and contain:

Column 1: The 1st character tells the type of file. The next 9 characters indicate permissions. File permissions are explained at length in Chapter 03 "File and Directory Permissions".
Column 2: Displays how many links the file or the directory has.
Column 3: Shows owner name of the file or directory.
Column 4: Displays group name that the owner of the file or directory belongs to.
Column 5: Gives file size in bytes. For directories, this number reflects number of blocks being used by the directory to hold information about its contents.
Column 6, 7 and 8: List month, day of the month and time the file or directory was created or last accessed/modified.
Column 9: Name of the file or directory.

Displaying File Contents

There are several commands that Linux offers to display file contents. Directory contents are simply the files and sub-directories within it. Use the *ll* or the *ls* command to view directory contents as explained earlier.

The *cat, more, less, head, tail, view, vi, vim, nano* and *strings* commands are available to display file contents. Following text explains each one of them.

Using the cat Command

The *cat* command displays the contents of a text file. In the example below, *.bash_profile* in *user1's* home directory is displayed using the *cat* command:

```
$ cat /home/user1/.bash_profile
# .bash_profile
# Get the aliases and functions
if [ -f ~/.bashrc ]; then
     . ~/.bashrc
fi
# User specific environment and startup programs
PATH=$PATH:$HOME/bin
export PATH
```

Using the more Command

The *more* command displays the contents of a long text file one page at a time from start to end. In the example below, */etc/profile* is shown with the *more* command. This command shows the percentage of the file being viewed in the last line.

```
$ more /etc/profile
# /etc/profile
# System wide environment and startup programs, for login setup
# Functions and aliases go in /etc/bashrc
. . . . . . . .
if [ "$EUID" = "0" ]; then
--More--(45%)
```

Navigation keys listed in Table 2-1 would be helpful when viewing a large file with *more*.

Key	Purpose
Spacebar / f	Scrolls to the next screen.
Enter	Scrolls one line at a time.
b	Scrolls to the previous screen.
d / u	Scrolls down / up half a screen.
h	Displays help.
q	Quits and returns to the shell prompt.
/string	Searches forward for string.
?string	Searches backward for string.
n / N	Finds the next / previous occurrence of string.

Table 2-1 Navigating with more

Using the less Command

The *less* command is the opposite of the *more* command. In the example below, */etc/profile* is shown with the *less* command:

```
$ less /etc/profile
# /etc/profile

# System wide environment and startup programs, for login setup
# Functions and aliases go in /etc/bashrc
if [ "$EUID" = "0" ]; then
/etc/profile
```

The navigation keys listed in Table 2-1 would be helpful when viewing a large file with *less*.

Using the head Command

The *head* command displays the first few lines of a text file. By default, the first 10 lines are displayed. The following example displays the first 10 lines from the */etc/profile* file:

$ head /etc/profile
\# /etc/profile

\# System wide environment and startup programs, for login setup
\# Functions and aliases go in /etc/bashrc

pathmunge () {
    if ! echo $PATH | /bin/egrep -q "(^|:)$1($|:)" ; then
     if ["$2" = "after"] ; then
      PATH=$PATH:$1
     else

Supply a number with the command as an argument to view a different number of lines. The following example displays the first three lines from the *etc/profile* file:

$ head –3 /etc/profile
\# /etc/profile

\# System wide environment and startup programs, for login setup

Using the tail Command

The *tail* command displays the last few lines of a file. By default, the last 10 lines are displayed. The following example shows the last 10 lines from the *etc/profile* file:

$ tail /etc/profile
export PATH USER LOGNAME MAIL HOSTNAME HISTSIZE INPUTRC

for i in /etc/profile.d/*.sh ; do
  if [-r "$i"]; then
   . $i
  fi
done

unset i
unset pathmunge

You can specify a numerical value to view a different set of lines. The following example displays the last 8 lines from *etc/profile*:

$ tail –8 /etc/profile
for i in /etc/profile.d/*.sh ; do
  if [-r "$i"]; then
   . $i
  fi
done

unset i
unset pathmunge

The *tail* command proves to be very useful when you wish to view a log file while it is being updated. The –f option enables this function. The following example shows how to view the RHEL system log file */var/log/messages* in this manner. Try running this command on your system and notice the behavior.

> **$ tail –f /var/log/messages**

Using the view, vi and vim Commands

These commands open up the specified text file in the *vi* editor for modification. Here is how to run them to open *.bash_profile* in *user1*'s home directory:

> **$ view /home/user1/.bash_profile**
> **$ vi /home/user1/.bash_profile**
> **$ vim /home/user1/.bash_profile**

See Chapter 04 "Text Editors and Processors" to get details on the *vi* and *vim* editors.

Using the nano Command

Many system administrators and users prefer to use a menu-driven text editor call *nano* (nano's another). Here is how you would run it to open */home/user1/.bash_profile* file:

> **$ nano /home/user1/.bash_profile**

See Chapter 04 "Text Editors and Processors" to get details on the nano editor.

Using the uniq Command

The *uniq* command identifies any duplicate line entries in a file or input provided. Without any options, this command prints unique lines and with –d option, it prints only the duplicate lines. You can specify –i option to instruct the command to ignore the letter case. Here is an example:

```
$ uniq /home/user1/.bash_profile
# .bash_profile

# Get the aliases and functions
if [ -f ~/.bashrc ]; then
    . ~/.bashrc
fi

# User specific environment and startup programs

PATH=$PATH:$HOME/bin

export PATH
```

Using the strings Command

The *strings* command finds and displays legible information embedded within a non-text or binary file. For example, when you run the *strings* command on */bin/cat*, you will observe output similar to the following. Although */bin/cat* is a non-text file, it does contain some legible information.

$ strings /bin/cat
/lib/ld-linux.so.2
__gmon_start__
libc.so.6
_IO_stdin_used
__printf_chk
setlocale
mbrtowc
optind
· · · · · · · ·

Copying Files and Directories

The copy operation duplicates a file or directory. There is a single command called *cp* which is used for this purpose. Here is how to use it.

Copying Files

The *cp* command copies one or more files to either current or another directory. If you want to duplicate a file in the same directory, you must give a different name to the target file. If you want to copy a file to a different directory, you can either use the same file name as the original file does or assign it a different name. Consider the following examples.

To copy *file1* as *newfile1* in the same directory:

$ cp file1 newfile1

To copy *file1* by the same name into another directory called *subdir1*:

$ cp file1 subdir1

By default, when you copy a file, the destination is overwritten and a warning message is not generated. In order to avoid such a situation use the –i option with the *cp* command, which prompts for confirmation before overwriting.

$ cp –i file1 file2
cp: overwrite `file2'?

Copying Directories

The *cp* command with –r (recursive) option copies a directory and its contents to another location. In the following example, *scripts1* directory is copied under *subdir1*:

$ cp –r scripts1 subdir1

You may wish to use the –i option with *cp* if needed.

Moving and Renaming Files and Directories

The move operation copies a file or directory to an alternate location and deletes the original file or directory. The rename operation simply changes the name of a file or directory. Here is how to perform these operations.

Moving and Renaming Files

The *mv* command is used to move or rename files. The –i option can be specified for user confirmation if the destination file exists. The following example moves *file1* to *subdir1* and prompts for confirmation if a file by the same name exists in *subdir1*:

$ mv –i file1 subdir1
mv overwrite: subdir1/file1? (y/n)

To rename *file3* as *file4*:

$ mv file3 file4

You may want to use the –i option with *mv* command if needed.

Moving and Renaming Directories

To move a directory along with its contents to some other directory location or simply change the name of the directory, use the *mv* command. For example, to move *scripts1* into *scripts2* (*scripts2* must exist), do the following:

$ mv scripts1 scripts2

To rename *scripts1* as *scripts10* (*scripts10* must not exist):

$ mv scripts1 scripts10

Removing Files and Directories

The remove operation deletes a file or directory. Here is how to do it.

Removing Files

You can remove a file using the *rm* command. The *rm* command deletes one or more specified files at once. The following example deletes *newfile*:

$ rm newfile

The –i option can be used to prevent accidental file removal. The option prompts for confirmation before removing. The following example prompts for confirmation before deleting *newfile*:

$ rm –i newfile
rm: remove regular file `newfile'? y

Removing Directories

There are two commands available to remove directories, and are demonstrated by the following examples.

To remove an empty directory, use the *rmdir* command:

$ rmdir subdir100

To remove a non-empty directory, use *rm* with –r option:

$ rm –r subdir1

Use *rm* with –i option to remove interactively:

$ rm –ri subdir1

Displaying File and Directory Statistics

The *stat* command can be used to display a file or file system statistical information. The following example displays *stat* output on *install.log* file:

 # stat install.log
```
  File: `install.log'
  Size: 37232          Blocks: 88        IO Block: 4096    regular file
Device: fd00h/64768d   Inode: 384002    Links: 1
Access: (0644/-rw-r--r--)   Uid: ( 0/  root)   Gid: ( 0/  root)
Access: 2009-03-10 22:09:37.000000000 -0400
Modify: 2008-10-15 08:43:37.000000000 -0400
Change: 2008-10-15 08:43:47.000000000 -0400
```

The output displays attributes of the *install.log* file. It shows the file name, its size, blocks occupied, I/O block size, type, device number in hexadecimal format, inode number, number of hard links, access mode in octal and symbolic notations, ownership, group membership, and access, modification and change times.

If this command is executed on a file system such as */usr*, the output will resemble the following:

 # stat –f /usr
```
  File: "/usr"
    ID: 0          Namelen: 255                Type: ext2/ext3
Block size: 4096    Fundamental block size: 4096
Blocks: Total: 1983848   Free: 1469060   Available: 1366660
Inodes: Total: 2048256   Free: 1962009
```

The output displays the file system name, its ID, maximum length of filenames that can be created, file system type, block size for data transfer, block size for block counts, total, free and available blocks, and total and free inodes.

Summary of File and Directory Operations

Table 2-2 lists commands for file and directory operations you have just learnt.

Command to	File	Directory
Create	*cat, touch, vi, vim, nano*	*mkdir*
List	*ll, ls*	*ll, ls*
Display contents	*cat, more, less, head, tail, view, vi, vim, nano, uniq, strings*	*ll, ls*
Copy	*cp*	*cp*
Move	*mv*	*mv*
Rename	*mv*	*mv*
Remove	*rm*	*rm −r, rmdir*
Display statistics	*stat*	*stat*

Table 2-2 Summary of File / Directory Operations

File and Directory Operations Using Nautilus File Manager

Nautilus file manager may be used to perform most file and directory operations discussed thus far. To start the tool, execute the *nautilus* command at the X terminal window prompt, click Applications → System Tools → File Browser or right click the Computer icon on the desktop. By default, Nautilus displays the home directory contents of the user who runs it. See Figure 2-3. Navigate through the interface and perform operations for practice.

Figure 2-3 Nautilus File Manager

Modifying File and Directory Control Attributes

There are certain control attributes that may be set on a file or directory to make it appendable only, unchangeable, undeletable and so on. For example, you can enable attributes on a critical system file or directory so that no users including *root* can delete or change it, disallow a backup utility such as the *dump* command to backup a specific file or directory, and so on. These attributes can only be set on files and directories that are located in an ext2 or ext3 file system. See Chapter 14 "File Systems and Swap" for details on ext2 and ext3 file system.

Table 2-3 lists common control attributes.

Attribute	Affect on File or Directory
a (append)	File can only be appended.
A	Prevents updating access time.
c (compressed)	File is automatically compressed.
d (dump)	File cannot be backed up with the *dump* command.
D	Changes on a directory are written synchronously to the disk.
i (immutable)	File cannot be changed, renamed or deleted.
j (journaling)	File has its data written to the journal before being written to the file itself. See Chapter 14 "File Systems and Swap" for details on journaling.
s (secure delete)	File has its blocks wiped.
S (synchronous)	Changes on a file are written synchronously to the disk.
u (undeletable)	File cannot be deleted.

Table 2-3 File and Directory Control Attributes

There are two commands *lsattr* and *chattr* that can be used to list and modify these attributes. Following demonstrates a few examples on the usage with an assumption that you are in the */root* directory and *install.log* file exists.

To list current attributes on *install.log*:

> # **lsattr install.log**
> ------------- install.log

The output indicates that presently there are no attributes set on the file.

To prevent *install.log* from deletion and any modications:

> # **chattr +i install.log**
> # **lsattr install.log**
> ----i-------- install.log

Now, try deleting this file as *root*:

> # **rm install.log**
> rm: remove write-protected regular file `install.log'? **y**
> rm: cannot remove `install.log': Operation not permitted

To allow only append operation on the file:

> # **chattr +a install.log**
> # **cat /etc/fstab >> install.log**

To unset both attributes:

> # **chattr –ia install.log**

To set both attributes in one go:

> # **chattr =ia install.log**

Pattern Matching

RHEL provides a powerful tool to search the contents of one or more text files, or input provided, for matching a pattern. This is referred to as *pattern matching* (a.k.a. *regular expression* or *globbing*). A pattern can be a single character, a series of characters, a word or a sentence. You must enclose the pattern in double quotes if it contains one or more white spaces.

The tool is called *grep* (*global regular expression print*) and it searches contents of one or more specified files for a regular expression. If found, it prints every line containing the expression on the screen without changing the original file contents. Consider the following examples.

To search for the pattern "user1" in the */etc/passwd* file:

$ grep user1 /etc/passwd
user1:x:503:503::/home/user1:/bin/bash

To search for all occurrences of the pattern "user1" in both the */etc/passwd* and */etc/group* files:

$ grep user1 /etc/passwd /etc/group
/etc/passwd:user1:x:503:503::/home/user1:/bin/bash
/etc/group:user1:x:503:

To display only the names of those files that contain the pattern "user1" from the specified file list, use the –l option:

$ grep –l user1 /etc/group /etc/passwd /etc/hosts
/etc/group
/etc/passwd

To look for the pattern "root" in the */etc/group* file along with associated line number(s), use the –n option:

$ grep –n root /etc/group
1:root:x:0:root
2:bin:x:1:root,bin,daemon
3:daemon:x:2:root,bin,daemon
4:sys:x:3:root,bin,adm
5:adm:x:4:root,adm,daemon
7:disk:x:6:root
11:wheel:x:10:root

To search for the pattern "root" in */etc/group* and exclude the lines in the output that contain this pattern, use the –v option:

$ grep –v root /etc/group
tty:x:5:
lp:x:7:daemon,lp
mem:x:8:
. . . .

To search for all lines in the */etc/passwd* file that begin with the pattern "root". The BASH shell treats the caret (^) sign as a special character which marks the beginning of a line or word. This is useful, for instance, if you want to know whether there are more than one users by that name.

$ grep ^root /etc/passwd
root:x:0:0:root:/root:/bin/bash

To list all lines from the */etc/passwd* file that end with the pattern "bash". The BASH shell treats the dollar ($) sign as a special character which marks the end of a line or word. This is useful, for example, to determine which users have their shells set to the BASH shell.

$ grep bash$ /etc/passwd
root:x:0:0:root:/root:/bin/bash
user1:x:503:503::/home/user1:/bin/bash
user2:x:504:504::/home/user2:/bin/bash
user3:x:505:505::/home/user3:/bin/bash
user4:x:506:506::/home/user4:/bin/bash

To search for all empty lines in the */etc/passwd* file:

$ grep ^$ /etc/passwd

To search for all lines in the */etc/passwd* file that contain only the pattern "root":

$ grep ^root$ /etc/passwd

To search for all lines in the */etc/passwd* file that contain the pattern "root". The –i option used with the *grep* command here ignores letter case. This is useful to determine if there are *root* user accounts with a combination of lowercase and uppercase letters.

$ grep –i root /etc/passwd
root:x:0:0:root:/root:/bin/bash

To print all lines from the output of the *ll* command that contain either "drwx" or "xin" pattern, run either of the following:

$ ll /etc | grep –E 'drwx|xin'
$ ll /etc | egrep 'drwx|xin'
-rw-r--r--   1 root root   1001 Dec 6 2006 xinetd.conf
drwxr-xr-x 2 root root   4096 Feb 19 14:08 xinetd.d

Comparing File Contents

The *diff* (difference) command finds differences between contents of text files and prints them line-by-line on the screen. Two options –i and –c are commonly used to ignore letter case and produce a list of differences in three sections.

For example, assume that you have two text files *testfile1* and *testfile2* with the following contents:

testfile1	testfile2
apple	apple
pear	tomato
mango	guava
tomato	mango
guava	banana

Run the *diff* command to display the results in three sections:

```
$ diff –c testfile1 testfile2
*** testfile1   2008-11-26 16:50:15.000000000 -0500
--- testfile2   2008-11-26 16:50:35.000000000 -0500
***************
*** 1,5 ****
  apple
- pear
- mango
  tomato
  guava
--- 1,5 ----
  apple
  tomato
  guava
+ mango
+ banana
```

The first section shows the file names being compared along with time stamps on them and some fifteen asterisk (*) characters to mark the end of this section.

The second section tells the number of lines in *testfile1* that differs from *testfile2* and the total number of lines *testfile1* contains. Then it prints the actual line entries from *testfile1*. Each line that differs from *testfile2* is preceded by the (−) symbol.

The third section tells the number of lines in *testfile2* that differs from *testfile1* and the total number of lines *testfile2* contains. Then it prints the actual line entries from *testfile2*. Each line that differs from *testfile1* is preceded by the (+) symbol.

Now, if you wish to make the contents of the two files identical, you will need to remove entries for pear and mango from *testfile1* and append entries for mango and banana to *testfile1*.

You can also use the *diff* command to find differences in directory contents. The syntax is the same.

Finding Files

Sometimes you need to find one or more files or directories in the file system structure based on a criterion. RHEL offers two tools to help you in that situation. These tools are called *find* and *locate*, and are explained in the following sub-sections.

Finding Files Using the find Command

The *find* command recursively searches the directory tree, finds files that match the specified criteria and optionally performs an action. This powerful tool can be customized to look for files in a number of ways. The search criteria may include searching for files by name, size, ownership, group membership, last access or modification time, permissions, file type and inode number. Here is the command syntax:

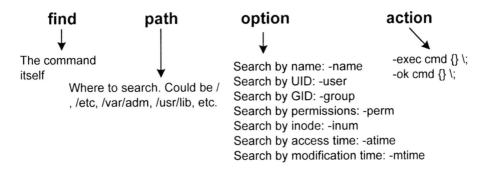

find — The command itself

path — Where to search. Could be / , /etc, /var/adm, /usr/lib, etc.

option —
Search by name: -name
Search by UID: -user
Search by GID: -group
Search by permissions: -perm
Search by inode: -inum
Search by access time: -atime
Search by modification time: -mtime

action —
-exec cmd {} \;
-ok cmd {} \;

With the *find* command, files that match the specified criteria are located and the full path to each file is displayed on the screen. Let us look at a few examples.

To search for *file2* in *user1*'s home directory */home/user1* (assuming *file2* exists):

```
$ cd
$ find . –name file2 –print
./file2
```

–print is optional. The *find* command, by default, displays results on the screen. You do not have to specify this option.

To search for files and directories in */dev* directory that begin with "vol" followed by any characters. The –i option forces the command to perform a case insensitive search.

```
# find /dev –iname vol*
/dev/VolGroup00
/dev/mapper/VolGroup00-lvol7
/dev/mapper/VolGroup00-lvol2
/dev/mapper/VolGroup00-lvol3
/dev/mapper/VolGroup00-lvol4
/dev/mapper/VolGroup00-lvol5
. . . . . . . .
```

To find files smaller than 1GB in size in *root*'s home directory:

```
# find ~ –size –1G
/root
. . . . . . . .
```

The tilde (~) character is used to represent a user's home directory. See Chapter 05 "The Shells" for details.

To find files larger than 100MB in size in */usr* directory:

> # **find /usr –size +100M**

To find files in */home* with both ownership and group membership set to *user1*:

> # **find /home –user user1 –group user1**
> /home/user1
> /home/user1/.lesshst
> . . . .

To find files in */home* with ownership set to *user1* and group membership set to any group but *user1*:

> # **find /home –user user1 –not –group user1**

To find all core files in */* that are not owned by *root*:

> # **find / –name core –not –user root**

To find files in */etc/rc.d* directory that were modified more than 120 days ago:

> # **find /etc/rc.d –mtime +120**
> /etc/rc.d/rc
> /etc/rc.d/rc.local
> . . . .

To find files in */etc/rc.d* directory that have not been accessed in the last 90 days:

> # **find /etc/rc.d –atime –90**
> /etc/rc.d
> /etc/rc.d/rc2.d
> . . . .

To find files in */etc/rc.d* directory that were modified exactly 10 days ago:

> # **find /etc/rc.d –mtime 10**

To search for character device files in */dev* directory with permissions 666:

> # **find /dev –type c –perm 666**
> /dev/full
> /dev/random
> . . . .

In the above example, two criteria are defined and files that match both criteria are displayed. The criteria are to look for files that are character device files with read and write permissions for all users.

To search for symbolic link files in *usr* directory with permissions 777:

 # find /usr –type l –perm 777
/usr/X11R6/bin/mkfontscale
/usr/X11R6/bin/mkfontdir

. . . .

To search for files in *usr* directory that have at least 444 permissions:

 # find /usr –perm –444
/usr
/usr/games

. . . .

To search for character device files in */dev* directory that are world writeable:

 # find /dev –type c –perm –222
/dev/full
/dev/random

. . . .

To search for block device files in */dev* directory that have write bit set at any of the three levels:

 # find /dev –type c –perm +222
/dev/md0
/dev/fd0u800
/dev/fd0u1120

. . . .

To search for *core* files in the entire directory tree and delete them as found without prompting for confirmation:

 # find / –name core –exec rm {} \;

 The pattern "{} \;" is part of the syntax and must be defined that way.

To search for *core* files in the entire directory tree and prompt to delete them as found:

 # find / –name core –ok rm {} \;

To search for *core* files in the entire directory tree and rename them as *core.old*:

 # find / –name core –exec mv {} {}.old \;

Finding Files Using the locate Command

The *locate* command is used for locating all occurrences of the specified string as it appears in file pathnames. It can also be used to locate files with certain extensions. The command searches the */var/lib/mlocate/mlocate.db* database file and displays matching occurrences. This file is updated automatically every day when the */etc/cron.daily/mlocate.cron* script is executed by the *cron* daemon. Alternatively, it can be updated manually with the *updatedb* command. The output is the absolute path of files and directories on which the user has access permissions. The security enhanced version of the *locate* command is the *slocate* command whose database file is */var/lib/slocate/slocate.db*. Here are a few examples to explain how the *locate* command works.

To locate all occurrences of the string "passwd":

> **$ locate passwd**
> /etc/passwd
> /etc/passwd-
> . . . .

Use the –n option to specify how many occurrences you wish to display:

> **$ locate –n 3 passwd**
> /etc/passwd
> /etc/passwd-
> /etc/pam.d/passwd

To locate all files with .sh extension and list the first five of them:

> **$ locate –n 5 .sh**
> /etc/X11/xinit/xinitrc.d/localuser.sh
> /etc/X11/xinit/xinitrc.d/sabayon-xinitrc.sh
> . . . .

Sorting File Contents

Sorting allows you to arrange columns of text in a specified order. The *sort* command is used for this purpose. This command sorts contents of one or more files and prints the result on the screen. You can sort file contents in either alphabetic (default) or numeric order.

Let us look at a few examples to understand the usage of *sort*.

Consider a file *file10* in *user1*'s home directory with the following text in two columns. The first column contains alphabets and the second numbers.

> Maryland 667
> Mississippi 662
> Pennsylvania 445
> Missouri 975
> Florida 772
> Montana 406
> Massachusetts 339

To sort this file alphabetically:

    $ sort file10
    Florida 772
    Maryland 667
    Massachusetts 339
    Mississippi 662
    Missouri 975
    Montana 406
    Pennsylvania 445

To sort this file numerically (–n option) on the second column (–k option):

    $ sort –k 2 –n file10
    Massachusetts **339**
    Montana **406**
    Pennsylvania **445**
    Mississippi **662**
    Maryland **667**
    Florida **772**
    Missouri **975**

To sort *file10* numerically but in reverse order (–r option):

    $ sort –k 2 –nr file10
    Missouri **975**
    Florida **772**
    Maryland **667**
    Mississippi **662**
    Pennsylvania **445**
    Montana **406**
    Massachusetts **339**

To sort the output of the *ll* command:

```
# ll / | sort
drwx------     2 root root 16384 Oct   9 12:57 lost+found
drwxrwxrwt  6 root root   4096 Nov 26 17:57 tmp
drwxr-xr-x  11 root root      0 Nov  5 18:03 sys
drwxr-xr-x  11 root root   3660 Nov 26 17:13 dev
drwxr-xr-x  12 root root   4096 Oct 16 12:48 lib
```

To sort on the 6th column (month) of the *ll* command output:

```
$ ll –a /etc/skel | sort –k 6M
total 64
drwxr-xr-x 95 root root  12288 Feb 20 00:44 ..
-rw-r--r--  1 root root    124 Feb  1 2008 .bashrc
-rw-r--r--  1 root root    176 Feb  1 2008 .bash_profile
```

```
-rw-r--r--    1 root root      33 Feb  1 2008 .bash_logout
drwxr-xr-x  4 root root    4096 Apr 28 2008 .mozilla
drwxr-xr-x  3 root root    4096 Oct 15 08:36 .
-rw-r--r--    1 root root     515 Dec 10 2007 .emacs
```

By default, the output of *sort* is displayed on the screen but if you like it to be redirected to a file, you can use the –o option. The example below saves the output in */tmp/sort.out* and does not display it on the screen:

> **$ ll /etc/skel | sort –k 6M –o /tmp/sort.out**

To sort on the 6th and then on the 7th column, do the following. This is an example of multi-level sorting.

```
$ ll –a /etc/skel | sort –k 6M –k 7
total 64
-rw-r--r--    1 root root      33 Feb  1 2008 .bash_logout
-rw-r--r--    1 root root     176 Feb  1 2008 .bash_profile
-rw-r--r--    1 root root     124 Feb  1 2008 .bashrc
drwxr-xr-x 95 root root 12288 Feb 20 00:44 ..
drwxr-xr-x  4 root root    4096 Apr 28  2008 .mozilla
drwxr-xr-x  3 root root    4096 Oct 15 08:36 .
-rw-r--r--    1 root root     515 Dec 10  2007 .emacs
```

There are numerous other options available with the *sort* command. Try them to build a better understanding. Refer to the command's man pages.

Linking Files and Directories

Each file in the system has a unique number assigned to it at the time it is created. This number is referred to as its *inode* (index node) number. All file attributes such as name, type, size, permissions, ownership, group membership and last access/modification time are maintained in that inode. Moreover, the inode points to the exact location in the file system where the file data is written. See Chapter 14 "File Systems and Swap" for details on inodes.

Linking files or directories means that you have more than one instance of them pointing to the same physical data location in the directory tree.

There are two types of links: *soft* links and *hard* links.

Soft Link

A *soft* link (a.k.a. *symbolic* link or *symlink*) makes it possible to associate one file with another. It is similar to a "shortcut" in MS Windows where the actual file resides somewhere in the directory structure but you may have multiple "shortcuts" or "pointers" with different names pointing to that file. This means accessing the file via the actual file name or any of the shortcuts would yield the same result. Each soft link has a unique inode number.

A soft link can cross file system boundaries and can be used to link directories.

To create a soft link for *file1* as *file10* in the same directory, use the *ln* command with –s option:

```
$ cd /home/user1
$ ln –s file1 file10
```

where:

> *file1* is an existing file
> *file10* is soft linked to *file1*

After you have created the link, do an *ll* with –i option. Notice the letter "l" as the first character in the second column of the output. Also notice an arrow pointing from the linked file to the original file. This indicates that *file10* is merely a pointer to *file1*. The –i option displays associated inode numbers in the first column.

```
$ ll –i
2453226 -rw-rw-r--  1  user1 user1 0 Jun 1 07:18 file1
2453227 lrwxrwxrwx 1  user1 user1 5 Jun 1 07:18 file10 -> file1
```

Run the *stat* command on the original and the linked file and compare the differences:

```
$ stat file1
  File: `file1'
  Size: 0            Blocks: 8          IO Block: 4096   regular empty file
Device: fd00h/64768d    Inode: 6389800     Links: 1
Access: (0664/-rw-rw-r--)  Uid: ( 500/ user1)    Gid: ( 500/ user1)
Access: 2009-06-01 07:18:38.000000000 -0400
Modify: 2009-06-01 07:18:38.000000000 -0400
Change: 2009-06-01 07:18:38.000000000 -0400
$ stat file10
  File: `file10' -> `file1'
  Size: 5            Blocks: 8          IO Block: 4096   symbolic link
Device: fd00h/64768d    Inode: 6389801     Links: 1
Access: (0777/lrwxrwxrwx)  Uid: ( 500/ user1)    Gid: ( 500/ user1)
Access: 2009-06-01 07:18:43.000000000 -0400
Modify: 2009-06-01 07:18:42.000000000 -0400
Change: 2009-06-01 07:18:42.000000000 -0400
```

If you remove the original file (*file1* in this example), the link (*file10*) stays but points to something that does not exist.

Hard Link

A *hard* link associates two or more files with a single inode number. This allows the files to have the same permissions, ownership, time stamp and file contents. Changes made to any of the files are reflected on the other linked files. All files will actually contain identical data.

A hard link cannot cross file system boundaries and cannot be used to link directories.

The following example uses the *ln* command and creates a hard link for *file2* located under */home/user1* to *file20* in the same directory. *file20* does not currently exist, it will be created.

```
$ cd /home/user1
$ ln file2 file20
```

After creating the link, do an *ll* with –i option:

```
$ ll –i
1179661  -rw-rw-r-- 2 user1 user1 0 Nov 26 20:46 file2
1179661  -rw-rw-r-- 2 user1 user1 0 Nov 26 20:46 file20
```

Look at the first and the third columns. The first column indicates that both files have identical inode numbers and the third column tells that each file has two hard links. *file2* points to *file20* and vice versa. If you remove the original file (*file2* in this example), you still will have access to the data through the linked file (*file20*).

The inode information can be confirmed with the *stat* command as well.

Summary

In this chapter, you got an overview of the RHEL file system structure and significant higher level sub-directories that consisted of either static or variable files and were logically grouped into lower level sub-directories. The files and sub-directories were accessed using path relative to either the top-most directory of the file system structure or your current location in the tree.

You learned about different types of files and a set of rules to adhere to when creating files or directories. You looked at several file and directory manipulation tools such as creating, listing, displaying, copying, moving, renaming and removing them.

Searching for text within files and searching for files within the directory structure using specified criteria provided you with an understanding and explanation of tools required to perform such tasks.

Finally, you studied how to sort contents of a text file or output generated by executing a command in ascending and descending orders. The last topic discussed creating soft and hard links between files and between directories.

## 03

File and Directory Permissions

This chapter covers the following major topics:

✓ File and directory permissions assigned to owners, members of owner's group, and others
✓ Types of permissions based on read, write and execute requirements
✓ Modes of permissions based on adding, revoking and assigning permissions
✓ Modify file and directory permissions using symbolic and octal notations, and Nautilus file manager
✓ Set default permissions on new files and directories
✓ Modify ownership and group membership on files and directories
✓ Configure special permissions on executable files and directories with setuid, setgid and sticky bits

Permissions are set on files and directories to prevent access by unauthorized

users. Users on the system are grouped into three distinct categories. Each user category is then assigned required permissions.

Determining Access Permissions

The following sub-sections elaborate on file and directory permissions.

Permission Classes

Users on the system are categorized into three distinct classes for the purpose of maintaining file security through permissions. These classes are described in Table 3-1.

Permission Class	Description
User (u)	Owner of file or directory. Usually, the creator of a file or directory is the owner of it.
Group (g)	A set of users that need identical access on files and directories that they share. Group information is maintained in the /etc/group file and users are assigned to groups according to shared file access needs.
Others (o)	All other users that have access to the system except the owner and group members. Also called *public*.

Table 3-1 Permission Classes

Permission Types

Permissions control what actions can be performed on a file or directory and by whom. There are four types of permissions as defined in Table 3-2.

Permission Type	Symbol	File	Directory
Read	r	Displays file contents or copies contents to another file.	Displays contents with the *ll* command.
Write	w	Modifies file contents.	Creates, removes, or renames files and sub-directories.
Execute	x	Executes a file.	*cd* into the directory.
Access Denied	-	None.	None.

Table 3-2 Permission Types

Permission Modes

A permission mode is used to add, revoke or assign a permission type to a permission class. Table 3-3 shows various permission modes.

Permission Mode	Description
Add (+)	Gives specified permission(s).
Revoke (-)	Removes specified permission(s).
Assign (=)	Gives specified permission(s) to owner, group members and public in one go.

Table 3-3 Permission Modes

The output of the *ll* command lists files and directories along with their type and permission settings. This information is shown in the first column of the output where 10 characters are displayed. The first character indicates the type of file: d for directory, – for regular file, l for symbolic link, c for character device file, b for block device file, n for named pipe, s for socket, and so on. The next nine characters – three groups of three characters – show read (r), write (w), execute (x) or none (-) permission for the three user classes: user, group and others, respectively.

Figure 3-1 illustrates the *ll* command output and its various components.

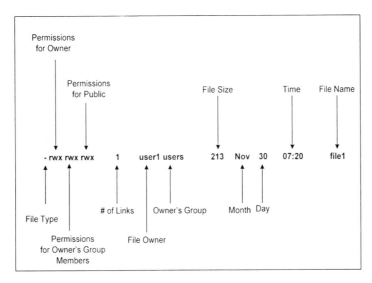

Figure 3-1 Permission Settings

From Figure 3-1, it is obvious who the owner (3rd column) of the file is and which group (4th column) the owner belongs to.

Changing Access Permissions

The *chmod* command is used to modify access permissions on files and directories. *chmod* can be used by *root* or file owner, and can modify permissions specified in one of two methods: *symbolic* or *octal*. Permissions can also be modified using the graphical Nautilus file manager.

Using Symbolic Notation

Symbolic notation uses a combination of letters and symbols to add, revoke or assign permissions to each class of users. The following examples and their explanation provide an understanding on how to set file permissions. It works in an identical fashion on directories.

Suppose there is a file called *file1* with read permission for the owner, group members and others. This file is owned by *user1* who will be modifying permissions in the following examples.

    -r--r--r-- 1 user1 user1 0 Nov 26 20:45 file1

To add execute permission for the owner:

   $ chmod u+x file1
   -r-xr--r-- 1 user1 user1 0 Nov 26 20:45 file1

To add write permission for the owner:

   $ chmod u+w file1
   -rwxr--r-- 1 user1 user1 0 Nov 26 20:45 file1

To add write permission for group members and public:

   $ chmod go+w file1
   -rwxrw-rw- 1 user1 user1 0 Nov 26 20:45 file1

To remove write permission for public:

   $ chmod o-w file1
   -rwxrw-r-- 1 user1 user1 0 Nov 26 20:45 file1

To assign read, write and execute permissions to all three user categories:

   $ chmod a=rwx file1
   -rwxrwxrwx 1 user1 user1 0 Nov 26 20:45 file1

Using Octal (or Absolute) Notation

The octal notation uses a three-digit numbering system that ranges from 0 to 7 to specify permissions for the three user classes. Octal values are given in Table 3-4.

Octal Value	Binary Notation	Symbolic Notation	Explanation
0	000	---	No permissions.
1	001	--x	Execute permission only.
2	010	-w-	Write permission only.
3	011	-wx	Write and execute permissions.
4	100	r--	Read permission only.
5	101	r-x	Read and execute permissions.
6	110	rw-	Read and write permissions.
7	111	rwx	Read, write and execute permissions.

Table 3-4 Octal Permission Notation

From Table 3-4, it is obvious that each "1" corresponds to an "r", a "w" or an "x", and each "0" corresponds to the "–" character for no permission at that level. Figure 3-2 shows weights associated with each digit location in the 3-digit octal numbering model. The right-most location has weight 1, the middle location carries weight 2 and the left-most location has 4. When you assign a permission of 6, for example, it would correspond to the two left-most digit locations. Similarly, a permission of 2 would mean only the middle digit location.

Figure 3-2 Permission Weights

The following examples and their explanation provide an understanding on how to set file permissions using octal method. It works in an identical fashion on directories.

Suppose you have a file called *file2* with read permission for the owner, group members and others. This file is owned by *user1* who will be modifying permissions in the following examples.

```
-r--r--r-- 1 user1 user1 0 Nov 26 21:19 file2
```

The current permissions on *file2* in the octal notation are 444, where each digit represents one class of users. The first 4 is for file owner, the second for owner's group members and the third for everyone else.

To add execute permission for the file owner:

$ chmod 544 file2
```
-r-xr--r-- 1 user1 user1 0 Nov 26 21:19 file2
```

To add write permission for the owner:

$ chmod 744 file2
```
-rwxr--r-- 1 user1 user1 0 Nov 26 21:19 file2
```

To add write permission for group members and others:

$ chmod 766 file2
```
-rwxrw-rw- 1 user1 user1 0 Nov 26 21:19 file2
```

To revoke write permission from public users:

$ chmod 764 file2
```
-rwxrw-r-- 1 user1 user1 0 Nov 26 21:19 file2
```

To assign read, write and execute permissions to all three user categories:

$ chmod 777 file2
```
-rwxrwxrwx 1 user1 user1 0 Nov 26 21:19 file2
```

Using Nautilus File Manager

Execute the *nautilus* command at the X terminal window prompt to start the Nautilus file manager. By default, Nautilus displays the home directory contents of the user who runs it. When Nautilus is up, right click on a file or directory, select Properties and then click the Permissions tab to view or modify permissions. See Figure 3-3.

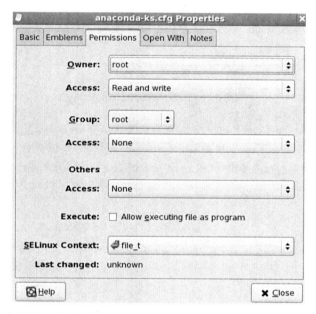

Figure 3-3 View/Modify Permissions with Nautilus File Manager

Setting Default Permissions

The system assigns *default permissions* to a file or directory when it is created. Default permissions are calculated based on the *umask* (user mask) permission value subtracted from a pre-defined value called *initial* permissions.

The umask is a three-digit value that refers to read/write/execute permissions for owner, group and others. Its purpose is to set default permissions on new files and directories. In RHEL, the default umask value is set to 0022 for the *root* user and 0002 for all regular users who use the BASH shell. Run the *umask* command without any options to display the current umask value:

$ **umask**
0002

Run the *umask* command with –S option to display the current umask in symbolic notation:

$ **umask –S**
u=rwx,g=rwx,o=rx

Different shells have different default umask values for regular users. For example, the Korn shell has 0022 and the C shell 22.

The pre-defined initial permission values are 666 (rw-rw-rw-) for files and 777 (rwxrwxrwx) for directories.

Calculating Default Permissions

Here is how you would calculate default permission values on files:

Initial Permissions	666	
umask	– 022	(subtract)
=========================		
Default Permissions	644	

This indicates that every new file will have read and write permissions assigned to owner, and read-only permission to owner's group members and public.

To calculate default permission values on directories:

Initial Permissions	777	
umask	– 022	(subtract)
=========================		
Default Permissions	755	

This indicates that every new directory will have read, write and execute permissions assigned to owner, and read and execute permissions to owner's group members and public.

If you wish to have different default permissions set on new files and directories, you need to modify umask. First determine what default values are needed. For example, if you want all your new files and directories to have 640 and 750 permissions, respectively, run *umask* and set the value to 027 as follows:

$ umask 027

The new umask value becomes effective right away. Note that the new umask is applied only on the files and directories created after the umask is changed. The existing files and directories will remain intact. Create a file *file10* and a directory *dir10* as *user1* under */home/user1* and test the effect of the change.

```
$ touch file10
$ ll file10
-rw-r----- 1 user1 user1    0 Nov 27 07:43 file10
$ mkdir dir10
$ ll –d dir10
drwxr-x--- 2 user1 user1 4096 Nov 27 07:43 dir10
```

The above examples show that new files and directories are created with different permissions. The files have (666 – 027 = 640) and directories have (777 – 027 = 750) permissions.

The umask value set at the command line is lost as soon as you log off. In order to retain the new setting, place it in one of the shell initialization files. Customizing shell initialization files is covered in Chapter 12 "Users and Groups".

Changing File Ownership and Group Membership

In RHEL, every file and directory has an owner associated with it. By default, the creator becomes the owner. The ownership can be altered if required, and allocated to some other user.

Similarly, every user is a member of one or more groups. A group is a collection of users with exact same privileges. By default, the owner's group is assigned to a file or directory.

For example, below is an output from the *ll* command ran on *file10*:

```
$ ll file10
-rw-r----- 1 user1 user1   0 Nov 27 07:43 file10
```

The output indicates that the owner of *file10* is *user1* who belongs to group *user1*. If you wish to view the corresponding UID and GID instead, run the *ll* command with –n option:

```
$ ll –n file10
-rw-r----- 1 500 500   0 Nov 27 07:43 file10
```

Use the *chown* and *chgrp* commands to alter ownership and group membership on files and directories. You must be *root* to make this modification. Consider the following examples.

To change ownership from *user1* to *user2*:

```
# chown user2 file10
# ll file10
-rw-r----- 1 user2 user1   0 Nov 27 07:43 file10
```

To change group membership from *user1* to *user2*:

```
# chgrp user2 file10
# ll file10
-rw-r----- 1 user2 user2   0 Nov 27 07:43 file10
```

To modify both ownership and group membership in one go:

```
# chown user1:user1 file10
# ll file10
-rw-r----- 1 user1 user1   0 Nov 27 07:43 file10
```

To modify recursively all files and sub-directories under *dir1* to be owned by *user2* and group *user2*:

```
# chown –R user2:user2 dir1
```

Special Permissions

There are three types of special permission bits that may be setup on executable files or directories if required. These permission bits are:

- ✓ *setuid* (set user identification) bit
- ✓ *setgid* (set group identification) bit
- ✓ *sticky* bit

The setuid Bit

The setuid bit is set on executable files at the file owner level. When this bit is enabled, the file will be executed by other users with exact same privileges as that of the file owner. For example, the *su* command is owned by *root* with group membership set to *root*. This command has setuid bit enabled on it by default. See the highlighted "s" in the owner's permission class below:

$ ll /bin/su
-rwsr-xr-x 1 root root 28336 Nov 30 2007 /bin/su

When a normal user executes this command, it will run as if *root* (the owner) is running it and, therefore, the user is able to run it successfully and gets the desired result.

The *su* (switch user) command allows a user to switch to some other user's account provided the switching user knows the password of the user he is trying to switch into.

Now, let us remove the bit from *su* and replace it with an "x":

 # chmod 755 /bin/su
-rwxr-xr-x 1 root root 28336 Nov 30 2007 /bin/su

The file is still executable, but when a normal user runs it, he will be running it as himself and not as *root*. Here is what will happen when *user1* tries to *su* into *user2* and enters a valid password:

$ su – user2
Password:
su: incorrect password

user1 gets the "incorrect password" message even though he entered correct login credentials.

To set setuid bit back on *su* or on some other file:

 # chmod 4755 /bin/su

When digit 4 is used with the *chmod* command in this manner, it sets the setuid bit on the file. Alternatively, you can use the symbolic notation to get exact same results:

 # chmod u+s /bin/su

To unset the setuid bit:

 # chmod u-s /bin/su

To search for all files in the system that have setuid bit set on them, use the *find* command:

```
# find / –perm –4000
```

The setgid Bit

The setgid bit is set on executable files at the group level. When this bit is enabled, the file will be executed by other users with exact same privileges that the group members have on it. For example, the *write* command is owned by *root* with group membership set to *tty*. This command has setgid bit enabled on it. See the highlighted "s" in the group's permission class below:

```
$ ll /usr/bin/write
-rwxr-sr-x  1  root  tty  14400  Mar  3  2008  /usr/bin/write
```

When a normal user executes this command, it will run as if a member of tty group is running it and, therefore, the user will be able to run it successfully and get the desired result.

To set the setgid bit on */home/user1/file10* you must either be the owner of the file or *root*:

```
$ chmod 2555 file10
$ ll
-r-xr-sr-x  1  user1  user1    0  Nov 27 07:43  file10
```

When digit 2 is used with the *chmod* command in this manner, it sets the setgid bit on the file. Alternatively, you can use the symbolic notation to get exact same results:

```
$ chmod g+s file10
```

To unset the setgid bit:

```
# chmod g-s /bin/su
```

To search for all files in the system that have setgid bit set, use the *find* command:

```
# find / –perm –2000
```

You may wish to setup setgid bit on a directory shared by members of a group. In this case you will need to create a group and add members to it who will need to share the directory. Let us call the directory */sdata1* and the group *sdata1grp*. Set appropriate permissions on the directory and add members to the group in the */etc/group* file. This will give the group members the ability to share files in the directory.

To set the setgid bit on the shared directory, issue the *chmod* command as follows:

```
$ mkdir /sdata1
$ chmod 2770 /sdata1
```

The Sticky Bit

The sticky bit is set on public writable directories to protect files and sub-directories of individual users from being deleted by other users. This bit is typically set on */tmp* and */var/tmp* directories.

Normally, all users are allowed to create and delete files and sub-directories in these directories. With default permissions, any user can remove any other user's files and sub-directories.

Here is how you would set sticky bit on */tmp* and */var/tmp*:

>   # **chmod 1777 /tmp**
>   # **chmod 1777 /var/tmp**

When digit 1 is used with the *chmod* command in this manner, it sets sticky bit on the specified directory. Alternatively, you can use the symbolic notation to do exactly the same:

>   # **chmod o+t /tmp**
>   # **chmod o+t /var/tmp**

After setting up sticky bits on the directories above, do an *ll* and you will notice the character "t" in other's permissions. This indicates that sticky bit is enabled.

>   # **ll –ld /tmp /var/tmp**
>   drwxrwxrwt 6 root root 4096 Nov 27 07:31 /tmp
>   drwxrwxrwt 2 root root 4096 Nov 5 18:01 /var/tmp

To search for all directories in the system that have sticky bit set, use the *find* command:

>   # **find / –type d –perm –1000**

Summary

In this chapter you learned about file and directory permissions assigned to their owners, members of the group that the owner belonged to, and other users. You looked at types and modes of permissions and how to modify them using symbolic and octal notations as well as the Nautilus file manager.

You studied how default permissions could be setup on new files and directories, and the role of umask value in determining new default permissions.

Then you saw how a user could alter his primary group membership temporarily and how a user or root could modify ownership and group membership on files and directories.

Finally, you learned about setting special permission bits on executable files and directories.

## 04

Text Editors and Processors

This chapter covers the following major topics:

- ✓ Modes of operation for the vi editor
- ✓ Start and quit the vi editor
- ✓ Navigate within vi
- ✓ Manipulate text
- ✓ Save modifications
- ✓ Customize vi settings
- ✓ Use nano text editor
- ✓ Manipulate columns of text using the awk text processor
- ✓ Manipulate rows of text using the sed text processor

As a system administrator you need to edit text files as required. RHEL provides several text editors for this purpose. Editors such as vi are very common among administrators. There are additional text editors that are included in RHEL. These include an enhanced and improved version of vi called *vim* (vi improved) and *nano* (nano's another).

The vim editor is basically the vi editor but provides several additional features such as multi-level undo, multi-window support, syntax highlighting, command line editing, tab completion, online help and visual selection.

Nano, on the other hand, is an enhanced editor of yet another text editor called *pico*. Nano provides simple editing functions similar to what the notepad tool provides in MS Windows.

The following sections provide details on the vi (also applicable to vim) and nano editors.

The vi (vim) Editor

The vi editor is an interactive *visual* text editor tool that enables a user to create and modify text files. It was written by Bill Joy in the mid 1970s. All text editing with the vi editor takes place in a buffer (a small chunk of memory used to hold updates being done to the file). Changes can either be written to the disk or discarded.

It is essential for system administrators to master the vi editor skills. The following sub-sections provide details on how to use and interact with vi.

Modes of Operation

The vi editor has three basic modes of operation:

1. Command mode
2. Edit mode
3. Last line mode

Command Mode

The *command* mode is the default mode of vi. The vi editor places you into this mode when you start it. While in the command mode, you can carry out tasks such as copy, cut, paste, move, remove, replace, change and search on text, in addition to performing navigational tasks. This mode is also known as the *escape* mode as the Esc key is pressed to enter it.

Input Mode

In *input* mode, anything you type at the keyboard is entered into the file as text. Commands cannot be run in this mode. The input mode is also called the *edit* mode or the *insert* mode. To retrun to the command mode, press the Esc key.

Last Line Mode

While in the command mode, you may carry out advanced editing tasks on text by pressing the colon (:) character, which places the cursor at the beginning of the last line of the screen and hence referred to as the *last line* mode. This mode is considered a special type of command mode.

Starting the vi Editor

The vi editor may be started in one of the ways described in Table 4-1. Use the *vimtutor* command to view the man pages of vi.

Method	Description
vi	Starts vi and opens up an empty screen for you to enter text. You can save or discard the text entered later as you wish.
vi *existing_file*	Starts vi and loads the specified file for editing or viewing.
vi *new_file*	Starts vi and creates the specified file when saved.

Table 4-1 Starting The vi Editor

Inserting text

To begin entering text, issue one of the commands described in Table 4-2 from the command mode to switch to the edit mode.

Command	Action
i	Inserts text before the current cursor position.
I	Inserts text at the beginning of the current line.
a	Appends text after the current cursor position.
A	Appends text at the end of the current line.
o	Opens up a new line below the current line.
O	Opens up a new line above the current line.

Table 4-2 Inserting Text

Press the Esc key when done to return to the command mode.

Navigating within vi

Table 4-3 elaborates key sequences that control cursor movement while you are in the vi editor. You must be in the command mode to move around.

Command	Action
h / left arrow / Backspace / Ctrl+h	Moves left (backward) one character.
j / down arrow	Moves down one line.
k / up arrow	Moves up one line.
l / right arrow / Spacebar	Moves right (forward) one character.
5 right arrow / Spacebar	Moves right (forward) five characters. Change the number to move that many characters.
5 left arrow	Moves left (backward) five characters. Change the number to move that many characters.
5 up / down arrow	Moves up / down five lines. Change the number to move that many lines.
W or w	Moves forward one word.
B or b	Moves backward one word.
E or e	Moves forward to the last character of the next word.

Command	Action
M	Moves to the line in the middle of the page.
$	Moves to the end of the current line.
0 (zero) or ^	Moves to the beginning of the current line.
Enter	Moves down to the beginning of the next line.
Ctrl+f / Page Down	Moves forward to the next page (scrolls down).
Ctrl+d	Moves forward one-half page (scrolls down).
Ctrl+b / Page Up	Moves backward to the previous page (scrolls up).
Ctrl+u	Moves backward one-half page (scrolls up).
G or]]	Moves to the last line of the file.
(	Moves backward to the beginning of the current sentence.
)	Moves forward to the beginning of the next sentence.
{	Moves backward to the beginning of the preceding paragraph.
}	Moves forward to the beginning of the next paragraph.
1G or [[or :1	Moves to the first line of the file.
:11 or 11G	Moves to the specified line number (such as line number 11).
Ctrl+g	Tells you what line number you are at.

Table 4-3 Navigating Within vi

Deleting Text

Commands listed in Table 4-4 are available to perform delete operations. You must be in the command mode to accomplish these tasks.

Command	Action
x	Deletes a character at the current cursor position. You may type a digit before this command to delete that many characters. For example, 2x would remove two characters, 3x would remove 3 characters and so on.
X	Deletes a character before the current cursor location. You may type a digit before this command to delete that many characters. For example, 2X would remove two characters, 3X would remove 3 characters and so on.
dw	Deletes a word or part of the word to the right of the current cursor location. You may type a digit before this command to delete that many words. For example, 2w would remove two words, 3w would remove 3 words and so on.
dd	Deletes the current line. You may type a digit before this command to delete that many lines. For example, 2dd would remove two lines, 3dd would remove 3 lines and so on.
d)	Deletes at the current cursor position to the end of the current sentence.
d(	Deletes at the current cursor position to the beginning of the last sentence.
d}	Deletes at the current cursor position to the end of the current paragraph.
d{	Deletes at the current cursor position to the beginning of the last paragraph.
D	Deletes at the current cursor position to the end of the current line.
:6,12d	Deletes lines 6 through 12.

Table 4-4 Deleting Text

Undoing and Repeating

Table 4-5 explains commands available to undo the last change you did and repeat the last command you ran. You must be in the command mode to perform the tasks.

Command	Action
u	Undoes the last command.
U	Undoes all changes at the current line.
:u	Undoes the previous last line mode command.
. (dot)	Repeats the last command that was run.
Ctrl+r	Repeats the last undone command.

Table 4-5 Undoing and Repeating

Searching and Replacing Text

Search and replace text functions are performed using commands mentioned in Table 4-6. You must be in command mode to do these tasks.

Command	Action
/string	Searches forward for string.
?string	Searches backward for string.
n	Finds next occurrence of string. This would only work if you have run either a forward or a backward string search.
N	Finds previous occurrence of string. This would only work if you have run either a forward or a backward string search.
:%s/old/new	Searches and replaces the first occurrence of *old* with *new*. For example, to replace first occurrence of "profile" with "Profile", you would use ":%s/profile/Profile".
:%s/old/new/g	Searches and replaces all occurrences of *old* with *new*. For example, to replace all occurrences of "profile" with "Profile" in the file, you would use ":%s/profile/Profile/g".

Table 4-6 Searching and Replacing Text

Copying, Moving and Pasting Text

The *co* command writes copied text into a temporary buffer. The *P* or *p* command reads text from the temporary buffer and writes it into current file at the specified location. You can also do move and copy functions from the last line mode. See Table 4-7 for further information.

Command	Action
yl	Yanks the current letter into buffer. You may specify a digit before this command to yank that many lines. For example, 2yl yanks two characters, 3yl yanks three characters and so on.
yw	Yanks the current word into buffer. You may specify a digit before this command to yank that many lines. For example, 2yw yanks two words, 3yw yanks three words and so on.
yy	Yanks the current line into buffer. You may specify a digit before this command to yank that many lines. For example, 2yy yanks two

Command	Action
	lines, 3yy yanks three lines and so on.
y)	Yanks the current sentence into buffer. You may specify a digit before this command to yank that many sentences. For example, 2y) yanks two sentences, 3y) yanks three sentences and so on.
y(	Yanks the previous sentence into buffer. You may specify a digit before this command to yank that many sentences. For example, 2y(yanks two previous sentences, 3y(yanks three previous sentences and so on.
y}	Yanks the current paragraph into buffer. You may specify a digit before this command to yank that many paragraphs. For example, 2y} yanks two paragraphs, 3y} yanks three paragraphs and so on.
y{	Yanks the previous paragraphs into buffer. You may specify a digit before this command to yank that many paragraphs. For example, 2y{ yanks two previous paragraphs, 3y{ yanks three previous paragraphs and so on.
p	Pastes yanked data below the current line.
P	Pastes yanked data above the current line.
:1,3co5	Copies lines 1 through 3 and pastes them after line 5.
:4,6m8	Moves lines 4 through 6 after line 8.

Table 4-7 Copying, Moving and Pasting Text

Changing Text

Use commands given in Table 4-8 to change text. Some of these commands take you to the edit mode. To return to the command mode, press the `Esc` key.

Command	Action
cl	Changes the letter at the cursor location.
cw	Changes a word (or part of a word) at the current cursor location to the end of the current word.
C	Changes at the current cursor position to the end of the current line.
r	Replaces character at the current cursor location with the character entered following this command.
R	Overwrites or replaces text on the current line.
s	Substitutes a string for character(s).
S or cc	Substitutes an entire line.
c)	Changes at the current cursor location to the end of the current sentence.
c(	Changes at the current cursor location to the beginning of the last sentence.
c}	Changes at the current cursor location to the end of the current paragraph.
c{	Changes at the current cursor location to the beginning of the last paragraph.
J	Joins the current line and the line below it.
xp	Switches position of the character at the current cursor position with the character to the right of it.
~	Changes letter case (uppercase to lowercase and vice versa) at the current cursor location.

Table 4-8 Changing Text

Importing Contents of Another File

While working in vi you may want to insert contents of some other file. The vi editor allows you to do that. You must be at the last line mode to accomplish this. See Table 4-9.

Command	Action
:r file2	Reads *file2* and inserts its contents below the current line.
:help	Displays help information.

Table 4-9 Importing Contents of Another File

Customizing vi Edit Sessions

The vi editor supports settings to customize edit sessions to display line numbers, invisible characters and so on. Use the *set* command to control these options. Consult Table 4-10.

Command	Action
:set nu	Shows line numbers.
:set nonu	Hides line numbers.
:set ic	Ignores letter case when carrying out searches.
:set noic	Does not ignore letter case when carrying out searches.
:set list	Displays invisible characters such as Tab and End Of Line (EOL).
:set nolist	Hides invisible characters such as Tab and EOL.
:set showmode	Displays current mode of operation.
:set noshowmode	Hides mode of operation.
:set	Displays current vi variable settings.
:set all	Displays all available vi variables and their current settings.

Table 4-10 Customizing vi Settings

Saving and Quitting vi

When you are done with modifications, you will want to save them (or discard them if you want to). Commands listed in Table 4-11 would help.

Command	Action
:w	Writes changes into file without quitting vi.
:w file3	Writes changes into a new file called *file3*.
:w!	Writes changes into file even if file owner does not have write permission on the file.
:wq or :x or ZZ	Writes changes to file and quits vi.
:wq! or :x!	Writes changes into file and quits vi even if file owner does not have write permission on the file.
:q	Quits vi if no modifications were made.
:q!	Quits vi if modifications were made, but you do not wish to save them.

Table 4-11 Saving and Quitting vi

Miscellaneous vi Commands

Table 4-12 describes additional commands available to perform specific tasks within vi.

Command	Action
Ctrl+l	Refreshes the vi screen, if proper terminal type is set.
:sh	Exits vi editor session temporarily. Type *exit* or Ctrl+d to come back.
:!cmd	Executes the specified command without quitting vi.

Table 4-12 Miscellaneous vi Commands

The nano Editor

Many users prefer to use the nano text editor. This editor displays a menu of commands at the bottom of the screen to help you edit a file efficiently. Figure 4-1 shows the interface that pops up when *nano* is executed on */home/user1/.bash_profile* file:

$ nano /home/user1/.bash_profile

Figure 4-1 Nano Text Editor

Several key combinations are available as commands within the editor to perform navigation and other tasks. Some of these are listed and described in Table 4-13.

Key (main screen)	Action
Ctrl+g	Displays help.
Ctrl+x	Exits nano.
Ctrl+o	Saves file.
Ctrl+j	Justifies current paragraph.
Ctrl+r	Reads a text file for insertion.
Ctrl+w	Searches for a pattern.
Ctrl+y	Takes you to the previous page.
Ctrl+v	Takes you to the next page.
Ctrl+k	Deletes the current line.
Ctrl+u	Undeletes the last deleted line.
Ctrl+c	Displays current cursor location.

Key (main screen)	Action
Ctrl+t	Checks spelling.

Table 4-13 nano Commands

The Text Processors

RHEL supports two famous UNIX text processors to perform various operations on columns and rows of text. These are known as *awk* and *sed*, and both work on input taken either from a specified file or the output of a command such as *ll*. Neither text processor makes any modifications to files provided as input, they only read input files and display results on the screen. If you wish to save the result, you need to use output redirection (See Chapter 05 "The Shells" on how to use output redirection). Let us take a look at both processors and understand them with the help of examples.

The awk Processor

The name *awk* was derived from the first initial of the last names of those who developed it: Alfred Aho, Peter Weinberger and Brian Kenigham.

awk works on columns of text to generate reports. It scans a file or input provided, one line at a time. It starts from the first line, searches for lines matching the specified pattern enclosed in quotes and curly braces, and performs selected action on those lines.

In order to understand the behavior of the *awk* utility, create a file by running the *ll* command and redirect its output to a file called *ll.out*. Then use this file as input to *awk* and examine results displayed on the screen. Before doing that, let us see how *awk* interprets columns. In other words how *awk* differentiates between columns. Let us run *ll* on *user1*'s home directory */home/user1*.

```
$ ll
total 0
-rw-rw-r-- 1 user1 user1   0 Nov 27 12:30 file1
-rw-rw-r-- 1 user1 user1   0 Nov 27 12:30 file2
-rw-rw-r-- 1 user1 user1   0 Nov 27 12:30 file3
-rw-rw-r-- 1 user1 user1   0 Nov 27 12:30 file4
```

awk automatically breaks a line into columns and assigns a variable to each column. A white space such as a tab is used as the default delimiter between columns to separate them.

Each line from the *ll* command output contains nine columns of text. Figure 4-2 shows how *awk* represents each column with respect to its position. The figure shows that $1 represents the first column, $2 represents the second column, $3 represents the third column and so on. All columns are collectively represented by $0.

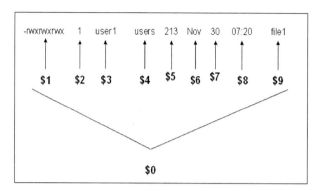

Figure 4-2 awk Command Arguments

Let us save the output of *ll* into *ll.out*:

$ **ll > ll.out**

The following examples help you develop an understanding on the usage of *awk*.

To display only the file name (column 9), file size (column 5) and file owner (column 3) in that sequence, do the following. Notice the space between variables in the *awk* statement. The output will not contain any spaces between columns. It will be printed as one single string of characters.

$ **awk '{print $9 $5 $3}' ll.out**

```
file10user1
file20user1
file30user1
file40user1
ll.out0user1
```

awk requires that you enclose the pattern in quotes and curly braces. The "print" function within the curly braces is part of the syntax. The above output does not contain any spaces between columns.

To place a single space between columns in the output, use a comma between variables:

$ **awk '{print $9, $5, $3}' ll.out**

```
file1 0 user1
file2 0 user1
file3 0 user1
file4 0 user1
ll.out 0 user1
```

To provide for exact alignment between columns, insert a tab or two:

$ awk '{print $9 " " $5 "   " $3}' ll.out

```
file1  0  user1
file2  0  user1
file3  0  user1
file4  0  user1
ll.out 0  user1
```

To re-arrange columns to display file owner, file size and file name in that order:

$ awk '{print $3,$5,$9}' ll.out

```
file1 0 user1
file2 0 user1
file3 0 user1
file4 0 user1
ll.out 0 user1
```

To add text between columns:

$ awk '{print $9,"was last modified/accessed on",$6,$7,"at",$8}' ll.out
```
was last modified/accessed on   at
file1 was last modified/accessed on Nov 27 at 12:30
file2 was last modified/accessed on Nov 27 at 12:30
file3 was last modified/accessed on Nov 27 at 12:30
file4 was last modified/accessed on Nov 27 at 12:30
ll.out was last modified/accessed on Nov 27 at 12:35
```

Note that when inserting text between columns, each text insert must be enclosed in double quotes and all but the last text inserted must be followed by a comma.

The sed Processor

Unlike *awk* that works on columns of text, the *sed* (stream editor) text processor works on rows of text. Following examples illustrate how *sed* works.

To search */etc/group* file for all lines containing the word "root" and hide them in the output. Note again that *sed* does not remove anything from the specified file. Let us first see what */etc/group* file contains:

$ cat /etc/group
```
root:x:0:root
bin:x:1:root,bin,daemon
daemon:x:2:root,bin,daemon
sys:x:3:root,bin,adm
adm:x:4:root,adm,daemon
tty:x:5:
. . . . . . . .
```

Now run *sed* to get the desired result:

$ sed '/root/d' /etc/group
tty:x:5:
lp:x:7:daemon,lp
mem:x:8:
kmem:x:9:
mail:x:12:mail
. . . .

/root/d is enclosed in single quotes. The "/root" portion of the command tells *sed* to search for the pattern "root" and the "/d" portion tells *sed* to delete that pattern from the output.

To remove all lines from the output of the *ll* command containing digit "4":

$ ll | sed '/4/d'
total 8
-rw-rw-r-- 1 user1 user1   0 Nov 27 12:30 file1
-rw-rw-r-- 1 user1 user1   0 Nov 27 12:30 file2
-rw-rw-r-- 1 user1 user1   0 Nov 27 12:30 file3
-rw-rw-r-- 1 user1 user1 619 Nov 27 13:03 group
-rw-rw-r-- 1 user1 user1 239 Nov 27 12:35 ll.out

To print all lines in duplicate that contain the pattern "root" from */etc/group* file. All other lines to be printed one time:

$ sed '/root/p' /etc/group
root:x:0:root
root:x:0:root
bin:x:1:root,bin,daemon
bin:x:1:root,bin,daemon
daemon:x:2:root,bin,daemon
daemon:x:2:root,bin,daemon
. . . .

To print only those lines that contain the pattern "root" in */etc/group* file:

$ sed –n '/root/p' /etc/group
root:x:0:root
bin:x:1:root,bin,daemon
daemon:x:2:root,bin,daemon
sys:x:3:root,bin,adm
adm:x:4:root,adm,daemon
disk:x:6:root
wheel:x:10:root

To append the character string "RHEL" to the end of every line in the output of the *ll* command. In the following command, "s" is used for substitute and "$" represents end of line. Run the command as *user1* on *user1*'s home directory */home/user1*:

```
$ ll | sed 's/$/ RHEL/'
total 8 RHEL
-rw-rw-r-- 1 user1 user1    0 Nov 27 12:30 file1 RHEL
-rw-rw-r-- 1 user1 user1    0 Nov 27 12:30 file2 RHEL
-rw-rw-r-- 1 user1 user1    0 Nov 27 12:30 file3 RHEL
-rw-rw-r-- 1 user1 user1    0 Nov 27 12:30 file4 RHEL
-rw-rw-r-- 1 user1 user1  619 Nov 27 13:03 group RHEL
-rw-rw-r-- 1 user1 user1  239 Nov 27 12:35 ll.out RHEL
```

To perform two edits on *etc/group* file where the first edit replaces all occurrences of "root" with "ROOT" and the second edit replaces "daemon" with "USERS":

```
$ sed -e 's/root/ROOT/g' -e 's/daemon/USERS/g' /etc/group
ROOT:x:0:ROOT
bin:x:1:ROOT,bin,USERS
USERS:x:2:ROOT,bin,USERS
sys:x:3:ROOT,bin,adm
adm:x:4:ROOT,adm,USERS
tty:x:5:
disk:x:6:ROOT
lp:x:7:USERS,lp
. . . . . . . .
```

You can perform multiple edits using this method.

Summary

Chapter 04 discussed the vi editor, nano editor and text processors. You learned various vi editor operating modes and methods of starting it. Within vi, you learned how to navigate, insert and delete text, undo and repeat previous commands, change text, search and replace text, copy, move and paste text, import contents from another file, customize vi settings, save modifications and exit out of it.

Next, you learned the nano editor, its benefits and how to use it.

At the end of the chapter you learned how to manipulate columns and rows of text using the *awk* and *sed* text processors, and saw several examples that explained their usage.

## 05

The Shells

This chapter covers the following major topics:

- ✓ Shells available in RHEL
- ✓ Features associated with the BASH shell
- ✓ Local and environment variables
- ✓ Set and unset variables
- ✓ View variable values
- ✓ Modify command prompt
- ✓ Get input from alternate source and send output and error messages to alternate destinations
- ✓ Tab completion, command line editing, command history, command aliasing and tilde substitution
- ✓ Special characters
- ✓ Pipes, and filters including tee, cut, pr and tr

In the Linux world, the *shell* is referred to as the command interpreter. It accepts instructions (or input) from users (or scripts), interprets them and passes to the kernel for processing. The kernel utilizes all hardware and software components required to process the instructions. When finished, the results are returned to the shell and displayed on the screen. The shell also produces appropriate error messages, if generated. In short, the shell operates as an interface between a user and the kernel.

The Shell

The shell provides many services such as I/O redirection, tab completion, pattern matching, environment variables, job control, command line editing, command aliasing, command history, tilde substitution, quoting mechanisms, conditional execution, flow control and writing shell scripts.

The shell is changeable providing a user with the flexibility to choose a command interpreter at any time.

Available Shells

There are several shells available in RHEL some of which are explained below:

The Bourne Again Shell (BASH)

The *Bourne Again SHell* is the default shell for all users including *root*. It is identified by the $ prompt and is located in the */bin/bash* file. It supports all the features listed above.

The Korn Shell

The *Korn* shell is similar to the BASH shell in terms of features. This shell was created by David Korn at the AT&T labs and its prompt is $. It resides in the */bin/ksh* file.

The C Shell

The *C* shell is mainly used by developers. It provides a programming interface similar to the C language and offers many BASH and Korn shell functions in addition to numerous other features. Created by Bill Joy at the University of California at Berkeley for early BSD UNIX releases, the prompt for the C shell is $ and it resides in the */bin/csh* file.

The TC Shell

The *TC* shell is backward compatible with the C shell with many enhancements. The prompt for the TC shell is $ and it resides in */bin/tcsh* file.

BASH Shell Features

The BASH shell offers many features that are discussed at length in the remainder of this chapter.

Variables

A *variable* is a temporary storage of data in memory. Variables contain information used for customizing the shell environment. Their values are used by many system and application processes to function properly. The shell allows you to store values into variables.

There are two types of variables: *local* and *environment*.

Local Variable

A local variable is private to the shell it is created in and its value cannot be used by processes that are not started in that shell. This introduces the concept of *current* shell and *sub*-shell (or *child* shell). The current shell is where you execute your programs from, whereas a sub-shell is created by a running program. The value of a local variable is available only in the current shell, and not in the child shell.

Environment Variable

The value of an environment variable, however, is passed from current shell to sub-shell. In other words, the value stored in an environment variable is passed from parent process to child process. The environment variable is also called *global* variable. Some variables are set automatically through system and user initialization files when you log in to the system. Variables may also be set in shell scripts or at the command line as required.

Setting, Unsetting and Viewing Variables

To set, unset or view shell variables, consult Table 5-1. Two variables – V1 and V2 – are used as examples. It is recommended that you use uppercase letters in variable names to distinguish them from the names of any commands or programs that you might have on the system.

Action	Local Variable	Environment Variable
Setting a variable	Syntax: V1=value Examples: **$ V1=college** **$ V2="I am using RHEL"**	Syntax: V1=value; export V1 OR export V1=value Examples: **$ V1=college; export V1** **$ V2="I am using RHEL"; export V2** or **$ export V1=college** **$ export V2="I am using RHEL"**
Listing variables and displaying their values	**$ echo $V1** **$ set**	**$ echo $V1** **$ set** **$ env** **$ export**
Unsetting a variable	**$ unset V1**	**$ unset V1**

Table 5-1 Setting, Unsetting and Viewing Variables

To set a local variable V1 to contain the value "college", simply define it as shown in Table 5-1. Note that there must not be any spaces either before or after the equal (=) sign. To make V1 a global variable, use the *export* command. Another example sets a variable V2 containing a series of space-separated words. Make sure to enclose them in double quotes.

To display the value of a variable, use the *echo*, *set*, *env* or *export* command.

The *set* command lists current values for all shell variables including local and environment variables. The *export* and *env* commands list only environment variables.

```
$ set
BASH=/bin/bash
BASH_ARGC=()
BASH_ARGV=()
BASH_LINENO=()
BASH_SOURCE=()
BASH_VERSINFO=([0]="3" [1]="2" [2]="25" [3]="1" [4]="release" [5]="x86_64-redhat-linux-gnu")
BASH_VERSION='3.2.25(1)-release'
. . . . . . . .
$ env
HOSTNAME=rhel01
TERM=xterm
SHELL=/bin/bash
HISTSIZE=1000
SSH_CLIENT=192.168.0.203 4538 22
SSH_TTY=/dev/pts/1
USER=user1
. . . . . . . .
$ export
declare -x G_BROKEN_FILENAMES="1"
declare -x HISTSIZE="1000"
declare -x HOME="/home/user1"
declare -x HOSTNAME="rhel01"
declare -x INPUTRC="/etc/inputrc"
. . . . . . . .
```

Finally, to unset (remove) a variable, use the *unset* command and specify the variable name to be unset.

Pre-Defined Environment Variables

Some environment variables are defined by the shell on login. You may define more environment variables as needed. Some of the common environment variables are DISPLAY, HISTFILE, HISTSIZE, HOME, LOGNAME, MAIL, PATH, PS1, PS2, PWD, SHELL and TERM. Here is a brief description of each one of these in Table 5-2.

Variable	Description
DISPLAY	Stores hostname or IP address to display graphics.
HISTFILE	Defines file name where shell stores a history of all commands as you execute them.

Variable	Description
HISTSIZE	Defines maximum size for HISTFILE to grow to.
HOME	Contains home directory path.
LOGNAME	Stores login name.
MAIL	Contains path to user mail directory. For example, it would be /var/spool/mail/user1 for user1.
PATH	Defines a colon separated list of directories to be searched when a user executes a command.
PS1	Defines primary command prompt. It is # for root by default.
PS2	Defines secondary command prompt. It it is > by default.
PWD	Stores current directory location.
SHELL	Holds absolute path of primary shell.
TERM	Holds terminal type value.

Table 5-2 Pre-Defined Environment Variables

Command and Variable Substitution

The primary command prompt for the *root* user is the # sign and that for the regular users is the $ sign. Customizing the primary command prompt to display useful information such as who you are, system you are currently logged on to and your current location in the directory tree, is a good practice. The examples below illustrate how to modify *user1*'s primary prompt using any of the following:

$ export PS1="< $LOGNAME@`hostname`:\$PWD > "
$ export PS1="< $LOGNAME@$(hostname):\$PWD > "

user1's command prompt will now look like:

< user1@rhel01:/home/user1 >

The value of the PWD variable will reflect the directory location in *user1*'s prompt as he navigates the directory tree. This is called *variable substitution*. For example, if *user1* moves to */usr/bin*, the prompt will change to:

< user1@rhel01:/usr/bin >

Also, the value of LOGNAME variable is used to display *user1*'s login name in this example.

Running the command *hostname* and assigning its output to a variable is an example of a shell feature called *command substitution*. Note that the command the output of which you want to assign to a variable must be either enclosed within single forward quotes or parentheses preceded by the $ sign.

Input, Output and Error Redirection

Many programs read input from the keyboard and write output to the terminal window where they were initiated. If any errors are encountered, they are displayed on the terminal window too. This is the default behavior. What if you do not wish to take input from the keyboard or write the output to the terminal window? The BASH shell allows you to redirect input, output and error messages to allow programs and commands to read input from something other than the keyboard and send output and errors to something other than the terminal window.

The default (or the standard) locations for input, output and error are referred to as *stdin*, *stdout* and *stderr*, respectively. Table 5-3 demonstrates that each of the three has an association with a symbol and a digit. These symbols and digits are used at the command line and in shell scripts for redirection purposes.

File Descriptor	Symbol	Associated Digit	Description
stdin	<	0	Standard input
stdout	>	1	Standard output
stderr	>	2	Standard error

Table 5-3 I/O/E Redirection Symbols

The following text explains how redirection of input, output and error takes place.

Redirecting Standard Input

Input redirection instructs a command to read required information from an alternate source such as a file, instead of the keyboard. For example, do the following to have the *mailx* command mail the contents of *file1* to *user2*:

$ mailx user2 < file1

In order for *mailx* to work properly, a mail server must be configured and running. See Chapter 27 "Internet Services and Electronic Mail" on how to configure a mail server and use it.

Redirecting Standard Output

Output redirection sends the output generated by a command to an alternate destination such as a file, instead of sending it to the terminal window. For example, do the following to direct the *sort* command to send the sorted output of *file1* to a file called *sort.out*. This will overwrite any *sort.out* file contents. If *sort.out* does not exist, it will be created.

$ sort file1 > sort.out

To direct the *sort* command to append output to *sort.out* file, use the >> symbols:

$ sort file1 >> sort.out

Redirecting Standard Error

Error redirection sends any error messages generated to an alternate destination such as a file, instead of sending them to the terminal window. For example, do the following to direct the *find* command to send any error messages generated to */dev/null*. The */dev/null* file is a special system file used to discard data.

$ find / –name core –print 2> /dev/null

This command will search for all occurrences of files by the name "core" in the entire root directory tree. Error messages will be generated when a directory where the user does not have rights is accessed with normal user privileges. These error messages will be discarded and sent to garbage.

Redirecting both Standard Output and Error

Do either of the following to redirect both stdout and stderr to a file called *testfile1*:

$ ls /etc /cdr 1> testfile1 2>&1
$ ls /etc /cdr &> testfile1

This example will produce a listing of the */etc* directory and save the result in *testfile1*. At the same time, it will generate an error message complaining about non-existence of */cdr* directory. This error message will also be sent to the same file and saved.

Tab Completion, Command Line Editing and Command History

Tab completion (a.k.a. *command line completion*) is a BASH shell feature whereby typing a partial filename at the command line and then hitting the Tab key twice, completes a filename if there are no other possibilities. If there exists multiple possibilities, it will complete up to the point they have in common.

Command line editing allows you to edit a line of text right at the command prompt. Pressing the Esc+k key combination or the up arrow key brings at the prompt the last command you executed. Pressing the letter k or the up arrow key repeatedly scrolls backward to previous commands in reverse chronological order. The letter j or the down arrow key scrolls forward through the command history in chronological order. When you get the desired command, you may edit it right at the command prompt using the vi editor commands (refer to Chapter 04 "Text Editors and Processors" to learn about the vi editor commands). If you do not wish to edit it or done with editing, simply press the Enter key to execute it.

Command history, or simply *history*, keeps a log of all commands that you run at the command prompt. The shell stores command history in a file located in user's home directory. You may retrieve these commands, modify them at the command line and re-run them using the command line editing feature.

There are three variables that enable the features you have just learnt. These variables are listed below along with sample values:

HISTFILE=~/.bash_history
HISTSIZE=1000
EDITOR=vi

The HISTFILE variable tells the BASH shell to store all commands run by a user in *.bash_history* file in that user's home directory. This file is created automatically if it does not exist. Each command, along with options and arguments, is stored on a separate line.

The HISTSIZE variable controls the maximum number of commands that can be stored in HISTFILE.

The EDITOR variable defines what text editor to use. If this variable is not set, issue the following to be able to use the tab completion, command line editing and command history features:

$ **set –o vi**

The three variables discussed may be defined in user or system initialization files. Refer to Chapter 12 "Users and Groups" on how to define variables in initialization files to customize the behavior.

RHEL provides the *history* command to display previously executed commands. It gets the information from the *.bash_history* file. By default, the last 500 entries are displayed.

$ **history**
```
1  man bash
2  history
3  cd
4  clear
5  ls -l
6  clear
. . . . . . . .
```

Let us use some of the *history* command options to alter its behavior.

To display this command and 17 commands preceding it:

$ **history 17**

To re-execute a command by its line number (line 38 for example) in the history file:

$ **!38**

To re-execute the most recent occurrence of a command that started with a particular letter or series of letters (ch for example), use any of the following:

$ **!ch**
$ **!?ch**

To repeat the last executed command, run any of the following:

$ **!!**
$ **!$**

Alias Substitution

A *command alias*, or simply an *alias*, allows you to create shortcuts for lengthy commands. When an alias is run, the BASH shell executes the corresponding command. This saves you time typing the same command repeatedly.

The BASH shell contains several pre-defined aliases that you can view by running the *alias* command. These aliases are typically defined in user or system initialization files. The *alias* command also displays aliases that you have defined.

```
$ alias
alias cp='cp -i'
alias l.='ls -d .* --color=tty'
alias ll='ls -l --color=tty'
alias ls='ls --color=tty'
alias mv='mv -i'
alias rm='rm -i'
alias which='alias | /usr/bin/which --tty-only --read-alias --show-dot --show-tilde'
```

These aliases are explained in Table 5-4.

Alias	Value	Definition
cp	cp –i	Runs the *cp* command interactively.
l.	ls –d .* --color=tty	Runs the *ls* command with –d .* and --color=tty options.
ll	ls –l --color=tty	Runs the *ls* command with –l and --color=tty options.
ls	ls --color=tty	Runs the *ls* command with --color=tty option.
mv	mv –i	Runs the *mv* command interactively.
rm	rm –i	Runs the *rm* command interactively.
which	alias	/usr/bin/which --tty-only --read-alias --show-dot --show-tilde	Runs the *which* command with the specified options.

Table 5-4 Pre-Defined Command Aliases

There are two commands – *alias* and *unalias* – available to work with aliases. The *alias* command displays and sets an alias while the *unalias* command unsets it. Let us look at a few examples.

Create an alias "f" to abbreviate the *find* command. Use either single or double quotes to enclose multiple words. Do not leave any spaces before and after the = sign.

$ alias f="find / –name core –exec rm {} \;"

Now, when you type the letter f at the command prompt and hit the Enter key, the shell will replace the alias "f" with what is stored in it. Basically, you have created a shortcut to that lengthy command.

Sometimes you create an alias by a name that matches the name of a system command. In this situation, the shell gives the alias precedence over the command. This means the shell will run the alias and not the command. For example, you know that the *rm* command deletes a file without giving any warning. To prevent accidental deletion of files with *rm*, you may create an alias by the same name.

$ alias rm="rm –i"
$ rm file1
file1: ? (y/n)

When you execute *rm* now, the shell will run what you have stored in the *rm* alias and not the command *rm*. If you wish to run the *rm* command, run it with a preceding \ character:

$ \rm file1

Use the *unalias* command to unset an alias if you no longer need it:

$ unalias f
$ unalias rm

Tilde Substitution

Tilde substitution (or *tilde expansion*) is performed on words that begin with the tilde ~ sign. The rules are:

1. If used as a standalone character, the shell refers to the $HOME directory of the user running the command. The following example displays the $HOME directory of *user1*:

   $ echo ~
   /home/user1

2. If used prior to the + sign, the shell refers to the current directory. For example, if *user1* is in */etc/init.d* directory and does ~+, the output will display the user's current directory location:

   $ echo ~+
   /etc/init.d

3. If used prior to the – sign, the shell refers to the last working directory. For example, if *user1* changes to */usr/share/man* directory from */etc/init.d* and does ~–, the output will display the user's last working directory location:

   $ echo ~–
   /etc/init.d

4. If used prior to a username, the shell refers to the $HOME directory of that user:

   $ echo ~user2
   /home/user2

You can use the tilde substitution with any commands such as *cd*, *ls* and *echo* that refer to location in the directory structure. Some more examples of tilde substitution are given in Chapter 01 "Overview of Linux".

Special Characters

Special characters are the symbols on keyboard that possess special meaning to the shell. These characters are also referred to as *metacharacters* or *wildcard* characters and are used for globbing purposes (See the topic on Pattern Matching in Chapter 02 "Files and Directories"). Some of these such as dash (–), tilde (~) and redirection symbols (< >) have already been discussed in this chapter. Four additional special characters: *asterisk* (*), *question mark* (?), *square brackets* ([ ]) and *semicolon* (;) will be discussed in this sub-section.

The Asterisk (*) Character

The asterisk character matches zero to unlimited number of any characters, except the leading period in a hidden file. See the following examples to understand its usage.

To list names of all files that begin with letters "fi" followed by any characters:

```
$ ls fi*
file1  file2  file3  file4
```

To list names of all files that begin with letter "d". You will notice in the output that contents of *dir1* and *dir2* sub-directories are also listed.

```
$ ls d*
dir1:
scripts1  scripts2

dir2:
newfile1  newfile2  newfile3  newfile4
```

To list names of all files that end with the digit "4":

```
$ ls *4
file4
```

To list names of all files that have a period followed by letters "out" at the end:

```
$ ls *.out
ll.out  sort.out
```

The Question Mark (?) Character

The question mark character matches exactly one character, except the leading period in a hidden file. See the following example to understand its usage.

To list all files that begin with characters "file" followed by one character only:

```
$ ls file?
file1  file2  file3  file4
```

The Square Bracket ([ ]) Characters

The square brackets can be used to match either a set of characters or a range of characters for a single character position.

When you specify a set of characters, order is unimportant, therefore, [xyz], [yxz], [xzy] and [yxz] are treated alike. The following example encloses two characters within square brackets. The output will include all files and directories that begin with either of the two characters followed by any number of characters.

```
$ ls [cf]*
car  car1  car2  file1  file2  file3  file4
```

A range of characters must be specified in proper order such as [a-z] or [0-9]. The following example matches all file and directory names that begin with any alphabet between "a" and "f":

```
$ ls [a–f]*
car car1 car2 file1 file2 file3 file4

dir1:
scripts1 scripts2

dir2:
newfile1 newfile2 newfile3 newfile4
```

The Semicolon (;) Character

The semicolon character separates commands and enables you to enter multiple commands on a single command line. The following example shows three commands: *cd*, *ls* and *date* separated by semicolon. The three commands will be executed in the order they are specified.

```
$ cd; ls fil*; date
file1 file2 file3 file4
Fri Nov 28 07:15:06 EST 2008
```

Masking Special Meaning of Some Special Characters

Sometimes you are in a situation where you want the shell to treat a special character as a regular character. There are three special characters that disable the meaning of other special characters when properly used with them. These characters are \, ' and ", and are described below.

The Backslash (\ ) Character

The backslash character forces the shell to mask the meaning of any special character that follows it. For example, if a file exists by the name * and you wish to remove it with the *rm* command, you will have to ensure that the \ character is specified right before *.

```
$ rm \*
```

If you forget \, all files in the directory will be deleted.

The Single Quote (') Character

The single quote character forces the shell to mask the meaning of all enclosed special characters. For example, LOGNAME is a variable and you use the *echo* command to display the value stored in it:

```
$ echo $LOGNAME
user1
```

If you enclose $LOGNAME within single quote characters, the *echo* command will display what is enclosed instead of the value of the variable.

```
$ echo '$LOGNAME'
$LOGNAME
```

Similarly, the backslash character is echoed when enclosed within single quotes.

```
$ echo '\'
\
```

The Double Quote (") Character

The double quote character forces the shell to mask the meaning of all but three special characters: \\, $ and '. These special characters retain their special meaning if used within double quotes. Look at the following examples to understand the concept.

```
$ echo "$SHELL"
/bin/bash
$ echo "\$PWD"
$PWD
$ echo "'\'"
'\'
```

Pipes and Filters

This section talks about pipes and filters often used at the command line and in shell scripts.

Pipes

The *pipe*, represented by the | character and resides with the \\ on the keyboard, is a special character that sends output of one command as input to another command.

The following example uses the *ll* command to display contents of the */etc* directory. The output is piped to the *more* command, which displays the listing one screen at a time.

```
$ ll /etc | more
total 3428
-rw-r--r--   1 root root     15288 Jan  15  2008 a2ps.cfg
-rw-r--r--   1 root root      2562 Jan  15  2008 a2ps-site.cfg
drwxr-xr-x  4 root root      4096 Oct    9 13:10 acpi
-rw-r--r--   1 root root        44 Oct 29 18:04 adjtime
drwxr-xr-x  4 root root      4096 Oct 15 08:35 alchemist
-rw-r--r--   1 root root      1512 Apr 25 2005 aliases
-rw-r-----   1 root smmsp 12288 Nov  5 18:04 aliases.db
drwxr-xr-x  4 root root      4096 Oct    9 13:10 alsa
drwxr-xr-x  2 root root      4096 Oct  15 08:42 alternatives
-rw-r--r--   1 root root       298 Dec 18  2006 anacrontab

. . . . . . . .
--More--
```

Another example runs the *who* command and pipe its output to the *nl* command to display associated line numbers:

```
$ who | nl
     1  user1   pts/1      2008-11-28 07:02 (192.168.0.201)
```

The following example creates a pipeline whereby the output of *ll* is sent to the first *grep* command, which filters out all lines that do not contain the pattern "root". The new output is then sent to the second *grep* command that filters out all lines that do not contain the pattern "apr". Finally, the output is numbered and displayed on the screen. A structure like this with multiple pipes is referred to as a *pipeline*.

```
$ ll /etc | grep root | grep –i may | nl
     1  -rw-r--r--  1 root root   1512 Apr 25  2005 aliases
     2  -rw-------  1 root root   2726 Apr  3  2008 autofs_ldap_auth.conf
     3  -rw-r--r--  1 root root    717 Apr  3  2008 auto.master
     4  -rw-r--r--  1 root root    581 Apr  3  2008 auto.misc
     5  -rwxr-xr-x  1 root root   1292 Apr  3  2008 auto.net
     6  -rwxr-xr-x  1 root root    715 Apr  3  2008 auto.smb
     7  -rw-r--r--  1 root root    178 Apr  9  2008 dhcp6c.conf
     8  -rw-r--r--  1 root root   4843 Apr 27  2007 enscript.cfg
     9  drwxr-xr-x  3 root root   4096 Apr 10  2008 hal
    10  -rw-r--r--  1 root root     74 Apr 29  2008 issue
    11  -rw-r--r--  1 root root     73 Apr 29  2008 issue.net
    12  -rw-r--r--  1 root root   2711 Apr  1  2008 multipath.conf
    13  drwxr-xr-x  2 root root   4096 Apr  1  2008 NetworkManager
    14  -rw-r--r--  1 root root   1895 Apr 11  2008 nscd.conf
    15  -rw-r--r--  1 root root     54 Apr 29  2008 redhat-release
    16  -rw-r--r--  1 root root    666 Apr 22  2008 scsi_id.config
```

The tee Filter

The *tee* filter is used to send output to more than one destination. It can send one copy of the output to a file and another to the screen (or some other program) if used with pipe.

In the following example, the output from *ll* is numbered and captured in */tmp/ll.out* file. The output is displayed on the screen too.

```
$ ll /etc | nl | tee /tmp/ll.out
```

Do a *cat* on */tmp/ll.out* and you will notice that the file contains the exact same information that was displayed on the screen when you executed the command.

By using –a with *tee*, the output is appended to the file, rather than overwriting existing contents.

```
$ date | tee –a /tmp/ll.out
```

The cut Filter

The *cut* filter is used to extract selected columns from a line. The default column separator used is white space such as a tab. The following example command cuts out columns 1 and 4 from the */etc/group* file as specified with the –f option. The colon character is used as a field separator.

```
$ cut –d: –f 1,4 /etc/group
root:root
bin:root,bin,daemon
daemon:root,bin,daemon
sys:root,bin,adm
. . . . . . . .
```

The pr Filter

The *pr* filter is used to format and display the contents of a text file. The output may be piped to a printer if one is configured.

By default, the *pr* command prints file name, time stamp on it, page number and file contents. For example, to display the contents of */etc/group* file:

$ pr /etc/group

```
2008-11-27 13:29              /etc/group              Page 1


root:x:0:root
bin:x:1:root,bin,daemon
daemon:x:2:root,bin,daemon
. . . . . . . .
```

Options listed in Table 5-5 are available with the *pr* command for enhanced readability.

Option	Purpose
+page	Begins printing from the specified page number: **$ pr +2 /etc/group**
–column	Prints the file in multiple columns: **$ pr –2 /etc/group**
–d	Prints with double line spacing: **$ pr –d /etc/group**
–l lines	Changes page length (default is 66 lines): **$ pr –l 20 /etc/group**
–m	Prints specified files side-by-side in separate columns: **$ pr –m /etc/group /etc/passwd /etc/hosts**
–h header	Replaces filename in the output.
–t	Suppresses the filename and time stamp on it.
–n	Assigns a number to each line in the output.

Table 5-5 pr Command Options

The following example prints the */etc/group* file in two columns with double spacing between lines, the header title "My PR Command Test" and the page length not more than 20 lines:

$ pr –2dh "My PR Command Test" –l 20 /etc/group

The tr Filter

The *tr* filter translates specified input characters and displays the output on the screen. Following are a few examples.

To remove all but one space between columns in the output of the *w* command. Note that there is a single space between double quotes in the command below:

```
$ w | tr –s ‘ ‘ “
07:40:01 up 22 days, 13:37, 1 user, load average: 0.00, 0.02, 0.00
USER TTY FROM LOGIN@ IDLE JCPU PCPU WHAT
user1 pts/1 192.168.0.203 07:02 0.00s 0.15s 0.00s w
```

To remove all digits from the output of the *w* command:

```
$ w | tr –d ‘[0-9]’
:: up days, :,  user, load average: ., ., .
USER    TTY    FROM         LOGIN@  IDLE  JCPU  PCPU WHAT
user   pts/   ...    :   .s .s .s w
```

To display all letters in uppercase:

```
$ w | tr ‘[a-z]’ ‘[A-Z]’
07:41:32 UP 22 DAYS, 13:39, 1 USER,  LOAD AVERAGE: 0.00, 0.01, 0.00
USER    TTY    FROM         LOGIN@  IDLE  JCPU  PCPU WHAT
USER1   PTS/1   192.168.0.203    07:02   0.00S 0.15S 0.00S W
```

Summary

Chapter 05 discussed shells and shell features in detail. You looked at shells available in RHEL; features of the BASH shells including setting, unsetting and displaying contents of local and environment variables, modifying command prompt to display useful information, getting input from non-default sources, sending output and error messages to alternate destinations, defining and undefining shortcuts to lengthy commands; using tilde substitution; setting required variables to enable tab completion, command line editing and command history features; and special characters.

Finally, you studied the use of the pipe character and several filter commands.

## 06

Basic Shell Scripting

This chapter covers the following major topics:

- ✓ What is shell scripting?
- ✓ Write scripts to display basic system information, set local and environment variables, use values of pre-defined environment variables, parse command outputs to variables, and understand usage of command line arguments and the role the shift command plays
- ✓ Execute and debug scripts
- ✓ Write interactive scripts

Shell scripts (a.k.a. *shell programs* or simply *scripts*) are text files that contain Linux commands and control structures to automate long, repetitive tasks. Commands are interpreted and run by the shell one at a time in the order they are listed in a script. Control structures are utilized for creating and managing logical and looping constructs. Comments are also usually included in shell scripts to add general information about the script such as author name, creation date, last modification date and purpose of the script.

Throughout this chapter, the approach will be to write scripts and examine them line-by-line. The chapter will begin with simple scripts and move forward to more complicated ones. As with any other programming languages, the scripting skill will develop overtime as you write, read and understand more and more scripts.

Scripts covered in this chapter are written for the BASH shell */bin/bash*. They can be used in Korn shell without any modifications, but not all of them can be run in C shell.

Shell scripting enables you to create programs for various purposes including automation of system and network administration tasks such as automating software package management, managing user accounts, manipulating physical volumes, volume groups, logical volumes and file systems, monitoring file system utilization, trimming log files, performing system backups, removing core, temporary and unnecessary files and generating reports.

The shell reads the contents of a script line by line when it is run. Each line is executed as if it is typed and executed at the command prompt. If the script encounters an error, the error message is displayed on the screen. There is nothing that you can place in a script but cannot run at the command prompt.

Scripts do not need to be compiled as many other programming languages do.

Creating Shell Scripts

Use the *vi* or *nano* editor to create example shell scripts presented in this chapter. This gives you an opportunity to practice them. The *nl* command is used to display the contents of the scripts along with associated line numbers. Following example scripts are created in the */usr/local/bin* directory.

Displaying Basic System Information

Let us create the first script called *sys_info.sh* and then examine it. Change directory into */usr/local/bin* and use *vi* or *nano* to construct the script. Type in what you see below excluding the line numbers:

```
# nl sys_info.sh
1    #!/bin/bash
2    # The name of this script is sys_info.sh.
3    # The author of this script is Asghar Ghori.
4    # The script is created on October 28, 2008.
5    # This script is last modified by Asghar Ghori on November 28, 2008.
6    # This script should be located in /usr/local/bin directory.
7    # The purpose of this script is to explain construct of a simple shell program.
```

```
8    echo "Display Linux Kernel Information"
9    echo "-------------------------------------------"
10   echo
11   echo "This machine is running the following kernel:"
12   /bin/uname –s
13   echo "This machine is running the following release of Linux kernel:"
14   /bin/uname –r
```

 Within vi, type :set nu to view line numbers associated with each line entry.

In this script, comments and commands are used.

The first line indicates the shell the script will use to run. This line must start with the "#!" character combination followed by the full pathname to the shell file.

The next six lines contain comments to include the script name, author name, creation time, the last modification time, default location to store and purpose. The # sign indicates that anything written to the right of this character is for informational purposes and will not be executed when the script is run. Note that line 1 uses this character too followed by the ! mark; this combination has a special meaning to the shell, which specifies the location of the shell file. Do not get confused between the two usages.

Line number 8 has the first command of the script. The *echo* command prints on the screen whatever follows it. In this case, you will see "Display Linux Kernel Information" printed.

Line number 9 underlines the "Display Linux Kernel Information" heading.

Line number 10 has the *echo* command followed by nothing. This means an empty line will be inserted in the output.

Line number 11 prints on the screen "The machine is running the following kernel:".

Line number 12 executes the *uname* command with –s option. This command returns the name of the Linux kernel currently being used.

Line number 13 prints on the screen "This machine is running the following release of Linux kernel:".

Line number 14 executes the *uname* command with –r option. This command returns the release of the Linux kernel being run.

Executing a Script

When you have a script constructed, it is usually not executable since the umask value is typically set to 0002, which allows read/write permissions to the owner and group members, and read permission to public on new files. You will need to run the script as follows while you are in */usr/local/bin*:

sh ./sys_info.sh

Alternatively, give the owner of the file execute permission:

 # chmod +x sys_info.sh

Now you can run the script using either its relative path or fully qualified path:

 # ./sys_info.sh
 # /usr/local/bin/sys_info.sh

If the */usr/local/bin* directory is not set in the PATH variable, define it in */etc/profile* file so whoever logs on to the system has this path set. Alternatively, the path to the directory may be added to *~/.bash_profile* file of users who need access to the directory. The following shows how to set the path at the command prompt:

 # export PATH=$PATH:/usr/local/bin

Let us run *sys_info.sh* and see what the output will look like:

 # sys_info.sh
Display Linux Kernel Information

This machine is running the following kernel:
Linux
This machine is running the following release of Linux kernel:
2.6.18-92.el5

Debugging a Shell Script

If you would like to use a basic debugging technique when you see that a script is not functioning the way it should be, you may want to append –x to "#!/bin/bash" in the first line of the script to look like "#!/bin/bash –x". Alternatively, you can execute the script as follows:

 # sh –x /usr/local/bin/sys_info.sh
+ echo 'Display Linux Kernel Information'
Display Linux Kernel Information
+ echo --

+ echo

+ echo 'This machine is running the following kernel:'
This machine is running the following kernel:
+ /bin/uname -s
Linux
+ echo 'This machine is running the following release of Linux kernel:'
This machine is running the following release of Linux kernel:
+ /bin/uname -r
2.6.18-92.el5

With the + sign, the actual line from the script is echoed on the screen followed in the next line by what it would produce in the output.

Using Local Variables

You have dealt with variables previously and seen how to use them. To recap, there are two types of variables: *local* (or *private*) and *global* (or *environment*). They are defined and used in scripts and at the command line in the exact same manner. A local variable defined in a script disappears once the script execution is finished, whereas, a global variable persists even after the execution finishes.

In the second script called *loc_var.sh,* a local variable is defined and its value displayed. After the script execution is complete, check the value of the variable again.

nl loc_var.sh
```
1    #!/bin/bash
2    # The name of this script is loc_var.sh.
3    # The author of this script is Asghar Ghori.
4    # The script is created on October 28, 2008.
5    # This script is last modified by Asghar Ghori on November 28, 2008.
6    # This script should be located in /usr/local/bin directory.
7    # The purpose of this script is to explain how a local variable is defined and used in a shell
8    # program.
9    echo "Setting a Local Variable".
10   echo "------------------------------"
11   echo
12   SYS_NAME=rhel01
13   echo "The hostname of this system is $SYS_NAME".
```

When you execute this script, the result will be:

loc_var.sh
```
Setting a Local Variable.
------------------------------

The hostname of this system is rhel01.
```

Now since it was a local variable and the script was run in a sub-shell, the variable disappeared after the script execution completed. Here is what you will see if you try to *echo* on the variable:

echo $SYS_NAME

Using Pre-Defined Environment Variables

In the next script called *pre_env.sh,* values of two pre-defined environment variables SHELL and LOGNAME are displayed:

nl pre_env.sh
```
1    #!/bin/bash
2    # The name of this script is pre_env.sh.
3    # The author of this script is Asghar Ghori.
4    # The script is created on October 28, 2008.
5    # This script is last modified by Asghar Ghori on November 28, 2008.
6    # This script should be located in /usr/local/bin directory.
```

7   # The purpose of this script is to explain how a pre-defined environment variable is used in a shell
8   # program.
9   echo "The location of my shell command is:"
10   echo $SHELL
11   echo "You are logged in as $LOGNAME".

The output will be:

 # pre_env.sh
The location of my shell command is:
/bin/bash
You are logged in as user1.

Setting New Environment Variables

In the next script *new_env.sh,* two environment variables SYS_NAME and OS_SYS are set during script execution. Once the script execution is done, you will see that the two variables still exist.

 # nl new_env.sh
1   #!/bin/bash
2   # The name of this script is new_env.sh.
3   # The author of this script is Asghar Ghori.
4   # The script is created on October 28, 2008.
5   # This script is last modified by Asghar Ghori on November 28, 2008.
6   # This script should be located in /usr/local/bin directory.
7   # The purpose of this script is to explain how environment variables are defined and used in a
8   # shell program.
9   echo "Setting New Environment Variables".
10   echo "--"
11   echo
12   SYS_NAME=rhel01
13   OS_SYS="RHEL 5"
14   export SYS_NAME OS_SYS
15   echo "The hostname of this system is $SYS_NAME".
16   echo "This system is running $OS_SYS Operating System software".

The output will be:

 # new_env.sh
Setting New Environment Variables.

The hostname of this system is rhel01.
This system is running RHEL 5 Operating System software.

The *export* command makes the specified variables environment variables. Even though the script was run in a sub-shell, both environment variables retained their values. Do an *echo* on them to check the values:

```
$ echo $SYS_NAME
rhel01
$ echo $OP_SYS
RHEL 5
```

Parsing Command Output

Shell scripts allow you to run a command and capture its output into a variable. For example, the following script called *cmdout.sh* is a modified version of the *new_env.sh* script. You must enclose the *hostname* and *uname* commands in forward quotes.

 # nl cmdout.sh

```
1    #!/bin/bash
2    # The name of this script is cmdout.sh.
3    # The author of this script is Asghar Ghori.
4    # The script is created on October 28, 2008.
5    # This script is last modified by Asghar Ghori on November 28, 2008.
6    # This script should be located in /usr/local/bin directory.
7    # The purpose of this script is to display how a command output is captured and stored in a
8    # variable.
9    echo "Parsing Command Output".
10   echo "----------------------------------"
11   echo
12   SYS_NAME=`hostname`
13   OS_VER=`uname –r`
14   export  SYS_NAME OS_VER
15   echo "The hostname of this system is $SYS_NAME".
16   echo "This system is running $OS_VER of RHEL Operating System kernel".
```

The output will be:

 # cmdout.sh

Parsing Command Output.

The hostname of this system is rhel01.
This system is running 2.6.18-92.el5 of RHEL Operating System kernel.

Using Command Line Arguments

Command line arguments (also called *positional parameters*) are the arguments specified at the command line with a command or script when it is executed. The locations at the command line of the arguments as well as the command or script itself, are stored in corresponding variables. These variables are special shell variables. Figure 6-1 and Table 6-1 help you understand them.

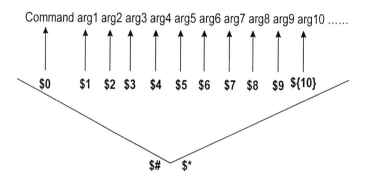

Figure 6-1 Command Line Arguments

Variable	Description
$0	Represents the command or script.
$1 to $9	Represents arguments 1 through 9.
${10} and so on	Represents arguments 10 and further.
$#	Represents total number of arguments.
$*	Represents all arguments.
$$	Represents the PID of a running script.

Table 6-1 Command Line Arguments

The script *com_line_arg.sh* shows the command line arguments supplied, a count of them, value of the first argument and the process ID of the script itself:

 # nl com_line_arg.sh
```
1    #!/bin/bash
2    # The name of this script is com_line_arg.sh.
3    # The author of this script is Asghar Ghori.
4    # The script is created on October 28, 2008.
5    # This script is last modified by Asghar Ghori on November 28, 2008.
6    # This script should be located in /usr/local/bin directory.
7    # The purpose of this script is to explain the usage of command line arguments.
8    echo "There are $# arguments specified at the command line".
9    echo "The arguments supplied are: $*"
10   echo "The first argument is: $1"
11   echo "The Process ID of the script is: $$"
```

When this script is executed with four arguments specified, the result will be:

 # com_line_arg.sh toronto chicago london washington
There are 4 arguments specified at the command line.
The arguments supplied are: toronto chicago london tokyo
The first argument is: toronto
The Process ID of the script is: 27322

Shifting Command Line Arguments

The *shift* command is used to move command line arguments one position to the left. The first argument gets lost. *com_line_arg_shift.sh* script below uses the *shift* command:

nl com_line_arg_shift.sh

```
1    #! /bin/bash
2    # The name of this script is com_line_arg_shift.sh.
3    # The author of this script is Asghar Ghori.
4    # The script is created on October 28, 2008.
5    # This script is last modified by Asghar Ghori on November 28, 2008.
6    # This script should be located in /usr/local/bin directory.
7    # The purpose of this script is to show you impact of the shift command on command line
8    # arguments.
9    echo "There are $# arguments specified at the command line".
10   echo "The arguments supplied are: $*"
11   echo "The first argument is: $1"
12   echo "The Process ID of the script is: $$"
13   shift
14   echo "The new first argument after the first shift is: $1"
15   shift
16   echo "The new first argument after the second shift is: $1"
```

Let us execute the script with four arguments. Notice that after each shift, a new value is assigned to $1.

com_line_arg_shift.sh toronto chicago london tokyo

```
There are 4 arguments specified at the command line.
The arguments supplied are: toronto chicago london tokyo
The first argument is: toronto
The Process ID of the script is: 27336
The new first argument after the first shift is: chicago
The new first argument after the second shift is: london
```

Multiple shifts in one attempt may be performed by furnishing a number to the *shift* command as an argument. For example, "*shift* 2" will carry out two shifts, "*shift* 3" will do three shifts and so on.

Writing an Interactive Script

Interactive shell scripts are written where you want the script to prompt for input and continue execution based on the input provided. The input gets stored into a variable. The *read* command is used for reading the input and is usually preceded by the *echo* command to display a message telling what is expected.

inter_read.sh lists files and prompts to enter a file name to be removed. Note a \c in the eleventh line. This is an example of *escape sequences*. It tells the *echo* command not to send carriage return and line feed after displaying "Enter name of file you want to remove:". When you enter a file name, you will be typing it on the same line right beside the colon character. Try running this script with and without \c. Also, a pre-defined environment variable called PWD is used in the script. This will display your location in the directory tree.

---

nl inter_read.sh

```
1   #! /bin/bash
2   # The name of this script is inter_read.sh.
3   # The author of this script is Asghar Ghori.
4   # The script is created on October 28, 2008.
5   # This script is last modified by Asghar Ghori on November 28, 2008.
6   # This script should be located in /usr/local/bin directory.
7   # The purpose of this script is to show you an example of how an interactive script works.
8   echo  "Here is a list of all files in $PWD directory:"
9   /bin/ls –l
10  echo
11  echo "Enter name of file you want to remove: \c".
12  read FILE
13  echo "Type 'y' to remove it, 'n' if you do not want to:"
14  /bin/rm –i $FILE
15  echo "The file is removed".
```

Let us assume that you are in *user1*'s home directory when this script is run. Here is what the *inter_read.sh* script will do:

$ inter_read.sh

```
. . . . . . . .
-rw-rw-r-- 1 user1 user1 2173 Nov 27 16:56 testfile1

Enter name of file you want to remove: \c.
testfile1
Type y to remove it, n if you do not want to:
/bin/rm: remove regular file `testfile1'? y
The file is removed.
```

There are some other escape sequences such as \t for tab, \n for new line, \a for beep, \f for form feed, \r for carriage return and \b for backspace that you can use in shell scripts to increase readability. Try using a few of them in *inter_read.sh* script.

Additional escape sequences such as \h, \u and \w may be used to display hostname, username and current working directory. For example, the following will change the primary command prompt to display the username, hostname and current working directory location:

```
# PS1="\u@\h:\w <\:>\$ "
root@rhel03:~ <\:>$
```

Summary

Shell scripting allows you to enclose one or more long and repetitive set of tasks into files called scripts, and run them when needed to accomplish desired results. This saves you a lot of typing. In this chapter you started off with an introduction to shell scripting. You were introduced to the components of a shell script. You wrote simple scripts to gather basic system information, define and manipulate local and environment variables, use and move command line arguments and prompt for user input. You looked at requirements to run scripts and how to debug them.

System Processes

This chapter covers the following major topics:

- ✓ Understand system and user executed processes
- ✓ Display processes
- ✓ View process states
- ✓ Nice value and how to start a process with a non-default nice value
- ✓ Modify nice value of a running process
- ✓ Run a command immune to hangup signals

A *process* is created in memory when a program or command is executed. A unique identification number, known as *process identification* (PID), is allocated to it, which is used by the kernel to manage the process until the program or command it is associated with, terminates. When a user logs on to the system, shell is started, which is a process. Similarly, when a user executes a command or opens up an application, a process is created. Thus, a process is any program, application or program that runs on the system.

Understanding Processes

Several processes are started at system boot up, many of which sit in memory and wait for an event to trigger a request to use their service. These background system processes are called *daemons* and are critical to system functionality.

Viewing System Processes

There are two commands commonly used to view currently running processes. These are *ps* (process status) and *top*.

The *ps* command without any options or arguments, lists processes specific to the terminal where the *ps* command is run:

```
$ ps
  PID  TTY   TIME     CMD
27934 pts/1  00:00:00 bash
27956 pts/1  00:00:00 ps
```

The output has four columns: PID of the process in the first column, terminal the process belongs to in the second column, cumulative time the process is given by the system CPU in the third column and actual command or program being executed in the last column.

Two options –e (every) and –f (full) are popularly used to generate detailed information on every process running in the system. Check the *ps* command man pages for more options.

```
# ps –ef
UID    PID PPID C STIME TTY  TIME    CMD
root     1   0  0 Nov05  ?   00:00:00 init [5]
root     2   1  0 Nov05  ?   00:00:00 [migration/0]
root     3   1  0 Nov05  ?   00:00:00 [ksoftirqd/0]
root     4   1  0 Nov05  ?   00:00:00 [watchdog/0]
root     5   1  0 Nov05  ?   00:24:44 [events/0]
root     6   1  0 Nov05  ?   00:00:00 [khelper]
root    37   1  0 Nov05  ?   00:00:00 [kthread]
. . . . . . . .
```

The output shows more details about running processes. Table 7-1 describes content type of each column.

Title Heading	Description
UID	User ID of process owner.
PID	Process ID of process.
PPID	Process ID of parent process.
C	Process priority.
STIME	Process start time.
TTY	Terminal where process was started. Console represents system console and ? indicates a daemon running in the background.
TIME	Cumulative execution time for process.
CMD	Command or process name.

Table 7-1 ps Command Output Explanation

Notice in the output of the *ps* command above that there are scores of daemon processes running in the background that have association with no terminals. Also notice PID and PPID numbers. The smaller the number, the earlier it is started. The process with PID 0 is started first at system boot, followed by the process with PID 1 and so on. Each PID has a PPID in the 3rd column. Owner of each process is also shown along with the command or program name.

Information of each running process is kept and maintained in a process table, which the *ps* and other commands read to display information.

The second method to view process information is the *top* command, which displays additional information including CPU and memory utilization. A sample output from a running *top* session is shown below:

```
$ top
top - 14:13:27 up 22 days, 20:10,  1 user,  load average: 0.00, 0.00, 0.00
Tasks: 82 total,  1 running, 81 sleeping,  0 stopped,  0 zombie
Cpu(s):  0.0%us,  0.1%sy,  0.0%ni, 99.9%id,  0.0%wa,  0.0%hi,  0.0%si,  0.0%st
Mem:  3866668k total,  960796k used,  2905872k free,  286744k buffers
Swap: 8421368k total,        0k used,  8421368k free,  475368k cached

PID USER  PR  NI  VIRT  RES  SHR S %CPU %MEM  TIME+  COMMAND
  1 root   15   0 10328  692  580 S  0.0   0.0  0:00.32 init
  2 root   RT  -5     0    0    0 S  0.0   0.0  0:00.00 migration/0
  3 root   34  19     0    0    0 S  0.0   0.0  0:00.00 ksoftirqd/0
  4 root   RT  -5     0    0    0 S  0.0   0.0  0:00.00 watchdog/0
  5 root   10  -5     0    0    0 S  0.0   0.0 24:45.03 events/0
  6 root   10  -5     0    0    0 S  0.0   0.0  0:00.00 khelper
 37 root   10  -5     0    0    0 S  0.0   0.0  0:00.00 kthread
 41 root   10  -5     0    0    0 S  0.0   0.0  0:00.02 kblockd/0
 42 root   20  -5     0    0    0 S  0.0   0.0  0:00.00 kacpid
 98 root   20  -5     0    0    0 S  0.0   0.0  0:00.00 cqueue/0
101 root   20  -5     0    0    0 S  0.0   0.0  0:00.00 khubd
103 root   10  -5     0    0    0 S  0.0   0.0  0:00.00 kseriod
169 root   25   0     0    0    0 S  0.0   0.0  0:00.00 pdflush
```

Press Ctrl+c to quit.

If *top* is run in an X terminal window, the screen will look similar to the one shown in Figure 7-1.

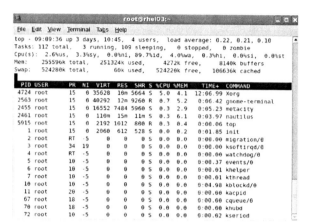

Figure 7-1 top in X Window

A third method to list, monitor and manage processes is a graphical tool called *system monitor* which can be started with the *gnome-system-monitor* command or by choosing (GNOME) System → Administration → System Monitor. A sample is displayed in Figure 7-2. An equivalent tool in KDE is called *kpm*.

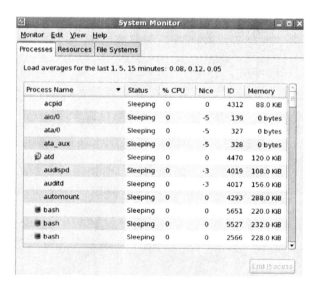

Figure 7-2 GNOME System Monitor

Listing a Specific Process

The *pidof* command can be used to list the PID of a specific process if you know the name of the process. For example, to list the PID of the *cupsd* daemon process, run the command as follows:

```
$ pidof cupsd
4312
```

Determining Processes by Ownership

Processes can be listed by their ownership or group membership. The *pgrep* command is used for this purpose. For example, to list all processes owned by *root*, use the –U option and specify the user name:

 # pgrep –U root
```
1
2
3
4
5
6
7
10
11
67
70
. . . . . . . .
```

With the –G option, this command lists all processes with the specified group name.

Process States

After a process is started, it does not run continuously. It may be in a non-running condition for a while or waiting for some other process to feed it with information so it continues to run. There are five process states: *running, sleeping, waiting, stopped* and *zombie*.

- ✓ The running state determines that the process is currently being executed by system CPU.
- ✓ The sleeping state shows that the process is currently waiting for input from user or another process.
- ✓ The waiting state means that the process has received input it has been waiting for and it is now ready to run as soon as its turn comes.
- ✓ The stopped state indicates that the process is currently halted and will not run even when its turn comes, unless it is sent a signal.
- ✓ The zombie state determines that the process is dead. A zombie process exists in process table just as any other process entry, but takes up no resources. The entry for zombie is retained until the parent process permits it to die. A zombie process is also called a *defunct* process.

Process Priority

Process priority is determined using the *nice* value. The system assigns a nice value to a process when it is initiated to establish priority.

A total of 40 nice values exists with -20 being the highest and +19 the lowest. Most system-started processes use the default nice value of 0. A child process inherits the nice value of its parent process.

Use the *ps* command and specify the –l option to determine nice values of running processes. See associated nice values for each process under the "NI" column in the following example:

```
# ps –efl
F S UID      PID PPID C PRI NI    ADDR  SZ    WCHAN STIME TTY TIME      CMD
4 S root      1    0   0  75  0    -     2582  -     Nov05 ?   00:00:00 init [5]
1 S root      2    1   0 -40  -    -     0     -     Nov05 ?   00:00:00 [migration/0]
1 S root      3    1   0  94 19    -     0     -     Nov05 ?   00:00:00 [ksoftirqd/0]
5 S root      4    1   0 -40  -    -     0     -     Nov05 ?   00:00:00 [watchdog/0]
. . . . . . . .
```

A different priority may be assigned to a program or command at the time it is initiated. For example, to run *system-config-users* with higher priority:

 # nice –2 system-config-users

The value assigned with *nice* is relative to the default nice value. The number –2 is added to 0, which means the specified program will run at a higher priority since its nice value is -2.

With no priority defined with the *nice* command, it adds 10 to the default priority to make it +10. Normal users can enhance their nice values but cannot reduce them.

To run the same program at a higher priority with nice value 18, use a pair of dash characters:

 # nice --2 system-config-users

The priority of a running program can be altered as well using the *renice* command. For example, to change the nice value of the running *system-config-users* program from -10 to +5, specify its PID (21342) with the *renice* command:

 # renice –n 5 21342
21342: old priority -10, new priority 5

Add 20 to –10 to get the previous nice value, which was +10. The new priority is actually 25 (20 + 5) but the system shows 5.

To alter nice values of all processes owned by members of a particular group, use the –g option with *renice*. Similarly, to alter nice values of all processes owned by a particular user, use the –u option with it. Check *renice* command's man pages on the usage.

Listing Open Files

A file is opened when the process or program stored in it is executed and closed when no longer required or the associated process or program is terminated. To determine information such as which files are open, which processes are using them and who the owners are, the *lsof* (list open files) command is used. Without any options, this command displays a list of all open files.

```
# lsof
COMMAND PID    USER  FD    TYPE  DEVICE  SIZE   NODE  NAME
init     1     root  cwd   DIR   253,0   4096   2     /
init     1     root  rtd   DIR   253,0   4096   2     /
init     1     root  txt   REG   253,0   38652  95475 /sbin/init
. . . . . . . .
```

The command generated nine columns in the output that are listed and explained in Table 7-2.

Column	Description
COMMAND	Displays the first nine characters of the command or process name.
PID	Displays the PID of the process.
USER	Displays the owner of the process.
FD	Displays the file descriptor of the file. Some of the values in this field would be: cwd = current working directory; rtd = root directory txt = text file; mem = memory-mapped file; pd = parent directory
TYPE	Displays the file's node type.
DEVICE	Displays the major and minor numbers of the device on which the file is located.
SIZE	Displays the file size or offset in bytes.
NODE	Displays the inode number of the file.
NAME	Displays the file name or the file system name where the file resides.

Table 7-2 lsof Command Output

Signals and Their Use

A system runs several processes simultaneously. Sometimes it becomes necessary to pass a notification to a process alerting it of an event. A user or the system uses a signal to pass that notification to a process. A signal contains a signal number and is used to control processes.

There are a number of signals available for use but most of the time you deal with only a few of them. Each signal is associated with a unique number, a name and an action. A list of available signals can be displayed with the *kill* command using the –l option:

```
# kill –l
 1) SIGHUP        2) SIGINT        3) SIGQUIT       4) SIGILL
 5) SIGTRAP       6) SIGABRT       7) SIGBUS        8) SIGFPE
 9) SIGKILL      10) SIGUSR1      11) SIGSEGV      12) SIGUSR2
13) SIGPIPE      14) SIGALRM      15) SIGTERM      16) SIGSTKFLT
17) SIGCHLD      18) SIGCONT      19) SIGSTOP      20) SIGTSTP
21) SIGTTIN      22) SIGTTOU      23) SIGURG       24) SIGXCPU
25) SIGXFSZ      26) SIGVTALRM    27) SIGPROF      28) SIGWINCH
29) SIGIO        30) SIGPWR       31) SIGSYS       34) SIGRTMIN
35) SIGRTMIN+1   36) SIGRTMIN+2   37) SIGRTMIN+3   38) SIGRTMIN+4
39) SIGRTMIN+5   40) SIGRTMIN+6   41) SIGRTMIN+7   42) SIGRTMIN+8
43) SIGRTMIN+9   44) SIGRTMIN+10  45) SIGRTMIN+11  46) SIGRTMIN+12
47) SIGRTMIN+13  48) SIGRTMIN+14  49) SIGRTMIN+15  50) SIGRTMAX-14
51) SIGRTMAX-13  52) SIGRTMAX-12  53) SIGRTMAX-11  54) SIGRTMAX-10
55) SIGRTMAX-9   56) SIGRTMAX-8   57) SIGRTMAX-7   58) SIGRTMAX-6
59) SIGRTMAX-5   60) SIGRTMAX-4   61) SIGRTMAX-3   62) SIGRTMAX-2
63) SIGRTMAX-1   64) SIGRTMAX
```

Table 7-3 describes signals that are used more oftenly.

Number	Name	Action	Response
1	SIGHUP	Hang up signal causes a phone line or terminal connection to be dropped. Also used to force a running daemon to re-read its configuration file.	Exit
2	SIGINT	Interrupt signal issued from keyboard, usually by ^c.	Exit
9	SIGKILL	Kills a process abruptly by force.	Exit
15	SIGTERM	Sends a process a soft TERMination signal to stop it in an orderly fashion. This signal is default.	Exit

Table 7-3 Key Signals

The commands used to pass a signal to a process are *kill* and *pkill*. These commands are usually used to terminate a process. Ordinary users can kill processes they own, while *root* can kill any process.

The syntax of the *kill* command to kill a process is:

kill PID
kill –s <signal name or number> PID

Specify multiple PIDs if you wish to kill all of them in one go.

The syntax of the *pkill* command to kill a process is:

pkill process_name
pkill –s <signal name or number> process_name

Specify multiple process names if you wish to kill all of them in one go.

Let us look at a few examples.

To pass the soft terminate signal to the printing daemon *cupsd*, use one of the following to determine PID of it:

```
# ps –ef | grep cupsd
root    4417    1  0 Nov05 ?      00:00:00 cupsd
# pgrep cupsd
4417
# pidof cupsd
4417
```

Now pass signal 15 to the process using any of the following:

```
# kill 4417                    # pkill cupsd
# kill –s 15 4417              # pkill –s 15 cupsd
# kill –15 4417               # pkill –15 cupsd
# kill –SIGTERM 4417          # pkill –SIGTERM cupsd
# kill –s SIGTERM 4417
```

Using the *kill* or *pkill* command without specifying a signal name or number sends default signal of 15 to the process. This signal usually causes the process to terminate.

Red Hat Certified Technician & Engineer

Some processes ignore signal 15 as they might be waiting for an input to continue processing. Such processes can be terminated by force using signal 9:

> **$ kill –s 9 4417**
> **$ pkill –9 cupsd**

You may wish to run the *killall* command to kill all running processes that match the specified criteria. Here is how you would kill all *cupsd* processes:

> **# killall cupsd**

Executing a Command Immune to Hangup Signals

When a command or program is executed, it ties itself to the terminal session where it is initiated. It does not release the control of the terminal session to the shell until the command or program finishes execution. During this time, if the terminal session is closed or terminated, the running command or program is also terminated. Imagine a large file transfer of several GBs was occurring and was about to finish when this unwanted termination occurred.

To avoid such a situation, use the *nohup* (no hang up) command to execute commands or programs that need to run for extended periods of time without being interrupted. For example, to copy */opt/data1* directory recursively containing 4GB of data to */opt/data2*, issue the *cp* command as follows:

> **# nohup cp –av /opt/data1 /opt/data2 &**

Summary

You studied about processes in this chapter. A good understanding of what user and system processes are running is vital for performance and general system administration. You learned how to display processes and about the five process states.

You studied nice values and how they were used to compute priority for a given process. You may either execute a process or command with the default nice value or assign one when you run it. You can always modify nice value of a process at any time in future while the process is still running.

Next, you looked at signals and understood what they did when passed to processes via the *kill* or *pkill* command.

Finally, you learned how to manage background jobs and run commands immune to hangup signals.

## 08

System Administration and Hardware

This chapter covers the following major topics:

- ✓ Responsibilities of a RHEL system administrator
- ✓ Help resources available to a RHEL system administrator
- ✓ Overview of PC hardware components
- ✓ Device files
- ✓ Major and minor numbers
- ✓ View hardware diagnostic messages
- ✓ Available hardware to work with

System administration is a series of management tasks that a person referred to as *system administrator*, is responsible for carrying out on a routine basis. The computing environment which the system administrator is responsible for may comprise one or more networked RHEL systems. Administration on standalone RHEL systems is referred to as *system administration* and administration of services that involve more than one systems is referred to as *network administration*. In the RHEL world, the term *system administrator* is commonly used for an individual that performs both system and network administration tasks.

System Administration Overview

The RHEL system administrator is responsible for installing, configuring, supporting and troubleshooting computers that run RHEL in a networked environment. This includes hardware integration and management, system virtualization and installation, as well as administration and support of software packages, users and groups, LVM and RAID, file systems and swap, system boot and kernel, backups and printing, scheduling and logging, network interfaces and routing, naming and internet services, email and time synchronization, resource sharing and automated installation, security and system hardening, and troubleshooting and resolving issues.

The system administrator requires an infrequent data center access and *root* user privileges to configure and support a RHEL based computing infrastructure.

System Administrator Resources

There are certain resources available to the system administrator to help perform system and network administration tasks effectively and efficiently. Some of the key resources are:

✓ Online *man* pages – loaded on the system as part of a RHEL installation. See Chapter 01 "Overview of Linux" on usage and details.
✓ */usr/share/doc* – contains documentation with basic information related to installed packages.
✓ *www.redhat.com/docs/manuals* – contains release notes, white papers, hardware compatibility list (HCL) and guides on installation, deployment, virtualization, etc. Visit this site to access up-to-date technical information.

In addition, there are thousands of linux support forums and websites on the Internet that you can use to obtain information and help.

Personal Computer Architecture and Components

This section briefly examines architecture and common hardware components found in personal computers (PCs). An understanding of these components is paramount in the sense that it would help you interact with a PC in a better way.

Even though RHEL runs on IBM mainframe systems (s390x) and other hardware architectures such as IBM PowerPC and Intel Itanium, PCs with 32-bit and 64-bit Intel and AMD processors are widely used in the industry for running RHEL.

In PCs, communication takes place via three key channels – *Interrupt Request* (IRQ), *Input/Output address* (I/O address) and *Direct Memory Address* (DMA). Modern PCs use a feature called *plug and play*, which allows operating systems such as RHEL to manage these communication channels automatically without human interaction.

An IRQ is a signal sent by a device to the CPU to request processing time. The requesting device may be a network interface, graphics adapter, mouse, modem, printer, keyboard, USB device or a serial port. Each device attached to a computer may require a dedicated IRQ. Newer devices such as USB devices can share IRQs. To check which IRQs are in use, view the */proc/interrupts* file:

```
# cat /proc/interrupts
         CPU0
  0: 2062990559   IO-APIC-edge  timer
  1:         11   IO-APIC-edge  i8042
  6:          5   IO-APIC-edge  floppy
  7:          0   IO-APIC-edge  parport0
  8:          0   IO-APIC-edge  rtc
  9:          0   IO-APIC-level acpi
 12:        107   IO-APIC-edge  i8042
 14:    7214895   IO-APIC-edge  ide0
169:     333194   IO-APIC-level ioc0
177:    1270165   IO-APIC-level eth0
. . . . . . . .
```

An I/O address is a memory storage location used for communication between different parts of a computer and the CPU. To check for a list of assigned I/O addresses, view the */proc/ioports* file:

```
# cat /proc/ioports
0000-001f : dma1
0020-0021 : pic1
0040-0043 : timer0
0050-0053 : timer1
0060-006f : keyboard
0070-0077 : rtc
0080-008f : dma page reg
00a0-00a1 : pic2
00c0-00df : dma2
00f0-00ff : fpu
01f0-01f7 : ide0
02f8-02ff : serial
. . . . . . . .
```

A DMA channel is used when a device has its own processor and can bypass the system CPU when exchanging data with other devices. Examples of such devices include sound card and fibre channel cards. There are eight (0 to 7) DMA channels. To check assigned DMA addresses, view the */proc/dma* file:

```
# cat /proc/dma
2: floppy
4: cascade
```

Slot

An *I/O slot* (or simply a *slot*) is a receptacle for installing an interface card. Figure 8-1 shows a system board with multiple I/O slots.

Figure 8-1 Slots

PC Card

PC card (originally called *PCMCIA card* and stood for *Personal Computer Memory Card International Association*) was designed to support memory expansion in laptop computers. Later, the scope enhanced and network and modem PC cards were also widely available in this form factor, which led to the name change to PC card (a.k.a. *CardBus* cards). In order to use these cards in RHEL, you need to install a software package called Card Services. Today, with a lot of enhancements, these cards are now called *ExpressCards*.

ExpressCards are much more versatile. They can accept FireWire, SATA, wireless, memory card reader, memory and several other types of devices with much faster connectivity to the system. ExpressCards are widely used in newer laptop computers, and are not backward compatible with PC cards or CardBus cards.

PCI and PCIe

PCI stands for *Peripheral Component Interconnect* and PCIe stands for *PCI express*. These technologies include a slot, an interface adapter that goes into the slot and the electronic circuitry that connects the slot to the system board. PCs come with a mix of both PCI and PCIe slots, and I/O cards that fit into them.

PCI provides a shared data path between CPUs and I/O adapters. It runs at 33MHz and 66MHz speeds and supports both 32-bit and 64-bit data paths. Figure 8-2 shows a picture of a PCI card.

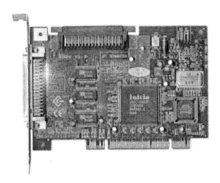

Figure 8-2 PCI Card

PCIe is an enhanced version of PCI and is backward compatible to it. PCIe runs at 133MHz and 266MHz speeds and supports both 32-bit and 64-bit data paths, but 64-bit are more common. The 64-bit PCIe slots and PCIe adapters are longer in size than their PCI counterparts and are almost twice as fast. These cards were designed to replace PCI, PCI-X, and AGP graphics cards.

Interface Card

An *interface card* is either integrated onto the system board or plugs into one of the system slots. It enables the system to communicate with external hardware devices. Different types of interface cards are available to connect fibre channel, SCSI, Ethernet and other types of external devices. Interface cards are also referred to as *host adapters, device adapters* and *controller cards*. Figures 8-2 through 8-6 show different types of interface cards.

Network Interface Card (NIC)

A *Network Interface Card* (NIC) connects a system to the network. It is usually built-in to the system board and also available as an interface card. It enables the system to talk to other systems on the network. You must have proper software driver installed in order to use it. Multiport NICs are also available that provide 2 or 4 ports on a single physical card. Figure 8-3 shows pictures of 1-port and 4-port NICs.

Figure 8-3 Network Interface Cards

By default, device files associated with network interfaces on RHEL are *eth0, eth1, eth2* and so on.

Small Computer System Interface (SCSI) Card

Small Computer System Interface (SCSI) (pronounced scuzzy) was developed in 1986 and has since been widely used in computers. SCSI is an I/O bus technology controlled by a set of protocols. It allows several peripheral devices including hard drives, tape drives and CD/DVD drives to be connected to a single SCSI controller card (a.k.a. SCSI *Host Bus Adapter* – HBA). Figure 8-4 shows a picture of a SCSI HBA.

Figure 8-4 SCSI Card

Many types of SCSI HBAs are available, and they differ based on factors such as bandwidth, data transfer speed and pin count on the connector. Table 8-1 lists and compares them.

Type	Bus Width	Max Speed
SCSI	8 bit	5MB/second
Wide SCSI	16 bit	10MB/second
Fast SCSI	8 bit	10MB/second
Fast Wide SCSI	16 bit	20MB/second
Ultra SCSI	8 bit	20MB/second
Ultra Wide SCSI	16 bit	40MB/second
Ultra2 SCSI	8 bit	40MB/second
Ultra2 Wide SCSI	16 bit	80MB/second
Ultra160 (Ultra 3)	16 bit	160MB/second
Ultra320	16 bit	320MB/second
Ultra640	16 bit	640MB/second

Table 8-1 SCSI Chart

When working with SCSI devices and SCSI cards, make sure that the two are of the same type. For example, an Ultra3 SCSI DVD drive requires that the HBA it is connected to is also Ultra3 SCSI.

Fibre Channel (FC) Card

A *Fibre Channel* (FC) *card* provides systems with optical connectivity to a fibre channel-based network and storage devices such as switches, disk storage and tape libraries.

FC cards are available in 1Gbps (*gigabits per second*), 2Gbps and 4Gbps speeds. The FC cards with 1Gbps speed have the connector type called *Siemens Connector* (SC); the higher speed cards have a different type of connector called *Lucent Connector* (LC).

The FC cards (a.k.a. FC HBAs) are available in single and dual port packaging. Figure 8-5 shows both types with LC connector interface.

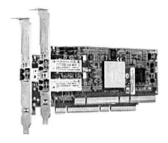

Figure 8-5 Fibre Channel Cards

Multi-I/O (MIO) Card

A *Multi-I/O* (MIO) *card* (a.k.a. a *combo card*) is a card that has the capability built-in to it to perform more than one functions concurrently. Such cards are commonly used in computers to save on slots. Some examples of MIO cards include:

✓ Cards with a combination of Ethernet and SCSI ports.
✓ Cards with a combination of Ethernet and fibre channel ports.
✓ Cards with a combination of SCSI and fibre channel ports.
✓ Cards with a combination of Ethernet and modem ports.

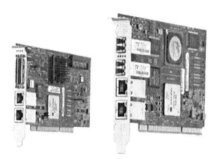

Figure 8-6 Multi-I/O Cards

Bus

All hardware components such as processors, memory and interface cards communicate with one another through electrical circuits called *buses*. Data flows between processor and memory, memory and disk, memory and interface cards and so on. Busses can be internal or external. Internal busses facilitate data movement within the system while external buses allow external devices to become part of the system through interface adapters.

Processor/Core

RHEL runs on several types of hardware architectures – Intel, AMD, Integrity, PowerPC and mainframe.

The Intel, AMD, Integrity and PowerPC processors are available in dual- and quad-core configurations meaning that a single processor chip has two or four independent processors on it that share the chip connections to the system board. To know what kind of CPUs your system has, check */proc/cpuinfo*:

```
# cat /proc/cpuinfo
processor       : 0
vendor_id       : GenuineIntel
cpu family      : 6
model           : 15
model name      : Intel(R) Xeon(R) CPU       E5345  @ 2.33GHz
stepping        : 8
cpu MHz         : 2333.186
cache size      : 4096 KB
fpu             : yes
fpu_exception   : yes
cpuid level     : 10
wp              : yes
flags           : fpu vme de pse tsc msr pae mce cx8 apic sep mtrr pge mca cmov pat pse36
clflush dts acpi mmx fxsr sse sse2 ss syscall lm constant_tsc up pni ds_cpl cx16 lahf_lm
bogomips        : 4672.72
clflush size    : 64
cache_alignment : 64
address sizes   : 36 bits physical, 48 bits virtual
power management:
```

Hard Drive

A hard drive is a mass storage device used for storing data. It is the device where RHEL is installed. There are several supported types of hard drives used in PCs. These are:

- ✓ PATA (*Parallel Advanced Technology Attachment*) drives: These drives are widely recognized as IDE (*Integrated Drive Electronics*) and EIDE (*Enhanced IDE*) drives. Up to 4 such drives are supported in a PC concurrently. Disks and CD/DVD drives are common.
- ✓ SATA (*Serial Advanced Technology Attachment*) drives: This drive technology is successor to PATA.
- ✓ Parallel SCSI drives: Up to 31 SCSI drives (disks, CD/DVD) are supported.
- ✓ SAS (*Serial Attached SCSI*) drives: A faster technology to replace SCSI drives. SAS devices include disks, CD/DVD, scanners, printers, etc.
- ✓ FireWire drives: These drives support installing Linux, but the boot files must be located either on a boot floppy or CD/DVD.
- ✓ USB (*Universal Serial Bus*) drives: These drives support installing Linux, but the boot files must be located either on a boot floppy or CD/DVD.

PCs support a mix of of all types of drives.

Serial Port

There are a number of serial port devices available on the market. These include external modems, printers and mice. When a device is attached to a serial port, RHEL assigns it a device file. For example, the default modem device file is */dev/ttyS0*. Protocols such as *Serial Line Internet Protocol* (SLIP) and *Point to Point Protocol* (PPP) can be configured on serial ports to connect a system to IP networks. Device files for SLIP would be */dev/slip0*, */dev/slip1* and so on and that for PPP would be */dev/ppp0*, */dev/ppp1* and so on.

Parallel Port

Several different types of peripheral devices can be attached to a parallel port. Most common among these is the printer. Other devices include an external hard drive. When a device is attached to a parallel port, RHEL assigns it a device file. For example, the default parallel printer device file is */dev/lp0*. If you wish to see what device file is associated with a printer, view the */etc/cups/printers.conf* file.

Universal Serial Bus (USB)

USB technology allows several peripheral devices to be connected to a single system port providing plug and play capability. The use of USB devices is rising rapidly. Flash drives, hard drives, printers, cameras, video camcorders, keyboards, mice, etc. are available for USB. RHEL recognizes and creates device files when a USB device is plugged in.

FireWire

FireWire is the famous name for the IEEE 1394 specification developed for applications such as movies that require data transfer at extremely high speeds. Another common name for FireWire is *iLink*. RHEL recognizes and creates device files when a FireWire device is plugged in.

Advanced Configuration and Power Interface (ACPI)

Advanced Configuration and Power Interface (ACPI) is a statndard for managing power consumption on computers. It allows the operating system such as RHEL and MS Windows to control computer power consumtion. ACPI is the successor to *Advanced Power Management* (APM) used earlier in computers to enable power management via system BIOS.

Hardware Management

Following sub-sections cover hardware device management including topics such as hardware abstraction layer, plug and play, hardware device files, probing and configuring devices, listing device information, major and minor numbers, and how to view hardware diagnostic messages.

Hardware Abstraction Layer and Plug and Play

The *Hardware Abstraction Layer* (HAL) is a piece of software implemented to function between the Linux kernel and the underlying system hardware. It hides differences in hardware from the kernel to enable it to run on a variety of hardware platforms.

The implementation of HAL in RHEL has enabled it to work on a variety of computer system hardware. The *hald* daemon runs on the system and maintains a list of devices. It automatically detects any new hardware added to the system on the fly. If the added hardware is a CD/DVD or a USB drive, the daemon mounts the device on the pre-defined mount point.

The *Plug and Play* (PnP) functionality uses HAL to allow a removable device added to the system to work with RHEL without any manual intervention. This ability autoconfigures necessary IRQs, I/O addresses and DMA settings for the device.

The *lshal* command displays a list of all detected hardware in the system:

```
# lshal
Dumping 48 device(s) from the Global Device List:
-------------------------------------------------
udi = '/org/freedesktop/Hal/devices/computer'
  info.callouts.add = {'hal-storage-cleanup-all-mountpoints'} (string list)
  org.freedesktop.Hal.Device.SystemPowerManagement.method_execpaths = {'hal-system-power-
suspend', 'hal-system-power-suspend-clear-error', 'hal-system-power-hibernate', 'hal-system-power-
hibernate-clear-error', 'hal-system-power-shutdown','hal-system-power-reboot', 'hal-system-power-set-
power-save'} (string list)
  org.freedesktop.Hal.Device.SystemPowerManagement.method_argnames = {'num_secon
ds_to_sleep', '', '', '', '', '', 'enable_power_save'} (string list)
  org.freedesktop.Hal.Device.SystemPowerManagement.method_signatures = {'i', '', '', '', '', '', 'b'} (string
list)
  org.freedesktop.Hal.Device.SystemPowerManagement.method_names = {'Suspend',
'SuspendClearError', 'Hibernate', 'HibernateClearError', 'Shutdown', 'Reboot', 'SetPowerSave'} (string list)
  info.interfaces = {'org.freedesktop.Hal.Device.SystemPowerManagement'} (string list)
  info.addons = {'hald-addon-acpi'} (string list)
  system.formfactor = 'unknown' (string)
  system.product = 'VMware Virtual Platform None' (string)
  system.vendor = 'VMware, Inc.' (string)
  system.chassis.type = 'Other' (string)
  system.chassis.manufacturer = 'No Enclosure' (string)
  system.firmware.release_date = '01/30/2008' (string)
  system.firmware.version = '6.00' (string)
. . . . . . . .
```

You can use the *hal-device* command to view hardware device information in text mode, or its graphical equivalent *hal-device-manager* as shown in Figure 8-7. You will need to load the hal-gnome package using one of the package installation methods outlined in Chapter 11 "Software Package Management" to access this tool.

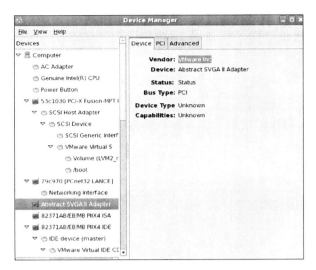

Figure 8-7 HAL Device Manager

Hardware Device Files

RHEL supports a wide variety of hardware devices such as hard drives, CD/DVD drives, USB drives, floppy drives, tape drives, printers, scanners, mice, keyboards, etc. and accesses them via device files which are automatically created in the *dev* directory when RHEL detects the presence of devices. Table 8-2 describes device files for various types of devices.

Device Category	Device Type	Device File
Hard drive and CD/DVD drives	PATA / IDE	*/dev/hda, /dev/hdb* and so on.
	SATA / SCSI / SAS / FireWire	*/dev/sda, /dev/sdb* and so on.
	Parallel	*/dev/pd1, /dev/pd2* and so on.
USB flash drives	USB	Usually device specific.
Floppy drive	PATA / IDE	*/dev/fd0, /dev/fd1* and so on.
Tape drive	Parallel	*/dev/pt1, /dev/pt2* and so on.

Table 8-2 Common Device Files

As an example the following output demonstrates that the CD drive at */dev/cdrom* is connected to the first PATA interface:

 # ll /dev/cdrom
```
lrwxrwxrwx  1  root  root  3  Nov  5 18:03  /dev/cdrom  ->  hda
```

Probing and Configuring Devices

Each time a system is rebooted, a startup script */etc/rc.d/init.d/kudzu* is executed which issues the *kudzu* command to probe the system hardware for any added or removed devices. The *kudzu* command scans the system and compares the devices found against the devices listed in the */etc/sysconfig/hwconf* file, which contains information about the devices detected and configured at the previous system boot or the last execution of the *kudzu* command. If no differences are found, the *kudzu* command takes no action. In case a new device is discovered, *kudzu* configures it and updates the *hwconf* file if you answer yes when prompted. In case *kudzu* is unable to detect a device which is listed in the *hwconf* file, it unconfigures the device and removes the associated entry from the file if you answer yes when prompted.

Certain key options such as –b, –c and –p are available with *kudzu* that can be used with the command if you wish to run it manually. With –b option, the command scans for devices on the specified hardware bus; with –c option, it probes for devices that belong to the specified class; and with –p option, the command probes the hardware without configuring or unconfiguring any devices.

 # kudzu –p

-
class: OTHER
bus: PCI
detached: 0
driver: i2c-piix4
desc: "Intel Corporation 82371AB/EB/MB PIIX4 ACPI"
vendorId: 8086
deviceId: 7113
subVendorId: 15ad
subDeviceId: 1976

. . . .

 # kudzu –p –b PCI

-
class: OTHER
bus: PCI
detached: 0
driver: i2c-piix4
desc: "Intel Corporation 82371AB/EB/MB PIIX4 ACPI"
vendorId: 8086
deviceId: 7113
subVendorId: 15ad
subDeviceId: 1976

. . . .

 # kudzu –p –c NETWORK

-
class: NETWORK
bus: PCI
detached: 0
device: eth0
driver: pcnet32
desc: "Advanced Micro Devices [AMD] 79c970 [PCnet32 LANCE]"
network.hwaddr: 00:0c:29:4f:cf:01
vendorId: 1022
deviceId: 2000
subVendorId: 1022
subDeviceId: 2000

. . . .

As part of configuring a new device, *kudzu* references files under the */usr/share/hwdata* directory and adds corresponding kernel module for the device. You may need to install or update the hwdata software package using one of the package management tools identified in Chapter 11 "Software Package Management".

Managing Device Files Dynamically with udev

All hardware device files are located in the */dev* directory and are added or removed if the associated device is detected or detached. This happens automatically and dynamically using a RHEL feature called *udev*. With udev, device management is performed via the *udevd* daemon that receives events directly from the kernel on device addition and deletion. It then adds or removes device files under */dev* as appropriate based on rules defined in files under the */etc/rules.d* directory. With udev, only those device files are present in the */dev* directory that have matching devices currently available, all other files are removed.

udev includes a daemon, configuration files and commands as listed and explained in Table 8-3.

	Description
Daemon	
udevd	Daemon that gets device add and delete information from kernel and passes it onto udev for processing.
Configuration Files	
/etc/udev/udev.conf	Specifies the locations for device files and udev rules, and an appropriate log level (err, info or debug). The defaults are /dev, /etc/udev/rules.d and err, respectively.
/etc/udev/rules.d	Contains rules to apply to devices being added or removed. Rules include device file name, ownership and group membership, symlink name and device file permissions in addition to the commands to be executed to complete the process.
Commands	
udevinfo	Queries and displays device information.
udevtest	Simulates a udev execution for the specified device.
udevmonitor	Displays kernel and udev events.
udevcontrol	Handles the udevd daemon.
udevtrigger	Requests kernel device events for cold plugged devices.

Table 8-3 udev Daemon, Configuration Files and Commands

An excerpt from a rules file */etc/udev/rules.d/50-udev.rules* is shown below:

```
# cat /etc/udev/rules.d/50-udev.rules
. . . . . . . .
KERNEL=="*", OWNER="root" GROUP="root", MODE="0600"

# all block devices
SUBSYSTEM=="block",        GROUP="disk", MODE="0640"
KERNEL=="root",            GROUP="disk", MODE="0640"

# console devices
```

```
KERNEL=="tty",            NAME="%k", GROUP="tty", MODE="0666", OPTIONS="last_rule"
KERNEL=="console",        NAME="%k", MODE="0600", OPTIONS="last_rule"
KERNEL=="tty[0-9]*",      NAME="%k", GROUP="tty", MODE="0660", OPTIONS="last_rule"
KERNEL=="vc/[0-9]*",      NAME="%k", GROUP="tty", MODE="0660", OPTIONS="last_rule"

# pty devices
# Set this to 0660 if you only want users belonging to tty group
# to be able to allocate PTYs
KERNEL=="ptmx",           NAME="%k", GROUP="tty", MODE="666", OPTIONS="last_rule"
KERNEL=="pty[pqrstuvwxyzabcdef][0123456789abcdef]", NAME="%k", GROUP="tty", MODE
="660", OPTIONS="last_rule"
KERNEL=="tty[pqrstuvwxyzabcdef][0123456789abcdef]", NAME="%k", GROUP="tty", MODE
="660", OPTIONS="last_rule"
KERNEL=="pty/m*",         NAME="%k", GROUP="tty", MODE="0660", OPTIONS="last_rule"

# serial+dialup devices
KERNEL=="ippp*",          NAME="%k", MODE="0660"
KERNEL=="isdn*",          NAME="%k", MODE="0660"
KERNEL=="isdnctrl*",      NAME="%k", MODE="0660"
KERNEL=="capi",           NAME="capi20", GROUP="uucp", MODE="0660"
KERNEL=="capi*",          NAME="capi/%n", GROUP="uucp", MODE="0660"
. . . . . . . .
```

This file contains rules for different kinds of devices such as block, console, pseudo terminal, serial, dialup, memory, tape, keyboard and USB devices. It defines file names, ownership, group membership and permission modes that will be assigned to device files.

To display all devices that are currently configured in the udev database, run the *udevinfo* command with –e option:

```
# udevinfo –e
P: /block/fd0
N: fd0
S: floppy
S: floppy-fd0

P: /block/hdc
N: hdc
S: cdrom
S: cdrom-hdc
S: disk/by-id/ata-VMware_Virtual_IDE_CDROM_Drive_10000000000000000001
S: disk/by-path/pci-0000:00:07.1-ide-0:0
E: ID_TYPE=cd
E: ID_MODEL=VMware_Virtual_IDE_CDROM_Drive
E: ID_SERIAL=10000000000000000001
E: ID_REVISION=00000001
E: ID_BUS=ata
E: ID_PATH=pci-0000:00:07.1-ide-0:0
. . . . . . . .
```

To query an individual device such as *\/dev\/sde*:

udevinfo –a –p /block/sde/sde
. . . .
  looking at device '/block/sde':
   KERNEL=="sde"
   SUBSYSTEM=="block"
   SYSFS{stat}=="   242   10   1552   109   0   0   0   0   0   109   109"
   SYSFS{size}=="8388608"
   SYSFS{removable}=="0"
   SYSFS{range}=="16"
   SYSFS{dev}=="8:64"

  looking at parent device '/devices/pci0000:00/0000:00:10.0/host0/target0:0:4/0:0:4:0':
   ID=="0:0:4:0"
   BUS=="scsi"
   DRIVER=="sd"
   SYSFS{ioerr_cnt}=="0xf"
   SYSFS{iodone_cnt}=="0x117"
. . . .

To display more information about a specific device such as *sde1*:

udevinfo –q all –n sde
P: /block/sde
N: sde
S: disk/by-path/pci-0000:00:10.0-scsi-0:0:4:0
E: ID_VENDOR=VMware,
E: ID_MODEL=VMware_Virtual_S
E: ID_REVISION=1.0
E: ID_SERIAL=
E: ID_TYPE=disk
E: ID_BUS=scsi
E: ID_PATH=pci-0000:00:10.0-scsi-0:0:4:0

Listing Device Information

Information about PCI, USB and PC card devices can be gathered and displayed using commands such as *lspci*, *lsusb* and *pccardctl* in addition to the *lshal* command.

The *lspci* command displays information about PCI buses and devices attached to them. Specify –v, –vv or –vvv for detailed output. With –m option, the command enhanced readability of the output.

lspci –m
00:00.0 "Host bridge" "Intel Corporation" "440BX/ZX/DX - 82443BX/ZX/DX Host bridge" -r01
"VMware Inc" "Virtual Machine Chipset"
00:01.0 "PCI bridge" "Intel Corporation" "440BX/ZX/DX - 82443BX/ZX/DX AGP bridge" -r01 "" ""
00:07.0 "ISA bridge" "Intel Corporation" "82371AB/EB/MB PIIX4 ISA" -r08 "VMware Inc" "Virtual
Machine Chipset"

00:07.1 "IDE interface" "Intel Corporation" "82371AB/EB/MB PIIX4 IDE" -r01 -p8a "VMware Inc" "Virtual Machine Chipset"
00:07.3 "Bridge" "Intel Corporation" "82371AB/EB/MB PIIX4 ACPI" -r08 "VMware Inc" "Virtual Machine Chipset"
00:0f.0 "VGA compatible controller" "VMware Inc" "Abstract SVGA II Adapter" "VMware Inc" "Abstract SVGA II Adapter"
00:10.0 "SCSI storage controller" "LSI Logic / Symbios Logic" "53c1030 PCI-X Fusion-MPT Dual Ultra320 SCSI" -r01 "" ""
00:11.0 "Ethernet controller" "Advanced Micro Devices [AMD]" "79c970 [PCnet32 LANCE]" -r10 "Advanced Micro Devices [AMD]" "PCnet - Fast 79C971"

The *lsusb* command displays information about USB buses and devices connected to them. Specify −v option for verbosity.

> # **lsusb**
> Bus 002 Device 001: ID 0000:0000
> Bus 003 Device 001: ID 0000:0000
> Bus 004 Device 001: ID 0000:0000
> Bus 005 Device 001: ID 0000:0000

The *pccardctl* command monitors and controls the state of PCMCIA sockets on a laptop computer. See its man pages for details.

Major and Minor Numbres

Every hardware device in the system has an associated device driver loaded in the kernel. Some of the hardware device types are disks, CD/DVD drives, tape drives, printers, terminals and modems. The kernel talks to hardware devices through their respective device drivers. Each device driver has a unique number called *major* number allocated to it by which the kernel recognizes its type.

Furthermore, there is a possibility that more than one devices of the same type are installed in the system. In this case the same driver is used to control all of them. For example, SAS device driver controls all SAS hard disks and CD/DVD drives. The kernel in this situation assigns another unique number called *minor* number to each individual device within that device driver category to identify it as a separate device. In summary, a major number points to the device driver and a minor number points to an individual device controlled by that device driver.

The major and minor numbers can be viewed using the *ll* command:

> # **ll /dev/sd***
> brw-r----- 1 root disk   8, 0 Nov 5 18:03 sda
> brw-r----- 1 root disk   8, 1 Nov 5 18:03 sda1
> brw-r----- 1 root disk   8, 2 Nov 5 18:03 sda2

Column 5 in the output shows the major number and column 6 shows the minor numbers. Major number 8 represents the block device driver for a SATA disk. All minor numbers are unique.

Viewing Hardware Diagnostic Messages

The *dmesg* (diagnostic messages) command gathers recent diagnostic messages from the */var/log/dmesg* file and displays them on the screen. These messages include messages generated when unusual events occur in the system and may prove helpful in troubleshooting.

dmesg
Linux version 2.6.18-92.el5 (brewbuilder@ls20-bc2-13.build.redhat.com) (gcc vers
ion 4.1.2 20071124 (Red Hat 4.1.2-41)) #1 SMP Tue Apr 29 13:16:15 EDT 2008
Command line: ro root=/dev/vg00/lvol1 rhgb quiet
BIOS-provided physical RAM map:
 BIOS-e820: 0000000000000000 - 000000000009f800 (usable)
 BIOS-e820: 000000000009f800 - 00000000000a0000 (reserved)
 BIOS-e820: 00000000000ca000 - 00000000000cc000 (reserved)
 BIOS-e820: 00000000000dc000 - 0000000000100000 (reserved)
 BIOS-e820: 0000000000100000 - 00000000efef0000 (usable)
 BIOS-e820: 00000000efef0000 - 00000000efeff000 (ACPI data)
 BIOS-e820: 00000000efeff000 - 00000000eff00000 (ACPI NVS)
 BIOS-e820: 00000000eff00000 - 00000000f0000000 (usable)
 BIOS-e820: 00000000fec00000 - 00000000fec10000 (reserved)
 BIOS-e820: 00000000fee00000 - 00000000fee01000 (reserved)
 BIOS-e820: 00000000fffe0000 - 0000000100000000 (reserved)
DMI present.
ACPI: RSDP (v000 PTLTD   ) @ 0x00000000000f6c60
. . . .

Available Hardware and Partitions to Work with

Beginning Chapter 09 "Installation" and through to the end of the book, several system, network and security administration topics will be covered along with procedures on how to implement, administer and troubleshoot them. Example commands will be executed and their outputs displayed. The following hardware and partitioning configuration will be used to explain procedures:

PC architecture:	Intel Dual Core
Memory in the PC:	3GB
Disk size:	250GB
Number of network interfaces:	2
Base operating system:	Windows XP
Virtualization software:	VMware server
Number of VM partitions:	3
Memory in each VM partition:	800MB
OS in each virtual partition:	RHEL 5 update 2
First virtual partition:	rhel01 with 192.168.0.201 on eth0 and 192.168.1.201 on eth1
Second virtual partition:	rhel02 with 192.168.0.202 on eth0 and 192.168.1.202 on eth1
Third virtual partition:	rhel03 with 192.168.0.203 on eth0 and 192.168.1.203 on eth1
Additional assumed systems:	rhel04 with 192.168.0.204 on eth0 and 192.168.1.204 on eth1
	rhel05 with 192.168.0.205 on eth0 and 192.168.1.205 on eth1
	rhel06 with 192.168.0.206 on eth0 and 192.168.1.206 on eth1

	rhel07 with 192.168.0.207 on eth0 and 192.168.1.207 on eth1
Disk space in rhel01:	1 x 30GB for OS and 5 x 4GB for disk management exercises
Disk spaces in rhel02 and rhel03:	1 x 30GB for OS

Summary

In this chapter you learned about the responsibilities of a system administrator in a RHEL-based computing environment. You looked at available resources to seek help when required.

The next set of topics covered in detail PC hardware components including slot, PCI and PCIe cards, interface card, network card, SCSI card, fibre channel card, multi-i/o card, bus, processor/core, hard drives, serial port, parallel port, USB port and FireWire port. You were presented with hardware abstraction layer, plug and play functionality and advanced configuration and power interface features.

You learned about device files and concepts surrounding major and minor numbers. You saw how to view hardware diagnostic messages. Finally, information on hardware and partitions that would be used to perform lab exercises in the book was provided.

## 09

Installation

This chapter covers the following major topics:

✓ Installation methods and requirements
✓ Plan installation
✓ Download RHEL installation software
✓ Install using local CD/DVD media in text mode
✓ Explain graphical mode installation specifics
✓ Perform post-installation configuration
✓ Describe installation log files
✓ Explain virtual consoles available during installation

This chapter

This chapter explains how to perform a fresh installation of RHEL 5 in a virtual VMware partition using local CD/DVD drive. The install process requires prior planning for system configuration. Key configuration items such as disk drive and disk management software to be used, types and sizes of file systems, and locale and networking information need to be identified before starting the load. This chapter covers text mode installation method which typically takes less time to finish than its graphical equivalent. For information purposes, graphical specifics are also discussed.

Available Installation Methods

There are several methods available to install RHEL. You can follow either text-based or graphical installation process with installation software located on a CD/DVD, a Linux partition on the same system or an NFS, HTTP or FTP server. For installation in a VMware partition, the installation software image can also be located in a Windows directory on the same system. For advanced installation methods using a configured NFS, HTTP or FTP server, refer to Chapter 28 "Network Installation" later in the book.

The RHEL installation program called *anaconda* is started automatically from the installation media, and in the graphical mode by default unless you type "linux text" at the boot: prompt to force it ro run in text mode. If you wish to perform a network installation instead, type "linux askmethod" at the boot: prompt, which will present you with five possible source options – local CD, local disk, HTTP, FTP and NFS – to choose from.

Installation Requirements

The first thing that you need to do is to identify the requirements for the installation. Critical items such as type of system and CPUs, amount of physical memory and types and sizes of hard disks need to be determined. Installation may fail or the system may not function as expected if any of these requirements are not met. The following sub-sections discuss these requirements.

System Requirements

There is a wide array of hardware platforms where RHEL can be loaded and run. The best place to check whether the hardware is certified for RHEL is to refer to the Red Hat's *Hardware Compatibility List* (HCL) available at *http://www.redhat.com/rhel/compatibility/hardware*. The HCL lists a number of computer system brands that have been tested and certified to work with RHEL. A large number of unbranded machines and laptop computers also work without any issues.

CPU Requirements

RHEL is supported on computers with 32-bit and 64-bit Intel and AMD processors as well as Itanium (IA64) and Power PC (zSeries, iSeries and pSeries) processors.

RHEL is generally used as a server operating system. Servers usually have several CPUs. In order for an operating system to be able to make use of all installed CPUs, the operating system must support that capability. RHEL comes standard with *Symmetric MultiProcessing* (SMP) software component, which allows the operating system to use any number of CPUs installed in the computer. RHEL 5 also supports software and hardware partitioning called *virtualization*. With software partitioning, you can create virtual machines using Red Hat's Xen-based kernel and with hardware partitioning, RHEL 5 allows you to install MS Windows (and other Intel-compatible operating systems) within RHEL, but it requires at least two processors in the system.

Physical Memory Requirements

Enough physical memory should be available in the system to support not only full RHEL software, but also applications that the system is purposed to run. For installation have a minimum of 256MB memory available; add more for better performance.

Planning Installation

Installation of RHEL 5 requires that you have the following configuration information handy. You will be asked to input this information during the installation process.

- ✓ Language to be used during installation.
- ✓ Type of keyboard.
- ✓ Installation number (optional).
- ✓ Partitioning type.
- ✓ Hard disk to be used in case there are more than one.
- ✓ Partition layout approach (standard partitioning, RAID partitioning or LVM partitioning).
- ✓ File system sizes, types and mount points.
- ✓ Size of swap space.
- ✓ Boot loader password (optional).
- ✓ Location of boot loader.
- ✓ Hostname.
- ✓ IP address.
- ✓ Subnet mask.
- ✓ Default gateway.
- ✓ Primary and seconday DNS server names or IP addresses (optional).
- ✓ Time Zone.
- ✓ Root password.
- ✓ Software packages to be loaded.
- ✓ Firewall information.
- ✓ SELinux information.
- ✓ Date and time, or NTP server information (optional).
- ✓ NIS domain and NIS server name (or IP address) (optional).
- ✓ LDAP server name or IP address (optional).

Downloading RHEL 5

If you do not already have the software on CDs/DVD, you need to download the ISO images and burn them on CDs/DVD. Follow the steps below to download the images to a Windows PC and burn them:

1. Go to *www.redhat.com* and click "Downloads" at the very top.
2. Under "Downloads Red Hat Enterprise Linux", there are two options. Click "Download your software here" if you have an active subscription or click either "Purchase from the Red Hat Store" or "Free 30-day evaluation subscription" as appropriate.

3. For option #1, you will be required to log on to the Red Hat Network with credentials you may already have or register to obtain. You will be placed directly on the "Download Software" page. For option #2, you will need to fill out a form to receive an email with instructions on how to download a free copy of the software.
4. Click "Red Hat Enterprise Linux (v. 5 for 32-bit x86)".
5. The next page will provide a list of binary disc ISO images for Red Hat Linux 5.2 Server (x86). There will be five CD images of which the first four contain core components. The fifth image contains cluster and virtualization products which we do not need for this demonstration. Alternatively, you can download the single DVD image.
6. Use any CD/DVD burner tool on your Windows PC to burn the images on blank CDs/DVD.

Installing Using Local CD/DVD – Text Mode

Here are the steps to follow for installing RHEL 5 in text mode in a virtual VMware partition via a local CD drive. This procedure assumes that a new virtual partition with 30GB of disk space and 800MB of physical memory is configured and available. The procedure also assumes that a CD/DVD drive is accessible from the virtual partition and the installation will take place using CDs (and not DVD).

1. Start (or power on) the virtual partition.
2. Insert RHEL 5 CD #1 into the drive.
3. Press the Esc key within 3 seconds to get to the Boot Menu. Highlight CDROM Drive and press the Enter key to boot.

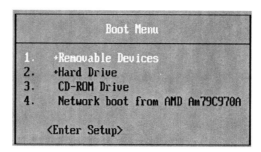

Figure 9-1 Installation – Boot Menu

4. Type "linux text" at the boot prompt as shown in Figure 9-2 and press the Enter key to begin installation in text mode. Text mode installation is also invoked automatically if a mouse is not detected.

Figure 9-2 Installation – Linux Boot Screen

5. Press "Skip" when asked to test the installation media.
6. The *anaconda* installer program will start and a welcome screen will appear. Press OK to continue.
7. Choose a language to be used during the installation process. The default is English. Make a selection and press OK.

Figure 9-3 Installation – Language Selection

8. Choose a keyboard model attached to the computer. The default is the US keyboard. Make a selection and press OK.

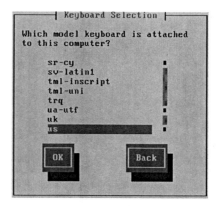

Figure 9-4 Installation – Keyboard Selection

9. Enter an Installation Number if you have one or choose "Skip entering Installation Number" if you do not. Press OK.

Figure 9-5 Installation – Installation Number

10. If you chose "Skip entering Installation Number" in the previous step, a message with disadvantages of not entering an installation number will appear. Press Skip to continue.
11. A warning message about initializing the disk and data loss will appear. Press Yes to continue.
12. The next screen will list four partitioning options:

   ✓ Remove all partitions on selected drives and create default layout.
   ✓ Remove linux partitions on selected drives and create default layout.
   ✓ Use free space on selected drives and create default layout.
   ✓ Create custom layout.

   This screen will also display detected hard drives. Choose "Create custom layout" for this demonstration. Select "sda" drive to install RHEL on. Press OK to continue.

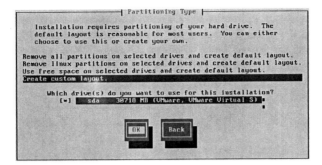

Figure 9-6 Installation – Partitioning Type

13. The next screen will show that the name of the selected disk drive is */dev/sda* and it is 30,720MB in size. Currently, all disk space is free.

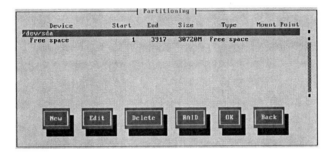

Figure 9-7 Installation – Current Partitioning

There are six menu options as depicted in Figure 9-7 across the bottom: New, Edit, Delete, RAID, OK and Back. These options allow you to create, edit and delete a partition, and configure a RAID partition. The last two options are self-explanatory.

Creating Standard Partitions

Steps 14 and 15 will explain how to create standard partitions on the disk.

14. Tab to New and press Enter to bring up Add Partition screen. See Figure 9-8.

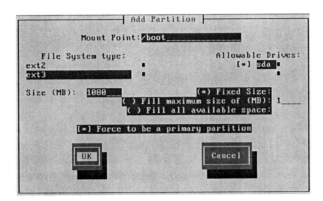

Figure 9-8 Installation – Add Standard Partition

Create partitions as per Table 9-1. Figure 9-8 shows how to fill in information for the */boot* partition. Repeat the same for the rest of the partitions but do not select "Force to be a primary partition" for any of them. Use the Tab key for navigation purposes.

Mount Point	File System Type	Size (MB)
/boot	ext3	1000
/	ext3	1000
/home	ext3	2000
/tmp	ext3	2000
/usr	ext3	5000
/var	ext3	5000
/opt	ext3	5000
N/A	Swap	8000

Table 9-1 Installation – File System Suggestions

For the swap partition, choose "swap" under "File System type". A swap partition does not have a mount point. A detailed discussion on swap is covered in Chapter 14 "File Systems and Swap".

15. A summary of all partitions created will be displayed including the available free space at the bottom. See Figure 9-9. Press OK to continue.

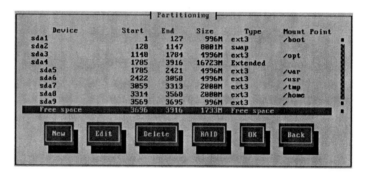

Figure 9-9 Installation – Standard Partitioning Summary

Go to "Remaining Installation Steps" to continue with the installation.

Creating Software RAID Partitions

Steps 16 through 18 will explain how to create and use software RAID partitions.

 Standard and software RAID partitions can co-exist on the same disk without any issues.

16. RHEL supports RAID 0, 1, 5 and 6. RAID is explained at length in Chapter 13 "Disk Partitioning". A RAID partition may be constructed using two or more standard partitions. For example, to construct */boot* in RAID 1 configuration, first create two standard partitions

as explained earlier but with file system type of "software RAID". Figure 9-10 shows two standard partitions of size 996MB each and are called sda1 and sda2.

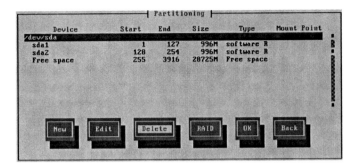

Figure 9-10 Installation – Standard Partitions for Software RAID

Now press RAID from the menu and create */boot* RAID 1 partition using both sda1 and sda2. As shown in Figure 9-11, you will need to specify the mount point, file system type, RAID level and the standard partitions. Leave "Number of spares" at default. Do not forget to select "Format partition?". Press OK when done.

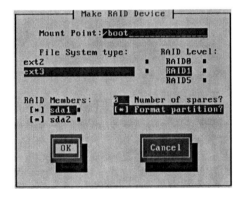

Figure 9-11 Installation – Add RAID Partition

17. Figure 9-12 shows the RAID device just created as RAID Device 0 of size 996MB with file system type ext3 and mount point */boot*.

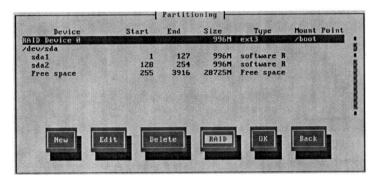

Figure 9-12 Installation – Example Software RAID Partition

18. Follow the same procedure for constructing other file systems. Press OK when done to continue.

Go to "Remaining Installation Steps" to continue with the installation.

Creating LVM Partitions

"Create custom layout" partitioning type chosen in step 12 does not allow creating LVM partitions. You will need to choose one of the first three options for this purpose. For this demonstration, let us select the first option "Remove all partitions on selected drives and create default layout". When you press OK a message will be displayed warning that all data on the disk will be removed. Press Yes to continue. Press Yes again on the "Review and modify partitioning layout" question. Figure 9-13 shows the default partitioning that will appear next.

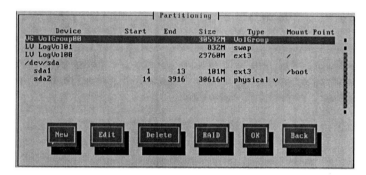

Figure 9-13 Installation – Default Partitioning

19. Highlight the */boot* partition and press Edit to increase its size to 1000MB and mark "Force to be the primary partition". Note that */boot* must be outside of LVM configuration, otherwise, the system will not recognize it.
20. Highlight "LV LogVol00" and "LV LogVol01" one at a time and press Delete to delete them. Now you have base LVM partitioning on the disk as shown in Figure 9-14.

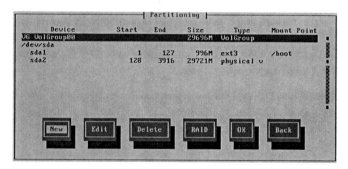

Figure 9-14 Installation – Base LVM Partitioning

21. Create logical volumes and file systems in the *VolGroup00* volume group as per information provided in Table 9-2.

Mount Point	File System Type	Size (MB)	Logical Volume
/boot	ext3	1000	N/A
/	ext3	1000	lvol1
/home	ext3	2000	lvol2
/tmp	ext3	2000	lvol3
/usr	ext3	5000	lvol4
/var	ext3	5000	lvol5
/opt	ext3	5000	lvol6
N/A	Swap	8000	lvol7

Table 9-2 Installation – File System Information

22. Press New to create the first logical volume in *VolGroup00*. A window as shown in Figure 9-15 will appear. Choose "logical volume" and press OK.

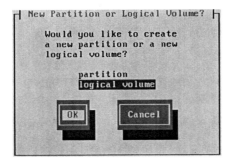

Figure 9-15 Installation – Create Partition or Logical Volume

23. Figure 9-16 displays the information that you will need to supply to create the first logical volume. As shown in the figure, the mount point will be / for the root file system with type ext3 to be created in *lvol1* logical volume of size 1000MB. Do not forget to mark "Format partition". Press OK to continue.

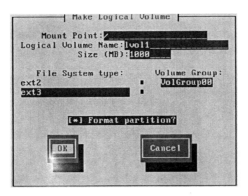

Figure 9-16 Installation – Make Logical Volume / File System

24. Repeat steps 22 and 23 for constructing */home*, */tmp*, */usr*, */var* and */opt* file systems. For the swap logical volume, use "swap" under "File System type". Figure 9-17 summarizes LVM partitions created based on the information provided in Table 9-2.

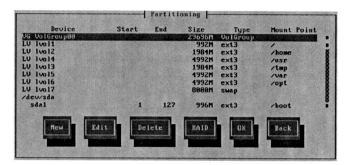

Figure 9-17 Installation – LVM Partitions

Press OK to continue with the installation process as outlined in the next sub-section.

Remaining Installation Steps

After the disk has been carved up using one or more disk management solutions explained earlier, follow the steps below to continue the installation process.

25. Press OK on the following screen to select "Use GRUB Boot Loader". GRUB stands for *Grand Unified Bootloader*. The "No Boot Loader" option is used when other Linux partitions also exist on the computer.

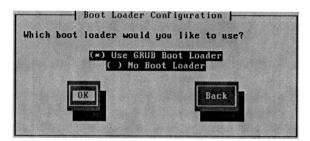

Figure 9-18 Installation – Boot Loader Selection

26. Specify any special options that you wish to pass on to the kernel each time the system will boot. For this demonstration, simply press the OK button.

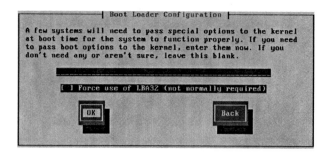

Figure 9-19 Installation – Boot Loader Option

27. Choose a boot loader password if you wish to. For this demonstration, press OK to continue without entering a password.

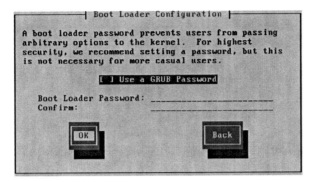

Figure 9-20 Installation – Boot Loader Password

28. The next screen will display the default boot label and its location on the disk. In case of a single installation on the computer, the list will contain only one boot label entry. For this demonstration, simply press the OK button. If you wish to modify the boot label, press Edit.

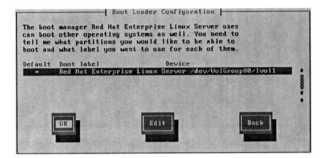

Figure 9-21 Installation – Boot Loader Label

29. The next screen will ask you to choose a location to install the boot loader. Two choices will be presented: *Master Boot Record* (MBR) and the first sector of the boot partition. Choose the first option for this demonstration and press OK.

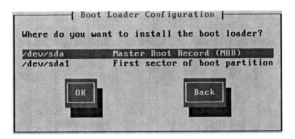

Figure 9-22 Installation – Boot Loader Location

30. The next screen will allow you to choose whether you wish to configure the first detected network interface *eth0* now. Select Yes for this demonstration. If you wish to only define a hostname or obtain it from a configured, active DHCP server and optionally add gateway and

DNS server information now, choose NO and follow the screens. Later, you can configure the interface using one of the methods explained in Chapter 21 "Network Interface Administration and Routing".

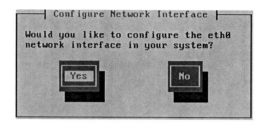

Figure 9-23 Installation – Network Interface Configuration

31. Select the two options as shown in Figure 9-24. The "Activate on boot" will automatically activate the network interface at each system reboot and "Enable IPv4 support" will enable support for IPv4 addresses. Select "Enable IPv6 support" also if required. Press OK to go to the next screen.

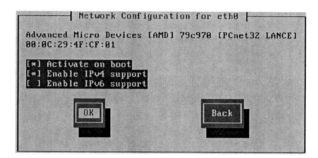

Figure 9-24 Installation – Network Interface Configuration

32. Two choices will appear on the next screen. If you wish the system to obtain IP address and netmask information for the interface from a configured, active DHCP server, choose "Dynamic IP configuration (DHCP)" option, otherwise, select "Manual address configuration" to supply the information manually. For this demonstration, choose the second option and enter IP and netmask values. Press OK when done.

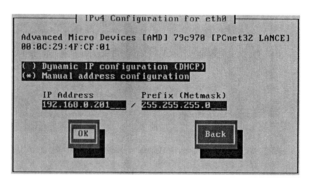

Figure 9-25 Installation – IPv4 Configuration

33. Input gateway address and primary and/or secondary DNS server information if available.

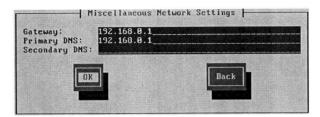

Figure 9-26 Installation – Miscellaneous Network Settings

34. Specify a hostname or choose "automatically via DHCP" if you wish to obtain it from DHCP.

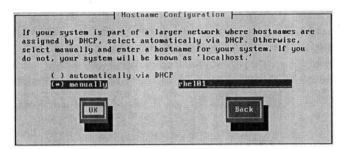

Figure 9-27 Installation – Hostname Configuration

35. Choose an appropriate time zone for the system. For this demonstration, select "America/New_York". Unselect "System clock uses UTC". Press OK to continue.

Figure 9-28 Installation – Time Zone Selection

36. Enter a password for the *root* user and press OK.

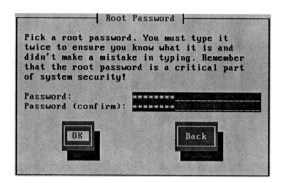

Figure 9-29 Installation – Root Password

37. The next screen will allow you to choose whether you wish to also install software development and web server software packages in addition to the default RHEL software. The other choice on the screen "Customize software selection" will allow you to choose whether you wish to select or unselect specific pacakges within software package group categories. Choose all three as shown in Figure 9-30 for this demonstration and press OK.

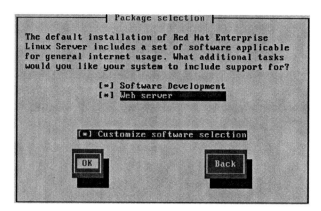

Figure 9-30 Installation – Package Selection

As per customize software selection chosen in Figure 9-30, Table 9-3 lists and describes available choices. Choosing a package group installs associated software described under the "Description" column.

Package Groups	Description	Part of
Administration Tools	Graphical administration tools such as authconfig-gtk, system-config-authentication, pirut, sabayon, setroubleshoot, system-config-date, system-config-kdump, system-config-keyboard, system-config-kickstart, system-config-language, system-config-lvm, system-config-network, system-config-rootpassword, system-config-soundcard and system-config-	Default

Package Groups	Description	Part of
	users. All these tools are installed by default.	
Authoring and Publishing	Documentation systems.	None
DNS Name Server	Support for DNS server.	None
Development Libraries	Library routines for adding and modifying programs.	Software Development
Development Tools	The make, gcc, perl, python and other useful compiler software packages.	Software Development
Editors	The vi editor and emacs.	Default
Engineering and Scientific	Scientific and mathematical tools.	None
FTP Server	Support for very secure FTP (vsFTP) service. This is RHEL's default FTP server.	None
GNOME Desktop Environment	Default graphical desktop.	Default
GNOME Software Development	Packages needed to develop additional GTK+ and GNOME graphical applications.	Software Development
Games and Entertainment	Games and other entertainment software.	Default
Graphical Internet	FireFox browser, XChat and gFTP client.	Default
Graphics	X windows system.	Default
Java Development	Packages needed to develop programs in Java.	None
KDE (K Desktop Environment)	Additional graphical desktop.	None
KDE Software Development	Packages needed to develop additional QT and KDE graphical applications.	None
Legacy Network Server	Support for rsh, telnet and tftp services.	None
Legacy Software Development	C and C++ compilers.	None
Legacy Software Support	Support for old software.	Default
Mail Server	Support for Sendmail and Postfix mail servers.	None
MySQL Database	Support for MySQL database.	None
Network Servers	Support for network services such as DHCP and NIS.	None
News Server	Support for News services.	None
Office/Productivity	Office productivity tools.	Default
OpenFabrics Enterprise Distribution	Support for high-performance networks.	None
PostgreSQL Database	Support for PostgreSQL database.	None
Printing Support	Support for the Common UNIX Printing System (CUPS). It supports Internet Printing Protocol (IPP). This	Default

Package Groups	Description	Part of
	support is added by default.	
Server Configuration Tools	Graphical server configuration tools such as system-config-bind, system-config-boot, system-config-httpd, system-config-nfs, system-config-samba, system-config-securitylevel, system-config-services and system-config-mail-gnome.	None
Sound and Video	Sound and video cards.	Default
System Tools	Support for ethereal network traffic reader, Z shell, SAMBA client, createrepo RPM, and so on.	None
Text-based Internet	links web browser, and fetchmail and mutt email readers.	Default
Web Server	Support for Apache and Squid.	Web Server
Windows File Server	Samba client and server components. This package is installed by default.	None
X Software Development	Packages needed to develop additional graphical applications.	Software Development
X Window System	Support for graphical fonts, libraries, and critical tools such as system-config-display. X Window system is required is you choose either GNOME or KDE desktops, or both.	Default

Table 9-3 Installation – Available Software Packages

38. The next screen will display all available software packages. Choose the ones you need, and press OK to continue.

Figure 9-31 Installation – Individual Package Selection

39. The installation program will perform a dependency check for the selected packages and will display the location of the installation log file. Press OK.

40. The last in the series of installation program screens will display the CD media required based on the software package selection. Press Continue to begin installation. Figure 9-32 depicts that the first four installation CDs will be required.

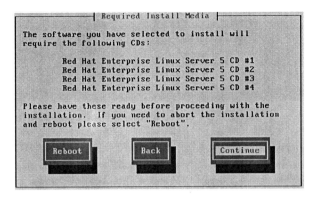

Figure 9-32 Installation – Media Required for Installation

As the installation continues, informational messages will appear on the screen apprising you of the progress. The installer will initialize the disk, create and format logical volumes and partitions, mount file systems, install selected packages and perform post install configuration.

41. During installation you will be asked to change CDs. Insert CDs as prompted.
42. After the installation is complete, you will be asked to remove any CDs in the drive and press the Reboot button to reboot the system.
43. Following the reboot, the system will initiate a program called *firstboot*, which will bring up *setup agent* on the screen by executing the *setup* command for you to customize authentication, firewall, keyboard, network, system services and timezone settings. Refer to sub-section "Firstboot in Graphical Mode" later in this chapter for details. Note that the setup agent comparatively provides more configuration choices in post-graphical mode installation.

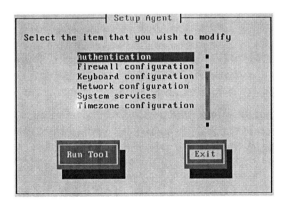

Figure 9-33 Firstboot – Setup Agent

44. Press Exit if you do not wish to make any modifications at this time (you may run this program later by executing the *setup* command or rebooting the system. To disable it permanently so it does not come up automatically at the following system reboots, set

RUN_FIRSTBOOT=NO in the *etc/sysconfig/firstboot* file and run *chkconfig firstboot off*). A login prompt will appear for you to log on to the system. Log in with *root* user credentials.

```
Red Hat Enterprise Linux Server release 5.2 (Tikanga)
Kernel 2.6.18-92.el5 on an i686

rhel01 login: root
Password:
[root@rhel01 ~]#
[root@rhel01 ~]#
[root@rhel01 ~]# _
```

Figure 9-34 Installation – root User Login

This completes the text-based step-by-step procedure for installing RHEL 5 via local CD/DVD media. At this point if you wish to run X Windows and bring up the graphical interface, execute the *startx* command at the command prompt. Figure 9-35 shows the main graphical desktop screen.

Figure 9-35 Installation – Graphical Desktop

Installing Using Local CD/DVD – Graphical Mode Specifics

The installation and initial configuration when installing RHEL in graphical mode is not too different from that in the text mode. You will need to press the Enter key at the boot: prompt rather than typing "linux text" to initiate graphical mode installation process.

In graphical mode, anaconda presents choices in a different format. For instance, choices for software packages are grouped into six categories as outlined in Table 9-4, and you will need to click on individual categories to view and select/unselect packages. The default (selected) packages are already checkmarked.

Category	Packages Included	Description	Part of
Desktop Environments	GNOME Desktop Environment	Default graphical desktop.	Default
	KDE (K Desktop Environment)	Additional graphical desktop.	None
Applications	Authoring and Publishing	Documentation systems.	None
	Editors	The vi editor and emacs.	Default

Category	Packages Included	Description	Part of
	Engineering and Scientific	Scientific and mathematical tools.	None
	Games and Entertainment	Games and other entertainment software.	Default
	Graphical Internet	FireFox browser, XChat and gFTP client.	Default
	Graphics	X windows system.	Default
	Office/Productivity	Office productivity tools.	Default
	Sound and Video	Sound and video cards.	Default
	Text-based Internet	links web browser, and fetchmail and mutt email readers.	Default
	Development Libraries	Library routines for adding and modifying programs.	Software Development
	Development Tools	The make, gcc, perl, python and other useful compiler software packages.	Software Development
	GNOME Software Development	Packages needed to develop additional GTK+ and GNOME graphical applications.	Software Development
Development	Java Development	Packages needed to develop programs in Java.	None
	KDE Software Development	Packages needed to develop additional QT and KDE graphical applications.	None
	Legacy Software Development	C and C++ compilers.	None
	Ruby	Programming language used for web development.	None
	X Software Development	Packages needed to develop additional graphical applications.	Software Development
Servres	DNS Name Server	Support for DNS server.	None
	FTP Server	Support for Very Secure FTP (vsFTP) service. This is RHEL's default FTP server.	None
	Legacy Network Server	Support for rsh, telnet and tftp services.	None
	Mail Server	Support for Sendmail and Postfix mail servers.	None
	MySQL Database	Support for MySQL database.	None
	Network Servers	Support for network services such as DHCP and NIS.	None
	News Server	Support for Internet Network News (INN) srevice.	None
	PostgreSQL Database	Support for PostgreSQL database.	None
	Printing Support	Support for the Common UNIX Printing System (CUPS). It supports Internet Printing Protocol (IPP). This support is	Default

Category	Packages Included	Description	Part of
		added by default.	
	Server Configuration Tools	Graphical server configuration tools such as system-config-bind, system-config-boot, system-config-httpd, system-config-nfs, system-config-samba, system-config-securitylevel, system-config-services and system-config-mail-gnome.	None
	Web Server	Support for Apache and Squid.	Web Server
	Windows File Server	Samba client and server components. This package is installed by default.	None
Base System	Administration Tools	Graphical administration tools such as authconfig-gtk, system-config-authentication, pirut, sabayon, setroubleshoot, system-config-date, system-config-kdump, system-config-keyboard, system-config-kickstart, system-config-language, system-config-lvm, system-config-network, system-config-rootpassword, system-config-soundcard and system-config-users. All these tools are installed by default.	Default
	Base	Packages required for basic RHEL functionality.	Default
	Dialup Networking Support	Network support over dialup lines such as telephone, ISDN & PPP.	Default
	Java	Support for Java software.	None
	Legacy Software Support	Support for old software.	None
	System Tools	Support for ethereal network traffic reader, Z shell, Samba client, createrepo RPM, etc.	None
	X Window System	Support for graphical font libraries and critical tools such as system-config-display. Required if GNOME and/or KDE desktops are chosen.	Default
Languages	List of several languages	Supports different language for installation purposes.	None

Table 9-4 Installation – Packages Displayed in Graphical Mode

Firstboot in Graphical Mode

The *firstboot* program (a.k.a. *Red Hat Setup Agent*) is started automatically following the first system reboot after the installation is finished. It allows you to perform certain post-installation configuration tasks, which are highlighted in this sub-section.

1. A Welcome screen will appear, which lists several options to be configured. Click Forward to go to the next screen.

Figure 9-36 Firstboot – Welcome Screen

2. The license agreement window will appear next. You must agree to the terms and conditions of use.
3. The next window will provide an opportunity to enable, disable and configure firewall. If you wish to enable specific network services to allow them to work through the firewall, select them from the list. The list includes FTP, Mail (SMTP), NFS4, SSH, Samba, Secure WWW (HTTPS), Telnet and WWW (HTTP). Click "Other ports" to open any other ports. If you do not wish to enable firewall at this time, you can configure it later using one of the methods described in Chapter 30 "System and Network Security".

Figure 9-37 Firstboot – Firewall Configuration

4. You can enable or disable enhanced Linux security called *SELinux* (Security Enhanced Linux) on this screen. SELinux enables enhanced protection for the system. The options are "enforcing" (enabled), "permissive" (enabled but without any protection) and "disabled". If you do not wish to enable SELinux at this point, you can do so later using one of the methods described in Chapter 30 "System and Network Security".

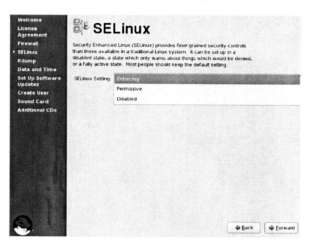

Figure 9-38 Firstboot – SELinux Configuration

5. The next window will allow you to configure kernel dump settings. You should reserve some memory for kernel crash dump purposes in the work environment. The dump can be helpful in determining the root cause of a system crash. By default, it is disabled. If you make any modifications here, the system will have to be rebooted for the changes to take effect. If you do not wish to enable Kdump at this point, you can do so later using the Kdump Configurator *system-config-kdump*.

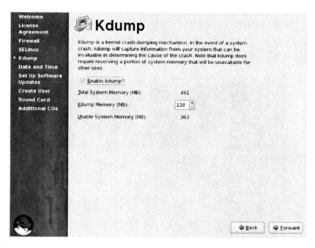

Figure 9-39 Firstboot – Kernel Dump Configuration

6. Set correct date and time for the system. If you wish to connect to an NTP server to obtain time, enable NTP, which will use default NTP servers listed there. You may specify hostname(s) or IP address(es) of your own NTP server(s). Figure 9-40 shows non-NTP date/time settings and

---

Figure 9-41 displays NTP settings. If you do not wish to set date/time at this point, you can do so later using one of the methods described in Chapter 25 "Network Time Protocol".

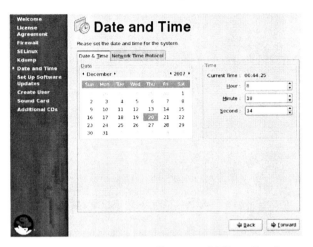

Figure 9-40 Firstboot – Date and Time Settings

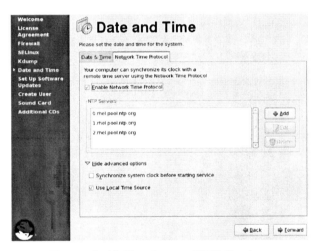

Figure 9-41 Firstboot – NTP Settings

7. If you have an active subscription, you should register the system with Red Hat Network to get benefits such as automatic software updates for the system. Choose "No, I prefer to register at a later time" if you do not wish to do so at this time. Refer to Chapter 11 "Software Package Management" for details on how to register.

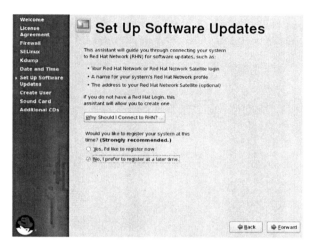

Figure 9-42 Firstboot – RHN Registration

8. Create a user account in addition to the default *root* user if you wish to. Supply username and password information. The password must not be less than six characters in length. If you have NIS or LDAP server in place for user account management, click "Use Network Login" and configure client functionality for the available service. Refer to Figures 9-43 through 9-48. If you do not wish to create a user account at this point, you can do so later using one of the methods described in Chapter 12 "Users and Groups".

Figure 9-43 Firstboot – User Creation

Figure 9-44 Firstboot – Network User Options

Figure 9-45 Firstboot – NIS User Creation

Figure 9-46 Firstboot – LDAP User Creation

Figure 9-47 Firstboot – Network User Authentication Options

Figure 9-48 Firstboot – User Authentication Options

9. If a sound card is detected, you will be asked to configure it. If you do not wish to configure it at this point, you can do so later using the Sound Card Configurator *system-config-soundcard*.
10. Insert a software CD and click Install if you wish to install any other software.
11. Click Finish to complete the firstboot process. A login screen will appear and you should now be able to log in either as *root* or the user that you have created.

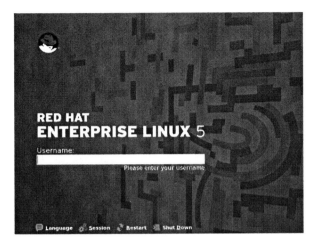

Figure 9-49 Firstboot – Login Screen

Installation Log Files

There are several log files created during the installation process. These files record configuration and status information. You can view their contents after the installation has been completed to check how the installation progressed. The files are listed and described in Table 9-5.

File	Description
/root/anaconda-ks.cfg	Records configuration entered during installation.
/root/install.log	Lists packages installed during installation.
/root/install.log.syslog	Stores messages generated during installation.
/tmp/anaconda.log	This file is moved to the */var/log* directory after installation is complete. Contains informational, debug and other messages generated during installation.
/tmp/anaconda.syslog	This file is moved to the */var/log* directory after installation is complete. Contains messages generated when the *dmesg* command is initially executed.
/tmp/anaconda.xlog	This file is moved to the */var/log* directory after installation is complete. Contains information about X during installation. This log file is created only if you have performed a graphical installation.

Table 9-5 Installation Log Files

Here are the contents of some of these files:

cat /root/anaconda-ks.cfg
\# Kickstart file automatically generated by anaconda.

install
cdrom
key --skip
lang en_US.UTF-8

keyboard us
xconfig --startxonboot
network --device eth0 --bootproto static --ip 192.168.0.201 --netmask 255.255.255.0 --gateway
192.168.0.1 --nameserver 192.168.0.1 --hostname rhel01
rootpw --iscrypted 1NONm5QUi$u6j2G96L7dEE2xtzQAwGg0
firewall --enabled --port=22:tcp
authconfig --enableshadow --enablemd5
selinux --enforcing
timezone --utc America/New_York
bootloader --location=mbr --driveorder=sda --append="rhgb quiet"
. . . .
%packages
@editors
@system-tools
@text-internet
@legacy-network-server
. . . .

cat /root/install.log
Installing libgcc - 4.1.2-42.el5.i386
warning: libgcc-4.1.2-42.el5: Header V3 DSA signature: NOKEY, key ID 37017186
Installing setup - 2.5.58-1.el5.noarch
Installing filesystem - 2.4.0-1.i386
Installing basesystem - 8.0-5.1.1.noarch
Installing tzdata - 2007d-1.el5.noarch
Installing glibc-common - 2.5-18.i386
Installing glibc - 2.5-18.i686
Installing glib2 - 2.12.3-2.fc6.i386
Installing zlib - 1.2.3-3.i386
Installing chkconfig - 1.3.30.1-1.i386
Installing atk - 1.12.2-1.fc6.i386
. . . .

cat /root/install.log.syslog
<86>Dec 2 08:42:57 groupadd[822]: new group: name=rpm, GID=37
<86>Dec 2 08:42:57 useradd[826]: new user: name=rpm, UID=37, GID=37, home=/var/lib/rpm,
shell=/sbin/nologin
<86>Dec 2 08:42:59 useradd[836]: new group: name=dbus, GID=81
<86>Dec 2 08:42:59 useradd[836]: new user: name=dbus, UID=81, GID=81, home=/, shell=/sbin/nologin
<86>Dec 2 08:43:29 groupadd[882]: new group: name=utmp, GID=22
<86>Dec 2 08:43:29 groupadd[886]: new group: name=utempter, GID=35
<86>Dec 2 08:43:53 useradd[974]: new group: name=avahi, GID=70
<86>Dec 2 08:43:53 useradd[974]: new user: name=avahi, UID=70, GID=70, home=/,shell=/sbin/nologin
<86>Dec 2 08:44:08 useradd[1021]: new group: name=mailnull, GID=47
. . . .

Virtual Console Screens

There are five text console screens available during text mode installation to manage and monitor
the installation process. If the installation process followed is graphical, a sixth screen will be
available as well to interact with the installation program. You can switch among the screens by

pressing a combination of keys. The information displayed on the consoles is captured in installation log files as well.

Console #1 (Alt-F1 in text mode, Ctrl-Alt-F1 in graphical mode)

This is the default text mode installation console screen.

Console #2 (Alt-F2 in text mode, Ctrl-Alt-F2 in graphical mode)

BASH shell interface for running commands.

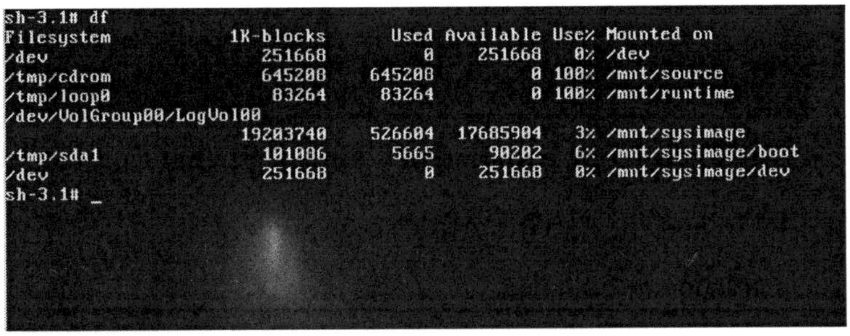

```
sh-3.1# df
Filesystem           1K-blocks     Used Available Use% Mounted on
/dev                    251668        0    251668   0% /dev
/tmp/cdrom              645200   645200         0 100% /mnt/source
/tmp/loop0               83264    83264         0 100% /mnt/runtime
/dev/VolGroup00/LogVol00
                      19203740   526604  17685904   3% /mnt/sysimage
/tmp/sda1               101086     5665     90202   6% /mnt/sysimage/boot
/dev                    251668        0    251668   0% /mnt/sysimage/dev
sh-3.1# _
```

Figure 9-50 Installation – Second Virtual Console

Console #3 (Alt-F3 in text mode, Ctrl-Alt-F3 in graphical mode)

Displays installation log, which is also stored in */tmp/anaconda.log*. Information on hardware detected is captured in this file, in addition to other information.

```
21:40:33 INFO    : formatting /boot as ext3
21:40:33 INFO    : Format command:  ['/usr/sbin/mke2fs', '/tmp/sda1', '-i', '409
6', '-j']
21:40:36 INFO    : trying to mount VolGroup00/LogVol00 on /
21:40:36 INFO    : set SELinux context for mountpoint / to system_u:object_r:roo
t_t:s0
21:40:36 INFO    : trying to mount sda1 on /boot
21:40:36 INFO    : set SELinux context for mountpoint /boot to system_u:object_r
:boot_t:s0
21:40:36 INFO    : trying to mount sys on /sys
21:40:36 INFO    : set SELinux context for mountpoint /sys to None
21:40:36 INFO    : trying to mount proc on /proc
21:40:36 INFO    : set SELinux context for mountpoint /proc to None
21:40:36 INFO    : moving (1) to step migratefilesystems
21:40:36 INFO    : moving (1) to step setuptime
16:50:43 INFO    : moving (1) to step preinstallconfig
16:50:57 WARNING : no dev package, going to bind mount /dev
16:50:57 INFO    : self.hostname = rhel01
16:50:57 INFO    : moving (1) to step installpackages
16:50:57 INFO    : Preparing to install packages
16:50:57 INFO    : switching from CD [1] to 1 for ('emacs-leim', 'i386', '0', '2
1.4', '19.el5')
```

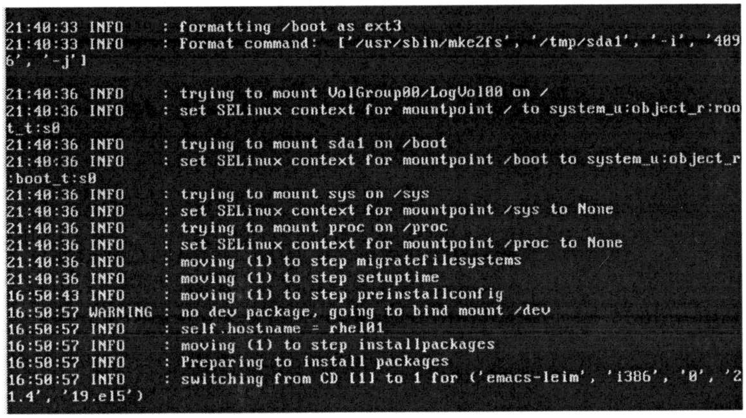

Figure 9-51 Installation – Third Virtual Console

Console #4 (Alt-F4 in text mode, Ctrl-Alt-F4 in graphical mode)

Displays kernel messages, which is also stored in */tmp/install.log.syslog*. Information on hardware detected is captured in greater detail in this file, in addition to other information.

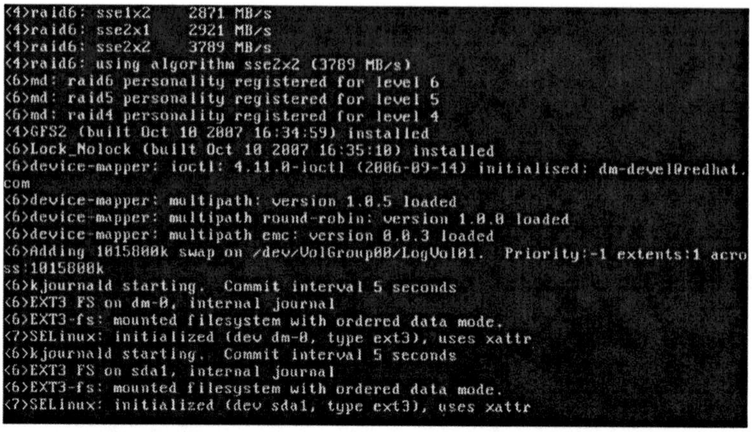

```
<4>raid6: sse1x2    2871 MB/s
<4>raid6: sse2x1    2921 MB/s
<4>raid6: sse2x2    3789 MB/s
<4>raid6: using algorithm sse2x2 (3789 MB/s)
<6>md: raid6 personality registered for level 6
<6>md: raid5 personality registered for level 5
<6>md: raid4 personality registered for level 4
<4>GFS2 (built Oct 10 2007 16:34:59) installed
<6>Lock_Nolock (built Oct 10 2007 16:35:10) installed
<6>device-mapper: ioctl: 4.11.0-ioctl (2006-09-14) initialised: dm-devel@redhat.
com
<6>device-mapper: multipath: version 1.0.5 loaded
<6>device-mapper: multipath round-robin: version 1.0.0 loaded
<6>device-mapper: multipath emc: version 0.0.3 loaded
<6>Adding 1015800k swap on /dev/VolGroup00/LogVol01.  Priority:-1 extents:1 acro
ss:1015800k
<6>kjournald starting.  Commit interval 5 seconds
<6>EXT3 FS on dm-0, internal journal
<6>EXT3-fs: mounted filesystem with ordered data mode.
<7>SELinux: initialized (dev dm-0, type ext3), uses xattr
<6>kjournald starting.  Commit interval 5 seconds
<6>EXT3 FS on sda1, internal journal
<6>EXT3-fs: mounted filesystem with ordered data mode.
<7>SELinux: initialized (dev sda1, type ext3), uses xattr
```

Figure 9-52 Installation – Fourth Virtual Console

Console #5 (Alt-F5 in text mode, Ctrl-Alt-F5 in graphical mode)

Displays file system creation information.

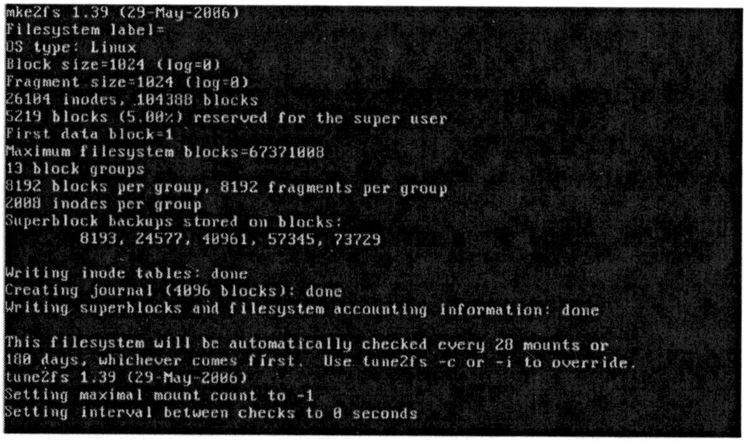

```
mke2fs 1.39 (29-May-2006)
Filesystem label=
OS type: Linux
Block size=1024 (log=0)
Fragment size=1024 (log=0)
26104 inodes, 104388 blocks
5219 blocks (5.00%) reserved for the super user
First data block=1
Maximum filesystem blocks=67371008
13 block groups
8192 blocks per group, 8192 fragments per group
2008 inodes per group
Superblock backups stored on blocks:
        8193, 24577, 40961, 57345, 73729

Writing inode tables: done
Creating journal (4096 blocks): done
Writing superblocks and filesystem accounting information: done

This filesystem will be automatically checked every 28 mounts or
180 days, whichever comes first.  Use tune2fs -c or -i to override.
tune2fs 1.39 (29-May-2006)
Setting maximal mount count to -1
Setting interval between checks to 0 seconds
```

Figure 9-53 Installation – Fifth Virtual Console

Console #6 (Ctrl-Alt-F6 in graphical mode)

This console is available only during graphical mode installation.

Summary

In this chapter you studied installation requirements and methods. You learned how to download the installation software and perform an installation using local CD/DVD media in text mode. You were also presented with differences in text mode and graphical mode installations. You performed several post-installation steps to further configure and modify key system settings. You looked at installation log files and view contents of some of them. Finally, you were presented with basic information on virtual consoles available during installation.

X Window System and Desktop Managers

This chapter covers the following major topics:

- ✓ Overview of X Window System
- ✓ X server and how to configure it
- ✓ X configuration files
- ✓ Manage start and stop of X font server
- ✓ X client applications and graphical desktop managers
- ✓ Configure default desktop manager
- ✓ Run X client applications over the network

Depending on the usage of a RHEL system, you may or may not need the X

Window software installed and configured. *X Window* (or simply *X*) provides the foundation for running graphical applications. Throughout this book you will be using several RHEL administration tools that require a graphical environment to operate. Additionally, RHEL provides graphical display and desktop managers called GNOME and KDE that require X capability to function. All these and other graphical applications are dependent on the X software loaded and configured properly on the system. Although not all RHEL systems require the presence of X, it is a good idea to have it just in case it is needed. The amount of disk space the software packages take is not much.

Overview

RHEL uses X Window System provided by *X.Org Foundation*, an open source organization whose focus is to manage the development of X and technologies surrounding it. X is based on client/server architecture whereby a software daemon runs on a system and serves graphical client requests initiated on local or networked systems. This means both client and server can run on one system or different. X server manages the graphics and associated video hardware and X client is any graphical application that communicates with the X server in order to funtion. You simply need to point to the computer where you wish the graphics to be displayed. A single X server daemon can handle as many X client applications as the system permits. All Red Hat graphical configuration tools are X clients of the X server.

X Server

The configuration for the X server and graphical desktops is performed during RHEL installation. The video hardware is detected and automatically configured for optimum performance and results.

In order for the X server and graphical desktops to run properly and efficiently, ensure that the system has enough memory and supported video hardware such as video card, monitor and mouse, installed. By default, X.Org supports a number of multivendor video cards, monitors and other video devices. Visit *www.x.org* or consult Red Hat's hardware compatibility documentation at *https://hardware.redhat.com* for detailed information. If a device that you intend to use is not on the hardware compatibility list, use built-in generic drivers such as generic VGA for the video card, and so on.

Configuring X Server

With hardware verified, execute the following or the Red Hat Display Configurator (a.k.a. X Configurator) to modify the display and video card settings:

> **# system-config-display --noui --reconfig --set-resolution=800x600 --set-depth=16**

This command executes the Display Configurator and creates the */etc/X11/xorg.conf* file with the supplied video settings.

The Display Configurator can be executed in graphical mode, which automatically probes the system for video hardware and selects appropriate drivers based on what it has detected. It displays a list of built-in, supported video cards if it cannot find a proper driver for the hardware found. Figure 10-1 shows the main screen for the Display Configurator.

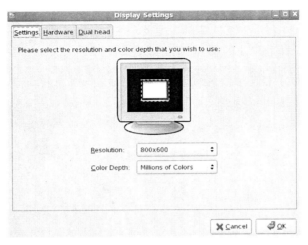

Figure 10-1 Display Configurator – Display Settings

There are three tabs available in the tool that allow you to configure video hardware. The Settings tab enables you to set monitor resolution and color depth. The Hardware tab allows you to configure Monitor Type and Video Card. Currently, the monitor is set to "autoconfigured" and video card to "VMWare SVGA PCI Display Adapter". These settings were automatically detected and set during installation. If you need to modify them click an appropriate Configure button and choose suitable hardware. For an unsupported piece of hardware, select a similar video card or use a generic card such as a VESA driver (update *etc/X11.xorg.conf* file accordingly), use any compatible VGA or SVGA card, or go to *www.x.org* and download the latest drivers.

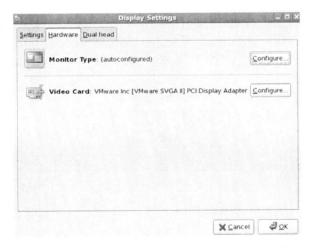

Figure 10-2 Display Configurator – Hardware Settings

In case you have dual display monitors connected to the system, you can configure the second monitor under the Dual Head tab. Basically, it requires you to choose the second monitor type, the video card it is attached to, monitor resolution, color depth and a layout of the desktop – individual or spanning. See Figure 10-3.

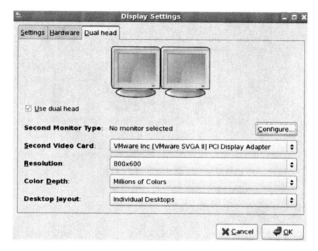

Figure 10-3 Display Configurator – Dual Head Settings

X Server Configuration File

Modifications made with the Display Configurator are saved in */etc/X11/xorg.conf*, which is the primary configuration file for the X server. The default contents look similar to the following:

```
# cat /etc/X11/xorg.conf
# Xorg configuration created by pyxf86config

Section "ServerLayout"
    Identifier     "Default Layout"
    Screen      0 "Screen0" 0 0
    InputDevice    "Keyboard0" "CoreKeyboard"
EndSection

Section "InputDevice"
    Identifier "Keyboard0"
    Driver     "kbd"
    Option     "XkbModel" "pc105"
    Option     "XkbLayout" "us"
EndSection

Section "Device"
    Identifier  "Videocard0"
    Driver      "vmware"
EndSection

Section "Screen"
    Identifier "Screen0"
    Device     "Videocard0"
```

```
        DefaultDepth    24
        SubSection "Display"
            Viewport  0 0
            Depth    24
        EndSubSection
    EndSection
```

The first line indicates that the file was created during installation and has not been updated since then. If you modify the configuration using the Display Configurator, the line will say "Xorg configuration created by system-config-display". By default, there are four sections in the file, and are enclosed within Section and EndSection keywords. These sections are explained below:

- ✓ The ServerLayout section begins with an identifier, which is set to Default Layout and points to the screen and the input devices being used. The identifier will change to "dual head configuration" if you have two monitors attached and configured.
- ✓ The InputDevice section defines configuration for the input device, which is the keyboard. It outlines the type of keyboard (US) and the number of keys (105) on it. It also tells you the driver being used for the keyboard (kbd).
- ✓ The Device section shows the video card detected at the time of RHEL installation and the driver it is using for the card.
- ✓ The Screen section uses the identifier and the device as defined in previous sections. It also defines the display characteristics.

Probing Hardware and Rebuilding X Server Configuration File

Alternative to running the Display Configurator to update the video hardware configuration in */etc/X11/xorg.conf*, you can use the *X* command in run level 3 to probe the graphics hardware and build a new *xorg.conf.new* file. You can then test the configuration and replace the original *xorg.conf* file with it. Follow the procedure below:

By default, a RHEL system boots up to run level 5 where all configured graphical programs including X are started. Run level 3 does not run X automatically. A detailed discussion on run levels is covered in Chapter 15 "Shutdown and Boot".

1. Execute the following to switch to run level 3. This will automatically stop all graphical programs currently running, as well as X.

    # **init 3**

2. Once you are in this run level, run the *X* command to probe the graphics hardware:

    # **X –probeonly**
    X Window System Version 7.1.1
    Release Date: 12 May 2006
    X Protocol Version 11, Revision 0, Release 7.1.1
    Build Operating System: Linux 2.6.9-67.0.7.ELsmp x86_64 Red Hat, Inc.
    Current Operating System: Linux caat0jp01 2.6.18-92.el5 #1 SMP Tue Apr 29 13:16:15 EDT 2008
    x86_64

Build Date: 02 April 2008

Build ID: xorg-x11-server 1.1.1-48.41.el5

    Before reporting problems, check http://wiki.x.org to make sure that you have the latest version.

Module Loader present

Markers: (--) probed, (**) from config file, (==) default setting,

    (++) from command line, (!!) notice, (II) informational,

    (WW) warning, (EE) error, (NI) not implemented, (??) unknown.

(==) Log file: "/var/log/Xorg.0.log", Time: Sat Dec 6 08:35:42 2008

(==) Using config file: "/etc/X11/xorg.conf"

3. Run the following to load all video driver modules, probe for available hardware and store the information found in the *xorg.conf.new* file:

    # X –configure

    . . . .

    List of video drivers:

        ati

        trident

        voodoo

        savage

        s3

    . . . .

    (++) Using config file: "/root/xorg.conf.new"

    Xorg detected your mouse at device /dev/input/mice. Please check your config if the mouse is still not operational, as by default Xorg tries to autodetect the protocol.

    Your xorg.conf file is /root/xorg.conf.new. To test the server, run 'X -config /root/xorg.conf.new'

4. Test the configuration in the */root/xorg.conf.new* file by running the following:

    # X –config /root/xorg.conf.new

    X Window System Version 7.1.1

    Release Date: 12 May 2006

    X Protocol Version 11, Revision 0, Release 7.1.1

    Build Operating System: Linux 2.6.9-67.0.7.ELsmp x86_64 Red Hat, Inc.

    Current Operating System: Linux caat0jp01 2.6.18-92.el5 #1 SMP Tue Apr 29 13:16:15 EDT 2008 x86_64

    Build Date: 02 April 2008

    Build ID: xorg-x11-server 1.1.1-48.41.el5

        Before reporting problems, check http://wiki.x.org

        to make sure that you have the latest version.

    Module Loader present

    Markers: (--) probed, (**) from config file, (==) default setting,

        (++) from command line, (!!) notice, (II) informational,

        (WW) warning, (EE) error, (NI) not implemented, (??) unknown.

    (==) Log file: "/var/log/Xorg.0.log", Time: Sat Dec 6 08:38:43 2008

    (++) Using config file: "/root/xorg.conf.new"

(WW) VMWARE(0): Failed to set up write-combining range (0xf8000000,0x400000)

Sat Dec 6 08:38:45 2008
vncext: VNC extension running!
. . . .

5. After testing the new configuration, copy the file into */etc/X11 as xorg.conf*. Bring the system back to run level 5 so the new configuration is used to bring up X:

init 5

Additional X Configuration Files

In addition to *xorg.conf*, there are several other configuration files that are referenced when X is started. Some of these are per-user while others are system-wide. The per-user files include *.Xclients*, *.xinitrc* and *.xsession*, and are located in user home directories. These files do not exist by default. The system-wide files are stored in the */etc/X11/xinit* directory and include *Xclients* and *xinitrc*, and in the */etc/X11/xinit/xinitrc.d* directory. The system-wide files are used when per-user files are unavailable. Table 10-1 lists and explains some key configuration files.

File	Description
Per-User	
~/.Xclients	Used when *.xinitrc* and *.xsession* files are unavailable.
~/.xinitrc	Defines client programs to run. This file can be created and the following text may be entered to bring *xterm* and *xclock* client programs up in specified window sizes and at specified screen locations. It will also start KDE desktop manager. xterm –g 80x24+0+0 & xclock –g 50x50-0+0 & exec startkde
~/.xserverrc	Defines the default server to run. If this file does not exist, X is started automatically as the default server.
~/.xsession	Defines the desktop environment to start.
System-Wide	
/etc/X11	Contains configuration files for X server and client.
/etc/X11/xorg.conf	Defines configuration settings for the X server.
/etc/X11/xinit/Xclients	Executed if ~/.Xclients is missing.
/etc/X11/xinit/xinitrc	Executed if ~/.xinitrc is missing. Calls ~/.Xclients or /etc/X11/xinit/Xclients, whichever appropriate. This script also runs programs stored in the /etc/X11/xinit/xinitrc.d directory.
/etc/X11/xinit/Xsession	Executed if ~/.xsession is missing.
/etc/X11/xinit/xinitrc.d	Scripts located here are executed by the *xinitrc* script.

Table 10-1 X Configuration Files

X Startup File

The *startx* script is used to manually start the X server if it is not already running. This script is the front-end to the *xinit* command, which starts the X server by calling the *X* (symbolically linked to the *Xorg* command) command. During the X startup process, configuration files such as */etc/X11/xorg.conf* and those located in the user's home directory and */etc/X11* are referenced. These files, as explained in Table 10-1, may be customized to alter the behavior of X. The *startx* (or *xinit*) also starts any defined graphical client programs such as GNOME or KDE desktop managers (as defined in *~/.xinitrc* or */etc/X11/xinit/xinitrc*) during the startup process. An excerpt from the *startx* script is displayed below:

```
# cat /usr/bin/startx
. . . . . . . .
userclientrc=$HOME/.xinitrc
sysclientrc=/etc/X11/xinit/xinitrc
userserverrc=$HOME/.xserverrc
sysserverrc=/etc/X11/xinit/xserverrc
defaultclient=xterm
defaultserver=/usr/bin/X
. . . . . . . .
```

The above output indicates that per-user files from *$HOME* and system-wide files from */etc/X11* are referenced during X startup.

X Font Server

X requires fonts to dispay the text properly. It works with the X font server to make this happen. The X font server is configured to autostart at system reboots. The font server configuration file is */etc/X11/fs/config* and the fonts are located in the */usr/share/X11/fonts* directory. You can perform some manual operations on the font server such as checking its operational status and starting, restarting and stopping it.

To check if the X font server is running:

```
# service xfs status
xfs (pid 2256) is running...
```

To start if not already running:

```
# service xfs start
Starting xfs:                            [ OK ]
```

To restart if already running:

```
# service xfs restart
Restarting xfs:
Shutting down xfs:                       [ OK ]
Starting xfs:                            [ OK ]
```

To stop if not needed:

 # service xfs stop
Shutting down xfs: [OK]

To check if it is configured to autostart at system reboots:

 # chkconfig --list xfs
xfs   0:off   1:off   2:on   3:on   4:on   5:on   6:off

To configure it to autostart at each system reboot if not already set:

 # chkconfig xfs on

X Clients

X clients are programs that require an active X server to be available. X client programs can be run on the same system where X server is running, or they can be run on remote systems. There are several such programs available in RHEL that you can invoke either from menu or command prompt. These programs include *xterm*, *xclock* and desktop managers such as GNOME and KDE.

Configuring a Sample X Client Program

Running X client programs at the command prompt via options allows you to control the size and location of the program window on the desktop screen, font to be used and so on. Table 10-2 lists and explains some common options.

Option	Description
–geometry Xsize x Ysize + Xoff + Yoff	Specifies a window size and its location on the desktop.
–background	Specifies a background window color.
–bordercolor	Specifies a window border color.
–borderwidth	Specifies a window border width in number of pixels.
–foreground	Specifies a foreground window color.
–font	Specifies the font to display text. You can choose from the */usr/share/X11/fonts* directory.
–title	Specifies a window title to be displayed.

Table 10-2 X Client Command Line Options

Based on options described in Table 10-2, the following example will run *xterm* in 100 pixel by 80 pixel window with 25 pixels horizontal and 50 pixels vertical offset from the upper left corner of the screen. It will use the blue color for the foreground, red color for the background and lucidasans-14 font for text. The *xterm* window will have the title "X Client Example" with green border of 10 pixels in width.

**# xterm –geometry 100x80+25+50 –foreground blue –background red –font lucidasans-14 **
–title "X Client Example" –bordercolor green –borderwidth 10

Alternatively, you can invoke *xterm* as (GNOME) Applications → Accessories → Terminal or (KDE) Main Menu → System → Terminal. This will start *xterm* with pre-defined defaults.

Display and Desktop Managers

A *display manager*, a.k.a. a *window manager*, and a *desktop manager* are GUI (*Graphical User Interface*) based applications for users to interact with the system in a convenient way. A display manager is started when the X server is up and running. Normally, when the system is booted into run level 5, the X server is autostarted followed by a pre-defined display manager. The display manager presents a login prompt in a graphical setting for you to enter user credentials. A pre-configured graphical *desktop manager* appears after the credentials are verified.

RHEL comes standard with support for two widely-used graphical managers referred to as GNOME (*GNU Network Object Model Environment*) and KDE (*K Desktop Environment*). Each one of these provides both display as well as desktop management capabilities, and are almost equally powerful, versatile and flexible from a user perspective. Normally, one desktop manager runs at a time, but you can invoke KDE from within GNOME, and vice versa.

There is one other desktop manager called TOM (*Tom's Window Manager*) that you might want to use instead, but it is not as powerful.

GNOME Display and Desktop Managers

GNOME is the default display and desktop management software in RHEL. It includes support for the GTK+ (GIMP) toolkit, and from several other projects such as GConf and ORBIT. The default login screen for GNOME is shown in Figure 10-4.

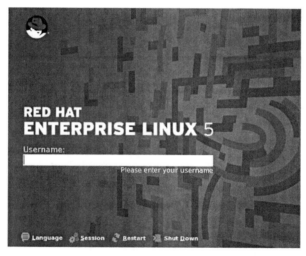

Figure 10-4 GNOME Display Manager

After you are successfully logged on, the default GNOME desktop manager appears as shown in Figure 10-5.

Figure 10-5 GNOME Desktop Manager

Individual user configuration files for GNOME are stored in user home directories under various sub-directories such as *.gconf*, *.gnome* and *.gnome2*.

Usually the look and feel, and features included in a desktop environment are similar to one another. If you are familiar with Microsoft Windows graphical interface, you should not have any difficulty using this interface. The default screen includes some icons on the desktop to open associated applications with a double-click of mouse. The desktop environment allows you to open several virtual desktops. The desktop and the menus are customizable and allow you to create icons for additional applications. Several tools such as GNOME Office are included by default.

There are control centers across the desktop screen at the top and bottom. The Red Hat icon at the top left hand corner is the Applications menu which contains a list of items and sub-items. You can access a variety of applications from here and add as many as you want. The Places menu next to Applications provides access to CD/DVD tools. The System menu is where all system, network and security administration tools, desktop setting tools and documentation are located. You can log off the session and shut down the system from this menu as well.

At the bottom on the right side is where you can switch from one virtual desktop to another. By default, you can open up to four, but add more if you need to.

KDE Display and Desktop Managers

KDE is another popular display and desktop management software available on RHEL. It is not auto-selected during RHEL installation. You have to choose it manually if you wish to load it. KDE is built on the Qt C++ cross-platform GUI toolkit. Figure 10-6 shows the KDE display manager interface.

Figure 10-6 KDE Display Manager

After you are successfully logged on, the default KDE desktop manager appears as shown in Figure 10-7.

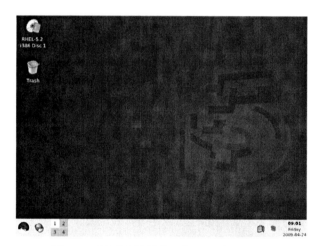

Figure 10-7 KDE Desktop Manager

Individual user configuration files for KDE are stored in user home directories under *.kde* sub-directory.

The look and feel of KDE is similar to the GUI interface of MS Windows'. It offers several features that MS Windows desktop also does. The KDE desktop includes a Main Menu button (a red hat) in the lower left corner of the desktop screen. Like GNOME, KDE allows you to open several virtual desktops. The desktop and the menus are customizable and allow you to create icons for additional applications.

There is a control center across the bottom. The Red Hat icon at the bottom left hand corner is the Main menu which contains a list of items and sub-items. You can access a variety of applications from here and add as many as you want. It contains all system, network and security administration tools, desktop setting tools and documentation as well. The Browser icon next to the Main menu opens up a browser window. The four numbered squares at the bottom allows you to switch from one virtual desktop to another. By default, you can open up to four, but add more if you need to.

Configuring System-Wide Default Display Manager

To change the default display manager permanently for all other users, edit or create the */etc/sysconfig/desktop* file and define a variable DISPLAYMANAGER. Valid values are GNOME, KDE and XDM. For example, to set it up to KDE, do the following:

# **vi /etc/sysconfig/desktop**
DISPLAYMANAGER=KDE

When X is restarted it will consult the */etc/X11/prefdm* file and check the DISPLAYMANAGER directive defined in the */etc/sysconfig/desktop* file, and will start the defined display manager.

Configuring Per-User Default Desktop

Use the *switchdesk* command or its GUI version *switchdesk-gui* (desktop switching tool) to set the default desktop. You need to load the switchdesk software package in order for this tool to function as the package is not installed by default. Use an appropriate package installation method as outlined in Chapter 11 "Software Package Management". Here is how to switch to GNOME assuming that you are currently running KDE:

$ **switchdesk gnome**
Red Hat Linux switchdesk 4.0
Copyright (C) 1999-2004 Red Hat, Inc
Redistributable under the terms of the GNU General Public License
Desktop now set up to run GNOME.

This command creates two files – *.Xclients* and *.Xclients-default* – in your home directory where this desktop is defined as the default upon subsequent logins. Each user on the system can run this command and set a different window manager for himself. If you wish to switch to an alternate desktop manager such as KDE, edit the *.Xclients-default* file and modify the WM directive value to KDE, and log out and log back in.

To do this via menu, choose (GNOME) System → Preferences → More Preferences → Desktop Switching Tool, or (KDE) Main Menu → Settings → Desktop Settings Wizard.

Configuring System-Wide Default Desktop Manager

To set default desktop manager for new users, edit or create the */etc/sysconfig/desktop* file and define a variable DESKTOP. Valid values are GNOME and KDE. For example, to set it up to GNOME, do the following:

# **vi /etc/sysconfig/desktop**
DESKTOP=GNOME

Running X Applications Remotely

As you know X is a client/server application and is capable of running in a networked environment. This allows you to run graphical administrative tools on a remote RHEL system or your desktop computer without having to connect to the console of that system. Here is how you would initiate an X session on *rhel02* from *rhel01*. This procedure assumes that you have X running on both systems.

1. Make sure that the *sshd* daemon is running on *rhel02*:

    # ps –ef | grep sshd | grep –v grep
    root   4545   1 0 09:17 ?   00:00:00 /usr/sbin/sshd

2. On *rhel01*, open an *xterm* and run the following at the command prompt to initiate an X session as *root* on *rhel02*:

    # ssh –X root@rhel02

3. Say yes if prompted to setup an encryption key.
4. Enter *root*'s password to log in.
5. Run a graphical application such as *system-config-display* or *system-config-selinux*. The display will appear on *rhel01*.

In case of any issues, switch to a virtual console and log in. Check error logs in *~/.xsession-errors*, */var/log/messages* and */var/log/Xorg.0.log* files, the status of the X font server and the setting of the DISPLAY variable (DISPLAY=localhost:0.0 or DISPLAY=:0.0 for localhost).

Summary

This chapter discussed X Window System and graphical desktop managers in detail. You were presented with an overview of the X Window system, X server and associated configuration files. You looked at how to configure an X server.

Next, you learned how to manage the start and stop of the X font server. You studied X client applications and graphical desktop managers. Finally, you saw how to configure the default desktop manager and run X client applications over the network.

## 11

Software Package Management

This chapter covers the following major topics:

- ✓ Software package concepts including naming convention, dependency, database and repository
- ✓ Red Hat Network and its benefits
- ✓ Administer software using RHN
- ✓ Package administration commands
- ✓ List, install, upgrade, freshen, query, remove, extract, validate and verify packages using rpm command
- ✓ Overview of yum repository and how to create one
- ✓ List, install, update, search, remove and check availability of packages as well as synchronize package header information using yum
- ✓ List, install, remove and upgrade packages using pirut
- ✓ Manage package upgrades using pup
- ✓ Build custom packages

RHEL provides a rich set of tools for installing and managing software packages on the system. Red Hat software packaging is based on a special format called *Redhat Package Manager* (RPM). All packages available in and for RHEL are in this format. An RPM package contains necessary files, as well as metadata structures such as ownership, permissions and directory location for each individual file included in the package.

Package Overview

There are several concepts associated with software package management and are touched upon in the following sub-sections.

Packages and Packaging

A software *package* is a set of files organized in a directory structure and makes up a Red Hat software application. Files contained in a package includes installable scripts, configuration files, commands and associated documentation. The documentation provides detailed instructions on how to install and uninstall the package, manual pages of the files and commands included and any other specific information pertaining to installation and usage.

All data related to packages is stored at a central location and includes information such as package versioning, location it is installed at and checksum values. This allows package management tools to efficiently handle package administration tasks by referencing this data.

Package Naming Convention

Red Hat software packages follow a standard naming convention. Typically, there are four parts to it. The first part contains the package name, the second includes the version of it, the third includes the package release (revision or build) and the last part tells the processor architecture the package is built for. An installable package name always has the .rpm extension. The extension is removed after the package has been installed. For example:

> sendmail-8.13.8-2.el5.i386.rpm   (package name before it is installed)
> sendmail-8.13.8-2.el5   (package name after it has been installed)

Here is a description of each part in the package name:

- ✓ **sendmail** – package name
- ✓ **8.13.8** – package version
- ✓ **2** – package release
- ✓ **el5** – stands for Enterprise Linux 5. Some packages have it, others do not.
- ✓ **i386** – processor architecture the package is built for. If you see "noarch" instead, the package will be platform-independent and can be installed on any hardware architecture. If you see "src", it will contain source code for the package.
- ✓ **.rpm** – the extension

Package Dependency

A package to be loaded may require the presence of certain files or other packages in order for a successful installation of it. Similarly, many software packages require certain files or other packages to be present in order for them to be able to run and operate smoothly. This is referred to as *package dependency* where a software depends on other software for a successful installation or run.

Package Database

Metadata information of installed package files is stored in the */var/lib/rpm* directory. This directory location is referred to as *package database*. This database is referenced by package management tools to obtain information such as ownership, permissions, timestamp and size of files. This database also contains information about package dependencies. The information contained herein help package management commands verify dependencies and file attributes, upgrade and uninstall an existing package, and add new packages.

Package Repository

A package *repository* is a storage location from where one or several software packages can be downloaded at cost or cost-free for installation. Red Hat maintains its own repositories for this purpose. In addition to accessing many other Internet-based repositories, you can create your own and add packages to it for later installation on one or more systems. It is advisable that you obtain packages from authentic and reliable sources such as Red Hat Network, as described in the next section, to prevent any damage to the system or software corruption.

Red Hat Network (RHN)

The *Red Hat Network* (RHN) at *www.rhn.redhat.com* is the Red Hat's web interface that allows the company's customers to subscribe to it and manage software updates, perform kickstart installations, schedule tasks for later execution and monitor the health of their systems remotely, efficiently and conveniently. To check available software updates and scheduled tasks, a daemon called *rhnsd* must be running on your system(s), which polls RHN every 4 hours as defined in the */etc/sysconfig/rhn/rhnsd* file and performs any required actions without human intervention. Alternatively, you can execute the *rhn_check* command to manually perform the check.

RHN Benefits

Several benefits are associated with RHN subscription. Some of them are:

- ✓ Schedule commands for later execution on one or more systems.
- ✓ Install, update and remove packages on one or more systems.
- ✓ Group systems based on requirements.
- ✓ Add and edit custom configuration files.
- ✓ Create kickstart installations.
- ✓ Create system snapshots.

Registering with RHN

In order to obtain the benefits RHN offers, you must register your system using an active subscription. Usually, you go through this registration process after the system reboots following a graphical installation of RHEL. This process does not automatically begin after text-based and network-based installations.

Here are the steps to register a system:

1. Run *rhn_register* at the command prompt in an X terminal window or choose (GNOME) Applications / (KDE) Main Menu → System Tools → Software Updater. The "Welcome to Red Hat Update Agent" screen will appear as shown in Figure 11-1. Click Forward.

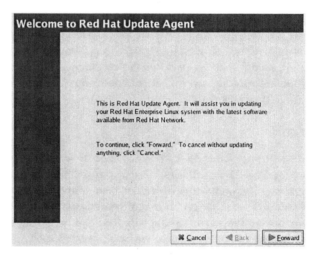

Figure 11-1 RHN Registration – Welcome Screen

2. On the subsequent screen, enter a username and password if you already have one registered, otherwise choose the second option "I don't have a Red Hat login. I need to create one." as shown in Figure 11-2 and click Forward.

Figure 11-2 RHN Registration – Login Screen

3. Fill out the form as shown in Figure 11-3 and click Forward.

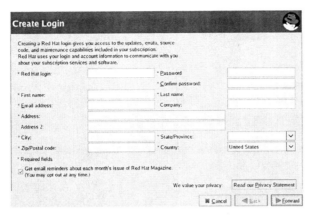

Figure 11-3 RHN Registration – User Account Creation

4. Enter a subscription number or choose "Use one of my existing, active subscriptions" in case you already have subscribed. Select "send basic hardware information" and "send package list" to enable RHN to check whether you need software and security updates for your system hardware type. Specify the system name in the window below. Click Forward when done. See Figure 11-4.

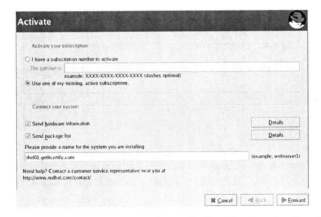

Figure 11-4 RHN Registration – Subscription Activation

5. Follow subsequent screens to complete the registration process.

Administering Software via RHN

After you have created a user account and registered the system, you can log in to the Red Hat Network website at *www.rhn.redhat.com* and manage the system remotely, which includes installing, updating and removing packages on the system automatically or manually, and viewing pending actions in addition to performing other management tasks. Ensure that the *rhnsd* daemon is running on the system by checking it with the following command:

service rhnsd status

If the daemon is not running, perform the below steps to start it manually and make certain that it gets started at each system reboot:

 # service rhnsd start
 # chkconfig rhnsd on

Package Administration Tools

Several commands are available to perform package management functions. Table 11-1 provides a list along with a short description of each.

Command	Description
rpm	Installs, removes, updates and verifies a package. This command does not automatically satisfy package dependencies.
rpm2cpio	Extracts packages.
rpmbuild	Builds new RPMs based on customization.
rpmquery	Queries on packages.
rpmverify	Verifies package attributes.
yum	Front-end to the rpm command. Installs, removes and updates packages from one or more repositories and automatically satisfies dependencies. Also allows to search and list package information. Supports globbing.
pup	Installs and updates packages.
pirut	Graphical tool to install and update packages.

Table 11-1 Package Management Commands

The sections to follow shed light on using the tools listed in Table 11-1.

Managing Packages with rpm

This section discusses package management tasks including listing, installing, upgrading, freshening, querying, removing, extracting, validating and verifying packages using the *rpm* command.

Before getting into details, let us take a look at Table 11-2, which provides a list of options commonly used with the *rpm* command. These options may be used in either way.

Option	Description
–a (--all)	Displays all packages.
–c (--configfiles)	Displays configuration files.
–d (--docfiles)	Displays documentation files.
–e (--erase)	Removes a package.
–f (--file)	Displays information about the specified file.
–F (--freshen)	Upgrades an existing package. An older version of the package must exist in order to upgrade it.
--force	Installs a package even if the same version already exists.
–h (--hash)	Displays progress of package installation / upgrade.
–i (--info)	Displays basic information about a package.
--import	Imports the specified public key.

Option	Description
–i (--install)	Installs a package.
–K (--checksig)	Validates the signature and also the package integrity.
–l (--list)	Lists files in a package.
–p (--package)	Verifies an installed package against an installable package.
–q (--query)	Queries and displays packages. You can use the *rpmquery* command instead.
--replacepkgs	Overwrites existing packages.
–R (--requires)	Lists dependencies without which a package cannot be installed.
–U (--upgrade)	Upgrades an existing package or installs if not already installed.
–v or –vv	Displays detailed information.
–V (--verify)	Verifies the integrity of package files. You can use the *rpmverify* command instead.

Table 11-2 rpm Command Options

Listing Installed Packages

Run either of the following to list all installed packages:

```
# rpm –qa
# rpmquery –a
glib2-2.12.3-2.fc6
mktemp-1.5-23.2.2
bzip2-libs-1.0.3-3
gdbm-1.8.0-26.2.1
beecrypt-4.1.2-10.1.1

. . . . . . . .
```

These commands list an updated list of all packages currently loaded on the system. Alternatively, you can view the contents of the */var/log/rpmpkgs* file, which maintains a list of installed packages. This file might not have the latest information as it is updated once a day.

Installing a Package

Installing a package creates directory structure for the package and installs the required files.

Use the *rpm* command to install a package. The following example attempts to install a package called sendmail-8.13.8-2.el5.i386.rpm with an assumption that the package is downloaded and is located in the */var/tmp* directory:

```
# rpm –ivh /var/tmp/sendmail-8.13.8-2.el5.i386.rpm
Preparing...        ########################################### [100%]
   1:sendmail        ########################################### [100%]
```

If this package requires the presence of other missing packages, you will see an error message that would say "failed dependencies". You must first install the missing packages in order for this package to be loaded successfully.

Alternatively, you may specify the --force option to forcibly install the package without satisfying the dependencies. This is something not recommended. This option also forcibly installs a package even if the same version of the package is already installed by overwriting existing files.

To install the sendmail package located in a remote repository such as *ftp.getitcertify.com* without downloading the package:

> # **rpm –ivh ftp://ftp.getitcertify.com/pub/outgoing/sendmail-8.13.8-2.el5.i386.rpm**
> # **rpm –ivh ftp://aghori:Welcome01@ftp.getitcertify.com/pub/outgoing/**
> **sendmail-8.13.8-2.el5.i386.rpm**

The first command logs in as *anonymous* user and the second uses username *aghori* and password Welcome01 to log in and install the package.

Upgrading a Package

Upgrading a package upgrades the specified package if an older version of the package is already installed. If an older version is not already there, it will go ahead and install it.

To upgrade a package called sendmail-8.13.8-2.el5, use the –U option with the *rpm* command:

> # **rpm –Uvh /var/tmp/sendmail-8.13.8-2.el5.i386.rpm**
> Preparing...   ## [100%]
>   package sendmail-8.13.8-2.i386.el5 is already installed

The command makes a backup of all affected configuration files during the upgrade process and adds the extension *.rpmsave* to them.

Freshening a Package

Freshening a package requires that an older version of the package must already exist.

To freshen a package called sendmail-8.13.8-2.el5.i386.rpm, use the –F option with the *rpm* command:

> # **rpm –Fvh /var/tmp/sendmail-8.13.8-2.el5.i386.rpm**

To freshen all existing packages, do the following:

> # **rpm –Fvh *.rpm**

Overwriting a Package

Overwriting a package replaces existing files associated with the package with the same version.

To overwrite an installed package called sendmail-8.13.8-2.el5.i386.rpm, use the --replacepkgs option with the *rpm* command:

> # **rpm –ivh --replacepkgs /var/tmp/sendmail-8.13.8-2.el5.i386.rpm**

Querying a Package

Querying one or all packages searches for information and displays on the screen. You can use either *rpm* or *rpmquery* command with –q or --query options.

To query whether a package is installed, run any of the following:

> # **rpm –q sendmail**
> # **rpmquery sendmail**
> sendmail-8.13.8-2.el5

To identify which package the specified file is associated with, run any of the following:

> # **rpm –qf /etc/mail/sendmail.cf**
> # **rpmquery –f /etc/mail/sendmail.cf**
> sendmail-8.13.8-2.el5

To list all configuration files in a package, run any of the following:

> # **rpm –qc sendmail**
> # **rpmquery –c sendmail**
> /etc/mail/Makefile
> /etc/mail/access
> . . . .

To list all documentation files in a package, run any of the following:

> # **rpm –qd sendmail**
> # **rpmquery –d sendmail**
> /usr/share/man/man1/mailq.sendmail.1.gz
> /usr/share/man/man1/newaliases.sendmail.1.gz
> . . . .

To display basic information about a package, run any of the following:

> # **rpm –qi sendmail**
> # **rpmquery –i sendmail**
> Name   : sendmail   Relocations: (not relocatable)
> Version   : 8.13.8   Vendor: Red Hat, Inc.
> Release   : 2.el5   Build Date: Tue 28 Nov 2006 09:59:05 AM EST
> Install Date: Mon 24 Dec 2007 12:22:26 PM EST   Build Host: ls20-bc1-14.build.redhat.com
> Group   : System Environment/Daemons   Source RPM: sendmail-8.13.8-2.el5.src.rpm
> Size   : 1370608   License: Sendmail
> Signature   : DSA/SHA1, Wed 17 Jan 2007 03:38:27 PM EST, Key ID 5326810137017186
> Packager   : Red Hat, Inc. <http://bugzilla.redhat.com/bugzilla>
> Summary   : A widely used Mail Transport Agent (MTA).
> Description :
> The Sendmail program is a very widely used Mail Transport Agent (MTA).
> . . . .

To list all files in a package, run any of the following:

```
# rpm –ql sendmail
# rpmquery –l sendmail
/etc/mail
/etc/mail/Makefile
/etc/mail/access
/etc/mail/domaintable
/etc/mail/helpfile
/etc/mail/local-host-names
. . . . . . . .
```

To list all dependencies without which the specified package cannot be installed, run any of the following:

```
# rpm –qR sendmail
# rpmquery –R sendmail
/bin/bash
/bin/mktemp
/bin/sh
. . . . . . . .
```

To query all installed packages, run any of the following:

```
# rpm –qa
# rpmquery –a
termcap-5.5-1.20060701.1
mktemp-1.5-23.2.2
libusb-0.1.12-5.1
readline-5.1-1.1
. . . . . . . .
```

Removing a Package

Removing a package uninstalls the package and all associated files and directory structure.

Use the *rpm* command with –e option to remove a package:

```
# rpm –e sendmail
```

This command performs a dependency check to see if there are any packages that require the existence of the package being removed, and will fail if it determines that another package has dependencies on it.

Extracting Files from a Package

RPM packages are created, and packaged for distribution using the *cpio* command. Each package contains several associated directories and files, and may be retrieved to replace a corrupted or lost command or a critical configuration file. For example, to extract a corrupted */etc/inittab* file, use the below command to determine what package contains it:

```
# rpm –qf /etc/inittab
initscripts-8.45.19.EL-1
```

Assuming that the package is located in the */var/tmp* directory, use the *rpm2cpio* command to extract (–i) all files from the initscripts package and create (–d) directory structure as required:

```
# cd /var/tmp
# rpm2cpio initscripts-8.45.19.EL-1 | cpio –id
```

Search for the *inittab* file under */var/tmp* and copy it to the */etc* directory.

Verifying Package Signature

A package may be checked for integrity (completeness and error-free state) and originality after it is copied to another location, downloaded from the web or obtained elsewhere, and before it is installed. You can use the MD5 checksum for package completeness and error-free state and the *GNU Privacy Guard* (GPG) public key signatures to ensure that the package is in fact an official Red Hat package. This will ensure that you are using an authentic piece of software.

Each package contains the GPG signature on the installation media, in the appropriate RPM-GPG-KEY-* file or in the */etc/pki/rpm-gpg* directory. RHEL 5 supports 6 GPG keys based on whether the package was released before or after November 2006. The RPM-GPG-KEY-redhat-former is used for packages released prior to November 2006 and the RPM-GPG-KEY-redhat-release and RPM-GPG-KEY-redhat-auxilliary are used for packages released after November 2006.

Here is how you would check the integrity and originality of a package such as sendmail-8.13.8-2.el5.i386.rpm located in the */var/tmp* directory. The first command will import the specified GPG key, the second verify that the import is successful, the third validate the signature and also the package integrity, and the last command will display detailed information about the key:

```
# rpm --import /etc/pki/rpm-gpg/RPM-GPG-KEY-redhat-release
# rpm –qa gpg-pubkey
gpg-pubkey-37017186-45761324
# rpm –K /var/tmp/Server/sendmail-8.13.8-2.el5.i386.rpm
sendmail-8.13.8-2.el5.i386.rpm: (sha1) dsa sha1 md5 gpg OK
# rpm –qi gpg-pubkey*
Name        : gpg-pubkey        Relocations: (not relocatable)
Version     : 37017186          Vendor: (none)
Release     : 45761324          Build Date: Wed 11 Mar 2009 11:31:00 AM EDT
Install Date : Wed 11 Mar 2009 11:31:00 AM EDT    Build Host: localhost
Group       : Public Keys       Source RPM: (none)
Size        : 0                 License: pubkey
Signature   : (none)
Summary     : gpg(Red Hat, Inc. (release key) <security@redhat.com>)
Description  :
-----BEGIN PGP PUBLIC KEY BLOCK-----
Version: rpm-4.4.2 (beecrypt-4.1.2)

mQGiBEV2EyQRBAD4/SR69qoLzK4HIa6g9iS+baiX0o3NjkLftFHg/xy+IMOMg//i4c5bUpLK
DTMH3+yT0G8qpul/RALUFOESKFkZm3/SlkJKuroXcB8U6s2dh5XX9DDBISqRwL7M5qB8rfDP
```

KHN+k/XwJ9CNpHMdNxnnc2WhnnmHNp6NrD/bUEH4vwCglMa0rFRXPaN7407DARGHvW/jugsE
ANFaeZsFwos/sajL1XQRfHZUTnvDjJgz31IFY+OLDlOVAOtV/NaECMwIJsMIhoisW4Luwp4m
75Qh3ogq3bwqSWNLsfJ9WFnNqXOgamyDh/F4q492z6FpyIb1JZLABBSH7LEQjHlR/s/Ct5JE
Wc5MyfzdjBi6J9qCh3y/IYL0EbfRA/4yoJ/fH9uthDLZsZRWmnGJvb+VpRvcVs8IQ4aIAcOM
bWu2Sp3U9pm6cxZFN7tShmAwiiGj9UXVtlhpj3lnquILMD9VqXGF0YgDOaQ7CP/99OEEhUjB
j/8o8udFgxc1i2WJjc7/sr8IMbDv/SNToi0bnZUxXa/BUjj92uaQ6/LupbQxUmVkIEhhdCwg
SW5jLiAocmVsZWFzZSBrZXkpIDxzZWN1cml0eUByZWRoYXQuY29tPohfBBMRAgAfBQJFdhMk
AhsDBgsJCAcDAgQVAggDAxYCAQIeAQIXgAAKCRBTJoEBNwFxhogXAKCDTuYeyQrkYXjg9Jm
OdTZvsIVfZgCcCWKJXtfbC5dbv0piTHI/cdwVzJo=
=mhzo
-----END PGP PUBLIC KEY BLOCK-----

Verifying Attributes of an Installed Package

Verifying an installed package compares several package attributes with the original attributes saved and stored in the package database at */var/lib/rpm* at the time the package was installed. The *rpm* or the *rpmverify* command can be used for package attribute verification purposes.

To verify attributes of all installed packages, run any of the following:

rpm –Va
rpm --verify –a
rpmverify –a
SM5DLUGT d /usr/share/info/history.info.gz
.......T d /usr/share/info/readline.info.gz
.......T d /usr/share/info/rluserman.info.gz
.......T d /usr/share/man/man3/history.3.gz
.......T d /usr/share/man/man3/readline.3.gz
. . . .

The commands perform a total of eight checks on each package as illustrated by the eight character codes in the first column of the output and display what, if any, changes have occurred since the file was installed or created. Each of these codes have an associated meaning. Table 11-3 lists the codes as they appear from left to right, and describes them. A dot character appears for an attribute that has not been modified.

Code	Description
S	Appears if file size is different.
M	Appears if permission or file type is altered.
5	Appears if MD5 checksum does not match.
D	Appears if the file is a device file and its major or minor number is changed.
L	Appears if the file is a symlink and its path is altered.
U	Appears if the ownership is modified.
G	Appears if the group membership is modified.
T	Appears if timestamp is changed.
.	Appears if no modification is detected.

Table 11-3 Package Verification Codes

The second column in the output above indicates a code that represents the type of file. Table 11-4 lists them.

File Type	Description
c	Configuration file.
d	Documentation file.
g	Ghost file.
l	License file.
r	Readme file.

Table 11-4 File Type Codes

To verify a single file, use any of the following. There will be no output if no modifications are detected.

```
# rpm –Vf /bin/cp
# rpm –V --file /bin/cp
# rpmverify –f /bin/cp
```

To verify an installed package against an installable package, use any of the following:

```
# rpm –Vp /var/tmp/sendmail-8.13.8-2.el5.i386.rpm
# rpm –V --package /var/tmp/sendmail-8.13.8-2.el5.i386.rpm
# rpmverify --package /var/tmp/sendmail-8.13.8-2.el5.i386.rpm
```

Managing Packages with yum

The *yum* command (*yellowdog updater modified*) is a text-based utility used for package management. This tool requires that your system has access to one or more configured software repositories such as RHN with a valid user account. Alternatively, packages to be installed may be downloaded and stored in a local yum repository. The location of the repository is then defined in the */etc/yum.repos.d* directory. The primary benefit of using this tool is that it performs dependency checks by itself and downloads any required packages automatically in order to successfully install the specified package. With multiple repositories defined, *yum* can extract the specified software package from wherever it finds it. The default yum repository is RHN. When the *yum* command is executed the first time on a system to connect to the RHN repository, it downloads header information associated with software packages and keep them in cache. The next time you access RHN via *yum*, it will download only the updated headers into cache.

Before getting into details, let us take a look at Table 11-5, which provides a list of options commonly used with the *yum* command.

Option	Description
check-upate	Checks if any updates are available for the installed packages.
clean	Synchronizes package header information.
groupinstall	Installs or updates a group of packages.
info	Displays package header information.
install	Installs the specified package(s) or updates them if already installed.
list	Lists packages that are installed or available for installation or update.

Option	Description
localinstall	Installs or updates packages located locally on the system.
provides (or whatprovides)	Searches for packages that contain the specified file.
remove	Removes the specified package(s).
search	Searches for packages that contain the specified string.
update	Updates package(s) if already installed.

Table 11-5 yum Command Options

YUM Repository

Although several yum repositories are available on the Internet, you can configure one for your network. This is a good practice if you have a large number of RHEL systems where you want to manage packages with proper dependencies satisfied. This also helps you maintain consistent packages installed across the board. If you have developed a new package or built one, it can be kept in that repository as well. You may create separate sub-directories within a yum repository to save dissimilar package versions.

Creating a YUM Repository

Here is how you would create a private yum repository for use on your network:

1. Download and install a package called createrepo if it is not already installed. With –y option, the command assumes that the answer is in affirmative.

```
# yum –y install createrepo
Loading "rhnplugin" plugin
Loading "security" plugin
rhel-i386-server-5        100% |===========================| 1.4 kB    00:00
Setting up Install Process
Parsing package install arguments
Resolving Dependencies
--> Running transaction check
---> Package createrepo.noarch 0:0.4.11-3.el5 set to be updated
--> Finished Dependency Resolution
Dependencies Resolved
```

```
===============================================================================
 Package           Arch      Version        Repository         Size
===============================================================================
Installing:
 createrepo        noarch    0.4.11-3.el5   rhel-i386-server-5  59 k

Transaction Summary
===============================================================================
Install       1 Package(s)
Update        0 Package(s)
Remove        0 Package(s)
```

```
Total download size: 59 k
Is this ok [y/N]: y
Downloading Packages:
(1/1): createrepo-0.4.11- 100% |=========================| 59 kB   00:00
Running rpm_check_debug
Running Transaction Test
Finished Transaction Test
Transaction Test Succeeded
Running Transaction
  Installing: createrepo                ######################## [1/1]
Installed: createrepo.noarch 0:0.4.11-3.el5
Complete!
```

2. Create a directory such as */var/yum/repos.d* and *cd* into it:

   # **mkdir –p /var/yum/repos.d && cd /var/yum/repos.d**

3. Move the packages to be made available into this directory. For this demonstration, a package called a2ps-4.13b-57.2.el5.src.rpm is copied.
4. Execute the *createrepo* command on the */var/yum/repos.d* directory. This command will remove header information from each package located in that directory, generate a sub-directory called *repodata*, generate XML files to describe the repository, *gzip* them and place them into this directory.

   ```
   # createrepo –v .
   1/1 - a2ps-4.13b-57.2.el5.src.rpm
   Saving Primary metadata
   Saving file lists metadata
   Saving other metadata
   # ll repodata
   -rw-r--r-- 1 root root   472 Mar  3 10:55 filelists.xml.gz
   -rw-r--r-- 1 root root 3575 Mar  3 10:55 other.xml.gz
   -rw-r--r-- 1 root root   893 Mar  3 10:55 primary.xml.gz
   -rw-r--r-- 1 root root   951 Mar  3 10:55 repomd.xml
   ```

5. Create a definition file such as */etc/yum.repos.d/rhel01.repo* for the repository. Specify the URL for the repository and the protocol to be used to access it:

   ```
   # vi /etc/yum.repos.d/rhel01.repo
   [rhel01]
   name=yum repository for rhel01
   baseurl=ftp://rhel01/var/yum/repos.d/
   enabled=1
   gpgcheck=1
   gpgkey=file:///etc/pki/rpm-gpg/RPM-GPG-KEY-redhat-release
   ```

YUM Configuration File

The key configuration file for *yum* is */etc/yum.conf*. The default contents are listed below:

```
# cat /etc/yum.conf
[main]
cachedir=/var/cache/yum
keepcache=0
debuglevel=2
logfile=/var/log/yum.log
distroverpkg=redhat-release
tolerant=1
exactarch=1
obsoletes=1
gpgcheck=1
plugins=1
# Note: yum-RHN-plugin doesn't honor this.
metadata_expire=1h
# Default.
# installonly_limit = 3
# PUT YOUR REPOS HERE OR IN separate files named file.repo
# in /etc/yum.repos.d
```

Table 11-6 explains various directives defined in the file.

Directive	Description
cachedir	Specifies the location to store *yum* downloads. Default is */var/cache/yum*.
keepcache	Specifies whether to store the cache of packages and headers following a successful installation. Default is 0 (disabled).
debuglevel	Specifies the level at which the debug is to be recorded in the logfile. Default is 2.
logfile	Specifies the location of the log file for *yum* activities. Default is */var/log/yum.log*.
pkgpolicy	Specifies the version to be downloaded/installed. Default is newest.
distroverpkg	Specifies where to get the version. Default is redhat-release, which obtains the information from */etc/redhat-release* file.
tolerant	Specifies whether to ignore minor errors. Default is 1 (enabled).
exactarch	Specifies the CPU architecture for the package to be downloaded. Default is 1 (enabled).
obsoletes	Checks and removes any obsolete packages. Default is 1 (enabled).
gpgcheck	Specifies whether to check the GPG signature for package authenticity. Default is 1 (enabled).
plugins	Specifies to include plug-ins with the packages to be downloaded. Default is 1 (enabled).
metadata_expire	Specifies a lifetime for header data downloaded from RHN. Default is 1 hour. The *yum* command automatically downloads the latest package header information if *yum* is not used for this long. This is to ensure that header data is up to date.

Table 11-6 Directives as Defined in /etc/yum.conf File

Listing Packages

To list packages available from the */var/yum/repos.d* repository:

```
# yum list available
Loading "security" plugin
Loading "rhnplugin" plugin
Available Packages
Deployment_Guide-as-IN.noarch      5.2-11         rhel-i386-server
. . . . . . . .
```

To list all packages including those that are already installed:

```
# yum list
. . . . . . . .
Installed Packages
Deployment_Guide-en-US.noarch      5.1.0-11       installed
Gconf2.i386                        2.14.0-9.el5   installed
. . . . . . . .
```

To list all packages available for installation from various repositories:

```
# yum list all
. . . . . . . .
Installed Packages
Deployment_Guide-en-US.noarch      5.2-9              installed
GConf2.i386                        2.14.0-9.el5       installed
ImageMagick.i386                   6.2.8.0-4.el5_1.1  installed
MAKEDEV.i386                       3.23-1.2           installed
```

To list all packages available from various repositories that you should be able to install:

```
# yum list available
. . . . . . . .
Available Packages
Deployment_Guide-as-IN.noarch      5.2-11         rhel-i386-server
. . . . . . . .
```

To list all packages available from various repositories that you should be able to update:

```
# yum list updates
. . . . . . . .
Updated Packages
Deployment_Guide-en-US.noarch      5.2-11           rhel-i386-server
NetworkManager.i386                1:0.7.0-3.el5    rhel-i386-server
. . . . . . . .
```

To list if a package ("bc" for instance) is installed or is available to be installed from any configured repository:

```
# yum list bc
. . . . . . .
Installed Packages
bc.i386                    1.06-21              installed
```

To list all installed packages that contain "gnome" in their names:

```
# yum list installed *gnome"
. . . . . . .
Installed Packages
NetworkManager-gnome.i386        1:0.6.4-8.el5        installed
bluez-gnome.xi386                0.5-5.fc6            installed
gnome-applets.i386               1:2.16.0.1-19.el5    installed
. . . . . . .
```

Installing and Updating Packages

To install or update the *system-config-samba* tool for instance, issue the following. Note that *yum* installs the specified package if it is not already installed and updates it to the latest available version if it is already loaded.

```
# yum –y install system-config-samba
. . . . . . .
rhel-i386-server-5    100% |=========================| 1.3 kB   00:00
Setting up Install Process
Parsing package install arguments
Resolving Dependencies
--> Running transaction check
--> Package system-config-samba.noarch 0:1.2.41-3.el5 set to be updated
--> Finished Dependency Resolution
Dependencies Resolved

================================================================================
 Package              Arch      Version       Repository        Size
================================================================================
Installing:
 system-config-samba  noarch    1.2.41-3.el5  rhel-i386-server-5 268 k

Transaction Summary
================================================================================
Install      1 Package(s)
Update       0 Package(s)
Remove       0 Package(s)

Total download size: 268 k
Is this ok [y/N]: y
Downloading Packages:
(1/1): system-config-samb 100% |=========================| 268 kB   00:00
Running rpm_check_debug
```

```
Running Transaction Test
Finished Transaction Test
Transaction Test Succeeded
Running Transaction
  Installing: system-config-samba      ######################### [1/1]
Installed: system-config-samba.noarch 0:1.2.41-3.el5
Complete!
```

Indicate the version information with the package name if you want to obtain and install a specific version of the package.

To install or update several packages:

yum install system-config-samba system-config-display system-config-user
```
Loading "security" plugin
Loading "rhnplugin" plugin
rhel-i386-server-5       100% |=========================| 1.3 kB   00:00
Setting up Install Process
Parsing package install arguments
Package system-config-samba - 1.2.41-3.el5.noarch is already installed.
Package system-config-display - 1.0.48-2.el5.noarch is already installed.
No package system-config-user available.
Nothing to do
```

To install or update a package such as system-config-display located locally on the system:

yum localinstall /var/yum/repos.d/system-config-display

To install or update a group of packages such as kde-desktop:

yum groupinstall kde-desktop

To update a package to the latest available version, issue the following. Note that *yum* will only update the package to the latest version. The command will fail if the specified package is not already installed.

yum update system-config-samba
```
. . . . . . . .
rhel-i386-server-5       100% |=========================| 1.3 kB   00:00
Setting up Update Process
Could not find update match for system-config-samba
No Packages marked for Update
```

To update all installed packages to the latest version:

yum update
```
. . . . . . .
rhel-i386-server-5       100% |=========================| 1.3 kB   00:00
Setting up Update Process
```

```
Resolving Dependencies
Skipping security plugin, no data
--> Running transaction check
---> Package stunnel.i386 0:4.15-2.el5.1 set to be updated
. . . . . . . .
```

To display package header information for the system-config-samba package:

yum info system-config-samba

```
. . . . . . .
rhel-i386-server-5        100% |=========================| 1.3 kB   00:00
Installed Packages
Name   : system-config-samba
Arch   : noarch
Version: 1.2.41
Release: 3.el5
Size   : 1.0 M
Repo   : installed
Summary: Samba server configuration tool
Description:
system-config-samba is a graphical user interface for creating,
modifying, and deleting samba shares.
```

Searching Packages

To search for all the packages that contain a specific file such as system-config-display, use either "provides" or "whatprovides" option with the *yum* command:

yum provides /usr/bin/system-config-display

```
. . . . . . .
Reading repository metadata in from local files
setuptool.i386                    1.19.2-1           installed
Matched from:
/etc/setuptool.d/98system-config-display
system-config-display.noarch      1.0.48-2.el5       installed
Matched from:
/etc/pam.d/system-config-display
/etc/security/console.apps/system-config-display
. . . . . . . .
```

Use the wildcard character to match all filenames:

yum provides /usr/bin/system-config*

```
. . . . . . .
Reading repository metadata in from local files
system-config-services.noarch     0.9.4-1.el5        installed
Matched from:
/etc/pam.d/system-config-services
. . . . . . . .
```

To search for all packages that contain the specified string in their name, description or summary:

yum search system-config

. . . .

system-config-lvm.noarch : A utility for graphically configuring Logical Volumes
system-config-securitylevel-tui.i386 : A text interface for modifying the system security level
system-config-language.noarch : A graphical interface for modifying the system language
system-config-netboot-cmd.noarch : network booting/install configuration utility

. . . .

Removing Packages

To remove the system-config-samba package and any packages that depend on it:

yum remove system-config-samba

. . . .

Setting up Remove Process
rhel-i386-server-5   100% |=========================| 1.3 kB   00:00
Resolving Dependencies
--> Running transaction check
---> Package system-config-samba.noarch 0:1.2.39-1.el5 set to be erased
--> Finished Dependency Resolution
Dependencies Resolved

===

Package   Arch   Version   Repository   Size
===

Removing:
 system-config-samba   noarch   1.2.39-1.el5   installed   1.0 M

Transaction Summary
===

Install   0 Package(s)
Update   0 Package(s)
Remove   1 Package(s)
Is this ok [y/N]: **y**
Downloading Packages:
Running rpm_check_debug
Running Transaction Test
Finished Transaction Test
Transaction Test Succeeded
Running Transaction
  Erasing   : system-config-samba   ######################### [1/1]
Removed: system-config-samba.noarch 0:1.2.39-1.el5
Complete!

Checking Availability of Updated Packages

To check whether any updates are available for packages installed on your system:

 # yum check-update

. . . .

Deployment_Guide-en-US.noarch	5.2-11	rhel-i386-server
NetworkManager.i386	1:0.7.0-3.el5	rhel-i386-server
NetworkManager-glib.i386	1:0.7.0-3.el5	rhel-i386-server

. . . .

Synchronizing Package Headers

By default, the header information associated with packages in the */var/cache/yum* cache directory is automatically synchronized with that in the Red Hat repositories every 30 minutes by the *yum* command if the system is registered. This default expiry period is defined in the */etc/yum.conf* file via the *metadata_expire* directive. If you wish to synchronize it instantly, do the following:

 # yum clean all

. . . .

Cleaning up Everything

Managing Packages with pirut

pirut (package install, remove and update tool) is a graphical front-end to the *yum* command, which can be used to install, remove and update a number of software packages on the system simultaneously and with dependencies satisfied automatically.

To start, execute the *pirut* command from the command prompt, run *system-config-packages* or choose (GNOME) Applications → Add/Remove Software or (KDE) Main Menu → System → Add/Remove Software. There are three tabs – Browse, Search and List – associated with package management as shown in Figure 11-5.

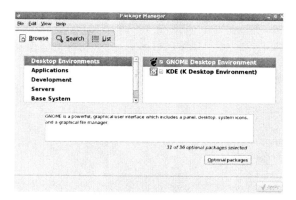

Figure 11-5 pirut – Browse tab

The Browse tab shows all available software package groups available from RHN or other repositories. You can expand the groups and choose the packages that you want installed or updated. This interface is the same that you interacted with during RHEL installation.

The Search tab allows you to search for a specific package and tells you whether it is already installed. See Figure 11-6 that shows the system-config-samba searched.

Figure 11-6 pirut – Search tab

The List tab displays all installed or available packages, or both. Packages that have a checkmark are either already installed or selected for installation.

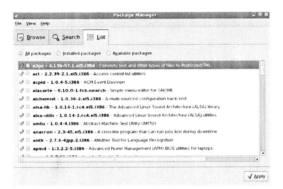

Figure 11-7 pirut – List tab

To obtain and install a package using *pirut*, perform the following steps:

1. Start *pirut*.
2. Select a package group in the Browse tab and click Optional Packages. This will display a list of all installed and available packages for that package group. Select a package to be installed and click Close. Another method is to go to the List tab and choose the ones that you want installed, and click Apply. The third method is to go to the Search tab and type a package name to be searched. If a checkmark appears beside the package name, it would mean that the package is already installed, otherwise you can click the box next to the package name and click Apply. Details of selected package(s) can be viewed under Package Details.
3. A window with a list of packages that you have selected for installation will appear. Click Continue.
4. If there are any dependencies, you will see a Dependencies Added window with a list of dependent packages to be included in the install. Review Details and click Continue.
5. *pirut* will download packages and install them.
6. Click OK when the process is finished.

Likewise, you can remove an installed software package from the system. In step 2 above, any packages that you wish to remove, simply uncheck the associated box and click Apply.

Updating Packages with pup

pup (*package updater*) is a graphical front-end to the *yum* command and is used only to manage the software updates on the system. It displays a list of updated packages from the RHN repository and allows you to select or unselect them. The selected packages will have their dependencies satisfied automatically, and will be downloaded and installed. The system must already be registered with RHN in order for this tool to function as desired, or else it will start up the registration process as soon as it is run. Execute the *pup* command from the command prompt or choose (GNOME) Applications / (KDE) Main Menu → System Tools → Software Updater to start it. Select or unselect desired updates and click Apply Updates to update selected packages. See Figure 11-8.

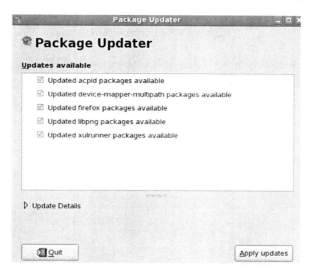

Figure 11-8 pup Interface

Building a Custom Package

A software package is in binary, installable format and is typically downloaded from the web. Sometimes it becomes necessary to build your own custom package. In that situation, you would want to obtain the source code for the package by downloading it at no charge under the *GNU Public License* (GPL). Source code for RHEL packages may be downloaded from *ftp.redhat.com*.

Follow the procedure below to download the source code for a specific package, build a package and install it. For this demonstration, let us get a2ps-4.13b-57.2.el5.src.rpm and work with it.

1. Change directory into where you wish the package to be downloaded. For example, to download in */var/tmp*, *cd* into it:

   # **cd /var/tmp**

2. Use the *ftp* command to get the package by logging in as *anonymous* user on *ftp.redhat.com*. Enter any password for *anonymous* user.

ftp ftp.redhat.com

. . . .

Name (ftp.redhat.com:root): **anonymous**

331 Please specify the password.

Password:

230 Login successful.

Remote system type is UNIX.

Using binary mode to transfer files.

ftp> **cd pub/redhat/linux/enterprise/5Server/en/os/SRPMS**

250 Directory successfully changed.

ftp> **dir a2ps-4.13b-57.2.el5.src.rpm**

227 Entering Passive Mode (209,132,176,30,52,22)

150 Here comes the directory listing.

-rw-rw-r-- 2 ftp ftp 2360917 Jan 17 2008 a2ps-4.13b-57.2.el5.src.rpm

226 Directory send OK.

ftp> **get a2ps-4.13b-57.2.el5.src.rpm**

local: a2ps-4.13b-57.2.el5.src.rpm remote: a2ps-4.13b-57.2.el5.src.rpm

227 Entering Passive Mode (209,132,176,30,47,82)

150 Opening BINARY mode data connection for a2ps-4.13b-57.2.el5.src.rpm (2360917 bytes).

226 File send OK.

2360917 bytes received in 4.7 seconds (4.9e+02 Kbytes/s)

ftp> **quit**

221 Goodbye.

Alternatively, use the *wget* command to download the package:

wget ftp.redhat.com/pub/redhat/linux/enterprise/5Server/en/os/SRPMS/
a2ps-4.13b-57.2.el5.src.rpm

--17:24:15-- ftp://ftp.redhat.com/pub/redhat/linux/enterprise/5Server/en/os/SRPMS/a2ps-4.13b-
57.2.el5.src.rpm

     => `a2ps-4.13b-57.2.el5.src.rpm'

Resolving ftp.redhat.com... 209.132.176.30

Connecting to ftp.redhat.com|209.132.176.30|:21... connected.

Logging in as anonymous ... Logged in!

==> SYST ... done.   ==> PWD ... done.

==> TYPE I ... done. ==> CWD /pub/redhat/linux/enterprise/5Server/en/os/SRPMS ... done.

==> SIZE a2ps-4.13b-57.2.el5.src.rpm ... 2360917

==> PASV ... done.   ==> RETR a2ps-4.13b-57.2.el5.src.rpm ... done.

Length: 2360917 (2.3M)

100%[===>] 2,360,917   431K/s   in 5.7s

17:24:22 (406 KB/s) - `a2ps-4.13b-57.2.el5.src.rpm' saved [2360917]

3. Execute the following to install the package. Make sure that */usr/src/redhat* directory exists.

rpm –ivh a2ps-4.13b-57.2.el5.src.rpm

  1:a2ps   ### [100%]

---

4. The source code is installed in the SOURCES and SPECS sub-directories under *usr/src/redhat*. The SOURCES sub-directory contains source files and the SPECS sub-directory contains a single specification file.

5. Edit the specification file *a2ps.spec* and customize the code. This file will be used to build a custom, installable package.

The spec file contains several sections that begin with the % sign. Some of them are listed and explained in Table 11-7.

Section	Description
%build	Specifies commands to compile the spec file and build sources.
%changelog	Specifies revision list.
%clean	Specifies a command or script to perform any required cleanup tasks.
%description	A short description of the package.
%files	Specifies files included in the package.
%install	Specifies commands to install the software.
%pre	Specifies any pre-installation scripts.
%preamble	Specifies package summary, version, group and any dependent packages.
%prep	Specifies any preparatory scripts to be run prior to building the source code.
%preun	Specifies any preparatory scripts to be run prior to uninstalling.
%post	Specifies any preparatory scripts to be run after building the source code.
%postun	Specifies any preparatory scripts to be run after uninstalling.
%verify	Specifies any verification checks to be included.

Table 11-7 SPEC File Sections

An excerpt from the file is shown below:

 # cat /usr/src/redhat/SPECS/a2ps.spec
Summary: Converts text and other types of files to PostScriptl.
Name: a2ps
Version: 4.13b
Release: 57.2%{?dist}
License: GPL
Group: Applications/Publishing
Source: ftp://ftp.enst.fr/pub/unix/a2ps/%{name}-%{version}.tar.gz
Source1: ftp://ftp.enst.fr/pub/unix/a2ps/i18n-fonts-0.1.tar.gz
Patch0: a2ps-4.13-conf.patch
Patch1: a2ps-4.13-etc.patch
. . . .

6. Create directory structure under *usr/src/redhat* if it does not already exist:

 # cd /usr/src/redhat && mkdir BUILD SRPMS RPMS

7. Build a binary package using the *rpmbuild* command:

 # rpmbuild –bb a2ps.spec

If you wish to build the source package as well, run the following instead:

rpmbuild –ba a2ps.spec

The first command will use the BUILD directory to create the binary package and store it in the RPMS directory and the second command will also create the source package and store it in the SRPMS sub-directory.

You will need to load any missing packages prior to running the *rpmbuild* command.

8. Test install the package using the *rpm* command after it has been created to make certain that it works.

This completes the process of building a custom package from source code.

Summary

This chapter discussed software package management. You learned concepts around packages, packaging, naming convention, dependency and database. You looked at the benefits of RHN and how to register a system with it to administer software. You performed various package management tasks using the rpm, yum, pirut and pup commands. You studied yum repository concepts and how to create one.

Finally, you looked at how to build a custom package using various tools and methods.

## 12

Users and Groups

This chapter covers the following major topics:

✓ Understand /etc/passwd, /etc/shadow, /etc/group and /etc/gshadow authentication files

✓ Verify /etc/passwd, /etc/shadow, /etc/group and /etc/gshadow file consistency

✓ Lock /etc/passwd, /etc/shadow, /etc/group and /etc/gshadow files while being edited

✓ Create, modify and delete user accounts

✓ Set password aging

✓ User password requirements

✓ Use su and sudo commands

✓ Display successful and unsuccessful user login attempts history

✓ Display currently and recently logged in users

✓ Create, modify and delete group accounts

✓ Explain default login parameters file

✓ Understand user initialization files

In order for an authorized person to gain access into the system, a unique *username* (aka *login name*) must be assigned and a user account must be created on the system. This user is assigned membership to one or more groups. Members of the same group have the same access rights on files and directories. Other users and members of other groups may or may not be given access to those files. User and group account information is recorded in several files. Password aging may be set on user accounts to control access. Several user initialization files are involved when a user logs in. This chapter is going to explain users and groups, and associated details.

Overview

RHEL supports three fundamental user account types – *root*, *normal* and *service*. The *root* user possesses full powers on the system. It is the superuser or the administrator that has full access to all services and administrative functions. This user is automatically created during RHEL installation. The normal users have user-level privileges. They cannot perform any administrative functions, but can run applications and programs that they are authorized to execute. The service accounts are responsible for taking care of the installed services. These accounts include apache, games, mail, printing and squid.

User account information is stored in four files – */etc/passwd, /etc/shadow, /etc/group* and */etc/gshadow*. These files are updated when a user account is created, modified or removed. The same files are referenced when a user attempts to log in to the system and, therefore, the files are referred to as user authentication files. The following sub-sections discuss them in detail.

User Authentication – The /etc/passwd File

The */etc/passwd* file contains vital user login data. Each line entry in the file contains information about one user account. There are seven fields per line entry separated by the colon (:) character. A sample entry from the file is displayed in Figure 12-1.

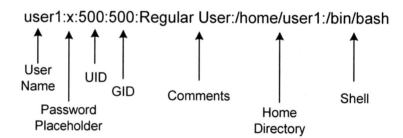

Figure 12-1 User Authentication File – /etc/passwd

Here is what is stored in each field:

✓ The first field contains a login name that a user uses to log in to the system. Usernames up to 255 characters are supported.
✓ The second field contains an "x" (points to the */etc/shadow* file for the actual password), an asterisk "*" character (denotes that the account is disabled) or a combination of random letters and numbers.

- The third field holds a unique number between 0 and approximately 2 billion. This number is known as *User ID* (UID). User ID 0 is reserved for the *root* user, UIDs between 1 and 499 are typically reserved for system accounts and UIDs 500 and beyond are used for all other users. By default, RHEL begins assigning UIDs to new users at 500.
- The fourth field holds a number referred to as *Group ID* (GID). This number corresponds with a group entry in the */etc/group* file. By default, RHEL creates a group for every new user by the same name as the username and the same GID as the user's UID. The GID defined in this field represents a user's primary group.
- The fifth field optionally contains general comments about a user that may include the user's name, phone number and location. This data may be viewed using commands such as *finger*.
- The sixth field defines the absolute path to a user home directory. A *home* directory is the location where a user is placed after logging in to a system, and is typically used to store personal files for the user. The default location for user home directories is */home*.
- The last field contains the absolute path of the shell file that the user will be using as his primary shell after logging in. Common shells are BASH (*/bin/bash*), Korn (*/bin/ksh*) and C (*/bin/csh*). The default shell assigned to users is BASH.

A sample *passwd* file is shown below:

cat /etc/passwd
root:x:0:0:root:/root:/bin/bash
bin:x:1:1:bin:/bin:/sbin/nologin
daemon:x:2:2:daemon:/sbin:/sbin/nologin
. . . .
user1:x:500:500::/home/user1:/bin/bash

 Permissions on */etc/passwd* should be 644 and the file must be owned by the *root* user.

User Authentication – The /etc/group File

The */etc/group* file contains group information. Each row in the file contains one group entry. Each user is assigned at least one group, which is referred to as the user's primary group. In RHEL, by default, a group name is same as the user name it is associated with. This group is known as *user's private group* (UPG) and it safeguards the user's files from other users' access. There are four fields per line entry in the file and are separated by the colon (:) character. A sample entry from the file is exhibited in Figure 12-2.

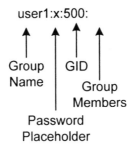

Figure 12-2 User Authentication File – /etc/group

Here is what is stored in each field:

- ✓ The first field contains a unique group name, which must start with an alphabet. By default, each user gets a unique group whose name is the same as the user name. Other common groups may be created and users assigned. Group names up to 255 characters are supported.
- ✓ The second field is not typically used and is left blank. It may, however, contain an encrypted group-level password (copied and pasted from /etc/shadow file) or an "x" which means that the actual password is defined in the /etc/gshadow file. You may set a password on a group if you want non-members to be able to change their group membership to this group using the newgrp command. The non-members must enter the correct password.
- ✓ The third field defines the GID, which is placed in the GID field of the /etc/passwd file. By default, groups are created with GIDs starting at 500 and match the username that they are assigned to. Several users can be members of one single group. Similarly, one user can be a member of several groups.
- ✓ The last field holds usernames that belong to the group. Note that a user's primary group is defined in the /etc/passwd file, and not here.

A sample *group* file is shown below:

```
# cat /etc/group
root:x:0:root
bin:x:1:root,bin,daemon
daemon:x:2:root,bin,daemon
sys:x:3:root,bin,adm
. . . . . . . .
user1:x:500:
```

 Permissions on the /etc/group file should be 644 and the file must be owned by the *root* user.

User Authentication – The /etc/shadow File

The implementation of shadow password mechanism in RHEL provides an added layer of user password security. With this mechanism in place, not only the user passwords are encrypted and stored at an alternate location in a more secure file /etc/shadow, but also certain limits on user passwords in terms of expiration, warning period, etc. can be implemented on a per-user basis. This is referred to as *password aging*. The *shadow* file is only readable by the *root* user, which makes the contents of the file concealed from everyone else.

With shadow password mechanism active, a user is initially checked in the *passwd* file and then in the *shadow* file for authenticity.

The *shadow* file contains extended user authentication information. Each row in the file corresponds to one entry in the *passwd* file. There are nine fields per line entry and are separated by the colon (:) character. A sample entry from this file is exhibited in Figure 12-3.

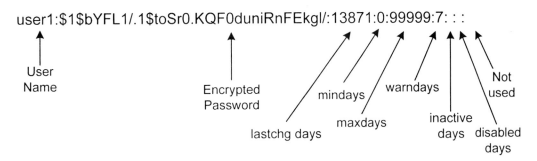

user1:1bYFL1/.1$toSr0.KQF0duniRnFEkgl/:13871:0:99999:7: : :

User Name

Encrypted Password

mindays

warndays

lastchg days

maxdays

inactive days

Not used

disabled days

Figure 12-3 User Authentication File – /etc/shadow

Here is what is stored in each field:

✓ The first field contains a login name as appeared in the */etc/passwd* file.
✓ The second field contains a combination of random letters and numbers, which represents a user password in an encrypted form.
✓ The third field contains the number of days since the epoch time (January 01, 1970) when the password was last modified.
✓ The fourth field contains the minimum number of days that must elapse before a user password can be changed. This field is set with –m or --mindays option of the *chage* command or –n option of the *passwd* command.
✓ The fifth field contains the maximum number of days of password validity before a user starts getting warning messages to change it. This field is set with –M or --maxdays option of the *chage* command or –x option of the *passwd* command.
✓ The sixth field contains the number of days a user gets warning messages to change password. This field is set with –W or --warndays option of the *chage* command or –w option of the *passwd* command.
✓ The seventh field contains the maximum allowable number of days of user inactivity. This field is set with –I or --inactive option of the *chage* command or –i option of the *passwd* command.
✓ The eighth field contains the number of days since the epoch time (January 01, 1970) after which the account gets expired. This field is set with –E or --expiredate option of the *chage* command.
✓ The last field is reserved for future use.

A sample *shadow* file is shown below:

cat /etc/shadow
root:1vcovVMMe$oZqiZ0gXlxcMibLZgy.XT0:13871:0:99999:7:::
bin:*:13871:0:99999:7:::
daemon:*:13871:0:99999:7:::
adm:*:13871:0:99999:7:::

. . . .
user1:1BqKmeXy3$6ziUK3CU.ImUpcvAhWxhj/:13871:0:99999:7:::

Permissions on the */etc/shadow* file should be 400 and the file must be owned by the *root* user.

User Authentication – The /etc/gshadow File

The shadow password implementation also provides an added layer of protection at the group level. With this mechanism activated, the group passwords are encrypted and stored at an alternate location in a more secure file /etc/gshadow, which is only readable by the *root* user, and, therefore, hides the contents from everyone else.

The *gshadow* file contains group encrypted password information. Each row in the file corresponds to one entry in the *group* file. There are four fields per line entry and are separated by the colon (:) character. A sample entry from this file is exhibited in Figure 12-4.

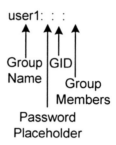

Figure 12-4 User Authentication File – /etc/gshadow

Here is what is stored in each field:

- ✓ The first field contains a group name as appeard in the /etc/group file.
- ✓ The second field may contain a combination of random letters and numbers if a group password is set using the *gpasswd* command. These characters hold the password in an encrypted form. If the field contains ! sign, it indicates that no users are allowed to access the group using the *newgrp* command; !! sign represents that a group password has never been set and no users are allowed to access the group using *newgrp*; and if the field is empty, it means that only group member(s) can change into this group with *newgrp*.
- ✓ The third field lists usernames of group administrators that are authorized to add or remove members to and from this group with the *gpasswd* command.
- ✓ The last field holds usernames that belong to the group.

A sample *gshadow* file is shown below:

```
# cat /etc/gshadow
root:::root
bin:::root,bin,daemon
daemon:::root,bin,daemon
sys:::root,bin,adm
. . . . . . . .
user1:!::
```

 Permissions on the /etc/gshadow file should be 400 and the file must be owned by the *root* user.

Red Hat Certified Technician & Engineer

Verifying Consistency of User Authentication Files

Sometimes inconsistencies occur in user authentication files. To check if the information in *passwd* and *shadow* files is valid and consistent, use the *pwck* command. This command checks and validates the number of fields in each line, login names, UIDs, GIDs and existence of login directory and shell, and reports any inconsistencies.

> # **pwck**
> user adm: directory /var/adm does not exist
> user news: directory /etc/news does not exist
> user uucp: directory /var/spool/uucp does not exist
> user gopher: directory /var/gopher does not exist
> user pcap: directory /var/arpwatch does not exist
> user sabayon: directory /home/sabayon does not exist
> pwck: no changes

To verify if the information in *group* and *gshadow* files is valid and consistent, use the *grpck* command. This command checks and validates the number of fields in each line and whether a user belonging to a group is missing from the *passwd* or *shadow* file, and reports any inconsistencies.

Locking User Authentication Files

Although not recommended, periodically it is imperative to modify the *passwd* file by hand using an editor; however, if another user attempts to change his password while *passwd* is being edited, the end result is a successful password modification for the user and the *passwd* file is updated to reflect the change. Unfortunately, this change will be lost when the file is saved by the person who opened it with an editor.

To prevent such an unwanted situation from happening, use the *vipw* command to edit *passwd* (and *shadow*). This command copies *passwd* file to a temporary file called */etc/ptmp* and disables write access to it. When another user attempts to change his password while you are editing the file, the user will be denied permission. When you quit *vipw*, some automatic checks are performed on *ptmp* to validate contents. If no errors are encountered, this file is saved as */etc/passwd*, otherwise, */etc/passwd* will remain unchanged. At this point, you are prompted whether you want to modify the *shadow* file as well. If your response is yes, the file will be opened as */etc/sptmp* and you will be able to edit it. After you quit the file, some automatic checks on *sptmp* will be performed to validate contents. If no errors are encountered, this file is saved as */etc/shadow*, otherwise, */etc/shadow* will remain unchanged. The files are now available for any modifications and the other user should be able to change his password.

Alternatively, if you do not wish to modify *shadow* by hand, you can simply run the *pwconv* command after manually modifying *passwd* to let the command reflect the changes in *shadow*.

Based on the above concept to prevent such an unwanted situation from happening to the *group* file, RHEL provides the *vigr* command to edit this file. This command copies *group* to a temporary file called */etc/gtmp* and disables write access to it. When another user attempts to modify the *group* file while you are editing it, he will be denied permission. When you quit *vigr*, some automatic checks are performed on *gtmp* to validate contents. If no errors are encountered, this file is saved as */etc/group*, otherwise, */etc/group* will remain intact. At this point, you are prompted whether you want to modify the *gshadow* file as well. If your response is yes, the file will be opened as */etc/sgtmp* and you will be able to edit it. After you quit the file, some automatic checks on *sgtmp* will be performed to validate contents. If no errors are encountered, this file is saved as */etc/gshadow*, otherwise, */etc/gshadow* will remain intact. The files are now available for any modifications.

Alternatively, if you do not wish to modify *gshadow* by hand, you can simply run the *grpconv* command after manually modifying *group* to let the command reflect the changes in *gshadow*.

Managing Password Shadowing

There are typically four commands that can be used for managing password shadowing. These are listed and described in Table 12-1.

Command	Description
pwconv	Creates/updates the *shadow* file and moves user passwords over from the *passwd* file.
pwunconv	Moves user passwords back to the *passwd* file and removes the *shadow* file.
grpconv	Creates/updates the *gshadow* file and moves group passwords over from the *group* file.
grpunconv	Moves group passwords back to the *group* file and removes the *gshadow* file.

Table 12-1 Password Shadowing Commands

Here are a few examples that will show the usage of the commands.

To enable password shadowing if it is not already enabled, execute the *pwconv* command:

 # pwconv

This command works quietly and does not display any output unless there is a problem. It creates the *shadow* file with read-only permission for *root* user:

 # ll /etc/shadow
```
-r-------- 1   root     root     1174   Dec   24   03:00   /etc/shadow
```

To enable password shadowing at the group level if it is not already enabled, execute the *grpconv* command:

 # grpconv

This command works quietly and does not display any output unless there is a problem. It creates the *gshadow* file with read-only permission for *root* user:

 # ll /etc/gshadow
```
-r-------- 1   root     root     572    Dec   24   03:01   /etc/gshadow
```

To disable password shadowing on user and group passwords, and remove the shadow files, execute the *pwunconv* and *grpunconv* commands, respectively.

Managing User Accounts and Password Aging

Managing user accounts involves creating, assigning passwords to, modifying and deleting user accounts. Managing password aging involves setting and modifying aging attributes on user accounts. You may use either command line or Red Hat User Manager to perform these tasks.

Table 12-2 lists and describes user account and password management commands.

Command	Description
useradd	Adds a user.
usermod	Modifies user attributes.
userdel	Deletes a user.
chage	Sets or modifies password aging attributes for a user.
passwd	Sets or modifies a user password, and some password aging attributes.

Table 12-2 User and Password Aging Commands

The following sub-sections explain the usage of these commands.

Creating a User Account

Use the *useradd* command to create a user account. This command adds entries to the *passwd* file and optionally to the *group* file. It also inserts entries to the *shadow* and *gshadow* files provided password shadowing is enabled. The command creates a home directory for the user and copies default user initialization files from the skeleton directory */etc/skel* into the user's home directory. There are several options available to the *useradd* command. Table 12-3 explains some of them.

Option	Description
–c (-- comment)	Defines useful comments or remarks.
–d (--home-dir)	Defines the absolute path to the user home directory.
–e (--expiredate)	Specifies a date after which a user account is automatically disabled.
–f (--inactive)	Denotes maximum days of inactivity before a user account is declared invalid.
–g (--gid)	Specifies the primary group. If this option is not used, a group account with the same name as the user name is created with GID the same as the user's UID. If you wish to assign some other GID, specify it with this option. Make sure that the group already exists.
–G (--groups)	Specifies membership to up to 20 supplementary groups. If this option is not specified, no supplementary groups will be added.
–k (--skel)	Specifies location of the skeleton directory (default is */etc/skel*), which contains user initialization template files. These files are copied to the user's home directory when it is created. Three BASH shell user initialization files – *.bash_profile*, *.bashrc* and *.bash_logout* – are available in this directory by default. You may customize these files or add more files to this directory so every new user gets all of them. Existing user home directories will not be affected by this change.

Option	Description
–M	Prevents the command from automatically creating a home directory for the user.
–m (--create-home)	Creates a home directory if it does not already exist.
–n	Prevents the command from automatically creating a private group for the user.
–o (--non-unique)	Means that the new user can share the UID with an existing user. When two users share a UID, both get identical rights on each other's files. This should only be done in specific situations.
–r	Creates a user account with a UID below 500 and with never expiring password.
–s (--shell)	Defines the absolute path to the shell file.
–u (--uid)	Indicates a unique user ID. The first UID assigned is 500. If this option is not specified, the next available UID from *etc/passwd* file is used.
login	Specifies a login name to be assigned to the new user account.

Table 12-3 useradd Command Options

Let us take a look at a few examples to understand the behavior of the command.

To create an account for user *aghori* with UID 501, home directory */home/aghori*, shell */bin/bash* and membership of *aghori* group with GID 501, do the following. Also make certain that the default initialization scripts from the skeleton directory are copied.

useradd –u 501 –m –d /home/aghori –k /etc/skel –s /bin/bash aghori

Create an initial password for *aghori* by running the *passwd* command:

passwd aghori
Changing password for user aghori.
New UNIX password:
Retype new UNIX password:
Passwd: all authentication tokens updated successfully.

The user account is created and now you can use it to log in to the system.

To create a user account via the Red Hat User Manager, follow the steps below:

☞Execute *system-config-users* at the command line, or click (GNOME) System / (KDE) Main Menu → Administration → Users and Groups. The main menu will appear as shown in Figure 12-5. Click Add User and fill out the form as shown in Figure 12-6. Click OK when done.

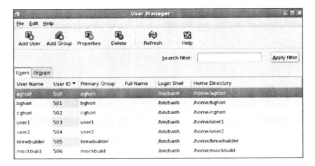

Figure 12-5 Red Hat User Manager – Main Menu

Figure 12-6 Red Hat User Manager – Create User

To create an account for user *bghori* with all defaults, do the following. The default values for this user will be *bghori* (primary group), */home/bghori* (home directory), */bin/bash* (shell) and no comments. It will also copy initialization files from */etc/skel*.

useradd bghori

To verify:

grep bghori /etc/passwd
bghori:x:501:501::/home/bghori:/bin/bash

Create an initial password for this user with the *passwd* command.

The command picked up the default values from the */etc/default/useradd* and */etc/login.defs* files. You can either view the *useradd* file contents with the *cat* command or do the following to view them:

```
# useradd –D
GROUP=100
HOME=/home
INACTIVE=-1
EXPIRE=
SHELL=/bin/bash
SKEL=/etc/skel
```

You may modify these defaults. For example, do the following to change the default base directory to */usr/home* so new user home directories are created in there:

 # useradd –D –b /usr/home

This modification will be reflected in the */etc/default/useradd* file.

The other file */etc/login.defs* contains additional directives that set defaults for user mail directory, password aging, UID/GID selection and so on. A *grep* on the uncommented lines is shown below:

```
# grep –v ^# /etc/login.defs
QMAIL_DIR          Maildir
MAIL_DIR           /var/spool/mail
MAIL_FILE          .mail
PASS_MAX_DAYS      99999
PASS_MIN_DAYS      0
PASS_MIN_LEN       5
PASS_WARN_AGE      7
UID_MIN            500
UID_MAX            60000
GID_MIN            500
GID_MAX            60000
USERDEL_CMD        /usr/sbin/userdel_local
CREATE_HOME        yes
UMASK              077
USERGROUPS_ENAB    yes
MD5_CRYPT_ENAB     yes
ENCRYPT_METHOD     MD5
```

Setting and Modifying Password Aging

The *chage* command is used to set and alter password aging parameters on a user account. Table 12-4 lists and describes key options available with this command.

Option	Description
–d (--lastday)	Specifies a date or number of days since the epoch time when the password was last modified. Corresponds to the third field in the *shadow* file.
–m (--mindays)	Specifies that the password cannot be changed before this many days are elapsed. Corresponds to the fourth field in the *shadow* file.

Option	Description
–M (--maxdays)	Denotes maximum days of validity of the password before a user starts getting warning messages to change password. Corresponds to the fifth field in the *shadow* file.
–W (--warndays)	Defines number of days a user gets warning messages to change password. Corresponds to the sixth field in the *shadow* file.
–I (--inactive)	Defines number of days of inactivity after a password is expired and before the account is locked. Corresponds to the seventh field in the *shadow* file.
–E (--expiredate)	Specifies a date or number of days since the epoch time on which the user account becomes deactivated. Corresponds to the eighth field in the *shadow* file.
–l	Lists password aging attributes set on a user account.

Table 12-4 chage Command Options

The following example sets password aging on user *bghori*. The "mindays" value is set to 7, the "maxdays" is set to 28, the "warndays" is set to 5 and the account will expire on December 31, 2009.

chage –m 7 –M 28 –W 5 –E 2009-12-31 bghori

Alternatively, you can use the *passwd* command to set some of these attributes. The following command performs what the *chage* command did except that it cannot set an expiration date:

passwd –n 7 –x 28 –w 5 bghori
Adjusting aging data for user bghori.
Passwd: Success

To list password aging parameters set on user *bghori*, run the *chage* command with –l option:

chage –l bghori
Last password change   : Jun 07, 2009
Password expires   : Jul 05, 2009
Password inactive   : never
Account expires   : Dec 31, 2009
Minimum number of days between password change   : 7
Maximum number of days between password change   : 28
Number of days of warning before password expires   : 5

To modify user *bghori* so that she cannot modify her password within five days after she changes her password:

chage –m 5 bghori

To modify user *bghori* so that she is forced to change her password at next login:

chage –d 0 bghori

To modify user *bghori* so that her account never expires:

> # **chage –E -1 bghori**

To set or modify password aging via the Red Hat User Manager, see the following sub-section.

Modifying a User Account

You can modify a user account with the *usermod* command. The syntax of the command is very similar to that of the *useradd* command. Majority of the options that this command accepts are identical to that of *useradd* command's, except with a few.

Let us look at a couple of examples.

To modify user *aghori*'s login name to *aghori1*, home directory to */home/aghori1* and login shell to */bin/ksh*:

> # **usermod –m –d /home/aghori1 –s /bin/ksh –l aghori1 aghori**

To verify:

> # **grep aghori /etc/passwd**
> aghori1:x:501:501::/home/aghori1:/bin/ksh

To reverse the previous change:

> # **usermod –m –d /home/aghori –s /bin/bash –l aghori aghori1**

To modify user *aghori*'s account to expire on December 31, 2009:

> # **usermod –e 2009-12-31 aghori**

To set */bin/ksh* as the default shell for user *aghori*:

> $ **chsh**
> Changing shell for aghori.
> Password:
> New shell [/bin/bash]: **/bin/ksh**
> Shell changed.

To verify:

> $ **grep aghori /etc/passwd**
> aghori:x:501:501:Asghar Ghori,2nd Floor,1-416-123-1234:/home/aghori:**/bin/ksh**

To reverse the previous change and set the default shell back to */sbin/bash*, run the *chsh* command again.

To modify comments associated with user *aghori*:

$ **chfn**
Changing finger information for aghori.
Password:
Name []: Asghar Ghori
Office []: 2nd Floor
Office Phone []: 1-416-123-1234
Home Phone []:

Finger information changed.

To verify, do either of the following:

$ **grep aghori /etc/passwd**
aghori:x:501:501:Asghar Ghori,2nd Floor,1-416-123-1234:/home/aghori:/bin/bash
finger aghori
Login: aghori   Name: Asghar Ghori
Directory: /home/aghori   Shell: /bin/bash
Office: 2nd Floor, 1-416-123-1234
Never logged in.
No mail.
No Plan.

To modify user *aghori* so that he also becomes a member of another group called *dba*:

$ **id**
uid=501(aghori) gid=501(aghori) groups=501(aghori)
# **usermod –G dba aghori**

The *id* command above displays the current group information for user *aghori* and the *usermod* command with –G option adds the user to the specified group.

Run the *id* command again to verify:

# **id**
uid=501(aghori) gid=501(aghori) groups=501(aghori),**508(dba)**

To add *aghori* to another supplementary group called *unixadm* while retaining existing memberships, use –a option:

usermod –a –G unixadm aghori

Note that without –a (append) option, the command will replace current supplementary group memberships with the one specified.

To lock user *aghori* so that he cannot log in to the system, run the *usermod* command with –L option. A ! sign will appear in the password field of the *shadow* file.

usermod –L aghori

To unlock:

 # usermod –U aghori

To modify a user account via the Red Hat User Manager, follow the steps below:

 Execute *system-config-users* at the command line, or click (GNOME) System / (KDE) Main Menu → Administration → Users and Groups. Highlight a user from the list that you wish to modify. Click Properties. Four tabs – User Data, Account Info, Password Info and Group – will appear on the screen as shown in Figure 12-7. Select User Data to modify general user information, select Account Info to enable and set account expiration or lock the user, choose Password Info to enable and set password aging, and choose Groups to modify user's group membership including its primary group. Click OK when done.

Figure 12-7 Red Hat User Manager – Modify User Properties

Switching Users

Even though you can log in to the system directly as *root*, it is recommended that you log in as yourself as a normal user and then use the *su* command to become *root* if necessary. This is a safer practice and ensures system security and protection.

For example, if user *bghori* needs to become *root*, she would have to know the *root* password:

$ su
Password:

If she specifies the dash (–) character with the *su* command, it would also execute *root* user's initialization files to define the environment including the PATH variable:

$ su –
Password:

If she wants to switch into another user's account such as user *aghori*, she will have to know that user's password:

$ su – aghori
Password:

The rule of knowing another user's password to switch into does not apply to *root*. If *root* wishes to *su* into a user account, he is not prompted for the user password.

Doing as Superuser

RHEL offers a way for normal users to be able to run privileged commands. This is done via a utility called *sudo* (superuser do). Any normal user that requires access to one or more administrative commands is defined in the */etc/sudoers* file. This file may be edited using the *visudo* command, which creates */etc/sudoers.tmp* file and apply the changes in there. When you save and quit, the contents are written to */etc/sudoers,* and */etc/sudoers.tmp* is removed. The syntax for user and group entries in the file looks like the following for user *user1* and group *dba*:

```
user1       ALL=(ALL)     ALL
%dba        ALL=(ALL)     ALL
```

These entries mean that *user1* and members of *dba* group have full privileges to run all administrative commands.

Follow the syntax above to add individual users and groups to the file.

Whenever *user1* or any member of *dba* group executes a command, he will be required to enter his own password:

$ sudo system-config-users
Password:

If you wish *user1* and members of *dba* group not to be prompted for password, you can modify their entries in the *sudoers* file to look like:

```
user1       ALL=(ALL)     NOPASSWD:     ALL
%dba        ALL=(ALL)     NOPASSWD:     ALL
```

To restrict *user1* and *dba* group members to be able to run only *system-config-display* and *system-config-users* commands with *root* privileges, modify the directives as follows:

```
user1       ALL=/usr/bin/system-config-display,/usr/bin/system-config-users
%dba        ALL=/usr/bin/system-config-display,/usr/bin/system-config-users
```

The *sudo* command logs information of commands being executed in the */var/log/messages* file as the user who runs it (and not as *root*).

Run the *visudo* command and read how User_Alias directive can be defined for a group of users that require access to run a set of commands as defined with the directive Cmnd_Alias.

Deleting a User Account

Deleting a user account deletes the user from the system. Execute the *userdel* command for this purpose. For example, the following will delete user *bghori* including her home and mail spool directories:

 # userdel –r bghori

Do not specify the –r option if you do not wish to delete the user's home and mail directories.

To delete a user account via the Red Hat User Manager, follow the steps below:

☞ Execute *system-config-users* at the command line, or click (GNOME) System / (KDE) Main Menu → Administration → Users and Groups. Highlight a user from the list and click Delete. See Figure 12-5 earlier.

Displaying Successful User Login Attempts History

The *last* command reports on successful user login attempts history and system reboots by reading the */var/log/wtmp* file. This file keeps a record of all login and logout activities including login time, duration a user stayed logged in and tty where the user session took place. Consider the following examples.

To list all login and logout activities, type the *last* command without any arguments:

```
# last
. . . . . . . .
root     pts/1    :0.0                 Wed Oct 15 12:57 - down   (01:09)
root     :0                            Wed Oct 15 12:57 - down   (01:10)
root     :0                            Wed Oct 15 12:57 - 12:57  (00:00)
reboot   system boot 2.6.18-92.el5     Wed Oct 15 12:53          (01:14)
reboot   system boot 2.6.18-92.el5     Wed Oct 15 08:45          (04:06)
wtmp begins Wed Oct 15 08:45:21 2008
```

To list only system reboot information:

```
# last reboot
reboot   system boot 2.6.18-92.el5   Fri Oct 24 20:03     (4+16:27)
reboot   system boot 2.6.18-92.el5   Fri Oct 17 17:51     (7+02:11)
reboot   system boot 2.6.18-92.el5   Thu Oct 16 11:37     (1+05:37)
reboot   system boot 2.6.18-92.el5   Wed Oct 15 18:48     (03:15)
reboot   system boot 2.6.18-92.el5   Wed Oct 15 18:41     (00:06)
reboot   system boot 2.6.18-92.el5   Wed Oct 15 18:16     (00:23)
reboot   system boot 2.6.18-92.el5   Wed Oct 15 14:09     (04:06)
reboot   system boot 2.6.18-92.el5   Wed Oct 15 12:53     (01:14)
reboot   system boot 2.6.18-92.el5   Wed Oct 15 08:45     (04:06)
wtmp begins Wed Oct 15 08:45:21 2008
```

There is another command that lists more detailed information on recent logins and reboots. This command is *utmpdump* and is executed the following way:

```
# utmpdump /var/log/wtmp
. . . . . . . .
[8] [15097] [    ] [        ] [pts/2 ] [              ] [0.0.0.0          ] [Wed Dec 10 17:09:51 2008 EST]
[8] [15356] [    ] [        ] [pts/1 ] [              ] [0.0.0.0          ] [Wed Dec 10 17:50:16 2008 EST]
[7] [15839] [ts/1] [root  ] [pts/1 ] [192.168.0.203] [192.168.0.203 ] [Wed Dec 10 20:15:42 2008 EST]
[8] [15837] [    ] [        ] [pts/1 ] [              ] [0.0.0.0          ] [Wed Dec 10 20:56:19 2008 EST]
[7] [17576] [ts/1] [root  ] [pts/1 ] [192.168.0.203] [192.168.0.203 ] [Thu Dec 11 07:57:13 2008 EST]
```

Displaying Unsuccessful User Login Attempts History

The *lastb* command reports on unsuccessful user login attempts history by reading the */var/log/btmp* file. This file keeps a record of all unsuccessful login attempt activities including login name, time and the tty where the attempt was made. Consider the following examples.

To list all unsuccessful login attempts, type the *lastb* command without any arguments:

```
# lastb
. . . . . . . .
user1   ssh:notty   192.168.0.203   Tue Nov 25 18:05 - 18:05  (00:00)
root    ssh:notty   192.168.0.204   Wed Oct 29 17:42 - 17:42  (00:00)
root    :0                          Wed Oct 15 12:57 - 12:57  (00:00)

btmp begins Wed Oct 15 12:57:22 2008
```

Alternatively, you can use the following command to display the above information:

```
# utmpdump /var/log/btmp
. . . . . . . .
[6] [19482] [   ] [root ] [ssh:notty ] [192.168.0.202  ] [192.168.0.202 ] [Sun Dec 07 15:26:35 2008 EST]
[6] [21767] [   ] [root ] [ssh:notty ] [192.168.0.202  ] [192.168.0.202 ] [Mon Dec 08 07:44:15 2008 EST]
[6] [15097] [   ] [root ] [ssh:notty ] [192.168.0.204  ] [192.168.0.204 ] [Wed Dec 10 14:34:55 2008 EST]
[6] [15837] [   ] [root ] [ssh:notty ] [192.168.0.204  ] [192.168.0.204 ] [Wed Dec 10 20:15:41 2008 EST]
```

Displaying Failed Login Attempts

The *faillog* command reports on failed user login attempts by reading the */var/log/faillog* file. This file keeps a record of all failed login attempt activities including login name, number of failed attempts made, maximum number of failed login attempts allowed before an account is disabled, the latest failed attempt and the location where the attempt was made. Consider the following examples.

To list all failed login attempts, run the *faillog* command without any arguments:

```
# faillog
Login    Failures Maximum  Latest          On
user1       4        0     06/28/09  05:59:38 -0400  192.168.0.2
user2       2        0     06/28/09  06:00:11 -0400  192.168.0.2
```

With –u option, this command displays failed login attempts information for a specific user:

```
# faillog –u user1
Login    Failures Maximum Latest          On
user1       4        0    06/28/09  05:59:38 -0400  192.168.0.2
```

In order for the system to be able to capture failed login attempt information, you will need to edit a PAM configuration file */etc/pam.d/system-auth* and add the following entries in the auth and account sections. See Chapter "System and Network Security" for details on Pluggable Authentication Modules (PAM).

auth	required	pam_tally.so	deny=2	unlock_time=600
account	required	pam_tally.so		

Once these entries are in place, any unsuccessful user login attempt will be recorded and the account will be locked for 10 minutes after two unsuccessful tries.

You can use the *pam_tally* command to reset the information for a specific user:

```
# pam_tally --user=aghori --reset
User aghori    (501)  had  4
```

Displaying Currently Logged In Users

The *who* command reads the */var/run/utmp* file, which keeps a record of all currently logged in users, and lists them on the screen:

```
# who
root   pts/1    2008-12-11  07:57  (192.168.0.204)
```

Displaying Recent User Logins

The *lastlog* command reads the */var/log/lastlog* file, which keeps a record of all recent user logins, and lists them on the screen:

```
# lastlog
Username     Port   From          Latest
root         pts/1  192.168.0.203  Thu Dec 11 07:57:13 -0500 2008
bin                 **Never logged in**
. . . . . . . .
user1        pts/1  192.168.0.203  Sat Nov 29 13:55:14 -0500 2008
user2        pts/1  192.168.0.203  Thu Nov 27 19:15:27 -0500 2008
user3               **Never logged in**
```

Managing Group Accounts

Managing group accounts involve creating and modifying groups, adding and deleting group administrators, and deleting groups. You can use commands or Red Hat User Manager to perform these tasks.

Table 12-5 lists group account management commands.

Command	Description
groupadd	Adds a group.
groupmod	Modifies group attributes.
groupdel	Deletes a group.
gpasswd	Add group administrators, adds or deletes group members, assigns or revokes a group password and disables access to a group via the *newgrp* command.

Table 12-5 Group Management Commands

Creating a Group Account

Use the *groupadd* command to add a new group account. Consider the following examples to understand usage.

To create a group called *sysadmin* and assign it GID 1000:

    # **groupadd –g 1000 sysadmin**

To verify:

    # **grep sysadmin /etc/group**
    sysadmin:x:1000:

The –o option may be specified to use a GID that is already in use by some other group account. When more than one groups share a GID, group members get identical rights on one another's files. This should be done only in specific situations.

To create a group account via the Red Hat User Manager, follow the steps below:

Execute *system-config-users* at the command line, or click (GNOME) System / (KDE) Main Menu → Administration → Users and Groups. The main menu will appear as was shown in Figure 12-5. Click Add Group and enter a group name and optionally a GID. See Figure 12-8. Click OK when done.

Figure 12-8 Red Hat User Manager – Add Group

Modifying a Group Account

You can modify a group account with the *groupmod* command. For example, to modify the group name from *dba* to *dba1* and GID to 2000, run the following:

    # **groupmod –g 2000 –n dba1 dba**

To verify:

    # **grep dba /etc/group**
    dba1:x:2000:

To modify a group account via the Red Hat User Manager, follow the steps below:

☞Execute *system-config-users* at the command line, or click (GNOME) System / (KDE) Main Menu → Administration → Users and Groups. The main menu will appear as was shown in Figure 12-5. Click Groups tab and then highlight a group to be modified. Click Properties and change the group name or membership. Click OK when done.

Managing Groups with gpasswd Command

The *gpasswd* command can be used to add group administrators, add or delete group members, assign or revoke a group password and disable access to a group via the *newgrp* command. The *root* user can perform all these tasks and a group administrator can perform only the last three. This command prompts to change a group's password if invoked by *root* or a group administrator on a group. There are several options available and are explained in Table 12-6.

Option	Description
–A	Adds a group administrator. Inserts an entry in the third field of the gshadow file.
–a	Adds a group member. Inserts an entry in the fourth field of both group and gshadow files. Can be done as either root or a group administrator.
–d	Deletes a group member.
–M	Substitutes all existing group members.
–R	Disables access to a group via the newgrp command.
–r	Revokes the password set on a group.

Table 12-6 gpasswd Command Options

Let us look at the following examples to understand the usage.

To add *user1* as a group administrator to the *dba1* group:

gpasswd –A user1 dba1

To add *user2* as a group member to the *dba1* group:

gpasswd –a user2 dba1
Adding user user2 to group dba1

To delete a group member *user2* from the *dba1* group:

gpasswd –d user2 dba1
Removing user user2 from group dba1

To substitute all existing group members of *dba1* with *user3* and *user4*:

gpasswd –M user3,user4 dba1

To assign *dba1* group a password:

gpasswd dba1
Changing the password for group dba1
New Password:
Re-enter new password:

To revoke the group password:

gpasswd –r dba1

To change into *dba1* as *user3*:

$ newgrp dba1
Password:

Enter the group's password when prompted. The *newgrp* command changes a user's primary group temporarily until either the *exit* command is run or Ctrl+d is pressed.

To disable access to the *dba1* group via the *newgrp* command:

gpasswd –R dba1

Deleting a Group Account

To delete a group account from the system, use the *groupdel* command. For example, to delete group *dba1*, perform the following:

groupdel dba1

Note that the system does not let you delete the primary group of an existing user. You have to remove the user to also remove the group.

To delete a group account via the Red Hat User Manager, follow the steps below:

☞ Execute *system-config-users* at the command line, or click (GNOME) System / (KDE) Main Menu → Administration → Users and Groups. The main menu will appear as was shown in Figure 12-5. Click Groups tab and highlight a group to be deleted. Click Delete and then OK to confirm the deletion.

Default Login Parameters

User and group management commands consult the */etc/login.defs* file to obtain some default information. Some key directives from the file are shown below:

```
# grep –v ^# /etc/login.defs
MAIL_DIR                /var/spool/mail
PASS_MAX_DAYS           99999
PASS_MIN_DAYS           0
PASS_MIN_LEN            5
PASS_WARN_AGE          7
UID_MIN                500
```

```
UID_MAX                 60000
GID_MIN                 500
GID_MAX                 60000
CREATE_HOME             yes
UMASK                   077
USERGROUPS_ENAB         yes
```

Several parameters are set in this file by default. These parameters include the mail directory location for the user (MAIL_DIR), password aging parameters for the user (PASS_MAX_DAYS, PASS_MIN_DAYS, PASS_MIN_LEN and PASS_WARN_AGE), range of UIDs and GIDs to be allocated to new user and group accounts (UID_MIN, UID_MAX, GID_MIN and GID_MAX), instruction for the *useradd* command to create a home directory for the user (CREATE_HOME), instruction for the *useradd* command to set the default umask for the user to 077 (UMASK) and instruction for the *userdel* command to delete groups with no members (USERGROUPS_ENAB).

User Initialization Files

In Chapter 05 "The Shells" you used local and environment variables. You modified the default command prompt and added useful information to it. You created shortcuts using aliases. In other words you modified the default shell environment to customize according to your needs. The changes you made were lost when you logged off the system. What if you wanted to make those changes permanent so each time you logged in they were there for you?

Modifications to the default shell environment can be stored in text files called *initialization* files, which are executed after a user is authenticated and before he gets the command prompt. There are two types of initialization files: *system-wide* and *per-user*.

System-wide Initialization Files

System-wide initialization files define general environment variables required by all or most users of the system. These files are maintained by the system administrator and can be modified to define any additional environment variables and customization needed by all system users.

Table 12-7 lists and describes system-wide initialization files for the BASH shell users.

System-wide Files	Comments
/etc/bashrc	Defines functions and aliases. This file sets umask value, command prompt, etc., and is called by the *~/.bashrc* file.
/etc/profile	Sets environment variables such as PATH, USER, LOGNAME, MAIL, HOSTNAME and HISTSIZE for users and startup programs.
/etc/profile.d	Scripts located here are called by the */etc/profile* file.

Table 12-7 System-wide Initialization Files

Sample *bashrc* and *profile* files, and a list of files in the *profile.d* directory are displayed below:

cat /etc/bashrc

```
# System wide functions and aliases
# Environment stuff goes in /etc/profile
# By default, we want this to get set.
# Even for non-interactive, non-login shells.
If [ $UID –gt 99 ] && [ "`id –gn`" = "`id –un`" ]; then
      umask 002
else
      umask 022
fi
# are we an interactive shell?
If [ "$PS1" ]; then
    case $TERM in
      xterm*)
. . . . . . . .
```

cat /etc/profile

```
# System wide environment and startup programs, for login setup
# Functions and aliases go in /etc/bashrc
. . . . . . . .
if [ -x /usr/bin/id ]; then
      USER="`id –un`"
      LOGNAME=$USER
      MAIL="/var/spool/mail/$USER"
fi
HOSTNAME=`/bin/hostname`
HISTSIZE=1000
if [ -z "$INPUTRC" –a ! –f "$HOME/.inputrc" ]; then
    INPUTRC=/etc/inputrc
fi
export PATH USER LOGNAME MAIL HOSTNAME HISTSIZE INPUTRC
for i in /etc/profile.d/*.sh ; do
    if [ -r "$i" ]; then
      . $i
. . . . . . . .
```

ll /etc/profile.d

```
total 39
-rwxr-xr-x 1 root root  713 Nov 27  2006 colorls.sh
-rwxr-xr-x 1 root root  192 Aug 30  2006 glib2.sh
. . . . . . . .
```

Per-user Initialization Files

Per-user initialization files override or modify system defaults set by system-wide initialization files. These files may be customized by individual users to suit their needs.

You may create additional per-user initialization files in your home directory to define additional environment variables or set additional shell properties.

Table 12-8 lists and describes per-user initialization files for the BASH shell users.

Per-user Files	Comments
~/.bashrc	Defines functions and aliases. This file is called by ~/.bash_profile file.
~/.bash_profile	Sets environment variables. This file is called by the profile file.
~/.bash_logout	Defines any specific commands to be executed prior to logout.

Table 12-8 Per-user Initialization Files

An excerpt from these files is shown below:

```
# cat ~/.bashrc
# .bashrc
# Source global definitions
if [ -f /etc/bashrc ]; then
    . /etc/bashrc
fi
# User specific aliases and functions
# cat ~/.bash_profile
# Get the aliases and functions
if [ -f ~/.bashrc ]; then
    . ~/.bashrc
fi
# User specific environment and startup programs
PATH=$PATH:$HOME/bin
export PATH
# cat ~/.bash_logout
# ~/.bash_logout
clear
```

Summary

In this chapter, you started off with building an understanding of /etc/passwd, /etc/shadow, /etc/group and /etc/gshadow files. You looked at what the files contained, the syntax, and how to verify consistency. You looked at ways to lock these files while being edited to avoid loosing changes done by other users during that time.

You studied password shadowing and password aging. You learned user management including creating, modifying and deleting user accounts. You looked at how to set and modify password aging attributes on user accounts. You learned a few simple tools that allowed you to switch into another user account, run privileged commands, view history of successful and unsuccessful user login attempts, display currently logged in users, and display recent user logins. Likewise, you studied group management including creating, modifying and deleting group accounts. Then you studied default login parameters that are used by user and group management commands.

Finally, you learned about the system-wide and per-user initialization files, and what these files contained.

## 13

Disk Partitioning

This chapter covers the following major topics:

✓ Disk management techniques
✓ Use fdisk and parted to create, modify and delete partitions
✓ Create, modify, recover and delete RAID arrays
✓ LVM concepts, components and structure
✓ Use LVM to initialize and uninitialize a physical volume; create, display, extend, reduce and remove a volume group; move physical extents; and create, display, extend, reduce, rename and remove a logical volume

Data is stored on disk drives that are logically divided into partitions at the operating system level. A partition can exist on an entire disk or it can span multiple disks. Each partition may contain a file system, a raw data space, a swap space or a dump space.

A file system holds files and directories, a raw data space is used by databases and other applications, a swap space supplements physical memory on the system and a dump space stores memory image after a system crash occurs.

RHEL offers three solutions for creating and managing disk partitions. These include solutions using *fdisk* and *parted* partitioning utilities, *software RAID* and the *Logical Volume Manager* (LVM). All three can be used concurrently on a single disk.

During RHEL installation, a disk partitioning program called *disk druid* is invoked to carve up disks based on requirements. This program allows you to use standard partitioning, software RAID partitioning or LVM partitioning technique, or a combination. The Disk Druid utility is available only during the installation process. You cannot run it after the installation is complete.

Disk Partitioning Using fdisk

The *fdisk* tool is commonly used to carve up disks on RHEL systems. This text-based, menu-driven program allows you to display, add, modify, verify and delete partitions. It allows up to three usable primary partitions and one extended partition. Within the extended partition, you can further add logical partitions. This partitioning information is stored in the *partition table,* which is located on the first sector of the disk.

The *fdisk* utility is invoked on a disk device file. To determine how many disks are available on the system and basic information about the disks, run the *fdisk* command with –l option:

```
# fdisk –l
Disk /dev/sda: 32.2 GB, 32212254720 bytes
255 heads, 63 sectors/track, 3916 cylinders
Units = cylinders of 16065 * 512 = 8225280 bytes

   Device Boot    Start     End    Blocks   Id System
/dev/sda1   *       1       127    1020096  83 Linux
/dev/sda2          128      3916   30435142+ 8e Linux LVM

Disk /dev/sdb: 8589 MB, 8589934592 bytes
255 heads, 63 sectors/track, 1044 cylinders
Units = cylinders of 16065 * 512 = 8225280 bytes

Disk /dev/sdb doesn't contain a valid partition table

Disk /dev/sdc: 8589 MB, 8589934592 bytes
255 heads, 63 sectors/track, 1044 cylinders
Units = cylinders of 16065 * 512 = 8225280 bytes

Disk /dev/sdc doesn't contain a valid partition table
```

Disk /dev/sdd: 8589 MB, 8589934592 bytes
255 heads, 63 sectors/track, 1044 cylinders
Units = cylinders of 16065 * 512 = 8225280 bytes

Disk /dev/sdd doesn't contain a valid partition table

Disk /dev/sde: 8589 MB, 8589934592 bytes
255 heads, 63 sectors/track, 1044 cylinders
Units = cylinders of 16065 * 512 = 8225280 bytes

Disk /dev/sde doesn't contain a valid partition table

The output indicates that there are five SCSI disks in the system: */dev/sda*, */dev/sdb*, */dev/sdc*, */dev/sdd* and */dev/sde*. */dev/sda* is 32gb in size and has two partitions in it. Each of the remaining four disks is 8.5gb in size, and currently none of them contain any partitions.

"sd" represents a SCSI disk and "hd" represents an IDE (PATA) disk. "a" represents the first disk, "b" represents the second disk and so on. "1" represents the first partition on the disk, "2" represents the second partition on the disk and so on. Therefore, */dev/sda1* represents the first partition on the first SCSI disk.

The main menu of *fdisk* can be invoked on any one of the five disks. Let us do that on */dev/sda*:

```
# fdisk /dev/sda
Command (m for help): m
Command      action
   a         toggle a bootable flag
   b         edit bsd disklabel
   c         toggle the dos compatibility flag
   d         delete a partition
   l         list known partition types
   m         print this menu
   n         add a new partition
   o         create a new empty DOS partition table
   p         print the partition table
   q         quit without saving changes
   s         create a new empty Sun disklabel
   t         change a partition's system id
   u         change display/entry units
   v         verify the partition table
   w         write table to disk and exit
   x         extra functionality (experts only)

Command (m for help):
```

There are several sub-commands in the main menu. Table 13-1 lists and describes them.

Command	Description
a	Toggles a bootable flag.
b	Edits BSD disk label.
c	Toggles the DOS compatibility flag.
d	Deletes a partition.
l	Lists known partition types.
m	Prints this menu.
n	Adds a new partition. There are two sub-options – extended (e) and primary (p) – available with this command. You can define upto 4 primary partitions with one of them must be selected as an extended partition. Within the extended partition, you can create upto 12 logical partitions.
o	Adds a new empty DOS partition table.
p	Prints (displays) partition table information.
q	Quits without saving changes.
s	Adds a new empty Sun disk label.
t	Changes a partition's system id.
u	Changes display/entry units.
v	Verifies the partition table.
w	Writes partition table information to disk and exits.
x	Extra functionality available to experts.

Table 13-1 fdisk Sub-Commands

Let us create, modify and delete partitions using *fdisk* to understand its usage.

Creating a Partition

To create a partition on the second SCSI disk */dev/sdb* to be used as a file system or raw database space, follow the steps below:

1. Execute the *fdisk* command on the */dev/sdb* disk:

   # **fdisk /dev/sdb**

2. Choose the sub-command *n* to add a new partition. It will ask if you wish to create an extended or a primary partition. For this demonstration, add primary partition #1. Your input is displayed in the following text in bold letters:

   Command (m for help): **n**
   Command action
     e   extended
     p   primary partition (1-4)
   p
   Partition number (1-4): **1**

3. Enter the cylinder number, say 1, where you wish the partition to begin:

   First cylinder (1-1044, default 1): **1**

4. Specify a partition size. You can enter an end cylinder number based on which *fdisk* will automatically calculate the size of the partition. Alternatively, you can enter the size in KBs or MBs. The default is to use all available disk space. For this demonistration, use 500MBs.

> Last cylinder or +size or +sizeM or +sizeK (1-1044,def 1044): **+500m**

5. Execute *p* to print the updated partition table:

> Command (m for help): **p**
> Disk /dev/sdb: 8589 MB, 8589934592 bytes
> 255 heads, 63 sectors/track, 1044 cylinders
> Units = cylinders of 16065 * 512 = 8225280 bytes

Device Boot	Start	End	Blocks	Id	System
/dev/sdb1	1	62	497983+	83	Linux

6. Write this information to the disk using the *w* sub-command and exit out of *fdisk*:

> Command (m for help): **w**
> The partition table has been altered!
> Calling ioctl() to re-read partition table.
> Syncing disks.

7. Execute the *partprobe* command at the command prompt to force the kernel to re-read the updated partition table information:

> # **partprobe**

8. Confirm the partition information using any of the following:

> # **fdisk –l /dev/sdb**
> Disk /dev/sdb: 8589 MB, 8589934592 bytes
> 255 heads, 63 sectors/track, 1044 cylinders
> Units = cylinders of 16065 * 512 = 8225280 bytes

Device Boot	Start	End	Blocks	Id	System
/dev/sdb1	1	62	497983+	83	Linux

> # **grep sdb /proc/partitions**

major	minor	#blocks	name
8	0	497983	sdb1

Creating a Swap Partition

To create a partition on the second SCSI disk */dev/sdb* to be used as a swap partition, follow the steps below:

1. Invoke the *fdisk* command on the */dev/sdb* disk:

> # **fdisk /dev/sdb**

2. Choose the sub-command *n* to add a new partition. It will ask if you wish to create an extended or a primary partition. For this demonstration, add primary partition #2. Your input is displayed in the following text in bold letters:

```
Command (m for help): n
Command action
   e   extended
   p   primary partition (1-4)
p
Partition number (1-4): 2
```

3. Enter the cylinder number, say 501, where you wish the partition to begin:

```
First cylinder (501-1044, default 501): 501
```

4. Specify a partition size. You can enter an end cylinder number based on which *fdisk* will automatically calculate the size of the partition. Alternatively, you can enter the size in KBs or MBs. The default is to use all available disk space. For this demonistration, use 500MBs.

```
Last cylinder or +size or +sizeM or +sizeK (63-522,def 522): +500m
```

5. Execute *l* to list known partition types; swap will be among them:

```
Command (m for help): l
```

0 Empty	1e Hidden W95 FAT1	80 Old Minix	be Solaris boot
1 FAT12	24 NEC DOS	81 Minix / old Lin	bf Solaris
2 XENIX root	39 Plan 9	**82 Linux swap / So**	c1 DRDOS/sec (FAT-
3 XENIX usr	3c PartitionMagic	83 Linux	c4 DRDOS/sec (FAT-
4 FAT16 <32M	40 Venix 80286	84 OS/2 hidden C:	c6 DRDOS/sec (FAT-
5 Extended	41 PPC PrEP Boot	85 Linux extended	c7 Syrinx
6 FAT16	42 SFS	86 NTFS volume set	da Non-FS data
7 HPFS/NTFS	4d QNX4.x	87 NTFS volume set	db CP/M / CTOS / .
8 AIX	4^e QNX4.x 2nd part	88 Linux plaintext	de Dell Utility
9 AIX bootable	4f QNX4.x 3rd part	8^e Linux LVM	df BootIt
a OS/2 Boot Manag	50 OnTrack DM	93 Amoeba	e1 DOS access
b W95 FAT32	51 OnTrack DM6 Aux	94 Amoeba BBT	e3 DOS R/O
c W95 FAT32 (LBA)	52 CP/M	9f BSD/OS	e4 SpeedStor
e W95 FAT16 (LBA)	53 OnTrack DM6 Aux	a0 IBM Thinkpad hi	eb BeOS fs
f W95 Ext'd (LBA)	54 OnTrackDM6	a5 FreeBSD	ee EFI GPT
10 OPUS	55 EZ-Drive	a6 OpenBSD	ef EFI (FAT-12/16/
11 Hidden FAT12	56 Golden Bow	a7 NeXTSTEP	f0 Linux/PA-RISC b
12 Compaq diagnost	5c Priam Edisk	a8 Darwin UFS	f1 SpeedStor
14 Hidden FAT16 <3	61 SpeedStor	a9 NetBSD	f4 SpeedStor
16 Hidden FAT16	63 GNU HURD or Sys	ab Darwin boot	f2 DOS secondary
17 Hidden HPFS/NTF	64 Novell Netware	b7 BSDI fs	fd Linux raid auto
18 AST SmartSleep	65 Novell Netware	b8 BSDI swap	fe LANstep
1b Hidden W95 FAT3	70 DiskSecure Mult	bb Boot Wizard hid	ff BBT
1c Hidden W95 FAT3	75 PC/IX		

6. Execute *p* to print the updated partition table:

```
Command (m for help): p
Disk /dev/sdb: 8589 MB, 8589934592 bytes
255 heads, 63 sectors/track, 1044 cylinders
Units = cylinders of 16065 * 512 = 8225280 bytes

   Device Boot    Start      End    Blocks    Id  System
/dev/sdb1            1        62    497983+   83  Linux
/dev/sdb2           63       124    498015    83  Linux
```

7. Execute *t* to change the partition type of */dev/sdb2* to swap (82):

```
Command (m for help): t
Selected partition 2
Hex code (type L to list codes): 82
Changed system type of partition 2 to 82 (Linux swap / Solaris)
```

8. Write this information to the disk using the *w* sub-command and exit out of *fdisk*:

```
Command (m for help): w
The partition table has been altered!

Calling ioctl() to re-read partition table.

Syncing disks.
```

9. Execute the *partprobe* command at the command prompt to force the kernel to re-read the updated partition table information:

   # **partprobe**

10. Confirm the partition information using any of the following:

    # **fdisk –l /dev/sdb**
    ```
    Disk /dev/sdb: 8589 MB, 8589934592 bytes
    255 heads, 63 sectors/track, 1044 cylinders
    Units = cylinders of 16065 * 512 = 8225280 bytes

       Device Boot    Start      End    Blocks  Id  System
    /dev/sdb1            1        62    497983+ 83  Linux
    /dev/sdb2           63       124    498015+ 82  Linux swap / Solaris
    ```
    # **grep sdb2 /proc/partitions**

Deleting a Partition

Deleting a partition deletes the partition information from the partition table. Let us delete both partitions *sdb1* and *sdb2* created earlier.

1. Execute the *fdisk* command on the */dev/sdb* disk:

    # **fdisk /dev/sdb**

2. Execute *p* to print the partition table:

    Command (m for help): **p**

    Disk /dev/sdb: 8589 MB, 8589934592 bytes
    255 heads, 63 sectors/track, 522 cylinders
    Units = cylinders of 16065 * 512 = 8225280 bytes

Device Boot	Start	End	Blocks	Id	System
/dev/sdb1	1	62	497983+	83	Linux
/dev/sdb2	63	124	498015	82	Linux swap / Solaris

3. Execute *d* to delete partitions 1 and 2:

    Command (m for help): **d1**
    Command (m for help): **d2**

4. Write this information to the disk using the *w* sub-command and exit out of *fdisk*:

    Command (m for help): **w**
    The partition table has been altered!

    Calling ioctl() to re-read partition table.

    Syncing disks.

5. Execute the *partprobe* command at the command probe to force the kernel to re-read the updated partition table information:

    # **partprobe**

6. Confirm the deletion using any of the following:

    # **fdisk –l /dev/sdb**
    Disk /dev/sdb: 8589 MB, 8589934592 bytes
    255 heads, 63 sectors/track, 1044 cylinders
    Units = cylinders of 16065 * 512 = 8225280 bytes

Device Boot	Start	End	Blocks	Id	System
    # **grep sdb /proc/partitions**

Disk Partitioning Using parted

parted is another tool for slicing disks. This text-based, menu-driven program allows you to display, add, check, modify, copy, resize and delete partitions. The main interface of the program looks like the following. It produces a list of sub-commands when you run *help* at the parted prompt:

parted
GNU Parted 1.8.1
Using /dev/sda
Welcome to GNU Parted! Type 'help' to view a list of commands.
(parted) **help**

check NUMBER	do a simple check on the file system
cp [FROM-DEVICE] FROM-NUMBER TO-NUMBER	copy file system to another partition
help [COMMAND]	prints general help, or help on COMMAND
mklabel,mktable LABEL-TYPE	create a new disklabel (partition table)
mkfs NUMBER FS-TYPE	make a FS-TYPE file system on partititon NUMBER
mkpart PART-TYPE [FS-TYPE] START END	make a partition
mkpartfs PART-TYPE FS-TYPE START END	make a partition with a file system
move NUMBER START END	move partition NUMBER
name NUMBER NAME	name partition NUMBER as NAME
print [free|NUMBER|all]	display the partition table, a partition, or all devices
quit	exit program
rescue START END	rescue a lost partition near START and END
resize NUMBER START END	resize partition NUMBER and its file system
rm NUMBER	delete partition NUMBER
select DEVICE	choose the device to edit
set NUMBER FLAG STATE	change the FLAG on partition NUMBER
toggle [NUMBER [FLAG]]	toggle the state of FLAG on partition NUMBER
unit UNIT	set the default unit to UNIT
version	displays the current version of GNU Parted and copyright information

There are several sub-commands in the main menu. Table 13-2 lists and describes them.

Command	Description
check	Checks the specified file system.
cp	Copies a file system to another partition.
help	Displays command help.
mklabel	Makes a new disk label.
mkfs	Makes the specified type of file system.
mkpart	Makes a partition without a file system in it.
mkpartfs	Makes a partition with a file system in it.
move	Moves partition number.
name	Assigns a name to a partition.
print	Displays partition table, a specific partition or all devices.
quit	Quits parted.
rescue	Recovers a lost partition.
resize	Resizes the specified partition number and file system within it.

Command	Description
rm	Removes the specified partition.
select	Selects a device to edit.
set	Sets FLAG on the specified partition number.
toggle	Toggles the state of FLAG on the specified partition number.
unit	Sets default unit.
version	Displays *parted* version.

Table 13-2 parted Sub-Commands

At the *parted* command prompt, you can invoke help on a specific sub-command. For example, to obtain help on *mklabel*, do the following:

```
(parted) help mklabel
   Mklabel,mktable LABEL-TYPE                     Create a new disklabel (partition table)
         LABEL-TYPE is one of: aix, amiga, bsd, dvh, gpt, mac, msdos, sun, loop
(parted)
```

Let us create, modify and delete partitions with *parted* to understand its usage. As noted in section "Disk Partitioning Using fdisk", there are four hard drives – */dev/sdb, /dev/sdc, /dev/sdd* and */dev/sde* – installed on the system. You will be able to use them to perform various tasks in this section.

Creating a Partition

To create a partition on the third SCSI disk */dev/sdc* to be used as a file system or raw database space, follow the steps below:

1. Execute the *parted* command on the */dev/sdc* disk:

    ```
    # parted /dev/sdc
    GNU Parted 1.8.1
    Using /dev/sdc
    Welcome to GNU Parted! Type 'help' to view a list of commands.
    ```

2. Assign the disk a label using *mklabel*. This must be done on a new disk.

    ```
    (parted) mklabel
    New disk label type? msdos
    ```

    There are several supported label types available that can be assigned to a disk. Some of them are msdos, bsd and sun.

3. Create a partition using *mkpart*. For this demonstration, create a 500MB partition:

    ```
    (parted) mkpart
    Partition type?  Primary/extended? primary
    File system type?  [ext2]?
    Start? 1
    End? 500m
    ```

4. Execute *print* to verify:

    (parted) **print**

    Model: Vmware, Vmware Virtual S (scsi)
    Disk /dev/sdc: 8590MB
    Sector size (logical/physical): 512B/512B
    Partition Table: msdos

Number	Start	End	Size	Type	File system	Flags
1	0.51kB	500MB	500MB	primary	ext2	

5. Exit out of *parted* and execute the *partprobe* command at the command prompt to force the kernel to re-read the updated partition table information:

    # **partprobe**

6. Confirm the partition information using any of the following:

    # **parted /dev/sdc print**
    Model: Vmware, Vmware Virtual S (scsi)
    Disk /dev/sdc: 8590GB
    Sector size (logical/physical): 512B/512B
    Partition Table: msdos

Number	Start	End	Size	Type	File system	Flags
1	0.51kB	500MB	500MB	primary	ext2	

    Information: Don't forget to update /etc/fstab, if necessary.
    # **grep sdcb /proc/partitions**

Creating a Swap Partition

To create a partition on the third SCSI disk */dev/sdc* for use as a swap partition, follow the steps:

1. Execute the *parted* command on the */dev/sdc* disk:

    # **parted /dev/sdc**
    GNU Parted 1.8.1
    Using /dev/sdc
    Welcome to GNU Parted! Type 'help' to view a list of commands.

2. Create a partition using *mkpart*. For this demonstration, create a 500MB partition:

    (parted) **mkpart**
    Partition type? Primary/extended? **primary**
    File system type? [ext2]? **linux-swap**
    Start? **501m**
    End? **1000m**

3. Execute *print* to verify:

    (parted) **print**

    Model: Vmware, Vmware Virtual S (scsi)
    Disk /dev/sdc: 8590MB
    Sector size (logical/physical): 512B/512B
    Partition Table: msdos

Number	Start	End	Size	Type	File system	Flags
1	0.51kB	500MB	500MB	primary	ext2	
2	500MB	1000MB	500MB	primary		

4. Exit out of *parted* and execute the *partprobe* command at the command prompt to force the kernel to re-read the updated partition table information:

    # **partprobe**

5. Confirm the partition information using any of the following:

    # **parted /dev/sdc print**
    Model: Vmware, Vmware Virtual S (scsi)
    Disk /dev/sdc: 8590GB
    Sector size (logical/physical): 512B/512B
    Partition Table: msdos

Number	Start	End	Size	Type	File system	Flags
1	0.51kB	500MB	500MB	primary	ext2	
2	500MB	1000MB	500MB	primary		

    Information: Don't forget to update /etc/fstab, if necessary.
    # **grep sdc /proc/partitions**

Deleting a Partition

Deleting a partition deletes the partition information from the partition table. Let us delete both partitions created earlier:

1. Execute the *parted* command on the */dev/sdc* disk:

    # **parted /dev/sdc**
    GNU Parted 1.8.1
    Using /dev/sdc
    Welcome to GNU Parted! Type 'help' to view a list of commands.

2. Execute *rm* to delete both partitions:

    (parted) **rm 1**
    (parted) **rm 2**

3. Execute *print* to verify:

    (parted) **print**

    Model: Vmware, Vmware Virtual S (scsi)
    Disk /dev/sdc: 8590MB
    Sector size (logical/physical): 512B/512B
    Partition Table: msdos

    Number Start   End   Size   Type   File system   Flags

4. Exit out of *parted* and execute the *partprobe* command at the command prompt to force the kernel to re-read the updated partition table information:

    # **partprobe**

5. Confirm the partition information using any of the following:

    # **parted /dev/sdc print**
    Model: Vmware, Vmware Virtual S (scsi)
    Disk /dev/sdc: 8590GB
    Sector size (logical/physical): 512B/512B
    Partition Table: msdos

    Number Start End   Size   Type   File system Flags

    Information: Don't forget to update /etc/fstab, if necessary.
    # **grep sdc /proc/partitions**

Disk Partitioning Using Software RAID

RAID, stands for *Redundant Array of Independent Disks*, is an arrangement of disk drives that is used to provide fault tolerance in case of a disk failure within the arrangement or to provide increased performance, or a combination. RAID provides fault tolerance using striping, mirroring or parity. There are two types of RAID – hardware and software. Hardware RAID is provided by storage sub-systems (small to enterprise disk devices). Software RAID, in contrast, is configured at the operating system level. Almost all operating systems today including RHEL 5, support software RAID.

RAID may be implemented using two or more partitions on a single disk, but it will not provide any benefits from fault tolerance and performance perspectives. It is highly recommended to use partitions from separate disks to create RAID arrays to get true benefits offered by this arrangement.

There are several RAID levels, but RHEL 5 supports only 0, 1, 5 and 6. These are explained below along with advantages associated with each one of them.

RAID 0 (Concatenation)

This arrangement allows disks to be added one after the other in such a way that a single large volume is formed. This setup requires at least two disks. A major disadvantage is that the entire volume stops working if one of the disks fails. In this configuration, data is written on the first disk and then on the second disk after the first one fills up. This type of RAID configuration is also referred to as *concatenation*.

RAID 0 (Striping)

This arrangement allows disks to be added one after the other in such a way that a single large volume is formed. This setup requires at least two disks. A major disadvantage is that the entire volume stops working if one of the disks fails, but at the same time this arrangement offers better speed. In this configuration, data is equally and alternately read and written to on all the disks in the arrangement. This type of RAID configuration is also referred to as *striping*.

RAID 1 (mirroring)

RAID 1 facilitates duplication of data on two disks. If one of the disks fails, the other disk continues to function normally. The disadvantage of using RAID 1 is that you need twice as much disk capacity, but the advantage is 100% redundancy. This RAID level offers slower write performance as compared to RAID 0 since it has to write the same data on two separate disks. The read performance is better. It is highly recommended to use disks located on separate controllers for improved performance and increased redundancy. RAID 1 is also referred to as *mirroring*.

RAID 5 (striping with parity)

RAID 5 supports both striping as well as redundancy in terms of data parity. It adds an additional disk to RAID 0 striped volume. RAID 5 survives a single disk failure by using the parity bit to recalculate and rebuild lost data on the replaced disk. This configuration requires at least 3 disks to setup. It distributes the parity bit evenly across all disks in the configuration. RAID 5 offers good read and write performance. In this configuration, 25% of the combined disk space is used to store the parity information. In other words, you have 75% of the total disk capacity available for use.

RAID 6

RAID 6 is an enhanced form of RAID 5. It requires at least 4 disks to be configured and uses double parity bits. This RAID level survives a concurrent failure of two disks, but does not perform as fast as RAID 5 because it has to write two parity bits, which requires some extra overhead.

As noted in section "Disk Partitioning Using fdisk", there are four hard drives – */dev/sdb*, */dev/sdc*, */dev/sdd* and */dev/sde* – installed on the system. You will be able to use them to perform various tasks in this section.

Creating a RAID Array

Creating a RAID array requires the needed number of hard disks for the RAID level that you wish to implement. Although you can create any RAID level on a single physical disk, it defeats the purpose of using RAID. Moreover, each disk in the configuration should be on a separate physical controller card. In this sub-section, you will configure RAID 1 and 5.

Software RAID uses existing standard partitions and it requires a minimum of two for RAID 1 and three for RAID 5. A software package called mdadm must be installed on the system to configure software RAID:

rpm –qa | grep mdadm
mdadm-2.6.4-1.el5

Creating a RAID 1 Array

Here are the steps for creating a RAID 1 array:

1. Create two partitions using either *fdisk* or *parted* as explained earlier in this chapter. For this demonstration, it is assumed that you have */dev/sdb1* and */dev/sdc1* partitions of size 1GB each, available with the partition ID type set to "fd" (Linux raid autodetect). You should be able to see the two partitions as follows:

   # **fdisk –l**
   . . . .
   Disk /dev/sdb: 8589 MB, 8589934592 bytes
   255 heads, 63 sectors/track, 1044 cylinders
   Units = cylinders of 16065 * 512 = 8225280 bytes

Device Boot	Start	End	Blocks	Id	System
/dev/sdb1	1	123	987966	fd	Linux raid autodetect

   Disk /dev/sdc: 8589 MB, 8589934592 bytes
   255 heads, 63 sectors/track, 1044 cylinders
   Units = cylinders of 16065 * 512 = 8225280 bytes

Device Boot	Start	End	Blocks	Id	System
/dev/sdc1	1	123	987966	fd	Linux raid autodetect

   . . . .

2. Execute the *mdadm* command to create a RAID 1 array. The command will create (–C) a raid array called */dev/md0* of type (–l) RAID 1 and will include two partitions (–n) */dev/sdb1* and */dev/sdc1*. The –v option is used for verbosity.

   # **mdadm –vC /dev/md0 –n=2 /dev/sdb1 /dev/sdc1 –l=1**
   mdadm: size set to 981248K
   mdadm: array /dev/md0 started.

3. Verify the array by listing the contents of the */proc/mdstat* file or running the *mdadm* command with –D (detail) option:

   # **cat /proc/mdstat**
   Personalities : [raid1]
   md0 : active raid1 sdc1[1] sdb1[0]
        981248 blocks [2/2] [UU]
   unused devices: <none>

```
# mdadm –D /dev/md0
/dev/md0:
        Version : 00.90.03
  Creation Time : Wed Dec 10 19:54:36 2008
     Raid Level : raid1
     Array Size : 981248 (958.41 MiB 1004.80 MB)
  Used Device Size : 981248 (958.41 MiB 1004.80 MB)
   Raid Devices : 2
  Total Devices : 2
Preferred Minor : 0
    Persistence : Superblock is persistent

    Update Time : Wed Dec 10 19:55:40 2008
          State : clean
  Active Devices : 2
 Working Devices : 2
  Failed Devices : 0
   Spare Devices : 0

        UUID : 2afd9446:bc8c4b06:c2deaaa3:ba36d256
      Events : 0.2

    Number  Major  Minor  Raid  Device State
       0      8      17     0    active sync  /dev/sdb1
       1      8      33     1    active sync  /dev/sdc1
```

Creating a RAID 5 Array

Here are the steps to create a RAID 5 array:

1. Create four partitions using either *fdisk* or *parted* as explained earlier in this chapter. For this demonstration, it is assumed that you have */dev/sdb1*, */dev/sdc1*, */dev/sdd1* and */dev/sde1* partitions of size 1GB each available with the partition ID type set to "fd" (Linux raid autodetect). You should be able to see the four partitions as follows:

```
# fdisk –l
. . . . . . . .
Disk /dev/sdb: 8589 MB, 8589934592  bytes
255 heads, 63 sectors/track, 1044 cylinders
Units = cylinders of 16065 * 512 = 8225280 bytes

   Device Boot    Start     End     Blocks   Id  System
/dev/sdb1           1       123     987966   fd  Linux raid autodetect

Disk /dev/sdc: 8589 MB, 8589934592 bytes
255 heads, 63 sectors/track, 1044 cylinders
Units = cylinders of 16065 * 512 = 8225280 bytes
```

Device Boot	Start	End	Blocks	Id	System
/dev/sdc1	1	123	987966	fd	Linux raid autodetect

Disk /dev/sdd: 8589 MB, 8589934592 bytes
255 heads, 63 sectors/track, 1044 cylinders
Units = cylinders of 16065 * 512 = 8225280 bytes

Device Boot	Start	End	Blocks	Id	System
/dev/sdd1	1	123	987966	fd	Linux raid autodetect

Disk /dev/sde: 8589 MB, 8589934592 bytes
255 heads, 63 sectors/track, 1044 cylinders
Units = cylinders of 16065 * 512 = 8225280 bytes

Device Boot	Start	End	Blocks	Id	System
/dev/sde1	1	123	987966	fd	Linux raid autodetect

2. Execute the following to create a RAID 5 array. The command will create (–C) a raid array called */dev/md1* of type (–l) RAID 5 and will include four partitions (–n) */dev/sdb1*, */dev/sdc1*, */dev/sdd1* and */dev/sde1*. The –v option is used for verbosity.

mdadm –vC /dev/md1 –n=4 /dev/sdb1 /dev/sdc1 /dev/sdd1 /dev/sde1 –l=5
mdadm: layout defaults to left-symmetric
mdadm: chunk size defaults to 64K
mdadm: size set to 987840K
Continue creating array? **y**
mdadm: array /dev/md1 started.

3. Verify the array by listing the contents of the */proc/mdstat* file or running the *mdadm* command with –D (detail) option:

cat /proc/mdstat
Personalities : [raid1] [raid6] [raid5] [raid4]
md1 : active raid5 sde1[3] sdd1[2] sdc1[1] sdb1[0]
    2963520 blocks level 5, 64k chunk, algorithm 2 [4/4] [UUUU]
mdadm –D /dev/md1
/dev/md1:
        Version : 00.90.03
  Creation Time : Wed Dec 10 23:51:53 2008
     Raid Level : raid5
     Array Size   : 2963520 (2.83 GiB 3.03 GB)
  Used Device Size   : 987840 (964.85 MiB 1011.55 MB)
    Raid Devices : 4
   Total Devices : 4
  Preferred Minor : 1
    Persistence   : Superblock is persistent

    Update Time : Wed Dec 10 23:54:15 2008
        State : clean

```
     Active Devices : 4
    Working Devices : 4
      ailed Devices : 0
     Spare Devices : 0

          Layout : left-symmetric
      Chunk Size : 64K

          UUID : 5634eda2:a61d50f2:41f2bce4:49d37d4f
         Events : 0.2

    Number  Major  Minor  Raid Device  State
       0      8     17     0    active sync  /dev/sdb1
       1      8     33     1    active sync  /dev/sdc1
       2      8     49     2    active sync  /dev/sdd1
       3      8     65     3    active sync  /dev/sde1
```

You need to format both */dev/md0* and */dev/md1* RAID devices, create mount points and mount them, or use them for swap. If you wish them to be automatically mounted at each system reboot, edit the */etc/fstab* file and add entries. Refer to Chapter 14 "File Systems and Swap" on how to perform these tasks.

Replacing a Failed Disk in a RAID Array

If a hardware failure occurs in one of the disks in a RAID array, replace the disk and add the new disk to the RAID configuration. For a demonstration purpose, run the following on */dev/sde1* partition in the RAID 5 array created in a previous sub-section to cause it to fail:

> # **mdadm /dev/md1 –f /dev/sde1**
> mdadm: set /dev/sde1 faulty in /dev/md1

Remove the failed partition from the array:

> # **mdadm /dev/md1 –r /dev/sde1**
> mdadm: hot removed /dev/sde1

You can perform both the above in one go:

> # **mdadm –v /dev/md1 –f /dev/sde1 –r /dev/sde1**
> mdadm: set /dev/sde1 faulty in /dev/md1
> mdadm: hot removed /dev/sde1

To confirm:

> # **mdadm –D /dev/md1**
> /dev/md1:
>   Version : 00.90.03
> Creation Time : Wed Dec 10 23:51:53 2008
>   Raid Level : raid5

```
      Array Size : 2963520 (2.83 GiB 3.03 GB)
 Used Device Size : 987840 (964.85 MiB 1011.55 MB)
     Raid Devices : 4
    Total Devices : 3
  Preferred Minor : 1
      Persistence : Superblock is persistent

      Update Time : Wed Dec 11 00:00:03 2008
            State : clean, degraded
   Active Devices : 3
  Working Devices : 3
   Failed Devices : 0
    Spare Devices : 0

           Layout : left-symmetric
       Chunk Size : 64K

             UUID : 5634eda2:a61d50f2:41f2bce4:49d37d4f
           Events : 0.6

    Number   Major   Minor   Raid   Device State
       0       8       17      0     active sync   /dev/sdb1
       1       8       33      1     active sync   /dev/sdc1
       2       8       49      2     active sync   /dev/sdd1
       3       0        0      3     removed
```

Install a new disk and use *fdisk* or *parted* to create */dev/sde1* on it with the same size as it was before. Now run the following to add the partition to the RAID 5 array:

> # **mdadm /dev/md1 –a /dev/sde1**
> mdadm: re-added /dev/sde1

Confirm the replacement using any of the following:

> # **mdadm –D /dev/md1**
> # **cat /proc/mdstat**

Deleting a RAID Array

Deleting a RAID array deletes all its configuration information from the system. Here is how to do it.

To delete RAID 1 array */dev/md0*, first stop it and then remove:

> # **mdadm –vS /dev/md0**
> mdadm: stopped /dev/md0
> # **mdadm –vr /dev/md0**

The sequence of commands would be the same to delete RAID 5 array */dev/md1*.

Check the */proc/mdstat* file. The entry for both should have been gone. At this point if you wish you can remove all the partitions created for these arrays.

Disk Partitioning Using Logical Volume Manager

The LVM solution is widely used for managing disk storage. LVM enables you to accumulate spaces taken from one or several disks (called *physical volumes*) to form a large logical container (called *volume group*), which can then be divided into partitions (called *logical volumes*). Figure 13-1 demonstrates LVM components.

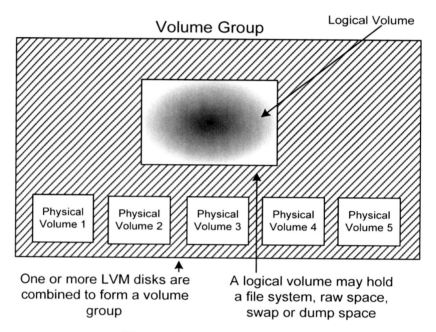

Figure 13-1 LVM Structure

LVM structure is made up of three key virtual objects called physical volume, volume group and logical volume that use *physical extents* (PEs) and *logical extents* (LEs) to further carve up the virtual objects. These components are explained in the following sub-sections.

Physical Volume

A physical volume (PV) is created when a standard partition, a software RAID partition or an entire disk is brought under LVM control by initializing the partition or disk, and constructing LVM data structures on it. A partition or disk must first be initialized before it can be used in a volume group.

Currently, there is one physical volume on the system, which was created during RHEL installation. Run the *pvs* command to view it:

```
# pvs
  PV          VG          Fmt    Attr   PSize   PFree
  /dev/sda2   VolGroup00  lvm2   a-     29.00G  1.72G
```

The output indicates that there is one physical volume */dev/sda2* of size 29GB in the *VolGroup00* volume group.

Volume Group

A volume group (VG) is created when at least one physical volume is added to it. The space from all physical volumes in a volume group is summed up to form a large pool of storage, which is then used to build one or more logical volumes. The default naming convention for volume groups is *VolGroup00, VolGroup01, VolGroup02* and so on, however, you may use any naming scheme you wish. For example, a volume group can be called *vg01, vgora, vgweb* and so on.

Currently, there is one volume group on the system, which was created during RHEL installation. Run the *vgs* command to view it:

```
# vgs
  VG              #PV   #LV   #SN   Attr    VSize    VFree
  VolGroup00      1     7     0     wz--n-  29.00G   1.72G
```

The output indicates that there is one volume group *VolGroup01* containing one physical volume.

Physical Extent

When a volume group is created, the physical volume added to it is divided into several smaller logical pieces known as physical extents (PEs). An extent is the smallest allocatable unit of space in LVM. At volume group creation time, you can either define the size of the PE or leave it to the default value, which is 4MB. This means an 8GB disk would contain approximately 2000 PEs. All physical volumes in a volume group must use the same PE size.

The following command displays physical extent size used in *VolGroup00* volume group:

```
# vgdisplay VolGroup00
  . . . . . . . .
  Format                lvm2
  Metadata Areas        1
  Metadata Sequence     No  8
  VG Access             read/write
  VG Status             resizable
  MAX LV                0
  Cur LV                7
  Open LV               7
  Max PV                0
  Cur PV                1
  Act PV                1
  VG Size               29.00 GB
  PE Size               32.00 MB
  Total PE              928
  Alloc PE / Size       873 / 27.28 GB
  Free  PE / Size       55 / 1.72 GB
  VG UUID               EPaUft-3G6K-riru-2txQ-rZCu-LQU7-25uvqz
```

Logical Volume

A volume group contains a pool of space taken from one or more physical volumes added to it. This volume group space is divided into one or more partitions called logical volumes (LVs).

A logical volume can be increased or decreased in size and can use space taken from several physical volumes inside the volume group.

The default naming convention for logical volumes is *lvol1, lvol2, lvol3* and so on, however, you may use any naming scheme you wish. For example, a logical volume can be called *system, undo, table* and so on. The following demonstrates device files for logical volumes in the *VolGroup00* volume group.

```
# ll /dev/VolGroup00
total 0
lrwxrwxrwx 1 root root 28 Dec 11 07:50 lvol1 -> /dev/mapper/VolGroup00-lvol1
lrwxrwxrwx 1 root root 28 Dec 11 07:50 lvol2 -> /dev/mapper/VolGroup00-lvol2
lrwxrwxrwx 1 root root 28 Dec 11 07:50 lvol3 -> /dev/mapper/VolGroup00-lvol3
lrwxrwxrwx 1 root root 28 Dec 11 07:50 lvol4 -> /dev/mapper/VolGroup00-lvol4
lrwxrwxrwx 1 root root 28 Dec 11 07:50 lvol5 -> /dev/mapper/VolGroup00-lvol5
lrwxrwxrwx 1 root root 28 Dec 11 07:50 lvol6 -> /dev/mapper/VolGroup00-lvol6
lrwxrwxrwx 1 root root 28 Dec 11 07:50 lvol7 -> /dev/mapper/VolGroup00-lvol7
```

Currently, there are seven logical volumes on the system, which were created during RHEL installation. Run the *lvs* command to view them:

```
# lvs
  LV      VG          Attr    LSize    Origin  Snap%  Move  Log   Copy%  Convert
  lvol1   VolGroup00  -wi-ao  992.00M
  lvol2   VolGroup00  -wi-ao  1.94G
  lvol3   VolGroup00  -wi-ao  1.94G
  lvol4   VolGroup00  -wi-ao  4.88G
  lvol5   VolGroup00  -wi-ao  4.88G
  lvol6   VolGroup00  -wi-ao  4.88G
  lvol7   VolGroup00  -wi-ao  7.81G
```

The output indicates that there is one volume group *VolGroup00* containing seven logical volumes.

Logical Extent

A logical volume is made up of extents called logical extents (LEs). Logical extents point to physical extents. The larger a logical volume is, the more LEs it will have.

The PE and LE sizes are usually kept the same within a volume group. A logical extent, however, can be smaller or larger than a physical extent. The default size for an LE is 4MB. The following command displays information about */dev/VolGroup00/lvol1* logical volume. The output does not indicate the LE size; however, you can divide the LV size by the Current LE count to get the LE size (which comes to 32MB in this example).

lvdisplay /dev/VolGroup00/lvol1

```
--- Logical volume ---
LV Name              /dev/VolGroup00/lvol1
VG Name              VolGroup00
LV UUID              e2ZQcd-se0g-LvuQ-CepS-7WM9-wTFl-7J0Wse
LV Write Access      read/write
LV Status            available
# open               1
LV Size              992.00 MB
Current LE           31
Segments             1
Allocation           inherit
Read ahead sectors   auto
 - currently set to  256
Block device         253:0
```

Managing Disk Space Using LVM

Managing disk space using LVM involves several tasks such as creating a physical volume, creating and displaying a volume group, creating and displaying a logical volume, extending a volume group, extending a logical volume, reducing a logical volume, renaming a logical volume, removing a logical volume, moving physical extents, reducing a volume group, removing a volume group and uninitializing a physical volume. You may either use LVM commands or the Red Hat LVM Configurator *system-config-lvm* to do the job.

Table 13-3 lists and describes some key LVM commands.

Command	Description
lvcreate	Creates a logical volume.
lvdisplay	Displays details of a logical volume.
lvextend	Extends a logical volume.
lvreduce	Reduces a logical volume.
lvremove	Removes a logical volume.
lvrename	Renames a logical volume.
lvresize	Resizes a logical volume.
pvcreate	Initializes a disk or partition for LVM.
pvdisplay	Displays details of a physical volume.
pvmove	Moves data from one PV to another.
pvremove	Uninitializes a physical volume.
vgcreate	Creates a volume group.
vgdisplay	Displays details of a volume group.
vgextend	Extends a volume group.
vgremove	Removes a volume group.

Table 13-3 LVM Commands

Overview of LVM Configurator

The LVM Configurator is a graphical interface for you to perform LVM management tasks such as:

- ✓ Display volume group, logical volumes and physical volumes, and their properties.
- ✓ Extend or reduce a volume group.
- ✓ Create or remove a logical volume.
- ✓ Display PE to LE mapping.

Figure 13-2 displays the main window that pops up when the LVM Configurator *system-config-lvm* is invoked. The Configurator may also be invoked as (GNOME) System / (KDE) Main Menu → Administration → Logical Volume Management. The main interface shows physical and logical views of each configured volume group, as well as all physical and logical volumes within each volume group. As you highlight a volume group, an unallocated volume or an uninitialized entity on the left hand side, a graphical representation of it is displayed in the middle window along with associated properties on the right hand side.

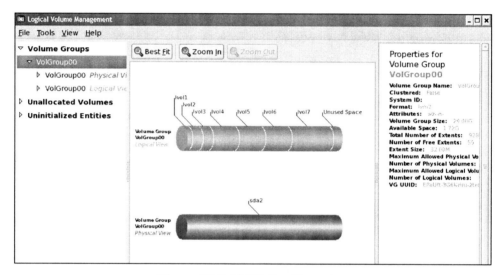

Figure 13-2 LVM Configurator

As noted in section "Disk Partitioning Using fdisk", there are four hard drives – */dev/sdb*, */dev/sdc*, */dev/sdd* and */dev/sde* – installed on the system. You will be able to use them to perform various tasks in this section. All LVM commands discussed in the remaining portion of this chapter support –v (or --verbose) option for verbosity. See man pages of commands for additional options and usage.

Creating a Physical Volume

A disk or partition must be initialized with the *pvcreate* command before it can be used in LVM. After initialization, the disk or partition is added to a volume group as a physical volume to create logical volumes. The following explains how a disk and a partition are initialized.

Make sure that LVM software packages are installed on the system:

```
# rpm –qa | grep lvm
system-config-lvm-1.1.3-2.0.el5
lvm2-2.02.32-4.el5
```

Table 13-4 provides short description of these packages.

Package	Description
system-config-lvm	Graphical LVM Configurator.
lvm2	Includes complete LVM product.

Table 13-4 LVM Package Description

Initialize */dev/sdb* disk:

 # pvcreate /dev/sdb
   Physical volume "/dev/sdb" successfully created

Initialize */dev/sdc1* partition. It is assumed that */dev/sdc1* partition already exists and was created with either *fdisk* (partition ID "8e" (Linux LVM)) or *parted* (file system flag "lvm").

 # pvcreate /dev/sdc1
   Physical volume "/dev/sdc1" successfully created

You can use the LVM Configurator to create a physical volume. Follow the steps below:

☞ Start LVM Configurator and go to Uninitialized Entities → /dev/sdb. Click Initialize Entity and then Yes to initialize the disk.

Creating and Displaying a Volume Group

The next step is to create a volume group. Follow the steps below to create a volume group *VolGroup01* with two physical volumes */dev/sdb and /dev/sdc1*:

 # vgcreate VolGroup01 /dev/sdb /dev/sdc1
   Volume group "VolGroup01" successfully created

There are several options available with *vgcreate* that you can use to specify non-default properties for the volume group. Some of these options are described in Table 13-5.

Option	Description
–l (--maxlogicalvolumes)	Limits the maximum number of LVs that can be created in a volume group. The default is 0 and the maximum is unlimited.
–p (--maxphysicalvolumes)	Limits the maximum number of PVs that can be added to a volume group. The default is 0 and the maximum is unlimited.
–s (--physicalextentsize)	Assigns the PE size, in KBs or MBs, to be used in a volume group. The default is 4MB and the maximum is unlimited.

Table 13-5 vgcreate Command Options

Execute the *vgdisplay* command to view what *vgcreate* has done. Run this command with and without the –v option. With –v, it reports in detail.

```
# vgdisplay −v VolGroup01
   Using volume group(s) on command line
   Finding volume group "VolGroup01"
   --- Volume group ---
   VG Name                    VolGroup01
   System ID
   Format                     lvm2
   Metadata Areas             2
   Metadata Sequence No       1
   VG Access                  read/write
   VG Status                  resizable
   MAX LV                     0
   Cur LV                     0
   Open LV                    0
   Max PV                     0
   Cur PV                     2
   Act PV                     2
   VG Size                    8.94 GB
   PE Size                    4.00 MB
   Total PE                   2288
   Alloc PE / Size            0 / 0
   Free  PE / Size            2288 / 8.94 GB
   VG UUID                    ZFRYws-jY1P-UyVC-eAE3-QkAN-v5vM-ZDgS1H

   --- Physical volumes ---
   PV Name                    /dev/sdb
   PV UUID                    x3jrs8-tOXa-d6f1-0ZiZ-ElT2-8r3t-QC084s
   PV Status                  allocatable
   Total PE / Free PE         2047 / 2047

   PV Name                    /dev/sdc1
   PV UUID                    nY17XC-oc0y-iyPv-D323-j0sV-xsNB-V7g8Kw
   PV Status                  allocatable
   Total PE / Free PE         241 / 241
```

The *vgdisplay* command shows that there are two physical volumes in the *VolGroup01* volume group with 2047 PEs in the first physical volume and 241 in the second. The PE size is 4MB. Currently, none of the PEs are allocated and no logical volumes exist. The last portion from the output under "Physical volumes" displays information about the physical volumes included in *VolGroup01*.

You can view detailed information about a physical volume using the *pvdisplay* command. Run it with and without the −v option on */dev/sdb*:

```
# pvdisplay /dev/sdb
   --- Physical volume ---
   PV Name        /dev/sdb
   VG Name        VolGroup01
   PV Size        8.00 GB / not usable 4.00 MB
```

Allocatable	yes
PE Size (KByte)	4096
Total PE	2047
Free PE	2047
Allocated PE	0
PV UUID	x3jrs8-tOXa-d6f1-0ZiZ-ElT2-8r3t-QC084s

You can use the LVM Configurator to create a volume group. Follow the steps below to create *VolGroup01*:

☞ Start LVM Configurator and go to Unallocated Volumes → /dev/sdb → Partition 1. Click Create New Volume Group. Enter volume group name and leave other values to defaults. Click OK.

Creating and Displaying a Logical Volume

At this point, you have a pool of storage space available within *VolGroup01* that you can use to construct logical volumes. Create a logical volume of size 2000MB using the *lvcreate* command:

lvcreate –L 2000 VolGroup01
  Logical volume "lvol0" created

The size can be specified in KBs (kilobytes), MBs (megabytes), GBs (gigabytes), TBs (terabytes), PBs (petabytes), EBs (exabytes) or LEs (logical extents), however, MB is the default. In the above example, the size specified is 2000MB. Alternatively, you can use the –l option and specify the size in multiples of LEs. For example, to create another logical volume of size 2000MB (which is equal to 500 LEs), run the above command as follows:

lvcreate –l 500 VolGroup01
  Logical volume "lvol1" created

Run the *vgdisplay* command to see what *lvcreate* has performed:

vgdisplay –v VolGroup01
  Using volume group(s) on command line
  Finding volume group "VolGroup01"
  --- Volume group ---

VG Name	VolGroup01
System ID	
Format	lvm2
Metadata Areas	2
Metadata Sequence No	3
VG Access	read/write
VG Status	resizable
MAX LV	0
Cur LV	2
Open LV	0
Max PV	0
Cur PV	2

Act PV	2
VG Size	8.94 GB
PE Size	4.00 MB
Total PE	2288
Alloc PE / Size	1000 / 3.91 GB
Free PE / Size	1288 / 5.03 GB
VG UUID	ZFRYws-jY1P-UyVC-eAE3-QkAN-v5vM-ZDgS1H

--- Logical volume ---

LV Name	/dev/VolGroup01/lvol0
VG Name	VolGroup01
LV UUID	t1KWaN-QBIu-t2GU-71cX-edjE-u7A7-xp6z6k
LV Write Access	read/write
LV Status	available
# open	0
LV Size	1.95 GB
Current LE	500
Segments	1
Allocation	inherit
Read ahead sectors	auto
- currently set to	256
Block device	253:7

--- Logical volume ---

LV Name	/dev/VolGroup01/lvol1
VG Name	VolGroup01
LV UUID	hHC2CO-Sz9J-pFr0-dHvA-yVNb-OHT2-h9ACgf
LV Write Access	read/write
LV Status	available
# open	0
LV Size	1.95 GB
Current LE	500
Segments	1
Allocation	inherit
Read ahead sectors	auto
- currently set to	256
Block device	253:8

--- Physical volumes ---

PV Name	/dev/sdb
PV UUID	x3jrs8-tOXa-d6f1-0ZiZ-ElT2-8r3t-QC084s
PV Status	allocatable
Total PE / Free PE	2047 / 1047

PV Name	/dev/sdc1
PV UUID	nY17XC-oc0y-iyPv-D323-j0sV-xsNB-V7g8Kw
PV Status	allocatable
Total PE / Free PE	241 / 241

Notice the change in the *vgdisplay* output before and after the creation of the logical volumes. The logical volumes constructed above have used the default logical volume names which are *lvol0* and *lvol1*.

The following example creates a 3150MB logical volume called *oravol* in *VolGroup01*:

lvcreate −L 3150 −n oravol VolGroup01
Rounding up size to full physical extent 3.08 GB
Logical volume "oravol" created

To display *oravol* logical volume information, use the *lvdisplay* command:

lvdisplay /dev/VolGroup01/oravol
--- Logical volume ---
LV Name	/dev/VolGroup01/oravol
VG Name	VolGroup01
LV UUID	LZWoh4-opWN-u8y7-ej81-dpya-c6xt-9rx0PI
LV Write Access	read/write
LV Status	available
# open	0
LV Size	3.08 GB
Current LE	788
Segments	1
Allocation	inherit
Read ahead sectors	auto
- currently set to	256
Block device	253:9

At this stage, you may want to view the file contents in the */etc/lvm/backup* directory where volume group information, along with physical volumes and logical volumes, is stored. Each volume group in the system has a sub-directory corresponding to its name.

ll /etc/lvm/backup
total 16
-rw------- 1 root root 2937 Dec   2 15:07 VolGroup00
-rw------- 1 root root 1931 Dec 11 13:11 VolGroup01

The contents of *VolGroup01* file is displayed below:

cat /etc/lvm/backup/VolGroup01
# Generated by LVM2 version 2.02.32-RHEL5 (2008-03-04): Thu Dec 11 13:11:29 2008
contents = "Text Format Volume Group"
version = 1
description = "Created *after* executing 'lvcreate -L 3150 -n oravol VolGroup01'"

creation_host = "rhel01"   # Linux rhel01 2.6.18-92.el5 #1 SMP Tue Apr 29 13:16:12 EDT 2008 i686
creation_time = 1229019089   # Thu Dec 11 13:11:29 2008

VolGroup01 {

```
id = "ZFRYws-jY1P-UyVC-eAE3-QkAN-v5vM-ZDgS1H"
seqno = 4
status = ["RESIZEABLE", "READ", "WRITE"]
extent_size = 8192          # 4 Megabytes
max_lv = 0
max_pv = 0

physical_volumes {

      pv0 {
              id = "x3jrs8-tOXa-d6f1-0ZiZ-ElT2-8r3t-QC084s"
              device = "/dev/sdb"     # Hint only

              status = ["ALLOCATABLE"]
              dev_size = 16777216     # 8 Gigabytes
              pe_start = 384
              pe_count = 2047 # 7.99609 Gigabytes
      }
. . . . . . . .
      logical_volumes {

          lvol0 {
              id = "t1KWaN-QBIu-t2GU-71cX-edjE-u7A7-xp6z6k"
              status = ["READ", "WRITE", "VISIBLE"]
              segment_count = 1
. . . . . . . .
```

You can use the LVM Configurator to create a logical volume. Follow the steps below to create *lvol1*:

☞ Start LVM Configurator and go to Volume Groups → VolGroup01 → VolGroup01 Logical View. Click Create New Logical Volume. Enter the logical volume name and size, and leave other values to defaults. Click OK.

Extending a Volume Group

Extending a volume group adds one or more physical volumes to it. Currently, *VolGroup01* includes two physical volumes */dev/sdb* and */dev/sdc1*. The following example adds to it another disk */dev/sdd*. Run *pvcreate* and then *vgextend* to achieve this:

```
# pvcreate /dev/sdd
 Physical volume "/dev/sdd" successfully created
# vgextend VolGroup01 /dev/sdd
 Volume group "VolGroup01" successfully extended
```

Do a *vgdisplay* with −v to see updated information about *VolGroup01*.

You can use the LVM Configurator to extend a volume group. Follow the steps below to extend *VolGroup01*:

☞ Start LVM Configurator and go to Volume Groups → VolGroup01 → VolGroup01 Physical View. Click Extend Volume Group. Highlight the partition or disk that you wish to add to the volume group and click OK.

Extending a Logical Volume

Extending a logical volume increases the logical volume in size. Currently, three logical volumes – *lvol0*, *lvol1* and *oravol* – with sizes 2000MB, 2000MB and 3150MB respectively, exist. The following example extends *lvol0* to 5000MB. Use the *lvextend* command to perform this activity. You can specify the size in either MBs or LEs. All of the following will generate an identical result:

```
# lvextend –L 5000 /dev/VolGroup01/lvol0
  Extending logical volume lvol0 to 4.88 GB
  Logical volume lvol0 successfully resized
# lvextend –L +3000 /dev/VolGroup01/lvol0
# lvextend –l 1250 /dev/VolGroup01/lvol0
# lvextend –l +750 /dev/VolGroup01/lvol0
```

Alternatively, you can use the *lvresize* command to extend a logical volume. For example, to double the size of *lvol1* to 4000MB, do any of the following:

```
# lvresize –L 4000 /dev/VolGroup01/lvol1
  Extending logical volume lvol1 to 3.91 GB
  Logical volume lvol1 successfully resized
# lvresize –L +2000 /dev/VolGroup01/lvol1
# lvresize –l 1000 /dev/VolGroup01/lvol1
# lvresize –l +500 /dev/VolGroup01/lvol1
```

Do a *vgdisplay* with –v to see updated information about *VolGroup01*. You can also use the *lvdisplay* command with –v option on the *lvol0* and *lvol1* logical volumes to view details.

You can use the LVM Configurator to extend a logical volume. Follow the steps below to extend *lvol1*:

☞ Start LVM Configurator and go to Volume Groups → VolGroup01 → VolGroup01 Logical View → lvol1. Click Edit Properties. Specify a new size and click OK.

Reducing a Logical Volume

Reducing a logical volume decreases the logical volume in size. Currently, *lvol0* is 5000MB. The following example reduces it to 1000MB. Use the *lvreduce* command to perform this activity. You can specify the size in either MBs or LEs. All of the following will do exactly the same:

```
# lvreduce –L 1000 /dev/VolGroup01/lvol0
  WARNING: Reducing active logical volume to 1000.00 MB
  THIS MAY DESTROY YOUR DATA (filesystem etc.)
Do you really want to reduce lvol0? [y/n]: y
  Reducing logical volume lvol0 to 1000.00 MB
  Logical volume lvol0 successfully resized
```

```
# lvreduce –L –4000 /dev/VolGroup01/lvol0
# lvreduce –l 125 /dev/VolGroup01/vol0
# lvreduce –l –1000 /dev/VolGroup01/lvol0
```

There is a risk involved when reducing the size of a logical volume, critical data may be lost. Always perform a backup of data in the logical volume before reducing it. See Chapter 17 "Backup, Restore and Compression" for details on how to perform backups.

You can use the LVM Configurator to reduce a logical volume. Follow the steps below to reduce *lvol1*:

☞ Start LVM Configurator and go to Volume Groups → VolGroup01 → VolGroup01 Logical View → lvol1. Click Edit Properties. Specify a new size and click OK.

Renaming a Logical Volume

Renaming a logical volume changes the name of the logical volume. The following example renames *lvol0* to *newlvol0*. Use the *lvrename* command to perform this activity:

```
# lvrename /dev/VolGroup01/lvol0 /dev/VolGroup01/newlvol0
  Renamed "lvol0" to "newlvol0" in volume group "VolGroup01"
```

You can use the LVM Configurator to rename a logical volume. Follow the steps below to rename *lvol1*:

☞ Start LVM Configurator and go to Volume Groups → VolGroup01 → VolGroup01 Logical View → lvol1. Click Edit Properties. Specify a new name and click OK.

Removing a Logical Volume

Removing a logical volume is a destructive task. Ensure that you perform a backup of any data in the target logical volume prior to deleting it. You will need to unmount the file system or disable swap in the logical volume. See Chapter 14 "File Systems and Swap" on how to unmount a file system and disable swap.

Use the *lvremove* command to remove *lvol0*:

```
# lvremove /dev/VolGroup01/lvol0
Do you really want to remove active logical volume "lvol0"? [y/n]: y
  Logical volume "lvol0" successfully removed
```

The command gives a warning message. Proceed with caution.

You can use the LVM Configurator to remove a logical volume. Follow the steps below to remove *lvol1*:

☞ Start LVM Configurator and go to Volume Groups → VolGroup01 → VolGroup01 Logical View → lvol1. Click Remove Logical Volume and then Yes to remove it.

Moving Physical Extents

If a physical volume with some PEs being used needs to be removed from a volume group, the data that resides in those PEs will need to be moved out to an available physical volume(s) in the same volume group. The destination physical volume(s) should have at least the same number of unused PEs available. The *pvmove* command is used for this purpose. The following example moves PEs from */dev/sdc1* to unused PEs available on any other physical volume in the volume group. Specify the name of a destination physical volume if you wish the PEs to be moved there. This operation can safely be performed on an online, busy logical volume.

    # **pvmove /dev/sdc1**
      /dev/sdc1: Moved: 8.0%
      /dev/sdc1: Moved: 17.9%
    . . . .
      /dev/sdc1: Moved: 100.0%

Issue *vgdisplay* and *pvdisplay* commands to view the updated information.

You can use the LVM Configurator to move PEs. Follow the steps below to move */dev/sdc1* PEs:

☞ Start LVM Configurator and go to Volume Groups → VolGroup01 → VolGroup01 Physical View → /dev/sdc → Partition 1. Highlight extents in the graphics and click Migrate Selected Extent(s) from Volume. Click Yes to confirm the move.

Reducing a Volume Group

Reducing a volume group removes one or more physical volumes from it. Currently, *VolGroup01* includes three physical volumes: */devsdb, /dev/sdc1* and */dev/sdd*. Use *vgreduce* to remove */dev/sdc1* from it. The physical volume must not be in use.

    # **vgreduce VolGroup01 /dev/sdc1**
      Removed "/dev/sdc1" from volume group "VolGroup01"

Issue *vgdisplay* with –v option to see the updated information about *VolGroup01*.

You can use the LVM Configurator to reduce a volume group. Follow the steps below to remove */dev/sdc1* to reduce *VolGroup01*:

☞ Start LVM Configurator and go to Volume Groups → VolGroup01 → VolGroup01 Physical View → /dev/sdc → Partition 1. Click Remove Volume from Volume Group and then Yes to remove it.

Removing a Volume Group

Removing a volume group removes all logical volumes within that volume group and then remove the volume group. Currently, you have *lvol1* and *oravol* logical volumes in *VolGroup01*. Use the *vgremove* command with –f (--force) option to remove the logical volumes and then the volume group itself:

```
# vgremove –f VolGroup01
Logical volume "lvol1" successfully removed
Logical volume "oravol" successfully removed
Volume group "VolGroup01" successfully removed
```

Remember to proceed with caution whenever you perform reduce and remove operations.

You can use the LVM Configurator to remove a volume group. Follow the steps below to remove *VolGroup01*.

☞ Start LVM Configurator and go to Volume Groups → VolGroup01 → VolGroup01 Logical View. Remove both logical volumes. Go to VolGroup01 Physical View → VolGroup01 and Click Remove Volume Group. Click Yes to remove the volume group.

Uninitializing a Physical Volume

Uninitializing a physical volume removes all LVM metadata information from it. Use the *pvremove* command:

```
# pvremove /dev/sdb
Labels on physical volume "/dev/sdb" successfully wiped
```

You can use the LVM Configurator to uninitialize a physical volume. Follow the steps below to uninitialize */dev/sdb*:

☞ Start LVM Configurator and go Unallocated Volumes → /dev/sdb → Partition 1. Click Remove Volume from LVM and then Yes to uninitialize /dev/sdb.

Summary

In this chapter, you looked at disk partitioning techniques available in RHEL, and features and benefits associated with them.

You performed partitioning tasks such as creating, modifying and deleting partitions using fdisk and parted utilities. You looked at various RAID levels and created, modified, recovered and deleted RAID array configurations.

Finally, you learned concepts, components and structure of LVM at length. You learned how to perform LVM management tasks using commands and graphical tool. You performed tasks including converting disks and partitions into physical volumes; creating, displaying, extending, reducing and removing volume groups; moving physical extents; creating, displaying, extending, reducing, renaming and removing logical volumes; and uninitializing a physical volume.

14

File Systems and Swap

This chapter covers the following major topics:

- ✓ File system concepts
- ✓ Supported file system types
- ✓ Manage file systems including creating, mounting, labeling, viewing, extending, reducing, unmounting and removing them
- ✓ Mount file systems automatically at each system boot
- ✓ Set extended file and directory permissions using Access Control List (ACL)
- ✓ Understand and configure disk quota
- ✓ Activate disk quota at each system reboot
- ✓ Check and repair file system structures
- ✓ Mount and unmount other types of file systems
- ✓ Use df and du to monitor file system space utilization
- ✓ Swap and paging concepts
- ✓ Device and file system swap
- ✓ Primary and secondary swap
- ✓ Create and enable device and file system swap
- ✓ View swap utilization
- ✓ List swap best practices

A *file system* is a logical container that holds files and directories. Each file system is created in a separate partition or logical volume. A typical RHEL system usually has numerous file systems. During installation, only two file systems are created by default – / (root) and */boot*, though you can choose custom partitioning and construct separate containers to store different types of information. Typical additional file systems created during installation are */home*, */opt*, */tmp*, */usr* and */var*. / (root) and */boot* are special file systems without which a system cannot boot.

Storing similar data in separate file systems versus storing all data in a single file system offers advantages such as you can:

✓ Make a file system accessible or inaccessible to users independent of other file systems. This hides or unhides information contained within that file system.
✓ Perform file system repair activities on individual file systems.
✓ Keep dissimilar data in separate file systems.
✓ Optimize or tune each file system independently.
✓ Grow or shrink a file system independently.
✓ Set user disk quotas at the individual file system level.

Moreover, some backup tools such as *dump* works only at the file system level.

File System Types

There are several different types of supported file systems, which may be categorized in three groups – disk-based, network-based and memory-based. Disk-based file systems are typically created on hard drives, CD/DVD drives, floppy disks, USB flash drives, ZIP drives and so on. Network-based file systems are basically disk-based file systems shared over the network. Memory-based file systems such as */proc* are virtual. They are created at system startup and destroyed when the system goes down. Table 14-1 lists and explains various common disk- and network-based file system types supported in RHEL 5.

File System	Type	Description
ext2	Disk	2nd generation of extended file system. The 1st generation is no longer supported. ext2 is the default file system type in RHEL 5. This file system type is also supported on Zip drives.
ext3	Disk	3rd generation of extended file system. Supports journaling which offers benefits such as faster recovery after system crash using metadata information from intent log (called *journal*), and superior reliability. This file system type is also supported on Zip drives.
ISO 9660	Disk	Used for CD and DVD file systems.
MS-DOS	Disk	Used for pre-Windows 95 file system formats.
NTFS	Disk	Used for post-Windows 95 file system formats on hard disks, USB drives and floppy disks. Supports security at the user login level.
VFAT	Disk	Same as NTFS but does not support security at the user login level. Supports FAT16 and FAT32 types as well.
NFS	Network	Network File System. See Chapter 26 "NFS and

File System	Type	Description
		AutoFS" for details.
AutoFS	Network	Auto File System. See Chapter 26 "NFS and AutoFS" for details.
CIFS	Network	Common Internet File System. See Chapter 27 "Samba" for details.

Table 14-1 File System Types

This chapter covers in detail ext2 and ext3 file systems on hard drives. It also covers mounting and unmounting of ISO 9660 and VFAT file systems. NFS, AutoFS and CIFS are covered in later chapters. Memory-based file systems, and MS-DOS and NTFS file systems are beyond the scope of this book.

Extended File Systems (ext2 and ext3)

Extended file systems have been supported in RHEL for several years. The 1st generation (ext) is obsolete and no longer supported. The second generation (ext2) has been supported for long time. The 3rd generation (ext3) is the latest in the series and supports what is called *journaling*.

The structure for an ext file system is built in a partition or logical volume when an extended file system is created in it, and is divided into two sets. One set that consists of not too many disk blocks, holds the file system's metadata information. The other set consisting of majority of file system disk blocks, holds actual data.

The metadata information includes the *superblock* which keeps vital file system structural information such as the type, size and status of file system, and number of data blocks in it. Since the superblock holds such critical information, a copy of it is automatically stored at various locations throughout the file system. The superblock at the beginning of the file system is referred to as the *primary superblock* and all others as *backup superblocks*. For any reasons, if the primary superblock is corrupted or lost, the file system becomes inaccessible. The metadata also contains the *inode table* which maintains a list of *index node* (inode) numbers. Each inode number is assigned to a file when it is created, and holds file related information such as the file type, permissions on it, ownership and group membership information, its size, last access/modification time and pointers to data blocks that store the file contents.

The ext3 file system is a journaling file system, which offers several benefits over conventional ext2 file system type. One major advantage is its ability to recover quickly following a system crash.

An ext3 file system keeps track of file system structural updates in a *journal*. Each metadata update is written in its entirety to the journal after it is complete. The system looks in the journal of each file system after it is rebooted following a crash, and recovers the file system rapidly using the updated structural information stored in its journal.

Managing File Systems

Managing file systems involves creating, mounting, labeling, viewing, extending, reducing, unmounting, automatically mounting, modifying attributes of, and removing a file system. There are several commands used for performing these tasks. Table 14-2 lists and describes them.

Command	Description
blkid	Displays block device attributes.
e2fsck	Checks an ext2 or ext3 file system.
e2label	Modifies the label on an ext2 or ext3 file system.
findfs	Finds a file system by label.
fuser	Lists processes using a file system.
lsof	Lists open files.
mkfs	Creates a file system.
mkfs.ext2	Creates an ext2 file system.
mkfs.ext3	Creates an ext3 file system.
mount	Mounts a file system for user access.
resize2fs	Resizes an ext2 or ext3 file system.
tune2fs	Tunes ext2 or ext3 file system attributes.
umount	Unmounts a file system.

Table 14-2 File System Management Commands

The following sub-sections explain how to perform various file system management operations.

Creating a File System

In Chapter 13, you learned disk management using standard, software RAID and LVM partitioning techniques. In order for a partition or logical volume to be able to store files and directories, it needs to be initialized as a file system, otherwise, it can only be used as a raw partition or swap. In RHEL, the command that is used to construct ext2 and ext3 file systems is *mkfs*.

Assume that there is a partition */dev/sdb1* of size 1GB and two logical volumes *lvol1* and *lvol2* in *VolGroup01* volume group of sizes 1GB and 2GB available. The following commands work identically on standard partitions, software RAID partitions and logical volumes. You simply need to specify the correct device file.

To create an ext2 file system in */dev/sdb1* partition, run any of the following:

```
# mkfs /dev/sdb1
# mkfs –t ext2 /dev/sdb1
# mkfs.ext2 /dev/sdb1
# mke2fs /dev/sdb1
mke2fs 1.39 (29-May-2006)
Filesystem label=
OS type: Linux
Block size=4096 (log=2)
Fragment size=4096 (log=2)
123648 inodes, 246991 blocks
12349 blocks (5.00%) reserved for the super user
First data block=0
Maximum filesystem blocks=255852544
8 block groups
32768 blocks per group, 32768 fragments per group
15456 inodes per group
Superblock backups stored on blocks:
```

32768, 98304, 163840, 229376

Writing inode tables: done
Writing superblocks and filesystem accounting information: done

This filesystem will be automatically checked every 28 mounts or
180 days, whichever comes first. Use tune2fs -c or -i to override.

To upgrade */dev/sdb1* ext2 file system to ext3, simpy add a journal to it using the *tune2fs* command:

tune2fs –j /dev/sdb1
tune2fs 1.39 (29-May-2006)
Creating journal inode: done
This filesystem will be automatically checked every 28 mounts or
180 days, whichever comes first. Use tune2fs -c or -i to override.

To create an ext3 file system in */dev/VolGroup01/lvol1* logical volume, run any of the following:

mkfs –t ext3 /dev/VolGroup01/lvol1
mkfs.ext3 /dev/VolGroup01/lvol1
mke2fs –j /dev/VolGroup01/lvol1
mke2fs 1.39 (29-May-2006)
Filesystem label=
OS type: Linux
Block size=4096 (log=2)
Fragment size=4096 (log=2)
128000 inodes, 256000 blocks
12800 blocks (5.00%) reserved for the super user
First data block=0
Maximum filesystem blocks=264241152
8 block groups
32768 blocks per group, 32768 fragments per group
16000 inodes per group
Superblock backups stored on blocks:
        32768, 98304, 163840, 229376

Writing inode tables: done
Creating journal (4096 blocks): done
Writing superblocks and filesystem accounting information: done

This filesystem will be automatically checked every 36 mounts or
180 days, whichever comes first. Use tune2fs -c or -i to override.

You can choose to create an ext2 or ext3 file system in a logical volume when you create the logical volume using the LVM Configurator. Follow the steps below to create ext3 file system in *lvol1*.

☞Execute *system-config-lvm* or (GNOME) System / (KDE) Main Menu → Administration → Logical Volume Management and go to Volume Groups → VolGroup01 → VolGroup01 Logical

View. Click Create New Logical Volume. Enter a logical volume name and size. Click to choose a file system type. Check the boxes beside "Mount" and "Mount when rebooted", and specify a mount point. Click OK. This will create the specified logical volume and initialize it with ext3 file system type. It will also create a mount point and mount the logical volume on it. Moreover, it will add an entry to the *etc/fstab* file so the file system is automatically mounted at each system reboot.

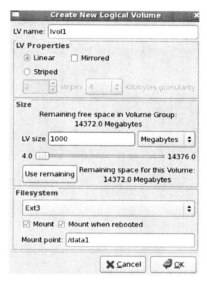

Figure 14-1 LVM Configurator – Create LV & File System

Mounting a File System

After a file system is constructed, it can be made accessible by connecting it to the root of the directory hierarchy. A directory needs to be created for this purpose, which will be referred to as *mount point* and then run the *mount* command to mount the file system on the mount point. Several options are available with the *mount* command. Some of them are described in Table 14-3.

Option	Description
async (sync)	All file system I/O to occur asynchronously (synchronously).
atime (noatime)	Updates (does not update) inode access time for each access.
auto (noauto)	Mounts (does not mount) the file system when –a option is specified with the *mount* command.
defaults	Accepts all defaults. Default options are rw, suid, dev, exec, auto, nouser and async.
dev (nodev)	Interprets (does not interpret) device files on the file system.
exec (noexec)	Permits (does not permit) binary file execution.
owner	Allows the owner of a file system to mount the file system.
remount	Remounts an already mounted file system.
ro (rw)	Mounts a file system read-only (read/write).
suid (nosuid)	Enables (disables) running setuid and setgid programs.
user (nouser)	Allows (disallows) a normal user to mount a file system.
users	Allows all users to mount and unmount a file system.

Table 14-3 mount Command Options

Currently, there are two file systems */dev/sdb1* and */dev/VolGroup01/lvol1* from the previous sub-section. Here is the procedure to mount them using appropriate options.

To mount */dev/sdb1* file system on */data0*:

> # **mkdir /data0**
> # **mount –t ext3 /dev/sdb1 /data0**

The "–t ext3" is optional and there is no need to specify it. The reason being that *mount* detects the file system type and automatically mounts an ext3 file system as ext3 and an ext2 file system as ext2. The *mount* command adds an entry to the */etc/mtab* file and the kernel adds an entry to the */proc/mounts* file after a file system is successfully mounted. Here are the entries from the files:

> # **grep data0 /etc/mtab**
> /dev/sdb1 /data0 ext3 rw 0 0
> # **grep data0 /proc/mounts**
> /dev/sdb1 /data0 ext3 rw,data=ordered 0 0

To mount */dev/VolGroup01/lvol1* file system on */data1*:

> # **mkdir /data1**
> # **mount /dev/VolGroup01/lvol1 /data1**

Labeling a File System

An ext2/ext3 file system may be associated with a label to make it unique among tens or hundreds of file systems on the system. A major benefit is that the label stays the same even if the device file associated with the file system is changed (for whatever reasons) at system reboots.

The *e2label* command is used to apply a label to an existing file system. For example, to apply the label *testvol* to */dev/VolGroup01/lvol1*, do the following:

> # **e2label /dev/VolGroup01/lvol1 testvol**

To verify:

> # **e2label /dev/VolGroup01/lvol1**
> testvol

Now you can mount the */dev/VolGroup01/lvol1* file system on */data1* as follows:

> # **mount LABEL=testvol /data1**

To check which device file is associated with a specific label, use the *findfs* command. The following example displays the associated device file for the label testvol:

> # **findfs LABEL=testvol**
> /dev/mapper/VolGroup01-lvol1

Another command called *blkid* can be used to display label associated with a file system:

 # blkid | grep testvol

/dev/mapper/VolGroup01-lvol1: **LABEL="testvol"** UUID="570bdaab-e3d4-41f5-878b-ff2b07007613"
SEC_TYPE="ext2" TYPE="ext3"
/dev/VolGroup01/lvol1: UUID="570bdaab-e3d4-41f5-878b-ff2b07007613" SEC_TYPE="ext2"
TYPE="ext3" **LABEL="testvol"**

 A label can also be applied to a file system at creation using –L option with the *mkfs* command or its variants.

See section "Mounting a File System at System Boot" later in this chapter on how to add entries to */etc/fstab* file to make file systems mounted automatically at each system reboot using device files and labels.

Viewing Mounted File Systems

There are several tools available to list mounted file systems, *df* and *mount* are more common and both read the */etc/mtab* file to display information.

Run the *df* command to view mounted file systems. Notice that */dev/sdb1* is mounted on */data0* and */dev/VolGroup01/lvol1* on */data1*.

 # df

Filesystem	1K-blocks	Used	Available	Use%	Mounted on
. . . .					
/dev/sdb1	972404	17632	905376	2%	/data0
/dev/mapper/VolGroup01-lvol1					
	1007896	17672	939024	2%	/data1

The *df* command may be executed with –h and –T options to display the output in a better format.

Run the *mount* command to view mounted file systems:

 # mount

. . . .
/dev/sdb1 on /data0 type ext3 (rw)
/dev/mapper/VolGroup01-lvol1 on /data1 type ext3 (rw)

Extending a File System

Extending a file system adds more space to it. Both ext2 and ext3 file systems can be extended. The first step is to grow the logical volume that contains the file system using the procedure outlined in Chapter 13 "Disk Partitioning" and then follow the steps below.

To extend the ext2 file system */dev/VolGroup01/lvol1* mounted on */data1* from 1000MB to 2000MB (assuming *lvol1* has already been extended to 2000MB), unmount the file system, run *e2fsck* command on it to check the metadata and extend it with the *resize2fs* command. When done, remount it and use *df* to verify the new size.

```
# umount /data1
# e2fsck –f /dev/VolGroup01/lvol1
e2fsck 1.39 (29-May-2006)
Pass 1: Checking inodes, blocks, and sizes
Pass 2: Checking directory structure
Pass 3: Checking directory connectivity
Pass 4: Checking reference counts
Pass 5: Checking group summary information
/dev/VolGroup01/lvol1: 11/128000 files (9.1% non-contiguous), 4342/256000 blocks
# resize2fs /dev/VolGroup01/lvol1
resize2fs 1.39 (29-May-2006)
Resizing the filesystem on /dev/VolGroup01/lvol1 to 2000 (4k) blocks.
The filesystem on /dev/VolGroup01/lvol1 is now 2000 blocks long.
# mount /dev/VolGroup01/lvol1 /data1
# df –k /data1
Filesystem        1K-blocks    Used Available Use% Mounted on
/dev/mapper/VolGroup01-lvol1
                  2015824     1512  1911912   1% /data1
```

To extend the ext3 file system */dev/VolGroup01/lvol2* mounted on */data2* from 1000MB to 2000MB (assuming *lvol2* has already been extended to 2000MB), use the *resize2fs* command on the mounted file system. When done, use the *df* command to verify the new size.

```
# resize2fs /dev/VolGroup01/lvol2
resize2fs 1.39 (29-May-2006)
Filesystem at /dev/VolGroup01/lvol2 is mounted on /data2; on-line resizing required
Performing an on-line resize of /dev/VolGroup01/lvol2 to 409600 (1k) blocks.
The filesystem on /dev/VolGroup01/lvol2 is now 409600 blocks long.
# df –k /data2
/dev/mapper/VolGroup01-lvol2
                  2015824    17920  1896744   1% /data2
```

For a file system that resides in a partition, you will have to destroy the partition, recreate it with a new size and reconstruct a file system in it.

You can choose to extend an ext2 or ext3 file system in a logical volume when you extend the logical volume using the LVM Configurator. Follow the steps below to extend ext2 or ext3 file system in *lvol2*.

☞ Execute *system-config-lvm* or (GNOME) System / (KDE) Main Menu → Administration → Logical Volume Management and go to Volume Groups → VolGroup01 → VolGroup01 Logical View → lvol2. Click Edit Properties. Enter a new size for the logical volume and click OK. This will extend the logical volume as well as the file system in it.

Reducing a File System

There are times when you need to reduce the size of a file system. It is possible to reduce an ext3 file system size but not possible with ext2 type. The only way to shrink an ext2 file system is to back it up, reduce the logical volume it resides in, run *mkfs* on the logical volume, mount the file system and restore the data in it.

To decrease */data2* ext3 file system from 2000MB to 1000MB, unmount the file system, reduce the size of the file system using the *resize2fs* command and then the logical volume that the file system resides in using the *lvreduce* command:

```
# umount /data2
# e2fsck –f /dev/VolGroup01/lvol2
e2fsck 1.39 (29-May-2006)
Pass 1: Checking inodes, blocks, and sizes
Pass 2: Checking directory structure
Pass 3: Checking directory connectivity
Pass 4: Checking reference counts
Pass 5: Checking group summary information
/dev/VolGroup01/lvol2: 11/256000 files (9.1% non-contiguous), 12524/512000 blocks
# resize2fs /dev/VolGroup01/lvol2 1000m
resize2fs 1.39 (29-May-2006)
Resizing the filesystem on /dev/VolGroup01/lvol2 to 256000 (4k) blocks.
The filesystem on /dev/VolGroup01/lvol2 is now 256000 blocks long.
# lvreduce –L 1000 /dev/VolGroup01/lvol2
  WARNING: Reducing active logical volume to 1000.00 MB
  THIS MAY DESTROY YOUR DATA (filesystem etc.)
Do you really want to reduce lvol2? [y/n]: y
  Reducing logical volume lvol2 to 1000.00 MB
  Logical volume lvol2 successfully resized
# mount /dev/VolGroup01/lvol2 /data2
/dev/mapper/VolGroup01-lvol2
          1007896    17672   949264   2% /data2
```

You can choose to reduce an ext2 or ext3 file system in a logical volume when you reduce the logical volume using the LVM Configurator. Follow the steps below to reduce ext2 or ext3 file system in *lvol2*.

☞ Execute *system-config-lvm* or (GNOME) System / (KDE) Main Menu → Administration → Logical Volume Management and go to Volume Groups → VolGroup01 → VolGroup01 Logical View → lvol2. Click Edit Properties. Enter a new size for the logical volume and click OK. This will reduce the logical volume as well as the file system in it.

Observe extreme caution when reducing a file system size. Any data sitting on the blocks being removed from the file system will be lost. It is highly recommended to do a file system backup prior to performing this action.

Unmounting a File System

Unmounting a file system makes the file system inaccessible to users by disconnecting it from the directory structure. The procedure to unmount both ext2 and ext3 file systems is identical. Use the *umount* command to unmount both file systems constructed earlier:

```
# umount /data1
# umount /data2
```

The *umount* command scans the */etc/mtab* file and determines the logical volume device file associated with the mount point to unmount it.

Occasionally, you get the "Device busy" message when attempting to unmount a file system:

```
# umount /data1
umount: /data1: device is busy
```

This message indicates that the specified file system is currently busy. A process or a user might be using it or a file in that file system is open.

To determine who or what processes are using the file system, use the *fuser* command:

```
# fuser –cu /data1
/data1:          5051c(root)
```

The –c option tells the process ID and –u gives the username who owns the process ID.

You can also use the *lsof* command to list open files for a specific file system or directory:

```
# lsof /data1
COMMAND  PID   USER  FD   TYPE DEVICE SIZE NODE NAME
bash     5051  root  cwd  DIR  253,7  4096  2    /data2
lsof     5554  root  cwd  DIR  253,7  4096  2    /data2
lsof     5555  root  cwd  DIR  253,7  4096  2    /data2
```

You can kill all the processes using the file system by running the *fuser* command with –k option:

```
# fuser –ck /data1
/data1:   5051c
```

Now you should be able to unmount */data1*.

At times, it becomes crucial to unmount all mounted file systems other than */var*, */usr* and */ that cannot be unmounted. Issue the *umount* command with –a option:

```
# umount –a
umount: /: device is busy
umount: /var: device is busy
umount: /usr: device is busy
```

Mounting a File System at System Boot

So far, you have mounted file systems from the command line. If the system reboots, none of them will remount automatically. To automate mounting of file systems at system reboots, proper entries must be placed in the */etc/fstab* file.

Another advantage with adding entries to the file is that if the file systems need to be mounted manually, you will need to specify only their mount points or the associated device files with the *mount* command, the rest will be obtained from this file.

The default *fstab* file contains entries only for file systems that make up the root volume. For LVM, this file looks similar to:

```
# cat /etc/fstab
/dev/VolGroup00/lvol1   /          ext3     defaults        1 1
/dev/VolGroup00/lvol4   /usr       ext3     defaults        1 2
/dev/VolGroup00/lvol2   /home      ext3     defaults        1 2
/dev/VolGroup00/lvol5   /var       ext3     defaults        1 2
/dev/VolGroup00/lvol3   /tmp       ext3     defaults        1 2
/dev/VolGroup00/lvol6   /opt       ext3     defaults        1 2
LABEL=/boot             /boot      ext3     defaults        1 2
tmpfs                   /dev/shm   tmpfs    defaults        0 0
devpts                  /dev/pts   devpts   gid=5,mode=620  0 0
sysfs                   /sys       sysfs    defaults        0 0
proc                    /proc      proc     defaults        0 0
/dev/VolGroup00/lvol7   swap       swap     defaults        0 0
```

There are six fields per line entry and are explained below:

- ✓ The first field defines either the device where the file system resides or the LABEL associated with it.
- ✓ The second field defines the mount point or "swap".
- ✓ The third field specifies the type of file system such as ext2, ext3, vfat, iso9660 or swap.
- ✓ The fourth field specifies any options to use when mounting the file system. Some of these options are listed and described in Table 14-2.
- ✓ The fifth field specifies whether to write the data to the file system when the system shuts down. A value of "0" disables it and a value of "1" enables it.
- ✓ The last field indicates a sequence number in which to run the *fsck* (file system check and repair) utility on the file system. By default, it is 1 for /, 2 for other local file systems and 0 for memory-based, remote and removable file systems.

Add */data0*, */data1* and */data2* file system entries to *fstab* using vi. The updated file will have the following additional entries:

```
# cat /etc/fstab
/dev/sdb1               /data0     ext3     defaults        1    2
/dev/VolGroup01/lvol1   /data1     ext3     defaults        1    2
/dev/VolGroup01/lvol2   /data2     ext3     defaults        1    2
```

After making the entries, run the following to mount all file systems listed in the file but are not currently mounted:

```
# mount –a
```

To mount only */data1*, do one of the following:

```
# mount /data1
# mount /dev/VolGroup01/lvol1
```

Remember, the *mount* command references the *fstab* file to mount file systems.

Removing a File System

Removing a file system is a destructive operation. It wipes out all data from the file system. To remove a file system, simply unmount it and remove the logical volume that holds it. The procedure is same for both ext2 and ext3 file systems. Use the *lvremove* command with –f option to remove *lvol0* from *VolGroup01*:

```
# lvremove –f /dev/VolGroup01/lvol0
  Logical volume "lvol0" successfully removed
```

For disk partitions, use the *fdisk* or *parted* command to remove the partition. It will also remove the file system in the partition.

When you remove a logical volume using the LVM Configurator, it also removes the file system in it. Follow the steps below to remove *lvol1* as well as ext2 or ext3 file system that it contains.

☞ Execute *system-config-lvm* or (GNOME) System / (KDE) Main Menu → Administration → Logical Volume Management and go to Volume Groups → VolGroup01 → VolGroup01 Logical View → lvol0. Click Remove Logical Volume and then Yes to remove the logical volume as well as the file system in it.

Access Control List (ACL)

Access Control List (ACL) provides an extended set of permissions that can be set on files and directories. These permissions are on top of the standard Linux file and directory permissions discussed earlier. The ACL allows you to define permissions for specific users and groups using either the octal or the symbolic notation.

There are two commands – *getfacl* and *setfacl* – available to work with ACL with the former displays permission information and the latter is used to set, modify, substitute and delete ACL entries.

Listing ACL Information

There are two commands *ll* and *getfacl* that help you determine if a file or directory has ACL set on it. The *ll* command displays a + sign right beside permissions to indicate if ACL is set. The *getfacl* command provides details:

```
$ getfacl file1
# file: file1
# owner: user1
# group: user1
user::rw-
group::r--
other::r--
```

The output indicates that currently there is no ACL set on *file1*. It shows that the file owner is *user1* who belongs to *user1* group. The owner has read and write permissions on the file, and group members and public read-only permission.

Changing ACL Information

Let us set ACL on *file1* with the *setfacl* command and then perform modify, substitute and delete functions to understand the behavior.

Before beginning, look at Table 14-4 to see how ACL entries are used with the *setfacl* command.

ACL Entry	Description
u[ser]::perm	Standard UNIX permissions for file or directory owner.
g[roup]::perm	Standard UNIX permissions for group members which the file or directory owner belongs to.
o[ther]:perm	Standard UNIX permissions for public.
m[ask]:perm	Maximum permissions a specific user or a specific group can have on a file or directory. If this is set to rw- for example, then no specific user or group can have more permissions than read/write.
u[ser]:UID:perm (or u[ser]:username:perm)	Permissions assigned to a specific user. The user must exist in */etc/passwd* file.
g[roup]:GID:perm (or g[roup]:groupname:perm)	Permissions assigned to a specific group. The group must exist in */etc/group* file.
d[efault]:u:perm	Default standard UNIX permissions for the owner set at the directory level.
d[efault]:u::perm	Default permissions for a specific user set at the directory level.
d[efault]:g:perm	Default standard UNIX permissions for owner's group members set at the directory level.
d[efault]:g::perm	Default permissions for a specific group set at the directory level.
d[efault]:o:perm	Default permissions for public set at the directory level.
d[efault]:m:perm	Default maximum permissions a user or group can have when the user or a group member creates a file in a directory where default ACL is set.

Table 14-4 ACL Entry Usage

Suppose you have *user1*, *user2*, *user3* and *user4* as members of *user1* group and *file1* owned by *user1* with 644 permissions and no ACL set.

```
-rw-r--r-- 1 user1 user1 0 Nov 27 10:11 file1
```

To allocate read/write/execute permissions to a specific user, *user2*, use *setfacl*. Before you can set extended permissions, you must ensure that the file system where the file or directory resides is mounted with the acl option. Suppose *file1* is located in the */home* file system, perform the following to check whether */home* has acl enabled:

```
# tune2fs –l /dev/mapper/VolGroup00-lvol2 | grep acl
Default mount options:   user_xattr acl
```

If not, run the following to remount */home* with acl activated:

mount –o remount,acl /home

On a file system created after RHEL installation, you will need to enable acl support and then mount or remout it. Here is how you would enable the option on */dev/sdb1*:

tune2fs /dev/sdb1 –o acl

Now, execute the *setfacl* command to set the permissions for *user2*:

$ **setfacl –m u:user2:7 file1**

The *ll* command reports:

$ **ll**
-rw-rwxr--+ 1 user1 user1 0 Nov 27 10:11 file1

Notice the + sign next to permissions. This indicates that *file1* has ACL set on it.

The *getfacl* command reports:

$ **getfacl file1**
# file: file1
# owner: user1
# group: user1
user::rw-
user:**user2**:rwx
group::r--
mask::rwx
other::r--

A row is added for *user2* showing rwx (7) permissions for him. Another row showing the mask is also added and is set to rwx (7) as well. The value of mask determines the maximum permissions assigned to a specific user or group. In this case, the maximum permissions allocated to *user2* is rwx and, therefore, mask is also set to rwx.

To modify these entries to have *user4* read/write permissions on *file1* as well, do the following:

$ **setfacl –m u:user4:rw file1**

The *getfacl* command reports:

$ **getfacl file1**
# file: file1
# owner: user1
# group: user1
user::rw-
user:**user2**:rwx
user:**user4**:rw-

```
group::r--
mask::rwx
other::r--
```

To delete the ACL entries for *user2*, use the –x option with *setfacl*:

```
$ setfacl –x u:user2 file1
$ getfacl file1
# file: file1
# owner: user1
# group: user1
user::rw-
user:user4:rw-
group::r--
mask::rw-
other::r--
```

Note that the maximum permissions are now reduced to read/write since that is what the maximum is for a specific user or group defined by mask.

To delete all the ACL entries set on *file1*, use the –b option with *setfacl*:

```
$ setfacl –b file1
```

To set ACL on *file1* to have rwx for the owner, rw for the group, r for public and rwx for *user3*, use the –m option with *setfacl*:

```
$ setfacl –m u::rwx,g::rw,o:r,u:user3:rwx file1
$ getfacl file1
# file: file1
# owner: user1
# group: user1
user::rwx
user:user3:rwx
group::rw-
mask::rwx
other::r--
```

The above command in octal notation will be:

```
$ setfacl –m u::7,g::6,o:4,u:user3:7 file1
```

Default ACL

Sometimes it is imperative for several users belonging to different groups to share the contents of a common directory. They want to have permissions setup on the directory in such a way that when files and sub-directories are created underneath, they inherit parent directory permissions. This way the users will not have to modify permissions on each new file and sub-directory created in there. Setting default ACL on a directory fulfills this requirement.

Default ACL can be described as the maximum discretionary permissions that can be allocated on a directory.

For example, to set default ACL on the */home/user3/project* directory for *user1* and *user2* so they have read and write permissions on the *project* directory, perform the following:

setfacl –m d:u:user1:6,d:u:user2:6 /home/user3/project

Use the *getfacl* command to verify.

Understanding Disk Quota

By default, users can create as many files as they want in a file system provided there is enough room available. This allows them to occupy a large chunk of file system space to store their files, which may include unnecessary data. With quota management, you can control which user can use how much space within a file system. Quota may be set at the user level, or at the group level so all users within that group share the allocated space.

Table 14-5 lists and describes quota management commands.

Command	Description
edquota	Edits/sets/copies user quota settings.
quota	Displays quota settings and usage status.
quotacheck	Checks quota usage.
quotaoff	Disables quota on a file system.
quotaon	Enables quota on a file system.
repquota	Reports quota usage.
setquota	Sets disk quota at the command line.

Table 14-5 Quota Management Commands

Quota can be set either by inodes (number of files a user can create) or disk size (amount of disk space a user can use). The kernel supports quota management by default. Do a *grep* on CONFIG_QUOTA in the */boot/config-`uname –r`* file and it will display the value "y" for the directive, which indicates that quota is enabled:

# **grep CONFIG_QUOTA /boot/config-`uname –r`**
CONFIG_QUOTA=y

When working with disk quota, the concepts of *soft* and *hard* limits are essential.

A soft limit defines the maximum amount of disk space that a user can use in a file system. In other words, soft limit acts as a upper-level threshold. If this threshold is met, the user is denied further access. If a grace period is set, the user must remove files within that time period to bring down his usage below this limit or will be denied access to further use the disk capacity.

A hard limit, on the other hand, is the absolute maximum limit beyond which a user cannot use any further disk space.

Configuring and Managing Disk Quota

The following sub-sections explain how to setup and manage disk quotas at user and group levels.

Configuring Disk Quota

Let us use the *home* file system to configure quota for a user and group. The following steps explain the procedure:

1. Ensure that the quota package is installed on the system. Run the *rpm* command to determine:

   # rpm –q quota
   quota-3.13-1.2.3.2.el5

2. Remount *home* with quota support enabled at user (usrquota) or group (grpquota) level, or both:

   # mount –o remount,acl,usrquota,grpquota /home

3. Confirm that *home* is mounted with quota support enabled:

   # mount –v | grep home
   /dev/mapper/VolGroup00-lvol2 on /home type ext3 (rw,**acl,usrquota,grpquota**)

4. Execute the *quotacheck* command on the file system to perform a quota scan for all users and groups. The first time this command is executed, you will see messages that will tell you that the command cannot find old quota files. Upon subsequent executions, no such messages will appear. The command creates *aquota.user* and *aquota.group* files in the file system on which quota is enabled and *quotacheck* command is executed.

   # quotacheck –cgmuv /home
   quotacheck: Scanning /dev/mapper/VolGroup00-lvol2 [/home] quotacheck: Cannot stat old user quota file: No such file or directory
   quotacheck: Cannot stat old group quota file: No such file or directory
   quotacheck: Cannot stat old user quota file: No such file or directory
   quotacheck: Cannot stat old group quota file: No such file or directory
   done
   quotacheck: Checked 3 directories and 2 files
   quotacheck: Old file not found.
   quotacheck: Old file not found.
   # quotacheck –cgmuv /home
   quotacheck: Scanning /dev/mapper/VolGroup00-lvol2 [/home] done
   quotacheck: Checked 3 directories and 4 files

   Options used with the *quotacheck* command are described in Table 14-6.

Option	Description
–c	Scans a file system for quota information.
–g	Checks group quota.

Red Hat Certified Technician & Engineer

Option	Description
–m	Does not try to remount a file system in read-only mode.
–u	Checks user quota. This is default.
–v	Displays detailed information.

Table 14-6 quotocheck Command Options

After you have executed the *quotacheck* command, check for the presence of *aquota.user* and *aquota.group* files:

 # ll /home | grep aquota
-rw------- 1 root root 6144 Dec 14 08:29 aquota.group
-rw------- 1 root root 6144 Dec 14 08:29 aquota.user

5. Activate quota on */home*:

    # quotaon –ugv /home
    /dev/mapper/VolGroup00-lvol2 [/home]: group quotas turned on
    /dev/mapper/VolGroup00-lvol2 [/home]: user quotas turned on

6. Set user quota by modifying the *aquota.user* file with the *edquota* command. The following sets a soft limit of 30MB and a hard limit of 35MB for user *aghori*:

    # edquota aghori
    Disk quotas for user aghori (uid 501):

Filesystem	blocks	soft	hard	inodes	soft	hard
/dev/mapper/VolGroup00-lvol2	96	30000	35000	12	0	0

    The *edquota* command opens up the *aquota.user* file in the vi editor. The above indicates that user *aghori* is currently using 96 blocks and 12 inodes in */home*. The value of 0 under soft and hard means that no limits are set.

    Alternatively, you can use the *setquota* command to modify the limits directly at the command prompt:

    # setquota –u aghori 30000 35000 0 0 /home

7. Log in as user *aghori* and try to make a file of size larger than 35MB in his home directory, and see the results. You may alternatively try copying some data over. For example, copy the contents of */etc* as follows:

    $ cp /etc/* ~
    . . . .
    dm-4: warning, user block quota exceeded.
    dm-4: write failed, user block limit reached.
    cp: writing `./termcap': Disk quota exceeded
    cp: cannot create regular file `./tux.mime.types': Disk quota exceeded
    . . . .

8. Next, set group quota by modifying the *aquota.group* file with the *edquota* command. The following sets a soft limit of 2000MB and a hard limit of 2500MB for *dba* group members:

edquota –g dba
Disk quotas for group dba (gid 1000):

Filesystem	blocks	soft	hard	inodes	soft	hard
/dev/mapper/VolGroup00-lvol2	0	2000000	2200000	0	0	0

With the *setquota* command, it would be:

setquota –g dba 2000000 2200000 0 0 /home

A few other usages of the *edquota* command are given below:

To modify the grace period from default of 7 days to 4 days for all users, use the –t option with the *edquota* command. This will allow users a grace period of up to 4 days to use the file system beyond the configured soft limit. Within this grace period users will have to move or remove files to bring the usage back under the soft limit in order to be able to continue to use the file system.

edquota –t
Grace period before enforcing soft limits for users:
Time units may be: days, hours, minutes, or seconds

Filesystem	Block grace period	Inode grace period
/dev/mapper/VolGroup00-lvol2	4days	4days

To modify the grace period for only user *aghori*, use the –T option with the *edquota* command:

edquota –T aghori

To modify the grace period for only group *dba*, specify either the group name or the GID:

edquota –Tg dba

You can perform the above three operations with the *setquota* command as well, but you will need to specify the period in seconds. Here are the equivalent commands for them:

setquota –ut 345600 345600 /home
setquota –uT aghori 345600 345600 /home
setquota –gT dba 345600 345600 /home

To replicate quota settings for one user to other users, use the *edquota* command. The following will copy user *aghori*'s quota settings to users *bghori* and *cghori*:

edquota –up aghori bghori cghori

Activating Quota Automatically at System Reboot

To activate disk quota settings on a file system each time the system is rebooted, define appropriate options in the */etc/fstab* file for it. Specify associated device file for the logical volume or partition.

For the *home* file system, the entry for both user (usrquota) and group (grpquota) quota settings will look like:

```
/dev/VolGroup00/lvol2    /home   ext3    acl,usrquota,grpquota    1   2
```

The */etc/rc.d/rc.sysinit* script is executed as part of the system boot process, which executes the *quotacheck* and *quotaon* commands on the file systems listed in the *fstab* file with quota options set.

Reporting on Quota Usage

To check which user or group is using how much space on a quota-enabled file system, use the *repquota* command. This command generates reports for all users and groups. You can specify the –a option to direct the *repquota* command to display a complete usage report. Here is an example that shows user quota:

```
# repquota –a
*** Report for user quotas on device /dev/mapper/VolGroup00-lvol2
Block grace time: 7days; Inode grace time: 7days
```

User		Block limits				File limits		
	used	soft	hard	grace	used	soft	hard	grace
root	--	35788	0	0	4	0	0	
aghori	+-	3200	3000	3200 6days	120	0	0	
bghori	--	96	3000	3200	12	0	0	
cghori	--	96	3000	3200	12	0	0	

To display group quata usage:

```
# repquota –ag
*** Report for group quotas on device /dev/mapper/VolGroup00-lvol2
Block grace time: 7days; Inode grace time: 7days
```

Group		Block limits				File limits		
	used	soft	hard	grace	used	soft	hard	grace
root	--	35788	0	0	4	0	0	
aghori	--	3200	0	0	120	0	0	
bghori	--	104	0	0	13	0	0	
cghori	--	96	0	0	12	0	0	

You may specify a file system name with *repquota* along with verbose option to check user quota on the file system:

```
# repquota –v /home
*** Report for user quotas on device /dev/mapper/VolGroup00-lvol2
Block grace time: 7days; Inode grace time: 7days
```

User		Block limits				File limits		
	used	soft	hard	grace	used	soft	hard	grace
root	--	35788	0	0	4	0	0	

```
aghori      +-   3200  3000  3200  6days   120  0   0
bghori      --     96  3000  3200           12  0   0
cghori      --     96  3000  3200           12  0   0
```

Statistics:
Total blocks: 7
Data blocks: 1
Entries: 4
Used average: 4.000000

To check group quota on */home*:

repquota –vg /home

```
*** Report for group quotas on device /dev/mapper/VolGroup00-lvol2
Block grace time: 7days; Inode grace time: 7days
                Block limits          File limits
    Group     used   soft  hard grace  used soft hard grace
    ---------------------------------------------------------
    root       --   35788   0    0          4   0   0
    aghori     --    3200   0    0        120   0   0
    bghori     --     104   0    0         13   0   0
    cghori     --      96   0    0         12   0   0
```

Statistics:
Total blocks: 7
Data blocks: 1
Entries: 4
Used average: 4.000000

To report quota for a specific user:

quota bghori

```
Disk quotas for user aghori (uid 501):
   Filesystem blocks  quota  limit  grace  files  quota  limit  grace
/dev/mapper/VolGroup00-lvol2
             3200*   3000   3200           120     0      0
```

Individual users can check their own usage with the *quota* command:

$ quota

```
Disk quotas for user bghori (uid 501):
   Filesystem blocks  quota  limit  grace  files  quota  limit  grace
/dev/mapper/VolGroup00-lvol2
               96    3000   3200            12     0      0
```

The *root* user can check usage of any user:

```
# quota cghori
Disk quotas for user cghori (uid 502):
    Filesystem blocks quota limit grace files quota limit grace
/dev/mapper/VolGroup00-lvol2
                    96    3000   3200           12    0     0
```

Disabling Disk Quota

Quota on a file system can be disabled by running the *quotaoff* command. The following command disables quota on all file systems for all users and groups:

```
# quotaoff –av
/dev/mapper/VolGroup00-lvol2 [/home]: group quotas turned off
/dev/mapper/VolGroup00-lvol2 [/home]: user quotas turned off
```

Specify the name of a file system if you wish to disable quota on a specific file system:

```
# quotaoff –ugv /home
/dev/mapper/VolGroup00-lvol2 [/home]: group quotas turned off
/dev/mapper/VolGroup00-lvol2 [/home]: user quotas turned off
```

Repairing a Damaged File System

The structure of a file system could be damaged when an abnormal system shutdown or crash occurs. To maintain file system integrity, a utility called *fsck* is used. This utility is called automatically when a reboot occurs following an abnormal system shutdown or crash. It performs multiple checks on file system structures, reports any inconsistencies as it finds and attempts to fix them. If an inconsistency cannot be resolved, it prompts for user intervention. The command can also be executed manually on a file system at the command line. It expects a "yes" or "no" response as it proceeds with trying to correct any inconsistencies. It takes longer to check and repair an ext2 file system than ext3. This utility actually calls the *e2fsck* command to perform the check and repair functions. Alternatively, you can run *e2fsck* directly.

The following example runs file system checks on an unmounted ext2 file system located in a logical volume (for partition, specify an associated device file):

```
# umount /data1
# fsck /dev/VolGroup01/lvol0 (or e2fsck /dev/VolGroup01/lvol0)
fsck 1.39 (29-May-2006)
e2fsck 1.39 (29-May-2006)
/dev/VolGroup01/lvol0: clean, 11/128000 files, 4342/256000 blocks
```

If the file system was not cleanly unmounted, the output will indicate that:

```
# fsck /dev/VolGroup01/lvol0 (or e2fsck /dev/VolGroup01/lvol0)
fsck 1.39 (29-May-2006)
e2fsck 1.39 (29-May-2006)
/dev/VolGroup01/lvol0 was not cleanly unmounted, check forced.
Pass 1: Checking inodes, blocks, and sizes
```

Pass 2: Checking directory structure
Pass 3: Checking directory connectivity
Pass 4: Checking reference counts
Pass 5: Checking group summary information

/dev/VolGroup01/lvol0: ***** FILE SYSTEM WAS MODIFIED *****
/dev/VolGroup01/lvol0: 11/76912 files (9.1% non-contiguous), 11777/307200 blocks

fsck may be invoked in *preen* mode by supplying the –p option with it. In this mode, the command performs an automatic repair without asking any questions.

fsck –p /dev/VolGroup01/lvol0 (or e2fsck –p /dev/VolGroup01/lvol0)

If the primary superblock is missing or corrupted, run the *dumpe2fs* command to display the list of backup superblock locations and then use one of the locations to repair the primary superblock using the *fsck* or *e2fsck* command:

dumpe2fs /dev/VolGroup01/lvol0
dumpe2fs 1.39 (29-May-2006)

Filesystem volume name:	<none>
Last mounted on:	<not available>
Filesystem UUID:	24a635b6-1a4b-4ff6-aeee-3ad7ab6e650e
Filesystem magic number:	0xEF53
Filesystem revision #:	1 (dynamic)
Filesystem features:	resize_inode dir_index filetype sparse_super large_file
Default mount options:	(none)
Filesystem state:	clean
Errors behavior:	Continue
Filesystem OS type:	Linux
Inode count:	128000
Block count:	256000
Reserved block count:	12800
Free blocks:	251658
Free inodes:	127989
First block:	0
Block size:	4096
Fragment size:	4096
Reserved GDT blocks:	62
Blocks per group:	32768
Fragments per group:	32768
Inodes per group:	16000
Inode blocks per group:	500
Filesystem created:	Sun Dec 14 14:16:40 2008
Last mount time:	n/a
Last write time:	Sun Dec 14 14:16:40 2008
Mount count:	0
Maximum mount count:	24
Last checked:	Sun Dec 14 14:16:40 2008
Check interval:	15552000 (6 months)

Red Hat Certified Technician & Engineer

Next check after:	Fri Jun 12 15:16:40 2009
Reserved blocks uid:	0 (user root)
Reserved blocks gid:	0 (group root)
First inode:	11
Inode size:	128
Default directory hash:	tea
Directory Hash Seed:	9b1272b8-cfdd-4a68-8cdc-e8d67fb1ecff

Group 0: (Blocks 0-32767)
  Primary superblock at 0, Group descriptors at 1-1
  Reserved GDT blocks at 2-63
  Block bitmap at 64 (+64), Inode bitmap at 65 (+65)
  Inode table at 66-565 (+66)
  32196 free blocks, 15989 free inodes, 2 directories
  Free blocks: 572-32767
  Free inodes: 12-16000
Group 1: (Blocks 32768-65535)
  Backup superblock at **32768**, Group descriptors at 32769-32769
  Reserved GDT blocks at 32770-32831
  Block bitmap at 32832 (+64), Inode bitmap at 32833 (+65)
  Inode table at 32834-33333 (+66)
  32202 free blocks, 16000 free inodes, 0 directories
. . . .
 # fsck –b 32768 /dev/VolGroup01/lvol0 (or **e2fsck –b 32768 /dev/VolGroup01/lvol0**)
fsck 1.39 (29-May-2006)
e2fsck 1.39 (29-May-2006)
/dev/VolGroup01/lvol0 was not cleanly unmounted, check forced.
Pass 1: Checking inodes, blocks, and sizes
Pass 2: Checking directory structure
Pass 3: Checking directory connectivity
Pass 4: Checking reference counts
Pass 5: Checking group summary information

/dev/VolGroup01/lvol0: ***** FILE SYSTEM WAS MODIFIED *****
/dev/VolGroup01/lvol0: 11/128000 files (9.1% non-contiguous), 4342/256000 blocks

While checking a file system, *fsck* may encounter a file with missing name. It moves the file to the *lost+found* directory located in that file system. This file is known as *orphan* file and is renamed to correspond to its inode number. You need to figure out the actual name of the file. Use the *file* command to determine the file's type. If it is a text file, use *cat* or *more* to view contents; otherwise, use the *strings* command to view legible contents in it. You can move the file to its correct directory location if you determine the whereabouts of it.

Managing Other Types of File Systems

Other than ext2 and ext3 file system types on hard disks, you may need to manage an ISO 9660 file system, a VFAT file system, or an ext2/ext3 file system on a Zip disk. Managing them involves mounting and unmounting them and checking their status. The following examples show how to mount a CD/DVD medium, a hard disk partition, and a USB, floppy and Zip drive.

To mount a CD/DVD medium with device file such as */dev/cdrom* (or */dev/hdc*) formatted with ISO 9660 file system type on */cdrom0* in read-only mode, run the following and then use the *df* or *mount* command to verify:

mkdir /cdrom0
mount −t iso9660 −o ro /dev/cdrom /cdrom0
df
/dev/hdc   93408   93408   0 100% /cdrom0

To unmount it, issue the *umount* command and supply either the mount point or the associated device file as an argument. If mount point is supplied, the command gets the device file name from the */etc/mtab* file.

umount /cdrom0
umount /dev/hdc

To mount a disk partition such as */dev/sdd1* formatted with VFAT file system type on */disk0*:

mkdir /disk0
mount −t vfat /dev/sdd1 /disk0

To mount a USB disk such as */dev/sdf* formatted with VFAT file system type on */usb0*:

mkdir /usb0
mount −t vfat /dev/sdf /usb0

To mount a floppy disk such as */dev/fd0* formatted with VFAT file system type on */floppy0*:

mkdir /floppy0
mount −t vfat /dev/fd0 /floppy0

Check their status with *df* or *mount*:

df
. . . .
/dev/sdd1   93408   93408   0 100% /disk0
/dev/sdf   93408   93408   0 100% /usb0
/dev/fd0   93408   93408   0 100% /floppy0

To unmount the VFAT file systems, issue the *umount* command and supply either the mount point or the associated device file as an argument:

umount /disk0
umount /usb0
umount /floppy0

To mount a Zip disk such as */dev/hdb1* formatted with ext3 file system type on */zip0*:

mkdir /zip0

```
# mount –t ext3 /dev/hdb1 /zip0
# df
/dev/hdb1          93408    93408    0 100%  /zip0
```

To unmount the Zip disk, issue any of the following:

```
# umount /zip0
# umount /dev/hdb1
```

If you are running GNOME or KDE, all removable media get automatically mounted under */media* directory when inserted in the drive.

Monitoring File System Space Utilization

File system space monitoring involves checking used and available file system space and inodes. It also includes watching space occupied by individual users. Several tools such as *df* and *du* are available to view this information in addition to a graphical tool called Disk Usage Analyzer. These tools are discussed in the following sub-sections.

Using df

df (disk free) reports on available file system blocks and inodes. It lists each file system with its corresponding logical volume or partition device file, free, used and available blocks/inodes, percentage of used blocks/inodes and mount point. By default, the *df* command displays the output in KBs.

To view the information in KBs:

```
# df
Filesystem                      1K-blocks    Used  Available Use%  Mounted on
/dev/mapper/VolGroup00-lvol1      983960    218124    715048   24%  /
/dev/mapper/VolGroup00-lvol4     4951688   2783696   1912404   60%  /usr
/dev/mapper/VolGroup00-lvol2     2984720     38640   2795360    2%  /home
/dev/mapper/VolGroup00-lvol5     4951688    198708   4497392    5%  /var
/dev/mapper/VolGroup00-lvol3     1967952     35828   1830544    2%  /tmp
. . . . . . . .
```

To view in MBs, use the –m option:

```
# df –m
Filesystem                      1M-blocks    Used  Available Use%  Mounted on
/dev/mapper/VolGroup00-lvol1         961      214       699   24%  /
/dev/mapper/VolGroup00-lvol4        4836     2719      1868   60%  /usr
/dev/mapper/VolGroup00-lvol2        2915       38      2730    2%  /home
/dev/mapper/VolGroup00-lvol5        4836      195      4392    5%  /var
/dev/mapper/VolGroup00-lvol3        1922       35      1788    2%  /tmp
. . . . . . . .
```

To view in human readable format, use the –h option:

```
# df –h
Filesystem                       Size   Used   Avail  Use%   Mounted on
/dev/mapper/VolGroup00-lvol1     961M   214M   699M   24%    /
/dev/mapper/VolGroup00-lvol4     4.8G   2.7G   1.9G   60%    /usr
/dev/mapper/VolGroup00-lvol2     2.9G   38M    2.7G   2%     /home
/dev/mapper/VolGroup00-lvol5     4.8G   195M   4.3G   5%     /var
/dev/mapper/VolGroup00-lvol3     1.9G   35M    1.8G   2%     /tmp
. . . . . . . .
```

To view by inodes, use the –i option:

```
# df –i
Filesystem                       Inodes    IUsed    IFree     IUse%   Mounted on
/dev/mapper/VolGroup00-lvol1     253952    5185     248767    3%      /
/dev/mapper/VolGroup00-lvol4     1277952   134583   1143369   11%     /usr
/dev/mapper/VolGroup00-lvol2     761856    158      761698    1%      /home
/dev/mapper/VolGroup00-lvol5     1277952   1303     1276649   1%      /var
/dev/mapper/VolGroup00-lvol3     507904    22       507882    1%      /tmp
. . . . . . . .
```

Try running *df* with "–t ext2" and "–t ext3" options also.

Using du

du (disk usage) calculates the amount of disk space a file, directory or file system is occupying:

```
# du –h /boot
16K    /boot/lost+found
312K   /boot/grub
6.2M   /boot
```

The –h option shows the count in KBs, MBs or GBs, as appropriate. Run this command without any options to see the output in KBs only and with –s option to display only the total.

Using Disk Usage Analyzer

Disk Usage Analyzer is a graphical tool that can be used to perform file system space analysis, and can be invoked by running the *baobab* command or choosing (GNOME) Applications → System Tools → Disk Usage Analyzer.

Figure 14-2 Disk Usage Analyzer

This tool scans local or remote directories and file systems, and reports on usage in terms of number of objects, used capacity, etc. in a tree-like format.

Understanding Swap

Physical memory in the system is a finite temporary storage resource used for loading the kernel and data structures, as well as running user programs and applications. The system divides the memory into smaller pieces called *pages*. A page is typically 4KB in size.

The size of swap should not be less than the amount of physical memory; however, depending on application requirements, it may be twice or even larger. Run the *free* command to view how much memory is installed, used and free in the system. You can use the –m or –g flag to list the values in MBs or GBs.

free

	total	used	free	shared	buffers	cached
Mem:	807708	795080	12628	0	183808	216776
-/+ buffers/cache:		394496	413212			
Swap:	8191992	60	8191932			

Alternatively, use the following to determine memory information:

cat /proc/meminfo

MemTotal:	807660 kB
MemFree:	138492 kB
Buffers:	169164 kB
Cached:	387492 kB
SwapCached:	0 kB
Active:	205116 kB
Inactive:	403384 kB
HighTotal:	0 kB
HighFree:	0 kB
LowTotal:	807660 kB
LowFree:	138492 kB
SwapTotal:	1638392 kB
SwapFree:	1638392 kB

. . . .

There is 800MB (MemTotal) of physical memory on this system. For performance enhancement reasons, the kernel uses as much memory as it can for caching data. As reads and writes occur constantly, the kernel struggles to keep the data in cache as pertinent as possible. The caching information is reported as the sum of the number of buffers and cached pages. The portion of the cache memory used by a certain process is released when the process is terminated, and is allocated to a new process as needed. The above output indicates that about half of 800MB (Inactive) is available for use by new processes. The output also displays the total amount of configured swap (SwapTotal) and how much it is used and available (SwapFree).

Swap Space and Demand Paging

Swap space is a region on a physical disk used for demand paging purposes. When a program or process is spawned, it requires space in the memory to run and be processed. Although many programs can run concurrently, but the physical memory cannot hold all of them at the same time. The kernel monitors free physical memory. As long as it is below a high threshold, no paging occurs. When the amount of free physical memory falls below that threshold, the system starts moving selected idle pages of data from physical memory to the swap space to make room to accommodate other programs. This is referred to as *page out*. Since system CPU performs process execution in a round-robin fashion, when the time comes for the paged out data to be executed, the CPU looks for that data in the physical memory and *page fault* occurs. The pages are then moved back into the physical memory from the swap space. The moving back into the physical memory of paged out data is referred to as *page in,* and the entire process of paging data out and in is known as *demand paging.*

RHEL systems with less physical memory but high memory requirements can become so busy doing paging out and in that they do not have enough time to carry out other useful tasks causing system performance to degrade. When this situation occurs, the system appears to be frozen. The excessive amount of paging that causes the system performance to go down is called *thrashing.*

When thrashing begins, or when the free physical memory falls below a low threshold, the system deactivates idle processes and prevents new processes from initiating. The idle processes only get reactivated and new processes are only started when the system discovers that available physical memory has climbed above the threshold level and thrashing has stopped.

Device and File System Swap

There are two types of swap space: *device swap* and *file system swap.*

A device swap is created and enabled in a logical volume or a disk partition, whereas, a file system swap is a portion in a mounted file system allocated and enabled for paging purposes.

When file system swap is enabled, a directory called *paging* is created at the root of that file system. Under the *paging* directory, files are created for each individual swap chunk used in file system paging. By default, a swap chunk is 2MB in size.

A file system swap can be defined and enabled dynamically. It may be defined to use a fixed or any amount of file system area. Remember, once a file system has been enabled for swapping, it is not possible to unmount it. You must reboot the system with the swap space line entry commented out in the */etc/fstab* file, if defined.

Primary and Secondary Swap

Primary swap is the device swap created during RHEL installation and becomes available each time the system boots up. It usually exists with OS file systems and shares the same physical disk.

In addition to the primary swap, one or more *secondary* swap spaces may be defined based on application requirements. It is recommended to always use device swap for improved performance, and create it on a physical disk with no other swap area.

If you must use a file system swap, always define it as secondary.

Secondary swap spaces can be enabled automatically at boot time provided an entry is defined in the */etc/fstab* file. They may also be added manually to a running system.

Managing Swap

Managing swap involves creating device and file system swap areas, enabling them and viewing their usage. The following sub-sections describe these operations.

Creating and Enabling a Device Swap

To create and enable a device swap called *swaplvol* of size 2000MB in *VolGroup01* volume group, perform the following steps. The first command creates the logical volume, the second creates swap structures and the third enables swapping in it.

1. Create a logical volume *swaplvol* in *VolGroup01* of size 2000MB with the *lvcreate* command:

    # lvcreate –L 2000 –n swaplvol VolGroup01
    Logical volume "swaplvol" created

2. Create swap structures in the logical volume using the *mkswap* command:

    # mkswap /dev/VolGroup01/swaplvol
    Setting up swapspace version 1, size = 2097147 kB

3. Enable swapping in the logical volume using the *swapon* command:

    # swapon /dev/VolGroup01/swaplvol
    Setting up swapspace version 1, size = 2097147 kB

4. Confirm new swap by running either *swapon* with –s option, or viewing the contents of the */proc/swaps* file:

    # swapon –s

Filename	Type	Size	Used	Priority
/dev/mapper/VolGroup00-lvol7	partition	8191992	0	-2
/dev/mapper/VolGroup01-swaplvol	partition	2047992	0	-3

    # cat /proc/swaps

You can also use the *vmstat* (virtual memory statistics) command to display information on virtual memory utilization. Here is the output from this command:

```
# vmstat
procs -------------memory------------- ----swap-- -------io---- ----system--- -----cpu-------------
 r  b   swpd   free    buff   cache     si   so    bi   bo     in    cs   us sy id wa st
 0  0    0    46824  50516 226836       0    0     52    6    1013   61    0  1 98  1  0
```

The output displays six pieces of information. The r and b under procs show the number of processes waiting for run time and in uninterruptible sleep; the swpd, free, buff and cache under memory indicate amount of used virtual memory, idle memory, memory used as buffers and cache; the si and so under swap determine amount of memory swapped in and out; the bi and bo under io display number of blocks in and out; the in and cs under system indicate numbers per second of interrupts and context switches; and us, sy, id, wa and st identify percentages of total CPU time spent in running non-kernel code, kernel code, idle state, waiting for I/O and stolen from a virtual machine.

The *vmstat* command can be run with the –s switch to display the output in a different format:

```
# vmstat –s
      807660  total memory
      474508  used memory
      157000  active memory
      285408  inactive memory
      333152  free memory
       44116  buffer memory
      337880  swap cache
     8323056  total swap
           0  used swap
     8323056  free swap
        1921  non-nice user cpu ticks
        1560  nice user cpu ticks
       12455  system cpu ticks
     3518551  idle cpu ticks
        2642  IO-wait cpu ticks
        1259  IRQ cpu ticks
         702  softirq cpu ticks
           0  stolen cpu ticks
      365301  pages paged in
       91452  pages paged out
           0  pages swapped in
           0  pages swapped out
    35801292  interrupts
     1730789  CPU context switches
  1237372139  boot time
        4048  forks
```

To create a device swap in a disk partition, construct a partition using *fdisk* or *parted* as explained in Chapter 13 "Disk Partitioning", and then perform steps 2 and 3 above on the partition device file.

If you wish to apply a label to a swap logical volume or partition, use the –L option with the *mkswap* or the *e2label* command. See earlier in this chapter on details.

Creating and Enabling a File System Swap

To create and enable a file system swap in */data2* file system, for example, by the name fs_swap1 and limit it to use 200MB for swap, follow the steps below:

1. Reserve 200MB of contiguous space with the *dd* command:

   # dd if=/dev/zero of=/data2/fs_swap1 bs=1024 count=204800
   204800+0 records in
   204800+0 records out
   209715200 bytes (210 MB) copied, 1.71204 seconds, 122 MB/s

2. Create swap structures in */data2/fs_swap1* using the *mkswap* command:

   # mkswap /data2/fs_swap1
   Setting up swapspace version 1, size = 209711 kB

   If you wish to assign this swap space a label, use –L option and supply a desired label name.

3. Enable swapping using the *swapon* command:

   # swapon /data2/fs_swap1

4. Confirm the new swap using either the *swapon* command with –s option or the *cat* command on the */proc/swaps* file:

   # swapon –s

Filename	Type	Size	Used	Priority
/dev/mapper/VolGroup00-lvol7	partition	8191992	0	-2
/dev/mapper/VolGroup01-swaplvol	partition	2047992	0	-3
/data2/fs_swap1	file	204792	0	-4

   # cat /proc/swaps

Enabling Swap Space at System Boot

In order to make all swap spaces activated when the system reboots, you need to define them in the */etc/fstab* file. During the boot process, the *swapon* command with –a flag is executed activating all swap spaces listed in the file.

Here is what needs to be added to the *fstab* file for the *swaplvol* (device) and */data2/fs_swap1* (file system) swap entries:

```
/dev/VolGroup01/swaplvol    swap    swap    defaults  0  0
/data2/fs_swap1             swap    swap    defaults  0  0
```

The first field lists the logical volume (or partition) device file or the file system swap location, the second and the third fields specify the type "swap", the fourth field directs to use all default options

---

and the last two fields are always 0 for swap since you will not want to run *fsck* on them. See subsection "Mounting a File System at System Boot" for more information.

Activating and Deactivating Swap Spaces Manually

To deactivate all unused swap spaces manually:

> # **swapoff –a**

To activate all swap spaces listed in the */etc/fstab* file manually:

> # **swapon –a**

Removing a Swap Space

To remove the device swap */dev/VolGroup01/swaplvol*, deactivate it and remove the logical volume. Do not forget to update the *fstab* file.

> # **swapoff /dev/VolGroup01/swaplvol**
> # **lvremove –f /dev/VolGroup01/swaplvol**
>   Logical volume "swaplvol" successfully removed

Replace the logical volume name with the partition device file to remove swap from it.

To remove the file system swap space in */data2/fs_swap1*, deactivate it and remove the file. Do not forget to update the *fstab* file.

> # **swapoff /data2/fs_swap1**
> # **rm /data2/fs_swap1**

Swap Best Practices

Following best practices should be adhered to when configuring a swap for better and improved performance:

- ✓ Do not configure more than one swap spaces on a single physical disk.
- ✓ Favor faster disks over slower.
- ✓ Two smaller, same size device swap areas on two separate physical disks are better than one large swap space on one single physical disk.
- ✓ Avoid using file system swap as much as possible. Use it only if there is absolutely no physical disk space left for building an additional device swap.
- ✓ Choose less utilized file systems over busier file systems if you must use file system swap.

Summary

In this chapter, you learned about file systems and swap. You learned concepts and supported file system types.

The chapter discussed managing file systems, which involved creating, mounting, labeling, viewing, extending, reducing, unmounting and removing them using both command line and GUI tools. You saw how file systems were defined for getting automounted at system reboots.

You learned about setting extended permissions on files and directories using Access Control List. You were presented with the concepts of disk quota that could be set at a user or group level to control file system space utilization. You performed tasks such as configuring quota, reporting on its usage and disabling it. You looked at how to add options to a file system entry in */etc/fstab* file to activate quota at each system reboot.

You were explained how to check and repair file system structures after a system crash automatically and manually. You looked at mounting, unmounting and viewing several other types of file systems, and also file system monitoring tools such as *df* and *du* to monitor their space utilization.

You studied concepts of swapping and paging. You saw how paging worked. Device and file system swap, and primary and secondary swap regions were discussed along with associated advantages and disadvantages.

You looked at managing swap that covered creating, enabling and viewing both device and file system swap. You saw how configured swap areas could be enabled manually and at system reboots. Finally, swap best practices were covered.

## 15

Shutdown and Boot

This chapter covers the following major topics:

- ✓ Understand run control levels
- ✓ Current and previous run levels
- ✓ Change run levels with shutdown, init, halt, poweroff and reboot commands
- ✓ System boot process – BIOS initialization, GRUB, kernel initialization and system initialization
- ✓ Boot the system manually from GRUB
- ✓ Understand GRUB configuration
- ✓ Understand key initialization file and virtual console screens
- ✓ Understand startup scripts, configuration files and sequencer directories
- ✓ Start, stop, restart and manage system services via commands, menu-driven program and graphically

RHEL systems need to be shutdown periodically for maintenance such as adding or removing hardware components. Sometimes, software is installed that affect kernel configuration and a reboot is required prior to the new configuration taking effect. There may be other situations when a shutdown or reboot of a server becomes necessary. There are several levels at which a system can run with each level providing a subset of services. A system has to go through several phases successfully in order to get to the point where users are able to access it.

Shutting Down

RHEL changes run levels when a system shutdown occurs. Similarly, run levels are changed when a system boot occurs. The following sub-sections discuss system run control levels and how to manipulate them.

Run Control Levels

System *run control* (rc) levels are pre-defined and determines the current state of the system. RHEL supports eight rc levels of which seven are currently implemented. Not all of them are commonly used though. The default rc level is 5. Table 15-1 describes various run levels.

Run Level	Description
0	RHEL is down and the system is halted.
s or S	Single user state with file systems mounted. The system can be accessed only at the system console.
1	Single user state with all file systems mounted and SELinux activated. Scripts located in the */etc/rc.d/rc1.d* directory are executed.
2	Multi-user state. Most system and network services, except NFS server and X window system, running.
3	Multi-user state. All system and network services including NFS server running. X window is not available.
4	Not implemented.
5	Fully operational multi-user state with X window and GUI desktop running. This is the default run level.
6	RHEL reboots.
emergency	Special boot mode to fix any system boot issues. The root file system is mounted in read-only mode.
rescue	Special boot mode to fix issues such as reinstalling a corrupted boot loader. The system needs to be booted with RHEL installation CD/DVD or a bootable USB or CD.

Table 15-1 System Run Levels

Table 15-1 tells that run levels 0 and 6 are used to shutdown and reboot the system. Run levels 1 and s bring the system up into the single user mode where only the system administrator can log in and perform administrative tasks that require all or most system services to be in the stopped state. Network connectivity does not start at these run levels though. Run levels 2 and 3 provide multi-user accessibility into the system. The difference between the two lies at the number of network services started up. Run level 3 has all networking capabilities up, in contrast with run level 2 which has fewer. If X Window software is not installed, run level 3 becomes the default. Run level

4 is not implemented; it may be defined and used in a future release of the operating system. Run level 5 is the default run level at which RHEL is fully functional with all services including networking and X/GUI are operational.

There are two special boot methods that are typically used to fix issues with an unbootable system. These are referred to as *emergency* and *rescue*.

Checking Current and Previous Run Control Levels

To check the current and previous rc levels of the system, use the *who* command with –r option:

who –r
     run-level 5 2008-12-15 10:02   last=3

The output indicates that the system is currently running at run level 5 and its last run level was 3. The output also displays the date and time of the last system run level change.

You may also use the *runlevel* command which displays the previous and current run levels:

runlevel
3 5

Changing Run Control Levels

Run control levels are also referred to as *init* levels because the system uses the *init* command to alter levels. The *shutdown, halt, reboot* and *poweroff* commands are also widely used to change system run levels.

The init Command

The *init* command is used to change run levels. If the system is currently in run level 5 and you want to switch to run level 3, issue the command as follows:

init 3

This command gracefully stops all services and daemons that should not be running at level 3. The command does not affect any other running processes and services.

Similarly, by initiating *init 1* from run level 3, most system services and daemons can be stopped for the system to transition into single user state.

To stop all system services gracefully and take the system to the halt state, pass 0 as an argument to the *init* command:

init 0

Likewise, to stop all system services gracefully, shut down the system and reboot it to the default run level, specify 6 as an argument to the *init* command:

init 6

If the system is running in run level 1 and you wish to bring it up to run level 5, do the following:

init 5

The shutdown Command

The *shutdown* command is more commonly used than the *init* command. It stops all services, processes and daemons in a sequential and consistent fashion as does the *init* command. It broadcasts a message to all logged in users and waits for one minute, by default, for users to log off, after which time it begins stopping services, processes and daemons. It unmounts file systems and proceeds as per the options specified at the command line.

The following examples show options and arguments that can be supplied with *shutdown*:

# **shutdown**	(broadcasts a message, waits for one minute, prompts for confirmation and then takes the system to single user mode).
# **shutdown –hy 300**	(broadcasts a message, waits for 5 minutes and then takes the system to the halt state).
# **shutdown –ry 300**	(broadcasts a message, waits for 5 minutes, stops all services gracefully, shuts down the system and reboots it automatically to the default run control level).
# **shutdown –ry 0**	(broadcasts a message, begins stopping services immediately and gracefully, shuts down the system and reboots it automatically to the default run control level).
# **shutdown –ry now**	(same as "shutdown –ry 0").
# **shutdown –fry now**	(same as "shutdown –ry 0", but will not run *fsck* on reboot).
# **shutdown –Fry now**	(same as "shutdown –ry 0", but will force run *fsck* on reboot).

When the *shutdown* command is initiated to halt the system, you will see messages similar to the following on the system console:

```
Red Hat Enterprise Linux Server release 5.1 (Tikanga)
Kernel 2.6.18-53.el5 on an i686

localhost login: Shutting down smartd:              [  OK  ]
Shutting down Avahi daemon:                          [  OK  ]
Stopping HAL daemon:                                 [  OK  ]
Stopping yum-updatesd:                               [  OK  ]
Stopping atd:                                        [  OK  ]
Stopping cups:                                       [  OK  ]
Stopping hpiod:                                      [  OK  ]
Stopping hpssd:                                      [  OK  ]
Shutting down xfs:                                   [  OK  ]
Shutting down console mouse services:                [  OK  ]
Stopping httpd:                                      [  OK  ]
Stopping sshd:                                       [  OK  ]
Shutting down sm-client:                             [  OK  ]
Shutting down sendmail:                              [  OK  ]
Stopping acpi daemon:                                [  OK  ]
Stopping crond:                                      [  OK  ]
Stopping autofs:   Stopping automount:               [  OK  ]
                                                     [  OK  ]
Shutting down ntpd:                                  [  OK  ]
Stopping system message bus:                         [  OK  ]
Stopping RPC idmapd:                                 [  OK  ]
. . . . . . . .
Turning off swap:                                    [  OK  ]
Turning off quotas:                                  [  OK  ]
Unmounting pipe file systems:                        [  OK  ]
Unmounting file systems:                             [  OK  ]
Halting system...
md: stopping all md devices.
```

Red Hat Certified Technician & Engineer

By default, only *root* can execute the *shutdown* command. If you wish to delegate this responsibility to other users of the system as well, you will need to add entries for the users in the */etc/shutdown.allow* file. This file controls which users can shutdown the system. For example, the following two entries will enable users *aghori* and *bghori* to bring *rhel01* down:

    aghori
    bghori

These users will need to use the –a option with the *shutdown* command, which will force the command to reference the *shutdown.allow* file, verify the username and run the command.

The *shutdown* command actually calls the *init* command behind the scenes to perform run level changes. You may use the *init* command instead. The only two features not available with *init* compared to *shutdown* are that *init* does not broadcast a message and does not wait for a period of time. It starts the run level change process immediately.

The halt, reboot, and poweroff Commands

The *halt* command without any options calls the *shutdown* command with –h signal to shutdown the system:

    # **halt**

The *reboot* command without any options calls the *shutdown* command with –r signal to shutdown and then reboot the system:

    # **reboot**

The *poweroff* command without any options calls the *shutdown* command with –h signal to shutdown the system. If the hardware supports, this command also turns the power of the system off.

    # **poweroff**

You can specify the –f option with any of these commands to shutdown the system immedialtely. This option calls the *kill* command with signal 9 to terminate all running processes, which makes the system go down quickly; however, it introduces the risk of damaging application files and file system structures. It is not recommended to use this option from any multi-user run control levels.

Booting into Specific Run Control Levels

RHEL can be booted into one of several run control levels as identified in Table 15-1. Two special methods of booting an unbootable system are *emergency* and *rescue*. Choosing to boot to a non-default rc level may be achieved either by modifying the initdefault directive in the */etc/inittab* file or entering an appropriate level at the boot loader prompt. Usually, booting into a non-default rc level is done to perform administrative tasks that either cannot be done or cannot be done properly in a multi-user system state. Such tasks may include backing up file systems such as / and */usr*, and troubleshooting a specific problem. For example, if the default rc level is set to 5 but the system does not start the X window system, you might want to boot into rc level 3 and work to fix the X window startup issue. If the system becomes unbootable because of a missing boot-time required command or configuration file, you will need to boot into maintenance or emergency mode. Levels 1 and s enable the system to mount the root file system, which is required to fix any issues related to such files as *etc/fstab* and *etc/inittab*. The rescue mode is typically used when the boot loader is corrupted and requires a repair.

The Boot Process – In a Nutshell

When the system is powered on or reset, it goes through the *boot* process until the login prompt appears. A step-by-step system boot process is presented below:

- ✓ Power on external devices.
- ✓ Power on the system (or virtual partition).
- ✓ System BIOS (*Basic Input/Output System*) is initiated, which runs *Power On Self Test* (POST) on the system hardware components such as processor, memory and I/O, and initializes them.
- ✓ System BIOS locates the boot device and loads the initial boot loader program called GRUB (*Grand Unified Bootloader*) into memory. GRUB is the default boot loader in RHEL 5 and typically resides on the *Master Boot Record* (MBR), which is located on the very first sector of the boot device. GRUB code located in the MBR is referred to as *stage 1*.

 GRUB may alternatively be installed on a disk partition such as /dev/sda1 at RHEL installation time.

- ✓ GRUB stage 1 may call GRUB *stage 1.5*, which understands an ext2 file system called e2fs_stage1_5, and refers to files such as fat_stage1_5, ffs_stage1_5, iso9660_stage1_5, jfs_stage1_5, ufs2_stage1_5, vstafs_stage1_5 and xfs_stage1_5. GRUB stage 1.5 consults the */boot/grub/grub.conf* file for boot directives such as available kernels, their locations, associated ramdisk image, the root file system location and the default kernel to boot.
- ✓ GRUB stage 1 or stage 1.5 calls and loads GRUB *stage 2*, which presents a list of available bootable operating systems to boot. Several commands are available at this point that can be executed from the grub> shell prompt for performing tasks such as booting the system interactively.
- ✓ GRUB stage 2 calls the default kernel, loads it into memory, decompresses and initializes it. It also loads the contents of the root directory into the ramdisk.
- ✓ The kernel initializes and configures hardware as it finds, loads required modules, starts the kernel swapper process called *kswapd*, initializes RAID and LVM virtual devices, creates a root device and mounts the root file system in read-only mode on /.
- ✓ The kernel calls the *init* command from the ramdisk and transfers the control over to it to initiate the system initialization process. The *init* process is also known as the *first process* and it always possesses PID 1.
- ✓ The *init* command references the *inittab* file to determine the default run level to boot into.
- ✓ The *init* command calls the */etc/rc.d/rc.sysinit* script to perform configuration tasks such as initializing the hardware clock, loading kernel modules, configuring kernel parameters, setting the hostname, remounting the root file system in read/write mode, checking and mounting local file systems, activating disk quotas, starting local swap spaces and activating SELinux.
- ✓ The *init* command calls the */etc/rc.d/rc* script to execute all startup scripts needed to bring the system to the default run level.

✓ The *init* command finally runs the */etc/rc.d/rc.local* script and spawns getty messages that display the login prompt. If the default run level is set to 5, the */etc/X11/prefdm* script is called to bring up the default display manager.

Booting – BIOS Initialization Phase

BIOS is a small memory chip in the system which stores the system date and time, list and sequence of boot devices and I/O. This information may be altered as required. Boot devices on newer computers support booting them via CD/DVD, USB drive and other media.

Depending on the computer manufacturer, you may have to press F2, F8, F10, ESC or DEL key to enter BIOS setup. Many computers allow you to press F12 to boot the system off a network-based boot server. Pressing the Esc key on systems displays a boot menu where you can choose a boot source to boot the system off of. The computer goes through the hardware initialization phase that involves detecting and diagnosing connected hardware devices. It runs POST on the devices as found. It installs graphics card and the attached monitor, and begins displaying system messages on the video hardware. It detects the boot device and passes the control over to the GRUB boot loader.

Booting – GRUB Phase

The GRUB boot loader may be installed in the MBR or the */boot* file system. You can interact with GRUB to perform any non-default boot-related tasks such as booting into single user mode, booting into any other non-default modes and booting via a non-default disk such as a CD/DVD or a USB drive. If you wish to boot the system using the default boot device with all configured default settings, do not press any key, as shown below, and let the system go through the autoboot process.

Booting Red Hat Enterprise Linux Server (2.6.18-92.el5) in 5 seconds...

If you choose to interrupt the autoboot process, you will get to the GRUB menu where you can perform a number of tasks such as searching for alternate boot devices, doing a manual boot from a non-default boot device or kernel, viewing or altering boot configuration and booting into a non-default rc level. Figure 15-1 displays the main GRUB menu.

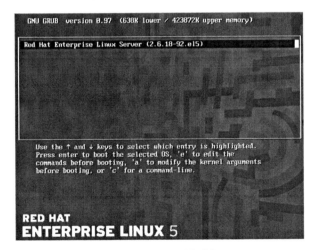

Figure 15-1 GRUB Menu

Three commands are available at the main menu along with the `Enter` key, which boots the highlighted operating system. The commands are listed and explained in Table 15-2.

Command	Description
a	Appends or modifies a kernel argument.
c	Takes you to the grub> command prompt.
e	Edits directives for the highlighted entry before booting.

Table 15-2 GRUB Main Menu Commands

Figure 15-2 shows a picture of boot directives displayed when *e* is typed in the GRUB menu.

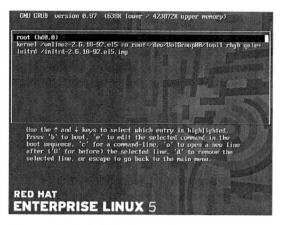

Figure 15-2 GRUB Menu Boot Information

A few commands are available at GRUB's edit menu and are listed and described in Table 15-3.

Command	Description
b	Boots the operating system.
c	Takes you to the grub> command prompt.
e	Edits the highlighted directive.
d	Deletes the highlighted line entry.
o	Opens a new line after the highlighted line entry.
O	Opens a new line before the highlighted line entry.
Esc	Takes you back to the main menu.

Table 15-3 GRUB Edit Menu Commands

Boot Examples

As described, the system can be booted into various rc levels from the GRUB menu. The following text explains how.

Booting into Single User Mode

Booting the system into single user mode allows you to perform maintenance tasks such as changing a forgotten *root* password, modifying a corrupted *passwd, shadow* or *fstab* file, or executing *fsck*. Follow the instructions below to boot into this mode:

Red Hat Certified Technician & Engineer

1. Press any key before the countdown ends to interact with GRUB.
2. Press *a* to go to append mode.
3. Press Spacebar and type *1, s* or *single* and then press Enter to boot.
4. Perform any required maintenance tasks.
5. Execute the *exit* command to boot to the default run level when done. Alternatively, issue the *reboot* or the *shutdown* command to reboot the system into the default rc level.

Booting into rc Level 2 or 3

Booting the system into rc level 2 or 3 starts most system services. Follow the instructions below:

1. Press any key before the countdown ends to interact with GRUB.
2. Press *a* to go to append mode.
3. Press Spacebar and enter the desired rc level. Press Enter to boot.

Booting into Emergency Mode

Booting the system into emergency mode allows you to perform certain maintenance tasks on an unbootable system. Follow the instructions below:

1. Press any key before the countdown ends to interact with GRUB.
2. Press *a* to go to append mode.
3. Press Spacebar and type *emergency*. Press Enter to boot. Enter *root* user password when prompted to get into the emergency mode.
4. Perform any required maintenance tasks.
5. Execute the *exit* command to boot to the default run level when done. Alternatively, issue the *reboot* or the *shutdown* command to reboot the system into the default rc level.

Booting into Rescue Mode

See section "Booting the System into Linux Rescue Mode" in Chapter "System, Network and Security Troubleshooting" for details.

Understanding GRUB Configuration File

It is important that you understand the contents of the GRUB configuration file *grub.conf* located in the */boot/grub* directory. This file has symlinks from */etc/grub.conf* and */boot/grub/menu.lst* files. Here is an excerpt from the default file:

```
# nl /boot/grub/grub.conf
. . . . . . . .
    10  default=0
    11  timeout=5
    12  splashimage=(hd0,0)/grub/splash.xpm.gz
    13  hiddenmenu
    14  title Red Hat Enterprise Linux Server (2.6.18-92.el5)
    15       root (hd0,0)
    16       kernel /vmlinuz-2.6.18-92.el5 ro root=/dev/VolGroup00/lvol1 rhgb quiet
    17       initrd /initrd-2.6.18-92.el5.img
```

The line contents from the file are explained below:

- ✓ Line #10: Sets default kernel, as defined with the corresponding "title" (line #14), to boot. If the value is set to 1, it would point to the next kernel associated with "title", and so on for subsequent values.
- ✓ Line #11: Gives you 5 seconds to interrupt the autoboot process to interact with the GRUB menu.
- ✓ Line #12: Sets the location of the graphical GRUB screen. The value indicates the first partition on the first disk located at /boot/grub/splash.xpm.gz.
- ✓ Line #13: Instructs the system to hide the GRUB menu until a key is pressed to interrupt the autoboot process.
- ✓ Line #14: Specifies a name or short description of an available kernel.
- ✓ Line #15: Sub-entry that points to the location of the boot partition. Entry from the file means the first partition on the first disk (as defined in /boot/grub/device.map file).

> # **cat /boot/grub/device.map**
> (hd0)   /dev/sda

- ✓ Line #16: Sub-entry that specifies the kernel file name and its location with respect to /boot. The entry further indicates that the kernel is loaded read-only from the root logical volume at /dev/VolGroup01/lvol1 and is booted in graphical mode "rhgb" (Red Hat Graphical Boot) with all non-critical boot messages hidden "quiet".
- ✓ Line #17: Sub-entry that initializes the RAM disk so the kernel starts up and mounts an initial root file system from /boot/initrd-2.6.18-92.el5.img. This file is created when the kernel is built. It may also be recreated if needed, using the *mkinitrd* command.

Managing GRUB

There are a number of commands accessible at the grub> prompt for GRUB and other pre-boot management tasks. Press the TAB key at the grub> prompt to see the list (Figure 15-3). Usage of some of these commands is demonstrated in this sub-section.

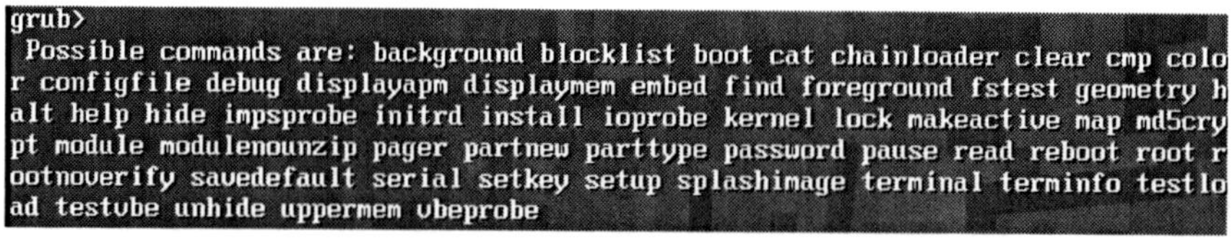

Figure 15-3 GRUB Management Commands

To find which disk and partition contains the *grub.conf* file in the /boot/grub directory:

> grub> **find /grub/grub.conf**
> (hd0,0)

To view the contents of the *grub.conf* file:

> grub> **cat /grub/grub.conf**

To obtain information about the root partition:

grub> **root**
(hd0,0): Filesystem type is ext2fs, partition type 0x83

To load the root partition that resides in the first partition on the first hard drive:

grub> **root (hd0,0)**
Filesystem type is ext2fs, partition type 0x83

To install GRUB in MBR if it has been corrupted. Specify (hd0) if GRUB is to be installed on the first partition of the first hard drive.

grub> **setup (hd0)**
Checking if "/boot/grub/stage1" exists... no
Checking if "/grub/stage1" exists... yes
Checking if "/grub/stage2" exists... yes
Checking if "/grub/e2fs_stage1_5" exists... yes
Running "embed /grub/e2fs_stage1_5 (hd0)"... 15 sectors are embedded.
succeeded
Running "install /grub/stage1 (hd0) (hd0)1+15 p (hd0,0)/grub/stage2 p /grub/grub.conf"... succeeded
Done.

Booting – Kernel Initialization Phase

GRUB initializes the kernel and loads it into the memory. Several messages appear on the console during kernel initialization depending on the hardware and system configuration. These messages are logged to the */var/log/dmesg* file and can be viewed later with a *more* on the file or the *dmesg* command. The messages include information about kernel version, memory, CPU, console, SELinux status, disks, root logical volume or partition, network interfaces and swap logical volumes/partitions.

An excerpt from the *dmesg* file is shown below:

cat /var/log/dmesg
Linux version 2.6.18-92.el5 (brewbuilder@hs20-bc2-3.build.redhat.com) (gcc versi
on 4.1.2 20071124 (Red Hat 4.1.2-41)) #1 SMP Tue Apr 29 13:16:12 EDT 2008
BIOS-provided physical RAM map:
 BIOS-e820: 0000000000000000 - 000000000009f800 (usable)
 BIOS-e820: 000000000009f800 - 00000000000a0000 (reserved)

. . . .
0MB HIGHMEM available.
416MB LOWMEM available.
found SMP MP-table at 000f6ce0
Memory for crash kernel (0x0 to 0x0) notwithin permissible range
disabling kdump
Using x86 segment limits to approximate NX protection
On node 0 totalpages: 106496
 DMA zone: 4096 pages, LIFO batch:0
 Normal zone: 102400 pages, LIFO batch:31
DMI present.

Using APIC driver default

. . . .

Allocating PCI resources starting at 20000000 (gap: 1a000000:e4c00000)
Detected 1993.825 MHz processor.
Built 1 zonelists. Total pages: 106496
Kernel command line: ro root=/dev/VolGroup00/lvol1 rhgb quiet

. . . .

Memory: 414448k/425984k available (2095k kernel code, 10920k reserved, 874k data
, 228k init, 0k highmem)
Checking if this processor honours the WP bit even in supervisor mode... Ok.
Calibrating delay using timer specific routine.. 4057.59 BogoMIPS (lpj=2028799)
Security Framework v1.0.0 initialized
SELinux: Initializing.
SELinux: Starting in permissive mode

. . . .

Adding 8191992k swap on /dev/VolGroup00/lvol7. Priority:-1 extents:1 across:8191992k
Adding 204792k swap on /data2/fs_swap1. Priority:-2 extents:52 across:207268k
SELinux: initialized (dev binfmt_misc, type binfmt_misc), uses genfs_contexts

The Linux kernel is modular. During loading in the memory, it loads device drivers for installed hardware as well as supporting software modules for components such as the ext3 filesystem type. The *lsmod* command can be used to list the loaded modules:

lsmod

Module	Size	Used by	
autofs4	24517	2	
hidp	23105	2	
rfcomm	42457	0	
l2cap	29505	10	hidp,rfcomm
bluetooth	53797	5	hidp,rfcomm,l2cap
sunrpc	144893	1	
ipv6	258273	16	
xfrm_nalgo	13765	1	ipv6
crypto_api	11969	1	xfrm_nalgo
dm_multipath	22089	0	
raid456	120145	0	
xor	18249	1	raid456
video	21193	0	
sbs	18533	0	
backlight	10049	1	video

. . . .

Booting – First Boot (init) Phase

The kernel calls the */sbin/init* command and transfers the control over to it to initiate the system initialization process known as *first process*. The *init* command looks into the */etc/inittab* file to determine the default run control level for the system to boot into. The file also contains the system initialization script */etc/rc.d/rc.sysinit*, virtual consoles, etc.

Understanding /etc/inittab File

A sample *inittab* file is shown below. The first uncommented line in the file defines the default run control level, which is 5.

 # cat /etc/inittab

```
. . . . . . . .
id:5:initdefault:

# System initialization.
si::sysinit:/etc/rc.d/rc.sysinit

l0:0:wait:/etc/rc.d/rc 0
l1:1:wait:/etc/rc.d/rc 1
l2:2:wait:/etc/rc.d/rc 2
l3:3:wait:/etc/rc.d/rc 3
l4:4:wait:/etc/rc.d/rc 4
l5:5:wait:/etc/rc.d/rc 5
l6:6:wait:/etc/rc.d/rc 6

# Trap CTRL-ALT-DELETE
ca::ctrlaltdel:/sbin/shutdown -t3 -r now

# When our UPS tells us power has failed, assume we have a few minutes
# of power left.  Schedule a shutdown for 2 minutes from now.
# This does, of course, assume you have powerd installed and your
# UPS connected and working correctly.
pf::powerfail:/sbin/shutdown -f -h +2 "Power Failure; System Shutting Down"

# If power was restored before the shutdown kicked in, cancel it.
pr:12345:powerokwait:/sbin/shutdown -c "Power Restored; Shutdown Cancelled"

# Run gettys in standard runlevels
1:2345:respawn:/sbin/mingetty tty1
2:2345:respawn:/sbin/mingetty tty2
3:2345:respawn:/sbin/mingetty tty3
4:2345:respawn:/sbin/mingetty tty4
5:2345:respawn:/sbin/mingetty tty5
6:2345:respawn:/sbin/mingetty tty6

# Run xdm in runlevel 5
x:5:respawn:/etc/X11/prefdm -nodaemon
```

As you can see, there are four fields per line entry separated by the colon character. The fields are:

- ✓ The first field defines a unique identification string containing 1–4 characters.
- ✓ The second field identifies run levels at which the entry is executed. An empty field is valid for all run levels.

✓ The third field determines an action to be taken. There are many possible actions, some of which are:

initdefault – this action determines the default run level for the system. The *init* command reads this line and boots the system to the specified run level.
sysinit – this action executes the specified process before *init* tries to access the system console.
wait – when an entry with this action is executed, other entries at the same run level wait for its completion before their turn comes.
respawn – restarts the specified process as soon as it dies. If the process is running, no action is taken.

✓ The fourth field defines the fully qualified pathname to the process or command that is to be executed along with any arguments.

If *inittab* is modified, you need to force the *init* process to re-read the updated information from the file by running any of the following as *root*:

 # init q
 # kill –HUP 1

Understanding Virtual Console Screens

In Chapter 09 "Installation" it is mentioned that five virtual console screens are available during text mode RHEL installation (and six in graphical mode), which can be switched by pressing a combination of keys. The same concept applies once RHEL is installed and is up and running. Unlike during installation, you can now invoke up to 12 virtual consoles of which 7 are pre-defined and the rest can be defined. The same key combination is used to switch among the consoles as described in Chapter 09. The seventh console screen is dedicated to display graphics only. Virtual consoles are defined in the *inittab* file:

```
# Run gettys in standard runlevels
1:2345:respawn:/sbin/mingetty tty1
2:2345:respawn:/sbin/mingetty tty2
3:2345:respawn:/sbin/mingetty tty3
4:2345:respawn:/sbin/mingetty tty4
5:2345:respawn:/sbin/mingetty tty5
6:2345:respawn:/sbin/mingetty tty6
```

Starting System and Network Services

Next, the *init* command executes the */etc/rc.d/rc.sysinit* script, which calls appropriate scripts and commands to configure networking, SELinux, keyboard mapping, hardware clock and hostname. The script activates swapping, runs *fsck* on file systems, mounts them, activates disk quota and loads kernel modules in addition to other tasks defined in it.

The *init* command then calls the */etc/rc.d/rc* script and passes the initdefault value from the *inittab* file as an argument to it. This script locates services to be started in the sequencer directories */etc/rc.d/rc#.d*, gets configuration information from the startup configuration files located in the */etc/sysconfig* directory, and starts them up from the initialization directory */etc/rc.d/init.d*.

Red Hat Certified Technician & Engineer

Here is a list of the sequencer and initialization directories along with other scripts located there:

ll /etc/rc.d
```
drwxr-xr-x 2 root root  4096 Dec 19 18:17 /etc/rc.d/init.d
-rwxr-xr-x 1 root root  2255 Sep 21  2006 /etc/rc.d/rc
drwxr-xr-x 2 root root  4096 Dec 19 18:17 /etc/rc.d/rc0.d
drwxr-xr-x 2 root root  4096 Dec 19 18:17 /etc/rc.d/rc1.d
drwxr-xr-x 2 root root  4096 Dec 20 00:44 /etc/rc.d/rc2.d
drwxr-xr-x 2 root root  4096 Dec 20 00:45 /etc/rc.d/rc3.d
drwxr-xr-x 2 root root  4096 Dec 20 00:44 /etc/rc.d/rc4.d
drwxr-xr-x 2 root root  4096 Dec 20 00:45 /etc/rc.d/rc5.d
drwxr-xr-x 2 root root  4096 Dec 19 18:17 /etc/rc.d/rc6.d
-rwxr-xr-x 1 root root   220 Jun 23  2003 /etc/rc.d/rc.local
-rwxr-xr-x 1 root root 26376 Jan 19  2007 /etc/rc.d/rc.sysinit
```

The following shows contents of the *rc0.d* directory. Notice that all scripts are mere symlinks to the actual start/stop scripts located in the */etc/rc.d/init.d* directory.

ll /etc/rc.d/rc0.d
```
total 268
lrwxrwxrwx 1 root root 28 Aug 16 07:34 K02cups-config-daemon -> ../init.d/cups-config-daemon
lrwxrwxrwx 1 root root 19 Aug 16 07:31 K02haldaemon -> ../init.d/haldaemon
lrwxrwxrwx 1 root root 24 Aug 23 08:29 K02NetworkManager -> ../init.d/NetworkManager
lrwxrwxrwx 1 root root 20 Aug 16 07:31 K03messagebus -> ../init.d/messagebus
lrwxrwxrwx 1 root root 15 Aug 16 07:32 K03rhnsd -> ../init.d/rhnsd
lrwxrwxrwx 1 root root 17 Aug 16 07:32 K05anacron -> ../init.d/anacron
lrwxrwxrwx 1 root root 13 Aug 16 07:32 K05atd -> ../init.d/atd
lrwxrwxrwx 1 root root 19 Aug 16 07:31 K05saslauthd -> ../init.d/saslauthd
lrwxrwxrwx 1 root root 14 Aug 16 07:33 K10cups -> ../init.d/cups
lrwxrwxrwx 1 root root 19 Aug 16 07:33 K10dc_server -> ../init.d/dc_server
  . . . . . . . .
```

The following lists directory contents of *rc5.d*:

ll /etc/rc.d/rc5.d
```
total 260
lrwxrwxrwx 1 root root 24 Aug 23 08:29 K02NetworkManager -> ../init.d/NetworkManager
lrwxrwxrwx 1 root root 19 Aug 16 07:31 K05saslauthd -> ../init.d/saslauthd
lrwxrwxrwx 1 root root 19 Aug 16 07:33 K10dc_server -> ../init.d/dc_server
lrwxrwxrwx 1 root root 16 Aug 16 07:32 K10psacct -> ../init.d/psacct
lrwxrwxrwx 1 root root 19 Aug 16 07:33 K12dc_client -> ../init.d/dc_client
lrwxrwxrwx 1 root root 13 Aug 16 07:32 K20nfs -> ../init.d/nfs
lrwxrwxrwx 1 root root 14 Aug 16 07:32 K24irda -> ../init.d/irda
lrwxrwxrwx 1 root root 15 Aug 16 07:33 K25squid -> ../init.d/squid
lrwxrwxrwx 1 root root 22 Aug 16 07:36 K30spamassassin -> ../init.d/spamassassin
lrwxrwxrwx 1 root root 18 Jan   2 14:09 K34dhcrelay -> ../init.d/dhcrelay
lrwxrwxrwx 1 root root 15 Jan   2 14:09 K35dhcpd -> ../init.d/dhcpd
  . . . . . . . .
```

There are six sequencer directories – *rc0.d, rc1.d, rc2.d, rc3.d, rc4.d, rc5.d* and *rc6.d* – corresponding to the six rc levels. There are two types of scripts located in these directories: *start* and *kill*. The names of the start scripts begin with an uppercase S and that for the kill scripts with an uppercase K. These scripts are symbolically linked to actual start/kill scripts located in the */etc/rc.d/init.d* directory. Each start/kill script contains "start", "stop", "status", "restart", "reload" and "condrestart" functions corresponding to service start, stop, status check, stop and start, configuration file re-read, and restart only if it is already running. The contents of one of the scripts */etc/rc.d/init.d/cups*, is shown below as an example:

cat /etc/rc.d/init.d/cups

```
. . . . . . . .
start () {
        echo -n $"Starting $prog: "

        # start daemon
        daemon $DAEMON
        RETVAL=$?
        echo
        [ $RETVAL = 0 ] && touch /var/lock/subsys/cups
        return $RETVAL
}

stop () {
        # stop daemon
        echo -n $"Stopping $prog: "
        killproc $DAEMON
        RETVAL=$?
        echo
        [ $RETVAL = 0 ] && rm -f /var/lock/subsys/cups
}

restart() {
        stop
        start
}

case $1 in
        start)
                start
        ;;
        stop)
                stop
        ;;
        restart)
                restart
        ;;
        condrestart)
                [ -f /var/lock/subsys/cups ] && restart || :
        ;;
```

```
reload)
    echo -n $"Reloading $prog: "
    killproc $DAEMON -HUP
    RETVAL=$?
    echo
;;
status)
    status $DAEMON
    RETVAL=$?
;;
restartlog)
    stop
    cat /dev/null >/var/log/cups/error_log
    start
;;
*)

    echo $"Usage: $prog {start|stop|restart|condrestart|reload|status}"
    exit 3
esac

exit $RETVAL
```

Majority of the scripts located in lower numbered sequencer directories are kill scripts and as you go to higher numbered directories, you will find increasing number of start scripts.

When the system comes up, S scripts are executed one after the other in the ascending numerical sequence from the *rc1.d*, *rc2.d*, *rc3.d* and *rc5.d* directories. Similarly, when the system goes down, K scripts are executed one after the other in the descending numerical sequence from the *rc5.d*, *rc3.d*, *rc2.d*, *rc1.d* and *rc0.d* directories.

The following lists configuration files for the start/kill scripts placed in the */etc/sysconfig* configuration directory:

 # ll /etc/sysconfig
```
total 488
-rw-r--r--   1 root root  4765 Aug 22  2006 apmd
drwxr-xr-x 2 root root  4096 Dec 19 08:47 apm-scripts
-rw-r-----   1 root root   514 Aug 20 14:33 auditd
-rw-r--r--   1 root root   245 Dec 19 18:18 authconfig
-rw-r--r--   1 root root  1419 Sep 25 11:20 autofs
-rw-r--r--   1 root root   232 Oct  2  2006 bluetooth
drwxr-xr-x 2 root root  4096 Dec 19 08:41 cbq
-rw-r--r--   1 root root   180 Dec 20 00:45 clock
-rw-r--r--   1 root root   903 Jun 28  2007 conman
drwxr-xr-x 2 root root  4096 Aug  7 11:51 console
-rw-r--r--   1 root root  2377 Jun 27  2007 cpuspeed
-rw-r--r--   1 root root   512 Jun 22  2007 crond
-rw-r--r--   1 root root     0 Dec 19 18:18 desktop
. . . . . . . .
```

The following listing from the */etc/rc.d/init.d* directory shows actual start/kill scripts:

```
# ll /etc/rc.d/init.d
total 812
-rwxr-xr-x 1 root root 1128 Oct 10  2006 acpid
-rwxr-xr-x 1 root root 1441 Dec 18  2006 anacron
-rwxr-xr-x 1 root root 1429 Aug 22  2006 apmd
-rwxr-xr-x 1 root root 1176 Aug 23  2006 atd
-rwxr-xr-x 1 root root 3114 Apr 20  2008 auditd
-rwxr-xr-x 1 root root 2461 Apr  3  2008 autofs
-rwxr-xr-x 1 root root 1848 Jan  8  2007 avahi-daemon
-rwxr-xr-x 1 root root 1789 Jan  8  2007 avahi-dnsconfd
-rwxr-xr-x 1 root root 1477 Oct  2  2006 bluetooth
-rwxr-xr-x 1 root root 1357 Nov 20  2007 capi
-rwxr-xr-x 1 root root 1470 Jun 28  2007 conman
-rwxr-xr-x 1 root root 7654 Mar  6  2008 cpuspeed
-rwxr-xr-x 1 root root 1904 Jun 22  2007 crond
-rwxr-xr-x 1 root root 1942 Mar 20  2008 cups
. . . . . . . .
```

System Boot Log File

Log information for each service startup at system boot is captured in the */var/log/boot.log* file. You may want to scroll through this file after the system has been booted up to view which services started up successfully and which did not. Here is a sample from the file:

```
# cat /var/log/boot.log
. . . . . . . .
Jan  4 14:49:08 rhel01 sysctl: net.ipv4.conf.default.rp_filter = 1
Jan  4 14:49:08 rhel01 sysctl: net.ipv4.conf.default.accept_source_route = 0
Jan  4 14:49:08 rhel01 sysctl: kernel.sysrq = 0
Jan  4 14:49:08 rhel01 sysctl: kernel.core_uses_pid = 1
Jan  4 14:49:08 rhel01 network: Setting network parameters:  succeeded
Jan  4 14:49:08 rhel01 network: Bringing up loopback interface:  succeeded
Jan  4 14:49:09 rhel01 ifup:
Jan  4 14:49:09 rhel01 ifup: Determining IP information for eth0...
. . . . . . . .
```

Managing Services

There are several system and network services that RHEL provides, which can be configured to start automatically at each system reboot. These services can also be configured to not start at system boot. Moreover, the automatic start and stop can be defined at individual rc levels. For example, you may want the NFS client service to start only at run levels 3 and 5, and remain inactive at 2. Besides, you can view the operational status of a service and can force it to reload its configuration. A service can also be restarted manually.

There are commands, a menu-driven program and a graphical tool available to manage service start and stop, and are explained in the following sub-sections.

Managing Service Start and Stop via Commands

RHEL provides the *chkconfig* and *service* commands to manage service start/stop at the command prompt. The *chkconfig* command gives you the ability to display service start and stop settings, and set a service to start and stop at appropriate rc levels. The *service* command allows you to start, stop, restart, check status of or conditionally start a service. This command also enables you to force the service to reload its configuration information if there has been any change.

Listing, Disabling and Enabling a Service

Following examples show how to use the *chkconfig* command to list, enable and disable a service.

To display the current startup configuration for the *ntpd* service:

> **# chkconfig --list ntpd**
> ntpd 0:off   1:off   2:off   3:on   4:on   5:on   6:off

The output indicates that *ntpd* service is set to start only at run levels 3, 4 and 5. Since run level 4 has no meaning, you can turn it off. Here is how you can set a service to not start at a particular rc level:

> **# chkconfig --level 4 ntpd off**

To confirm:

> **# chkconfig --list ntpd**
> ntpd   0:off   1:off   2:off   3:on   **4:off**   5:on   6:off

To list run level start/stop assignments for all services on the system:

> **# chkconfig --list**
> NetworkManager   0:off   1:off   2:off   3:off   4:off   5:off   6:off
> NetworkManagerDispatcher 0:off   1:off   2:off   3:off   4:off   5:off   6:off
> acpid   0:off   1:off   2:off   3:on   4:on   5:on   6:off
> anacron   0:off   1:off   2:on   3:on   4:on   5:on   6:off
> . . . .
> xinetd based services:
>   chargen-dgram: off
>   chargen-stream: off
>   cvs: off
> . . . .

To enable or disable a service at all run levels, do the following. The first command enables the *ntpd* service to start at all run levels and the second disables it from starting at all run levels. Note that a service need not be defined to start at run levels 0, 1 and 6. In fact, the *chkconfig* command does not affect these levels when run the following way:

> **# chkconfig ntpd on**
> **# chkconfig --list ntpd**
> ntpd   0:off   1:off   2:on   3:on   4:on   5:on   6:off

```
# chkconfig ntpd off
# chkconfig --list ntpd
ntpd              0:off      1:off      2:off      3:off      4:off      5:off      6:off
```

The *chkconfig* command can also be used to add a new service or delete an existing service using the --add or --delete option, respectively. The service must already be available for the add or delete operation.

Checking Service Operational Status

The *service* command can be used to list the operational status (running or stopped) of all system services. The command below depicts that information:

```
# service --status-all
acpid (pid 4548) is running...
anacron is stopped
atd (pid 4706) is running...
auditd (pid 4252) is running...
automount (pid 4529) is running...
Avahi daemon is running
Avahi DNS daemon is not running
hcid (pid 4425) is running...
sdpd (pid 4431) is running...
capi not installed - No such file or directory (2)
conmand is stopped
cpuspeed is stopped
crond (pid 4654) is running...
cupsd (pid 4590) is running...
. . . . . . . .
```

Starting and Stopping a Service Manually

Following examples show how to use the *service* command to start and stop a service.

Run one of the following without any arguments to check available switches:

```
# service ntpd
# /etc/rc.d/init.d/ntpd
Usage: /etc/rc.d/init.d/ntpd {start|stop|restart|condrestart|status}
```

The command displays the usage of the script. There are five options – start the service, stop the service, stop and then start the service in one go, restart the service conditionally and check the operational status of the service.

To start the *ntpd* service, do one of the following:

```
# service ntpd start
# /etc/rc.d/init.d/ntpd start
Starting ntpd:                                    [ OK ]
```

To stop the service, do one of the following:

```
# service ntpd stop
# /etc/rc.d/init.d/ntpd stop
Shutting down ntpd:                              [ OK ]
```

To stop and start the service in one go, do one of the following:

```
# service ntpd restart
# /etc/rc.d/init.d/ntpd restart
Shutting down ntpd:                              [ OK ]
Starting ntpd:                                   [ OK ]
```

To check the operational status of the service, do one of the following:

```
# service ntpd status
# /etc/rc.d/init.d/ntpd status
ntpd (pid 5205 5203) is running...
```

Managing Service Start and Stop via Menu-Driven Program

RHEL provides a menu-driven program called *ntsysv* to manage service start/stop. Here is an example to demonstrate the usage of this tool.

To enable several services at run levels 2 and 3, run the *ntsysv* command as follows. It will bring up a window as shown in Figure 15-4 that will list all available services. Select the ones you want to enable and press OK.

```
# ntsysv --level 23
```

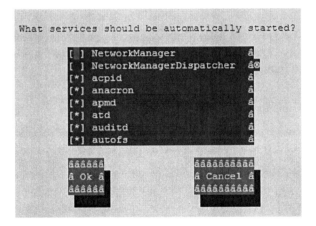

Figure 15-4 Service Management via Menu-Driven Program

By specifying run levels at the command prompt this way, you are directing *ntsysv* to modify start/stop only at those run levels for the services that you are going to be selecting.

Managing Service Start and Stop via Service Configurator

Figure 15-5 displays the Red Hat Service Configurator interface, which is invoked via either the *serviceconf* or the *system-config-services* command in an X terminal window. Alternatively, you can invoke the program as (GNOME) System / (KDE) Main Menu → Administration → Server Settings → Services.

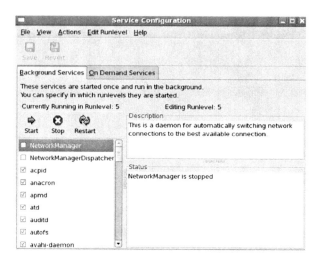

Figure 15-5 Service Management via Service Configurator

Click "Edit Runlevel" at the top and choose a run level to configure start/stop of one or more services. Scroll up or down to look for desired services in the left hand window pane and check or uncheck the boxes as needed. This ensures that the service will start and stop at appropriate run levels. As well, you can highlight a service and start, stop or restart it by clicking a button above it.

The other tab in the Service Configurator allows you to configure on-demand services as defined in the */etc/xinetd.d* directory. Detailed information on the on-demand services is covered in Chapter 24 "Internet Services and Electronic Mail".

Summary

In this chapter, you learned how to shutdown a RHEL system using tools at your disposal. You saw different run control levels that a system could run at, and how to switch from one to another.

You learned system boot process that covered pre-boot administration tasks, and kernel and system initialization. Pre-boot administration included interacting with BIOS and GRUB, and booting into specific run levels. Kernel initialization included viewing messages generated during system startup, and system initialization included an explanation of key initialization file, virtual console screens, and an understanding of sequencer directories, startup scripts and configuration files that were run to bring a system to a fully functional state.

You examined how to configure one or more services to autostart or remain stopped at specific rc levels using commands, a menu-driven program and a graphical interface.

## 16

Linux Kernel

This chapter covers the following major topics:

- ✓ Overview of Linux kernel
- ✓ Anatomy of kernel version
- ✓ Kernel directory structure
- ✓ Load and unload modules
- ✓ Update, upgrade and patch kernel
- ✓ Obtain and install kernel source code
- ✓ Modify or create kernel configuration file
- ✓ Build a new kernel
- ✓ Copy kernel files to create boot CD

The kernel controls everything inside-out on a system that runs the Linux operating system. It controls system hardware including memory, processors, disks and I/O devices; runs, schedules and manages processes and service daemons; enforces security and access controls; and so on. The kernel receives instructions from the shell, engages appropriate hardware resources and acts as instructed.

Overview

The Linux kernel is a set of software components called *modules* that work together coherently as a single unit to enable programs, services and applications to run smoothly and efficiently on the system. Modules are basically *device drivers* used for controlling hardware devices such as controller cards and peripheral devices, as well as software components such as LVM, file systems and RAID. Some of these modules are static to the kernel while others are loaded automatically and dynamically as necessary.

When the system is booted, the kernel is loaded into memory with all static modules. The dynamic modules are separately and individually loaded when needed. A linux kernel that comprises of static modules only is referred to as a *monolithic* kernel and a linux kernel that includes dynamic modules as well is known as a *modular* kernel.

A monolithic kernel is typically larger in size than a modular kernel since it includes all components that may or may not be required at all times. This makes a monolithic kernel occupy more physical memory and less efficient.

A modular kernel, on the other hand, is made up of mere critical and essential components, and loads dynamic modules automatically as and when needed. This makes a modular kernel occupy less physical memory as compared to a monolithic kernel, faster and more efficient in terms of overall performance, and less vulnerable to crashes. Another benefit of a modular kernel is that software driver updates only require the associated module recomplile without a system reboot. It does not need an entire kernel recompile.

RHEL distributions come standard with several types of kernels that are designed for diverse processor architectures such as 32-bit and 64-bit Intel/AMD (i386/i686), 64-bit Itanium 2 (ia64), 64-bit PowerPC, and IBM System z and 390 mainframes. The *uname* command with –m option tells the architecture of the system. At RHEL installation, the installer program automatically chooses the regular kernel that best suits the processor architecture. Files related to kernel architectures are installed in */boot* directory. The regular kernel supports not more than 4GB of physical memory on a system with one or more processors. Additional kernels – kernel-PAE and kernel-xen – are also available for each supported architecture, which provide support for systems with multiple processors and physical memory beyond 4GB (up to 64GB), and allow for constructing several virtual machines on a single system. Optional software packages such as kernel-devel and kernel-headers may also be loaded to get device drivers and associated header information. RHEL distribution also includes source code for the kernel.

The default kernel installed during installation is usually adequate for most system needs; however, it requires a rebuild when a new functionality is added or removed. The new functionality may be introduced by updating or upgrading the kernel, installing a new hardware device or changing a critical system component. Likewise, an existing functionality that is no longer needed may be removed to make the kernel smaller resulting in improved performance and reduced memory utilization.

To control the behavior of the modules, and the kernel in general, several tunable parameters are set, which define a baseline for the kernel functionality. Some of these parameters must be tuned to allow certain applications and database software to be installed smoothly and function properly.

RHEL allows you to generate and store several custom kernels with varying configuration and required modules included, but only one of them active at a time. Other kernels may be loaded by rebooting the system and selecting an alternate kernel.

Checking and Understanding Kernel Version

To check the version of the kernel, run the *uname* or the *rpm* command:

```
# uname –r
2.6.18-92.el5
# rpm –q kernel
kernel-2.6.18-92.el5
```

The output indicates that the kernel version currently in use is 2.6.18-92.el5. An anatomy of the version is displayed in Figure 16-1 and explained below.

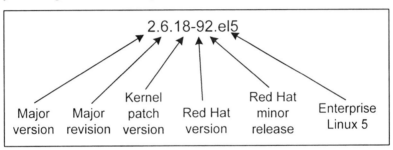

Figure 16-1 Kernel Version Anatomy

From left to right:

✓ (2) indicates that this is the second major version of the Linux kernel. The major number changes when there are significant alterations, enhancements and updates to the previous major version.
✓ (6) indicates that this is the sixth major revision of the second major version.
✓ (18) indicates that this is the eighteenth patched version of this kernel to fix minor bugs and security holes, add minor enhancements and so on.
✓ (9) indicates that this is the ninth version of Red Hat customized kernel.
✓ (2) indicates that this is the second build of the ninth version of the Red Hat customized kernel.
✓ (el5) indicates that this kernel is for Red Hat Enterprise Linux 5.

A further analysis indicates that 2.6.18 holds general Linux kernel version information and the following letters and numbers represent Red Hat specific information.

Understanding Kernel Directory Structure

Kernel files are stored at different locations in the system directory hierarchy of which four locations – */boot*, */proc*, */lib/modules* and */usr/src* – are of significance, and are explained in subsequent sub-sections.

The /boot File System

The */boot* file system is created at system installation time and its purpose is to store kernel-related information including current working kernel and associated files. This file system also stores any updated or modified kernel data. An *ll* on */boot* displays the following information:

```
# ll /boot
total 27575
-rw-r--r--   1 root root     64551 Oct  10 16:43 config-2.6.18-92.el5
drwxr-xr-x 2 root root      1024 Jan  17 21:12 grub
-rw-------  1 root root 3104359 Dec 19 18:18 initrd-2.6.18-92.el5.img
drwx------ 2 root root     12288 Dec 19 08:34 lost+found
-rw-r--r--   1 root root     87586 Oct  10 16:44 symvers-2.6.18-92.el5.gz
-rw-r--r--   1 root root   903969 Oct  10 16:43 System.map-2.6.18-92.el5
-rw-r--r--   1 root root 1791572 Oct  10 16:43 vmlinuz-2.6.18-92.el5
```

The output indicates that the current kernel is *vmlinuz-2.6.18-92.el5*, its boot image is stored in the *initrd-2.6.18-92.el5.img* file and configuration is located in the *config-2.6.18-92.el5* file.

A sub-directory */boot/grub* contains GRUB information as shown below:

```
# ll /boot/grub
total 304
-rw-r--r--    1 root root        63 Dec 12 03:39 device.map
-rw-r--r--    1 root root      7584 Dec 12 03:39 e2fs_stage1_5
-rw-r--r--    1 root root      7456 Dec 12 03:39 fat_stage1_5
-rw-r--r--    1 root root      6720 Dec 12 03:39 ffs_stage1_5
-rw-------   1 root root       621 Dec 12 03:39 grub.conf
-rw-r--r--    1 root root      6720 Dec 12 03:39 iso9660_stage1_5
-rw-r--r--    1 root root      8192 Dec 12 03:39 jfs_stage1_5
lrwxrwxrwx 1 root root        11 Dec 12 03:39 menu.lst -> ./grub.conf
-rw-r--r--    1 root root      6880 Dec 12 03:39 minix_stage1_5
-rw-r--r--    1 root root      9248 Dec 12 03:39 reiserfs_stage1_5
-rw-r--r--    1 root root     32428 Jan   4 2007 splash.xpm.gz
-rw-r--r--    1 root root       512 Dec 12 03:39 stage1
-rw-r--r--    1 root root 104988 Dec 12 03:39 stage2
-rw-r--r--    1 root root      7072 Dec 12 03:39 ufs2_stage1_5
-rw-r--r--    1 root root      6272 Dec 12 03:39 vstafs_stage1_5
-rw-r--r--    1 root root      8896 Dec 12 03:39 xfs_stage1_5
```

The key file in */boot/grub* is *grub.conf*, which maintains a list of available kernels and defines the default kernel to load at boot. Here is an excerpt from this file:

```
# cat /boot/grub/grub.conf
. . . . . . . .
default=0
timeout=5
splashimage=(hd0,0)/grub/splash.xpm.gz
hiddenmenu
title Red Hat Enterprise Linux Server (2.6.18-92.el5)
        root (hd0,0)
        kernel /vmlinuz-2.6.18-92.el5 ro root=/dev/VolGroup00/lvol1 rhgb quiet
        initrd /initrd-2.6.18-92.el5.img
```

For an explanation of line items in this file, refer to Chapter "Shutdown and Boot".

The /proc File System

/proc is a virtual file system that is created in memory. Its contents are created at system boot and destroyed when the system is shut off. Underneath this file system lie current hardware configuration and status information. A directory listing of */proc* is provided below:

```
# ll /proc
. . . . . . . .
dr-xr-xr-x   5  root  root  0  Jan  2 21:13  1
dr-xr-xr-x   5  root  root  0  Jan  2 21:14 10
dr-xr-xr-x   5  root  root  0  Jan  2 21:14 11

. . . . . . . .
dr-xr-xr-x   5  root  root  0  Jan  2 22:32 72
dr-xr-xr-x  11  root  root  0  Jan  2 22:33 acpi
-r--r--r--   1  root  root  0  Jan  2 23:19 buddyinfo
dr-xr-xr-x   6  root  root  0  Jan  2 22:32 bus
-r--r--r--   1  root  root  0  Jan  2 23:19 cmdline
-r--r--r--   1  root  root  0  Jan  2 23:19 cpuinfo
-r--r--r--   1  root  root  0  Jan  2 23:19 crypto
-r--r--r--   1  root  root  0  Jan  2 23:19 devices
. . . . . . . .
```

The output displays several files and sub-directories. Some sub-directory names are numerical and contain information about a specific process with process ID matching the sub-directory name. Within each sub-directory, there are files and further sub-directories, which include information such as memory segment specific to that particular process. Other files and sub-directories contain configuration data for system components. If you wish to view configuration information for a specific item such as the CPU or memory, *cat* the contents of *cpuinfo* and *meminfo* files as shown below:

```
# cat /proc/cpuinfo
processor          : 0
vendor_id          : GenuineIntel
cpu family         : 6
model              : 15
```

```
model name        : Intel(R) Core(TM)2 Duo CPU    T7250  @ 2.00GHz
stepping          : 8
cpu MHz           : 1993.883
cache size        : 2048 KB
fdiv_bug          : no
hlt_bug           : no
f00f_bug          : no
coma_bug          : no
. . . . . . . .
```

cat /proc/meminfo

```
MemTotal:     807660 kB
MemFree:      138492 kB
Buffers:      169164 kB
Cached:       387492 kB
SwapCached:        0 kB
Active:       205116 kB
Inactive:     403384 kB
HighTotal:         0 kB
HighFree:          0 kB
LowTotal:     807660 kB
LowFree:      138492 kB
SwapTotal:   1638392 kB
SwapFree:    1638392 kB
Dirty:            84 kB
Writeback:         0 kB
AnonPages:     51860 kB
Mapped:        21508 kB
Slab:          52628 kB
PageTables:     1772 kB
. . . . . . . .
```

The data stored in files in the *proc* file system is used by a number of system utilities including *top*, *uname* and *vmstat* to display information.

The /lib/modules Directory

This directory holds information about kernel modules. Underneath this directory, there are sub-directories specific to the kernels available on the system. For example, the *ll* output on */lib/modules* below shows that there are four kernel configurations stored on this system:

ll /lib/modules

```
total 32
drwxr-xr-x 6 root root 4096 Jan 17 21:17 2.6.18-92.el5
drwxr-xr-x 6 root root 4096 Jan 17 21:12 2.6.18-92.el5debug
drwxr-xr-x 6 root root 4096 Jan 17 21:10 2.6.18-92.el5PAE
drwxr-xr-x 6 root root 4096 Jan 17 21:09 2.6.18-92.el5xen
```

Now do an *ll* on the default kernel sub-directory *2.6.18-92.el5*:

```
# ll /lib/modules/2.6.18-92.el5
total 1140
lrwxrwxrwx 1 root root       43 Dec 19 08:44 build -> ../../../usr/src/kernels/2.6.18-92.el5-i686
drwxr-xr-x 2 root root     4096 Oct 10 16:44 extra
drwxr-xr-x 9 root root     4096 Dec 19 08:44 kernel
-rw-r--r-- 1 root root 245095 Jan 17 21:17 modules.alias
-rw-r--r-- 1 root root       69 Jan 17 21:17 modules.ccwmap
-rw-r--r-- 1 root root 185925 Jan 17 21:17 modules.dep
-rw-r--r-- 1 root root      147 Jan 17 21:17 modules.ieee1394map
-rw-r--r-- 1 root root      375 Jan 17 21:17 modules.inputmap
-rw-r--r-- 1 root root     2160 Jan 17 21:17 modules.isapnpmap
-rw-r--r-- 1 root root       74 Jan 17 21:17 modules.ofmap
-rw-r--r-- 1 root root 179642 Jan 17 21:17 modules.pcimap
-rw-r--r-- 1 root root      589 Jan 17 21:17 modules.seriomap

. . . . . . . .
```

There are several files and a few sub-directories displayed in the output above. These files and sub-directories hold module specific information. Browse the directory tree to get yourself familiarized.

One of the key sub-directories is *lib/modules/2.6.18-92.el5/kernel/drivers* where modules categorized in groups are stored in various sub-directories as shown in the listing below:

```
# ll /lib/modules/2.6.18-92.el5/kernel/drivers
total 280
drwxr-xr-x 2 root root 4096 Dec 19 08:44 acpi
drwxr-xr-x 2 root root 4096 Dec 19 08:44 ata
drwxr-xr-x 2 root root 4096 Dec 19 08:44 atm
drwxr-xr-x 4 root root 4096 Dec 19 08:44 block
drwxr-xr-x 2 root root 4096 Dec 19 08:44 bluetooth
drwxr-xr-x 2 root root 4096 Dec 19 08:44 cdrom
drwxr-xr-x 7 root root 4096 Dec 19 08:44 char
drwxr-xr-x 2 root root 4096 Dec 19 08:44 cpufreq
drwxr-xr-x 2 root root 4096 Dec 19 08:44 crypto
drwxr-xr-x 2 root root 4096 Dec 19 08:44 dma
drwxr-xr-x 2 root root 4096 Dec 19 08:44 edac
drwxr-xr-x 2 root root 4096 Dec 19 08:44 firewire
drwxr-xr-x 2 root root 4096 Dec 19 08:44 firmware
drwxr-xr-x 2 root root 4096 Dec 19 08:44 hwmon
drwxr-xr-x 5 root root 4096 Dec 19 08:44 i2c
drwxr-xr-x 3 root root 4096 Dec 19 08:44 ide
drwxr-xr-x 6 root root 4096 Dec 19 08:44 infiniband
drwxr-xr-x 8 root root 4096 Dec 19 08:44 input
drwxr-xr-x 8 root root 4096 Dec 19 08:44 isdn
drwxr-xr-x 2 root root 4096 Dec 19 08:44 leds
drwxr-xr-x 2 root root 4096 Dec 19 08:44 md
drwxr-xr-x 5 root root 4096 Dec 19 08:44 media
drwxr-xr-x 4 root root 4096 Dec 19 08:44 message
drwxr-xr-x 3 root root 4096 Dec 19 08:44 misc

. . . . . . . .
```

Several module categories such as ata, block, syslogd, cdrom, char, firewire, ide, input, net, parport, pci, scsi, serial, usb and video exist. These categories contain driver modules to control hardware devices associated with them.

The /usr/src Directory

This directory contains source code for kernel. All information related to building a new kernel from the source code is located here. The */usr/src* directory contains two sub-directories as shown below:

```
# ll /usr/src
total 16
drwxr-xr-x  5 root root 4096 Aug 16 10:25 kernels
drwxr-xr-x  7 root root 4096 Jan   30  2007 redhat
```

The *kernels* sub-directory contains the current kernel information and the *redhat* sub-directory contains the associated source code. Five sub-directories under *redhat* are created as shown below:

```
# ll /usr/src/redhat
total 40
drwxr-xr-x  2 root root 4096 Jan 30  2007 BUILD
drwxr-xr-x  4 root root 4096 Jan 30  2007 RPMS
drwxr-xr-x  2 root root 4096 Jan 30  2007 SOURCES
drwxr-xr-x  2 root root 4096 Jan 30  2007 SPECS
drwxr-xr-x  2 root root 4096 Jan 30  2007 SRPMS
```

The purpose and use of these sub-directories are explained later in this chapter.

Managing Modules and the Kernel

Managing modules includes tasks such as listing, building, installing, loading and unloading modules, and managing the kernel involves tasks such as updating, upgrading and patching it. These tasks are explained in the following sub-sections.

Listing a Module

RHEL provides the *lsmod* command to view currently loaded modules. Alternatively, you can view them by displaying the contents of the */proc/modules* file. Both methods show module names, their sizes, how they are being used and dependent modules.

```
# lsmod
Module            Size     Used by
. . . . . . . .
e1000             119505   0
autofs4           24517    2
hidp              23105    2
rfcomm            42457    0
bluetooth         53797    5       hidp,rfcomm,l2cap
. . . . . . . .
```

```
# cat /proc/modules
. . . . . . . .
e1000                   119505  0 – Live 0xe03b3000
pcspkr                    7105  0 – Live 0xda93c000
i2c_piix4                12237  0 – Live 0xda938000
i2c_core                 23745  2 i2c_ec,i2c_piix4, Live 0xda96d000
ide_cd                   40033  1 – Live 0xda962000
. . . . . . . .
```

Building and Installing a New Module

RHEL detects most hardware and loads appropriate modules automatically; however, there may be instances when a device is left undetected or added online (as in the case of SAN disk allocation). In such a situation, execute the *depmod* command to force the system to scan the hardware, find appropriate modules for the new devices and update the */lib/modules/2.6.18-92.el5/modules.dep* file in addition to creating or updating several corresponding map files in that directory.

```
# depmod
```

Here is a listing of the module files in the */lib/modules/2.6.18-92.el5* directory:

```
# ll /lib/modules/2.6.18-92.el5 | grep modules
-rw-r–r-- 1  root root 245095 Jan 17 21:17  modules.alias
-rw-r–r-- 1  root root     69 Jan 17 21:17  modules.ccwmap
-rw-r–r-- 1  root root 185925 Jan 17 21:17  modules.dep
-rw-r–r-- 1  root root    147 Jan 17 21:17  modules.ieee1394map
-rw-r–r-- 1  root root    375 Jan 17 21:17  modules.inputmap
-rw-r–r-- 1  root root   2160 Jan 17 21:17  modules.isapnpmap
-rw-r–r-- 1  root root     74 Jan 17 21:17  modules.ofmap
. . . . . . . .
```

Loading and Unloading a Module

Now you can load the new module just built and installed using the *modprobe* command. This command ensures that any dependent modules are loaded prior to loading the specified module. The following example loads the Intel Ethernet network card module called *e1000*:

```
# modprobe e1000
```

Add an entry to the */etc/modprobe.conf* file to make the module get automatically loaded at each system reboot when the */etc/rc.d/rc.sysinit* script is executed and references this file. An excerpt from */etc/modprobe.conf* is shown below:

```
# cat /etc/modprobe.conf
alias eth0 e1000
alias scsi_hostadapter mptbase
alias scsi_hostadapter1 mptspi
alias scsi_hostadapter2 ata_piix
```

The *etc/modprobe.conf* file supports several directives, some of which are explained in Table 16-1.

Directive	Description
alias	Specifies the association of logical device and module. In the file excerpt above, e1000 is a module associated with the network interface logical device *eth0*.
install	Executes the specified command on a module instead of running the *insmod* command.
options	Specifies options for a module.
post-install	Executes the specified command after installing a module.
post-remove	Executes the specified command after removing a module.
pre-install	Executes the specified command prior to installing a module.
pre-remove	Executes the specified command prior to removing a module.
remove	Executes the specified command on a module instead of running the *rmmod* command.

Table 16-1 modprobe.conf Directives

To unload the *e1000* module along with all unused dependent modules, run either the *modprobe* or the *rmmod* command:

 # modprobe –r e1000
 # rmmod e1000

If you wish to load all modules specific to a particular hardware category, use the *modprobe* command. Here is an example on how to load modules for usb hardware. The –l option lists modules being loaded and the –t option forces the command to load only the modules specific to the category.

 # modprobe –lt usb
/lib/modules/2.6.18-92.el5/kernel/drivers/usb/storage/usb-storage.ko
/lib/modules/2.6.18-92.el5/kernel/drivers/usb/input/acecad.ko
/lib/modules/2.6.18-92.el5/kernel/drivers/usb/input/wacom.ko
/lib/modules/2.6.18-92.el5/kernel/drivers/usb/input/ati_remote.ko
/lib/modules/2.6.18-92.el5/kernel/drivers/usb/input/kbtab.ko
/lib/modules/2.6.18-92.el5/kernel/drivers/usb/input/appletouch.ko
/lib/modules/2.6.18-92.el5/kernel/drivers/usb/input/powermate.ko

. . . .

To display information about a specific module such as e1000, use the *modinfo* command:

 # modinfo e1000
filename: /lib/modules/2.6.18-92.el5/kernel/drivers/net/e1000/e1000.ko
version: 7.3.20-k2-NAPI
license: GPL
description: Intel(R) PRO/1000 Network Driver
author: Intel Corporation, <linux.nics@intel.com>
srcversion: 61E17F062F789856DE3DC58
alias: pci:v00008086d000010B5sv*sd*bc*sc*i*

alias:	pci:v00008086d00001099sv*sd*bc*sc*i*
alias:	pci:v00008086d0000108Asv*sd*bc*sc*i*
alias:	pci:v00008086d0000107Csv*sd*bc*sc*i*
alias:	pci:v00008086d0000107Bsv*sd*bc*sc*i*
alias:	pci:v00008086d0000107Asv*sd*bc*sc*i*
alias:	pci:v00008086d00001079sv*sd*bc*sc*i*

. . . .

depends:	
vermagic:	2.6.18-92.el5 SMP mod_unload 686 REGPARM 4KSTACKS gcc-4.1
parm:	TxDescriptors:Number of transmit descriptors (array of int)
parm:	TxDescPower:Binary exponential size (2^X) of each transmit descriptor (array of int)
parm:	RxDescriptors:Number of receive descriptors (array of int)
parm:	Speed:Speed setting (array of int)
parm:	Duplex:Duplex setting (array of int)
parm:	AutoNeg:Advertised auto-negotiation setting (array of int)
parm:	FlowControl:Flow Control setting (array of int)
parm:	XsumRX:Disable or enable Receive Checksum offload (array of int)
parm:	TxIntDelay:Transmit Interrupt Delay (array of int)
parm:	TxAbsIntDelay:Transmit Absolute Interrupt Delay (array of int)
parm:	RxIntDelay:Receive Interrupt Delay (array of int)
parm:	RxAbsIntDelay:Receive Absolute Interrupt Delay (array of int)
parm:	InterruptThrottleRate:Interrupt Throttling Rate (array of int)
parm:	SmartPowerDownEnable:Enable PHY smart power down (array of int)
parm:	KumeranLockLoss:Enable Kumeran lock loss workaround (array of int)
parm:	copybreak:Maximum size of packet that is copied to a new buffer on receive (uint)
parm:	debug:Debug level (0=none,...,16=all) (int)
module_sig:	883f350497eb5d576c8145391998811279 2409e3d6bc658a373a7c9136a890ed

3462ac69e5d3709cba52b79e4cabe2f2d5e898dac6aefc31bfe995

Adding a Module to Initial RAM Disk

As you know GRUB initializes the RAM disk so the kernel starts up, mounts an initial root file system and loads modules. The RAM disk is located in a compressed file */boot/initrd-2.6.18-92.el5.img* on *rhel01* and contains module and device information. The RAM disk file is created when the kernel is built, and may also be created if you wish to add or remove support for a specific module. The following procedure demonstrates how you would add to it a module called Bluetooth so it becomes available at the next system reboot with support for Bluetooth devices.

1. Change directory into */boot* and list the file:

    # cd /boot && ll initrd-*
    -rw------- 1 root root 3209762 Apr 24 14:50 initrd-2.6.18-92.el5.img

2. Run the following to list the contents of the file:

    # zcat initrd* | cpio –itv
    | drwx------ | 2 root | root | 0 Apr 24 14:50 sys |
    | lrwxrwxrwx | 1 root | root | 3 Apr 24 14:50 sbin -> bin |
    | drwx------ | 2 root | root | 0 Apr 24 14:50 proc |

```
drwx------      3 root    root           0 Apr 24 14:50 etc
drwx------      2 root    root           0 Apr 24 14:50 etc/lvm
-rw-------      1 root    root       15911 Apr 24 14:50 etc/lvm/lvm.conf
drwx------      3 root    root           0 Apr 24 14:50 lib
-rw-------      1 root    root       42648 Apr 24 14:50 lib/mptscsih.ko
-rw-------      1 root    root       29144 Apr 24 14:50 lib/ohci-hcd.ko
-rw-------      1 root    root      176832 Apr 24 14:50 lib/scsi_mod.ko
-rw-------      1 root    root       17756 Apr 24 14:50 lib/dm-log.ko
-rw-------      1 root    root      146056 Apr 24 14:50 lib/ext3.ko
-rw-------      1 root    root       26600 Apr 24 14:50 lib/dm-snapshot.ko
-rw-------      1 root    root       30024 Apr 24 14:50 lib/uhci-hcd.ko
-rw-------      1 root    root        7764 Apr 24 14:50 lib/dm-zero.ko
. . . . . . . .
```

3. Generate a new file called *initrd-bluetooth-`uname –r`* with Bluetooth support for the kernel specified with the *uname* command with –r flag using the *mkinitrd* command:

    # **mkinitrd --with=bluetooth initrd-bluetooth-`uname –r` `uname –r`**

4. Update the */boot/grub/grub.conf* file and change the initrd entry to reflect the new name:

    initrd /initrd-bluetooth-2.6.18-92.el5

5. Reboot the system and validate the new module with the *lsmod* command:

    # **lsmod | grep bluetooth**
    bluetooth   53797 5 hidp,rfcomm,l2cap

Updating the Kernel

Kernel updates are needed when there are any deficiencies or bugs in the existing kernel hampering the kernel's smooth operation. An updade addresses such issues and adds bug fixes, security updates and new features to the kernel without changing its version. You can use either the *yum* or the *rpm* command to update the kernel. Here is how you would do it using an updated kernel package from Red Hat.

To update with *yum* if the package is located in RHN repository, use the update option. Remember that this option overwrites existing kernel configuration.

```
# yum –y update kernel
Loading "rhnplugin" plugin
Loading "security" plugin
rhel-i386-server-5      100% |=============================| 1.3 kB    00:00
Skipping security plugin, no data
Setting up Update Process
Resolving Dependencies
Skipping security plugin, no data
--> Running transaction check
---> Package kernel.i686 0:2.6.18-128.1.6.el5 set to be installed
```

```
--> Processing Conflict: kernel conflicts ecryptfs-utils < 44
--> Restarting Dependency Resolution with new changes.
--> Running transaction check
---> Package ecryptfs-utils.i386 0:56-8.el5 set to be updated
--> Finished Dependency Resolution


Dependencies Resolved


================================================================================
 Package          Arch    Version        Repository        Size
================================================================================

Installing:
 kernel           i686    2.6.18-128.1.6.el5  rhel-i386-server-5   15 M
Updating for dependencies:
 ecryptfs-utils   i386    56-8.el5            rhel-i386-server-5  127 k


Transaction Summary
================================================================================
Install     1 Package(s)
Update      1 Package(s)
Remove      0 Package(s)


Total download size: 15 M
Is this ok [y/N]: Downloading Packages:
Running rpm_check_debug
Running Transaction Test
Finished Transaction Test
Transaction Test Succeeded
Running Transaction
  Updating   : ecryptfs-utils        ######################### [1/3]
  Installing : kernel                ######################### [2/3]
  Cleanup    : ecryptfs-utils        ######################### [3/3]


Installed: kernel.i686 0:2.6.18-128.1.6.el5
Dependency Updated: ecryptfs-utils.i386 0:56-8.el5
Complete!
```

The output indicates that the Linux kernel 2.6.18 is updated to a higher Red Hat version 128.1.6.

To update with *rpm* if the same package is located in a local */var/yum/repos.d/kernel* repository:

 # rpm –Uvh /var/yum/repos.d/kernel/kernel-2.6.18-128.1.6.el5.rpm

You will need to install any dependent packages as reported by the *rpm* command.

Either of the above two commands updates the existing kernel and associated files and save them in different files.

Upgrading the Kernel

Upgrading the kernel changes the current Linux kernel version to a higher version and brings new features such as security enhancements, support for additional hardware devices and major bug fixes. The process for kernel upgrade is similar to updating it. Either *yum* or *rpm* can be used. Here is how you would do it from Red Hat Network.

To upgrade with *yum* if the new package is located in RHN repository:

```
# yum –y install kernel
Loading "rhnplugin" plugin
Loading "security" plugin
rhel-i386-server-5        100% |==========================| 1.3 kB   00:00
Setting up Install Process
Parsing package install arguments
Resolving Dependencies
--> Running transaction check
---> Package kernel.i686 0:2.6.18-128.1.6.el5 set to be installed
--> Finished Dependency Resolution

Dependencies Resolved

==================================================================
Package          Arch     Version          Repository        Size
==================================================================
Installing:
kernel           i686     2.6.18-128.1.6.el5  rhel-i386-server-5   15 M

Transaction Summary
==================================================================
Install      1 Package(s)
Update       0 Package(s)
Remove       0 Package(s)

Total download size: 15 M
Downloading Packages:
(1/1): kernel-2.6.18-128. 100% |==========================| 15 MB   00:34
Running rpm_check_debug
Running Transaction Test
Finished Transaction Test
Transaction Test Succeeded
Running Transaction
  Installing: kernel                    ######################### [1/1]

Installed: kernel.i686 0:2.6.18-128.1.6.el5
Complete!
```

To upgrade with *rpm* if the new package is located in a local */var/yum/repos.d/kernel* repository:

Red Hat Certified Technician & Engineer

rpm –ivh /var/yum/repos.d/kernel/kernel-2.6.18-128.1.6.el5.rpm

You will need to install any dependent packages as reported by the *rpm* command.

Either of the above two commands upgrades the kernel and associated files and save them in different files. Neither of them affects the existing kernel or associated configuration files. Both updates the *grub.conf* file and appends an entry for the upgraded kernel.

Always install (–i) a new kernel even though you want to upgrade (–U) an existing kernel. This will ensure that you can go back to the previous kernel if needed.

You might also need to update the *grub.conf* file and append an entry for the new kernel. If you wish to make this kernel the default, change the default directive value to point to this new kernel.

Patching the Kernel

Kernel patching is performed to fix issues with any existing feature or functionality that is preventing the kernel from functioning properly. Kernel patches may be downloaded from Red Hat's website, *ftp.kernel.org/pub/linux/kernel/v2.6* or any other public site. The following example demonstrates patching the kernel to 2.6.28. Assume that the patch *patch-2.6.28.gz* has already been downloaded and is located in the */var/run* directory. Change into */var/run*, *gunzip* the patch file and run the *patch* command to apply the patch:

```
# cd /var/tmp
# gunzip patch-2.6.28.gz
# patch –p0 patch-2.6.28
```

With –p option, the command retains the original path of the files as defined in the patch file.

Modifying Kernel Parameters

There are hundreds of kernel parameters whose values affect the overall behavior of the kernel, and the running system in general. Runtime values of these parameters are stored in files in the */proc/sys* directory and can be altered on the fly by changing associated files, which will then remain effective until either the value is readjusted or the system is rebooted. The changes can be made using either the *sysctl* or the *echo* command. To make the change persistent across reboots, the values will have to be defined in the */etc/sysctl.conf* file.

The default contents of *sysctl.conf* are displayed below:

```
# cat /etc/sysctl.conf
# Kernel sysctl configuration file for Red Hat Linux
#
# For binary values, 0 is disabled, 1 is enabled.  See sysctl(8) and
# sysctl.conf(5) for more details.
# Controls IP packet forwarding
net.ipv4.ip_forward = 0
# Controls source route verification
net.ipv4.conf.default.rp_filter = 1
```

```
# Do not accept source routing
net.ipv4.conf.default.accept_source_route = 0
# Controls the System Request debugging functionality of the kernel
kernel.sysrq = 0
# Controls whether core dumps will append the PID to the core filename
# Useful for debugging multi-threaded applications
kernel.core_uses_pid = 1
# Controls the use of TCP syncookies
net.ipv4.tcp_syncookies = 1
# Controls the maximum size of a message, in bytes
kernel.msgmnb = 65536
# Controls the default maxmimum size of a mesage queue
kernel.msgmax = 65536
# Controls the maximum shared segment size, in bytes
kernel.shmmax = 68719476736
# Controls the maximum number of shared memory segments, in pages
kernel.shmall = 4294967296
```

As you can see, there are certain kernel parameters configured, other default settings automatically take effect when the kernel is loaded at system boot. Run the *sysctl* command with –a option to list all parameters with their values currently being used:

```
# sysctl –a
sunrpc.max_resvport = 1023
sunrpc.min_resvport = 665
sunrpc.tcp_slot_table_entries = 16
sunrpc.udp_slot_table_entries = 16
sunrpc.nlm_debug = 0
sunrpc.nfsd_debug = 0
sunrpc.nfs_debug = 0
sunrpc.rpc_debug = 0
abi.vsyscall32 = 1
dev.parport.parport0.devices.active = none
dev.parport.parport0.modes = PCSPP,TRISTATE
. . . . . . . .
```

Let us take a look at the following example to understand how to display and alter the value of a kernel parameter called net.ipv4.tcp_abc. Run *sysctl* to determine the current value of this parameter:

```
# sysctl net.ipv4.tcp_abc
net.ipv4.tcp_abc = 0
```

The value is stored in the */proc/sys/net/ipv4/tcp_abc* file and can be viewed with *cat*:

```
# cat /proc/sys/net/ipv4/tcp_abc
0
```

Use either *sysctl* or *echo* to change the value from 0 to 10:

```
# sysctl –w net.ipv4.tcp_abc=10
net.ipv4.tcp_abc = 10
# echo 10 > /proc/sys/net/ipv4/tcp_abc
```

At this point if the system is rebooted, this value will revert to its original setting. To make the value persistent across reboots, edit *sysctl.conf* and append the following line entry:

```
net.ipv4.tcp_abc = 10
```

Now, run the *sysctl* command again to load the new value if it is not already loaded:

```
# sysctl –p
net.ipv4.tcp_abc = 10
```

Similarly, if you wish to modify the kernel parameter net.ipv4.icmp_echo_ignore_all to prevent ICMP requests from striking your system, run the following:

```
# sysctl –w net.ipv4.icmp_echo_ignore_all=1
net.ipv4.icmp_echo_ignore_all = 1
```

Follow the rules as explained above to make this change permanent if needed.

Building a New Kernel from Source Code

Sometimes it becomes necessary to build a new kernel based on specific system requirements using source code obtained and unpacked in the */usr/src/redhat* directory. The following sub-sections guide you on the process of doing this.

Obtaining Kernel Source Code

The first step toward building a new kernel is to obtain the source code and store it in the */var/tmp* directory. There are scores of sources where you can download the code. These sources include the original RHEL CDs/DVD that you got, the Red Hat's HTTP site at *www.redhat.com*, Red Hat's FTP site at *ftp.redhat.com/pub/redhat/linux/enterprise/5Server/en/os/SRPMS, www.kernel.org* and *ftp.kernel.org*. If you are registered with RHN, you can obtain the code from there too using *yum*. Run *uname –a* on the system to determine the kernel level, kernel type and processor type for which you wish to obtain the source code (you may wish to obtain source code for a later kernel version too). For example, if the command returns *2.6.18-92.el5*, the kernel source code RPM package name would be *kernel-2.6.18-92.el5.src.rpm*. Furthermore, you will need the tools to successfully build a new kernel. The packages that you may need are listed in Table 16-2.

Package	Description
binutils	Binary utilities.
cpp	Preprocessor for the C language.
gcc	GNU C language compiler.
glib2-devel	Glib2 header files.
glibc-devel	C library files.
glibc-headers	Header files for the kernel.
gtk2-devel	TK X window files.

Package	Description
libglade2-devel	Libglade2 library files.
ncurses	Required for menuconfig screen.
ncurses-devel	Ncurses library files.
qt-devel	QT library files.
tcl	Scripting language.

Table 16-2 Packages Required to Build a New Kernel

Use the *yum* command to obtain and install the packages identified in Table 16-2, as well as any other required packages. As always, the *yum* command is preferred as it automatically downloads and installs dependencies. For example, the following obtains and installs all packages listed in the table from RHN or other available repository:

**# yum –y install binutils cpp gcc glib2-devel glibc-devel glibc-headers gtk2-devel \
libglade2-devel ncurses ncurses-devel gt-devel tcl**

Installing Kernel Source Code

Perform the following steps to install the source code RPM and build a new source code for target platform:

1. Install the kernel source code RPM. The *rpm* command will create two sub-directories under */usr/src/redhat* called *SOURCES* and *SPECS* with *SOURCES* getting all the source code and *SPECS* the associated specification file. Ignore messages pertaining to non-existence of certain user and group.

    # cd /var/tmp
    # rpm –ivh kernel-2.6.18-92.el5.src.rpm
    1:kernel   ### [100%]

2. Create *BUILD* sub-directory under */usr/src/redhat*:

    # mkdir /usr/src/redhat/BUILD

3. Modify the *kernel-2.6.spec* file located in the */usr/src/redhat/SPECS* directory if necessary.
4. Build source code for i386 platform in the */usr/src/redhat/BUILD/kernel-2.6.18/linux-2.6.18.i386* directory with vanilla version of it going into */usr/src/redhat/BUILD/kernel-2.6.18/vanilla* using the *kernel-2.6.spec* specification file:

    # cd /usr/src/redhat/SPECS
    # rpmbuild –bp --target=i386 kernel-2.6.spec
    Building target platforms: i386
    Building for target i386
    Executing(%prep): /bin/sh -e /var/tmp/rpm-tmp.18619
    + umask 022
    + cd /usr/src/redhat/BUILD
    + LANG=C
    + export LANG

```
+ unset DISPLAY
+ '[' '!' -d kernel-2.6.18/vanilla ']'
+ rm -f pax_global_header
+ cd /usr/src/redhat/BUILD
+ rm -rf kernel-2.6.18
+ /bin/mkdir -p kernel-2.6.18
+ cd kernel-2.6.18
+ /usr/bin/bzip2 -dc /usr/src/redhat/SOURCES/linux-2.6.18.tar.bz2
. . . . . . . .
```

Creating Configuration File

Now you need to create a configuration file that will be used for building a new kernel. The configuration file should include support for only the required hardware and software components. For this demonstration, copy the existing kernel configuration file */boot/config-2.6.18-92.el5* as *.config* to the */usr/src/redhat/BUILD/kernel-2.6.18/linux-2.6.18.i386* directory and edit it using one of the options of the *make* command as listed in Table 16-3.

Option	Description
config	Builds a new file based on responses entered. Answer M if you need a module to be loaded dynamically, answer Y if you wish the module to be static and answer N if you do not wish a specific module support included in the new kernel. Default choices are displayed in uppercase letter. Press Enter to accept the default.
menuconfig	Builds/modifies the file with text-based, menu-driven interface.
gconfig	Builds/modifies the file with graphical interface. Requires GNOME library files.
xconfig	Builds/modifies the file with graphical interface. Requires KDE library files.

Table 16-3 Configuration File Build Options

Here is how the four interfaces look like:

The make config Interface

```
scripts/kconfig/conf arch/i386/Kconfig
*
* Linux Kernel Configuration
*
* Code maturity level options
*
Prompt for development and/or incomplete code/drivers (EXPERIMENTAL) [Y/n/?] y
*
* General setup
*
Local version - append to kernel release (LOCALVERSION) []
. . . . . . . .
```

The make menuconfig Interface

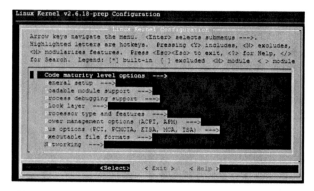

Figure 16-2 Text-Based Menu-Driven Interface

The make gconfig Interface

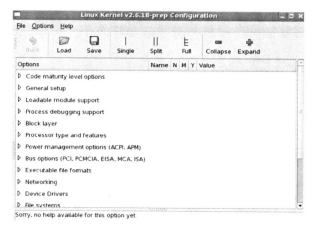

Figure 16-3 Graphical Interface Using GNOME Libraries

The make xconfig Interface

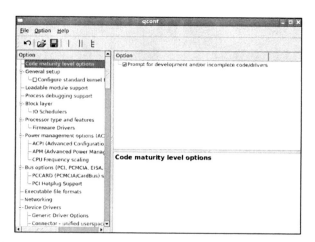

Figure 16-4 Graphical Interface Using KDE Libraries

Table 16-4 touches upon some of the common options configured in the *.config* file.

Option	Description
Block Layer	Enables support for diversified block devices.
Bus Options	Includes support for PCI, PCMCIA, EISA, MCA and ISA bus adapters. The "PCCARD Support" and "PCI Hotplug Support" options are related.
Code Maturity Level	Allows you to add development code or drivers to the kernel.
Cryptographic	Includes support for various types of encryption.
Device Drivers	Plenty of options are available to define varying device driver configurations. These options include support for parallel port, plug and play, IDE, ATA/ATAPI, SCSI, PCMCIA, RAID, LVM, wireless, network cards, ISDN, RAM/ROM/Flash chip, input devices (keyboard, mouse, touchscreen), NAND, IEEE 1394 (FireWire), video cards, serial ports, multimedia devices, USB devices (pen drives, printers, input devices, cameras, scanners), sound card devices, MMC/SD, InfiniBand and system hardware clock.
File Systems	Includes support for a variety of file system types such as ext2, ext3, DOS/FAT/NTFS, psedo file systems and Network File Systems.
Firmware Drivers	Includes support for firmware drivers for hardware devices.
General Setup	Contains basic hardware such as power management and networking, and kernel configuration options.
Library Routines	Includes support for various compression tools.
Loadable Module Support	Enables the kernel to automatically load a module as soon as a hardware associated with it, is detected.
Networking	Includes support for various network hardware devices and their configuration. Additional options such as "Networking Options", "TCP Congestion Control" and several IP related settings are available for granular control.
Partition Types	Includes support for disk partitioning types such as MSDOS, BSD, MINIX, Solaris, SGI, Sun, etc.
Power Management (ACPI and APM)	Supports power management using *Advanced Configuration and Power Interface* (ACPI), *Advanced Power Management* (APM) and processor frequency scaling.
Process Debugging Support	Enables debugging a variety of kernel events.
Processor Type and Features	Includes support for various processor types.
Security	Includes support for securing the system via SELinux, IPSec, etc.

Table 16-4 Kernel Configuration Options

Building a New Kernel

Now that you have a configuration file on hand, follow the steps below to build a new kernel based on that file:

1. Change into the kernel source code directory where the *.config* file resides:

   # **cd /usr/src/redhat/BUILD/kernel-2.6.18/linux-2.6.18.i386**

2. Edit *Makefile* file (the *make* command's source file) and set the value of the EXTRAVERSION directive as follows to give the kernel a unique name:

   EXTRAVERSION = -New-Kernel-1

3. Execute the *make* command to clean up the directory tree and prepare it to store new configuration and build:

   # **make mrproper**
   ```
   CLEAN   scripts/basic
   CLEAN   scripts/kconfig/lxdialog
   CLEAN   scripts/kconfig
   CLEAN   include/config
   CLEAN   .config .config.old
   ```

4. Execute the *make* command again to create a new kernel with settings defined in the *.config* file. The new kernel will be created in the */usr/src/redhat/RPMS/i386* directory.

   # **make**
   ```
   HOSTCC  scripts/basic/fixdep
   HOSTCC  scripts/basic/docproc
   HOSTCC  scripts/kconfig/conf.o
   HOSTCC  scripts/kconfig/kxgettext.o
   HOSTCC  scripts/kconfig/mconf.o
   SHIPPED scripts/kconfig/zconf.tab.c
   SHIPPED scripts/kconfig/lex.zconf.c
   SHIPPED scripts/kconfig/zconf.hash.c
   HOSTCC  scripts/kconfig/zconf.tab.o
   HOSTLD  scripts/kconfig/conf
   scripts/kconfig/conf -s arch/i386/Kconfig
   . . . . . . . .
   ```

5. Execute the *make* command again to install modules in their proper directory location:

   # **make modules_install**
   ```
   HOSTCC  scripts/basic/fixdep
   HOSTCC  scripts/basic/docproc
   HOSTCC  scripts/kconfig/conf.o
   HOSTCC  scripts/kconfig/kxgettext.o
   HOSTCC  scripts/kconfig/mconf.o
   SHIPPED scripts/kconfig/zconf.tab.c
   SHIPPED scripts/kconfig/lex.zconf.c
   . . . . . . . .
   ```

6. Execute the *make* command to copy the new kernel into */boot* and add a new boot string to the *grub.conf* file:

make install
sh /usr/src/redhat/BUILD/kernel-2.6.18/linux-2.6.18.i386/arch/i386/boot/install.sh 2.6.18-New-Kernel-1 arch/i386/boot/bzImage System.map "/boot"

7. Verify the new boot string in the *grub.conf* file:

cat /boot/grub/grub.conf
. . . .
default=1
timeout=5
splashimage=(hd0,0)/grub/splash.xpm.gz
hiddenmenu
title Red Hat Enterprise Linux Server (2.6.18-New-Kernel-1)
    root (hd0,0)
    kernel /vmlinuz-2.6.18-New-Kernel-1 ro root=/dev/VolGroup00/LogVol00 rhgb quiet
    initrd /initrd-2.6.18-New-Kernel-1.img
title Red Hat Enterprise Linux Server (2.6.18-92.el5)
    root (hd0,0)
    kernel /vmlinuz-2.6.18-92.el5 ro root=/dev/VolGroup00/LogVol00 rhgb quiet
    initrd /initrd-2.6.18-92.el5.img

As you can see the file now contains two boot strings. The first one is for the new kernel and the second one is the original boot entry and is still the default (default=1). If you wish to make the new kernel default, change the value of the variable to 0.

8. Create an initial RAM disk. All modules configured will be available at boot time.

mkinitrd /boot/initrd-2.6.18-New-Kernel-1.img 2.6.18-New-Kernel-1

9. Reboot the system and choose the new kernel to test boot it.

This completes the procedure to configure, build and test a new kernel.

Creating a Boot CD

You can create a boot CD so it can be used to boot a system when needed. There are two steps involved. In the first step an ISO image of a desired kernel is created using the *mkbootdisk* command and in the second step the image is burnt to a CD using the *cdrecord* command. Follow the procedure below to create a boot image on a CD:

1. Create an ISO image called *test.iso* in the */var/tmp* directory for kernel 2.6.18-92.el5 using the *mkbootdisk* command. The ISO image will contain the kernel file, grub configuration file and other supported files.

```
# mkbootdisk --verbose --iso --device /var/tmp/test.iso 2.6.18-92.el5
Installing isolinux... done
Copying /boot/vmlinuz-2.6.18-92.el5... done.
Copying /boot/initrd-2.6.18-92.el5.img... done.
Configuring bootloader... done.
```

2. Insert a blank CD in the drive and burn the image on it using the *cdrecord* command. The following assumes that the CD device is 0,0,0.

```
# cdrecord dev=0,0,0 -v /var/tmp/test.iso
```

3. Mount the CD on */mnt/cdrom* and list the contents of it:

```
# mount /mnt/cdrom
# ls /mnt/cdrom/isolinux
boot.cat  boot.msg  initrd-2.6.18-92.el5.img  isolinux.bin  isolinux.cfg   TRANS.TBL  vmlinuz-
2.6.18-92.el5
```

4. Check what the *isolinux.cfg* file contains:

```
# cat /mnt/cdrom/isolinux/isolinux.cfg
default linux
prompt 1
display boot.msg
timeout 100
label linux
     kernel vmlinuz
     append initrd=initrd.img ro  root=/dev/hda2
```

Reboot the system with the CD in the drive; the system will boot off the kernel on the CD.

Summary

This chapter talked about kernel, its management and how to build one from source code. You got an overview of Linux kernel. You learned about monolithic and modular kernels and the difference between them. You looked at how to check and understand kernel version.

You studied directory locations where kernel-related information is stored. You learned how to use tools to load and unload a module and update, upgrade and patch the kernel.

Finally, you were presented with details on generating a new kernel from source code, which included tasks such as obtaining and installing kernel source code, creating configuration file and building a new kernel based on that file. The very last topic of the chapter explained how to create a bootable ISO image and burn it on a CD to make it a bootable CD.

## 17

Backup, Restore and Compression

This chapter covers the following major topics:

- ✓ Reasons to perform backups
- ✓ Backup, archive, restore and recovery definitions
- ✓ Backup types – full, incremental and differential
- ✓ Backup levels
- ✓ Backup schedule
- ✓ Restore from multi-level backups
- ✓ Perform backups and restores using tools such as dump/restore, tar, rsync, cpio, dd and mkisofs/cdrecord
- ✓ Use compression tools to compress one or more files

Backing up system and data files is a vital function of system administration. Backups are performed to copy data and use it to restore in case the original data is corrupted, deleted or lost. The media containing the backups are stored at an alternate, secure location geographically distant from the system. The alternate location may be another room, building or city.

Basics of Backup

In order to save valuable data on external media, a *backup strategy* needs to be developed. A backup strategy is based on several factors. The following sub-sections highlight backup, archive, restore and recovery functions, and some critical backup strategy components.

Backup, Archive, Restore and Recovery Functions

Backup is a function of duplicating hard disk data to an alternative media for extended storage, emergency and safety purposes. The alternative media could be a tape, a hard drive on a remote system, a dedicated storage device or a re-writeable optical disc. For small data backup jobs, a flash or Jaz drive may also be used. Backups are typically meant to be recycled and over-written with updated data.

Archive is a function that is similar to backup, but the backed up data is intended to be kept for a longer period of time for historical purposes without being recycled or over-written. Archives may be made on any media that is also used for backups. Throughout this book the terms backup and archive are used interchangeably.

Restore is the opposite function of backup. Restore retrieves data from the alternative media and places it back to where it is supposed to be on the hard disk.

A similar function called *recovery* recovers a crashed system to its previous normal state. It may require restoring lost data files from alternative media.

Types of Backup

There are three common backup types, and are referred to as *full*, *incremental* and *differential*.

A full backup copies selected data and it is self-contained. This type of backup normally takes more time to complete than other backup methods, and is usually scheduled to occur every week and once every month.

An incremental backup copies only the data that has been modified since its last full, incremental or differential backup was done. This type of backup usually takes the least amount of time to complete. An incremental backup is usually scheduled to happen on a daily basis.

A differential backup copies only the data that has been modified since it was last backed up as part of a full backup. This type of backup normally takes more time to finish than an incremental backup. A differential backup may be scheduled to occur on a daily basis in place of an incremental backup, or on a weekly basis in place of a full backup. In the latter situation, full backups are then scheduled to run once per month.

Levels of Backup

There are certain pre-defined levels that can be specified to make backups full, incremental or differential. These levels are relative to one another. There are 10 supported levels as listed in Table 17-1.

Backup Level	Description
0	Corresponds to a full backup. This is the default level.
1	Corresponds to an incremental or differential backup since the last level 0 backup occurred.
2	Represents an incremental backup since the last level 1 backup was performed and corresponds to a differential backup since the last level 0 backup occurred.
3	Represents an incremental backup since the last level 2 backup was performed and corresponds to a differential backup since the last level 0 backup occurred.
4	Represents an incremental backup since the last level 3 backup was performed and corresponds to a differential backup since the last level 0 backup occurred.
5 – 9	Follow the same rule as above for subsequent backup levels.

Table 17-1 Backup Levels

What to Backup

From an operating system standpoint, /, /boot, /home, /tmp, /opt, /usr and /var file systems should be backed up on a regular basis. File systems that are virtual, contain temporary data, NFS mounts and mount points of removable media should not be included in backups. These file systems include /dev/shm, /proc, /misc, /sys, /mnt and /media.

Sample Backup Schedule

The example below explores setting up a backup schedule for a file system called /opt/oracle with the following scheduling requirements:

- ✓ A monthly full backup on the first Sunday of each month.
- ✓ A weekly differential backup on each Sunday, other than the first Sunday of each month.
- ✓ A daily incremental backup, except on Sundays, to backup all data that has changed since its last incremental or differential backup, whichever is more recent, occurred.

To develop a backup schedule to meet the above requirements, use level 0 for full, level 1 for differential and level 2 for incremental backup representations. The following displays a schedule for five weeks to accomplish the above:

```
Date:  1 2 3 4  5 6 7 8 9 10 11 12 13 14 15 16 17 18 19 20 21 22 23 24 25 26 27 28 29 30 1  2  3 4 5 6
Day:   s m t w  t f s s m t  w  t  f  s  s  m  t  w  t  f  s  s  m  t  w  t  f  s  s  m t w t f s s
Level: 0 2 2 2  2 2 2 1 2 2  2  2  2  1  2  2  2  2  2  2  1  2  2  2  2  2  2  1  2  2 2 2 2 2 2 0
```

Restore Procedure for the Sample Backup

From a restore perspective, if the data becomes corrupted on Wednesday the 18th before the Wednesday backup is commenced, you will need to perform restores in the following sequence to get the data back to the Tuesday the 17th state:

- ✓ Restore the full backup from Sunday the 1st.
- ✓ Restore the differential backup from Sunday the 15th.
- ✓ Restore the incremental backup from Monday the 16th.
- ✓ Restore the incremental backup from Tuesday the 17th.

This will bring the data in */opt/oracle* file system to the state where it was on Tuesday the 17th.

Managing Backups and Restores

There are many native tools in RHEL that can be utilized to do backups and restores of data. These tools include *dump/restore, tar, rsync, cpio, dd* and *mkisofs/cdrecord*. The following sub-sections discuss them in detail.

Performing Backups Using dump/restore

The *dump* command can be used to perform full, incremental and differential backups of ext2 and ext3 file systems. This command does not backup individual files or directories, it works at the file system level. The *dump* command is recommended to be used on unmounted and read-only file systems only.

Some essential options *dump* supports are listed in Table 17-2. The – sign before an option is not mandatory.

Option	Description
–f	Specifies a device to be used for backup.
–level	Defines a backup level as described in the previous table.
–S	Estimates number of tapes required for a backup.
–u	Updates */etc/dumpdates* file at each successful backup completion. Information written includes start and end backup time stamps, level of backup performed and name of the graph file used.
–v	Displays verbose information.

Table 17-2 dump Command Options

Some essential options *restore* supports are listed in Table 17-3. The – sign before an option is not mandatory.

Option	Description
–f	Specifies a device to be used for backup.
–i	Runs the command in interactive mode. Sub-commands include *add, cd, delete, extract, ls* and *pwd*.
–r	Restores an entire file system.
–t	Lists backed up contents.
–v	Displays verbose information.

Option	Description
−x	Extracts specified files and directories.

Table 17-3 restore Command Options

Let us look at a few examples to understand the working of *dump*.

To estimate the amount of space needed to perform a level 0 backup of the */boot* file system:

dump 0S /boot
6443008

To perform a level 0 backup on Sunday of */boot* file system to the tape device at */dev/pt1* and update the *dumpdates* file:

dump 0uvf /dev/pt1 /boot
   DUMP: Date of this level 0 dump: Mon Dec 22 19:36:39 2008
   DUMP: Dumping /dev/sda1 (/boot) to /dev/pt1
   DUMP: Excluding inode 8 (journal inode) from dump
   DUMP: Excluding inode 7 (resize inode) from dump
   DUMP: Label: /boot
   DUMP: Writing 10 Kilobyte records
   DUMP: mapping (Pass I) [regular files]
   DUMP: mapping (Pass II) [directories]
   DUMP: estimated 6292 blocks.
   DUMP: Volume 1 started with block 1 at: Mon Dec 22 19:36:41 2008
   DUMP: dumping (Pass III) [directories]
   DUMP: dumping directory inode 2
. . . .
   DUMP: Volume 1 transfer rate: 3195 kB/s
   DUMP: 6390 blocks (6.24MB) on 1 volume(s)
   DUMP: finished in 2 seconds, throughput 3195 kBytes/sec
   DUMP: Date of this level 0 dump: Mon Dec 22 19:36:39 2008
   DUMP: Date this dump completed: Mon Dec 22 19:36:43 2008
   DUMP: Average transfer rate: 3195 kB/s
   DUMP: DUMP IS DONE

The *dumpdates* file will contain the following after the backup is complete:

cat /etc/dumpdates
/dev/sda1 0 Mon Dec 22 19:36:39 2008 -0500

To perform an incremental backup of */boot* for the next six days (Monday to Saturday):

dump 2uvf /dev/pt1 /boot

To perform a differential backup of */boot* on the following Sunday:

dump 1uvf /dev/pt1 /boot

To perform the level 0 backup on the tape device at */dev/pt2* on *rhel02* system:

> # **dump 0uvf rhel02:/dev/pt1 /boot**

To list the contents of tape:

> # **restore tf /dev/pt1**
> Dump   date: Mon Dec 22 19:39:35 2008
> Dumped from: the epoch
> Level 0 dump of /boot on rhel01:/dev/sda1
> Label: /boot
>   2 .
>   11 ./lost+found
> 159521 ./grub
> 159523 ./grub/grub.conf
> 159522 ./grub/splash.xpm.gz
> 159524 ./grub/menu.lst
> 159525 ./grub/device.map
> 159526 ./grub/stage1
> 159527 ./grub/stage2
> 159528 ./grub/e2fs_stage1_5
> 159529 ./grub/fat_stage1_5
> 159530 ./grub/ffs_stage1_5
> 159531 ./grub/iso9660_stage1_5
> 159532 ./grub/jfs_stage1_5
> . . . .

To restore the entire */boot* file system contents in the */tmp* directory:

> # **cd /tmp**
> # **restore rf /dev/pt1**

To restore a specific file such as */boot/grub/grub.conf* into */var/tmp*:

> # **cd /var/tmp**
> # **restore xf /dev/pt1 ./grub/grub.conf**
> You have not read any volumes yet.
> Unless you know which volume your file(s) are on you should start
> with the last volume and work towards the first.
> Specify next volume # (none if no more volumes): 1
> set owner/mode for '.'? [yn] n

To restore files interactively, run the *restore* command with –i option. Run *help* at the restore> prompt to list available commands.

restore if /dev/pt1
restore > **help**
Available commands are:
> ls [arg] - list directory
> cd arg - change directory
> pwd - print current directory
> add [arg] - add `arg' to list of files to be extracted
> delete [arg] - delete `arg' from list of files to be extracted
> extract - extract requested files
> setmodes - set modes of requested directories
> quit - immediately exit program
> what - list dump header information
> verbose - toggle verbose flag (useful with ``ls")
> prompt - toggle the prompt display
> help or `?' - print this list

If no `arg' is supplied, the current directory is used

Using tar

The *tar* (tape archive) command archives, lists and extracts files to and from a single file called *tar* file. A tar file can be created as a regular file on disk or tape.

tar supports several options, some of which are summarized in Table 17-4.

Switch	Definition
–c	Creates an archive.
–f	Specifies archive destination.
–j	Compresses the archived contents with *bzip2* command.
–t	Lists archive contents.
–v	Verbose mode.
–x	Extracts from an archive.
–z	Compresses the archived contents with *gzip* command.

Table 17-4 tar Command Options

A few examples follow to explain how *tar* works. Note that the – character may or may not be used with an option.

To create an archive at */dev/pt1* of the */home* directory:

```
# tar cvf /dev/pt1 /home
/home/
/home/aquota.user
/home/aghori/
/home/aghori/inputrc
/home/aghori/modprobe.conf
/home/aghori/dovecot.conf
/home/aghori/profile
/home/aghori/host.conf
. . . . . . . .
```

To create the above on a tape device at */dev/pt2* on *rhel02* system:

    # **tar cvf rhel02:/dev/pt1 /home**

To create a single archive file called */tmp/files.tar* containing files – *file1*, *file2*, *file3* and *file4*:

    # **tar cvf /tmp/files.tar file1 file2 file3 file4**

To list tape contents at */dev/pt1*:

    # **tar tvf /dev/pt1**
    drwxr-xr-x root/root   0 2008-12-21 16:28:44 home/
    -rw------- root/root   7168 2008-12-14 09:02:10 home/aquota.user
    drwx------ aghori/aghori   0 2008-12-15 23:18:43 home/aghori/
    -rw-r--r-- aghori/aghori 758 2008-12-14 08:42:35 home/aghori/inputrc
    -rw-r--r-- aghori/aghori 112 2008-12-14 08:42:35 home/aghori/modprobe.conf
    -rw-r--r-- aghori/aghori 42747 2008-12-14 08:42:35 home/aghori/dovecot.conf
    . . . .

To list *files.tar* contents:

    # **tar tvf /tmp/files.tar**
    -rw-r--r-- root/root   0 2008-12-24 19:21:42 file1
    -rw-r--r-- root/root   0 2008-12-24 19:21:43 file2
    -rw-r--r-- root/root   0 2008-12-24 19:21:44 file3
    -rw-r--r-- root/root   0 2008-12-24 19:21:45 file4

To restore */home* from */dev/pt1*:

    # **tar xvf /dev/pt1**

To extract files from */tmp/files.tar*:

    # **tar xvf /tmp/files.tar**

To create an archive at */dev/pt1* of the */home* directory and compress it with *gzip*:

    # **tar cvzf /dev/pt1 /home**

To create an archive at */dev/pt1* of the */home* directory and compress it with *bzip2*:

    # **tar cvjf /dev/pt1 /home**

Using rsync

The *rsync* (remote synchronization) command works in a manner similar to the *cp*, *rcp* and *scp* commands to copy data from source to destination. With *rsync*, the source and destination could be on the same system or different. The first initiation of *rsync* copies all data from the specified source to the specified destination with subsequent initiations of it on the same source and destination copies only the updated data and leaves the unmodified data intact. If the copy operation is performed between hosts, the *rsync* command by default uses the ssh protocol for file transfer.

The following examples explain the usage of *rsync*.

To copy a sinlge file such as *grub.conf* to */tmp* on the same system:

> **# rsync –avz /boot/grub/grub.conf /tmp**
> building file list ... done
> grub.conf
>
> sent 719 bytes received 42 bytes 1522.00 bytes/sec
> total size is 621 speedup is 0.82

The –a option instructs the command to perform an archive operation and preserve all file properties such as permissions, ownership, symlinks and timestamps, the –v option is used for verbosity and the –z option compresses the data.

Subsequent invocations of the above would produce an output similar to the following if the file has not been modified:

> **# rsync –av /boot/grub/grub.conf /tmp**
> building file list ... done
>
> sent 52 bytes received 20 bytes 144.00 bytes/sec
> total size is 621 speedup is 8.62

To push copy *grub.conf* to */tmp* on a remote system *rhel02*:

> **# rsync –av /boot/grub/grub.conf rhel02:/tmp**

To pull copy *grub.conf* from *rhel02* to */tmp* on *rhel01*:

> **# rsync –av rhel02:/boot/grub/grub.conf /tmp**

To copy entire */boot* directory to */var/bootbak* on the same system:

> **# rsync –av /boot /var/bootbak**

To push copy the entire */boot* directory to */var/bootbak* on a remote system *rhel02*:

> **# rsync –av /boot rhel02:/var/bootbak**

To pull copy the entire */boot* directory from *rhel02* to */var/bootbak*:

> **# rsync –av rhel02:/boot /var/bootbak**

The *rsync* command is very powerful and has a host of options. Refer to man pages for details.

Using cpio

The *cpio* (copy in/out) command copies, lists and extracts files to and from a tape or single file.

Certain options available with *cpio* are summarized in Table 17-5. The *cpio* command requires that o, i or p option must be specified.

Option	Description
–o	Copies data.
–i	Extracts from a copy.
–t	Lists copy contents.
–v	Verbose mode.
–p	Reads from a copy to get pathnames.
–a	Resets access times on files after they are copied.

Table 17-5 cpio Command Options

Here are a few examples to undersand the usage.

To copy current directory contents to the */dev/pt1* tape device:

```
# find . | cpio –ov > /dev/pt1
.
./file2
./.nautilus
./.nautilus/metafiles
./.nautilus/metafiles/x-nautilus-desktop:%2F%2F%2F.xml
./.nautilus/savedu0bFSM
./.gnome2
. . . . . . . .
```

To copy to a file called */tmp/mod.cpio* only those files in the current directory that have changed within the last week:

```
# find . –mtime –7 | cpio –ov > /tmp/mod.cpio
```

To list the two files just created:

```
# cpio –itv < /dev/pt1
# cpio –itv < /tmp/mod.cpio
```

To restore files from */tmp/mod.cpio:*

```
# cpio –iv < /tmp/mod.cpio
```

Using dd

The *dd* command performs a bit for bit duplication. This command is useful in limited situations only and is technically not a backup command. Here is how it works.

To duplicate everything that resides under */dev/VolGroup00/lvol1* to */dev/VolGroup01/lvol1*:

Red Hat Certified Technician & Engineer

dd if=/dev/VolGroup00/lvol1 of=/dev/VolGroup01/lvol1 bs=8k
126976+0 records in
126976+0 records out
1040187392 bytes (1.0 GB) copied, 61.5426 seconds, 16.9 MB/s

where:

"if" stands for input file, "of" for output file and bs specifies the size of data blocks read and written.

The destination /dev/VolGroup01/lvol1 must be either of the same size as /dev/VolGroup00/lvol1 or larger. View man pages of *dd* for details.

Using mkisofs / cdrecord

The *mkisofs* (make ISO file system) command is used to create an ISO image of data, which can then be recorded on a writeable CD or DVD using the *cdrecord* command.

The following example shows a basic usage of the two commands to create an ISO image of the /opt/oracle directory and record it on a CD/DVD device located at /dev/cdrom. The command will eject the medium after the operation is complete.

mkisofs –r /opt/oracle | cdrecord dev=/dev/cdrom –v –eject –
cdrecord: No write mode specified.
cdrecord: Asuming -tao mode.
cdrecord: Future versions of cdrecord may have different drive dependent defaults.
cdrecord: Continuing in 5 seconds...
INFO: UTF-8 character encoding detected by locale settings.
      Assuming UTF-8 encoded filenames on source filesystem, use -input-charset to override.
Total translation table size: 0
Total rockridge attributes bytes: 1565
Total directory bytes: 10240
Path table size(bytes): 88

. . . .
TOC Type: 1 = CD-ROM
scsidev: '/dev/cdrom'
devname: '/dev/cdrom'
scsibus: -2 target: -2 lun: -2
. . . .

Compression Tools

Compression tools are used to compress the size of an archive to save space. Once a compressed archive is created, it can be copied to a remote system faster than a non-compressed archive. These tools may be used with archive commands such as *tar* to create a single compressed archive of hundreds of files and directories. RHEL provides a number of tools such as *zip* (*unzip*), *bzip2* (*bunzip2*) and *gzip* (*gunzip*) that can be used for compression purposes. RHEL also offers a graphical tool called Archive Manager that can be used instead.

Using zip and unzip

The *zip* command is a popular compression utility available on a number of operating system platforms. This command adds the *.zip* extension to a zipped file.

The following example compresses three files into one called *file1.zip*. The first file name specified on the command line is automatically chosen as the name of the resultant compressed file.

```
# zip file1 file2 file3
# ll file1.zip
-rw-r--r-- 1 root root 262 Jan  1 09:43 file1.zip
```

The *unzip* command performs the opposite of what *zip* does. It uncompresses a zipped file and restores the files to their original state.

To uncompress the three files:

```
# unzip file1.zip
```

Using gzip and gunzip

The *gzip* command creates a compressed file of each file specified at the command line and adds the *.gz* extension to each of them.

To compress three files:

```
# gzip file1 file2 file3
# ll | grep file
-rw-r--r-- 1 root root    26 Jan  1 09:43 file1.gz
-rw-r--r-- 1 root root    26 Jan  1 09:43 file2.gz
-rw-r--r-- 1 root root    26 Jan  1 09:43 file3.gz
```

To uncompress the files, run either of the following on each file:

```
# gunzip file1.gz
# gzip –d file1.gz
```

Using bzip2 and bunzip2

The *bzip2* command creates a compressed file of each file specified at the command line and adds the *.bz2* extension to each one of them.

To compress three files:

```
# bzip2 file1 file2 file3
# ll | grep file
-rw-r--r-- 1 root root    14 Jan  1 09:43 file1.bz2
-rw-r--r-- 1 root root    14 Jan  1 09:43 file2.bz2
-rw-r--r-- 1 root root    14 Jan  1 09:43 file3.bz2
```

To uncompress the files, run either of the following on each file:

```
# bunzip2 file1.bz2
# bzip2 –d file1.bz2
```

Using Archive Manager

The Archive Manager can be invoked using the *file-roller* command in an X terminal window or by choosing (GNOME) Applications → Accessories → Archive Manager or (KDE) Utilities → File → Ark. The interface in KDE is a little different.

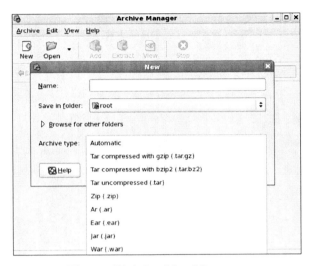

Figure 17-1 Archive Manager

Summary

In this chapter, you looked at reasons to perform backups of data files. You learned definitions of backup, archive, restore and recovery functions. You saw backup types such as full, incremental and differential that were based on backup levels you defined when configuring or running a backup.

You looked at various tools such as *dump/restore*, *tar*, *rsync*, *cpio*, *dd* and *mkisofs/cdrecord*. You used these tools to perform data backups and restores.

Finally, you learned compression tools such as *zip*, *unzip*, *gzip*, *gunzip*, *bzip2* and *bunzip2* and looked at how to use them to compress and decompress one or more files.

## 18

Print Services

This chapter covers the following major topics:

- ✓ CUPS concepts and directory tree
- ✓ Types of printer configurations – local, remote and network
- ✓ Printer classes
- ✓ Manage start and stop of cupsd
- ✓ Configure local, remote and network printers
- ✓ Administer printers – set default print destination, enable and disable a printer, allow and disallow users to submit print requests, check printer status and remove a printer
- ✓ Administer print requests – submit, list, modify, move and remove a print request

The printing system in RHEL is a set of utilities to manage printers and user print requests. It is based on the client/server architecture where a print client sends a file to a print server for printing. The print client is typically the *lp* or the *lpr* command that submits a file to the print server. The print server is the print scheduler daemon called *cupsd*, which is started when the system enters run level 2 and runs the */etc/rc.d/rc2.d/S56cups* script. Similarly, when the system changes run level to 1 or shuts down, a script called */etc/rc.d/rc1.d/K10cups* is executed to terminate the daemon. Both scripts are symbolically linked to the */etc/rc.d/init.d/cups* file and corresponds to the "start" and "stop" functions in the file.

Understanding the Printing System

Common UNIX Printing System (CUPS) is the standard printing service available in RHEL 5. CUPS has succeeded the *line printer daemon* (lpd) and the *Line Printer next generation* (LPRng) services. CUPS offers browser-based and GUI-based configurators for printer management. You may alternatively use commands or modify configuration files in the */etc/cups* directory.

CUPS is the UNIX/Linux implementation of the *Internet Printing Protocol* (IPP). It also supports the *PostScript Printer Definition* (PPD) files.

Types of Printer Configuration

Printers are normally configured in three ways, referred to as *local, remote* and *network* setups. Figure 18-1 illustrates four systems (*rhel01, rhel02, rhel03* and *rhel04*) and one printer (*prn2*) connected to the network. There is another printer (*prn1*) connected directly to *rhel01*.

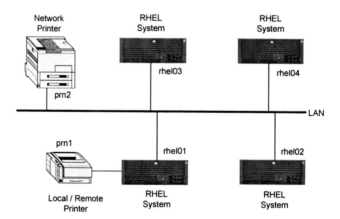

Figure 18-1 Types of Printer Setup

Local Printer

A printer attached physically to a system's parallel, serial or USB port, and accessed by users of that system only is called a local printer. In Figure 18-1, *prn1* is a local printer to users on *rhel01*.

Remote Printer

A local printer acts as a remote printer to users on remote systems. In Figure 18-1, *prn1* acts as a remote printer to *rhel02, rhel03* and *rhel04* users.

Network Printer

A network printer has a network card installed, is physically connected to a network port and has its own hostname and IP address. It is configured on the system after which it becomes accessible to users. In Figure 18-1, *prn2* is a network printer and accessible to users of all four systems.

CUPS Directory Hierarchy

The CUPS directory hierarchy comprises of two types of files: *static* and *dynamic*. Static files reside in */etc* and */usr* directories and include configuration files, commands, interface scripts and model scripts. Dynamic files reside in */var* directory and include status and log files. The dynamic directory structure also holds print requests temporarily in a spool directory before they are sent for printing.

Table 18-1 lists and explains some key CUPS configuration files and sub-directories.

File / Sub-directory	Purpose
Static	
/etc/cups/	Parent directory for all printer-related configuration.
/etc/cups/classes.conf	Contains information about printer classes.
/etc/cups/client.conf	Defines the default CUPS server.
/etc/cups/cupsd.conf	Main CUPS configuration file.
/etc/cups/mime.convs	Contains file format filters.
/etc/cups/mime.types	Defines file types.
/etc/cups/pdftops.conf	Defines language-specific PDF fonts.
/etc/cups/printers.conf	Stores printer configuration defined via the CUPS browser-based tool.
/etc/cups/pstoraster.convs	Contains a conversion filter for PostScript printers.
/etc/cups/snmp.conf	Defines parameters for discovery of network printers.
/etc/cups/ppd/	Contains custom printer settings.
/etc/cups/ssl/	Contains SSL certificates.
/etc/cups/interfaces/	Contains one file per configured printer that includes interface program to be used for the printer.
/etc/printcap	Defines SAMBA-shared printers.
/usr/bin/	Contains user-specific print commands such as *lp*, *lpr*, *lpstat* and *lprm*.
/usr/sbin/	Contains *root*-specific print administration commands such as *lpadmin*, *lpmove*, *accept* and *reject*.
Dynamic	
/var/spool/cups/	Parent directory for CUPS. Information about printer status, print requests, etc. is located here.
/var/spool/cups/tmp/	Print requests are temporarily held here before being sent to a printer for printing.
/var/log/cups/	Contains CUPS log files.

Table 18-1 CUPS Directory Hierarchy

SELinux Requirements for CUPS

If SELinux is enforced, you need to disable its protection for CUPS service to ensure smooth functionality. Use the *setsebool* command as demonstrated below, or the Red Hat SELinux Configurator *system-config-selinux* as explained in Chapter 30 "System and Network Security". Specify only those Booleans that need to be disabled, leave others intact.

> **# setsebool –P cupsd_config_disable_trans=1 cupsd_disable_trans=1 \
> cupsd_lpd_disable_trans=1 hplip_disable_trans=1**

Use the *getsebool* command to verify:

> **# getsebool cupsd_config_disable_trans cupsd_disable_trans cupsd_lpd_disable_trans \
> hplip_disable_trans**
> cupsd_config_disable_trans --> on
> cupsd_disable_trans --> on
> cupsd_lpd_disable_trans --> on
> hplip_disable_trans --> on

Managing CUPS Start and Stop

The *cupsd* daemon can be started, restarted, reloaded and stopped manually. It can also be configured to start automatically at specific run levels.

To start *cupsd*:

> **# service cups start**
> Starting cups: [OK]

To restart *cupsd*:

> **# service cups restart**
> Stopping cups: [OK]
> Starting cups: [OK]

To force *cupsd* to re-read its configuration:

> **# service cups reload**
> Reloading cups: [OK]

To stop *cupsd*:

> **# service cups stop**
> Stopping cups: [OK]

To enable *cupsd* to start at each system reboot:

> **# chkconfig cups on**

To check the status of *cupsd*:

```
# service cups status
cupsd (pid 21217) is running...
```

Configuring Printers

The printing system may be configured and managed via commands, the Red Hat Printer Configurator or the browser-based tool. Table 18-2 lists and explains the commands and tools.

Command/Tool	Description
lpadmin	Adds, modifies and removes printers and printer classes. Also sets default print destination.
lp / lpr	Sends user print request to a print destination.
lpc	Displays print queue status information.
lprm	Removes a submitted print request.
lpq	Displays print queue status.
lpstat	Displays print system status.
system-config-printer	Red Hat's graphical Printer Configurator tool for managing the printing system.

Table 18-2 Printing System Management Tools

The commands are installed by default as part of RHEL installation, whereas, the Printer Configurator and the browser-based tools are installed when you select the CUPS printing support during the installation. In case they were not selected at install time, you can use one of the methods described in Chapter 11 "Software Package Management" to install them.

Configuring a Local Printer via Command

To configure a local printer *prn1* (–p) on *rhel01* with "laserjet.ppd" printer model (–m) on parallel port parallel:/dev/lp0 (–v) and description "Test Room Laser Printer" (–D) using the *lpadmin* command. The –E option is specified to enable the printer to accept print requests.

 # lpadmin –p prn1 –m laserjet.ppd –v parallel:/dev/lp0 –D "Test Room Laser Printer" –E

Configuring a Local Printer via Printer Configurator

To configure a local printer *prn1* on *rhel01* with "HP LaserJet 5Si" duplexed printer model and */dev/lp0* as the parallel port device file using the Printer Configurator:

1. Execute *system-config-printer* in an X terminal window or choose (GNOME) System / (KDE) Main Menu → Administration → Printing. The Printer Configurator screen will open up as shown in Figure 18-2.

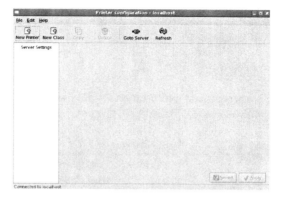
Figure 18-2 Configuring a New Printer (1)

2. Click New Printer and specify *prn1* as the printer name, "HP Laserjet 5Si with duplexer" as description and "Test Room" as location. Click Forward.

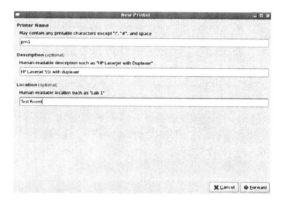
Figure 18-3 Configuring a New Printer (2)

3. Choose "LPT #1" as the parallel port and click Forward. For adding a serial printer, choose an appropriate serial port as shown in Figure 18-4. If a printer is connected and powered on, CUPS will detect its presence as well as type.

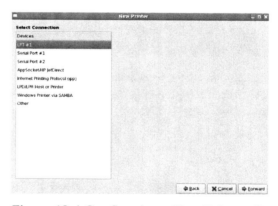
Figure 18-4 Configuring a New Printer (3)

4. The next screen will display a list of printer manufacturers. Choose HP from the list and click Forward. If the printer you are adding is a post script printer and you have its driver software, you may choose "Provide PPD file" and specify the location of the driver to be installed.

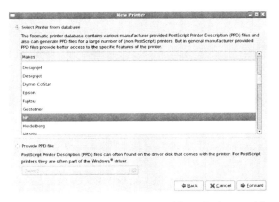

Figure 18-5 Configuring a New Printer (4)

5. Choose "Laserjet 5Si" printer model and the recommended driver. If you wish to select an alternate driver, highlight it. Click Forward.

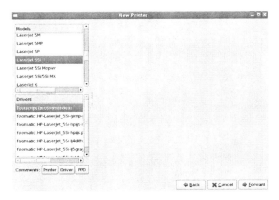

Figure 18-6 Configuring a New Printer (5)

6. Click Apply on the next screen to create *prn1* on */dev/lp0*. Figure 18-7 shows the details of the new printer just configured. Besides the parameters you entered, the figure also shows if the printer is default and whether it is enabled, accepting print requests and shared. You can go to other tabs and view more information.

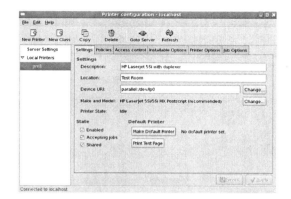

Figure 18-7 Configuring a New Printer – Summary

Configuring a Remote Printer via Command

To add access to *prn1* from another system *rhel02*, run the *lpadmin* command on *rhel02* and assign the printer a name such as *prn1* (same as on *rhel01*) and the ipp location as the device file (–v):

    # **lpadmin –p prn1 –v ipp://rhel01/printers/prn1 –E**

Configuring a Remote Printer via Printer Configurator

To add access to *prn1* on *rhel01* from another RHEL system *rhel02*, follow the steps below:

1.   Start the Printer Configurator as explained earlier on *rhel02*.
2.   Click "Server Settings" as shown in Figure 18-8. You will see five options:

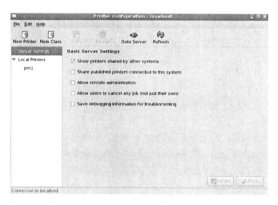

Figure 18-8 Configuring a Remote Printer (1)

  ✓ The "Show printers shared by other systems" option performs an automatic search on the network for any shared printers.
  ✓ The "Share published printers connected to this system" option enables remote servers to be able to access printers defined on this system.
  ✓ The "Allow remote administration" option enables administrators from remote systems to manage printers on this system.

✓ The "save debugging information for troubleshooting" option adds detailed information to the cups log files.

Select the "Show printers shared by other systems" option. Click Refresh and the Printer Configurator will search for any shared printers on the network and display them. Choose the printer that you wish to be defined as a remote printer for *rhel02* users, otherwise click "New Printer" and choose one of the three choices in the "Select Connection" window.

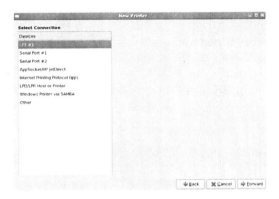

Figure 18-9 Configuring a Remote Printer (2)

The three choices available to configure a remote printer are:

1. *Internet Printing Protocol* (IPP)
2. LPD / LPR Host or Printer
3. Windows Printer via SAMBA

The first two choices require that you enter the hostname (*rhel01*) and printer name (*prn1*). The third choice allows you to choose a SAMBA-shared printer. You will need to enter a username and password to access it. Click Forward to add access to the printer.

Configuring a Network Printer via Printer Configurator

To configure a network printer, choose "AppSocket / HP JetDirect" as shown in Figure 18-10, and enter the hostname of the printer. Use the default 9100 port number.

Figure 18-10 Configuring a Network Printer

Click Forward and follow the screens to complete the configuration.

Configuring a Printer Class

You can create a printer class with a minimum of one printer as its member using the *lpadmin* command, the Printer Configurator or the browser-based tool. A printer class is a set of similar printers grouped together to form a single print destination for increased availability and better utilization of printers. When a print request is sent to a class of printers, the first available printer in the class prints it.

To configure a printer class *prn_class* on *rhel01* and define and add to it another local printer *prn2* with "laserjet" printer model and */dev/lp1* device file:

lpadmin –p prn2 –m laserjet.ppd –v parallel:/dev/lp1 –c prn_class –E

To add *prn1* to *prn_class* class:

lpadmin –p prn1 –c prn_class

To perform the same as above using the Printer Configurator, click "New Class" and supply a unique class name, optional description and location. Choose members on the next screen and click Forward. Click Apply to create the class. When done, click the printer class to view the properties of it. See Figure 18-11 which shows the details of *prn_class*.

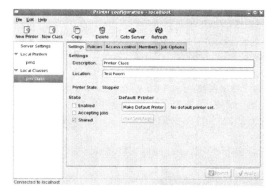

Figure 18-11 Configuring a Printer Class

The figure also displays if the printer class is default and whether it is enabled, accepting print requests and shared. You can go to other tabs and view more information.

Configuring a Printer Using Browser-Based Tool

The other graphical method to configure and manage printers is the CUPS browser-based program. This section only briefly explains the tool and does not show how to configure a printer since similar information covered earlier is required to achieve it.

Open up a browser window and type the URL *http://localhost:631* (631 is the default port). The main CUPS window will appear as shown in Figure 18-12.

Red Hat Certified Technician & Engineer

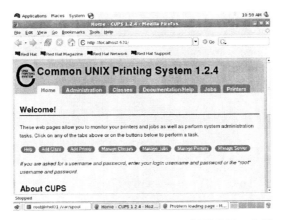

Figure 18-12 Browser-Based CUPS Tool (1)

The Home page displays introductory information about CUPS. There are seven buttons – Help, Add Class, Add Printer, Manage Classes, Manage Jobs, Manage Printers and Manage Server – under the Welcome! banner. You can either make a choice here or click one of the five tabs across the top and beside the Home tab for making a selection. The five tabs are:

- ✓ Administration – allows you to add and manage printers, printer classes and print requests.
- ✓ Classes – allows you to view and manage printer classes.
- ✓ Documentation / Help – gives you access to CUPS documentation.
- ✓ Jobs – allows you to display and manage print jobs.
- ✓ Printers – allows you to manage printers.

Click Administration and you will see a screen similar to the one shown in Figure 18-13 to add and manage a printer, add and manage printer classes, manage submitted print jobs, manually edit printer configuration file, view logs, change settings and so on.

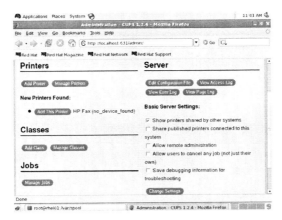

Figure 18-13 Browser-Based CUPS Tool (2)

Administering Printers via Commands

Printer administration includes tasks such as setting default print destination, enabling and disabling a printer, making a printer accept or reject print requests, checking printer status and removing a printer. The following sub-sections elaborate on how to perform these tasks using commands.

Setting Default Print Destination

A printer, or a printer class, can be defined as the default print destination for all user print requests. Here is how you would do it.

To make *prn1* the default printer, use the –d option with the *lpadmin* command:

> # **lpadmin –d prn1**

To make *prn_class* the default print destination, use the –d option with the *lpadmin* command:

> # **lpadmin –d prn_class**

Enabling and Disabling a Printer

A printer must be activated before it can print. The *cupsenable* command activates the specified printer and enables it to print requests. The *cupsdisable* command deactivates the specified printer and disables it from printing requests.

To enable *prn1*:

> # **cupsenable prn1**

To disable *prn1*:

> # **cupsdisable prn1**

To disable *prn1* and specify a reason for disabling it, use the –r option with *cupsdisable*. The reason will be displayed on user terminals when they attempt to submit print requests to this printer.

> # **cupsdisable –r "prn1 is disabled for maintenance for 1 hour" prn1**

Accepting and Rejecting Print Requests

A printer must be accepting requests in its queue before it can actually print them. The *accept* command allows user print requests to be queued for printing. The *reject* command denies queuing user print requests.

To accept user print requests in *prn1* or *prn_class* queue:

> # **accept prn1**
> # **accept prn_class**

To reject user print requests from being queued in *prn1* and *prn_class*:

 # reject −r "prn1 is down for 15 minutes for toner replacement" prn1
 # reject prn_class

The −r option allows you to specify some text to explain a reason for rejecting user requests. This text is displayed on user terminals when they attempt to send print requests to the printer or class.

Checking Printer Status

To view information about the status of configured printers and submitted user print requests, use the *lpstat* command. This command has several options, some of which are listed in Table 18-3.

Option	Description
−a	Displays accept/reject status.
−d	Displays default destination printer or printer class.
−o	Displays queued print requests only.
−p	Displays enable/disable status.
−r	Displays *cupsd* status.
−s	Displays summary information.
−t	Displays detailed information about all configured printers, printer classes and queued requests.
−v	Displays printer device file.

Table 18-3 lpstat Command Options

```
# lpstat −t
scheduler is running
system default destination: prn_class
members of class prn_class:
        prn2
        prn1
device for prn1: parallel:/dev/lp0
device for prn2: parallel:/dev/lp1
device for prn_class: ///dev/null
prn1 accepting requests since Thu 26 Feb 2009 09:50:56 PM EST
prn2 accepting requests since Thu 26 Feb 2009 09:51:40 PM EST
prn_class accepting requests since Thu 26 Feb 2009 09:53:37 PM EST
printer prn1 is idle.  enabled since Thu 26 Feb 2009 09:50:56 PM EST
printer prn2 is idle.  enabled since Thu 26 Feb 2009 09:51:40 PM EST
printer prn_class is idle.  enabled since Thu 26 Feb 2009 09:53:37 PM EST
```

Removing a Printer

Removing a printer removes all configuration information for the printer from the system. The *lpadmin* command is used for this purpose with −x option.

Prior to removing a printer, you need to run the *reject* and *cupsdisable* commands on it. Follow the steps below to remove *prn1*:

 # reject prn1
 # cupsdisable prn1

lpadmin –x prn1

Administering Printers via Printer Configurator and Browser-Based Tool

Printer administration can also be performed via Printer Configurator and the browser-based tool. Refer to Figures 18-8, 18-12 and 18-13 that self explain how to perform administration on configured printers and printer classes.

Administering Print Requests

Administering print requests involves submitting, listing, modifying, moving and removing a print request. The following sub-sections describe how to perform these tasks.

Submitting a Print Request

Print requests are submitted to a printer or printer class using the *lp* or *lpr* command. Both commands support several options, some of which are captured in Table 18-4.

lp (lpr) Option	Description
–d (–P)	Sends a print request to the specified destination.
–h (–H)	Sends a print request to a destination on the specified host.
–m	Notifies the user by sending a mail when a print request submitted by that user is finished printing.
–n (–#)	Defines number of copies to print.
–t (–T)	Specifies a title to be printed on the first page (default is submitting user's name).

Table 18-4 lp (lpr) Command Options

Let us take a look at some examples.

To print *group* file on the default printer *prn1*, run any of the following:

```
# lpr /etc/group
# lp /etc/group
request id is prn1-0 (1 file(s))
```

The output indicates that prn1-0 is the first print request submitted to this printer.

To print *passwd* file on a non-default printer *prn2*, run any of the following:

```
# lpr –Pprn2 /etc/passwd
# lp –dprn2 /etc/passwd
request id is prn2-1 (1 file(s))
```

To submit *passwd* file to *prn_class*:

```
# lpr –Pprn_class /etc/passwd
```

lp –dprn_class /etc/passwd
request id is prn_class-4 (1 file(s))

Listing a Print Request

To list all print requests submitted to all defined printer queues on the system, use the *lpstat* command with –o option. Additional commands – *lpc* and *lpq* – are also available that show similar information.

```
# lpstat –o
prn1-0          root          5120   Thu 26 Feb 2009 09:57:18 PM EST
prn2-1          root          5120   Thu 26 Feb 2009 09:57:35 PM EST
prn_class-4     root          5120   Thu 26 Feb 2009 09:59:02 PM EST
# lpc status
prn1:
    printer is on device 'parallel' speed -1
    queuing is enabled
    printing is enabled
    1 entries
    daemon present
prn2:
    printer is on device 'parallel' speed -1
    queuing is enabled
    printing is enabled
    1 entries
    daemon present
prn_class:
    printer is on device '///dev/null' speed -1
    queuing is enabled
    printing is enabled
    1 entries
    daemon present
# lpq
prn_class is ready
no entries
```

Moving a Print Request

Submitted print requests can be moved from one printer queue to another using the *lpmove* command. For example, to move all print requests from *prn1* to *prn2*, run the following:

lpmove prn1 prn2

To move only prn1-0 print request from *prn1* to *prn2*:

lpmove prn1-0 prn2

Removing a Print Request

To remove a single print request, use the *lprm* command as follows:

> # **lprm prn1-0**
> # **lprm prn2-1**

To remove all print requests queued on *prn2* and *prn_class*, use the *lprm* command as follows:

> # **lprm –P prn2**
> # **lprm –P prn_class**

Administering a Printer or Printer Class Remotely

Either graphical tool can be used to administer a printer or printer class from another RHEL system. You will need to enable remote printer administration in the Printer Configurator by checkmarking "Allow remote administration" box under Server Settings. The browser-based tool does not require any modifications except that the system where the printer or printer class is defined has to have port 631 open in the firewall.

Summary

You learned about printing in this chapter. You developed a good understanding of printing system, CUPS and CUPS directory structure. You looked at local, remote and network printer definitions, and reasons behind grouping printers into classes. You looked at managing the start and stop of the CUPS daemon automatically and manually. You configured local, remote and network printers using commands, and graphical and browser-based tools.

You studied printing system administration that involved setting default print destination, enabling and disabling a printer, allowing and disallowing users to submit print requests, checking printer status and removing a printer from the system. You performed these tasks using commands, and graphical and browser-based tools.

Finally, you learned how to submit, list and modify print requests, move submitted print requests to another printer or printer class, remove a submitted request and administer a printer or printer class from another system.

## 19

Job Scheduling and System Logging

This chapter covers the following major topics:

- ✓ Understand job scheduling
- ✓ SELinux requirements for Cron
- ✓ Manually manage scheduling daemons start and stop
- ✓ Allow and disallow users to schedule jobs
- ✓ Log cron activities
- ✓ Schedule, list and remove at jobs
- ✓ Understand crontab
- ✓ Schedule, list and remove cron jobs
- ✓ What is anacron?
- ✓ Introduction to system logging
- ✓ SELinux requirements for logging daemons
- ✓ Understand system log configuration files
- ✓ Types of messages and levels of criticality
- ✓ Maintain and manage log files
- ✓ Understand system log file

Job scheduling

Job scheduling is a feature that allows a user to schedule a command for execution at a specified time in future. The execution of the command could be one time in future or at regular intervals based on a pre-determined time schedule. All this is taken care of by two daemons – *atd* and *crond*. While the *atd* daemon manages jobs scheduled to run one time in future, the *crond* daemon takes care of jobs scheduled to run at pre-specified time. The *atd* daemon is started when the system enters run level 3 and runs the */etc/rc.d/rc3.d/S95atd* script and terminated when the system changes run level to 2, 1, 0 or 6, or shuts down, and calls the */etc/rc.d/rc#.d/K05atd* script. Likewise, the *crond* daemon is started when the system enters run level 2 and runs the */etc/rc.d/rc2.d/S90crond* script and terminated when the system changes run level to 1, 0 or 6, or shuts down, and calls the */etc/rc.d/rc#.d/K60crond* script. These scripts are symbolically linked to corresponding */etc/rc.d/init.d/atd* and */etc/rc.d/init.d/crond* files, which include "start" and "stop" functions coinciding with service startup and termination.

Understanding Job Scheduling

Jobs in future can be scheduled to run once or periodically. Usually, one-time execution is scheduled for an activity that is to be performed at times of low system usage. One example of such an activity is to run a lengthy shell program.

In contrast, recurring activities could include performing backups, trimming log files and removing unwanted files from the system.

SELinux Requirements for Cron

If SELinux is enforced, you need to disable its protection for Cron service to ensure smooth functionality. Use the *setsebool* command as demonstrated below, or the SELinux Configurator *system-config-selinux* as explained in Chapter 30 "System and Network Security".

> # **setsebool –P crond_disable_trans=1**

Use the *getsebool* command to verify:

> # **getsebool crond_disable_trans**
> crond_disable_trans --> on

There is no SELinux requirements for *atd* daemon.

Managing Scheduling Daemons Start and Stop

The *atd* and *crond* daemons can be started, restarted, reloaded and stopped manually, and can also be configured to start automatically at specific run levels. The following examples demonstrate performing these operations on *crond*. The commands and procedure can be identically followed for *atd*.

To start *crond*:

> # **service crond start**
> Starting crond: [OK]

To restart *crond*:

> # **service crond restart**
> Stopping crond: [OK]
> Starting crond: [OK]

To force *crond* to re-read its configuration:

> # **service crond reload**
> Reloading crond: [OK]

To stop *crond*:

> # **service crond stop**
> Stopping crond: [OK]

To enable *crond* to start at each system reboot:

> # **chkconfig crond on**

To check the status of *crond*:

> # **service crond status**
> crond (pid 4571) is running...

Controlling User Access

Which users can or cannot submit an *at* or *cron* job is controlled through files located in the */etc* directory. For *at* job control, the *at.allow* and *at.deny* files are used, and that for *cron*, the *cron.allow* and *cron.deny* files are used.

The syntax of all four files is identical. You only need to list usernames that need to be permitted or denied access to these tools. Each file takes one username per line. The *root* user is always allowed to use these tools and is neither impacted by the existence or non-existence of these files nor by the presence or absence of an entry for it in these files.

Table 19-1 shows various combinations and the impact on user access.

at.allow / *cron.allow*	*at.deny* / *cron.deny*	Impact
Exists, and contains user entries	Existence does not matter	All users listed in *.allow files are permitted.
Exists, but empty	Existence does not matter	No users are permitted.
Does not exist	Exists, and contains user entries	All users, other than those listed in *.deny files, are permitted.
Does not exist	Exists, but empty	All users are permitted.
Does not exist	Does not exist	No users are permitted.

Table 19-1 Controlling User Access

By default, the *.deny* files exist and are empty, and *.allow* files do not exist.

The following message will appear on the screen if you attempt to execute the *at* command, but are not authorized:

> You do not have permission to use at.

The following message will appear on the screen if you attempt to execute the *crontab* command, but are not authorized:

> You (user1) are not allowed to use this program (crontab)
> See crontab(1) for more information

Cron Log File

All activities involving the *crond* daemon are logged to the */var/log/cron* file. Information such as owner and start time for each invocation of *crontab* is captured. The file also keeps track of when the *crond* daemon was started, PID associated with it, spooled *cron* jobs, etc. Sample entries from the log file are shown below:

```
# cat /var/log/cron
Jan  6 16:26:49 rhel01 anacron[2317]: Job `cron.daily' terminated
Jan  6 16:29:35 rhel01 anacron[2317]: Job `cron.weekly' started
Jan  6 16:34:55 rhel01 anacron[2317]: Job `cron.weekly' terminated
Jan  6 16:34:55 rhel01 anacron[2317]: Normal exit (2 jobs run)
Jan  6 17:01:01 rhel01 crond[9495]: (root) CMD (run-parts /etc/cron.hourly)
Jan  6 18:01:01 rhel01 crond[9769]: (root) CMD (run-parts /etc/cron.hourly)
Jan  7 13:38:01 rhel01 crond[2278]: (CRON) STARTUP (V5.0)
Jan  7 13:38:03 rhel01 anacron[2320]: Anacron 2.3 started on 2008-01-07
Jan  7 13:38:03 rhel01 anacron[2320]: Will run job `cron.daily' in 65 min.
Jan  7 13:38:03 rhel01 anacron[2320]: Jobs will be executed sequentially
Jan  7 14:01:01 rhel01 crond[2664]: (root) CMD (run-parts /etc/cron.hourly)
Jan  7 14:43:03 rhel01 anacron[2320]: Job `cron.daily' started
Jan  7 14:44:14 rhel01 anacron[2320]: Job `cron.daily' terminated
. . . . . . . .
```

Job Scheduling Using at

The *at* command is used to schedule a one-time execution of a program in future. All submitted jobs are spooled in the */var/spool/at* directory and executed by the *atd* daemon when the scheduled time arrives.

Scheduling an at Job

To understand scheduling an *at* job, consider the following examples.

To schedule an *at* job to run the *find* command tonight at 11pm to look for all *core* files in the system and remove them:

> # at 11pm

at> **find / –name core –exec rm {} \;**
at> **Ctrl+d**
job 5 at 2009-01-08 23:00

You have to press Ctrl+d to submit the *at* job. A file is created in the */var/spool/at* directory, which will include all variable settings to be used when the job will actually run. These variables will establish the user's shell environment so that the job is properly carried out. This file will also include the name of the command or script to be executed. The following shows an *ll* on */var/spool/at* and the contents of the spooled file with the *cat* and *at* commands:

 # ll /var/spool/at
-rwx------ 1 root root 1636 Jan 8 10:37 a0000501392dd4
 # cat /var/spool/at/a0000501392dd4
at –c 5
#!/bin/sh
atrun uid=0 gid=0
mail   root 0
umask 22
HOSTNAME=rhel01; export HOSTNAME
SHELL=/bin/bash; export SHELL
HISTSIZE=1000; export HISTSIZE

. . . .

find / -name core -exec rm {} \;

There are multiple ways of specifying an execution time with the *at* command. Some examples are:

at 11am	(executes the task at next 11 am)
at 23:00	(executes the task at 11 pm tonight)
at 17:30 tomorrow	(executes the task at 5:30 pm next day)
at now + 5 days	(executes the task at this time after 5 days)
at now + 2 hours	(executes the task after 2 hours)
at now + 1 week	(executes the task at this time after 1 week)
at now + 2 minutes	(executes the task after 2 minutes)
at 3:00 8/13/09	(executes the task at 3 am on August 13, 2009)

 When year is not mentioned, the current year is assumed; when no date is mentioned, today's date is assumed.

If you wish to run a series of commands or scripts from a file, supply the file's name as input to *at* using the –f option. Here is how you would do it:

 # at –f file1 now + 5 days

In the above example, the contents of *file1* will be executed at the current time after 5 days.

Listing and Removing at Jobs

Use the *at* command with –l option or the *atq* command to list spooled *at* jobs:

```
# at –l
# atq
5      2009-01-08 23:00 a root
```

To remove a spooled *at* job, use the *at* command with –d option or the *atrm* command and specify the job ID you want to remove:

```
# at –d 5
# atrm 1
```

Job Scheduling Using crontab

Using the *crontab* command is the other method for scheduling tasks for execution in future. Unlike *at*, *crontab* executes jobs on a regular basis and at specified time defined in the master crontab file */etc/crontab*. Crontab files for users are located in the */var/spool/cron* directory. Each user, who is allowed and has scheduled a cron job, has a file by his login name created in this directory. The third location where cron files can be stored is the */etc/cron.d* directory. The *crond* daemon scans entries in */etc/crontab* file and the files at the two directory locations to determine job execution times. The daemon runs the commands or scripts at the specified time and puts a log entry into the */var/log/cron* file.

The *crontab* command is used to edit, list and remove crontab files.

Syntax of the User crontab File

Each line in the user crontab file that contains an entry for a scheduled job comprises of six fields. These fields must be in a precise sequence in order for the *crond* daemon to interpret them correctly. See Figure 19-1 for syntax of the crontab file.

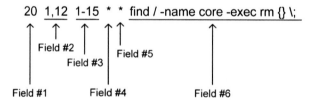

Figure 19-1 Syntax of the crontab File

A description of each field is given in Table 19-2.

Field #	Field Content	Description
1	Minute of the hour	Valid values are 0 (represents exact hour) to 59. This field can have one specific value (see Field #1 for usage), multiple comma-separated values (see Field #2 for usage), a range of values (see Field #3 for usage) or the * character that represents every minute of the hour (see Field #4 and #5 for usage).

Red Hat Certified Technician & Engineer

Field #	Field Content	Description
2	Hour of the day	Valid values are 0 (represents midnight) to 23, and are defined exactly the way they are defined for Field #1, except that the * character represents every hour of the day.
3	Date of the month	Valid values are 1 to 31, and are defined exactly the way they are defined for Field #1, except that the * character represents every day of the month.
4	Month of the year	Valid values are 1 to 12, and are defined exactly the way they are defined for Field #1, except that the * character represents every month of the year.
5	Day of the week	Valid values are 0 to 6, with 0 represents Sunday, 1 represents Monday and so on. Values are defined exactly the way they are defined for Field #1, except that the * character represents every day of the week.
6	Command or script to execute	Specifies the full path name of the command or script to be executed.

Table 19-2 crontab File Description

In addition, step values can be specified with * and ranges in the crontab files. Step values allow you to specify number of skips to be done for a given value. For example, */2 in the minute field would mean every 2nd minute, */3 would mean every 3rd minute, 0-59/4 would mean every 4th minute and so on. Step values are also supported in the same manner in the hour, date of month, month of year and day of week fields.

The default contents of the master crontab file */etc/crontab* are displayed below:

```
# cat /etc/crontab
SHELL=/bin/bash
PATH=/sbin:/bin:/usr/sbin:/usr/bin
MAILTO=root
HOME=/
# run-parts
01 * * * *  root  run-parts  /etc/cron.hourly
02 4 * * *  root  run-parts  /etc/cron.daily
22 4 * * 0  root  run-parts  /etc/cron.weekly
42 4 1 * *  root  run-parts  /etc/cron.monthly
```

The output indicates that there are four pre-defined schedules located in the */etc/cron.hourly*, */etc/cron.daily*, */etc/cron.weekly* and */etc/cron.monthly* directories run by the *run-parts* command on an hourly, daily, weekly and monthly basis. Each of these schedules contains one or several scripts executed at specified time. The contents tell that the hourly scripts run past one minute every hour, the daily scripts run every day at 4:02am, the weekly scripts run every Sunday at 4:22am and the monthly scripts run on the first of every month at 4:42am.

Also notice that there are four variables – SHELL, PATH, MAILTO and HOME – set in the file. These variables define the shell to be used to execute the programs, set the search path for programs, send a notification to the specified user or email address, and set the home directory, respectively. You may define additional variables as needed.

Do an *ll* on the */etc/cron.daily* directory, for instance, to see what scripts it contains:

```
# ll /etc/cron.daily
total 24
-rwxr-xr-x   1 root root    133 Jul 12  2006 00webalizer
-rwxr-xr-x   1 root root    379 Dec 18  2006 0anacron
lrwxrwxrwx 1 root root      39 Dec 24 12:25 0logwatch -> /usr/share/logwatch/scripts/logwatch.pl
-rwxr-xr-x   1 root root   1042 Aug 17  2006 certwatch
-rwxr-xr-x   1 root root    118 Aug  6 11:08 cups
-rwxr-xr-x   1 root root    180 Oct  1  2006 logrotate
-rwxr-xr-x   1 root root    418 Jul 13  2006 makewhatis.cron
-rwxr-xr-x   1 root root    137 Nov 26  2006 mlocate.cron
-rwxr-xr-x   1 root root   2181 Jun 21  2006 prelink
-rwxr-xr-x   1 root root    114 Aug 24 15:18 rpm
-rwxr-xr-x   1 root root    290 Nov 26  2006 tmpwatch
```

All these programs and scripts are scheduled to run once every day. If you wish to schedule your own scripts or programs to run once every hour, day, week or month, simply copy the script in the appropriate directory. There is no need to bounce the *crond* daemon.

Scheduling a cron Job

In addition to the pre-configured scripts in the */etc/crontab* file, normal users and *root* can create their own crontab files, which are stored in the */var/spool/cron* directory with their names correspond to owner names.

To schedule a cron job, execute the *crontab* command with –e (edit) option:

$ crontab –e

This will open the crontab file for the user who has executed this command based on permissions defined for that user in the *cron.allow* or *cron.deny* file. The *root* user can modify the contents of any other user's crontab file. For example, do the following to edit the crontab file of *user1* as *root*:

 # crontab –u user1 –e

> You do not have to be in the */var/spool/cron* directory to open crontab files. In fact, you can be anywhere in the directory structure.

Let us put the following entry in the *root* user's crontab file:

 # crontab –e
20 1,12 1-15 * * find / -name core –exec rm {} \;

This entry tells the *crond* daemon to execute the *find* command at 1:20am and 12:20pm every day from the 1st of the month to the 15th.

If you wish this command to run at 1:20am, 1:40am, 2:20pm and 2:40pm every day from the 1st of the month to the 15th:

```
# crontab –e
*/20 1,12 1-15 * * find / -name core –exec rm {} \;
```

Listing and Removing cron Jobs

Use the *crontab* command to list and remove cron jobs. See the examples below to understand the usage.

To list contents of the crontab file of *user1*, use –l (list) option:

```
$ crontab –l
```

To remove the crontab file of *user1*, use –r (remove) option:

```
$ crontab –r
```

What is anacron?

Anacron is a service that checks at every system reboot for any *cron* and *at* scheduled jobs that were missed from running while the system was down. It checks its configuration file */etc/anacrontab* and determines which jobs were not executed. It waits for a specified period of time and then executes them automatically. A typical */etc/anacrontab* file is displayed below:

```
# cat /etc/anacrontab
. . . . . . . .
1    65    cron.daily      run-parts /etc/cron.daily
7    70    cron.weekly     run-parts /etc/cron.weekly
30   75    cron.monthly    run-parts /etc/cron.monthly
```

The first column represents the period in days, the second specifies the delay in minutes, the third identifies the job, the fourth lists the command that will execute contents of the scripts directory indicated in the fifth column.

For each job, anacron checks whether the job was run in the past specified days (column 1) and executes it after waiting for the number of minutes (column 2) if it was not.

Anacron may be run manually at the command prompt. For example, to run all the jobs that are scheduled in */etc/anacrontab* file and were missed:

```
# anacron
```

To run all the jobs that are scheduled in */tmp/missed_cron* file and were missed:

```
# anacron –t /tmp/missed_cron
```

Anacron stores its execution date in the */var/spool/anacron* directory for each defined schedule.

System Logging

System logging is performed to keep track of messages generated by kernel, daemons, commands, user activities and so on. There are two daemons – *klogd* and *syslogd* – responsible for logging, with the former captures kernel messages and events, and the latter all other activities. Both daemons are started when the system enters run level 2 and runs the */etc/rc.d/rc2.d/S12syslog* script and terminated when the system changes run level to 1, 0 or 6, or shuts down, and calls the */etc/rc.d/rc#.d/K88syslog* script. These scripts are symbolically linked to */etc/rc.d/init.d/syslog* file, which includes "start" and "stop" functions corresponding with service startup and termination. The daemons read their configuration file */etc/syslog.conf* when coming up.

The two daemons can be started or stopped manually. Here is how:

```
# service syslog start
Starting system logger:                    [ OK ]
Starting kernel logger:                    [ OK ]
# service syslog stop
Shutting down kernel logger:               [ OK ]
Shutting down system logger:               [ OK ]
```

Process IDs are assigned to the daemons when they are started and stored in */var/run/klogd.pid* and */var/run/syslogd.pid* files.

SELinux Requirements for Logging Daemons

If SELinux is enforced, you need to disable its protection for the logging daemons to ensure smooth functionality. Use the *setsebool* command as demonstrated below, or the SELinux Configurator *system-config-selinux* as explained in Chapter 30 "System and Network Security".

```
# setsebool –P klogd_disable_trans=1 syslogd_disable_trans=1
```

Use the *getsebool* command to verify:

```
# getsebool klogd_disable_trans syslogd_disable_trans
klogd_disable_trans --> on
syslogd_disable_trans --> on
```

The System Log Configuration File

The system log configuration file is located in the */etc* directory and is called *syslog.conf*. The contents of the default file are shown below:

```
# cat /etc/syslog.conf
# Log all kernel messages to the console.
# Logging much else clutters up the screen.
#kern.*                                    /dev/console
# Log anything (except mail) of level info or higher.
# Don't log private authentication messages!
*.info;mail.none;authpriv.none;cron.none   /var/log/messages
# The authpriv file has restricted access.
```

```
authpriv.*                                  /var/log/secure
# Log all the mail messages in one place.
mail.*                                      -/var/log/maillog
# Log cron stuff
cron.*                                      /var/log/cron
# Everybody gets emergency messages
*.emerg                                     *
# Save news errors of level crit and higher in a special file.
uucp,news.crit                              /var/log/spooler
# Save boot messages also to boot.log
local7.*                                    /var/log/boot.log
```

Notice that each uncommented line entry consists of two fields. The left field is called *selector* and the right one is referred to as *action*. The selector field is further divided into two sub-fields, which are separated by the period character. The left sub-field, called *facility*, represents various system process categories that generate messages. Multiple facilities can be defined, with each facility separated from the other by the semicolon character. The right sub-field, called *severity level* or *priority*, represents severity associated with the message. The action field determines the destination to send the message to.

Some of the facilities are kern, authpriv, mail and cron. The asterisk character represents all of them.

In the same way, there are multiple severity levels such as emergency (emerg), alert (alert), critical (crit), error (err), warning (warning), notice (notice), informational (info), debug (debug) and none. The sequence provided is in descending order. The asterisk character represents all of them. If a lower severity level is selected, the daemons will log all messages of the service at that and higher levels.

Some example entries are listed and explained below:

```
1.  authpriv.*        /var/log/secure
2.  mail.*            /var/log/maillog
3.  cron.*            /var/log/cron
4.  *.emerg           *
5.  uucp,news.crit    /var/log/spooler
6.  local7.*          /var/log/boot.log
7.  kern.err          @rhel02
```

In the first line entry, facility is "authpriv" which is related to authentication, severity level is * and the action field is */var/log/secure*. This tells the *syslogd* daemon to log all messages generated by the authentication service to the */var/log/secure* file.

Similar to the first entry, the second, third and the sixth line entries tell the daemon to capture and log all messages generated by the mail, cron and local7 facilities to the */var/log/maillog*, */var/log/cron* and */var/log/boot.log* files, respectively.

The fourth line indicates that the *syslogd* daemon will display all emergency messages on the terminals of all logged in users.

In the fifth line entry, two facilities are defined, which tell the daemon to capture critical messages generated by uucp and news facilities and log them to */var/log/spooler* file.

The last line entry tells the *klogd* daemon to forward all kernel error messages to the *klogd* daemon running on another system *rhel02* to handle them. Likewise, you can have messages from any or all facilities redirected to some other system on the network. You will need to set the SYSLOGD_OPTIONS directive as follows and restart *syslogd* to give the system the ability to receive messages from other systems, and log them.

```
# grep SYSLOGD_OPTIONS /etc/sysconfig/syslog
SYSLOGD_OPTIONS="–m 0 –rx"
# service syslog restart
Shutting down kernel logger:                    [ OK ]
Shutting down system logger:                    [ OK ]
Starting system logger:                         [ OK ]
Starting kernel logger:                         [ OK ]
```

The –m option changes the mark timestamp to 0 minutes, or, in other words, disables it; the –r option enables the system to receive messages from other systems; and the –x option disables DNS lookups on receiving messages.

Maintaining and Managing Log Files

In RHEL, all system log files are stored in the */var/log* directory. Do an *ll* on the directory to list the contents:

```
# ll /var/log
total 2044
-rw-r-----  1 root  root    6077 Jan   7 09:01 acpid
-rw-------  1 root  root  493198 Dec 19 18:18 anaconda.log
-rw-------  1 root  root   17215 Dec 19 18:18 anaconda.syslog
-rw-------  1 root  root   31044 Dec 19 18:18 anaconda.xlog
drwxr-x---  2 root  root    4096 Dec 20 00:39 audit
-rw-------  1 root  root       0 Jan   7 10:07 boot.log
-rw-------  1 root  root      83 Jan   1 18:08 boot.log.1
-rw-------  1 root  root       0 Dec 20 00:39 boot.log.2
-rw-------  1 root  utmp       0 Dec 19 08:43 btmp
drwxr-xr-x  2 root  root    4096 Jun 28  2007 conman
drwxr-xr-x  2 root  root    4096 Jun 28  2007 conman.old
-rw-------  1 root  root     395 Jan   7 11:39 cron
-rw-------  1 root  root    6915 Jan   7 10:06 cron.1
-rw-------  1 root  root    9293 Dec 30 04:02 cron.2
drwxr-xr-x  2 lp    sys     4096 Jan   7 10:07 cups
-rw-r--r--  1 root  root   17563 Jan   7 08:57 dmesg
-rw-------  1 root  root   12048 Dec 24 04:00 faillog
drwxr-xr-x  2 root  root    4096 Jan   7 09:01 gdm
drwx------  2 root  root    4096 Aug  6 07:23 httpd
-rw-r--r--  1 root  root  146584 Jan   7 10:57 lastlog
drwxr-xr-x  2 root  root    4096 Dec 19 08:44 mail
-rw-------  1 root  root       0 Jan   7 10:07 maillog
-rw-------  1 root  root   11654 Jan   7 10:07 maillog.1
-rw-------  1 root  root    8497 Dec 30 04:02 maillog.2
```

```
-rw-------   1 root  root        118 Jan   7 10:59 messages
-rw-------   1 root  root     418140 Jan   7 10:07 messages.1
-rw-------   1 root  root     194273 Dec 30 03:59 messages.2
drwxr-xr-x 2 root  root       4096 Dec 19 08:47 pm
drwx------  2 root  root       4096 Dec  1 2006 ppp
drwxr-xr-x 2 root  root       4096 Dec 24 02:48 prelink
-rw-r--r--  1 root  root      25115 Jan   7 10:09 rpmpkgs
-rw-r--r--  1 root  root      25115 Jan   5 11:25 rpmpkgs.1
-rw-r--r--  1 root  root      25115 Dec 29 04:02 rpmpkgs.2
drwx------  2 root  root       4096 Jul  9 18:23 samba
-rw-r--r--  1 root  root      62111 Dec 19 18:16 scrollkeeper.log
-rw-------   1 root  root        290 Jan   7 11:33 secure
-rw-------   1 root  root       9814 Jan   7 09:04 secure.1
-rw-------   1 root  root       7008 Dec 29 15:33 secure.2
drwxr-xr-x 2 root  root       4096 Jan   7 10:07 setroubleshoot
-rw-------   1 root  root          0 Jan   7 10:07 spooler
-rw-------   1 root  root          0 Dec 30 04:02 spooler.1
-rw-------   1 root  root          0 Dec 19 08:44 spooler.2
drwxr-x--- 2 squid squid      4096 Mar 23 2007 squid
-rw-------   1 root  root          0 Dec 19 08:43 tallylog
drwxr-xr-x 2 root  root       4096 Dec 18 2006 vbox
-rw-rw-r--  1 root  utmp      75648 Jan   7 10:57 wtmp
-rw-rw-r--  1 root  utmp     184704 Jan   1 15:37 wtmp.1
-rw-r--r--  1 root  root      30998 Jan   7 09:01 Xorg.0.log
-rw-r--r--  1 root  root      30998 Jan   6 15:58 Xorg.0.log.old
-rw-r--r--  1 root  root          0 Dec 20 00:39 yum.log
```

The output indicates that there are different log files for different services. Depending on the number of messages generated and captured, log files may fill up the file system where the directory is located very quickly. Also, if a log file grows to a very large size, it becomes troublesome to load and read it.

In RHEL 5, a script */etc/cron.daily/logrotate* runs the *logrotate* command once a day to rotate log files by sourcing the */etc/logrotate.conf* file and configuration files from the */etc/logrotate.d* directory. These files may be modified to perform additional tasks such as removing, compressing and emailing identified log files.

Here is what the */etc/cron.daily/logrotate* file contains:

cat /etc/cron.daily/logrotate
```
#!/bin/sh
/usr/sbin/logrotate /etc/logrotate.conf
EXITVALUE=$?
If [ $EXITVALUE != 0 ]; then
    /usr/bin/logger –t logrotate "ALERT exited abnormally with [$EXITVALUE]"
fi
exit 0
```

The */etc/logrotate.conf* file contains the following information:

```
# cat /etc/logrotate.conf
# see "man logrotate" for details
# rotate log files weekly
weekly
# keep 4 weeks worth of backlogs
rotate 4
# create new (empty) log files after rotating old ones
create
# uncomment this if you want your log files compressed
#compress
# RPM packages drop log rotation information into this directory
include /etc/logrotate.d
# no packages own wtmp -- we'll rotate them here
/var/log/wtmp {
    monthly
    minsize 1M
    create 0664 root utmp
    rotate 1
}
# system-specific logs may be also be configured here.
```

The *etc/logrotate.d* directory includes a number of configuration files for individual log files. Log files for services listed in this directory are rotated automatically.

```
# ll /etc/logrotate.d
total 152
-rw-r--r--1 root root    144 Oct 10  2006 acpid
-rw-r--r--1 root root    288 Jun 28  2007 conman
-rw-r--r--1 root root     71 Aug  6 11:08 cups
-rw-r--r--1 root root    167 Aug  6 07:23 httpd
-rw-r--r--1 root root     61 Jun 11 2007 kdm
-rw-r--r--1 root root    571 Aug 21 2006 mgetty
-rw-r----1 root named  163 Jul 19 08:23 named
-rw-r--r--1 root root    136 Dec  1  2006 ppp
-rw-r--r--1 root root    323 Jul 12 2006 psacct
-rw-r--r--1 root root     61 Aug 24 15:18 rpm
-rw-r--r--1 root root    232 Jul  9 18:23 samba
-rw-r--r--1 root root     68 Jun 11 2007 sa-update
-rw-r--r--1 root root    121 Feb  6  2007 setroubleshoot
-rw-r--r--1 root root    543 Mar 23 2007 squid
-rw-r--r--1 root root    228 Jun 20 2007 syslog
-rw-r--r--1 root root     48 Aug 23 2006 tux
-rw-r--r--1 root root     32 Dec  6  2006 up2date
-rw-r--r--1 root root     95 Jan 17 2007 vsftpd.log
-rw-r--r--1 root root     89 Jan 10 2007 yum
```

A log watch command called *tmpwatch* can be scheduled to run periodically, such as on a daily basis via */etc/cron.daily* to remove old temporary files from */tmp* and */var/tmp* directories, as well as any other specified directories. This action prevents the file systems from filling up quickly.

The System Log File

The default system log file is */var/log/messages*. This is a plain text file and can be viewed with any file display utility such as *cat, more, less, head* or *tail*. This file may be viewed in real time using the *tail* command with –f switch. The *messages* file captures time stamp, hostname, daemon or command executed, PID of the process and a short description of what is being logged.

The following shows some sample entries from the file:

cat /var/log/messages
Jan 6 16:25:39 rhel01 syslogd 1.4.1: restart.
Jan 6 18:10:38 rhel01 gconfd (root-2726): Exiting
Jan 6 18:10:39 rhel01 gdm[2541]: Master halting...
Jan 6 18:10:39 rhel01 shutdown[2541]: shutting down for system halt
Jan 6 18:10:41 rhel01 smartd[2494]: smartd received signal 15: Terminated
Jan 6 18:10:41 rhel01 smartd[2494]: smartd is exiting (exit status 0)
Jan 6 18:10:41 rhel01 avahi-daemon[2364]: Got SIGTERM, quitting.
Jan 6 18:10:41 rhel01 avahi-daemon[2364]: Leaving mDNS multicast group on interface eth0.Ipv6 with address fe80::20c:29ff:fe71:c688.
Jan 6 18:10:41 rhel01 avahi-daemon[2364]: Leaving mDNS multicast group on interface eth0.Ipv4 with address 192.168.0.201.
Jan 6 18:10:44 rhel01 restorecond: Will not restore a file with more than one hard link (/etc/resolv.conf) Invalid argument
Jan 6 18:10:44 rhel01 xinetd[2223]: Exiting...
Jan 6 18:10:48 rhel01 hcid[2042]: Got disconnected from the system message bus
Jan 6 18:10:48 rhel01 rpc.statd[1975]: Caught signal 15, un-registering and exiting.
. . . .

Summary

You learned two system administration areas in this chapter. First, you learned how to schedule commands and scripts to run automatically at pre-determined time in future, which included the *at* and *crontab* tools that used *atd* and *crond* daemons. Normal users could automate their own tasks, if they were permitted. You looked at ways to permit and prohibit users to use the tools. Furthermore, you were presented with security requirements for *crond*, how to manually start and stop scheduling daemons, examples of listing and removing spooled jobs, and a brief introduction to anacron.

Second part of the chapter presented the system activity logging functionality, its security requirements, configuration files, types of messages captured and associated criticality. You looked at how to maintain and manage log files, and the */var/log/messages* file where all system activities were logged based on defined configuration.

## 20

Basic Networking

This chapter covers the following major topics:

- ✓ What is a Network?
- ✓ Types of networks
- ✓ Network topologies – bus, star, ring and hybrid
- ✓ Introduction to OSI Reference Networking Model
- ✓ The seven layers of the OSI Model
- ✓ Basic network terminology – gateway, protocol, port, socket, router, switch, bridge, repeater and hub
- ✓ Understand packet encapsulation and de-encapsulation
- ✓ What is peer to peer networking?
- ✓ Introduction to the TCP/IP protocol stack and the TCP/IP layers
- ✓ Understand and use hardware addresses, ARP and RARP
- ✓ Understand and define a system's hostname
- ✓ Understand IP addresses and network classes
- ✓ Divide a network into multiple, smaller sub-networks
- ✓ The role of subnet mask
- ✓ IP aliasing

A *network* is formed when two or more computers are interconnected to share resources and information. The computers may be interlinked via wired or wireless means. You need a cable, connectors, network ports and the software that support the connectivity. To interconnect several computers so that they can talk to one another, you need an interconnect device such as a hub, switch, router or a gateway, in addition to cables and connectors. A network also typically has other shared devices such as printers, plotters, disk storage and tape libraries. Throughout this and subsequent chapters, a term *node* is used to refer to shared networked devices including computers and printers. Figure 20-1 illustrates five nodes – four computers and one printer.

Network Types

There are two types of networks – *Local Area Network* (LAN) and *Wide Area Network* (WAN).

A LAN is composed of nodes usually located at a single physical location such as a building or campus. Figure 20-1 illustrates a typical LAN.

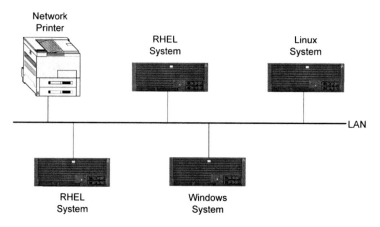

Figure 20-1 Local Area Network

LANs typically use *Ethernet* protocol to transfer data from one node to another. Ethernet was developed in the late 1970s and is presently the global standard for data transmission in today's computer networks. Some of the reasons for its popularity include support for a variety of cable types and topologies, affordability and scalability, and native support in almost all network operating systems out there. The data transmission speed on an Ethernet LAN ranges from 10Mbps (*megabits per second*) to 10Gbps (*gigabits per second*).

A WAN is composed of individual nodes or entire LANs that may be located geographically apart in different cities, countries or continents. Devices such as routers and gateways are employed to form a WAN using leased lines, phone lines, satellite links, wireless or other means. Figure 20-2 shows a typical WAN.

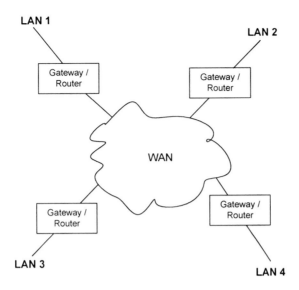

Figure 20-2 Wide Area Network

Network Topologies

A *network topology* refers to how nodes, interconnect devices and physical media are coupled together. There are three common types of physical topologies: *bus*, *star* and *ring*. The fourth type is a combination of bus and star, and is known as *hybrid*.

The following sub-sections discuss these topologies.

Bus Topology

The bus topology consists of a main backbone cable with a terminator connector at either end. All nodes are attached to the backbone. This type of topology is relatively inexpensive and easy to implement. Figure 20-1 shows a bus topology network diagram with a line across representing a backbone cable.

The primary disadvantage with this topology is that a break in the backbone cable or fault in one of the terminators might shut the entire network down.

Star Topology

The star topology uses an interconnect device called *switch* (or *hub*), with each node connected directly to it. Data packets must pass through this device to reach their destination. This topology is widely used in Ethernet networks. Figure 20-3 illustrates a star topology based network diagram.

Star topology networks are easier to deploy and manage, and are highly scalable. Nodes can be attached or detached without any disruption to the function of the network. If there is a broken cable, only the node using it is affected; however, if an interconnect device is down, all nodes connected to it become inaccessible.

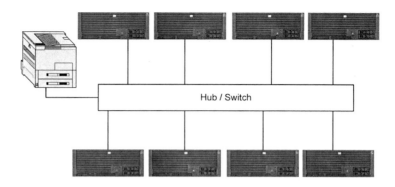

Figure 20-3 Star Topology

Ring Topology

The ring topology is a wiring scheme that allows information to pass from one node to another in a circle or ring. Nodes are joined in the shape of a closed loop so that each node is joined directly to two other nodes, one on either side of it. Figure 20-4 shows a ring topology network diagram.

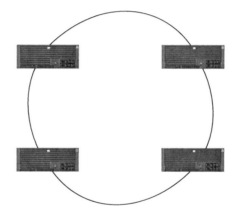

Figure 20-4 Ring Topology

The disadvantage with the ring topology is that if one of the cables in the ring breaks, all nodes in the ring become unreachable. This type of topology is more difficult to configure and wire than other topologies. The token ring protocol uses this topology on token ring networks.

Hybrid Topology

Corporate networks are generally formed using a combination of bus and star topologies. Interconnect devices are installed on different floors of a building or in different buildings and campuses using the bus topology scheme. The star topology is employed to join individual nodes to the interconnect devices.

Introduction to OSI Reference Model

The *Open Systems Interconnection* (OSI) is a reference networking model developed in the early 1980s by the *International Organization for Standardization* (universally abbreviated as ISO) to provide guidelines to networking product manufacturers. These guidelines have enabled them to develop products able to communicate and work with one another's software and hardware products in a heterogeneous computing environment. The OSI reference model is defined and divided for ease in seven layers (Figure 20-5), with each layer performing a unique function independent of other layers.

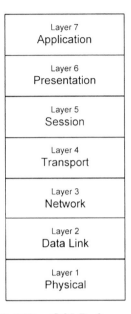

Figure 20-5 The OSI Reference Model

Each layer in the model interacts directly with two layers, one above it and one below it, except the top and the bottom layers. Functionality provided by the seven layers can be divided into three categories: application (such as ftp or telnet), set of transport/network protocols (such as TCP and IP) and related software and hardware (such as cables).

The function of the seven layers can be segregated into two groups. One group, containing the upper three layers (5 to 7), relates to user applications such as formatting of data. The other group, containing the lower four layers (1 to 4), add transport information such as address of the destination node.

Each layer of the OSI reference model is explained in the following sub-sections.

Layer 7: The Application Layer

The *application* layer is where a user or program requests initiation of some kind of service on a remote node. Utilities and programs that work at this layer include *ftp*, *telnet*, *rlogin*, *rcp*, SNMP, SMTP, HTTP, TFTP, NFS, DHCP, secure shell and X Window. On the remote node, server daemons for these services (*ftpd*, *telnetd*, *rlogind* and so on) respond by providing access to the requested services. In other words, client and server programs for *ftp*, *telnet*, *http*, etc. work at this layer.

Gateway

A *gateway* is a device that links two networks running completely different protocols, viz., TCP/IP and NetBEUI, or TCP/IP and IPX/SPX, and enables them to talk to each other. This device works at the application layer. Actually, it works in such a way that it covers all seven layers.

Protocol

A *protocol* is a set of rules governing the exchange of data between two nodes. These rules include how data is formatted, coded and controlled. The rules also provide error handling, speed matching and data packet sequencing. In other words, a protocol is a common language that all nodes on the network speak and understand. Some common protocols are TCP, IP, ICMP, Ethernet, NetBEUI and AppleTalk. Protocols are defined in the */etc/protocols* file, a sample of which is shown below:

```
# cat /etc/protocols
 . . . . . . . .
ip          0      IP          # internet protocol, pseudo protocol number
hopopt      0      HOPOPT      # hop-by-hop options for ipv6
icmp        1      ICMP        # internet control message protocol
igmp        2      IGMP        # internet group management protocol
ggp         3      GGP         # gateway-gateway protocol
ipencap     4      IP-ENCAP    # IP encapsulated in IP (officially ``IP'')
st          5      ST          # ST datagram mode
tcp         6      TCP         # transmission control protocol
cbt         7      CBT         # CBT, Tony Ballardie <A.Ballardie@cs.ucl.ac.uk>
egp         8      EGP         # exterior gateway protocol
igp         9      IGP         # any private interior gateway (Cisco: for IGRP)
 . . . . . . . .
```

The first column lists a protocol's official name, the second column shows the protocol number and the third column identifies any associated aliases.

Layer 6: The Presentation Layer

The *presentation* layer converts incoming data from the application layer into a format understandable by the remote node where this message is destined. The layer manages the presentation of the data to be independent of the node hardware architecture.

Layer 5: The Session Layer

The *session* layer sets up, synchronizes, sequences and terminates a communication session established between a client program at source node and the corresponding server program at the destination node. This layer deals with session and connection coordination between source and destination nodes.

Layer 4: The Transport Layer

The *transport* layer manages end-to-end data transfer reliability. It makes sure that data from source to destination arrives error-free, otherwise it retransmits it. The protocols that work at this layer are *Transmission Control Protocol* (TCP) and *User Datagram Protocol* (UDP).

TCP

TCP is reliable, connection-oriented, point-to-point, but slow. When a stream of packets is sent to the destination node using TCP, the destination node checks for errors and packet sequencing upon its arrival. Each packet contains information such as IP addresses for both source and destination nodes, port numbers, the data, a sequence number and checksum fields. The TCP protocol at the source node establishes a point-to-point connection with the peer TCP protocol at the destination. When the packet is received by the receiving TCP, an acknowledgement is sent back. If the packet contains an error or is lost in transit, the destination node requests the source node to resend the packet. This ensures guaranteed data delivery and makes TCP reliable. Due to acknowledgment and handshaking, some overhead signals are added to TCP, making it slow. TCP is analogous to a telephone communication session between two parties.

UDP

UDP is unreliable, connectionless, multi-point and faster than TCP. If a packet is lost or contains errors upon arrival at the destination node, the source node is unaware of it. The destination node does not send an acknowledgement back to the source node. UDP is normally used for broadcast purposes. There are no overhead signals involved, which makes UDP faster than TCP. UDP is analogous to a radio broadcast where there is no connection between parties.

TCP vs. UDP

Differences between TCP and UDP are summarized in Table 20-1.

TCP	UDP
Reliable	Unreliable
Connection-oriented	Connectionless
Point-to-point	Multipoint
Slow	Fast
Sequenced	Unsequenced
Acknowledgement	No acknowledgement
Uses TCP window for flow control	N/A

Table 20-1 TCP vs. UDP

Ports and Sockets

Both TCP and UDP use ports and sockets for data transmission between a client and its associated server program. A port is either well-known or private. A well-known port is pre-defined for a specific application for use by that application only. It is standardized across all network operating systems including RHEL. Well-known ports are defined in the */etc/services* file, an excerpt of which is shown below:

```
# cat /etc/services
# service-name  port/protocol [aliases ...]   [# comment]

tcpmux      1/tcp     # TCP port service multiplexer
tcpmux      1/udp     # TCP port service multiplexer
rje         5/tcp     # Remote Job Entry
rje         5/udp     # Remote Job Entry
```

echo	7/tcp	
echo	7/udp	
discard	9/tcp	sink null
discard	9/udp	sink null
systat	11/tcp	users
systat	11/udp	users
daytime	13/tcp	
daytime	13/udp	
qotd	17/tcp	quote
qotd	17/udp	quote

. . . .

The first column lists the official name of a network service, the second column contains associated well-known port number and the transport layer protocol the service uses, and the third column identifies any associated aliases.

Some common services and the ports they listen on are: *telnet* on port 23, *ftp* on 21, *sendmail* on 25, *http* on 80 and *ntp* on 123.

A private port, on the other hand, is a random number generated when a client application attempts to establish a communication session with its server process.

When a *telnet* request is initiated on *rhel01* (source node with IP address 192.168.0.201) to get into *rhel02* (destination node with IP address 192.168.0.202), a private port number (4352 for example) is generated and appended to the IP address of *rhel01* to form a source-side socket. This socket information is included in data packets carrying the *telnet* request to *rhel02*. Similarly, the IP address of *rhel02* is appended by the well-known *telnet* port number from the */etc/services* file to form a destination-side socket. This socket information too is added to data packets. Here is what the two sockets will look like:

Source node (*rhel01*):   192.168.0.201.4352 (IP address + private port number)
Destination node (*rhel02*):   192.168.0.202.23 (IP address + well-known port number)

A combination of the two sockets distinctively identifies this *telnet* communication session among several other possible *telnet* sessions established at that time.

Layer 3: The Network Layer

The network layer routes and forwards data packets to the right destination using the right network path. This layer manages data addressing and delivery functions. Protocols that work at this level are *Internet Protocol* (IP), *Address Resolution Protocol* (ARP), *Reverse Address Resolution Protocol* (RARP), *Internet Control Message Protocol* (ICMP), *Serial Line Internet Protocol* (SLIP), *Point to Point Protocol* (PPP), etc.

Router

A *router* is a device that works at the network layer, routing data packets from one network to another. The source and destination networks may be located thousands of miles apart. A router is widely employed on corporate networks and the Internet.

Layer 2: The Data Link Layer

The *data link* layer manages the delivery of data packets beyond the physical network. This layer does packet framing and provides error detection functionality. Protocols available at this layer include *Ethernet, IEEE 802.3, fast Ethernet, gigabit Ethernet, token ring, IEEE 802.5, Fibre Distributed Data Interchange* (FDDI).

Switch and Bridge

Network devices *switches* and *bridges* work at the data link layer.

A switch looks at the MAC address contained within each incoming packet and determines the output port to forward the packet to. Once it has that information, it switches the packet to the port and the packet ultimately reaches the destination node. A switch offers dedicated bandwidth to data flow.

A bridge is used to join LANs provided they use a common protocol (for example, Ethernet-Ethernet or token ring-token ring). A bridge examines MAC address contained within each data packet. If a match is found on the local network, the packet is passed to it, otherwise, it is forwarded to the destination node on the other LAN.

Layer 1: The Physical Layer

The *physical* layer transmits data packets through the network. It describes network hardware characteristics including electrical, mechanical, optical and functional specifications to ensure compatibility between communicating nodes. Protocols available at this layer include 10Base-T, 100Base-T and 1000Base-T.

Repeater and Hub

Network devices *repeaters* and *hubs* work at this layer. Also fall under the physical layer are cables, connectors and LAN interfaces.

A repeater is a network device that takes data signals as input, filters out unwanted noise, amplifies the signals and regenerates them to cover extended distances.

A hub is a network device that receives data from one or more directions and forwards it to one or more directions. The bandwidth of a hub is shared among connected, active nodes. For example, the speed per port on a 100Mbps 12-port hub is 100/12, which is approximately equal to 8Mbps. This means each node can communicate at 8Mbps. This calculation is based on the assumption that all ports on the hub have nodes hooked up and being used.

Summary of OSI Layers

Table 20-2 summarizes OSI layer functions.

OSI Layer	Description
Application (7)	Requests initiation of service on a remote system.
Presentation (6)	Manages presentation of data to be independent of node hardware architecture.
Session (5)	Establishes, synchronizes, sequences and terminates communication session setup between source and destination nodes.

OSI Layer	Description
Transport (4)	Manages end-to-end data transfer reliability.
Network (3)	Manages data addressing and delivery functions.
Data Link (2)	Performs packet framing and provides error detection functionality.
Physical (1)	Describes network hardware characteristics including electrical, mechanical, optical and functional specifications.

Table 20-2 OSI Layer Summary

Encapsulation and De-encapsulation

Data transmission from source node to destination node takes place in the form of packets. When a message is created at the application layer, subsequent layers add header information to the message as it passes down through to the physical layer. Headers contain layer-specific information. When the message along with header information, reaches the physical layer, it is referred to as *packet*. The process of forming a packet through the seven layers is called *encapsulation*.

The packet is transmitted as a stream of 1s and 0s through the medium to the destination node where the physical layer receives the data stream and a reverse process begins. Headers are detached at each subsequent layer as the message passes up through to the application layer. This reverse process is referred to as *de-encapsulation*. Figure 20-6 illustrates encapsulation and de-encapsulation processes.

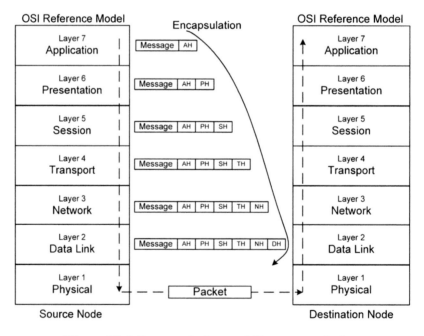

Figure 20-6 Encapsulation and De-encapsulation

Peer-to-Peer Model

Each layer on the source node acts as a peer layer to its corresponding layer on the destination node, making the OSI model *peer-to-peer*. Header information attached at the application layer can only

Red Hat Certified Technician & Engineer

be read, understood and removed by the application layer on the receiving side. Similarly, header attached at the session layer can only be read, understood and removed by the session layer on the receiving node, and so on for the other layers.

Introduction to TCP/IP

The *Transmission Control Protocol / Internet Protocol* (TCP/IP) is a suite of protocols developed by the US Department of Defense in 1969. Today, it is the global standard of information exchange. Although there are scores of protocols within the TCP/IP suite, the name is derived from the two key protocols: Transmission Control Protocol (TCP) and Internet Protocol (IP).

TCP/IP uses the client/server model of communication in which a client program on a source node requests a service and the server program on the destination node responds. TCP/IP communication is primarily point-to-point, meaning each communication session is between two nodes.

TCP/IP Layers

TCP/IP is layered similar to the OSI model. It is, in fact, based on the OSI reference model. Some vendors have defined the TCP/IP suite in four layers, while others in five. Figure 20-7 shows the suite in four layers, and compares it with the OSI reference model.

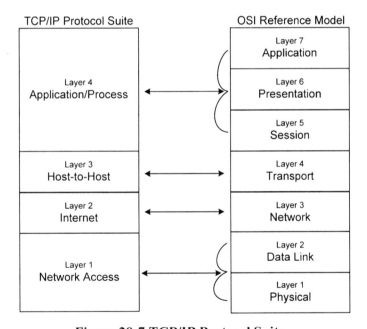

Figure 20-7 TCP/IP Protocol Suite

The figure illustrates the TCP/IP protocol stack on the left and compares it with the OSI reference model on the right. Notice that the bottom four layers are the same, only the names are dissimilar. The difference lies at the top three layers where TCP/IP merges the application, presentation and session layer functionalities into one layer, collectively referred to as the *application* layer. For a detailed understanding of each layer and how they interact, refer to the earlier sub-section "Introduction to OSI Reference Model".

Hardware Address

Hardware address is a unique 48-bit address used to identify the correct destination node for data packets transmitted from a source node. The data packets include hardware addresses for both the source and destination nodes. A network protocol called ARP, maps a hardware address to the destination node's IP address. Hardware address is also referred to as *Ethernet* or *physical* address.

Use the *ifconfig* or *ip* command to list all network interfaces available on the system along with associated hardware addresses:

```
# ifconfig | grep Ethernet
eth0      Link encap:Ethernet  HWaddr 00:0C:29:E1:D7:F5
eth1      Link encap:Ethernet  HWaddr 00:03:47:3B:EB:6E
# ip addr
. . . . . . . .
2: eth0: <BROADCAST,MULTICAST,UP,LOWER_UP> mtu 1500 qdisc pfifo_fast qlen 100
    link/ether 00:0c:29:e1:d7:f5 brd ff:ff:ff:ff:ff:ff
    inet 192.168.0.201/24 brd 192.168.0.255 scope global eth0
3: eth1: <BROADCAST,MULTICAST,UP> mtu 1500 qdisc pfifo_fast qlen 1000
    link/ether 00:03:47:3b:eb:6e brd ff:ff:ff:ff:ff:ff
    inet 192.168.1.201/24 brd 192.168.1.255 scope global eth1
# ip link
. . . . . . . .
2: eth0: <BROADCAST,MULTICAST,UP,LOWER_UP> mtu 1500 qdisc pfifo_fast qlen 100
    link/ether 00:0c:29:e1:d7:f5 brd ff:ff:ff:ff:ff:ff
3: eth1: <BROADCAST,MULTICAST,UP> mtu 1500 qdisc pfifo_fast qlen 1000
    link/ether 00:03:47:3b:eb:6e brd ff:ff:ff:ff:ff:ff
```

Address Resolution Protocol (ARP)

As you know that IP and hardware addresses work hand in hand with each other and a combination of both is critical to identifying the correct destination node. A protocol called *Address Resolution Protocol* (ARP) is used to enable IP and hardware addresses to work together. ARP determines the hardware address of the destination node when its IP address is already known.

ARP broadcasts messages over the network requesting each alive node to reply with its hardware and IP addresses. The addresses received are cached locally by the node in a special memory area called *ARP cache*, and can be viewed with the *arp* command as follows:

```
# arp –a
? (192.168.0.202) at 00:00:0C:07:AC:A2 [ether] on eth0
? (192.168.0.203) at 00:00:0C:07:AC:3E [ether] on eth0
```

Entries in the ARP cache are normally kept for 10 minutes and then removed. These entries can be added to or removed/modified using the *arp* command.

To remove an entry from the ARP cache for the host *rhel02*:

```
# arp –d rhel02
```

To determine the hardware address of *rhel02* from *rhel03*, issue the *arp* command on *rhel03*:

arp rhel02
rhel02 (**192.168.0.202**) at **00:00:0C:07:AC:A2** [ether] on eth0

The *arp* command proves useful when you suspect duplicate IP addresses on the network. Check its output for any duplicate entries.

Reverse Address Resolution Protocol (RARP)

The reverse of ARP is possible with the *Reverse Address Resolution Protocol* (RARP). This protocol gets the IP address of a remote node if you already know the hardware address of it. RARP is typically used by DHCP.

Hostname

A *hostname* is a unique alphanumeric name assigned to a node. It is normally allotted based on the purpose and primary use of the node, although any naming standard can be followed in accordance with corporate IT naming convention policy. For example, the hostname "rhdbp001" in a multi-vendor environment can be assigned to the first RHEL production database server and *sndbd003* can be given to the third SUN Solaris database server used for testing purposes.

A hostname is defined in the startup configuration file */etc/sysconfig/network* via the HOSTNAME directive. A hostname can be changed temporarily using the *hostname* command or permanently by either modifying the HOSTNAME directive in the *network* file or running the Red Hat Network Configurator *system-config-network*.

To display the current hostname of the system:

hostname
rhel01

To change the hostname of the system to *rhel10* on a temporary basis:

hostname rhel10
hostname
rhel10

To change the hostname of the system to *rhel10* on a permanent basis, set the HOSTNAME directive in the *network* file and reboot the system:

# **vi /etc/sysconfig/network**
HOSTNAME=rhel10
# **shutdown −ry now**

Whenever you modify the system hostname, make sure that you update the */etc/hosts* file to reflect the new hostname by changing the corresponding entry.

To change the hostname of the system back to *rhel01* using the Network Configurator, follow the steps below:

☞ Run *system-config-network* or choose (GNOME) System / (KDE) Main Menu →
Administration → Network. Click the DNS and Hosts tabs and modify the hostname. See Figure
20-8.

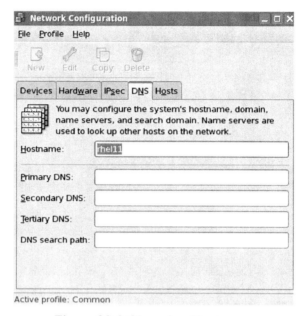

Figure 20-8 Changing Hostname

IP Address

IP stands for *Internet Protocol* and represents a unique 32-bit software address that every single
node on the network must have in order to communicate with other nodes. IP addresses can be
assigned temporarily or permanently. Temporary addresses are referred to as *dynamic* addresses
and are typically leased from a DHCP server for a specific period of time. Permanent addresses are
called *static* addresses and are not changed unless there is a requirement. Every data packet sent out
from a source node contains the destination node's IP address to determine the correct recipient of
the packet and the route to be taken to reach that destination. Hardware and IP addresses work
together to identify the correct network interface.

An IP address consists of four 8-bit octets separated by the period character. Each octet can have
values between 0 and 255 (00000000 to 11111111) inclusive, based on 2^8 (2x2x2x2x2x2x2x2=256)
formula. An IP address can be determined in both binary and decimal notations. Given an address
in binary, you can convert it into decimal, and vice versa. For instance, an address 192.168.123.102
is shown below in both notations:

```
   11000000   .   10101000   .   01111011   .   01100110   (binary)
    128+64        128+32+8   64+32+16+8+2+1  64+32+4+2
      192     .     168      .     123       .    102       (decimal)
```

Each bit in an octet has a weight based on its position in the octet. Figure 20-9 depicts that as either
0 or 1.

Red Hat Certified Technician & Engineer

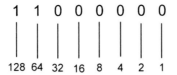

Figure 20-9 Binary to Decimal Conversion

The two left-most bits in the first octet of the IP address given above are 1. Based on the formula, they add up to 192. The second octet has the 1st, 3rd and the 5th left-most bits set to 1, which sum up to 168, and so on for the last two octets.

To view IP addresses assigned to network interfaces, use the *ifconfig* or *ip* command:

ifconfig
eth0   Link encap:Ethernet HWaddr 00:0C:29:E1:D7:F5
        inet addr:**192.168.0.201** Bcast:192.168.0.255 Mask:255.255.255.0
        UP BROADCAST RUNNING MULTICAST MTU:1500 Metric:1
        RX packets:200568 errors:0 dropped:0 overruns:0 frame:0
        TX packets:173189 errors:0 dropped:0 overruns:0 carrier:0
        collisions:0 txqueuelen:100
        RX bytes:18629316 (17.7 MiB) TX bytes:28834054 (27.4 MiB)
        Base address:0x1070 Memory:e8820000-e8840000
eth1   Link encap:Ethernet HWaddr 00:03:47:3B:EB:6E
        inet addr:**192.168.1.201** Bcast:192.168.1.255 Mask:255.255.255.0
        UP BROADCAST RUNNING MULTICAST MTU:1500 Metric:1
        RX packets:132133 errors:1 dropped:0 overruns:0 frame:1
        TX packets:78477 errors:0 dropped:0 overruns:0 carrier:0
        collisions:7 txqueuelen:1000
        RX bytes:9061553 (8.6 Mb) TX bytes:6604103 (6.2 Mb)
        Interrupt:16 Base address:0x3000 Memory:f6700000-f6700038
. . . .
ip addr
. . . .
2: eth0: <BROADCAST,MULTICAST,UP,LOWER_UP> mtu 1500 qdisc pfifo_fast qlen 100
    link/ether 00:0c:29:e1:d7:f5 brd ff:ff:ff:ff:ff:ff
    inet **192.168.0.201**/24 brd 192.168.0.255 scope global eth0
3: eth1: <BROADCAST,MULTICAST,UP> mtu 1500 qdisc pfifo_fast qlen 1000
    link/ether 00:03:47:3b:eb:6e brd ff:ff:ff:ff:ff:ff
    inet **192.168.1.201**/24 brd 192.168.1.255 scope global eth1

You can use the Network Configurator to view configured IP addresses. Follow the steps below:

☞Run *system-config-network* or choose (GNOME) System / (KDE) Main Menu →
Administration → Network. Click the Devices tab and double click one of the devices to view assigned IP address. See Figure 20-10.

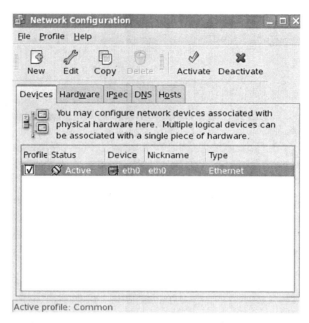

Figure 20-10 View Configured IP Addresses

IPv6 Address

With the explosive growth of the Internet, the presence of an extremely large number of nodes and an ever increasing demand for additional addresses, the conventional IP address space, which is 2^{32} (four octets) and provides approximately 4.3 billion addresses, is almost used up. To meet the future demand, a new version of IP address space has been introduced and is now available for use. This new version is referred to as *IPv6* (IP version 6). IPv6 addresses are 128-bit and provide 2^{128} (16 octets) additional IP addresses. Also, IPv6 provides simplified packet header format, better routing capabilities, enhanced security controls, more autoconfiguration options and many other new and enhanced features as compared to the conventional IP address space.

By default, IPv6 is disabled via the NETWORKING_IPV6 directive as defined in the */etc/sysconfig/network* file. This directive needs to be set to yes to enable the support. Additional directives such as IPV6INIT, IPV6ADDR and IPV6_DEFAULTGW may need to be set appropriately in interface configuration files located in */etc/sysconfig/network-scripts* directory. The same directory also holds interface-specific static IPv6 route files, which may need to be updated as well if required. An enhanced version of DHCP called DHCPV6 is now available and being used to autofurnish IPv6 network configuration, in addition to a new breed of commands such as *ping6*, *traceroute6* and *tracepath6* to complement existing network configuration and troubleshooting tools. The *ip* and the *host* commands are also IPv6 aware.

Network Classes

Each IP address is divided into two portions: a *network* portion and a *node* portion. The network portion identifies the correct destination network and the node portion identifies the correct destination node on that network.

Based on how many bits are allocated to the network portion, there are five useable IP address classes: A, B, C, D and E. Classes A, B and C are widely used, while classes D and E are dedicated for multicast networks and scientific purposes only. The following provides an explanation of classes A, B and C.

Class A

Class A addresses are used for networks with an extremely large number of nodes. The first octet defines the network address and the rest are allocated to nodes. Figure 20-11 displays the division of bits in a class A address.

Figure 20-11 Class A Address

The total number of useable network addresses in class A can be up to $2^{8-1} - 2$ (126) and the total number of useable node addresses up to $2^{24} - 2$ (16,777,214). Two is subtracted from both calculations because addresses with all 0s in the first octet and all 1s in the last octet are reserved. Also, one network bit is subtracted from 8 to get 2^7 network numbers since 0 is reserved. The network address range for class A networks is between 0 and 127 (**00000000** to **01111111**). See the example below that also shows reserved addresses:

    00001010.01111001.00110011.11010001 (binary notation)
       10 . 121 . 51 . 209   (decimal notation)

    10.121.51.**0**   (network address)
    10.121.51.**255**   (broadcast address)

0 and 255 in the decimal notation are network and broadcast addresses and are always reserved. Class A addresses always start with 0 as shown in the binary notation.

Class B

Class B addresses are used for mid-sized networks. The first two octets define the network address and the remaining are allocated to nodes. See Figure 20-12.

Figure 20-12 Class B Address

The total number of useable network addresses in class B can be up to 2^{16-2} (16,384) and the total number of useable node addresses up to $2^{16} - 2$ (65,534). The first two bits in class B network addresses are reserved and, therefore, not used in calculation. The network address range for class B networks is between 128 and 191 (**10000000** to **10111111**). See the example below that also shows reserved addresses:

    10100001.01111001.00110011.11010001 (binary notation)
       161 . 121 . 51 . 209   (decimal notation)

    161.121.51.**0**   (network address)
    161.121.51.**255**   (broadcast address)

Class B addresses always begin with 10 as shown in the binary notation.

Class C

Class C addresses are used for small networks with not more than 254 nodes. The first three octets define the network address and the fourth is allocated to nodes. Refer to Figure 20-13.

Figure 20-13 Class C Address

The total number of useable network addresses in class C can be up to 2^{24-3} (2,097,152) and the total number of useable node addresses up to $2^8 - 2$ (254). The first three bits in the network address are reserved and, therefore, not used in calculation. The network address range for class C networks is between 192 and 223 (**11000000** to **11011111**). See the example below that also shows reserved addresses:

11010111.01111001.00110011.11010001 (binary notation)
  215 .   121 . 51 . 209   (decimal notation)

215.121.51.**0**   (network address)
215.121.51.**255**   (broadcast address)

Class C addresses always begin with 110 as shown in the binary notation.

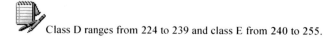 Class D ranges from 224 to 239 and class E from 240 to 255.

Subnetting

Subnetting is a method by which a large network address space can be divided into several smaller and more manageable logical sub-networks, commonly referred to as *subnets*. Subnetting usually results in reduced network traffic, improved network performance, and de-centralized and easier administration, among other benefits.

Subnetting does not touch the network bits, it makes use of the node bits only.

The following should be kept in mind when working with subnetting:

✓ Subnetting does not increase the number of IP addresses in a network. In fact, it reduces the number of useable IP addresses.
✓ All nodes in a given subnet must have the same subnet mask.
✓ Each subnet acts as a separate network and requires a router to talk to other subnets.
✓ The first and the last IP address in a subnet (similar to a network) are reserved. The first address points to the subnet itself and the last is the broadcast address.

Subnetting employs using required number of node bits. For example, if you wish to divide a class C network address of 192.168.12.0 with default netmask of 255.255.255.0 into 6 useable subnets each with 30 useable node addresses, you need 3 left-most node bits (highlighted) from the right-most octet (node octet), as shown below:

Red Hat Certified Technician & Engineer

```
192 . 168 . 12 . 0
11000000.10101000.00001100.00000000
```

Here is the formula to calculate useable subnets. 2 subnet bits give $2^2 - 2 = 2$ subnets, 3 subnet bits give $2^3 - 2 = 6$ subnets, 4 subnet bits give $2^4 - 2 = 14$ subnets, 5 subnet bits give $2^5 - 2 = 30$ subnets, 6 subnet bits give $2^6 - 2 = 62$ subnets and 7 subnet bits give $2^7 - 2 = 126$ subnets. This formula is applicable to determine number of useable subnets created out of a class A, B or C network address.

Similarly, use the formula to determine number of useable node addresses. 2 node bits give $2^2 - 2 = 2$ addresses, 3 node bits give $2^3 - 2 = 6$ addresses, 4 node bits give $2^4 - 2 = 14$ addresses, 5 node bits give $2^5 - 2 = 30$ addresses, 6 node bits give $2^6 - 2 = 62$ addresses and 7 node bits give $2^7 - 2 = 126$ addresses. This formula is applicable to determine number of useable node addresses created out of a class A, B or C network address.

As an example, suppose you have 3 subnet bits available to work with. The 3 bits would generate eight combinations – 000, 001, 010, 011, 100, 101, 110 and 111. The first and the last set of values (000 and 111) are reserved for network and broadcast addresses. This leaves the remaining 6 combinations useable. Table 20-3 lists the combinations along with subnet IP, range of useable IP addresses available within the subnet that can be assigned to nodes, and broadcast subnet addresses.

Subnet Bits	Subnet IP	First Useable IP	Last Useable IP	Broadcast Subnet IP
000	Reserved for subnet address			
001	192.168.12.32	192.168.12.33	192.168.12.62	192.168.12.63
010	192.168.12.64	192.168.12.65	192.168.12.94	192.168.12.95
011	192.168.12.96	192.168.12.97	192.168.12.126	192.168.12.127
100	192.168.12.128	192.168.12.129	192.168.12.158	192.168.12.159
101	192.168.12.160	192.168.12.161	192.168.12.190	192.168.12.191
110	192.168.12.192	192.168.12.193	192.168.12.222	192.168.12.223
111	Reserved for subnet broadcast address			

Table 20-3 Subnetting

Subnet Mask

After a network address is subnetted, you need to determine something called *subnet mask* or *netmask*. The subnet mask is the network portion plus the subnet bits. In other words, the subnet mask segregates the network bits from the node bits. It is used by routers to identify the start and end of the network/subnet portion and the start and end of the node portion of a given IP address.

The subnet mask, like an IP address, can be represented in either decimal or binary notation. The 1s in the subnet mask identify the subnet bits and 0s identify the node bits. The default subnet masks for class A, B and C networks are 255.0.0.0, 255.255.0.0 and 255.255.255.0, respectively.

To determine the subnet mask for the class C address 192.168.12.0 in the example earlier, set all network and subnet bits to 1 and all node bits to 0. This means the first 3 octets in the network portion plus the first 3 left-most bits in the node portion are set to 1 and the remaining 5 right-most node bits to 0.

```
11111111.11111111.11111111.11100000
 255  .  255  .  255  .  224
```

This gives the netmask of 255.255.255.224. In class A networks, there are 22 valid netmasks. Consult Table 20-4.

Subnet Mask	# of Subnet Bits	Useable Subnets	Nodes per Subnet
255.128.0.0	1	1	8,388,606
255.192.0.0	2	2	4,194,302
255.224.0.0	3	6	2,097,150
255.240.0.0	4	14	1,048,574
255.248.0.0	5	30	524,286
255.252.0.0	6	62	262,142
255.254.0.0	7	126	131,070
255.255.0.0	8	254	65,534
255.255.128.0	9	510	32,766
255.255.192.0	10	1,022	16,382
255.255.224.0	11	2,046	8,190
255.255.240.0	12	4,094	4,094
255.255.248.0	13	8,190	2,046
255.255.252.0	14	16,382	1,022
255.255.254.0	15	32,766	510
255.255.255.0	16	65,534	254
255.255.255.128	17	131,070	126
255.255.255.192	18	262,142	62
255.255.255.224	19	524,286	30
255.255.255.240	20	1,048,574	14
255.255.255.248	21	2,097,150	6
255.255.255.252	22	4,194,302	2

Table 20-4 Subnet Masks for Class C

In class B networks, there are 14 valid netmasks. Consult Table 20-5.

Subnet Mask	# of Subnet Bits	Useable Subnets	Nodes per Subnet
255.255.128.0	1	1	32,766
255.255.192.0	2	2	16,382
255.255.224.0	3	6	8,190
255.255.240.0	4	14	4,094
255.255.248.0	5	30	2,046
255.255.252.0	6	62	1,022
255.255.254.0	7	126	510
255.255.255.0	8	254	254
255.255.255.128	9	510	126
255.255.255.192	10	1,022	62
255.255.255.224	11	2,046	30
255.255.255.240	12	4,094	14
255.255.255.248	13	8,190	6
255.255.255.252	14	16,382	2

Table 20-5 Subnet Masks for Class B

In class C networks, there are 6 valid netmasks. Consult Table 20-6.

Subnet Mask	# of Subnet Bits	Useable Subnets	Nodes per Subnet
255.255.255.128	1	1	126
255.255.255.192	2	2	62
255.255.255.224	3	6	30
255.255.255.240	4	14	14
255.255.255.248	5	30	6
255.255.255.252	6	62	2

Table 20-6 Subnet Masks for Class C

To determine the subnet address for a given IP address such as 192.168.12.72 with netmask 255.255.255.224, write the IP address in binary format and then write the subnet mask in binary format with all network and subnet bits set to 1 and all node bits set to 0. Now perform a logical AND operation. For each matching 1 you get 1, otherwise 0. The following highlights ANDed bits:

```
11000000.10101000.00001100.01001000    (IP address)
11111111.11111111.11111111.11100000    (subnet mask)
================================
11000000.10101000.00001100.01000000    (subnet IP in binary format)
   192  .  168  .  12  .  64           (subnet IP in decimal format)
```

This calculation enables you to determine subnet address from a given IP address and subnet mask.

IP Aliasing

A single physical network interface can have multiple IP addresses assigned to it to create multiple logical interfaces. Each IP address can then be assigned to a unique hostname. Binding multiple IP addresses to a single physical network interface is referred to as *IP aliasing* or *IP multiplexing*.

IP aliasing enables a single system with single network interface to be seen as multiple systems, with each one of them having a unique IP address and hostname. This functionality allows several applications to run on one system, but appears to users as if they are running on separate, physical systems.

Each logical interface uses a unique logical instance number. For instance, the first logical interface on *eth0* would be *eth0:1*, the second would be *eth0:2* and so on. In this naming convention, "eth" refers to the Ethernet network interface associated with a numerical index for the physical interface within its class in the system, and ":1" and ":2" represent logical instances corresponding to logical interfaces for the specified physical interface. The default is 0. The interface name *eth0* is the same as *eth0:0*.

The first logical instance *eth0:0* is known as the *initial* interface, which must be configured before any subsequent logical interfaces such as *eth0:1*, *eth0:2* and *eth0:3* can be configured. Logical interfaces do not need to be assigned in sequence; in fact, *eth0:3* can be configured even if *eth0:1* and *eth0:2* do not exist.

Summary

In this chapter you were introduced to basics of networking. The chapter started off with providing an understanding of network, types of network and various common network topologies being employed in the industry.

The next section covered the OSI reference networking model in detail. You learned about the layers of the model, how packets were encapsulated and de-encapsulated, and the peer-to-peer nature of the model. You looked at a few other sub-topics including key transport protocols, concepts of ports and sockets, and definitions of devices such as gateways, routers, switches, repeaters and hubs.

The TCP/IP protocol stack and related concepts were discussed in detail. Topics such as TCP/IP layers, hardware address, ARP, RARP, hostname, IP address, network classes and IP aliasing provided you with a good understanding of the basics of TCP/IP. Finally, you were explained what the concepts of subnetting and subnet mask were, how to divide a network address into multiple sub-networks and the role a subnet mask played.

Network Interfa

Administration i

In order for a system to c
interfaces must be conf
parameters. Also, if t
configured as well
modified by ha
that the syst

Un

This chapter covers the following major topics:

- ✓ Understand network configuration files and commands
- ✓ Configure a network interface and assign a single IP address
- ✓ Configure a network interface and assign multiple IP addresses
- ✓ Enable network and logical interfaces to activate at system reboots
- ✓ Activate and deactivate network and logical interfaces manually
- ✓ The role of the /etc/hosts file
- ✓ Add, modify and delete network and logical interfaces via Network Configurator
- ✓ Modify network interface speed, duplex mode, etc.
- ✓ What is routing?
- ✓ Add, delete and display routes using commands and Network Configurator
- ✓ Understand network connectivity troubleshooting concepts
- ✓ Perform network connectivity troubleshooting using tools such as ping, netstat, traceroute, tracepath, mtr and tcpdump

ommunicate with other nodes on the network, one of its network
gured with a unique IP address, hostname and other required network
e system is required to access nodes on other networks, routing needs to be
. There are several files involved in networking configuration and can be
d or using a graphical tool. Once networking is configured, testing is done to ensure
m is able to successfully communicate with other networked nodes.

derstanding Configuration Files and Commands

HEL includes several configuration files, scripts and commands that are critical to performing
configuration and administration tasks on network interfaces. Following sub-sections explain key
files, scripts and commands.

Network Configuration Files and Scripts

When performing network interface administration, several configuration files and scripts are
involved. These files are located in the */etc/sysconfig* and */etc/sysconfig/network-scripts* directories,
and are explained below.

The /etc/sysconfig/network File

This file contains a minimum of two critical directives as shown below:

```
# cat /etc/sysconfig/network
NETWORKING=yes
HOSTNAME=rhel01
```

A short description of these and other directives that may be defined in this file is given in Table
21-1.

Directive	Description
HOSTNAME	Sets the hostname of the system.
GATEWAY	Defines the default gateway address. This directive can alternatively be defined in individual interface configuration files in the */etc/sysconfig/network-scripts* directory.
GATEWAYDEV	Specifies the network interface device such as *eth0*, associated with the default gateway.
NETWORKING	Enables or disables IPv4 networking.
NETWORKING_IPV6	Enables or disables IPv6 networking.
NISDOMAIN	Defines the name of NIS domain if configured.

Table 21-1 Directives in /etc/sysconfig/network File

The /etc/sysconfig/network-scripts Directory

This directory stores information about all configured network interfaces. Doing an *ll* on the
directory displays the following:

```
# ll /etc/sysconfig/network-scripts
total 380
-rw-r--r--    3 root root   112 Jan  1 18:07 ifcfg-eth0
-rw-r--r--    3 root root   112 Jan  1 18:08 ifcfg-eth1
-rw-r--r--    1 root root   254 Jun 20 2001 ifcfg-lo
lrwxrwxrwx 1 root root    20 Dec 19 08:43 ifdown -> ../../../sbin/ifdown
-rwxr-xr-x  1 root root   625 Sep 11 2006 ifdown-bnep
-rwxr-xr-x  1 root root  4421 Jan  4 2007 ifdown-eth
-rwxr-xr-x  1 root root   827 Apr 15 2005 ifdown-ippp
-rwxr-xr-x  1 root root  2159 Sep 11 2006 ifdown-ipsec
-rwxr-xr-x  1 root root  4473 Sep 11 2006 ifdown-ipv6
lrwxrwxrwx 1 root root    11 Dec 19 08:43 ifdown-isdn -> ifdown-ippp
-rwxr-xr-x  1 root root  1481 Sep 11 2006 ifdown-post
-rwxr-xr-x  1 root root  1084 Sep 11 2006 ifdown-ppp
. . . . . . . .
```

Several configuration files are located in this directory, some of which are briefly explained below.

The /etc/sysconfig/network-scripts/ifcfg-eth0 File

This file holds networking information for the first Ethernet interface. For additional interfaces, the file names would be *ifcfg-eth1*, *ifcfg-eth2* and so on. Here are the current contents of *ifcfg-eth0*:

```
# cat /etc/sysconfig/network-scripts/ifcfg-eth0
# Intel Corporation 82545EM Gigabit Ethernet Controller (Copper)
DEVICE=eth0
BOOTPROTO=none
BROADCAST=192.168.0.255
HWADDR=00:0C:29:E1:D7:F5
IPADDR=192.168.0.201
NETMASK=255.255.255.0
NETWORK=192.168.0.0
ONBOOT=yes
TYPE=Ethernet
```

These and other directives that may be defined in the file are described in Table 21-2.

Directive	Description
BOOTPROTO	Defines a boot protocol to be used. Values include "dhcp" to obtain IP information from a DHCP server, "bootp" to boot off a network boot server and get IP information from there, and "none" to use a static IP address defined in the file with IPADDR.
BROADCAST	Specifies a broadcast IP address.
DEVICE	Specifies the device name of the network interface.
DNS	Places an entry for a DNS server in the /etc/resolv.conf file if PEERDNS directive is set to "yes" in this file.
HWADDR	Defines the hardware address of the interface.
IPADDR	Specifies an IP address assigned to the interface.
IPV6INIT	Enables or disables the use of IPv6. Values can be "yes" or "no".

Directive	Description
NETMASK	Sets a netmask address.
ONBOOT	Activates the interface at system boot or leave it deactivated. Values can be "yes" or "no".
ONPARENT	Used with IP aliasing. Activates all logical interfaces with the parent physical interface or leave them deactivated. Values can be "yes" or "no".
PEERDNS	Modifies DNS client resolver file /etc/resolv.conf or leaves the file intact. Default is "yes" if BOOTPROTO=dhcp is set.
PEERNIS	Modifies NIS client configuration or leaves it intact. Values can be "yes" or "no".
PEERNTP	Modifies NTP client configuration or leaves it intact. Values can be "yes" or "no".
USERCTL	Allows or disallows non-root users to activate the interface. Values can be "yes" or "no".
TYPE	Interface type.

Table 21-2 Network Interface File Directives

There are other directives that may be defined in this file depending on the type of interface connection used.

Some additional files from /etc/sysconfig/network-scripts directory are described in Table 21-3.

File	Description
ifcfg-lo	Holds configuration for the loopback interface.
ifup-*	Activates specific network interface.
ifdown-*	Deactivates specific network interface.
network-functions	Contains functions sourced by many IPv4 network scripts.
network-functions-ipv6	Contains functions sourced by many IPv6 network scripts.

Table 21-3 Miscellaneous Network Files

The /etc/sysconfig/networking Directory

This directory stores current networking information and is maintained by the Network Configurator. Doing an *ll* with –R on the directory displays the following:

```
# ll –R /etc/sysconfig/networking
/etc/sysconfig/networking:
total 16
drwxr-xr-x 2 root root 4096 Jan   4 23:43 devices
drwxr-xr-x 3 root root 4096 Dec 11 22:36 profiles
/etc/sysconfig/networking/devices:
total 8
-rw-r--r-- 3 root root 264 Jan  4 23:43 ifcfg-eth0
-rw-r--r-- 3 root root 264 Jan  4 23:43 ifcfg-eth1
/etc/sysconfig/networking/profiles:
total 8
drwxr-xr-x 2 root root 4096 Jan  3 04:23 default
```

```
/etc/sysconfig/networking/profiles/default:
total 24
-rw-r--r-- 2 root root 177 Jan  4 23:42 hosts
-rw-r--r-- 3 root root 264 Jan  4 23:43 ifcfg-eth0
-rw-r--r-- 3 root root 264 Jan  4 23:43 ifcfg-eth1
-rw-r--r-- 1 root root   0 Jan  4 23:42 network
-rw-r--r-- 2 root root   0 Jan  4 23:42 resolv.conf
```

The output displays two sub-directories: *devices* and *profiles*. The *devices* sub-directory contains a hard link of each configured network interface file and the *profiles* sub-directory contains a directory structure that maintains a hard link of each configured network interface file, current */etc/hosts* file and the */etc/resolv.conf* DNS resolver file.

You can define multiple profiles based on requirements, and activate only one of them at a time with the *system-config-network-cmd* command. Currently, one profile called default is configured. Having multiple profiles defined is particularly beneficial for users who work from more than one locations.

Network Interface Administration Commands

There are certain commands that can be used to administer network interfaces. These commands are described in Table 21-4.

Command	Description
ethtool	Configures interface settings such as speed and duplex mode.
ifconfig	Configures, activates and deactivates an interface, and displays information about it.
ifdown	Brings an interface down.
ifup	Brings an interface up.
system-config-network-cmd	Displays details of configured interfaces.
system-config-network or *system-config-network-gui*	Graphical Red Hat Network Configurator tool for network interface administration.
system-config-network-tui	Text equivalent of Red Hat Network Configurator tool.

Table 21-4 Network Interface Administration Commands

Configuring Network Interfaces

Configuring network interfaces includes assigning IP address, subnet mask and broadcast address to an interface, defining IP aliasing, activating and deactivating an interface manually, autoactivating at system reboots, updating */etc/hosts* file and modifying interface settings. These tasks may be performed using either commands or the Network Configurator.

Configuring a Network Interface

To successfully configure a network interface *eth2* on *rhel01* with class C IP address 192.168.2.201, default netmask 255.255.255.0 and broadcast address 192.168.2.255, run the *ifconfig* command as follows:

ifconfig eth2 192.168.2.201 netmask 255.255.255.0 192.168.2.255

Run the command again to verify the new IP assignments:

ifconfig eth2
```
eth2    Link encap:Ethernet  HWaddr 00:03:47:3B:EB:6F
        inet addr:192.168.2.201  Bcast:192.168.2.255  Mask:255.255.255.0
        UP BROADCAST RUNNING MULTICAST  MTU:1500  Metric:1
        RX packets:98863 errors:0 dropped:0 overruns:0 frame:0
        TX packets:20 errors:0 dropped:0 overruns:0 carrier:0
        collisions:1 txqueuelen:1000
        RX bytes:5511313 (5.2 Mb)  TX bytes:880 (880.0 b)
        Interrupt:29 Base address:0x3020 Memory:f6701000-f6701038
```

Configuring IP Aliasing

If there is a plan to run multiple applications on a single system, you can have multiple IP addresses and hostnames assigned to a single physical network interface (assuming there is only one in the system). Users of each application will be given a different hostname and IP address for access. The *ifconfig* command below assigns three IP addresses to *eth2* with default netmask:

ifconfig eth2:1 192.168.3.201 netmask 255.255.255.0 192.168.3.255
ifconfig eth2:2 192.168.4.201 netmask 255.255.255.0 192.168.4.255
ifconfig eth2:3 192.168.5.201 netmask 255.255.255.0 192.168.5.255

Run the *ifconfig* or *ip* command to check the results:

ifconfig
```
. . . . . . . .
eth2    Link encap:Ethernet  HWaddr 00:03:47:3B:EB:6F
        inet addr:192.168.2.201  Bcast:192.168.2.255  Mask:255.255.255.0
        UP BROADCAST RUNNING MULTICAST  MTU:1500  Metric:1
        RX packets:98863 errors:0 dropped:0 overruns:0 frame:0
        TX packets:20 errors:0 dropped:0 overruns:0 carrier:0
        collisions:1 txqueuelen:1000
        RX bytes:5511313 (5.2 Mb)  TX bytes:880 (880.0 b)
        Interrupt:29 Base address:0x3020 Memory:f6701000-f6701038
eth2:1    Link encap:Ethernet  HWaddr 00:03:47:3B:EB:6F
        inet addr:192.168.3.201  Bcast:192.168.3.255  Mask:255.255.255.0
        UP BROADCAST RUNNING MULTICAST  MTU:1500  Metric:1
        Interrupt:29 Base address:0x3020 Memory:f6701000-f6701038
eth2:2    Link encap:Ethernet  HWaddr 00:03:47:3B:EB:6F
        inet addr:192.168.4.201  Bcast:192.168.4.255  Mask:255.255.255.0
        UP BROADCAST RUNNING MULTICAST  MTU:1500  Metric:1
        Interrupt:29 Base address:0x3020 Memory:f6701000-f6701038
eth2:3    Link encap:Ethernet  HWaddr 00:03:47:3B:EB:6F
        inet addr:192.168.5.201  Bcast:192.168.5.255  Mask:255.255.255.0
        UP BROADCAST RUNNING MULTICAST  MTU:1500  Metric:1
        Interrupt:29 Base address:0x3020 Memory:f6701000-f6701038
. . . . . . . .
```

ip addr
. . . .
4: eth2: <BROADCAST,MULTICAST,UP> mtu 1500 qdisc pfifo_fast qlen 1000
   link/ether 00:03:47:3B:EB:6F brd ff:ff:ff:ff:ff:ff
    inet 192.168.2.201/24 brd 192.168.2.255 scope global eth2
    inet 192.168.3.201/24 brd 192.168.3.255 scope global eth2:1
    inet 192.168.4.201/24 brd 192.168.4.255 scope global eth2:2
    inet 192.168.5.201/24 brd 192.168.5.255 scope global eth2:3

Now users can access the system with any of the four IP addresses.

Setting Network Interfaces to Activate at System Boot

The network interface configuration performed in previous sub-sections will not survive at the next system reboot. To preserve the settings across system reboots and get them automatically assigned to the interfaces, you need to create files – *ifcfg-eth2*, *ifcfg-eth2:1*, *ifcfg-eth2:2* and *ifcfg-eth2:3* – in the */etc/sysconfig/network-scripts* directory for each interface. These files will be sourced by the */etc/rc.d/init.d/network* startup script, which is executed at boot time when the system enters run level 2. This script reads the interface configuration files and executes *ifup* command on configured interfaces.

File contents for *eth2* and *eth2:1* are shown below:

```
# cat /etc/sysconfig/network-scripts/ifcfg-eth2
DEVICE=eth2
BOOTPROTO=none
BROADCAST=192.168.2.255
HWADDR=00:03:47:3B:EB:6F
IPADDR=192.168.2.201
NETMASK=255.255.255.0
NETWORK=192.168.2.0
ONBOOT=yes
TYPE=Ethernet
# cat /etc/sysconfig/network-scripts/ifcfg-eth2:1
DEVICE=eth2:1
BOOTPROTO=none
BROADCAST=192.168.3.255
HWADDR=00:03:47:3B:EB:6F
IPADDR=192.168.3.201
NETMASK=255.255.255.0
NETWORK=192.168.3.0
ONBOOT=yes
ONPARENT=yes
TYPE=Ethernet
```

Activating and Deactivating Network Interfaces Manually

Network interfaces can be activated or deactivated manually using the *ifup* and *ifdown* commands.

To deactivate *eth2*, run any of the following:

```
# ifdown eth2
# ifdown ifcfg-eth2
```

Execute any of the following to reactivate *eth2*:

```
# ifup eth2
# ifup ifcfg-eth2
```

To deactivate *eth2:1*, run any of the following:

```
# ifdown eth2:1
# ifdown ifcfg-eth2:1
```

Execute any of the following to reactivate *eth2:1*:

```
# ifup eth2:1
# ifup ifcfg-eth2:1
```

Adding IP Addresses and Hostnames to the /etc/hosts File

You need to choose hostnames to be assigned to each individual IP address. For example, the four IP addresses configured on *eth2* require unique hostnames such as *server1*, *server2*, *server3* and *server4*. These entries will need to be added to the */etc/hosts* file as shown below:

```
192.168.2.201   server1   db01  # first logical server
192.168.3.201   server2   db02  # second logical server
192.168.4.201   server3   db03  # third logical server
192.168.5.201   server4   db04  # fourth logical server
```

Each line in the file contains an IP address in the first column followed by an official (or *canonical*) hostname in the second column. You may also define one or more aliases per entry (*db01*, *db02*, *db03* and *db04* in the above example). The official hostname and one or more aliases allow you to have multiple hostnames assigned to a single IP address. This enables the system to be accessed using any of the hostnames.

The */etc/hosts* file is typically used if you need to access systems on the local network only. This file must be maintained on each individual system and be edited whenever an update is required.

Configuring Network Interfaces via Network Configurator

To successfully configure a network interface *eth2* on *rhel01* with class C IP address 192.168.2.201, default netmask 255.255.255.0 and broadcast address 192.168.2.255, follow the steps below using the Network Configurator:

1. Run *system-config-network* or choose (GNOME) System / (KDE) Main Menu →
    Administration → Network. The Network Configurator dialog box as shown in Figure 21-1 will appear. Click New to configure a new interface.

Figure 21-1 Network Configurator – Main Menu

There are five tabs on the main window. The Devices tab shows configured interfaces, which can be modified by clicking the Edit botton at the top; the Hardware tab allows you to modify hardware parameters such as memory location, DMA and IRQ associated with an interface; the IPsec tab allows you to configure secure tunnels between systems; the DNS tab is where you can define the system hostname, one or more (up to 3) DNS servers and DNS search path; and the Hosts tab displays the *etc/hosts* file contents and allows you to add or modify entries.

2. Select a device type to be used. For this demonstration, select "Ethernet Connection".

Figure 21-2 Network Configurator – Select Device Type

3. The Network Configurator will display a list of all network cards installed on the system. For this demonstration, choose AMD Ethernet card as shown in Figure 21-3 and click Forward.

Figure 21-3 Network Configurator – Select Ethernet Device

4. The next screen will allow you to choose a source to obtain IP information from. You can either opt to add the information manually or get it from a configured DHCP server. The "bootp" and "dialup" options are available to choose if you wish the system to obtain IP information from them. You can also choose whether you wish to obtain DNS information from a DHCP server.

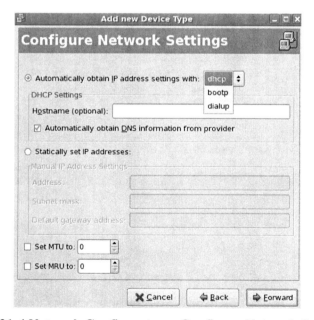

Figure 21-4 Network Configurator – Configure Network Settings I

5. If you do not wish to use DHCP, click "Statically set IP addresses" and enter IP, subnet mask and default gateway addresses. Click Forward when done.

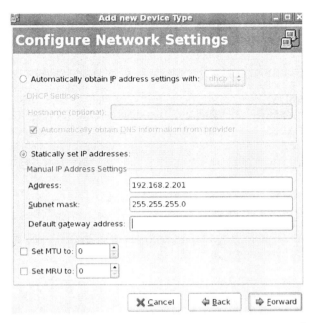

Figure 21-5 Network Configurator – Configure Network Settings II

6. The next screen will display a summary of choices made. Click Apply to configure the network interface as shown in Figure 21-6 or click Back to make any modifications.

Figure 21-6 Network Configurator – Create Ethernet Device

7. Now you are back to the Devices tab and you will see an entry for the interface in there. Highlight the entry for the interface and click Activate to activate it. Save the configuration when prompted. A file named *eth2* will be created in the */etc/sysconfig/network-scripts* directory and information supplied will be saved in it.

8. Go to the command prompt and run *ifconfig* or *ip* command to verify the settings.

Configuring IP Aliasing via Network Configurator

To successfully configure a logical interface *eth2:1* on *rhel01* with class C IP address 192.168.3.201, default netmask 255.255.255.0 and broadcast address 192.168.3.255 using the Network Configurator, highlight the entry that corresponds with *eth2* in the Devices tab and click New. Follow the instructions provided in the previous sub-section to add the IP assignments. The system will automatically add the new interface as logical interface *eth2:1*.

Managing Network Interface Attributes

RHEL provides a tool called *ethtool* that allows you to display and modify certain interface attributes such as transfer speed, negotiation method and duplex mode on a network interface. The following examples explain the usage of this command.

To display current settings for *eth1*:

```
# ethtool eth1
Settings for eth1:
        Supported ports: [ TP ]
        Supported link modes:   10baseT/Half 10baseT/Full
                                100baseT/Half 100baseT/Full
                                1000baseT/Full
        Supports auto-negotiation: Yes
        Advertised link modes:  10baseT/Half 10baseT/Full
                                100baseT/Half 100baseT/Full
                                1000baseT/Full
        Advertised auto-negotiation: Yes
        Speed: 100Mb/s
        Duplex: Half
        Port: Twisted Pair
        PHYAD: 1
        Transceiver: internal
        Auto-negotiation: off
        Supports Wake-on: d
        Wake-on: d
        Link detected: yes
```

The output shows supported parameters and current settings for *eth1*. Current settings include the speed (100Mb/s), duplex status (Half), port type (Twisted Pair) and auto-negotiation method (off). The last line indicates that the interface is linked to the network.

To modify the speed of the interface from 100Mb/s to 1000Mb/s, duplex mode from Half to Full and auto-negotiation from off to on, follow the sequence of commands:

```
# ifdown eth1
# ethtool –s eth1 speed 1000 duplex full autoneg on
# ifup eth1
```

To verify the change:

```
# ethtool eth1
. . . . . . . .
        Speed: 1000Mb/s
        Duplex: Full
        Port: Twisted Pair
        PHYAD: 1
        Transceiver: internal
        Auto-negotiation: on
        Supports Wake-on: d
        Wake-on: d
        Link detected: yes
```

These settings will be lost when the system is rebooted. To make them permanent, edit the associated interface file */etc/sysconfig/network-scripts/ifcfg-eth1* and append the following line to it:

ETHTOOL_OPTS="speed 1000 duplex full autoneg on"

Routing

Routing refers to the process of choosing a path over which to send a data packet. To perform the routing function, a routing device is needed. The routing device can be a specialized and sophisticated hardware device called *router* or it can be a RHEL system with more than one network interfaces installed. The RHEL system can perform the routing function, but it will not be as sophisticated. The following sub-sections discuss the basics of routing.

Routing Concepts

When nodes on two separate networks (or subnets) communicate with each other, proper route(s) must be setup in order for the nodes to be able to talk to each other. For instance, if a node on network A sends a data packet to a node on network B, one or more routing devices get involved to route the packet to the correct destination network. The two networks can be located in the same data center or thousands of miles apart. Once the data packet reaches a router, the router selects the next router along the path toward the destination node. The packet passes from router to router until it reaches the router that is able to deliver the packet directly to the destination node. Each router along the path is referred to as a *hop*.

One of the three rules is followed to determine the correct route:

✓ If both the source and destination nodes are on the same network (or subnet), the packet is sent directly to the destination node.
✓ If the source and destination nodes are on two different networks, all defined routes are tried one after the other. If a proper route is found, the packet is forwarded to it, which then forwards the packet to the destination node.

✓ If the source and destination nodes are on two different networks but no routes are defined, the packet is forwarded to the *default router* (or *default gateway*), which tries to find an appropriate route to the destination. If found, the packet is delivered to the destination node.

Routing Table

The *routing table* maintains information about available routes and their status. It is maintained by the kernel in memory. The routing table can be viewed with the *netstat* command using –r option or the *route* command. With –n option, the commands display address information in numerical format.

netstat –rn
route –n

Kernel IP routing table

Destination	Gateway	Genmask	Flags	Metric	Ref	Use	Iface
192.168.0.0	*	255.255.255.0	U	0	0	0	eth0
192.168.1.0	*	255.255.255.0	U	0	0	0	eth1
192.168.2.0	*	255.255.255.0	U	0	0	0	eth2
169.254.0.0	*	255.255.0.0	U	0	0	0	eth0
127.0.0.0	*	255.0.0.0	U	0	0	0	lo
default	192.168.0.1	0.0.0.0	UG	0	0	0	eth0

The output is organized in eight columns, which are explained in Table 21-5:

Column	Description
Destination	Route to a destination host or network.
Gateway	Packets are routed to the destination host or network via this address.
Genmask	Subnet mask for the destination network. It would be 255.255.255.255 for a host destination and 0.0.0.0 for the default route.
Flags	Displays route type. Following are various flags: U – route is up and it is a network route. H – route is a host route. UH – route is up and it is a host route. G – route is through a gateway. D – route is created dynamically. M – gateway route has been modified. ? – gateway route is unknown.
MSS	*Maximum Segment Size* for TCP connections.
Window	Window size for TCP connections.
irtt	Kernel uses *Initial Round Trip Time* to guess the best TCP parameters without waiting for an answer.
Iface	Network interface used by the route.

Table 21-5 netstat Command Output Description

You can also use the *ip* command to view the routing table:

```
# ip route
192.168.0.0/24 dev eth0 proto kernel scope link src 192.168.0.201
192.168.1.0/24 dev eth1 proto kernel scope link src 192.168.1.201
192.168.2.0/24 dev eth2 proto kernel scope link src 192.168.2.201
169.254.0.0/16 dev eth0 scope link
default via 192.168.0.1 dev eth0
```

Managing Routes

Managing routes involves adding a route, modifying a route, deleting a route and setting a default route. The *route* command or the Network Configurator can be used to perform these tasks. Alternatively, you can create/edit interface specific *route-eth** files in the */etc/sysconfig/network-scripts* directory to add, modify or delete route entries. Entries added with the *route* command are lost when the system is rebooted, whereas entries added with the Network Configurator or by editing *route-eth** files are permanent and available across system reboots. The Network Configurator automatically updates the corresponding *route-eth** file to reflect the add, modify and delete operations.

Adding Default and Static Routes

A route can be set to a network or host using commands, direct file edit or the Network Configurator.

To add a static route to a network such as 192.168.2.0 on *eth0* device with default class C netmask and gateway 192.168.0.1, use any of the following:

```
# route add –net 192.168.2.0 netmask 255.255.255.0 gw 192.168.0.1 1 dev eth0
# ip route add 192.168.2.0/24 via 192.168.0.1 dev eth0
```

To add a static route to a host such as 192.168.3.31 with default class C netmask and gateway 192.168.0.1, use any of the following:

```
# route add –host 192.168.3.31 netmask 255.255.255.0 gw 192.168.0.1 1 dev eth0
# ip route add 192.168.3.31/24 via 192.168.0.1 dev eth0
```

To make the routes permanent, edit the */etc/sysconfig/network-scripts/route-eth0* file and add the entries to it:

```
# vi /etc/sysconfig/network-scripts/route-eth0
GATEWAY0=192.168.0.1
NETMASK0=255.255.255.0
ADDRESS0=192.168.2.0
GATEWAY1=192.168.0.1
NETMASK1=255.255.255.0
ADDRESS1=192.168.3.31
```

Three directives GATEWAY, NETMASK and ADDRESS are defined for each route entry configured for *eth0* with an associated sequence number.

Execute the *ifup-routes* command to activate these routes if they are not already activated:

/etc/sysconfig/network-scripts/ifup-routes eth0

Run the *netstat*, *route* or *ip* command and verify the new settings.

If you wish to deactivate all the route entries defined in the file, execute the *ifdown-routes* command:

/etc/sysconfig/network-scripts/ifdown-routes eth0

Deleting a Route

To delete the two routes you just added:

route del –net 192.168.2.0 192.168.0.1 dev eth0
ip route del 192.168.2.0/24
route del –host 192.168.3.31 192.168.0.1 dev eth0
ip route del 192.168.3.31/24

Run the *netstat* or *route* command to confirm.

Adding, Modifying and Deleting a Route via Network Configurator

With the Network Configurator, you can add a new route or modify and delete an existing one. Start the Network Configurator, highlight an interface entry from the Devices tab and click Edit. A window similar to the one shown in Figure 21-7 will appear. Select the Route tab and click Add, Edit or Delete as appropriate.

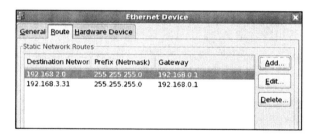

Figure 21-7 Network Configurator – Add/Edit/Delete a Route

Network Connectivity Troubleshooting

Network problems usually involve physical connectivity or incorrect configuration issues. Physical connectivity issues may include network card not seated properly in the slot, cable plugged into wrong network interface, a broken cable, bad or loose connectors at cable ends, cable too long, router, switch or hub not functioning or malfunctioning and so on.

Configuration issues may involve network card software driver not installed, duplicate IP addresses on the network, wrong IP address assignments, incorrect subnet mask, incorrect routing table entries, IP address and other network parameters lost at system reboot, network interface not in UP state and so on.

In the following sub-sections various network troubleshooting tools are presented that aid in troubleshooting physical connectivity issues. These tools include *ping*, *netstat*, *traceroute*, *tracepath*, *mtr* and *tcpdump*. Several other tools such as *arp* and *ifconfig* can also be used for troubleshooting purposes and were discussed earlier in this and the previous chapter. For problems related to incorrect configuration, check network assignments in key configuration files such as */etc/hosts* and files in */etc/sysconfig/network-scripts* directory.

Using ping

ping (packet internet gropper) tests connectivity at the TCP/IP level when the physical connectivity is ok and proper IP address and network assignments are in place. It sends out a series of 64-byte (56-byte plus 8-byte header) *Internet Control Message Protocol* (ICMP) test packets to a destination IP address and waits for a response. With –c option, you can specify the number of packets to be sent.

```
# ping –c3 192.168.0.202
PING rhel02 (192.168.0.202) 56(84) bytes of data.
64 bytes from rhel02 (192.168.0.202): icmp_seq=1 ttl=64 time=0.430 ms
64 bytes from rhel02 (192.168.0.202): icmp_seq=2 ttl=64 time=0.159 ms
64 bytes from rhel02 (192.168.0.202): icmp_seq=3 ttl=64 time=0.047 ms

--- rhel02 ping statistics ---
3 packets transmitted, 3 received, 0% packet loss, time 2002ms
rtt min/avg/max/mdev = 0.047/0.212/0.430/0.160 ms
```

At the bottom of the output under "rhel02 ping statistics", the number of packets transmitted, received and lost are shown. The packet loss should be 0% and the round trip time should not be high. You can ping the system's own IP, the loopback address (127.0.0.1), the default route, a node on the local network and a node on another network to check if the system is properly set to communicate to itself, nodes on local network and nodes beyond the local network.

Another item to notice in the output is that the first ICMP reply took longer to come back than the subsequent replies. This is based on the fact that the command broadcasts the destination interface's hardware address over the network using the *arp* command and the node with that hardware address replies. This process takes additional time and results in a delayed reply. It might not be the case always though.

If *ping* fails in any of the situations, check if the network card seated in the slot properly, its driver installed, network cable secured appropriately, IP and subnet mask are set correctly (use *ifconfig*), the default route configured right (use *netstat* or *route*) and there are no firewall restrictions between the source and the destination system. Verify the entries in the */etc/hosts* file and files in the */etc/sysconfig/network-scripts* directory.

Using netstat

netstat (network statistics) reports network interface statistics including their status. When this command is executed with –i option, it displays incoming and outgoing packet information per each configured interface. Examine its output when you suspect an issue with an interface.

```
# netstat –i
```
Kernel Interface table

Iface	MTU	Met	RX-OK	RX-ERR	RX-DRP	RX-OVR	TX-OK	TX-ERR	TX-DRP	TX-OVR	Flg
eth0	1500	0	135773	1	0	0	80591	0	0	0	BMRU
eth1	1500	0	109896	0	0	0	21	0	0	0	BMRU
eth2	1500	0	9234	0	0	0	12	0	0	0	BMRU
lo	16436	0	5905	0	0	0	5905	0	0	0	LRU

The *netstat* command with –r option displays the routing information:

```
# netstat –r
```
Kernel IP routing table

Destination	Gateway	Genmask	Flags	Metric	Ref	Use	Iface
192.168.0.0	*	255.255.255.0	U	0	0	0	eth0
192.168.1.0	*	255.255.255.0	U	0	0	0	eth1
192.168.2.0	*	255.255.255.0	U	0	0	0	eth2
169.254.0.0	*	255.255.0.0	U	0	0	0	eth0
127.0.0.0	*	255.0.0.0	U	0	0	0	lo
default	192.168.0.1	0.0.0.0	UG	0	0	0	eth0

Above output in numerical format would be:

```
# netstat –rn
```
Kernel IP routing table

Destination	Gateway	Genmask	Flags	MSS	Window	irtt	Iface
192.168.0.0	0.0.0.0	255.255.255.0	U	0	0	0	eth0
192.168.1.0	0.0.0.0	255.255.255.0	U	0	0	0	eth1
192.168.2.0	0.0.0.0	255.255.255.0	U	0	0	0	eth2
169.254.0.0	0.0.0.0	255.255.0.0	U	0	0	0	eth0
127.0.0.0	0.0.0.0	255.0.0.0	U	0	0	0	lo
0.0.0.0	192.168.0.1	0.0.0.0	UG	0	0	0	eth0

With –a option, the command displays status of socket connections:

```
# netstat –a
```
Active Internet connections (servers and established)

Proto	Recv-Q	Send-Q	Local Address	Foreign Address	State
tcp	0	0	*:sunrpc	*:*	LISTEN
tcp	0	0	*:x11	*:*	LISTEN
tcp	0	0	*:x11	*:*	LISTEN
tcp	0	0	*:ssh	*:*	LISTEN
tcp	0	0	rhel01:ssh	[UNKNOWN]:4656	ESTABLISHED
tcp	0	0	rhel01:ssh	[UNKNOWN]:4822	ESTABLISHED
udp	0	0	*:sunrpc	*:*	

Active UNIX domain sockets (servers and established)

Proto	RefCnt	Flags	Type	State	I-Node	Path
unix	2	[ACC]	STREAM	LISTENING	12070	/tmp/.X11-unix/X0

. . . .

With –s option, it displays network activity statistics:

 # netstat –s
Ip:
    43936 total packets received
    5792 with invalid addresses
    0 forwarded
    0 incoming packets discarded
    10727 incoming packets delivered
    11219 requests sent out
    9 dropped because of missing route
Icmp:
    8 ICMP messages received
    0 input ICMP message failed.
    ICMP input histogram:
        destination unreachable: 8
    54 ICMP messages sent
    0 ICMP messages failed
    ICMP output histogram:
        destination unreachable: 54
Tcp:
    123 active connections openings
    7 passive connection openings
    120 failed connection attempts
    2 connection resets received
    1 connections established
    9983 segments received
    10342 segments send out
    24 segments ☐yslogd☐ter☐d
    0 bad segments received.
    120 resets sent
Udp:
    735 packets received
    1 packets to unknown port received.
    0 packet receive errors
    . . . .

From a network connectivity troubleshooting perspective, use this command to check if proper routes and IP addresses are set, identify the direction of packet flowing, determine ports applications are listening on and list sources for established connections.

Using traceroute and tracepath

traceroute and *tracepath* commands are used to trace flow of network traffic to a destination host. These commands can be used to help isolate and troubleshoot connectivity issues with the destination host when *ping* fails. Both commands work similarly except that *traceroute* requires *root* privileges to function correctly. The commands require the destination system's hostname or IP address to be specified. You also need to ensure that there are no firewall restrictions between the source and the destination host if one is employed.

To trace route from *rhel01* to *rhel03* using the default interface chosen from the routing table:

> # **traceroute rhel03**
> traceroute to rhel03 (192.168.0.203), 30 hops max, 38 byte packets
> 1 rhel03 (192.168.0.203) 3.761 ms !X   3.847 ms !X   0.936 ms !X
> # **tracepath rhel03**
> 1: rhel01 (192.168.0.201)   3.547ms pmtu 1500
> 1: rhel03 (192.168.0.203)   1.567ms !H
>   Resume: pmtu 1500

To trace route from *rhel01* to *rhel03* using *eth1* interface:

> # **traceroute –i eth1 rhel03**
> traceroute to rhel03 (192.168.0.203), 30 hops max, 38 byte packets
> 1 rhel03 (192.168.0.203) 4.124 ms !X   4.237 ms !X   0.921 ms !X

Using mtr

mtr offers in a single tool what the *ping* and *traceroute* commands provide separately. This tool sends packets to a destination host and reports on response statistics. *mtr* can be used for network diagnostic purposes.

Without any options, this command continues to report on response statistics until `Ctrl+c` is pressed:

> # **mtr rhel03**
>   My traceroute [v0.71]
> rhel01 (0.0.0.0)   Sat Apr 18 01:07:59 2009
> Keys: Help Display mode Restart statistics Order of fields quit
>   Packets   Pings
> Host   Loss% Last Avg Best Wrst StDev
> 1. 192.168.0.203   0.0% 1.1   1.1 1.1   1.1 0.0

You can supply –r option to run *mtr* in report mode and specify the number of times it sends packets to the specified host with –c option:

> # **mtr -r -c 3 rhel03**
> rhel01   Snt: 3   Loss% Last Avg Best Wrst StDev
> rhel03   0.0% 0.9 1.0 0.9 1.2 0.3

With –p option, the above command will generate output similar to the following:

> # **mtr -r -c 3 rhel03 –p**
> 1 192.168.0.203 0 1 1 0 0 0
> 1 192.168.0.203 0 2 2 0 1 1

The six numerical values in the last columns correspond to the six columns of output as displayed in the previous two examples.

Using tcpdump

tcpdump is a common tool for capturing (*sniffing*) TCP packets on a network interface to be used for debugging purposes. The command can be run to display the dump on the screen or capture in a file. Let us take a look at a few examples to understand its usage.

To sniff all packets between *rhel01* and any other host that is currently communicating with this host on the default interface *eth0*:

tcpdump

. . . .

18:11:12.450128 IP rhel01.ssh > 192.168.0.201.redstorm_find: P 142776:142924(148) ack 51689 win 8576
18:11:12.451002 IP rhel01.ssh > 192.168.0.201.redstorm_find: P 143056:143204(148) ack 51689 win 8576
18:11:12.451132 IP 192.168.0.201.redstorm_find > rhel01.ssh: . ack 143056 win 62940
Ctrl+c
1228 packets captured
4501 packets received by filter
1810 packets dropped by kernel

You will need to press `Ctrl+c` to terminate the execution of *tcpdump*.

To sniff 5 packets between *rhel01* and *rhel02* on interface *eth1*:

tcpdump –i eth1 –c 5 –v host rhel02

tcpdump: listening on eth1, link-type EN10MB (Ethernet), capture size 96 bytes
02:11:29.465534 arp who-has rhel02 (Broadcast) tell 192.168.0.1
02:11:29.470568 arp reply rhel02 is-at 00:0c:29:10:b9:d7 (oui Unknown)
02:11:40.777897 arp who-has rhel02 (Broadcast) tell 192.168.0.1
02:11:40.778074 arp reply rhel02 is-at 00:0c:29:10:b9:d7 (oui Unknown)
02:11:52.354012 arp who-has rhel02 (Broadcast) tell 192.168.0.1
5 packets captured
7 packets received by filter
0 packets dropped by kernel

To sniff 5 packets between *rhel01* and *rhel02* on the default interface *eth0* and capture the output in a file called */tmp/tcpdump.out*:

tcpdump –c 5 host rhel02 –w /tmp/tcpdump.out

tcpdump: listening on eth0, link-type EN10MB (Ethernet), capture size 96 bytes
5 packets captured
10 packets received by filter
0 packets dropped by kernel

To read the dump captured in */tmp/tcpdump.out*:

tcpdump –r /tmp/tcpdump.out

reading from file /tmp/as, link-type EN10MB (Ethernet)
02:12:27.218169 arp who-has rhel02 (Broadcast) tell 192.168.0.1
02:12:27.218184 arp reply rhel02 is-at 00:0c:29:10:b9:d7 (oui Unknown)
02:12:38.541788 arp who-has rhel02 (Broadcast) tell 192.168.0.1

```
02:12:38.542048 arp reply rhel02 is-at 00:0c:29:10:b9:d7 (oui Unknown)
02:12:50.154928 arp who-has rhel02 (Broadcast) tell 192.168.0.1
```

Summary

In this chapter, you looked at various network configuration files and commands. You learned how to assign network parameters to a network interface including assigning it a single IP address and multiple IP addresses using commands as well as the Network Configurator. You looked at how to edit files so the interfaces were activated whenever a system reboot occurred. You performed activation and deactivation of interfaces manually, and defined IP addresses and hostnames in /etc/hosts database. You used a command line tool to modify the speed and other attributes of a network interface.

The next major topic in the chapter was on routing. You studied routing concepts and how it worked. You understood the concept of default route. You added, modified, deleted and displayed routes using commands as well as the Network Configurator.

You then studied network connectivity troubleshooting concepts and basic troubleshooting techniques using tools such as *ping, netstat, traceroute, tracepath, mtr* and *tcpdump.*

## 22

DNS and DHCP

This chapter covers the following major topics:

- ✓   What is name resolution?
- ✓   Name resolution approaches
- ✓   DNS concepts and components – name space, domain, zone, zone files, master server, slave server, caching server, forwarding server and DNS client
- ✓   Understand DNS boot and zone files
- ✓   Configure master DNS server
- ✓   Configure slave, caching and forwarding DNS servers
- ✓   Configure DNS client
- ✓   Verify DNS functionality with dig, host and nslookup
- ✓   Use rndc utility
- ✓   Overview of DHCP
- ✓   SELinux requirements for DHCP
- ✓   Configure a DHCP server and client

Name

Name resolution is a technique for determining the IP address of a system by providing its hostname. In other words, name resolution is a way of mapping a hostname with its IP address. Name resolution is used on the Internet and corporate networks. When you enter the address of a website in a browser window, you actually specify the hostname of a remote machine that exists somewhere in the world. You do not know its exact location, but you do know its hostname. There is a complex web of hundreds of thousands of routers configured on the Internet. These routers maintain information about other routers closer to them. When you hit the Enter key after entering a website name, the hostname (the website name) is passed to a DNS server, which tries to get the IP address associated with the website's hostname. Once it gets that information, the request to access the website is forwarded to the web server hosting the website from one router to another until the request reaches the destination system. Determining an IP address by providing a hostname is referred to as *name resolution* (a.k.a. *name lookup* or *DNS lookup*), determining a hostname by providing an IP address is referred to as *reverse name resolution* (a.k.a. *reverse name lookup* or *reverse DNS lookup*) and the service employed to perform name resolution is called *Domain Name System* (DNS). DNS is platform-independent and is supported on a wide array of operating systems including RHEL. DNS is commonly recognized by the name *Berkeley Internet Name Domain* (BIND) in the Linux and UNIX world. In fact, BIND is an implementation of DNS on Linux and UNIX platforms, and was developed at the University of California, Berkeley. The two terms are used interchangeably throughout this chapter.

Name Resolution Approaches

There are three methods available for hostname resolution, and are explained below.

The /etc/hosts File

The */etc/hosts* file is typically used when there are not too many systems on the network. This file is maintained locally on individual systems.

Each line in the *hosts* file contains an IP address in the first column, followed by an official (or *canonical*) hostname in the second column. You may also define one or more aliases per entry. Aliases are nicknames. The official hostname and one or more aliases allow you to assign multiple hostnames to a single IP address. This way the same system can be accessed using any of those names. A few sample entries below from the file display *rhel01, rhel02, rhel03, rhel04* and *rhel05* systems with IP addresses 192.168.0.201, 192.168.0.202, 192.168.0.203, 192.168.0.204 and 192.168.0.205, and aliases *r1, r2, r3, r4* and *r5*, respectively.

```
192.168.0.201    rhel01    r1     # Production database server
192.168.0.202    rhel02    r2     # Development web server
192.168.0.203    rhel03    r3     # Production application server
192.168.0.204    rhel04    r4     # Production application server
192.168.0.205    rhel05    r5     # Production backup server
```

Since the *hosts* file is maintained locally, it must be updated manually on each system to maintain consistency whenever a system is added or removed, or its IP or hostname is modified.

Network Information Service

An NIS server can serve only the systems on its local network. NIS clients send out broadcasts to locate and bind to an NIS server. Each NIS server is able to respond to hostname queries on its local network.

NIS is not used for hostname resolution because of limitations and security concerns.

Domain Name System

DNS is the de facto standard for name resolution used on the Internet and on corporate networks. Systems using DNS send name resolution requests to a DNS server instead of the *hosts* file or NIS.

The remainder of this chapter furnishes detailed information on DNS and how to set it up.

DNS Concepts and Components

This sections explains DNS concepts, identifies components, describes roles and explains how it works.

DNS Name Space and Domains

The DNS *name space* is a hierarchical organization of all the domains on the Internet. The root of the name space is represented by the dot character. The hierarchy right below the root is divided into top-level (first-level) domains such as com, gov, edu, mil, net, org, biz, tv, info and two-character country-specific domains such as ca, uk and au. A DNS *domain* is a collection of one or more systems. Sub-domains fall under domains. For example, the com domain consists of second-level sub-domains such as redhat, hp and ibm. Sub-domains can then be further divided into multiple, smaller third-level sub-domains, each of which may contain one or several systems. For example, *redhat.com* may contain *ca.redhat.com* sub-domain. Within a domain, any number of sub-domains can be defined.

Figure 22-1 exhibits the hierarchical structure of the DNS name space. It also shows domain levels.

At the deepest level of the hierarchy are the *leaves* (systems) of the name space. For example, a system *rhel01* in *ca.redhat.com* will be represented as *rhel01.ca.redhat.com*. If a dot is appended to the name to look like *rhel01.ca.redhat.com.*, it will be referred to as the *Fully Qualified Domain Name* (FQDN) for *rhel01*.

A system in the DNS name space may be a computer, a router, a switch, a network printer or any other device with an IP address.

The hierarchical structure of DNS enables the division of a single domain into multiple sub-domains with the management responsibility of each sub-domain delegated to different groups of administrators. This type of configuration allows each sub-domain to have its own DNS server with full authority on the information that the sub-domain contains. This distributed management approach simplifies overall DNS administration in large and complex environments.

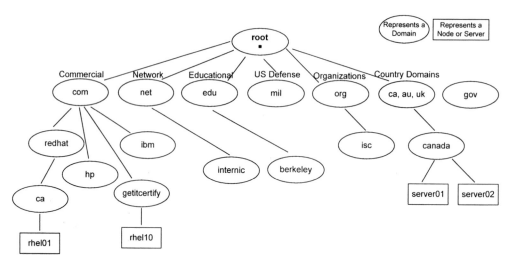

Figure 22-1 DNS Hierarchy

To run a server directly facing the Internet, you must get a domain name registered for it. Contact one of the accredited domain registrars licensed by the *Internet Corporation for Assigned Names and Numbers* (ICANN). Visit *www.icann.com* to obtain a list of licensed registrars or simply contact an ISP to get a domain registered.

DNS Zones and Zone Files

Every DNS server maintains complete information about the portion of the DNS name space it is responsible for. This information includes a complete set of authoritative data files. The portion of the name space for which a DNS server has a complete set of authoritative data files is known as the server's *zone* and the set of authoritative data files is known as *zone files* or *zone databases*.

DNS Roles

A role is a function that a system performs from a DNS standpoint. A system is typically configured to function as one of the three types of DNS servers, or as a client.

Master DNS Server

A *master DNS server* has the authority for its domain (or sub-domain) and contains that domain's data. Each domain must have one master server, which may delegate responsibility of one or more sub-domains to other DNS servers, referred to as slave and caching DNS servers.

Slave DNS Server

A *slave DNS server* also has the authority for its domain and stores that domain's zone files; however, the zone files are copied over from the master server. When updates are made to zone files on the master server, the slave server gets the updated files automatically. This type of DNS server is normally setup for redundancy purposes in case the master server fails, and for sharing master server's load. It is highly recommended to have at least one slave server per domain to supplement the master.

Caching DNS Server

A *caching DNS server* has no authority for any domains. It gets data from a master or slave server and caches it locally in its memory. Like a slave server, a caching server is normally used for redundancy and load-sharing purposes. The replies to queries from a caching server are normally quicker than the replies from either one of the other two. This is because a caching server keeps data in memory and not on disk. This type of DNS server is typically used by ISPs where hundreds of thousands of queries for name resolution arrive every minute.

Forwarding DNS Server

A *forwarding DNS server* has no authority for any domains. It simply forwards an incoming query to a specified DNS server.

DNS Client

A *DNS client* has a few files configured that are used for resolving hostname queries by referencing information defined in them.

Understanding BIND Software Packages

There are several software packages that need to be installed on the system in order for it to be configured as a DNS server or client, or both. Some of the packages are optional. Table 22-1 describes the packages.

Package	Description
bind	Contains BIND server software.
bind-chroot	Contains directory structure to cordone off BIND in case DNS is compromised. This package is not required for normal BIND functionality, but recommended to be used.
bind-devel	Contains BIND development libraries.
bind-libbind-devel	Contains BIND resolver library.
bind-libs	Contains supported library files for bind and bind-utils packages.
bind-sdb	Contains support for LDAP and other such databases.
bind-utils	Contains tools such as *dig* and *host*.
caching-nameserver	Contains caching DNS server files.
system-config-bind	The Red Hat graphical BIND Configurator tool.

Table 22-1 BIND Software Packages

If bind-chroot package is also installed, the BIND configuration files */etc/named.conf*, */etc/rndc.key* and */etc/rndc.conf* are relocated to the */var/named/chroot/etc* directory and all zone files to the */var/named/chroot/var/named* directory. The system then creates a symlink for each of these files from */etc* and */var/named* directories, which allows accessing the files using their pre-chrooted or post-chrooted locations.

The chroot feature enables BIND to work in a chroot jail environment by disabling the ability of the *named* daemon to see files that it is not supposed to by making the daemon think that the root directory is */var/named/chroot* and not */*. This secures the system from people gaining unauthorized access into the system by hiding higher level directories from them. The explanation and procedures provided in this chapter use chroot environment.

Understanding DNS Server Configuration and Zone Files

When working with DNS servers, several configuration and zone files are involved. The syntax of most zone files is similar. Table 22-2 describes the files.

File	Description
Configuration and Zone Template Files	
/usr/share/doc/bind-9*/sample/	Contains configuration and zone file templates.
Startup Configuration Files	
/etc/sysconfig/named	BIND startup configuration file.
/etc/rc.d/init.d/named	BIND startup script.
Configuration Files with respect to /var/named/chroot/etc directory	
named.conf	Defines the location of zones to be served.
named.caching-nameserver.conf	Default configuration file for a caching server. Renamed as *named.conf* and copied to caching server.
named.rfc1912.zones	Defines default zones for caching server.
rndc.key	Contains authentication key.
rndc.conf	Default configuration file for rndc.
Pre-Defined Zone Files with respect to /var/named/chroot/var/named directory	
localhost.zone	Contains forward mappings for the localhost.
named.local	Contains reverse mappings for the localhost.
localdomain.zone	Zone file for localhost's domain.
named.broadcast	Contains broadcast information for the localhost.
named.ca	Contains informtion about top level root servers.

Table 22-2 DNS Configuration and Zone Files

The */usr/share/doc/bind-9*/sample* directory contains templates for DNS configuration and zone files. You can copy them as required to proper locations and modify. A listing of the directory structure is given below:

```
# ll /usr/share/doc/bind-9*/sample
total 16
drwxr-xr-x 2 root root 4096 Jan 16 22:57 etc
drwxr-xr-x 3 root root 4096 Jan 16 22:57 var
# ll /usr/share/doc/bind-9*/sample/etc
total 32
-rw-r--r--   1 root  root 4212  Jul 10 2008   named.conf
-rw-r--r--   1 root  root  775  Mar 29 2006   named.rfc1912.zones
-rw-r--r--   1 root  root  524  Mar 29 2006   named.root.hints
-rw-r--r--   1 root  root    0  Jan  6 08:34  rndc.conf
# ll /usr/share/doc/bind-9*/sample/var/named
total 88
drwxr-xr-x 2 root root 4096 Jan  6 08:34 data
-rw-r--r-- 1 root root  198 Mar  6 2006 localdomain.zone
-rw-r--r-- 1 root root  195 Mar  6 2006 localhost.zone
-rw-r--r-- 1 root root   56 Jan  6 08:34 my.external.zone.db
-rw-r--r-- 1 root root   56 Jan  6 08:34 my.internal.zone.db
-rw-r--r-- 1 root root  427 Mar  6 2006 named.broadcast
```

```
-rw-r--r-- 1 root root  424 Mar  6 2006 named.ip6.local
-rw-r--r-- 1 root root  426 Mar  6 2006 named.local
-rw-r--r-- 1 root root 1892 Feb 26 2008 named.root
-rw-r--r-- 1 root root  427 Mar  6 2006 named.zero
drwxr-xr-x 2 root root 4096 Jan 16 22:57 slaves
```

Let us look at some configuration and zone files and see what kind of information they store.

The /etc/sysconfig/named File

This file defines the location of the root directory where the DNS zone files are stored, any options to be passed to the daemon when it is started, and so on. With chroot package installed, the default ROOTDIR is set to */var/named/chroot*. If you wish to store information elsewhere, you will need to specify that directory location here, create that directory and move files in there. The default contents of this file in a chrooted setting are shown below:

cat /etc/sysconfig/named

```
. . . . . . . .
# OPTIONS="whatever"   -- These additional options will be passed to named at startup.
# ENABLE_ZONE_WRITE=yes -- If SELinux is disabled, then allow named to write
#                its zone files and create files in its $ROOTDIR/var/named
#                directory, necessary for DDNS and slave zone transfers.
#                Slave zones should reside in the $ROOTDIR/var/named/slaves
#                directory, in which case you would not need to enable zone
#                writes. If SELinux is enabled, you must use only the
#                'named_write_master_zones' variable to enable zone writes.
. . . . . . . .
ROOTDIR=/var/named/chroot
```

The named.conf File

This is the primary DNS configuration file and is read each time the DNS server daemon *named* is started or restarted at boot time, or manually after the system is up. This file provides the DNS server with the names and location of zone databases with respect to ROOTDIR for all domains that this server serves. The file typically contains options, zone and include statements. Each statement begins with a { and ends in };. Both forward and reverse zone statements can be defined and there are typically scores of them. A sample *named.conf* file is shown below followed by an explanation:

cat /etc/named.conf

```
. . . . . . . .
options {
    listen-on port 53 { 127.0.0.1; 192.168.0.201; };
    allow-query { 127.0.0.1; 192.168.0.0/24; };
    allow-recursion { 127.0.0.1; 192.168.0.0/24; };
    allow-transfer { 192.168.0.203/24; };
    directory "/var/named";
    dump-file "/var/named/data/cache_dump.db";
    statistics-file "/var/named/data/named_stats.txt";
    memstatistics-file  "data/named_mem_stats.txt";
    pid-file "/var/run/named/named.pid";
```

```
            notify yes
            /*
. . . . . . . .
            */
            // query-source address * port 53;
;};

zone "getitcertify.com.zone" IN {
    type master;
    file "getitcertify.com.zone";
    allow-update { any; };
};

zone "0.168.192.in-addr.arpa." IN {
    type master;
    file "getitcertify.com.revzone";
    allow-update { any; };
};

zone "." IN {
    type hint;
    file "named.root";
};

zone "localhost." IN {
    type master;
    file "localhost.zone";
    allow-update { none; };
};

zone "0.0.127.in-addr.arpa." IN {
    type master;
    file "named.local";
    allow-update { none; };
};

include "/etc/rndc.key";
```

In this file, comments begin with // or can be enclosed within /* and */. Options can be defined at both global (within Options statement) and individual levels (within individual zone statements) as required. Individual options override global options. The listen-on directive defines the port 53, which the DNS server uses to listen to queries on the localhost interface and the interface configured with 192.168.0.201 address. The systems, or for that matter networks or domains, defined within { } and separated by the semicolon character are called *match-list* and can alternatively be defined using the acl directive. In addition to stating specific addresses, hostnames and domains, four pre-configured values – none, any, localhost (or 127.0.0.1) and localnets – are available, which signify matching no addresses, any addresses, any addresses of the server itself and addresses of the directly connected systems, respectively. It is recommended to always include the localhost or 127.0.0.1 in the match-list for ease of troubleshooting when required. Within the match-list, the ! character can also be used with a name or address to denote an exclusion. By default, if the listen-on directive is missing, the DNS server listens on all configured network interfaces. The allow-query directive defines a match-list, which enables the specified systems to query the DNS server for hosts in the *getitcertify.com* domain. You can restrict queries to one or more networks by specifying IP addresses of the networks. Add similar statements for other domains if you wish this DNS server to serve them too. If this directive is missing, the DNS server entertains all queries. The allow-recursion directive instructs the DNS server to chase referrals as defined in the match-list if an answer for a query is not found in the local cache. If this directive is missing, the DNS server chases any and every referrals for an answer. The allow-transfer directive allows systems as defined in the match-list to be able to transfer zone files and act as slave DNS servers. In case this directive is missing, any system on the network can act as a slave server. The directory directive identifies the location of the zone files with respect to ROOTDIR.

 BIND does not use TCP Wrappers for access control.

There are several zone statements defined in the file. The getitcertify.com.zone is a custom zone and information about it is stored in the *getitcertify.com.zone* file, which is located in the *ROOTDIR/var/named* directory. The allow-update directive specifies a match-list, which includes hosts that are allowed to dynamically update information in their zones. The 0.168.192.in-addr.arpa. stored in *getitcertify.com.revzone* is a custom zone for reverse lookups for the *getitcertify.com* domain. The zone " . " defines the root servers for query as defined in the *named.ca* file. The localhost. and 0.0.127.in-addr.arpa. zones define forward and reverse zones for the localhost, where localhost represents the server itself. The location of the zone files are with respect to the directory directive setting.

Within each zone statement, there is a type directive, which sets the zone type as one of the following:

- ✓ "master" designates the system to act as the master DNS server for this zone.
- ✓ "slave" designates the system to act as a slave DNS server for this zone.
- ✓ "forward" designates the system to act as a forwarding DNS server for this zone.
- ✓ "hint" points to root DNS servers for resolving queries.

The include directive at the very bottom of the file specifies any additional files to be referenced by *named*. The default entry is for the *rndc.key* file.

The named.caching-nameserver.conf Configuration File

This file is available only if the caching-nameserver package is installed, and needs to be customized if you want to use a caching DNS server. The structure of the file is similar to that of the */etc/named.conf* file. A custom file is shown below:

```
# cat /etc/named.caching-nameserver.conf
. . . . . . . .
options {
    listen-on port 53 { 127.0.0.1; 192.168.0.201 ; } ;
    directory     "/var/named";
```

```
        dump-file       "/var/named/data/cache_dump.db";
        statistics-file "/var/named/data/named_stats.txt";
        memstatistics-file "/var/named/data/named_mem_stats.txt";
        query-source    port 53 ;
        allow-query     { localhost ; } ;
} ;
logging {
    channel default_debug {
        file "data/named.run";
        severity dynamic;
    };
};
view localhost_resolver {
    match-clients      { localhost; };
    match-destinations { localhost; };
    recursion yes;
    syslogd "/etc/named.rfc1912.zones";
};
```

Similar to the *named.conf* file, this file also has options statement where you can define global options. The query-source directive within options specifies the port number to be used for querying other DNS servers. The logging statement defines logging-related settings. The "view localhost_resolver" statement sets the localhost as the caching DNS server for lookup queries.

The localhost.zone Forward Zone File

Each DNS server is authoritative of the network 127.0.0 and has the zone file *localhost.zone*. This file includes the resource record that maps 127.0.0.1 to the name of the loopback (localhost) address. In other words, this file contains a pointer to the localhost. You will need to reload the *named* daemon after this zone file is changed.

```
# cat /var/named/localhost.zone
$TTL    86400
@          IN SOA  @      root (
                        42          ; serial (d. adams)
                        3H          ; refresh
                        15M         ; retry
                        1W          ; expiry
                        1D )        ; minimum

        IN NS       @
        IN A        127.0.0.1
```

There are several entries in this file and are known as *resource records*. Table 22-3 explains them.

Record	Description
$TTL	*Time To Live* value is the time period for which the information in the zone is considered valid. The default is 86,400 seconds (24 hours).
@	Specifies the zone's origin as defined in *named.conf* in the zone statement.

Record	Description
IN	Specifies a class type with Internet zone as the default. The other two types are HS (Hesoid zone) and CHAOS (CHAOSnet zone).
SOA	*Start Of Authority.* Designates start of domain. It indicates the FQDN of the DNS server (*rhel01.getitcertify.com.*) authoritative for the domain as specified in *named.conf*, the address (*root.hel01.getitcertify.com*) of the user responsible for the DNS server and the following values: Serial: Denotes the zone file version. It is incremented each time the files are refreshed. Slave servers look at this number and compare with theirs. If the number is higher on the master, a transfer of the updated files takes place. Refresh: Indicates, in seconds, how often a slave server refreshes itself with the master. Retry: Indicates, in seconds, how often a slave server retries to get updates from the master after the previous refresh attempt fails. Expire: Indicates, in seconds, the duration a slave server can use the zone data before the data is considered expired. Minimum ttl: Indicates, in seconds, the minimum amount of time (*time to live*) to keep an entry.
NS	*Name Server.* Lists DNS servers, and domains they have authority for.
A	*Address.* Assigns IP address to the corresponding system.
CNAME	*Canonical Name.* Official hostname (FQDN) of a system.
PTR	*Pointer.* Defines IP address to hostname mapping.
MX	*Mail eXchanger.* Specifies a weighted list of systems to try when sendmail'ing to a destination on the Internet. MX data points to one or more other systems that accept mail for the target system if it is down or unreachable.

Table 22-3 Resource Records Description

The named.local Reverse Zone File

There is a corresponding zone file for *localhost.zone* called *named.local* that contains reverse lookup information for 127.0.0. You will need to reload the *named* daemon after this zone file is changed. The default contents of the file are shown below and resource records are described in Table 22-3.

```
# cat /var/named/named.local
$TTL   86400
@    IN    SOA    localhost. root.localhost. (
                  1997022700 ; Serial
                  28800      ; Refresh
                  14400      ; Retry
                  3600000    ; Expire
                  86400 )    ; Minimum
     IN    NS     localhost.
1    IN    PTR    localhost.
```

The named.ca Zone File

The *named.ca* file lists servers for the root domain. There are 13 super-authoritative root DNS servers, one of which is queried when a local DNS server is unable to resolve a hostname query from its local maps or cache. Every Internet-facing DNS server must have a copy of this file. Following are the default contents from this file:

```
; root "." zone hints file, queried of a.root-servers.net. by system-config-bind
; version of root zone: 2009011601
.                    518400  IN    NS    J.ROOT-SERVERS.NET.
.                    518400  IN    NS    L.ROOT-SERVERS.NET.
.                    518400  IN    NS    A.ROOT-SERVERS.NET.
.                    518400  IN    NS    D.ROOT-SERVERS.NET.
.                    518400  IN    NS    H.ROOT-SERVERS.NET.
.                    518400  IN    NS    K.ROOT-SERVERS.NET.
.                    518400  IN    NS    G.ROOT-SERVERS.NET.
.                    518400  IN    NS    C.ROOT-SERVERS.NET.
.                    518400  IN    NS    I.ROOT-SERVERS.NET.
.                    518400  IN    NS    E.ROOT-SERVERS.NET.
.                    518400  IN    NS    F.ROOT-SERVERS.NET.
.                    518400  IN    NS    M.ROOT-SERVERS.NET.
.                    518400  IN    NS    B.ROOT-SERVERS.NET.
A.ROOT-SERVERS.NET.  3600000 IN    A     198.41.0.4
A.ROOT-SERVERS.NET.  3600000 IN    AAAA  2001:503:ba3e::2:30
B.ROOT-SERVERS.NET.  3600000 IN    A     192.228.79.201
C.ROOT-SERVERS.NET.  3600000 IN    A     192.33.4.12
D.ROOT-SERVERS.NET.  3600000 IN    A     128.8.10.90
E.ROOT-SERVERS.NET.  3600000 IN    A     192.203.230.10
F.ROOT-SERVERS.NET.  3600000 IN    A     192.5.5.241
F.ROOT-SERVERS.NET.  3600000 IN    AAAA  2001:500:2f::f
G.ROOT-SERVERS.NET.  3600000 IN    A     192.112.36.4
H.ROOT-SERVERS.NET.  3600000 IN    A     128.63.2.53
H.ROOT-SERVERS.NET.  3600000 IN    AAAA  2001:500:1::803f:235
I.ROOT-SERVERS.NET.  3600000 IN    A     192.36.148.17
J.ROOT-SERVERS.NET.  3600000 IN    A     192.58.128.30
J.ROOT-SERVERS.NET.  3600000 IN    AAAA  2001:503:c27::2:30
```

Using acl Directive for Access Control

Access control, as explained earlier in sub-section "Understanding DNS Server Configuration and Zone Files", may be grouped within separate acl directives that specify match-lists containing IP addresses and/or hostnames, network names or domain names. The acl directives are typically defined at the beginning of the file and can be used individually where access control is required such as with listen-on, listen-on-v6, allow-query, allow-recursion, allow-transfer, match-clients and match-destinations directives. For example, the following defines three acl directives named personal, trusted and untrusted:

```
acl "personal"       { 127.0.0.1; 192.168.0.201; };
acl "trusted"        { 192.168.1.0/24; };
```

```
acl "untrusted"          { 192.168.2.0/24; };
```

Now the allow-query, allow-recursion and allow-transfer directives can use them as follows:

```
listen-on               { personal; };
allow-query             { personal; trusted; untrusted; };
allow-recursion         { personal; trusted; !untrusted; };
allow-transfer          { trusted; };
```

See sub-section "Understanding DNS Server Configuration and Zone Files" earlier in this chapter for an explanation. Defining access control this way is supported in *named.conf* as well as zone files.

Configuring DNS

DNS configuration for master, slave, caching and forwarding servers can be done by either editing files and starting the *named* daemon or using the BIND Configurator. Note that a single system can perform one or more of these roles depending on how zones are declared in the *named.conf* file.

SELinux Requirements for DNS

If SELinux is enforced, you need to disable its protection for DNS service to ensure smooth functionality. Use the *setsebool* command as demonstrated below, or the SELinux Configurator *system-config-selinux* as explained in Chapter 30 "System and Network Security". Specify only those Booleans that need to be disabled, leave others intact.

 # setsebool –P named_disable_trans=1 named_write_master_zones=1

Use the *getsebool* command to verify:

 # getsebool named_disable_trans named_write_master_zones
```
named_disable_trans --> on
named_write_master_zones --> on
```

Configuring a Master DNS Server

To configure *rhel01* to act as a master DNS server for domain *getitcertify.com*, perform the following steps:

1. Get *getitcertify.com* domain name registered.
2. Check whether the required BIND software packages are installed:

    # rpm –qa | grep bind
    ```
    bind-9.3.3-10.el5
    bind-devel-9.3.3-10.el5
    bind-libbind-devel-9.3.3-10.el5
    bind-libs-9.3.3-10.el5
    bind-sdb-9.3.3-10.el5
    bind-utils-9.3.3-10.el5
    ```

```
caching-nameserver-9.3.3-10.el5
system-config-bind-4.0.3-2.el5
bind-chroot-9.3.3-10.el5
```

Install any missing packages if they are not already loaded using one of the software package installation methods described in Chapter 11 "Software Package Management".

3. Create or update the *ROOTDIR/etc/named.conf* file as explained in section "Understanding DNS Server Configuration and Zone Files".
4. Create appropriate zone files in *ROOTDIR/var/named* directory.
5. Change ownership and group membership on *named.conf* and all zone files to root:named:

   # cd /var/named/chroot
   # chown root:named etc/named.conf
   # chown root:named var/named/*

6. Run the *named-checkconf* command to ensure that there are no syntax errors in *named.conf*. For checking a specific zone, you can use the *named-checkzone* command and specify a zone name and the associated file.

   # named-checkconf –v
   9.3.4-P1
   # named-checkzone getitcertify.com.zone var/named/getitcertify.com.zone
   zone getitcertify.com.zone/IN: loaded serial 42
   OK
   # named-checkzone 0.168.192.in-addr.arpa. var/named/getitcertify.com.revzone
   zone 0.168.192.in-addr.arpa/IN: loaded serial 1997022700
   OK

   You can also use the *service* command to check *named.conf* and all zones defined in it:

   # service named configtest
   zone getitcertify.com.zone/IN: loaded serial 42
   zone 0.168.192.in-addr.arpa/IN: loaded serial 1997022700
   zone localhost/IN: loaded serial 42
   zone 0.0.127.in-addr.arpa/IN: loaded serial 1997022700

7. Allow only the BIND daemon to be able to read *named.conf* by altering the SELinux file context to named_conf_t using the *chcon* command:

   # chcon –t named_conf_t named.conf

8. Execute the following to make BIND service autostart at each system reboot:

   # chkconfig named on

9. Allow BIND traffic on port 53 to pass through the firewall, or simply stop and disable the firewall if it is not used. Consult Chapter 30 "System and Network Security" on how to perform these tasks.

10. Start (or restart) the *named* daemon:

    # **service named start**

11. Execute the following to check the operational status of BIND service:

    # **service named status**
    bind (pid 2302) is running...

Skip steps 10 and 11 and go to step 12 if you wish to control the BIND service via *rndc*, otherwise, this completes a master DNS server setup.

Using rndc to Control BIND

rndc (remote name daemon control) offers a secure method to control the BIND daemon. It uses authentication keys and accepts several arguments such as those listed and described in Table 22-4. *rndc* is not required in order for BIND to function, it provides a better overall control. It stores the security keys in the *ROOTDIR/etc/rndc.key* file, which are checked when *named* is started or stopped via *rndc*. If the keys match, the daemon is started or stopped, otherwise, an error message is generated.

Argument	Description
flush	Flushes the server's cache.
halt	Stops *named* immediately.
querylog	Enables / disables query logging.
reconfig	Reloads configuration file and any new zones.
refresh	Schedules maintenance for the specified zone.
reload	Reloads the configuration file and one or all zones.
restart	Restarts *named*.
stats	Writes server statistics to the log file.
status	Displays server status.
stop	Saves any pending updates and stops *named*.
trace / notrace	Enables / disables debugging level.

Table 22-4 rndc Command Arguments

12. Execute the following to create (if not already exist) *rndc.conf* file:

    # **cd /var/named/chroot/etc && rndc-confgen > rndc.conf**
    # Start of rndc.conf
    key "rndckey" {
        algorithm hmac-md5;
        secret "5d4caxIv0/MKBearSQ5bYA==";
    };

    options {
        default-key "rndckey";
        default-server 127.0.0.1;
        default-port 953;

```
};
# End of rndc.conf

# Use with the following in named.conf, adjusting the allow list as needed:
# key "rndckey" {
#       algorithm hmac-md5;
#       secret "5d4caxIv0/MKBearSQ5bYA==";
# };
#
# controls {
#       inet 127.0.0.1 port 953
#             allow { 127.0.0.1; } keys { "rndckey"; };
# };
# End of named.conf
```

The output of the command was redirected into a file with an assumption that the file did not already exist. The command generated a random secret key id for key "rndckey" and an encryption algorithm to be used for the key. The only encryption method currently supported is hmac-md5. The options statement includes default-key, default-server and default-port directives. The default-key determines the key id of the key to be used, the default-server specifies the IP address of the nameserver for communication between the *rndc* and *named* daemons, and the default-port defines the port number for this communication.

13. Execute the *dns-keygen* command to generate a new secret key to be shared between *rndc* and *named* for digitally signing control traffic:

    # **dns-keygen**
    80W0rJVyu40NLJGcmUxpUMSKOVKmkDnnd9UsQlbDUW7eCyT446iuuFcHxD7x

14. Edit */etc/rndc.key* file and replace the default secret key with the new key just generated:

    secret 80W0rJVyu40NLJGcmUxpUMSKOVKmkDnnd9UsQlbDUW7eCyT446iuuFcHxD7x;

15. Allow only the BIND daemon to be able to read the *rndc.key* and *rndc.conf* files by altering SELinux file context to named_conf_t using the *chcon* command:

    # **chcon −t named_conf_t rndc.key rndc.conf**

16. Create symlinks for the two files in the */etc* directory if they do not already exist:

    # **ln −s /var/named/chroot/etc/rndc.conf /etc/rndc.conf**
    # **ln −s /var/named/chroot/etc/rndc.key /etc/rndc.key**

17. Ensure that the include directive is added to the *named.conf* file and is pointing to the *rndc.key* file:

    # **grep include /etc/named.conf**
    include "/etc/rndc.key";

---

18. Edit /etc/named.conf file and add the following. Also modify any other information as required.

```
controls {
    inet 127.0.0.1 port 953
        allow { 127.0.0.1; } keys { "rndckey"; };
};
```

The controls directive defines the network address and port to be used for rndc, the address of the host or network rndc control is allowed from and the file name that contains rndc keys.

19. Allow rndc traffic on port 953 to pass through the firewall, or simply stop and disable the firewall if it is not used. Consult Chapter 30 "System and Network Security" on how to perform these tasks.

20. Run the *service* command to verify the syntax:

    # **service named configtest**

21. Start (or restart) the *named* daemon:

    # **service named start**

22. Execute the following to check the operational status:

    # **rndc status**

Configuring a Slave DNS Server

A slave server may be configured to provide load balancing and high-availability functionalities. It consults the master server at predefined intervals and fetches updated zone information.

To configure *rhel02* as a slave DNS server for getitcertify.com and 0.168.192.in-addr.arpa zones, do the following:

1. Check with the *dig* command if the master server will allow this server to slave the zone data:

    # **dig −t axfr getitcertify.com @rhel01**

2. Copy *named.rfc1912.zones* file as *named.conf* in the *ROOTDIR/etc* directory:

    # **cd /var/named/chroot/etc && cp named.rfc1912.zones named.conf**

3. Edit *named.conf* and define slave zone statements. For demonstration purposes, use the getitcertify.com.zone and its reverse as slave zones. The type and file directives were explained in section "Understanding DNS Server Configuration and Zone Files" earlier. The masters directive specifies the IP address of the master DNS server where these zone maps are stored. Add other information as appropriate from the master server's *named.conf* file. All zone data fetched from the master server will be stored in *ROOTDIR/var/named/slaves* directory. Remove any unnecessary information from the file.

```
zone "getitcertify.com.zone" IN {
    type slave;
    file "slaves/getitcertify.com.zone";
    masters { 192.168.0.201; };
};

zone "0.168.192.in-addr.arpa" IN {
    type slave;
    file "slaves/getitcertify.com.revzone";
    masters { 192.168.0.201; };
};
```

4. Perform steps 5 through 22 from "Configuring a Master DNS Server" and "Using rndc to Control BIND" as appropriate to successfully configure a slave DNS server.

Configuring a Caching DNS Server

To configure *rhel03* as a caching DNS server, perform the following steps:

1. Copy *named.caching-nameserver.conf* file as *named.conf* in the *ROOTDIR/etc* directory:

   # cd /var/named/chroot/etc && cp named.caching-nameserver.conf named.conf

2. Edit *named.conf* and modify directives as per requirement. See section "Understanding DNS Server Configuration and Zone Files" earlier in this chapter for contents and explanation.
3. Perform steps 5 through 22 from "Configuring a Master DNS Server" and "Using rndc to Control BIND" as appropriate to successfully configure a caching DNS server.

Configuring a Forwarding DNS Server

To configure *rhel04* as a forwarding DNS server, perform the following steps:

1. Perform step 1 from "Configuring a Caching DNS Server".
2. Edit *named.conf* file and define the following information for forwarding servers. The forwarders directive instructs the server to forward all hostname queries to systems in the order in which they are listed on the match-list. If the forward directive is set to "only", only match-list servers will be queried; if it is set to "first", the DNS server will contact match-list servers for query and fall back to a root nameserver if it cannot find an answer. If forwarders directive is defined but forward directive is missing, the default behavior will be "forward first". Remove any unnecessary information from the file.

   ```
   options {
       directory "/var/named";
       forwarders { 192.168.0.220/24; 192.168.0.221/24;
       forward first; };
   };
   ```

3. Perform steps 5 through 22 from "Configuring a Master DNS Server" and "Using rndc to Control BIND" as appropriate to successfully configure a forwarding DNS server.

Configuring DNS via BIND Configurator

The BIND Configurator allows you to configure a DNS server, zones, views, ACLs, security keys, controls and DNSSEC trusted keys graphically. The following demonstrates how to perform some of these tasks.

1. Execute *system-config-bind* in an X terminal window or choose (GNOME) System / (KDE) Main Menu → Administration → Server Settings → Domain Name System. The BIND Configurator will open up as shown in Figure 22-2.

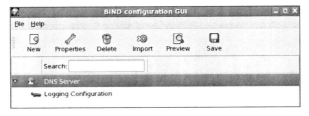

Figure 22-2 BIND Configurator – Main Screen

2. Click New and a sub-menu will appear as shown in Figure 22-3.

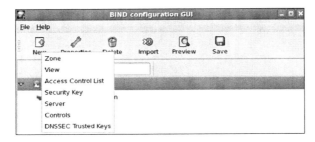

Figure 22-3 BIND Configurator – Add Configuration

3. Select Server to add a new server. A screen will open up as shown in Figure 22-4. Enter IP address of the server and click OK to add it.

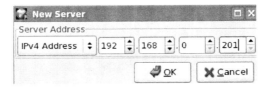

Figure 22-4 BIND Configurator – Add a New Server

4. Select Zone to add a new zone. Choose a Class, an Origin Type and a Zone Type. Click OK under Origin Type and modify properties such as cache time to live, authoritative nameserver name, administrator email and SOA information. Click OK when done.

Figure 22-5 BIND Configurator – Add a New Zone

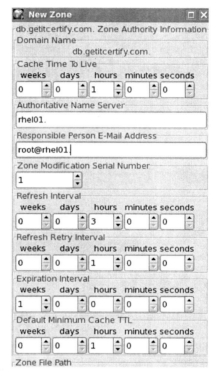

Figure 22-6 BIND Configurator – Add a New Zone - Properties

5. Highlight DNS Server in the main menu and right click Edit. Set or modify any options for the DNS server. The current options are listed in the left pane and all available options in the right pane. Highlight an option under All Options and click + to add it to Current Options. Similarly, hightlight an option under Current Options and click – to remove it from Current Options. As you highlight an option, a short description of it is displayed at the bottom. Click OK when done.

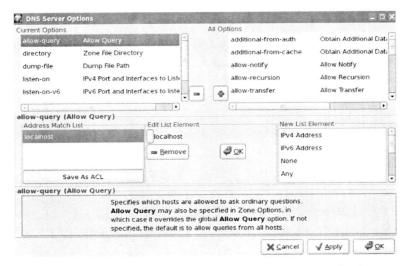

Figure 22-7 BIND Configurator – Set DNS Server Options

6. Click New in the main menu and choose DNS Controls. Set or modify any options and click OK when done.

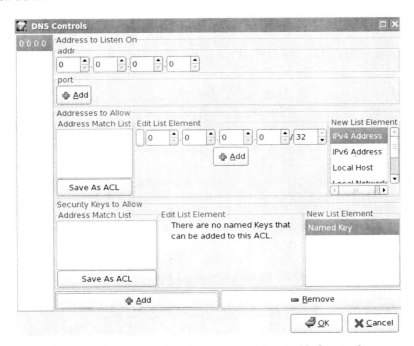

Figure 22-8 BIND Configurator – Set DNS Controls

Configuring a DNS Client

To setup a system to act as a DNS client, you need to configure three files */etc/nsswitch.conf,* */etc/host.conf* and */etc/resolv.conf* on the system. Note that there is no need to modify any SELinux Booleans for DNS client to work.

The /etc/nsswitch.conf File

In RHEL, more than one sources can be employed for hostname lookups. For example, host information can be obtained from */etc/hosts* file, NIS or DNS. Which of these sources to obtain information from and in what order, is determined in the *name service switch* configuration file called *nsswitch.conf* located in the */etc* directory. This file is referenced if */etc/host.conf* file does not exist.

An example entry below from the file consults the local *hosts* file first and then a DNS server for hostname resolution:

    hosts: files   dns

There are four keywords available for use when more than one potential source is referenced in the *nsswitch.conf* file. These keywords are listed in Table 22-5 with their meanings.

Keyword	Meaning
SUCCESS	Information found.
UNAVAIL	Source down or not responding.
NOTFOUND	Information not found.
TRYAGAIN	Source busy, try again later.

Table 22-5 Name Service Source Status

Based on the status code for a source, one of two actions given in Table 22-6, take place.

Action	Meaning
continue	Try the next source listed.
return	Do not try the next source.

Table 22-6 Name Service Source Actions

As an example, if the "hosts" entry looks like the following, the search will terminate when the required information is not found in DNS. The "files" source will be ignored.

    hosts: dns [NOTFOUND=return] files

Each keyword defined in Table 22-6 has a default action associated. If no keyword/action combination is specified, actions listed in Table 22-7 are assumed.

Keyword	Default Action
SUCCESS	return
UNAVAIL	continue
NOTFOUND	continue
TRYAGAIN	continue

Table 22-7 Name Service Source Default Actions

The /etc/host.conf File

This is a resolver configuration file and is referenced by the *dig* and *host* commands. The default entry from the file is shown below:

cat /etc/host.conf
order hosts,bind

This file typically has a single line entry, which tells the *named* daemon to use the *hosts* file for any name resolution and then contact a DNS server. You may alter the sequence. If this file does not exist, the *nsswitch.conf* file is referenced.

The /etc/resolv.conf File

The *resolv.conf* file is the DNS resolver file where you can define three keywords, as described in Table 22-8.

Keyword	Description
domain	Specifies the default domain name to be searched for queries. This keyword is defined when there are more than one domains, and is not needed for a single domain environment.
nameserver	Specifies up to three DNS server IP addresses to be used one at a time in the order in which they are listed. If none specified, the local DNS server is assumed.
search	Specifies up to six domain names with the first must be the local domain. The resolver appends these domain names one at a time in the order in which they are listed to the hostname specified when constructing queries.

Table 22-8 resolv.conf File Description

In your case, the DNS client will have the following entries in *nsswitch.conf* and *resolv.conf* files:

nsswitch.conf file:	hosts:	dns files	
resolv.conf file:	search	getitcertify.com	
	nameserver	192.168.0.201	# IP address of the master DNS server
	nameserver	192.168.0.202	# IP address of the slave DNS server

If the client gets IP information from a DHCP server, edit the associated network interface file in the */etc/sysconfig/network-scripts* directory and set the PEERDNS directive to "no" to prevent the DHCP server from supplying and overwriting DNS server information in the *resolv.conf* file.

Configuring a DNS Client via Network Configurator

To configure a DNS client using the Network Configurator, follow the steps below:

☞Run *system-config-network* or choose (GNOME) System / (KDE) Main Menu → Administration → Network. Click the DNS tab and enter up to three DNS server names or IP addresses, and search path. This information will be stored in the *resolv.conf* file.

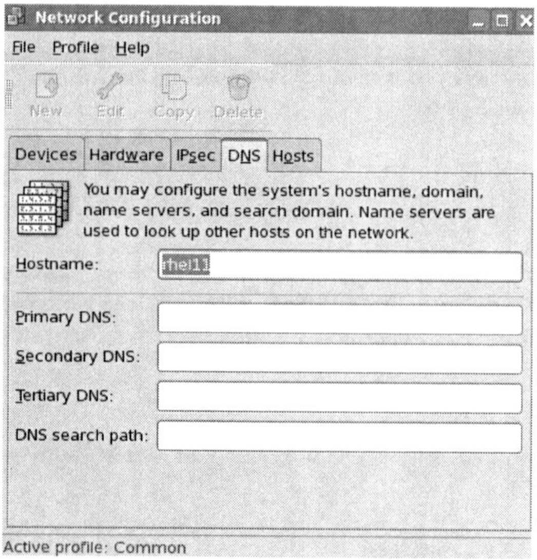

Figure 22-9 DNS Client Configuration – Network Configurator

Verifying DNS Functionality

RHEL provides three utilities – *dig*, *host* and *nslookup* – to test DNS functionality. These utilities are explained below.

Using dig

dig (domain information groper) is a lookup utility and may be used for troubleshooting DNS issues as well. This command looks in the *resolv.conf* file to determine DNS server information. If the information is not available or if the server is unavailable, it contacts one of the root DNS servers listed in the *named.root* file and tries to obtain the requested information from there. This command does not reference the *nsswitch.conf* file for source order determination, rather it uses the *host.conf* file.

To perform a forward lookup to obtain IP address of a system such as *rhel05*:

    # dig rhel05
    ; <<>> DiG 9.3.4-P1 <<>> rhel05
    ;; global options: printcmd
    ;; Got answer:
    ;; ->>HEADER<<- opcode: QUERY, status: NXDOMAIN, id: 58231
    ;; flags: qr rd ra; QUERY: 1, ANSWER: 0, AUTHORITY: 1, ADDITIONAL: 0

    ;; QUESTION SECTION:
    ;rhel01.   IN   A

    ;; AUTHORITY SECTION:
    .   10800 IN   SOA   a.root-servers.net. nstld.verisign-grs.com. 2009011800 1800 900 604800 86400

```
;; Query time: 39 msec
;; SERVER: 192.168.0.1#53(192.168.0.1)
;; WHEN: Sat Jan 17 17:20:51 2009
;; MSG SIZE  rcvd: 99
```

To perform a forward lookup to obtain IP address of *www.getitcertify.com*:

```
# dig www.getitcertify.com
; <<>> DiG 9.2.4 <<>> www.getitcertify.com
;; global options:  printcmd
;; Got answer:
;; ->>HEADER<<- opcode: QUERY, status: NOERROR, id: 59987
;; flags: qr rd ra; QUERY: 1, ANSWER: 1, AUTHORITY: 2, ADDITIONAL: 0

;; QUESTION SECTION :
;www.getitcertify.com.          IN      A

;; ANSWER SECTION:
www.getitcertify.com.  86400  IN    A     216.157.146.128

;; AUTHORITY SECTION:
getitcertify.com.      86400  IN    NS    ns2.vectorsolution.com.
getitcertify.com.      86400  IN    NS    ns3.vectorsolution.com.

;; Query time: 189 msec
;; SERVER: 199.81.11.53#53(199.81.11.53)
;; WHEN: Fri Feb  1 10:18:01 2008
;; MSG SIZE  rcvd: 105
```

To perform a reverse lookup on *www.getitcertify.com*, use –x option with the command:

```
# dig –x www.getitcertify.com
; <<>> DiG 9.3.4-P1 <<>> -x www.getitcertify.com
;; global options:  printcmd
;; Got answer:
;; ->>HEADER<<- opcode: QUERY, status: FORMERR, id: 30259
;; flags: qr aa rd ra; QUERY: 1, ANSWER: 0, AUTHORITY: 0, ADDITIONAL: 0

;; QUESTION SECTION:
;com.getitcertify.www.in-addr.arpa. IN  PTR

;; Query time: 10 msec
;; SERVER: 192.168.0.1#53(192.168.0.1)
;; WHEN: Wed Apr 22 03:17:40 2009
;; MSG SIZE  rcvd: 51
```

To perform an MX lookup on *www.getitcertify.com*, use –t option with the command:

---

dig –t mx www.getitcertify.com

```
; <<>> DiG 9.3.4-P1 <<>> -t mx www.getitcertify.com
;; global options:  printcmd
;; Got answer:
;; ->>HEADER<<- opcode: QUERY, status: NOERROR, id: 63062
;; flags: qr rd ra; QUERY: 1, ANSWER: 0, AUTHORITY: 1, ADDITIONAL: 0

;; QUESTION SECTION:
;www.getitcertify.com.          IN      MX

;; AUTHORITY SECTION:
getitcertify.com.     10800  IN    SOA     ns3.vectorsolution.com. support.vectorsolution.com.
2006080204 10800 3600 604800 86400

;; Query time: 53 msec
;; SERVER: 192.168.0.1#53(192.168.0.1)
;; WHEN: Wed Apr 22 03:18:10 2009
;; MSG SIZE  rcvd: 101
```

To perform an SOA lookup on *www.getitcertify.com*, use –t option with the command:

dig –t soa www.getitcertify.com

```
; <<>> DiG 9.3.4-P1 <<>> -t soa www.getitcertify.com
;; global options:  printcmd
;; Got answer:
;; ->>HEADER<<- opcode: QUERY, status: NOERROR, id: 31105
;; flags: qr rd ra; QUERY: 1, ANSWER: 0, AUTHORITY: 1, ADDITIONAL: 0

;; QUESTION SECTION:
;www.getitcertify.com.          IN      SOA

;; AUTHORITY SECTION:
getitcertify.com.     10800  IN    SOA     ns3.vectorsolution.com. support.vectorsolution.com.
2006080204 10800 3600 604800 86400

;; Query time: 51 msec
;; SERVER: 192.168.0.1#53(192.168.0.1)
;; WHEN: Wed Apr 22 03:18:27 2009
;; MSG SIZE  rcvd: 101
```

To query the name server directly, specify either its hostname or IP address:

dig @192.168.0.1

```
; <<>> DiG 9.3.4-P1 <<>> @192.168.0.1
; (1 server found)
;; global options:  printcmd
;; Got answer:
;; ->>HEADER<<- opcode: QUERY, status: NOERROR, id: 47732
;; flags: qr rd ra; QUERY: 1, ANSWER: 13, AUTHORITY: 0, ADDITIONAL: 14
```

```
;; QUESTION SECTION:
;.                      IN    NS
;; ANSWER SECTION:
.              431447  IN    NS    F.ROOT-SERVERS.NET.
.              431447  IN    NS    K.ROOT-SERVERS.NET.
.              431447  IN    NS    A.ROOT-SERVERS.NET.
.              431447  IN    NS    H.ROOT-SERVERS.NET.
.              431447  IN    NS    D.ROOT-SERVERS.NET.
.              431447  IN    NS    C.ROOT-SERVERS.NET.
.              431447  IN    NS    E.ROOT-SERVERS.NET.
.              431447  IN    NS    J.ROOT-SERVERS.NET.
.              431447  IN    NS    L.ROOT-SERVERS.NET.
.              431447  IN    NS    M.ROOT-SERVERS.NET.
.              431447  IN    NS    B.ROOT-SERVERS.NET.
.              431447  IN    NS    G.ROOT-SERVERS.NET.
.              431447  IN    NS    I.ROOT-SERVERS.NET.

;; ADDITIONAL SECTION:
K.ROOT-SERVERS.NET.    359028  IN    A      193.0.14.129
K.ROOT-SERVERS.NET.    211868  IN    AAAA   2001:7fd::1
A.ROOT-SERVERS.NET.    354914  IN    A      198.41.0.4
A.ROOT-SERVERS.NET.    347266  IN    AAAA   2001:503:ba3e::2:30
H.ROOT-SERVERS.NET.    196338  IN    A      128.63.2.53
H.ROOT-SERVERS.NET.    200839  IN    AAAA   2001:500:1::803f:235
D.ROOT-SERVERS.NET.    201825  IN    A      128.8.10.90
C.ROOT-SERVERS.NET.    200007  IN    A      192.33.4.12
E.ROOT-SERVERS.NET.    198633  IN    A      192.203.230.10
J.ROOT-SERVERS.NET.    198330  IN    A      192.58.128.30
J.ROOT-SERVERS.NET.    216865  IN    AAAA   2001:503:c27::2:30
L.ROOT-SERVERS.NET.    363587  IN    A      199.7.83.42
L.ROOT-SERVERS.NET.    232331  IN    AAAA   2001:500:3::42
M.ROOT-SERVERS.NET.    360248  IN    A      202.12.27.33

;; Query time: 19 msec
;; SERVER: 192.168.0.1#53(192.168.0.1)
;; WHEN: Wed Apr 22 02:52:28 2009
;; MSG SIZE  rcvd: 512
```

Using host

This command does not reference the *nsswitch.conf* file to determine the order for name resolution sources, rather it uses the *host.conf* file for that purpose. To perform a forward lookup to obtain IP address of *www.getitcertify.com*:

 # host www.getitcertify.com
www.getitcertify.com has address 216.157.146.128

To perform a reverse lookup to obtain hostname of the IP address 216.157.146.128:

 # host 216.157.146.128
128.146.157.216.in-addr.arpa domain name pointer hsphere.cc.

To perform an MX lookup on *getitcertify.com*:

 # host –t mx getitcertify.com
getitcertify.com mail is handled by 10 mail6.vectorsolution.com.

To perform an SOA lookup on *getitcertify.com*:

 # host –t soa getitcertify.com
getitcertify.com has SOA record ns3.vectorsolution.com. support.vectorsolution.com. 2006080204 10800 3600 604800 86400

To obtain detailed information, use –v option:

 # host –v www.getitcertify.com
Trying "www.getitcertify.com"
;; ->>HEADER<<- opcode: QUERY, status: NOERROR, id: 64141
;; flags: qr rd ra; QUERY: 1, ANSWER: 1, AUTHORITY: 2, ADDITIONAL: 0

;; QUESTION SECTION:
;www.getitcertify.com.   IN   A

;; ANSWER SECTION:
www.getitcertify.com. 84848 IN   A   216.157.146.128

;; AUTHORITY SECTION:
getitcertify.com.   84848 IN   NS   ns3.vectorsolution.com.
getitcertify.com.   84848 IN   NS   ns2.vectorsolution.com.

Received 105 bytes from 192.168.0.1#53 in 25 ms
Trying "www.getitcertify.com"
;; ->>HEADER<<- opcode: QUERY, status: NOERROR, id: 53520
;; flags: qr rd ra; QUERY: 1, ANSWER: 0, AUTHORITY: 1, ADDITIONAL: 0

;; QUESTION SECTION:
;www.getitcertify.com.   IN   AAAA

;; AUTHORITY SECTION:
getitcertify.com.   10626 IN   SOA   ns3.vectorsolution.com. support.vectorsolution.com.
2006080204 10800 3600 604800 86400

Received 101 bytes from 192.168.0.1#53 in 15 ms
Trying "www.getitcertify.com"
;; ->>HEADER<<- opcode: QUERY, status: NOERROR, id: 60328
;; flags: qr rd ra; QUERY: 1, ANSWER: 0, AUTHORITY: 1, ADDITIONAL: 0

;; QUESTION SECTION:

;www.getitcertify.com.   IN   MX

;; AUTHORITY SECTION:
getitcertify.com.   10626 IN   SOA   ns3.vectorsolution.com. support.vectorsolution.com.
2006080204 10800 3600 604800 86400

Received 101 bytes from 192.168.0.1#53 in 16 ms

Using nslookup

To obtain IP address of a system such as *rhel05*, use the *nslookup* (name server lookup) command:

> # **nslookup rhel05**
> Server: 192.168.0.201
> Address: 192.168.0.201#53
>
> Non-authoritative answer:
> Name: rhel05
> Address: 192.168.0.205

To perform a reverse lookup:

> # **nslookup 192.168.0.205**
> Server: 192.168.0.201
> Address: 192.168.0.201#53
>
> Name: rhel05
> Address: 192.168.0.205

The *nslookup* command can be run in an interactive mode as well:

> # **nslookup**
> >

At the > prompt, you can run the *server* command to force *nslookup* to use the specified DNS server for query. For example, to resolve hostnames using the slave DNS server *rhel02* instead of the master, do the following:

> > server rhel02

Type a system name for lookup:

> rhel05
> Name Server: getitcertify.com
> Addresses: 192.168.0.202
>
> Name: rhel05.getitcertify.com
> Address: 192.168.0.205

Type exit to quit *nslookup*.

To perform a lookup on *www.getitcertify.com*:

> **# nslookup www.getitcertify.com**
> Server: 199.82.72.18
> Address: 199.82.72.18#53
> Non-authoritative answer:
> Name: www.getitcertify.com
> Address: 216.157.146.128

Dynamic Host Configuration Protocol (DHCP)

Dynamic Host Configuration Protocol (DHCP) enables a system that acts as a *DHCP server* to provide IP address and other network parameters including subnet mask, default gateway, DNS/NIS/NTP server IP and domain name to other systems automatically. These other systems are referred to as *DHCP clients*.

When a RHEL system with DHCP client functionality enabled boots up, it broadcasts a DHCPDISCOVER message on the network requesting an available DHCP server to provide IP address and network parameter information. An available DHCP server receives the DHCPDISCOVER message and responds by sending a DHCPOFFER message back to the client. The DHCPOFFER message includes all the required information that the client requires to configure itself. The client evaluates the information and returns a DHCPREQUEST message to the server requesting it to lease the IP address for a fixed amount of time. The server reserves the address for the client and confirms by sending a DHCPACK message back to the client. The client stores the lease information in the */var/lib/dhcpd/dhcpd.leases* file and configures itself with the IP and other information. The IP address is auto-renewable at client request.

DHCP offloads you of IP configuration and maintenance tasks and it is an ideal solution for PC, workstation and laptop users. The DHCP client functionality should not be used on systems that require static IP settings.

Understanding DHCP Server Configuration File

The configuration file for DHCP server is */etc/dhcpd.conf*. This file does not contain any directives by default. You may copy the template *dhcpd.conf.sample* from */usr/share/doc/dhcp** directory into */etc* and rename it to *dhcpd.conf*. A slightly customized version of this file is shown below:

> **# cat /etc/dhcpd.conf**
> ddns-update-style none;
> ignore client-updates;
> subnet   192.168.0.0
> netmask   255.255.255.0 {
> # --- default gateway
>   option routers   192.168.0.1;
>   option subnet-mask   255.255.255.0;
>   option nis-domain   "nis_domain";
>   option domain-name   "testdom ";
>   option domain-name-servers   192.168.0.201;

```
        option time-offset              -18000; # Eastern Standard Time
        option ntp-servers              192.168.0.201;
. . . . . . . .
        range dynamic-bootp             192.168.0.2  192.168.0.20;
        default-lease-time              21600;
        max-lease-time                  43200;
        #  we want the nameserver to appear at a fixed address
        host rhel01 {
            next-server                 rhel02.getitcertify.com;
            hardware ethernet           00:0C:29:EC:5D:99;
            fixed-address               192.168.0.250;
        }
    }
```

Table 22-9 lists and explains various directives from this file.

Entry	Explanation
ddns-update-style	Specifies how close this server is to the current DDNS standard. Supported options are:
	interim: Standards are still in the development phase.
	none: Specifies whether the DHCP server should attempt to update DNS when a lease is accepted or released.
ignore	client-updates: Prevents normal users from changing system's name.
subnet	Specifies a network to be served.
netmask	Specifies an associated subnet mask.
option	Supports several options such as:
	routers: Specifies a default gateway to be used by the clients.
	subnet-mask: Specifies a subnet mask.
	nis-domain: Specifies an NIS domain name.
	domain-name: Specifies a DNS domain name.
	domain-name-servers: Specifies one or more addresses of available DNS servers.
	time-offset: Specifies offset in seconds from UTC.
	ntp-servers: Specifies one or more addresses of available NTP servers.
	netbios-name-servers: Specifies one or more addresses of available WINS servers.
	netbios-node-type 2: Specifies a node type for WINS servers.
range	dynamic-bootp: Reserves a range of addresses for BootP clients.
default-lease-time	Specifies a default time in seconds for an address lease.
max-lease-time	Specifies the maximum time in seconds for an address lease.
host	Reserves IP address for a specific system:
	next-server: Specifies the hostname or IP address of a BootP server.
	hardware: Specifies a client's Ethernet address.
	fixed-address: Specifies a static address.

Table 22-9 dhcpd.conf Directives

Configuring DHCP

Let us look at step-by-step procedures on how to configure a DHCP server and client.

SELinux Requirements for DHCP

If SELinux is enforced, you need to disable its protection for DHCP service to ensure smooth functionality. Use the *setsebool* command as demonstrated below, or the SELinux Configurator *system-config-selinux* as explained in Chapter 30 "System and Network Security".

> # **setsebool –P dhcpd_disable_trans=1**

Use the *getsebool* command to verify:

> # **getsebool dhcpd_disable_trans**
> dhcpd_disable_trans --> on

Configuring a DHCP Server

To configure *rhel06* to act as a DHCP server, perform the following steps:

1. Check whether the required DHCP software package is installed:

   > # **rpm –q dhcp**
   > dhcp-3.0.5-18.el5

   Install the package if it is not already loaded using one of the software package installation methods described in Chapter 11 "Software Package Management".

2. Copy */usr/share/doc/dhcp-*/dhcpd.conf.sample* to */etc* directory as *dhcpd.conf*:

   > # **cat /usr/share/doc/dhcp-*/dhcpd.conf.sample > /etc/dhcpd.conf**

3. Modify *dhcpd.conf* file appropriately.
4. Execute the following to check the file's syntax:

   > # **service dhcpd configtest**
   > Syntax: OK

5. Execute the following to make DHCP autostart at each system reboot:

   > # **chkconfig dhcpd on**

6. Allow DHCP traffic on port 67 to pass through the firewall, or simply stop and disable the firewall if it is not used. Consult Chapter 30 "System and Network Security" on how to perform these tasks.
7. Start (or restart) the *dhcpd* daemon:

   > # **service dhcpd start**
   > Starting dhcpd: [OK]

8. Execute the following to check the operational status of DHCP service:

   # service dhcpd status
   dhcpd (pid 1914) is running...

Configuring a DHCP Client

To configure *rhel07* as a DHCP client to use *eth0* network interface, perform the following steps:

1. Edit the */etc/sysconfig/network-scripts/ifcfg-eth0* file and make certain that the following directives are set:

   DEVICE=eth0
   BOOTPROTO=dhcp
   ONBOOT=yes
   PEERDNS=yes

2. Stop and restart the interface:

   # ifdown eth0
   # ifup eth0
   Determining IP information for eth0... done.   [OK]

3. Run the *ifconfig* command and check if the network interface has picked up IP assignments from the DHCP server. If PEERDNS is set to "yes", the *resolv.conf* file will be populated as well with DNS server information.

Alternatively, you can either use the Network Configurator or the *dhclient* command.

With the Network Configurator, execute *system-config-network* in an X terminal window or click (GNOME) System / (KDE) Main Menu → Administration → Network. Click Devices, highlight the network interface, click Edit and select "Automatically obtain IP address settings with dhcp". If you wish to obtain DNS information as well, select "Automatically obtain DNS information from provider". See Figure 22-10.

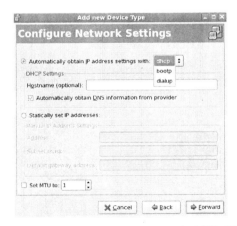

Figure 22-10 Network Configurator – DHCP Client Setup

Another method for configuring a DHCP client is to use the *dhclient* command. This command reads settings from the *dhcpd.conf* file and broadcasts a message on the network for IP information. A configured DHCP server responds and returns the information, which the command uses to configure one or more network interfaces.

 # dhclient

```
. . . . . . . .
Listening on LPF/eth0/00:0c:29:4f:cf:01
Sending on   LPF/eth0/00:0c:29:4f:cf:01
Sending on   Socket/fallback
DHCPREQUEST on eth0 to 255.255.255.255 port 67
DHCPACK from 192.168.0.1
bound to 192.168.0.201 -- renewal in 110785 seconds.
```

All information is recorded in the system log file */var/log/messages*.

Summary

This chapter introduced you to name resolution, DNS and DHCP. You learned name resolution concepts, how it worked and what methods were available.

You studied DNS components including name space, domain, zone, zone files, master server, slave server, caching server, and client. You were presented with step-by-step procedures on how to setup master, slave and caching DNS servers. You looked at the contents of boot and zone files, and files involved in DNS client setup. You used commands to verify DNS functionality.

The last topic was on DHCP. An overview of DHCP was provided followed by procedures on how to configure a DHCP server and client.

## 23

NIS and LDAP

This chapter covers the following major topics:

- ✓ NIS concepts and components – domain, maps, master server, slave server, client, daemons, and startup and configuration files
- ✓ SELinux requirements for NIS client
- ✓ Configure an NIS client using commands and Authentication Configurator
- ✓ Test client functionality and modify a user password
- ✓ Display and search NIS maps
- ✓ Manually bind to another server
- ✓ Introduction to LDAP
- ✓ Features and benefits of using LDAP
- ✓ LDAP terminology – directory, entry, attribute, matching rule, object class, schema, LDIF, DN / RDN and LDAP roles
- ✓ Configure an LDAP client using commands and Authentication Configurator

Every networked RHEL system requires some administrative work to be performed on it to stay current, and up and running. For example, if a user requires access to all networked RHEL systems, an account is created on each individual machine for the user. Likewise, if a new system needs to be added to the network, the *hosts* file is updated on all systems on the network with the hostname and IP address of the new system. As long as the number of users, systems and other system management requirements are low, administrative work can be done without much difficulty; however, when this number grows or requirements increase, system administration and updates to administrative data become tedious and time consuming. RHEL offers two services that help manage administrative data in large environments. These are referred to as NIS and LDAP.

NIS Concepts and Components

Rather than managing user accounts, hostnames, etc. on each individual system, a service called *Network Information Service* (NIS) may be used to maintain administrative files for these and several other services centrally on a single system. Other systems can then be configured to reference the central system to obtain user information, hostnames and so on. In an NIS environment, a new user account is setup on the central management system (and not on individual systems). This allows the user to log on to any system on the network with user credentials authenticated by the central system.

Another key advantage with central management of administrative files is that the data remains consistent and uniform across all systems.

NIS was derived from *yellow pages* service developed by the British Telecom in the UK. Most NIS commands and daemon names precede "yp" (for yellow pages).

When working with NIS, certain components and roles are used. These are explained in the following sub-sections.

NIS Domain

An *NIS domain* is a set of NIS-managed systems sharing common NIS-converted administrative data files called *NIS maps*.

NIS maps are stored under a sub-directory beneath */var/yp* on an NIS server, and is created when the NIS server is setup. The name of the sub-directory matches the name of the NIS domain.

 There is no relationship between NIS domain and DNS domain.

NIS Maps

There are numerous administrative files on the system, and most of them are located in the */etc* directory. These files are text files and can be modified with a text editor or system commands.

When a master NIS server is created, the information in these files is converted into a special NIS format and saved into new files under the domain directory located under */var/yp*. These special files are called *NIS maps*.

NIS Server

There are two types of NIS server setups: *master NIS server* and *slave NIS server*.

A master NIS server is the system where the original administrative files are kept and maintained. These files are translated into NIS maps and stored under the domain directory in */var/yp*. Any modifications to NIS maps must be made in the administrative files on the master NIS server.

A slave NIS server is not required for NIS functionality, having at least one on the network is highly recommended for redundancy and load balancing. Each slave server has an identical directory structure under */var/yp* containing a copy of NIS maps pulled from the master server.

NIS Client

An *NIS client* does not store a copy of the master server's administrative files or NIS maps locally; it does have its own administrative files, which may or may not be referenced when the client functionality is invoked on the system. NIS client binds itself with a configured NIS server at startup and pulls from it any required data as needed.

NIS Daemons

When the NIS functionality is initiated on a client system, a daemon called *ypbind* begins to run and binds itself with a server daemon called *ypserv* to fetch requested information. Binding information is stored in the */var/yp/binding/<domainname>* file. This daemon dynamically binds itself to another NIS server should the one it is bound to fails.

NIS Startup and Configuration Files

The startup NIS file is */etc/sysconfig/network* and the key configuration file is */etc/yp.conf*. The contents of the files are discussed in the next section.

Configuring an NIS Client

An NIS client can be configured either with commands or the Red Hat User Authenticator. Both methods are explained in the following sub-sections.

SELinux Requirements for NIS Client

If SELinux is enforced, you need to disable its protection for NIS client service to ensure smooth functionality. Use the *setsebool* command as demonstrated below, or the SELinux Configurator *system-config-selinux* as explained in Chapter 30 "System and Network Security". Specify only those Booleans that need to be disabled, leave others intact.

```
# setsebool –P allow_ypbind=1 ypbind_disable_trans=1 yppasswdd_disable_trans=1
```

Use the *getsebool* command to verify:

```
# getsebool allow_ypbind ypbind_disable_trans yppasswdd_disable_trans
allow_ypbind --> on
ypbind_disable_trans --> on
yppasswdd_disable_trans --> on
```

Configuring an NIS Client Using Commands

To configure *rhel05* to function as an NIS client of a pre-configured NIS server *rhel01* in *nis_domain* domain, perform the following steps on *rhel05*:

1. Check whether the required client software packages are installed:

   # **rpm –qa | egrep 'portmap|ypbind'**
   ypbind-1.19-8.el5
   portmap-4.0-65.2.2.1

   The ypbind package provides NIS client services and the portmap package is used for RPC-based communication, which NIS uses for its operation. Install the packages if they are not already loaded using one of the software package installation methods described in Chapter 11 "Software Package Management".

2. Edit */etc/yp.conf* and define the NIS domain and server:

   # **vi /etc/yp.conf**
   domain nis_domain   server rhel01

3. Edit */etc/sysconfig/network* and set the NISDOMAIN directive:

   # **vi /etc/sysconfig/network**
   NISDOMAIN=nis_domain

   Instead of running steps 2 and 3, you can run the following to update the files:

   # **authconfig --nisserver=rhel01 --nisdomain=nis_domain --update**

4. Edit */etc/sysconfig/authconfig* and set the USENIS directive to yes:

   # **vi /etc/sysconfig/authconfig**
   USENIS=yes

5. Edit */etc/nsswitch.conf* and ensure that sources for user authentication are listed in the below order. Consult Chapter 22 "DNS and DHCP" for details on the *nsswitch.conf* file.

   # **vi /etc/nsswitch.conf**
   passwd: nis files
   shadow: nis files
   group: nis files

6. Edit */etc/pam.d/system-auth-ac* and append the following line to have all password change requests served by the *rpc.yppasswdd* daemon running on the master NIS server:

   # **vi /etc/pam.d/system-auth-ac**
   password   sufficient   pam_unix.so   md5   shadow   nis   nullok   try_first_pass   use_authtok

---

7. Run the following to enable NIS client functionality to autostart at each system reboot:

   # **chkconfig portmap on**
   # **chkconfig ypbind on**

8. Start *portmap* and *ypbind* daemons:

   # **service portmap start**
   Starting portmap: [OK]
   # **service ypbind start**
   Turning on allow_ypbind SELinux boolean
   Binding to the NIS domain: [OK]
   Listening for an NIS domain server.............   [OK]

This completes the procedure for NIS client configuration at the command line.

If you wish to enable NIS authentication for members of one or more specific groups only, you will need to edit a PAM configuration file */etc/pam.d/system-auth-ac* and add the following line entry to the auth section right after the "auth required pam_env.so". See Chapter "System and Network Security" for details on Pluggable Authentication Modules (PAM).

   auth required pam_listfile.so item=group sense=allow file=/etc/security/groups.allow

Now create */etc/security/groups.allow* file and add group entries one per line.

Configuring an NIS Client via Authentication Configurator

To configure *rhel05* to function as an NIS client of a pre-configured NIS server *rhel01* in *nis_domain* domain, perform the following steps on *rhel05* using the Red Hat Authentication Configurator:

1. Execute *system-config-authentication* in an X terminal window (run *authconfig-tui* for its text equivalent or use the command *authconfig*) or choose (GNOME) System / (KDE) Main Menu → Administration → Authentication. The Authentication Configurator screen will open up as shown in Figure 23-1.

Figure 23-1 Authentication Configurator – NIS Client Configuration

2. Select Enable NIS Support under User Information and click Configure NIS. Enter the NIS domain and server names. Click OK when done.

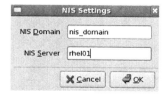

Figure 23-2 Authentication Configurator – NIS Settings

This sets the NIS client functionality and starts *ypbind* daemon on *rhel05*.

Managing NIS Client

Some of the NIS client management tasks include testing the NIS client functionality, modifying a user password, displaying and searching NIS maps for user information, and manually binding a client to another NIS server.

Testing NIS Client Functionality

To test which NIS server a client is bound to, run the *ypwhich* command without any options. Note that every system in an NIS domain including master and slave servers, is an NIS client. With –m option, this command also displays what maps are available from which server:

> # **ypwhich**
> rhel01
> # **ypwhich –m**
> netid.byname rhel01
> passwd.byuid rhel01
> group.bygid rhel01
> protocols.byname rhel01
> services.byservicename rhel01
> group.byname rhel01
> rpc.bynumber rhel01
> ypservers rhel01
> mail.aliases rhel01
> hosts.byname rhel01
> services.byname rhel01
> passwd.byname rhel01
> protocols.bynumber rhel01
> rpc.byname rhel01
> hosts.byaddr rhel01

Modifying a User Password

Once an NIS environment is established, use the *yppasswd* command to change a user password. For example, if user *aghori* wants to change his password, he will run the command, enter his existing password and then the new password that he wants to set:

```
$ yppasswd
```
Changing NIS account information for aghori on rhel01.
Please enter old password:
Changing NIS password for aghori on rhel01.
Please enter new password:
Please retype new password:
The NIS password has been changed on rhel01.

Displaying and Searching NIS Maps

The administrative data files are in plain ascii text. Translating them into NIS generates map files, which contain data in non-text format. These map files require a different set of commands to be viewed and searched. These commands are *ypcat* and *ypmatch*. In addition, there are a couple of other commands called *getent* and *yppoll* that are used to display and search the contents of an NIS map or a source text file, and display time stamps of the creation of maps, respectively. None of the four commands require that you specify the location of the map or file. Here is how you would use these tools.

To display the contents of the "passwd" map, use the *ypcat* command. This command performs an equivalent function to the *cat* command.

```
# ypcat passwd
brewbuilder:!!:505:505::/home/brewbuilder:/bin/bash
cghori:!!:502:502::/home/cghori:/bin/bash
aghori:$1$HXJxjHYp$GgsQ3mzkAxK2kRHrkUvxp/:500:500::/home/aghori:/bin/bash
user2:!!:504:504::/home/user2:/bin/bash
bghori:!!:501:501::/home/bghori:/bin/bash
mockbuild:!!:506:506::/home/mockbuild:/bin/bash
user1:$1$PAOK1lIC$lIfzCgWEcRuflgaTpOF6J.:503:503::/home/user1:/bin/bash
user3:!!:507:507::/home/user3:/bin/bash
```

To search for a group "user2" in the "group" map, use the *ypmatch* command. This command performs an equivalent function to the *grep* command.

```
# ypmatch user2 group
user2:!:504:
```

To display "group" information from the first available source as specified in the *nsswitch.conf* file, use the *getent* command:

```
# getent group
brewbuilder:x:505:
cghori:x:502:
aghori:x:500:
user2:x:504:
bghori:x:501:
mockbuild:x:506:
user1:x:503:
user3:x:507:
```

To search for a group "user2" in the first available source as specified in the *nsswitch.conf* file:

> # **getent group user2**
> user2:x:504:

To display the time stamp on a map, use the *yppoll* command. The time displayed is the offset in seconds from the epoch time.

> # **yppoll passwd.byuid**
> Domain nis_domain is supported.
> Map passwd.byuid has order number 1139927840.
> The master server is rhel01.

Manually Binding a Client to Another NIS Server

In order for a client system to be able to reference NIS information, it must be bound to an NIS server. This binding is set automatically when NIS client functionality is started either at system reboot or manually.

To manually alter the binding to another NIS server such as *rhel03*, use the *ypset* command:

> # **ypset rhel03**

Verify the change with the *ypwhich* or *yppoll* command.

Introduction to LDAP

More powerful, diversified and flexible than NIS, *Lightweight Directory Access Protocol* (LDAP) is a trivial, simplified networking protocol for obtaining directory information such as email messaging, user authentication and calendar services over the network. LDAP was derived from *Directory Access Protocol* (DAP), which is one of the protocols within X.500 specification developed jointly by the *International Telecommunication Union* (ITU) and the *International Organization for Standardization* (ISO). One of the major disadvantages with DAP was that it required too much computing resources to work efficiently. LDAP (also referred to as *X.500 Lite*), on the other hand, is thinner and requires less client-side computing resources. This protocol is platform-independent, which makes it available on a variety of vendor hardware platforms running heterogeneous operating system software.

LDAP is hierarchical and is similar to the structure of the Linux/UNIX directory tree and DNS. It can be based on logical boundaries defined by geography or organizational arrangement. A typical LDAP directory structure for a company ABC with domain *abc.com* and offices located in Canada, USA, UK and Australia, is shown in Figure 23-3.

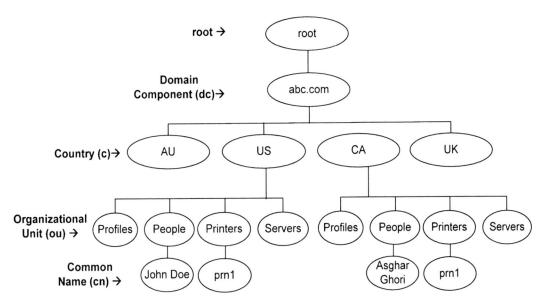

Figure 23-3 LDAP Directory Hierarchy

The top of the company is referred to as the *root* of the LDAP directory hierarchy. Underneath it, is located *domain component* (dc), which is usually the name of the company. *country* (c) falls under domain component. *organizational units* (ou) separate categories of directory information and may be country-specific. The actual information is at the lowest level of the hierarchy, which may include resources such as users, profiles, people, printers, servers, photos, text, URLs, pointers to information, binary data and public key certificates.

Features and Benefits of Using LDAP

Some of the features of LDAP and key benefits of using it are listed below:

- ✓ Has a hierarchical directory structure that provides organizations with information and resources in a logical fashion.
- ✓ Allows the consolidation of common information such as user information within an OU.
- ✓ Has lower overhead than X.500 DAP.
- ✓ Provides users and applications with a unified, standard interface to a single, extensible directory service making it easier to rapidly develop and deploy directory-enabled applications.
- ✓ Reduces the need to enter and coordinate redundant information in multiple services scattered across an enterprise.
- ✓ Enables fast searches, cost-effective management of users and security, and a central integration point for multiple applications and services.
- ✓ Maintains directory-wide consistent information.

LDAP Client Configuration Files

On RHEL, an open source LDAP implementation software called OpenLDAP is used to provide server and client functionalities. The key configuration files are */etc/ldap.conf* and

/etc/openldap/ldap.conf of which the former contains PAM and NSS LDAP module information and the latter holds the default LDAP configuration.

LDAP Terminology

To comprehend LDAP thoroughly, a grasp of the following key terms is essential.

Directory

An LDAP *directory*, a.k.a. *Directory Information Tree* (DIT), is like a specialized database that stores information about objects such as people, profiles, printers and servers. It organizes information in such a way that it becomes easier to find and retrieve needed information. It lists objects and gives details about them. An LDAP directory is similar in concept to the Linux/UNIX directory hierarchy.

Entry

An *entry* is a building block for an LDAP directory and represents a specific record in it. In other words, an entry is a collection of information consisting of one or more attributes for an object. An LDAP directory, for instance, might include entries for employees, printers and servers.

Attribute

An *attribute* contains two pieces of information – *attribute type* and *attribute values* – and is associated with one or more entries. The attribute type such as jobTitle represents the type of information the attribute contains. An attribute value is the specific information contained in that entry. For instance, a value for the jobTitle attribute type could be "director". Table 23-1 lists some common attribute types.

Attribute Type	Description
CommonName (cn)	Common name of an entry such as cn=John Doe
DomainComponent (dc)	Distinguished name (DN) of a component in DNS such as dc=ca, dc=abc, dc=com.
Country (c)	Country such as c=ca.
Mail (mail)	Email address.
Organization (o)	Name of an organization such as o=abc.
OrganizationalUnit (ou)	Name of a unit within an organization such as ou=Printers.
Owner (owner)	Owner of an entry such as cn=John Doe, ou=Printers, dc=abc, c=ca.
Surname (sn)	Person's last name such as Doe.
TelephoneNumber (telephoneNumber)	Telephone number such as (123) 456-7890 or 1234567890.

Table 23-1 Common LDAP Attribute Types

 Long names and corresponding abbreviations can be used interchangeably.

Matching Rule

A *matching rule* matches the attribute value sought against the attribute value stored in the directory in a search and compare task.

For example, matching rules associated with the telephoneNumber attribute could cause "(123) 456-7890" to match with either "(123) 456-7890" or "1234567890", or both. A matching rule is associated with an attribute when the attribute is defined.

Object Class

Each entry belongs to one or more *object classes*. An object class is a group of required and optional attributes that define the structure of an entry.

For example, an organizationalUser object class may include commonName and Surname as required attributes and telephoneNumber, UID, streetAddress and userPassword as optional attributes. Minimum required attributes must be defined when an entry is defined.

Schema

schema is a collection of attributes and object classes along with matching rules and syntax, and other related information.

LDAP Data Interchange Format (LDIF)

LDAP Data Interchange Format (LDIF) is a special format for importing and exporting LDAP records between LDAP servers. The data is in text format and consists of entries or alterations to entries, or a combination.

Each record is represented as a group of attributes with each attribute listed on a separate line comprising "name:value" pair. The following is a sample directory entry with attributes representing a record in LDIF:

```
dn: cn=John Doe,ou=People, c=ca,dc=abc
objectClass: inetLocalMailRecipient
sn: Doe
mail: john.doe@abc.com
cn: John Doe
givenName: John
uid: jdoe
telephoneNumber: (416) 123-4567
```

Distinguished Name and Relative Distinguished Name

A *Distinguished Name* (DN) uniquely identifies an entry in the entire directory tree. It is similar in concept to the absolute pathname of a file in the Linux directory hierarchy.

A *Relative Distinguished Name* (RDN), in contrast, represents individual components of a DN. It is similar in concept to the relative pathname of a file in the Linux directory hierarchy.

As an example, the DN for the printer *prn1* under Printers located in Canada (See Figure 23-1) is:

cn=prn1,ou=Printers,c=ca,dc=abc

In this example, the RDN for *prn1* is cn=prn1. Similarly, the RDN for Printers is ou=Printers, the RDN for ca is c=ca, and that for abc is dc=abc. A DN is thus a sequence of RDNs separated by commas.

LDAP Roles

There are four roles – *server*, *replica*, *client* and *referral* – that systems within an LDAP environment may perform. One system may be configured to execute more than one role.

LDAP Server

An LDAP server is a system that holds the LDAP directory information. It may be referred to as the *master* LDAP server. There must be one such server configured to offer directory services.

LDAP Replica

An LDAP replica is a system that contains a copy of the information that the LDAP server maintains. A replica may be referred to as a slave LDAP server. It is recommended that at least one replica be configured together with an LDAP server to achieve enhanced availability and load balancing.

LDAP Client

An LDAP client is a system that binds itself with a server or replica to establish a communication session to perform queries on directory entries and carry out necessary modifications.

LDAP Referral

An LDAP referral is an entity on a server that redirects an LDAP client's request to some other LDAP server or replica if it does not contain the requested information. A referral contains names and locations of other LDAP servers where requested information might be found.

Configuring an LDAP Client

An LDAP client can be configured at the command prompt or using the Authentication Configurator. Both methods are discussed in the following sub-sections.

Configuring an LDAP Client at the Command Prompt

To setup a system such as *rhel03* to act as an LDAP client of an LDAP server *rhel04*, perform the following on *rhel03*:

1. Ensure that the following packages are installed in order for the LDAP client functionality to work:

    ```
    # rpm –qa | grep ldap
    openldap-2.3.27-8
    openldap-clients-2.3.27-8
    nss_ldap-253-5.el5
    ```

2. Edit */etc/ldap.conf* file and insert entries as shown:

 # vi /etc/ldap.conf

host 192.168.0.204	# ldap server IP address
base dc=abc,dc=com	# defines the default DN
ssl start_tls	# encrypts passwords while in transit
pam_password md5	# Use md5 PAM password management

3. Edit */etc/openldap/ldap.conf* file and insert entries as shown:

 # vi /etc/openldap/ldap.conf

URI ldap://192.168.0.204	# ldap server
BASE dc=abc,dc=com	# sets default base DN

4. Edit */etc/sysconfig/authconfig* file and set the USELDAP and USELDAPAUTH directives to yes:

 # vi /etc/sysconfig/authconfig
USELDAP=yes
USELDAPAUTH=yes

5. Edit */etc/nsswitch.conf* file and ensure that user authentication is first referenced in LDAP:

 # vi /etc/nsswitch.conf

passwd:	ldap files
shadow:	ldap files
group:	ldap files

6. Edit */etc/pam.d/system-auth-ac* file and append the following lines to direct all authentication requests to be served by the LDAP server:

 # vi /etc/pam.d/system-auth-ac

auth	sufficient	pam_ldap.so use_first_pass
account	[default=bad success=ok user_unknown=ignore] pam_ldap.so	
password	sufficient	pam_ldap.so use_authtok
session	optional	pam_ldap.so

7. Run the following to enable the LDAP client facility to autostart at each system reboot:

 # chkconfig ldap on

8. Start the LDAP client service:

 # service ldap start

Checking configuration files for slapd: config file testing succeeded	[OK]
Starting slapd:	[OK]

This completes the procedure to configure an LDAP client at the command prompt. Restart the *sshd* service and use the *ssh* command to log in to the system to test authentication. You can use the *ldapsearch* command to pull user information from the LDAP server and the *openssl* command to test TLS (if configured):

ldapsearch –x –Z
openssl s_client –connect rhel04

Configuring an LDAP Client Using Authentication Configurator

To setup the system *rhel03* to act as an LDAP client of *rhel04* LDAP server, perform the following steps on *rhel03* using the Authentication Configurator.

1. Execute *system-config-authentication* in an X terminal window (run *authconfig-tui* for its text equivalent or use the command *authconfig*) or choose (GNOME) System / (KDE) Main Menu → Administration → Authentication. The Authentication Configurator screen will open up as shown in Figure 23-4.

Figure 23-4 Authentication Configurator – LDAP Client Configuration

2. Select Enable LDAP Support under User Information and click Configure LDAP. Enter LDAP Search Base DN and LDAP Server information. Click OK when done.

Figure 23-5 Authentication Configurator – LDAP Settings

3. Go to the Authentication tab and select Enable LDAP Support and click Configure LDAP. Enter LDAP Search Base DN and LDAP Server information. Click OK when done.
4. Go to the Options tab and choose appropriate options. Click OK when done. The tool will take a while to perform the requested configuration. It will also set the LDAP client

functionality to start at each system reboot at appropriate run levels. It will start the client right after that.

Figure 23-6 Authentication Configurator – LDAP Client Options

This sets up the LDAP client functionality and starts *slapd* daemon on *rhel03*.

Summary

In this chapter, you learned about NIS and LDAP. You looked at NIS concepts and components – domain, maps, master server, slave server and client. You performed configuration of an NIS client and were presented with procedures on how to test it. You displayed NIS map contents and searched through them for text using special commands. You saw how a user password could be modified in an NIS environment. You looked at procedures to manually bind a client with an alternate NIS server.

The second major topic in the chapter was LDAP. You were provided with an introduction and features and benefits associated with it. You were presented with definitions of LDAP components such as directory, entry, attribute, matching rule, object class, schema, LDIF, DN, RDN, server, replica, client and referral. Finally, you configured an LDAP client using commands as well as the Authentication Configurator.

## 24

Internet Services and Electronic Mail

This chapter covers the following major topics:

- ✓ Introduction to the Internet services
- ✓ The role of the Internet services daemon (xinetd)
- ✓ Internet services configuration files
- ✓ Enable/disable xinetd-controlled services and logging
- ✓ Introduction to very secure File Transfer Protocol (vsFTP)
- ✓ SELinux requirements, configuration file and access control
- ✓ Configure and test a vsFTP server
- ✓ Introduction to electronic mail
- ✓ How the mail system works
- ✓ Configure basic sendmail and postfix mail servers
- ✓ Sendmail and postfix configuration files and key macros/directives
- ✓ Check mail statistics and update aliases file
- ✓ Set a default MTA
- ✓ Configure non-secure and secure dovecot incoming mail servers
- ✓ Verify mail server functionality

RHEL internet services enable a system to function as a provider of one or more services to remote client systems over the network. These services include allowing users on the remote systems to log in, transfer files, send and receive mail, execute commands without logging in, get list of logged in users, synchronize time and so on.

There are several mail software programs supported on RHEL that allow you to configure a system as a server or client for sending and receiving mail. These software include sendmail and Postfix as outgoing mail servers, Dovecot as incoming mail server and several client programs.

The Internet Services

When services are used over the network, two pieces of a software program called *client* and *server* are involved. The client program requests for a service running on a remote system. The server program (or daemon) on the remote system responds to and serves the client request, establishing a client/server communication channel. At any given time, a system can act as both a server and a client. It can provide services to other systems and may use their services as a client.

Server programs are started in one of two ways: via startup scripts located in sequencer directories or via the master server program daemon called *xinetd* (*extended internet daemon*). *xinetd* is also referred to as a super-server. A detailed discussion on the startup scripts and sequencer directories is covered in Chapter 15 "Shutdown and Boot".

The *xinetd* daemon itself is started by one of the startup scripts when the system boots up into run level 3. This daemon reads its configuration file */etc/xinetd.conf* and sits in the memory listening on ports listed in the */etc/services* and */etc/rpc* files for services defined and enabled in the */etc/xinetd.d* directory. It waits for a client request to come in requesting one of the *xinetd*-controlled services. When one such request arrives on a particular port, this daemon starts the server program corresponding to that port. It hooks the client and server pieces up, gets itself out of that communication and starts listening on that port again on behalf of that server program. Every service uses a unique port number defined in the *services* or the *rpc* file.

Common Internet Services

There are two major categories of the Internet services: one developed at the University of California at Berkeley and referred to as *Berkeley* services and the other developed for the US Department of Defense's *Advanced Research Projects Agency* and referred to as *ARPA* services.

The Berkeley services include BIND (DNS), sendmail, *finger, rexec, rcp, rlogin, rsh, rup, ruptime* and *rwho*. These services were primarily developed to run on the UNIX platform; however, most of them today are also available on non-UNIX platforms such as Linux and Microsoft Windows. The names of most Berkeley services begin with an "r" and, therefore, may also be referred to as "r" commands.

The ARPA services, on the other hand, include *ftp* and *telnet*, which can be used on both Linux and non-Linux platforms.

Table 24-1 lists and describes some common Internet services.

Service	Description
fingerd	Enables the *finger* command to display information about users on local and remote systems. The *fingerd* daemon is started by *xinetd* and it uses port 79.
ftpd	Enables file transfer with other Linux and non-Linux systems. The client program is *ftp* or one of its variants. The *ftpd* daemon is started by *xinetd* and it uses port 21.
gssftp	Kerberos-based secure FTP service.
named	Enables hostname-to-IP and IP-to-hostname resolution. The *named* daemon responds to lookup commands such as *nslookup*, *dig* and *host*.
ntpd	Keeps the system clock in sync with a more reliable and accurate time source.
rcp	Enables you to perform a file copy. This protocol uses port 469.
rexecd	Enables executing a command on a remote system. The daemon is started by *xinetd*.
rsync	Enables you to perform a file copy using the differential method. This daemon is started by *xinetd* and it uses port 873.
sendmail	Sendmail is the most widely used mail transport agent on large networks and the Internet. It works with various client mail programs, and uses port 25.
telnetd	Enables a user to log in to a remote system. The client program is *telnet*. *telnetd* is started by *xinetd* and it uses port 23.
tftpd	Works with *bootps* to enable diskless systems and Kickstart clients to transfer files containing boot and other configuration data. The client program is *tftp*. *tftpd* is started by *xinetd* and it uses port 69.

Table 24-1 Internet Services

The xinetd Daemon, /etc/xinetd.conf File and /etc/xinetd.d Directory

The *xinetd* daemon is the master daemon for many Internet services. This daemon is started automatically at system boot when the */etc/rc.d/init.d/xinetd* script is executed. It listens for connection requests on behalf of the services listed in the */etc/xinetd.d* directory and in the */etc/xinetd.conf* file over the ports defined in the *services* and *rpc* files, and starts up an appropriate server process when a request arrives. Any time a change is made to the *xinetd.conf* file or a file in the *xinetd.d* directory, or a file is added to or removed from the *xinetd.d* directory, you will need to reload the configuration using the following:

service xinetd reload

And, if the daemon needs to be started, stopped or restarted manually, execute the above and pass the start, stop or restart argument as appropriate. You also need to ensure that the daemon is configured to autostart at each system reboot by running the following:

chkconfig --list xinetd
xinetd   0:off   1:off   2:off   3:on   4:on   5:on   6:off

Run the following if it is not:

chkconfig xinetd on

The default contents of *xinetd.conf* file look similar to the following:

```
# cat /etc/xinetd.conf
. . . . . . . .
defaults
{
# The next two items are intended to be a quick access place to
# temporarily enable or disable services.
#       enabled     =
#       disabled    =
# Define general logging characteristics.
        log_type          = SYSLOG daemon info
        log_on_failure    = HOST
        log_on_success    = PID HOST DURATION EXIT
# Define access restriction defaults
#       no_access   =
#       only_from   =
#       max_load    = 0
        cps               = 50 10
        instances         = 50
        per_source        = 10
# Address and networking defaults
#       bind        =
#       mdns        = yes
        v6only            = no
# setup environmental attributes
#       passenv     =
        groups            = yes
        umask             = 002
# Generally, banners are not used. This sets up their global defaults
#       banner          =
#       banner_fail     =
#       banner_success  =
}
includedir /etc/xinetd.d
```

Directives defined in the default section of the file are applicable to all services listed in the *xinetd.d*
directory, but any directive that is also defined in an *xinetd.d* directory configuration file, overrides
it. Here is an explanation of key directives from the *xinetd.conf* file:

✓ The defaults directive encloses all the default settings that are available to *xinetd*-controlled
  services when they start. The beginning and end are marked with curly braces { }.
✓ The enabled and disabled directives should not be uncommented unless you wish to perform
  some sort of testing, in which case you will need to specify names of services with these
  directives and uncomment them as appropriate. This will enable or disable services based on
  the setting of the disable directive in individual service scripts defined in the *xinetd.d*
  directory. When the testing is finished, comment them out so the enable and disable decision
  is made by the disable directive defined within each individual script in the *xinetd.d* directory.
✓ The logging related information is controlled via three directives – log_type, log_on_failure
  and log_on_success. The log_type directive directs the daemon to use *syslogd* for capturing
  connection information messages generated by the daemon facility in the */var/log/messages*

file. The log_on_failure directive specifies to capture hostname or IP address of the system from where a failed login attempt is made. The log_on_success directive defines to capture the process ID of the process, the hostname or IP address, the duration of service connection and the service termination time if the connection was established successfully. An example successful entry from the *messages* file is shown below for reference:

Jan 31 11:21:12 rhel01 xinetd[3192]: EXIT: ssh status=1 pid=3121 duration=102 (sec)

✓ The next set of directives defines the default access restrictions. With only_from and no_access directives, you can specify one or more hostnames or IP addresses associated with hosts, networks or domains from where you want incoming service requests allowed or denied. This level of access may also be defined at the individual service level in the *xinetd.d* directory scripts, and is evaluated after access is granted by TCP Wrappers as both *xinetd* and TCP Wrappers use the same library */usr/lib/libwrap.so* for this purpose. Refer to TCP Wrappers in Chapter 30 "System and Network Security" for detailed information. The max_load directive defines a load average number, after reaching which *xinetd* no longer accepts new connections. The cps directive limits incoming connections to 50 per second. If this limit is surpassed, the daemon waits for 10 seconds before restarting to entertain new requests. The instances and per_source directives control the number of active connections per service; the default is set to 50 from not more than 10 sources.

✓ The bind, mdns and v6only directives set address and networking defaults. With the bind directive, you can specify the IP address of one of the system's interfaces to be used for listening for incoming requests; the mdns directive is unavailable for now and the third directive can be set to either yes to restrict to the use of IPv6 addresses only or no to allow both IPv4 and IPv6 addresses.

✓ The next set of directives – passenv, groups and umask – defines environmental attributes. With passenv, global variables are specified whose values are used by a service when an incoming request attempts to establish a connection into that service. The groups directive can have one or more groups set as defined in the */etc/group* file, which provides the owner of a starting service access to those groups. The umask directive sets the default user mask.

✓ The includedir directive indicates the directory where service configuration files are located. The default is */etc/xinetd.d*.

The following output lists files located in the *xinetd.d* directory for each service currently installed and managed by *xinetd*:

```
# ll /etc/xinetd.d
total 152
-rw-r--r--1 root root 1157 Dec  6 2006 chargen-dgram
-rw-r--r--1 root root 1159 Dec  6 2006 chargen-stream
-rw-r--r--1 root root 1157 Dec  6 2006 daytime-dgram
-rw-r--r--1 root root 1159 Dec  6 2006 daytime-stream
-rw-r--r--1 root root 1157 Dec  6 2006 discard-dgram
-rw-r--r--1 root root 1159 Dec  6 2006 discard-stream
-rw-r--r--1 root root 1148 Dec  6 2006 echo-dgram
-rw-r--r--1 root root 1150 Dec  6 2006 echo-stream
-rw-r--r--1 root root  323 Sep  9 2004 eklogin
-rw-r--r--1 root root  347 Sep  6 2005 ekrb5-telnet
-rw-r--r--1 root root  326 Sep  9 2004 gssftp
```

```
-rw-r--r--1 root root   310 Sep  9 2004 klogin
-rw-r--r--1 root root   323 Sep  9 2004 krb5-telnet
-rw-r--r--1 root root   308 Sep  9 2004 kshell
-rw-r--r--1 root root   267 Sep  6 2006 ktalk
-rw-r--r--1 root root   317 Jul 12 2006 rsync
-rw-r--r--1 root root  1212 Dec  6 2006 tcpmux-server
-rw-r--r--1 root root  1149 Dec  6 2006 time-dgram
-rw-r--r--1 root root  1150 Dec  6 2006 time-stream
```

Majority of the services are disabled by default. Here are the contents of the *klogin* service file with some added directives:

```
# cat /etc/xinetd.d/klogin
# default: off
# description: The kerberized rlogin server accepts BSD-style rlogin sessions, \
#              but uses Kerberos 5 authentication.
Service klogin
{
        flags        = REUSE
        socket_type  = stream
        wait         = no
        user         = root
        server       = /usr/kerberos/sbin/klogind
        server_args  = -5
        no_access    = 192.168.3.0
        only_from    = 192.168.1.0
        disable      = yes
}
```

There are nine directives defined as shown in the output above. The flags directive specifies how the service is to be used. The default is REUSE, which forces the service to be used continuously. The socket_type directive defines the type of socket to be used for communication; the wait directive with "no" value allows several application connections to occur concurrently; the user directive specifies the owner for the service; the server and server_args directives specify the absolute path of the service and any associated arguments; the no_access and only_from directives were explained earlier in the *xinetd.conf* file explanation; and the disable directive disables (yes) or enables (no) the service.

Enabling an xinetd-controlled Service

To enable a service to start now and at each system reboot, run the following pair of commands:

```
# chkconfig klogin on
# service xinetd reload
Reloading configuration:                                    [ OK ]
```

The *chkconfig* command changes the value of the disable directive from yes to no in the */etc/xinetd.d/klogin* file and the second command forces the *xinetd* daemon to re-read all service configuration files located in the *xinetd.d* directory.

Alternatively, you can use the Red Hat Service Configurator *system-config-services* or the *ntsysv* command to enable the required service.

Disabling an xinetd-controlled Service

To stop a service now and disable it from autostarting at system reboots, run the following pair of commands:

 # chkconfig klogin off
 # service xinetd reload
Stopping configuration: [OK]

The *chkconfig* command changes the value of the disable directive from no to yes in the */etc/xinetd.d/klogin* file and the second command forces the *xinetd* daemon to re-read all service configuration files located in the *xinetd.d* directory.

Alternatively, you can use the Service Configurator *system-config-services* or the *ntsysv* command to disable the required service.

The services and rpc Files

The two key files that define service names and associated ports and protocols that they use are */etc/services* and */etc/rpc*. Line entries for some of the Internet services are extracted from the *services* file and displayed below. The output shows service name in the first column, port number and protocol in the second column, associated alias in the third column followed by comments in the last column.

 # cat /etc/services
```
. . . . . . . .
# service-name  port/protocol [aliases ...]  [# comment]

ftp          21/tcp
ftp          21/udp  fsp fspd
ssh          22/tcp   # SSH Remote Login Protocol
ssh          22/udp   # SSH Remote Login Protocol
telnet       23/tcp
telnet       23/udp
# 24 - private mail system
lmtp         24/tcp   # LMTP Mail Delivery
lmtp         24/udp   # LMTP Mail Delivery
smtp         25/tcp   mail
smtp         25/udp   mail
time         37/tcp   timserver
time         37/udp   timserver
rlp          39/tcp   resource      # resource location
rlp          39/udp   resource      # resource location
nameserver   42/tcp   name          # IEN 116
nameserver   42/udp   name          # IEN 116
. . . . . . . .
```

Line entries for some RPC-based services are extracted from the *rpc* file and displayed below. It shows service name in the first column, followed by port number and associated aliases.

```
# cat /etc/rpc
. . . . . . . .
portmapper    100000    portmap sunrpc rpcbind
rstatd        100001    rstat rup perfmeter rstat_svc
rusersd       100002    rusers
nfs           100003    nfsprog
ypserv        100004    ypprog
mountd        100005    mount showmount
ypbind        100007
walld         100008    rwall shutdown
yppasswdd     100009    yppasswd
etherstatd    100010    etherstat
rquotad       100011    rquotaprog quota rquota
sprayd        100012    spray
. . . . . . . .
```

File Transfer Protocol (FTP)

File Transfer Protocol (FTP) is the standard protocol for transferring files on the Internet and has been used on Linux, UNIX and other operating system platforms for years. In RHEL 5, an enhanced implementation of FTP called *very secure File Transfer Protocol* (vsFTP) is used as the default. This enhanced version is faster, more stable and more powerful than the standard FTP and at the same time allows you to enable, disable and set security controls on incoming requests. The vsFTP daemon called *vsftpd* listens on port 21 for communication as defined in the *services* file.

SELinux Requirements for FTP

If SELinux is enforced, you need to disable its protection for *ftpd* service to ensure smooth functionality. Use the *setsebool* command as demonstrated below, or the SELinux Configurator *system-config-selinux* as explained in Chapter 30 "System and Network Security". Specify only those Booleans that need to be disabled, leave others intact.

```
# setsebool –P ftp_is_daemon=1 allow_ftpd_full_access=1 allow_ftpd_anon_write=1 \
allow_ftpd_use_cifs=1 allow_ftpd_use_nfs=1 ftp_home_dir=1 ftpd_disable_trans=1
```

Use the *getsebool* command to verify:

```
# getsebool ftp_is_daemon allow_ftpd_full_access allow_ftpd_anon_write \
allow_ftpd_use_cifs allow_ftpd_use_nfs ftp_home_dir ftpd_disable_trans
allow_ftpd_anon_write --> on
allow_ftpd_full_access --> on
allow_ftpd_use_cifs --> on
allow_ftpd_use_nfs --> on
ftp_home_dir --> on
ftpd_disable_trans --> on
ftpd_is_daemon --> on
```

Understanding vsFTP Configuration File

The primary configuration file for vsFTP is */etc/vsftpd/vsftpd.conf* in which a number of directives can be defined to control the behavior of the *vsftpd* daemon. The default uncommented directives are shown below:

 # grep –v ^# /etc/vsftpd/vsftpd.conf
anonymous_enable=YES
local_enable=YES
write_enable=YES
local_umask=022
dirmessage_enable=YES
xferlog_enable=YES
connect_from_port_20=YES
xferlog_std_format=YES
listen=YES
pam_service_name=vsftpd
userlist_enable=YES
tcp_wrappers=YES

These and some other key directives are listed and explained in Table 24-2.

Variable	Description
anonymous_enable	Default is YES. Enables / disables anonymous FTP access. If enabled, anonymous users are logged in to the */var/ftp* directory by default. Alternatively, you can create a directory and define it with the anon_root directive.
anon_upload_enable	Disabled by default. Enables / disables anonymous users to be able to upload files.
anon_umask	Disabled by default. Automatically sets the umask on uploaded files.
chown_uploads	Disabled by default. Automatically changes the ownership on uploaded files.
chown_username	Disabled by default. Automatically changes the ownership on uploaded files to the specified username.
local_enable	Default is YES. Enables / disables local users to be able to log in via FTP.
write_enable	Default is YES. Enables / disables remote users to be able to write.
local_umask	Default is 022. Sets the *umask* value for local users.
dirmessage_enable	Default is YES. Enables / disables displaying the contents of the ~/.message file to logged in users.
xferlog_enable	Default is YES. Logs file transfer activities to */var/log/xferlog* file.
connect_from_port_20	Default is YES. Ensures that port transfer connections originate from TCP port 20.
xferlog_std_format	Default is YES. Logs file transfer activities in standard xferlog format.
listen	Default is YES. Enables *vsftpd* to listen on IPv4 sockets.
pam_service_name	Default is vsftp. Defines the service name for which PAM is to be enabled.

Variable	Description
userlist_deny	Default is YES. Enables / disables users listed in the /etc/vsftpd/user_list file to be able to log in via FTP.
userlist_enable	Default is YES. Enables / disables *vsftp* to consult /etc/vsftpd/user_list.
tcp_wrappers	Default is YES. Allows / disallows *vsftpd* access to incoming requests based on /etc/hosts.allow and /etc/hosts.deny file contents.

Table 24-2 vsftpd.conf Directives

Controlling Who Can Use vsFTP

There are two files that control which users can or cannot log in with FTP. These files are located in the */etc/vsftpd* directory and are called *ftpusers* and *user_list*. Both files contain a list of users one line per user name. Default entries are for system users including *root*, *bin*, *daemon*, *adm*, *lp*, *sync*, *shutdown*, *halt*, *mail*, *news*, *uucp*, *operator*, *games* and *nobody*. The *ftpusers* file lists users that are denied FTP access and the *user_list* file lists users that are allowed or denied access based on the NO or YES value of the userlist_deny directive in the *vsftpd.conf* file. The *user_list* file is only consulted if the userlist_enable directive is set to YES, otherwise it is ignored.

vsFTP uses TCP Wrappers for access control.

Configuring a vsFTP Server

To configure the vsFTP service on a system such as *rhel01* for specific user access, perform the following:

1. Check whether vsFTP software package is installed:

   # **rpm –qa | grep vsftpd**
   vsftpd-2.0.5-12.el5

   Install the package if it is not already loaded using one of the software package installation methods described in Chapter 11 "Software Package Management".

2. Execute the following to make vsFTP autostart at system reboots:

   # **chkconfig vsftpd on**

3. Configure TCP Wrappers files /etc/hosts.allow or /etc/hosts.deny appropriately for *vsftpd* access control. Consult Chapter 30 "System and Network Security" for details.
4. Allow vsFTP traffic on port 21 to pass through the firewall, or simply stop and disable the firewall if it is not used. Consult Chapter 30 "System and Network Security" on how to perform these tasks.
5. Update /etc/vsftpd/ftpusers or /etc/vsftpd/user_list file and enter names of users such as *aghori* to be allowed FTP access.
6. Start (or restart) the *vsftpd* daemon:

   # **service vsftpd start**
   Starting vsftpd for vsftpd: [OK]

This completes the setup for specific user access to vsFTP.

Configuring a vsFTP Server for Anonymous Access

To configure the vsFTP service on a system such as *rhel02* for downloading and uploading files as an anonymous user, perform the following:

1. Perform steps 1 through 4 from sub-section "Configuring a vsFTP Server".
2. Create a directory such as */var/ftp/incoming* for uploading files. The system uses */var/ftp* for downloading files by default.

   # **cd /var/ftp && mkdir incoming**

3. Change ownership and group membership on the directory to root:ftp:

   # **chown root:ftp incoming**

4. Change directory permissions so anonymous users are able to write to the directory:

   # **chmod 730 incoming**

5. Set anonymous_enable, anon_upload_enable and chown_uploads directives to YES, chown_username directive to bin and anon_umask to 077 in the *vsftp.conf* file. These directives enable anonymous users to be able to upload files and automatically change ownership to user *bin* with permissions 600.
6. Start (or restart) the *vsftpd* daemon:

   # **service vsftpd start**
   Starting vsftpd for vsftpd: [OK]

This completes the setup for anonymous user access to vsFTP.

Testing the Functionality

Once the vsFTP server is configured, use a client program such as *ftp* or *lftp* to test it. *lftp* is more powerful and includes more features than the standard *ftp* client program. Alternatively, you can use a browser and type in the IP address of the system or simply *localhost* in the URL and press Enter.

The procedure to use *lftp* is such that you specify the hostname or IP address of the remote machine you want to access. You can execute this command from another RHEL system. For example, the following runs *lftp* from *rhel02* to enter *rhel01* with IP address 192.168.0.201 as user *aghori*:

   $ **lftp 192.168.0.201 −u aghori**

As soon as *lftp* contacts *rhel01* on port 21, the *vsftpd* daemon comes into action and sends the requester a login prompt to enter username. It engages TCP Wrappers to check whether the remote system is allowed. It then checks for the validity of the user in the */etc/passwd* file and references *ftpusers* and *user_list* files whether the user is allowed. It prompts the user to enter password and consults */etc/shadow* file for validation. The daemon establishes a communication session with *lftp* if both the system and the user are validated.

To log in as an anonymous user for file transfers, run the *lftp* command as follows and type in *anonymous* as the user name and an email address as password:

$ lftp rhel01

Available commands at the *lftp:~>* prompt can be listed by typing *?*:

```
lftp:~> ?
    !<shell-command>              (commands)
    alias [<name> [<value>]]      anon
    bookmark [SUBCMD]             cache [SUBCMD]
    cat [-b] <files>              cd <rdir>
    chmod [OPTS] mode file...     close [-a]
    [re]cls [opts] [path/][pattern]  debug [<level>|off] [-o <file>]
    du [options] <dirs>           exit [<code>|bg]
    get [OPTS] <rfile> [-o <lfile>]  glob [OPTS] <cmd> <args>
    help [<cmd>]                  history -w file|-r file|-c|-l [cnt]
    jobs [-v]                     kill all|<job_no>
    lcd <ldir>                    lftp [OPTS] <site>
    ls [<args>]                   mget [OPTS] <files>
    mirror [OPTS] [remote [local]]  mkdir [-p] <dirs>
    module name [args]           more <files>
    mput [OPTS] <files>           mrm <files>
    mv <file1> <file2>           [re]nlist [<args>]
    open [OPTS] <site>            pget [OPTS] <rfile> [-o <lfile>]
    put [OPTS] <lfile> [-o <rfile>]  pwd [-p]
    queue [OPTS] [<cmd>]          quote <cmd>
    repeat [delay] [command]      rm [-r] [-f] <files>
    rmdir [-f] <dirs>            scache [<session_no>]
    set [OPT] [<var> [<val>]]     site <site_cmd>
    source <file>                user <user|URL> [<pass>]
    version                       wait [<jobno>]
    zcat <files>                  zmore <files>
```

Commands such as *cd, ls, pwd* and *quit* work the same way as they do at the Linux shell prompt. The *get* and *put* commands are used to download and upload a single file and their enhanced versions *mget* and *mput* for several files. These commands support wildcard characters and tab completion. You can run the *cd, ls* and *pwd* commands by preceding them with the ! character to run them at the Linux command prompt.

To quit, use the *quit* or *bye* command at the lftp> prompt.

All file transfer activities are recorded in the */var/log/xferlog* file by default.

RHEL also provides a graphical FTP client called *gFTP*, which can be invoked using *gftp* at the command prompt or (GNOME) Applications → Internet → gFTP. The interface of gFTP is shown in Figure 24-1.

Figure 24-1 Graphical FTP Client

The wget Utility

wget is a non-interactive file download utility that allows you to retrieve a single file, multiple files or an entire directory structure from an FTP or HTTP source. Certain options are important when working with *wget*, and are listed and explained in Table 24-3. For additional options and details, refer to the command's man pages.

Option	Description
–P	Specifies the directory location to save the files being retrieved. The default is the current directory.
–T	Specifies number of seconds before the command times out.
–d	Turns debug mode on.
–i	Downloads files from URLs listed in the specified file.
–nv	Hides verbose output except error messages and basic information.
–o	Logs messages to the specified output file.
–q	Hides output and any errors.
–r	Turns recursive retrieval on.
–t	Specifies number of retries.
–v	Displays verbose output. This is default.
--user	Specifies username for FTP and HTTP accesses.
--password	Specifies associated password for --user option.

Table 24-3 wget Command Options

Let us take a look at a couple of examples to understand the behavior of the command.

To download a kernel package in the current directory from *ftp.kernel.org* with verbose mode on:

wget ftp.kernel.org/pub/linux/kernel/v2.6/linux-2.6.27.1.tar.gz
--17:44:03-- http://ftp.kernel.org/pub/linux/kernel/v2.6/linux-2.6.27.1.tar.gz
Resolving ftp.kernel.org... 204.152.191.37, 149.20.20.133
Connecting to ftp.kernel.org|204.152.191.37|:80... connected.

HTTP request sent, awaiting response... 200 OK
Length: 63720029 (61M) [application/x-gzip]
Saving to: `linux-2.6.27.1.tar.gz.2'

100%[===>] 63,720,029   465K/s   in 2m 16s

17:46:20 (457 KB/s) - `linux-2.6.27.1.tar.gz.2' saved [63720029/63720029]

To download the same package and store at */var/tmp*:

wget ftp.kernel.org/pub/linux/kernel/v2.6/linux-2.6.27.1.tar.gz –P /var/tmp

To download the same package with output redirected to a file called */tmp/wget.out*:

wget ftp.kernel.org/pub/linux/kernel/v2.6/linux-2.6.27.1.tar.gz –o /tmp/wget.out
Setting --output-file (logfile) to wget.out

To download *index.html* file from *www.redhat.com* with debug mode on:

wget –d www.redhat.com
DEBUG output created by Wget 1.10.2 (Red Hat modified) on linux-gnu.

--17:54:46-- http://www.redhat.com/
Resolving www.redhat.com... 209.8.104.112
Caching www.redhat.com => 209.8.104.112
Connecting to www.redhat.com|209.8.104.112|:80... connected.
Created socket 3.
Releasing 0x084ebf00 (new refcount 1).

---request begin---
GET / HTTP/1.0
User-Agent: Wget/1.10.2 (Red Hat modified)
Accept: */*
Host: www.redhat.com
Connection: Keep-Alive

---request end---
HTTP request sent, awaiting response...
---response begin---
HTTP/1.0 200 OK
Server: Apache
Content-Type: text/html; charset=ISO-8859-1
Expires: Tue, 14 Apr 2009 11:58:21 GMT
Cache-Control: max-age=0, no-cache, no-store
Pragma: no-cache
Date: Tue, 14 Apr 2009 11:58:21 GMT
Content-Length: 13121
Connection: keep-alive
Set-Cookie: Apache=67.131.237.10.1239710301081308; path=/; expires=Sun, 13-Apr-14 11:58:21 GMT

```
---response end---
200 OK
hs->local_file is: index.html.1 (not existing)
Registered socket 3 for persistent reuse.

Stored cookie www.redhat.com -1 (ANY) / <permanent> <insecure> [expiry 2014-04-13 07:58:21]
Apache 67.131.237.10.1239710301081308
TEXTHTML is on.
Length: 13121 (13K) [text/html]
Saving to: `index.html.1'

100%[===========================================>] 13,121     --.-K/s   in 0.04s

17:54:46 (328 KB/s) - `index.html.1' saved [13121/13121]
```

Electronic Mail

Email is an essential part of RHEL, which enables a system to be used as both a mail server and a mail client. In RHEL 5, *sendmail* is the default mail server for sending mail and *dovecot* is the default mail server for receiving mail.

A fully functional mail system requires three key elements – *Mail Transport Agent* (MTA), *Mail Delivery Agent* (MDA) and *Mail User Agent* (MUA). An MTA is responsible for transporting a message from a sending mail server and another MTA is responsible for accepting the message at a receiving mail server. The primary protocol used between the mail servers is called *Simple Mail Transport Protocol* (SMTP) (Extended SMTP called ESMTP is also available now with enhanced features). The most widely used MTA at the sending end is sendmail, with Postfix and Exim being alternatives providing increased security and improved performance over sendmail. Example of an MTA responsible for receiving mail messages is Dovecot, which invokes an MDA to forward the message to a mail spool location and store it there until an MUA at the receiving end fetches the message into the inbox of the user via either *Post Office Protocol* (POP) or *Internet Message Access Protocol* (IMAP) for the user to read it. Examples of MDA are *Local Delivery Agent* (LDA), *procmail* and *maildrop*, with LDA comes as part of the Dovecot software. MUA is any mail client program that is used to write and read mail messages. An MUA uses either POP or IMAP to access mail. Examples of MUA are *mail, mailx, elm, mutt, fetchmail, evolution, thunderbird, squirrelmail, Microsoft Outlook* and *eudora*.

How Mail System Works

Here is how the mail system works. A user composes a mail message using an MUA on his computer. The user presses the Send button and the message leaves the system via port 25 to a configured outgoing MTA. The MTA checks the destination address in DNS and locates an associated MX record for the destination system's domain. The message is eventually transported to the receiving MTA, which invokes an MDA to forward the message to a mail spool location and store it there until an MUA at the receiving end pulls it into the inbox of the user. If the message is destined to a local user, the MTA simply places it into the mailbox of that user without having to engage DNS, from where the message is retrieved by the user via an MUA.

Depending on the location of the sending and receiving MUAs, the message may be transported on a large internal corporate network or over the Internet using tens or hundreds of routing devices. In either case, a DNS server is employed for name resolution. For small networks, *hosts* file may be used.

In subsequent sections, Sendmail, Postfix and Dovecot are covered at length in addition to a few MUAs. Other tools mentioned above are beyond the scope of this book.

Configuring Sendmail

This section is going to provide detailed information on sendmail and present how a RHEL system can be configured for use as a sendmail server.

Sendmail uses TCP Wrappers for access control.

Sendmail Configuration Files

Sendmail configuration files are located in the */etc/mail* directory with the exception of the startup and aliases files that are located in */etc/sysconfig* and */etc* directories, respectively. The key files are listed and described in Table 24-4.

File	Description
/etc/sysconfig/sendmail	Startup configuration file. There are two directives – DAEMON and QUEUE – defined by default of which the former specifies whether to run *sendmail* as a daemon and the latter sets a time delay for the daemon to check the mail queue.
/etc/aliases	Defines user aliases one per line for incoming domains listed in */etc/mail/local-host-names* file. Contents of this file are used to regenerate the */etc/mail/aliases.db* file. For instance, mail sent to user *user1* will be forwarded to a local user *asghar* and that for group *admin* to *asghar.ghori@yahoo.com*. user1: asghar admin: asghar.ghori@yahoo.com
/etc/aliases.db	Defines mail user aliases.
/etc/mail/sendmail.cf	Defines configuration rules for incoming mail. Regenerated when *sendmail* daemon is started or restarted if *sendmail.mc* is found modified.
/etc/mail/sendmail.mc	Contains macros. Contents of this file are used to regenerate the *sendmail.cf* file when *sendmail* service is started or restarted.
/etc/mail/submit.cf	Defines configuration rules for outgoing mail. Regenerated when *sendmail* daemon is started or restarted if *submit.mc* is found modified. Ususally not modified.
/etc/mail/submit.mc	Contains macros. Contents of this file are used to regenerate the *submit.cf* file when *sendmail* service is started or restarted.
/etc/mail/access	Contains access control information to REJECT, DISCARD or RELAY mail for specified systems and networks. Contents of this file are used to regenerate the *access.db* file.
/etc/mail/access.db	Contains access control information.

File	Description
/etc/mail/domaintable	Contains domain mappings to forward mail destined for one domain to an alternative domain. Contents of this file are used to regenerate the *domaintable.db* file.
/etc/mail/domaintable.db	Contains domain mappings.
/etc/mail/local-host-names	Contains hostnames or domain names for which the local system acts as an outgoing mail server.
/etc/mail/Makefile	Compiles the *sendmail.mc* macro file.
/etc/mail/spamassassin	Directory location to store spam configuration information.
/etc/mail/trusted-users	Contains usernames who could send email without generating any warning messages.
/etc/mail/mailertable	Defines routing information to a specific domain. Contents of this file are used to regenerate the *mailertable.db* file.
/etc/mail/mailertable.db	Defines routing information.
/etc/mail/virtusertable	Virtual user table. Defines mail forwarding for individual external users, an entire domain or a mailing list entry in */etc/aliases* file. Contents of this file are used to regenerate the *virtusertable.db* file.
/etc/mail/virtusertable.db	Allows mail forwarding for external users.

Table 24-4 Sendmail Configuration Files

Key Macros

Several macros are defined in the *sendmail.mc* and *submit.mc* files. These macros are processed through m4 processor when the *make* or *m4* command is executed to regenerate the corresponding configuration files. Some key macros are listed and described in Table 24-5.

Macro	Description
dnl (delete to new line)	Defines comments and is used to disable directives.
DAEMON_OPTIONS	Defines options for the *sendmail* daemon.
Define	Specifies directives to be included.
EXPOSED_USER	States usernames that should not be masqueraded.
FEATURE	Defines specific features to be included.
Include	Adds the specified file contents during processing.
LOCAL_DOMAIN	Lists hostnames by which this mail server is known. Any mail sent to any of these hostnames is treated as local mail.
MAILER	Indicates a mailer program such as local, smtp and procmail to be used.
MASQUERATE_DOMAIN	States a hostname to be used with outgoing mail as if the mail is coming from that hostname.
OSTYPE	Sets the name of the operating system.
VERSIONID	Records the version of the sendmail configuration.

Table 24-5 Key Macros

Mapping Virtual Addresses

The virtual user table file called *virtusertable* in the */etc/mail* directory stores mail forwarding information for external users or entire domains to local or other external addresses. The information can be stored one alias per domain or one alias per all email addresses for a specific domain. For example, the first column below shows external sources mapped to destination addresses in the second column:

aghori@getitcertify.com	asghar	# user email to a local user
bghori@getitcertify.com	bghori@yahoo.com	# user email to another external user
@getitcertify.com	asghar.ghori@yahoo.com	# all domain emails to an external user
john@	asghar.ghori@yahoo.com	# emails to user *john* on any domain to an external user

The first example entry will forward a user's mail to a local user, the second entry will forward a user's mail to an external user, the third example will forward all emails destined to a domain to an external user and the fourth example entry will forward emails to a specific user on any domain to an external user.

In order for mail forwarding to function, you will need to ensure that the following line entry is uncommented in the */etc/mail/sendmail.mc* file:

    FEATURE(`virtusertable', `hash –o /etc/mail/virtusertable.db')dnl

Configuring a sendmail Server

To configure a system such as *rhel02* to function as a sendmail server for both incoming and outgoing mail, follow the steps below. Make sure that only users on localhost, 192.168.2, 192.168.3 and *getitcertify.com* are allowed access and users on 192.168.4 and *example.net* are denied access. Note that the user mail is temporarily spooled in the */var/spool/mail* directory before it is sent out.

1. Check whether the required sendmail software packages are installed:

       # **rpm –qa | grep sendmail**
       sendmail-8.13.8-2.el5
       sendmail-cf-8.13.8-2.el5

   Install the packages if they are not already loaded using one of the software package installation methods described in Chapter 11 "Software Package Management".

2. Check whether sendmail is configured as the current MTA:

       # **alternatives --display mta | grep current**
       link currently points to /usr/sbin/sendmail.sendmail

3. Open the *sendmail.mc* file and disable the following line entry to allow other systems to be able to submit their mail to this mail server for transport:

       dnl DAEMON_OPTIONS(`Port=smtp,Addr=127.0.0.1, Name=MTA')dnl

4. Edit the *access* file and add the hostnames or IP addresses of the systems, domains or networks, or a combination, to be allowed or denied access to relay their mail using this sendmail server. Some example entries are:

localhost	RELAY
192.168.2	RELAY
192.168.3	RELAY
getitcertify.com	RELAY
192.168.4	REJECT
@example.net	DISCARD

5. Edit the *local-host-names* file and add hostnames and domain names this system will act as an outgoing mail server for. In other words, the system will have its own hostname and aliases, as well as names of other hosts and domains, defined here. This way this mail server will be recognized by all these names. Some example entries are:

```
rhel02
db02
getitcertify.com
rhel02.example.com
```

6. Edit the *aliases and virtusertable* files and define any local and virtual aliases, if needed. Refer to Table 24-4 for information on *aliases* file and sub-section "Mapping Virtual Addresses" for *virtusertable* file.
7. Run the following to regenerate the modified files:

 # make –C /etc/mail
make: Entering directory `/etc/mail'
make: Leaving directory `/etc/mail'

8. Execute the following to enable sendmail to autostart at each system reboot:

 # chkconfig sendmail on

9. Make certain that DNS or */etc/hosts* file is configured properly.
10. Allow traffic on port 25 to pass through the firewall, or simply stop and disable the firewall if it is not used. Consult Chapter 30 "System and Network Security" on how to perform these tasks.
11. Start (or restart) the *sendmail* daemon, which will read the *sendmail.cf* and *submit.cf* files:

 # service sendmail start
Starting sendmail: [OK]
Starting sm-client: [OK]

12. Execute the following to check the operational status of sendmail:

 # service sendmail status
sendmail (pid 2393 2383) is running...

All messages are logged to the */var/log/maillog* file. Doing a *tail* on the file produces an output similar to the following:

 # tail /var/log/maillog
Feb 5 19:57:21 rhel01 sendmail[5817]: alias database /etc/aliases rebuilt by root
Feb 5 19:57:21 rhel01 sendmail[5817]: /etc/aliases: 79 aliases, longest 17 bytes, 809 bytes total

Checking Mail Statistics

To check the statistics on the usage of the mail server, use the *mailstats* command. This command extracts information from the */var/log/mail/statistics* file.

 # mailstats
```
Statistics from Fri Jan 16 23:45:20 2009
 M  msgsfr bytes_from  msgsto  bytes_to msgsrej msgsdis msgsqur Mailer
 4    2      8K          0       0K        0       0       0     esmtp
 9   29     130K         8      39K        0       0       0     local
=================================================================
 T   31     138K         8      39K        0       0       0
 C   15                  0                 0
```

The output displays several columns that are listed and explained in Table 24-6.

Column	Description
M	Lists the mailer number.
mgsfr	Number of messages received from the mailer.
btes_from	KBs received from the mailer.
mgsto	Number of messages sent to the mailer.
bytes_to	KBs sent to the mailer.
mgsrej	Number of messages rejected.
mgsdis	Number of messages discarded.
msgsqur	Number of messages quarantined.
Mailer	Name of the mailer.

Table 24-6 mailstats Command Output

Configuring Postfix

This section furnishes detailed information on Postfix and presents how a RHEL system can be configured as a Postfix mail server. Postfix is sendmail compatible, easier to administer, supports pattern matching for filtering out unwanted mail and supports several virtual mail domains on a single system.

Postfix Daemons

The primary daemon for Postfix is known as *master*, which is located in the */usr/libexec/postfix* directory. The daemon starts sub-daemons – *nqmgr*, *pickup* and *smtpd* – to work as agents on its behalf. The *nqmgr* daemon is responsible for mail transmission, relay and local delivery, the *pickup* daemon transfers mail messages from */var/spool/mqueue* to */var/spool/mail* directory, and the *smtpd* daemon directs the incoming mail to */var/spool/mail* directory.

Postfix Configuration Files

Postfix has two key configuration files called *master.cf* and *main.cf* and both are located in the */etc/postfix* directory. The *master.cf* file contains settings to control the *master* daemon. It lists services needed by Postfix and starts them appropriately. An excerpt from *master.cf* is shown below:

 # cat /etc/postfix/master.cf

```
. . . . . . . .
# service    type    private  unpriv  chroot   wakeup maxproc        command + args
#            (yes)   (yes)    (yes)   (never)  (100)
# ================================================================================
smtp         inet    n        -       n        -      -              smtpd

. . . . . . . .
pickup       fifo    n        -       n        60     1              pickup
cleanup      unix    n        -       n        -      0              cleanup
qmgr         fifo    n        -       n        300    1              qmgr
. . . . . . . .
```

For each service listed in the first column, there are seven associated columns, which define how the service will be used. These columns are listed and explained in Table 24-7.

Column	Description
service	Name of the service.
type	Transport mechanism to be used.
private	Whether the service is to be used by Postfix only.
unpriv	Whether the service is to be run by non-*root* users.
chroot	Whether the service is to be chrooted for the mail queue.
wakeup	Wake up interval for the service.
maxproc	Maximum number of threads the service can start.
command	Command associated with the service plus any arguments.

Table 24-7 master.cf File Contents

The *main.cf* file is the primary Postfix configuration file, which defines global settings for Postfix operation. These settings include host, domain and network to be served, mail owner, network interfaces to listen on, etc. The default contents of this file are shown below. Note that the order in which the directives appear in the file is important.

 # cat /etc/postfix/main.cf

```
. . . . . . . .
# SOFT BOUNCE
# The soft_bounce parameter provides a limited safety net for
# testing.  When soft_bounce is enabled, mail will remain queued that
# would otherwise bounce. This parameter disables locally-generated
# bounces, and prevents the SMTP server from rejecting mail permanently
```

```
# (by changing 5xx replies into 4xx replies). However, soft_bounce
# is no cure for address rewriting mistakes or mail routing mistakes.
#soft_bounce = no
# LOCAL PATHNAME INFORMATION
# The queue_directory specifies the location of the Postfix queue.
# This is also the root directory of Postfix daemons that run chrooted.
# See the files in examples/chroot-setup for setting up Postfix chroot
# environments on different UNIX systems.
queue_directory = /var/spool/postfix
. . . . . . . .
```

Several directives may be set in the *main.cf* file. Table 24-8 lists and explains some of them.

Directive	Description
myhostname	Specifies the full hostname of the Postfix server.
mydomain	Specifies the domain name of the Postfix server.
myorigin	Specifies the domain name the outgoing mail appears to originate from.
inet_interfaces	Specifies network interfaces to be used for receiving mail.
mydestination	Specifies domains for which Postfix accepts mail.
mynetworks	Specifies IP addresses of trusted networks.
virtual_alias_maps	Defines virtual aliases in */etc/postfix/virtual* file for incoming mail. Same rules apply as in sendmail's */etc/mail/virtusertable* file.

Table 24-8 Key main.cf Directives

Displaying and Modifying /etc/postfix/main.cf

The *postconf* command is a Postfix configuration utility that can be used to display and modify the *main.cf* file contents. For example, to display the default and non-default settings, run the command with –d and –n option, respectively:

```
# postconf –d
2bounce_notice_recipient = postmaster
access_map_reject_code = 554
address_verify_default_transport = $default_transport
address_verify_local_transport = $local_transport
address_verify_map =
address_verify_negative_cache = yes
address_verify_negative_expire_time = 3d
address_verify_negative_refresh_time = 3h
address_verify_poll_count = 3
address_verify_poll_delay = 3s
address_verify_positive_expire_time = 31d
address_verify_positive_refresh_time = 7d
address_verify_relay_transport = $relay_transport
address_verify_relayhost = $relayhost
address_verify_sender = postmaster
. . . . . . . .
```

postconf –n

alias_database = hash:/etc/aliases
alias_maps = hash:/etc/aliases
command_directory = /usr/sbin
config_directory = /etc/postfix
daemon_directory = /usr/libexec/postfix
debug_peer_level = 2
html_directory = no
inet_interfaces = localhost
mail_owner = postfix
mailq_path = /usr/bin/mailq.postfix
manpage_directory = /usr/share/man
mydestination = $myhostname, localhost.$mydomain, localhost
newaliases_path = /usr/bin/newaliases.postfix
queue_directory = /var/spool/postfix
readme_directory = /usr/share/doc/postfix-2.3.3/README_FILES
sample_directory = /usr/share/doc/postfix-2.3.3/samples
sendmail_path = /usr/sbin/sendmail.postfix
setgid_group = postdrop
unknown_local_recipient_reject_code = 550

As an example, if you want to modify the value of the directive queue_directory from */var/spool/postfix* to */var/spool/defaultmail*, run the command as follows:

postconf –e queue_directory=/var/spool/defaultmail

Configuring a Postfix Server

To configure a system such as *rhel03* to function as a Postfix server, follow the steps below. Note that the user mail is temporarily spooled in the */var/spool/postfix* directory before it is sent out.

1. Check whether Postfix software package is installed:

    # **rpm –qa | grep postfix**
    postfix-2.3.3-2.1.el5_2

    Install the package if it is not already loaded using one of the software package installation methods described in Chapter 11 "Software Package Management".

2. Open the *main.cf* configuration file and set or modify the following directives:

    myhostname = rhel03.getitcertify.com
    mydomain = getitcertify.com
    myorigin = $getitcertify.com
    inet_interfaces = all
    mydestination = rhel03, db03, localhost.$getitcertify.com, $getitcertify.com, localhost
    mynetworks = 192.168.0.0/24, 127.0.0.0/8

---

3. Edit the */etc/postfix/access* file and add the hostnames or IP addresses of the remote systems, domains or networks to be allowed or denied access to relay their mail using this Postfix server:

192.168.2	RELAY
192.168.3	RELAY
getitcertify.com	RELAY
192.168.4	REJECT

4. Execute the following to make Postfix autostart at each system reboot:

    # **chkconfig postfix on**

5. Make certain that DNS or */etc/hosts* file is configured properly.
6. Allow traffic on port 25 to pass through the firewall, or simply stop and disable the firewall if it is not used. Consult Chapter 30 "System and Network Security" on how to perform these tasks.
7. Start (or restart) the Postfix daemon:

    # **service postfix start**
    Starting postfix: [OK]

8. Execute the following to check the operational status of Postfix:

    # **service postfix status**
    master (pid 1901) is running...

All messages are logged to the */var/log/maillog* file. Doing a *tail* on the file produces an output similar to the following:

tail /var/log/maillog
Mar 5 11:20:14 rhel03 postfix/postfix-script: starting the Postfix mail system
Mar 5 11:20:14 rhel03 postfix/master[1901]: daemon started – version 2.2.10, configuration /etc/postfix

Setting Default MTA

In case you have both sendmail and Postfix configured on the system, you should be able to activate one of them as the default mail server for outgoing mail using either the *alternatives* or the *system-switch-mail* command.

Here is how you would do it with *alternatives*.

To list which MTA is currently configured as the default, use the --display option with the command:

alternatives --display mta|grep current
link currently points to /usr/sbin/sendmail.sendmail

You can also use the --config option to display or change the default MTA:

alternatives --config mta
There are 2 programs which provide 'mta'.

```
  Selection    Command
-----------------------------------------------
* 1            /usr/sbin/sendmail.sendmail
+ 2            /usr/sbin/sendmail.postfix
```

Enter to keep the current selection[+], or type selection number:

The asterisk character besides the first selection tells that that mail server is currently the default. If you wish to keep the setting, simply press Enter or type a number corresponding to the other selection and press Enter to make that mail server the default. The selection updates all run levels in which the selected mail server is configured to autostart at reboots. Also, if an alternate selection is made, the *alternatives* command stops the current mail server and starts the selected one. Check the setting with the *alternatives* command (do not make any changes now; simply press Enter) or check the run levels in which it is set to autostart at reboots using the *chkconfig* command and the operational status using the *service* command:

chkconfig --list sendmail
```
sendmail       0:off  1:off  2:on   3:on   4:on   5:on   6:off
```
service sendmail status
```
sendmail (pid 2393 2383) is running...
```

You can use the *alternatives* command in the following way too to set the default MTA. The following shows how to change the default to Postfix:

alternatives --set mta /usr/sbin/sendmail.postfix

Alternatively, the *system-switch-mail* tool may be used for this purpose. Figure 24-2 shows the graphical interface of it.

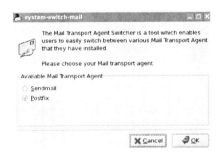

Figure 24-2 Mail Server Selection

Make an appropriate selection and click OK. You need to install the system-switch-mail package using one of the package installation methods explained in Chapter 11 "Software Package Management" as it is not installed by default.

Verifying Mail Server Functionality

You can verify that mail servers have been setup properly by mailing a test message. The following provides common testing procedures for both sendmail and Postfix.

To test local mail functionality, mail a message to a local user such as *user1* with subject "Local Mail Test":

> # **date | mail –s "Local Mail Test" user1**

To test network mail functionality, mail a message to a remote user such as *user2* on *rhel01*:

> # **date | mail –s "Remote Mail Test" user2@getitcertify.com**
> $ **mail**
> Mail version 8.1 6/6/93. Type ? for help.
> "/var/spool/mail/user2": 1 message 1 new
> >N 1 user2@getitcertify.com Wed Mar 5 11:44 18/835 "Remote Mail Test"
> &

A normal user can send mail to another user such as *aghori* using the *mail* command:

> $ **cal | mail –s "Test Mail from user1" aghori**

To mail the contents of a file such as */etc/group* to a user *aghori* on the local system and on a remote system *rhel01*:

> $ **mail aghori@localhost –s "Contents of /etc/group for your reference" < /etc/group**
> $ **mail aghori@rhel01 –s "Contents of /etc/group for your reference" < /etc/group**

Sent out mail is stored temporarily in the mail queue directory */var/spool/mqueue*. You can use the *mailq* command with –v option to display the contents:

> # **mailq –v**

At the destination, the mail is received by the mail server. *user1* can read the mail using the *mail* or *mailx* command and can reply to the sender, delete the message or forward it to other recipients. If not deleted, the mail is automatically saved in the */var/spool/mail/user1* file for sendmail and in the */var/spool/postfix* directory for Postfix.

> $ **mail**
> Mail version 8.1 6/6/93. Type ? for help.
> "/var/spool/mail/user1": 1 message 1 unread
> >U 1 root@rhel03.getitcertify.com Wed Mar 5 11:35 19/821 "Local Mail Test"
> &

A *cat* on the */var/spool/mail/user1* file produces the following output:

```
$ cat /var/spool/mail/user1
From root@rhel03.getitcertify.com  Wed Mar  5 11:35:23 2009
Return-Path: <root@rhel03.getitcertify.com>
X-Original-To: user1@rhel03.getitcertify.com
Delivered-To: user1@rhel03.getitcertify.com
Received: from rhel03.getitcertify.com (localhost.localdomain [127.0.0.1])
        by rhel03.getitcertify.com (Postfix) with ESMTP id 19C256F269
        for <user1@rhel03.getitcertify.com>; Wed,  5 Mar 2009 11:35:23 -0500 (EST)
Received: (from root@localhost)
        by rhel03.getitcertify.com (8.13.1/8.13.1/Submit) id m25GZNY6002831
        for user1; Wed, 5 Mar 2009 11:35:23 -0500
Date: Wed, 5 Mar 2009 11:35:23 -0500
From: root <root@rhel03.getitcertify.com>
Message-Id: <200903051635.m25GZNY6002831@rhel03.getitcertify.com>
To: user1@rhel03.getitcertify.com
Subject: Local Mail Test
Status: O

Wed Mar  5 11:35:23 EST 2009
```

Graphical mail client programs are also available that you can use for client mail management. These programs include Novell Evolution and Mozilla Thunderbird.

For Postfix, *postqueue* command is available to view queued mail (–p) and flush (–f) it.

Updating /etc/aliases File for Sendmail and Postfix

The *aliases* file contains aliases with associated user or group addresses. Both sendmail and Postfix reference this file for alias settings, and their associated daemons need to be informed of any modifications made to this file. The *newaliases* command is used for this purpose. Here is what this command would do when executed without any switches:

```
# newaliases
/etc/aliases: 79 aliases, longest 17 bytes, 809 bytes total
```

An excerpt from *aliases* is displayed below:

```
# cat /etc/aliases
. . . . . . . .
# General redirections for pseudo accounts.
bin:            root
daemon:         root
adm:            root
lp:             root
sync:           root
shutdown:       root
. . . . . . . .
# Person who should get root's mail
#root:          marc
```

The default contents show that any messages generated by system users will be forwarded to the *root* user. You can do similar setup for other users too. For example, if there was a user named *user1* who was setup on this system and was receiving mail has been removed, you can forward that user's incoming mail to one or more other users such as *aghori* and *bghori@getitcertify.com*. Modify the *aliases* file and add the following:

    user1:   aghori, bghori@getitcertify.com

You can create a mailing group of several users so that when a mail is sent to that group, it will go to all group members. Here is how to create a mailing group called *linuxadmteam* with users *aghori*, *bghori*, *user1* and *user2* as members. Add the following line to the *aliases* file:

    linuxadmteam: aghori, bghori, user1, user2

Do not forget to run the *newaliases* command after these modifications are done. Alternatively, you can restart the sendmail or Postfix service, which will automatically regenerate the *aliases* database.

Configuring Dovecot

Dovecot is an open-source mail server software used to handle incoming mail. It uses the POP and IMAP protocols, and supports their secure cousins as well. The current version of POP is 3 and that of IMAP is 4, and their secure versions that use SSL encryption over TCP to encrypt authentication and data are referred to as POP3s and IMAPs. The primary difference between the two protocols is that POP3 deletes the mail after it has been retrieved, whereas IMAP4 keeps it on the mail server unless it is specifically deleted. IMAP4 also supports improved login mechanism in addition to a few other benefits over POP3.

Dovecot uses TCP Wrappers for access control.

Dovecot Configuration File

The key configuration file for Dovecot is */etc/dovecot.conf*. This file contains scores of directives that you can set based on requirements. Some key directives are listed and explained in Table 24-9.

Directive	Description
base_dir	Directory location to store runtime information.
protocols	Specifies one or more protocols to be served. Options are pop3 (default port 110), pop3s (default port 995), imap (default port 143) and imaps (default port 993).
listen	IP address and port number to listen for non-secure incoming requests in case there are more than one network interfaces. No need to specify a port if using the default port.
ssl_disable	IP address and port number to listen for secure incoming requests in case there are more than one network interfaces. No need to specify a port if using the default port.
syslogd_facility	Syslog facility to be used for logging via *syslogd* daemon.
mail_location	Location of user inboxes.

Table 24-9 dovecot.conf Directives

Configuring a Non-Secure POP3 Dovecot Server

You can configure a system such as *rhel04* as a non-secure Dovecot server for receiving mail using POP3 by following the steps below:

1. Check whether Dovecot software package is installed:

    # **rpm –qa | grep dovecot**
    dovecot-1.0.7-2.el5

    Install the package if it is not already loaded using one of the software package installation methods described in Chapter 11 "Software Package Management".

2. Open the *dovecot.conf* file and set the following directives to use pop3 protocol and 192.168.0.204 IP address on the default port with user mailboxes located in the */var/spool/mail* directory:

    protocols = pop3
    listen = 192.168.0.204
    ssl_disable = yes
    mail_location = /var/spool/mail

3. Configure TCP Wrappers files */etc/hosts.allow* or */etc/hosts.deny* appropriately for *dovecot* access control. Consult Chapter 30 "System and Network Security" for details.
4. Execute the following to make Dovecot autostart at each system reboot:

    # **chkconfig dovecot on**

5. Disable SELinux protection for Dovecot and verify with the *getsebool* command:

    # **setsebool –P dovecot_disable_trans 1**
    # **getsebool dovecot_disable_trans**
    dovecot_disable_trans --> on

6. Make certain that DNS or */etc/hosts* file is configured properly.
7. Allow traffic on port 110 to pass through the firewall, or simply stop and disable the firewall if it is not used. Consult Chapter 30 "System and Network Security" on how to perform these tasks.
8. Start (or restart) the *dovecot* daemon::

    # **service dovecot start**
    Starting Dovecot Imap: [OK]

9. Execute the following to check the operational status of Dovecot service:

    # **service dovecot status**
    dovecot (pid 9117) is running...

Configuring a Secure IMAP Dovecot Server

You can configure a RHEL system such as *rhel05* as a secure Dovecot server for receiving mail using IMAPs by following the steps below:

1. Perform step 1 from sub-section "Configuring a Non-Secure POP3 Dovecot Server".
2. Open the *dovecot.conf* file and set the following directives to use imaps protocol, 192.168.0.205 IP address on the default port, user mailboxes in the */var/spool/mail* directory and custom SSL certificate information located in the */etc/pki/dovecot* directory:

   > protocols = imaps
   > listen = 192.168.0.205
   > ssl_disable = no
   > ssl_cert_file = /etc/pki/dovecot/certs/dovecot.pem
   > ssl_key_file = /etc/pki/dovecot/private/dovecot.pem
   > mail_location = /var/spool/mail

3. Open the *dovecot-openssl.cnf* file and modify entries as shown below, leave other entries intact:

   > # **cat /etc/pki/dovecot/dovecot-openssl.cnf**
   > C=CA
   > ST=Ontario
   > L=Toronto
   > O=getitcertify
   > OU=IMAP server
   > CN=imap.getitcertify.com
   > emailAddress=postmaster@getitcertify.com

   Some key directives that you may want to modify are listed and explained in Table 24-10.

Directive	Description
C	Country. Specifies a two-letter country code.
ST	State. Specifies the name of a state or province.
L	Location. Specifies the name of a city.
O	Organization. Specifies an organization or company name.
OU	Organizational Unit. Specifies an organizational unit name within the organization or company.
CN	Common Name. Specifies the name of a mail server.
emailAddress	Specifies an administrator email address.

   Table 24-10 Dovecot OpenSSL Configuration File

4. Rename the default certificate and key files:

   > # **cd /etc/pki/dovecot/certs && mv dovecot.pem dovecot.pem.old**
   > # **cd /etc/pki/dovecot/private && mv dovecot.pem dovecot.pem.old**

5. Execute the following script to generate a new private key based on the above configuration:

```
# /usr/share/doc/dovecot-1.0.7/examples/mkcert.sh
Generating a 1024 bit RSA private key
....................++++++
...............................++++++
writing new private key to '/etc/pki/dovecot/private/dovecot.pem'
-----
subject= /C=CA/ST=Ontario/L=Toronto/O=getitcertify/OU=IMAP
server/CN=imap.getitcertify.com/emailAddress=postmaster@getitcertify.com
SHA1 Fingerprint=D1:48:22:36:D5:21:7B:DF:65:B2:03:F2:81:21:5D:8F:91:53:2A:8C
```

6. Perform steps 3 through 6 from sub-section "Configuring a Non-Secure POP3 Dovecot Server".
7. Repeat step 7 for port 993 and perform steps 8 and 9 from sub-section "Configuring a Non-Secure POP3 Dovecot Server".

Verifying Dovecot Functionality

To verify Dovecot functionality, several graphical and textual mail client management programs are available. These programs include Novell Evolution, Mozilla Thunderbird, mutt and fetchmail of which the first two are graphical and the rest text-based. You can also use simple tools such as the *telnet* and the *openssl* command for testing purposes.

You will need to obtain the graphical tools to use them. The *mutt* command can be used with –f option to connect to the specified user mailbox such as that of user *aghori* on *rhel04* using pop and imap protocols and on *rhel05* using their secure cousins on default ports:

```
# mutt –f pop://aghori@rhel04:110
# mutt –f imaps://aghori@rhel05:993
```

The *telnet* command can be used as follows. You will need to enter the username and associated password. The *list* sub-command lists available messages and *quit* takes you out of the interface.

```
# telnet rhel04 pop3
. . . . . . . .
+OK Dovecot ready..
user aghori
+OK
pass Welcome01
+OK Logged in.
list
+OK 0 messages:
quit
+OK Logging out.
Connection closed by foreign host.
```

Summary

This chapter introduced you to the Internet and mail services.

You learned about common Internet services, Internet services daemon and related configuration files. You looked at how to activate and deactivate them. The next major topic talked about very secure FTP service and associated SELinux requirements and configuration file. It explained how to control user access. You studied how to configure a vsFTP server and test it with lftp client.

Next, you studied email systems including sendmail, postfix, dovecot and a few mail client programs. You learned the components of the mail system, the protocols used and how the mail system worked. You looked at various directives and macros defined in mail server configuration files. You were presented with step-by-step procedure on how to configure basic sendmail and postfix outgoing mail servers. You looked at how to set a default mail system. You then performed steps to configure non-secure and secure Dovcecot incoming mail servers. You sent mail messages to local and network users to verify client/server component functionality. You used mutt and telnet to connect to user mailboxes.

25

Network Time Protocol

This chapter covers the following major topics:

- ✓ NTP concepts and components
- ✓ SELinux requirements for NTP
- ✓ Configure an NTP server
- ✓ Configure an NTP peer
- ✓ Configure an NTP client using commands and Date/Time Configurator
- ✓ Use ntpdate to update system clock
- ✓ Query NTP servers
- ✓ Trace NTP server roots

The *Network Time Protocol* (NTP) service maintains the clock on the system and keeps it synchronized with a more accurate and reliable time source. Providing accurate and uniform time for systems on the network allows time-sensitive applications such as backup software, job scheduling tools and billing systems to perform correctly and precisely. It also aids logging daemons to capture information accurately in the log files. NTP uses port 123 for operation.

NTP Concepts and Components

In order to understand NTP, a discussion of NTP components and roles is imperative. The following sub-sections explain them.

Time Source

A *time source* is a server that synchronizes its time with *Universal Coordinated Time* (UTC). Care should be taken when choosing a time source for a network and preference be given to a time server that is physically close and takes the least amount of time to send and receive NTP packets.

The most common time sources available are:

- ✓ A local system clock.
- ✓ An Internet-based public time server.
- ✓ A radio clock.

Local System Clock

You can arrange for one of the RHEL systems on the network to function as a provider of time for other systems. This requires the maintenance of correct time on this local server either manually or automatically via *cron*. Keep in mind, however, that since this server is using its own system clock, it has no way of synchronizing itself with a more reliable and accurate external time source. Therefore, using a local system that relies on its own clock as a time server is the least recommended option.

Internet-Based Public Time Server

Several public time servers that can be employed for the provision of correct time are available via the Internet. One of the systems on the network must be connected to one or more such time servers. To make use of such a time source, a port in the firewall may need to be opened to allow for the flow of NTP traffic. Internet-based public time servers are typically operated by government organizations and universities. This option is more popular than using a local time server.

Several public time servers are available for access on the Internet. Visit *www.ntp.org* to obtain a list.

Radio Clock

A radio clock is considered the most accurate source of time. Some popular radio clock methods include *Global Positioning System* (GPS), *National Institute of Science and Technology* (NIST) radio broadcasts in Americas and DCF77 radio broadcasts in Europe. Of theses, GPS-based sources are the most accurate. In order to use them, some hardware must be added to one of the local systems on the network.

Stratum Levels

As you are aware that there are numerous time sources available to synchronize the system time with. These time sources are categorized into *stratum levels* based on their reliability and accuracy. There are 15 stratum levels ranging from 1 to 15 with 1 being the most accurate. The radio clocks are at stratum 1 as they are the most accurate. Stratum 1 time sources, however, cannot be used on a network directly. Therefore, one of the systems on the network at stratum 2, for instance, needs to be configured to get time updates from a stratum 1 server. The stratum 2 server then acts as the primary source of time for secondary servers and/or clients on the network. It can also be configured to provide time to stratum 3 or lower-reliability time servers.

> If a secondary server is also configured to get time from a stratum 1 server directly, it will act as a peer to the primary server.

NTP Roles

A role is a function that a system performs from an NTP standpoint. A system can be configured to assume one or more of the following roles:

Primary NTP Server

A *primary NTP server* gets time from one of the time sources mentioned above and provides time to one or more secondary servers or clients, or both. It can also be configured to broadcast time to secondary servers and clients.

Secondary NTP Server

A *secondary NTP server* receives time from a primary server or directly from one of the time sources mentioned above. It can be used to provide time to a set of clients to offload the primary server or as a redundant time server when the primary becomes unavailable. Having a secondary server is optional, but highly recommended. It can be configured to broadcast time to clients and peers.

NTP Peer

An *NTP peer* provides time to an NTP server and receives time from that server. They usually work at the same stratum level. Both primary and secondary servers can be peers of each other.

NTP Client

An *NTP client* receives time from either a primary or a secondary time server. A client can be configured in one of the following two ways:

- ✓ As a *polling* client that contacts a primary or secondary NTP server directly to get time updates to synchronize its system clock.
- ✓ As a *broadcast* client that listens to time broadcasts by a primary or secondary NTP server. A broadcast client binds itself with the NTP server that responds to its requests and synchronizes its clock with it. The NTP server must be configured in broadcast mode in order for the broadcast client to be able to bind to it.

Configuring NTP

The following sub-sections provide step-by-step procedures on how to configure an NTP server, peer and client.

SELinux Requirements for NTP

If SELinux is enforced, you need to disable its protection for NTP service to ensure smooth functionality. Use the *setsebool* command as demonstrated below, or the SELinux Configurator *system-config-selinux* as explained in Chapter 30 "System and Network Security".

> # **setsebool –P ntpd_disable_trans 1**

Use the *getsebool* command to verify:

> # **getsebool ntpd_disable_trans**
> ntpd_disable_trans --> on

Configuring NTP Server and Peer

To configure an NTP server or peer (primary or secondary) on *rhel01*, follow the steps below:

1. Check whether NTP software package is installed:

    > # **rpm –q ntp**
    > ntp-4.2.2p1-7.el5

    Install the package if it is not already loaded using one of the software package installation methods described in Chapter 11 "Software Package Management".

2. Select an appropriate time source. Refer to *www.ntp.org* for a list of public time servers.
3. Add the time source information to the */etc/ntp.conf* configuration file:

    For the local system clock, use the 127.127.1.0 reserved IP address. The fudge keyword defines the stratum level. Add the following two lines:

    > server   127.127.1.0
    > fudge   127.127.1.0   stratum   10

    For an Internet-based time server, specify either the fully qualified hostname or IP address of the server. For example, the entry for IP address 11.59.99.3 will look like:

    > server   11.59.99.3

    For a radio clock-based source of time, connect special hardware device to the system's serial port and add the following line to the file. The first three octets of the IP address (127.127.4) indicate that an external source of time is used. The last octet of the address (2) means that the radio clock hardware is connected to the second serial port of the system.

    > server   127.127.4.2

To setup a peer, specify the hostname or IP address of the NTP server with the keyword "peer". For example, enter the following to define that this system is a peer of *rhel03*:

```
peer          rhel03
```

It is recommended to choose a minimum of two time servers physically located apart and accessed via different network routes for redundancy purposes. NTP automatically starts using the secondary server should the primary becomes unavailable. The servers can act as peers of each other if they are at the same stratum level.

Besides, you may want to consider leaving the following line uncommented or modify it to look like the one below it:

```
restrict default kod nomodify notrap nopeer noquery
restrict 192.168.0.0 mask 255.255.255.0
```

The first restrict directive sets default restrictions on all incoming time requests. Several defaults are defined with the directive including kod, nomodify, notrap, nopeer and noquery options. The kod option prevents the server from being attacked with the *kiss of death* packets, which might cause the server to crash; the nomodify option disallows any modifications by other NTP servers; the notrap option disables messages from being trapped; the nopeer option prevents other NTP servers from establishing a peer relationship with this server; and the noquery option disallows all queries coming in from other NTP servers for time synchronization.

The second restrict directive sets the default restrictions on time requests that are coming in from systems on the 192.168.0 network with the default class C netmask. You may take any or all unneeded options out.

4. Execute the following to make NTP autostart at system reboots:

    # **chkconfig ntpd on**

5. Allow NTP traffic on port 123 to pass through the firewall, or simply stop and disable the firewall if it is not used. Consult Chapter 30 "System and Network Security" on how to perform these tasks.
6. Start (or restart) *ntpd* daemon manually:

    # **service ntpd start**
    Starting ntpd: [OK]

Configuring an NTP Client

To configure an NTP client, follow the steps below:

1. Add the following lines to the */etc/ntp.conf* file:

    To setup a system as a polling client to synchronize time with NTP server *rhel01*:

    ```
    server        rhel01
    driftfile     /var/lib/ntp/drift
    ```

The *ntpd* daemon computes the clock frequency error in the local system every 64 seconds by default. It may take *ntpd* hours after it is started to compute a good estimate of the error. The current error value is stored in the */var/lib/ntp/drift* file (or any other file or directory location specified with the driftfile keyword). This allows *ntpd* to reinitialize itself to the estimate stored in the driftfile, saving time in recomputing a good frequency estimate. In short, the use of a driftfile helps *ntpd* track local system clock accuracy. A driftfile is not required, but recommended.

To setup the client as a broadcast client:

```
broadcastclient        yes
driftfile              /var/lib/ntp/drift
```

To setup a broadcast client, define the broadcast network address in */etc/ntp.conf* on the NTP server and restart *ntpd*. An example entry would be "broadcast 11.69.99.255".

2. Execute the following to make NTP autostart at system reboots:

   # chkconfig ntpd on

3. Start (or restart) the *ntpd* daemon:

   # service ntpd start
   ```
   Starting ntpd:                                              [ OK ]
   ```

Configuring an NTP Client Using Date/Time Configurator

To configure an NTP client using the Red Hat Date/Time Configurator, follow the steps below:

1. Execute *system-config-date* (or *system-config-time*) in an X terminal window or choose (GNOME) System / (KDE) Main Menu → Administration → Date & Time. The Date/Time Configurator screen will open up as shown in Figure 25-1.
2. Click Network Time Protocol tab and then select Enable Network Time Protocol. Under NTP Servers, there are three public NTP servers listed by default. You can add your own if you wish. You also have the option to edit or delete any of the listed servers. Under Show/Hide advanced options, choose the first option if you want the time on the system to be brought at par with one of the configured NTP servers before bringing up the *ntpd* service. The second option allows the system to use its own clock as the source of time. For this demonstration, add the NTP server *rhel01*, and select the first option and leave the second one unchecked. Click OK when done.

This sets up NTP client functionality and starts *ntpd* daemon.

Figure 25-1 Date/Time Configurator – NTP Client Configuration

Managing NTP

Managing NTP involves updating system clock manually, querying NTP servers and tracing roots of an NTP server.

Updating System Clock Manually

You can run the *ntpdate* command anytime to bring the system clock close to the time on an NTP server. The *ntpd* daemon must not be running when this command is executed to obtain the desired results. Run *ntpdate* manually and specify either the hostname such as *rhel01.ntp.org* or IP address of the time server:

ntpdate rhel01.ntp.org
4 Mar 08:45:54 ntpdate[6615]: adjust time server rhel01.ntp.org offset -0.040837 sec

Querying NTP Servers

NTP servers may be queried for time synchronization and server association status using the *ntpq* command. This command sends out requests to and receives responses from NTP servers. The command may be run in interactive mode.

Run *ntpq* with –p option to print a list of NTP servers known to the system along with a summary of their states:

ntpq –p

remote	refid	st	t	when	poll	reach	delay	offset	jitter
*19.33.42.222	rhel01.ntp.org	2	u	180	1024	377	28.95	-0.437	0.000

Each column from the output is explained in Table 25-1.

Column	Description
remote	Shows IP addresses or hostnames of all NTP servers and peers. Each IP/hostname may be preceded by one of the following characters: * Indicates the current source of synchronization. # Indicates the server selected for synchronization, but distance exceeds the maximum. o Displays the server selected for synchronization. + Indicates the system considered for synchronization. x Designated false ticker by the intersection algorithm. . Indicates the systems picked up from the end of the candidate list. - Indicates the system not considered for synchronization. Blank Indicates the server rejected because of high stratum level or failed sanity checks.
refid	Shows the current source of synchronization.
st	Shows the stratum level of the server.
t	Shows available types: l = local (such as a GPS clock), u = unicast, m = multicast, b = broadcast and - = netaddr (usually 0).
when	Shows time, in seconds, since a response was received from the server.
poll	Shows polling interval. Default is 64 seconds.
reach	Shows number of successful attempts to reach the server. The value 001 indicates that the most recent probe was answered, 357 indicates that one probe was not answered and the value 377 indicates that all recent probes were answered.
delay	Shows how long, in milliseconds, it took for the reply packet to come back in response to a query sent to the server.
offset	Shows time difference, in milliseconds, between the server and the client clocks.
jitter	Shows how much the "offset" measurement varies between samples. This is an error-bound estimate.

Table 25-1 ntpq Command Output Description

Tracing Roots of an NTP Server

The roots of a specified NTP server can be traced using the *ntptrace* command. For example, the following will locate the NTP server where *rhel01.ntp.org* is getting time from:

 # ntptrace rhel01.ntp.org
rhel01.ntp.org: stratum 1, offset 0.000247, synch distance 0.00607, refid 'GPS'

The output indicates that *rhel01.ntp.org* is at stratum 1 and using GPS.

Summary

This chapter provided an introduction to Network Time Protocol and how to set it up. You learned concepts and components of it. You looked at configuring an NTP server, a peer and a client. You saw how to update the system clock manually, query NTP servers and trace roots of an NTP server.

Red Hat Certified Technician & Engineer

## 26

NFS and AutoFS

This chapter covers the following major topics:

- ✓ Understand NFS concepts and benefits
- ✓ Understand NFS versions, security, daemons, commands, related files and startup scripts
- ✓ How NFS client and server interact with each other
- ✓ Configure NFS server and client
- ✓ Display exported and mounted NFS resources
- ✓ Unmount and unexport a resource
- ✓ Monitor NFS activities
- ✓ Understand AutoFS
- ✓ Features and benefits
- ✓ How AutoFS works
- ✓ AutoFS configuration file
- ✓ Configure AutoFS maps – master, special, direct and indirect
- ✓ Mount user home directories

The *Network File System* (NFS) service is based on the client/server architecture whereby users on one system access files, directories and file systems (let us collectively call them *resources*) residing on a remote system as if they exist locally on their system. The remote system that makes its resources available to be accessed over the network is called an *NFS server*, and the process of making them accessible is referred to as *exporting*. The resources exported by the NFS server can be accessed by one or more systems. These systems are called *NFS clients*, and the process of making the resources accessible on clients is referred to as *mounting*. Resources may be kept mounted until either they are unmounted manually or the system is rebooted. The other method unmounts them automatically after a pre-determined time is elapsed.

Understanding Network File System (NFS)

A system can function as both an NFS server and an NFS client at the same time. When a directory or file system resource is exported, the entire directory structure beneath it becomes available for mounting on the client. A sub-directory or the parent directory of an exported resource cannot be re-exported if it exists in the same file system. Similarly, a resource mounted by an NFS client cannot be exported further by the client. A single exported file resource is mounted on a directory mount point.

NFS is built on top of *Remote Procedure Call* (RPC) and *eXternal Data Representation* (XDR) to allow a server and client to communicate. They provide a common "language" that both the server and client understand. This is standardized based on the fact that the NFS server and client may be running two completely different operating systems on different hardware platforms. RPC uses program numbers defined in the */etc/rpc* file.

The following data is extracted from the *rpc* file. It shows official service names in the first column, followed by program numbers and associated alias names in subsequent columns:

```
# cat /etc/rpc
. . . . . . . .
portmapper   100000  portmap sunrpc rpcbind
rstatd       100001  rstat rup perfmeter rstat_svc
rusersd      100002  rusers
nfs          100003  nfsprog
ypserv       100004  ypprog
mountd       100005  mount showmount
ypbind       100007
walld        100008  rwall shutdown
yppasswdd    100009  yppasswd
etherstatd   100010  etherstat
rquotad      100011  rquotaprog quota rquota
sprayd       100012  spray
. . . . . . . .
llockmgr     100020
nlockmgr     100021
. . . . . . . .
```

Benefits

Some benefits associated with using NFS are listed below:

- ✓ Supports heterogeneous operating system platforms including all Linux and UNIX versions out there, as well as Microsoft Windows.
- ✓ Several client systems can access a single exported resource simultaneously.
- ✓ Enables sharing common application binaries and read-only information such as the *man* pages, instead of loading them on each single system. This results in reduced overall disk storage cost and administration overhead.
- ✓ Gives users access to uniform data.
- ✓ Useful when many users exist on many systems with their home directories located on every single host. In such a situation, create user home directories on a single system under */home* for example, and export */home*. Now, whichever system a user logs on to, his home directory becomes available there. This way the user will need to maintain only one home directory, and not a lot.

NFS Statelessness

NFS is *stateless* by design, meaning that the server does not keep track of what a client system is doing on a shared resource. If the client is crashed and rebooted, it will reestablish a connection to the server. You do not have to do anything on the NFS server. Similarly, if the NFS server is crashed and rebooted, the NFS client will continue accessing the resource after the server is back up to normal. The only exception is that the client is unable to access the server for the period of time the server was down or unavailable. In this case too, there is nothing that needs to be done on the NFS server.

NFS Versions

RHEL 5 comes with version 4 of NFS protocol (NFS v4), which is an *Internet Engineering Task Force* (IETF) standard protocol that provides enhanced security, scalability, encrypted transfers, better cross-platform interoperability, works better through firewalls and on the Internet, and is more efficient than NFS v3. NFS v4 maintains all other features and benefits of NFS v3 including support for TCP and files of sizes up to 128GB (64-bit). NFS v4 uses usernames and groupnames rather than UIDs and GIDs when sharing files.

NFS v3 is still the default protocol for NFS in RHEL 5; however, NFS v4 can be used instead to take advantage of the benefits listed above.

NFS Security

NFS security is paramount in v4 to ensure that NFS operates securely in a WAN environment. In older versions, authentication was performed at the NFS client side. In contrast, an exchange of information takes place in v4 between the client and server for identification, authentication and authorization. Identification establishes identity of systems and users that will be accessing the shares, authentication confirms the identity and authorization controls what information systems and users will have access to. Exchange of information in transit between the client and server is encrypted to prevent eavesdropping and unauthorized access to private data.

NFS Daemons, Commands, Configuration Files and Scripts

When working with NFS, several daemons, commands, configuration files and scripts are involved. The tables given below list and explain them.

Table 26-1 describes NFS daemons.

Daemon	Description
portmap	Server- and client-side daemon responsible for forwarding incoming RPC requests to appropriate RPC daemons. Access to this daemon can be controlled via TCP Wrappers using */etc/hosts.allow* and */etc/hosts.deny* files. See Chapter 30 "System and Network Security" for details.
rpc.idmapd	Server- and client-side daemon that controls mappings of UIDs and GIDs with their corresponding usernames and groupnames. Its configuration file is */etc/idmapd.conf*.
rpc.lockd	Server- and client-side daemon that keeps an eye on the NFS client that has requested a lock on files to make sure the client is up and running. If the client is rebooted unexpectedly, this daemon removes all locks placed on the files so that other NFS clients may use them.
rpc.mountd	Server-side daemon that responds to client requests to mount a resource and provide status of exported and mounted resources. Access to this daemon can be controlled via TCP Wrappers using */etc/hosts.allow* and */etc/hosts.deny* files. See Chapter 30 "System and Network Security" for details.
rpc.nfsd	Server-side daemon that responds to client requests to access files.
rpc.rquotad	Server-side daemon that provides statistics on disk quota to clients.
rpc.statd	Server- and client-side daemon that works with *rpc.lockd* to provide crash and recovery services.

Table 26-1 NFS Daemons

Table 26-2 describes NFS commands.

Command	Description
exportfs	Server-side command that exports resources listed in the */etc/exports* file and displays exported resources listed in the */var/lib/nfs/etab* file.
showmount	Server- and client-side command that displays which resources are exported to which clients by consulting the */var/lib/nfs/etab* file and displays which clients have those resources mounted by consulting the */var/lib/nfs/rmtab* file.
mount	Client-side command that mounts a resource specified at the command line or listed in the */etc/fstab* file followed by adding an entry to client's */etc/mnttab* file, and server's */var/lib/nfs/rmtab* file via the *rpc.mountd* daemon. It also displays mounted resources listed in the */etc/mnttab* file.
umount	Client-side command that unmounts a single resource specified at the command line or listed in the */etc/mnttab* file followed by removing corresponding entry from this file and server's */var/lib/nfs/rmtab* file via the *rpc.mountd* daemon.
rpcinfo	Server-side command that checks whether NFS server daemons are registered with RPC.

Command	Description
nfsstat	Server- and client-side command that displays NFS and RPC statistics.

Table 26-2 NFS Commands

Table 26-3 describes NFS configuration and functional files.

File	Description
/etc/exports	Server-side file that contains a list of resources to be exported.
/var/lib/nfs/etab	Server-side file that contains a list of exported resources whether or not they are remotely mounted. This file is updated when a resource is exported or unexported, and is maintained by the *rpc.mountd* daemon.
/var/lib/nfs/rmtab	Server-side file that contains a list of exported resources, which have been mounted by clients. This file is updated when a resource is remotely mounted or unmounted, and is maintained by the *rpc.mountd* daemon.
/etc/fstab	Client-side file that contains a list of resources to be mounted at system reboots or manually with the *mount* command.
/etc/mtab	Client-side file that contains a list of mounted resources. The *mount* and *umount* commands update this file.
/etc/sysconfig/nfs	Server- and client-side configuration file used by NFS startup scripts.

Table 26-3 NFS Configuration and Functional Files

Table 26-4 describes NFS startup and shutdown scripts.

Scripts	Description
/etc/rc.d/init.d/nfs	Server-side script that starts (run levels 3 and up) and stops (run levels 2 and below) the *rpc.nfsd*, *rpc.rquotad*, *rpc.idmapd* and *rpc.mountd* daemons. Sources the */etc/sysconfig/nfs* file for configuration information.
/etc/rc.d/init.d/nfslock	Server- and client-side script that starts (run levels 3 and up) and stops (run levels 2 and below) the *rpc.lockd* and *rpc.statd* daemons. Sources the */etc/sysconfig/nfs* file for configuration information.
/etc/rc.d/init.d/protmap	Server- and client-side script that starts (run levels 3 and up) and stops (run levels 2 and below) the *portmap* daemon.

Table 26-4 NFS Startup and Shutdown Scripts

How NFS Works?

The following outlines the process of exporting and mounting a resource:

✓ The contents of */etc/exports* file are evaluated for any syntax problems and access issues.
✓ Each resource listed in this file is exported and an entry is added to the */var/lib/nfs/etab* file on the server. The *showmount* command looks into this file to display exported resource information.

- ✓ The client issues the *mount* command on the NFS client to request the NFS server to provide file handle for the requested resource.
- ✓ The request goes to the *rpc.mountd* daemon on the NFS server through the *portmap* daemon that runs on both the server and the client.
- ✓ The *rpc.mountd* daemon consults TCP Wrappers and performs an access check to validate if the client is authorized to mount the resource.
- ✓ The *rpc.mountd* daemon sends a file handle for the requested resource to the client.
- ✓ The client mounts the resource if the correct *mount* command syntax is used. To automate the mount process, an entry for the resource can be added to the */etc/fstab* file, which ensures that the resource will get automatically mounted when the client reboots.
- ✓ The *mount* command tells the *rpc.mountd* daemon on the NFS server that the resource has been mounted successfully. Upon receiving a confirmation, the daemon adds an entry to the */var/lib/nfs/rmtab* file. The *showmount* command uses this file to display remotely mounted NFS resources. When the resource is unmounted on the client, the *umount* command sends a request to the *rpc.mountd* daemon to remove the entry from this file.
- ✓ The *mount* command also adds an entry to the */etc/mtab* file for the mounted resource on the client. The *mount* and *df* commands reference this file to display information about mounted resources. The *mount* and *umount* commands update this file whenever they are executed successfully.
- ✓ Any file access request by the client on the mounted resource is now going to be handled by the server's *rpc.nfsd* daemon.
- ✓ The *rpc.lockd* and *rpc.statd* daemons are involved when the client requests the server to place a lock on a file.

SELinux Requirements for NFS

If SELinux is enforced, you need to disable its protection for NFS service to ensure smooth functionality. Use the *setsebool* command as demonstrated below, or the SELinux Configurator *system-config-selinux* as explained in Chapter 30 "System and Network Security". Specify only those Booleans that need to be disabled, leave others intact.

> # **setsebool –P nfs_export_all_ro=1 nfs_export_all_rw=1 nfsd_disable_trans=1 **
> **use_nfs_home_dirs=1**

Use the *getsebool* command to verify:

> # **getsebool nfs_export_all_ro nfs_export_all_rw nfsd_disable_trans use_nfs_home_dirs**
> nfs_export_all_ro --> on
> nfs_export_all_rw --> on
> nfsd_disable_trans --> on
> use_nfs_home_dirs --> on

Configuring NFS

This section discusses procedures on configuring NFS server and client.

Configuring an NFS Server

Let us look at the step-by-step procedure for configuring *rhel02* as an NFS server and export several resources. Prior to setting up an NFS environment, ensure that UIDs and GIDs are consistent across all systems that will be configured and used as NFS servers and clients.

1. Make sure that the following NFS software packages are installed:

    # rpm –qa | egrep 'portmap|nfs'
    portmap-4.0-65.2.2.1
    nfs-utils-1.0.9-33.el5
    system-config-nfs-1.3.23-1.el5

     The portmap package is not needed for NFS v4.

2. Ensure NFS support is included in the kernel by running the *lsmod* command:

    # lsmod | grep nfs
    nfsd   285193 5
    exportfs   38849 1 nfsd
    lockd   99057 1 nfsd
    nfs_acl   36673 1 nfsd
    auth_rpcgss   81889 1 nfsd
    sunrpc   198025 8 nfsd,lockd,nfs_acl,auth_rpcgss

3. Edit */etc/exports* file and insert the following entries one per line. Create this file if it does not already exist.

    # vi /etc/exports
    /usr/share/man rhel03(ro,sync) rhel04(ro,sync)
    /home   *.getitcertify.com(rw,sync)
    /var/opt   *(rw,sync,no_root_squash)
    /usr/local/bin *(rw,sync,no_root_squash)

    The first line entry will export */usr/share/man* directory to *rhel03* and *rhel04* servers in read-only mode. The sync option instructs *rpc.nsfd* to reply to client requests only after the changes have been committed. The second line entry will export */home* to all systems in the *getitcertify.com* domain in read-write mode. The third and fourth line entries will export the specified directories in read-write mode to any server that will attempt to mount them. The no_root_squash option will allow the *root* user to be able to access the shares on the client. Refer to Table 26-5 for details on these and additional options.

4. Edit */etc/sysconfig/nfs* file and define static ports for NFS daemons, otherwise the daemons will use random ports which might become an issue with the firewall. If the firewall is going to be shut off permanently, skip this and the next three steps.

```
# vi /etc/sysconfig/nfs
# TCP port rpc.lockd should listen on.
LOCKD_TCPPORT=6001
# UDP port rpc.lockd should listen on.
LOCKD_UDPPORT=6001
# Port rpc.statd should listen on.
STATD_PORT=6002
# Port rpc.mountd should listen on.
MOUNTD_PORT=6003
# Port rquotad should listen on.
RQUOTAD_PORT=6004
```

5. Edit */etc/services* file and define the ports in it. Ensure that the ports are not already in use by other applications or services.

```
# vi /etc/services
lockd       6001/tcp
lockd       6001/udp
statd       6002/tcp
mountd      6003/tcp
rquotad     6004/tcp
```

6. Configure TCP Wrappers files */etc/hosts.allow* or */etc/hosts.deny* appropriately for *portmap* and *rpc.mountd* access control. Consult Chapter 30 "System and Network Security" for details.
7. Allow NFS traffic on ports 111 (*portmapper*), 6001, 6002, 6003 and 6004 to pass through the firewall, or simply stop and disable the firewall if it is not used. Consult Chapter 30 "System and Network Security" on how to perform these tasks.
8. Execute the following to make NFS processes autostart at system reboots:

```
# chkconfig portmap on
# chkconfig nfslock on
# chkconfig nfs on
```

9. Start (or restart) the *portmap* process, and check its status:

```
# service portmap start
Starting portmap:                    [ OK ]
# service portmap status
portmap (pid 4348) is running...
```

10. Start NFS file locking service if it is not already running, and check its status:

```
# service nfslock start
Starting NFS statd:                  [ OK ]
# service nfslock status
rpc.statd (pid 5663) is running...
```

11. Start NFS server processes if they are not already running, and check their status:

---

service nfs start
Starting NFS services: [OK]
Starting NFS quotas: [OK]
Starting NFS daemon: [OK]
Starting NFS mountd: [OK]
service nfs status
rpc.mountd (pid 6715) is running...
nfsd (pid 6712 6711 6710 6709 6708 6707 6706 6705) is running...

If the processes are already running, simply execute the following:

exportfs –avr
exporting rhel03:/usr/share/man
exporting rhel04:/usr/share/man
exporting *.getitcertify.com:/home
exporting *:/usr/local/bin
exporting *:/var/opt

The –avr options instruct the command to export all resources listed in the */etc/exports* file, display details and update */var/lib/nfs/etab* file.

12. Run the *rpcinfo* command to verify that all the daemons identified in Table 26-1 are running:

rpcinfo –p
```
program vers proto   port
 100000  2  tcp   111  portmapper
 100000  2  udp   111  portmapper
 100024  1  udp   611  status
 100024  1  tcp   614  status
 100011  1  udp  6004  rquotad
 100011  2  udp  6004  rquotad
 100003  2  udp  2049  nfs
 100003  3  udp  2049  nfs
 100003  4  udp  2049  nfs
 100021  1  udp  6001  nlockmgr
 100021  3  udp  6001  nlockmgr
 100021  4  udp  6001  nlockmgr
 100021  1  tcp  6001  nlockmgr
 100021  3  tcp  6001  nlockmgr
 100021  4  tcp  6001  nlockmgr
 100003  2  tcp  2049  nfs
 100003  3  tcp  2049  nfs
 100003  4  tcp  2049  nfs
 100005  1  udp  6003  mountd
 100005  1  tcp  6003  mountd
 100005  2  udp  6003  mountd
 100005  2  tcp  6003  mountd
 100005  3  udp  6003  mountd
 100005  3  tcp  6003  mountd
```

Note that you can run the *exportfs* command with –i option and specify a resource to be exported temporarily without adding an entry for it to the */etc/exports* file. This way the resource will remain exported until it is either manually unexported or the server is rebooted. For example, to export */usr/share/man* with the options mentioned above, run the *exportfs* command as follows:

exportfs –o ro,sync –i rhel03:/usr/share/man rhel04:/usr/share/man

Common options that can be used when exporting a resource are described in Table 26-5.

Option	Description
*	Represents all possible matches. In the examples above, * means that any client can mount the exported resource and *.getitcertify.com (or .getitcertify.com) means that any client system on the getitcertify.com domain can mount the resource. You can specify one or more hostnames, IP addresses, domain names or network addresses, or a combination.
all_squash / no_all_squash (default=no_all_squash)	all_squash treats users on client systems as anonymous users and no_all_squash does not.
anongid=GID (default=65534)	Assigns the GID to anonymous groups.
anonuid=UID (default=65534)	Assigns the UID to anonymous users.
mp	Exports only if the specified directory is a file system.
root_squash / no_root_squash (default=root_squash)	root_squash prevents *root* users on an NFS client from gaining *root* access on a mounted NFS resource by mapping *root* to a special, unprivileged user called *nfsnobody* with UID 65534. no_root_squash allows *root* access. It is recommended to use the default to prevent unauthorized *root* access on clients.
rw / ro (default=ro)	rw (read/write) allows file modifications and ro (read-only) prevents doing it.
secure / insecure (default=secure)	secure allows access on ports lower than 1024 and insecure allows access on ports beyond 1024.
secure_locks / insecure_locks (default=secure_locks)	secure_locks checks file permissions on older NFS clients and insecure_locks does not.
subtree_check / no_subtree_check (default=no_subtree_check)	Enables / disables permission checking on higher level directories of an exported resource.
sync / async (default=sync)	Changes are written to disk before / after a command is complete.
wdelay / no_wdelay (default=wdelay)	wdelay delays data writes to the resource and no_wdelay writes data right away.

Table 26-5 exports Options

Configuring an NFS Server Using NFS Configurator

To configure an NFS server using the Red Hat NFS Configurator, follow the steps below:

Red Hat Certified Technician & Engineer

1. Execute *system-config-nfs* in an X terminal window or choose (GNOME) System / (KDE) Main Menu → System → NFS. The NFS Configurator screen will open up as shown in Figure 26-1. The Add button allows you to export a new resource and Server Settings (Figure 26-2) allows you to define any specific ports that you wish to use for NFS server daemons instead of the pre-defined ports.

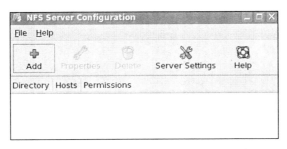

Figure 26-1 NFS Configurator – Main Screen

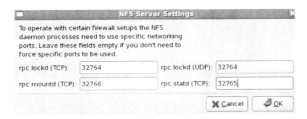

Figure 26-2 NFS Configurator – NFS Server Settings

2. There are three tabs – Basic, General Options and User Access – on the main screen. The Basic tab is where you input a resource name to be exported, hostname or IP address of the server, domain or network to be exported to (or an * for all hosts) and permissions. The General Options and User Access tabs allow you to modify some of the options listed in Table 26-5. In the Basic tab specify a resource name such as */usr/share/man* to be exported to *rhel03* and *rhel04*. Leave options in the other two tabs to their default values. Click OK when done. The system uses the *exportfs* command with –r option to export the resource. See Figure 26-3.

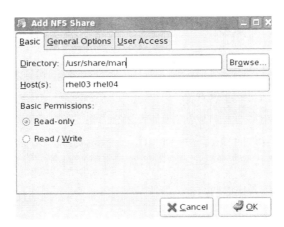

Figure 26-3 NFS Configurator – Add NFS Share

Configuring an NFS Client

Here is the procedure to configure an NFS client successfully:

1. Execute the following on the NFS server to determine available exported resources:

   # **showmount –e**
   Export list for rhel02:
   /var/opt   *
   /usr/local/bin   *
   /home   *.getitcertify.com
   /usr/share/man   rhel03,rhel04

   Alternatively, use the *exportfs* command or a *cat* on the */var/lib/nfs/etab* file:

   # **exportfs**
   /usr/share/man   rhel03
   /usr/share/man   rhel04
   /home   *.getitcertify.com
   /usr/local/bin   <world>
   /var/opt   <world>
   # **cat /var/lib/nfs/etab**
   /usr/share/man   rhel03(ro,sync,wdelay,hide,nocrossmnt,secure,root_squash,no_all_squash,
   no_subtree_check,secure_locks,acl,mapping=identity,anonuid=65534,anongid=65534)
   /usr/share/man   rhel04(ro,sync,wdelay,hide,nocrossmnt,secure,root_squash,no_all_squash,
   no_subtree_check,secure_locks,acl,mapping=identity,anonuid=65534,anongid=65534)
   /home   *.getitcertify.com(rw,sync,wdelay,hide,nocrossmnt,secure,root_squash,no_all_squash,
   no_subtree_check,secure_locks,acl,mapping=identity,anonuid=65534,anongid=65534)
   /usr/local/bin   *(rw,sync,wdelay,hide,nocrossmnt,secure,no_root_squash,no_all_squash,
   no_subtree_check,secure_locks,acl,mapping=identity,anonuid=65534,anongid=65534)
   /var/opt   *(rw,sync,wdelay,hide,nocrossmnt,secure,no_root_squash,no_all_squash,
   no_subtree_check,secure_locks,acl,mapping=identity,anonuid=65534,anongid=65534)

2. Execute the following on the client to determine available resources from the server *rhel02*:

   # **showmount –e rhel02**
   Export list for rhel02:
   /var/opt   *
   /usr/local/bin   *
   /home   *.getitcertify.com
   /usr/share/man   rhel03,rhel04

3. Execute the following on the client to make *portmap* and NFS file locking daemons autostart at system reboots:

   # **chkconfig portmap on**
   # **chkconfig nfslock on**

4. Start (or restart) the *portmap* and NFS file locking processes on the client:

```
# service portmap start
Starting portmap:                        [ OK ]
# service nfslock start
Starting NFS statd:                      [ OK ]
```

5. Edit */etc/fstab* and add the following entries for the resources. This is done to ensure the NFS resources get automatically mounted when this client is rebooted.

```
rhel02:/usr/share/man      /usr/share/man      nfs      ro,sync      0  0
rhel02:/home               /home               nfs      rw,sync      0  0
rhel02 :/var/opt           /var/opt            nfs      rw,sync      0  0
rhel02:/usr/local/bin      /usr/local/bin      nfs      rw,sync      0  0
```

6. Create required mount points with the *mkdir* command if they do not already exist.
7. Execute the *mount* command with "–at nfs" options to mount all the remote resources:

```
# mount –at nfs
```

Alternatively, you can manually mount the resources in one of three ways. Repeat the first command below for each resource and specify correct options with –o switch, run the second command that will obtain additional required information from the */etc/fstab* file or execute the third command that will mount all configured NFS resources as listed in the */etc/fstab* file:

```
# mount –t nfs –o ro,sync rhel02:/usr/share/man /usr/share/man
# mount /usr/share/man
# service netfs start
Mouting other filesystems:               [ OK ]
```

A mount point should be empty when an attempt is made to mount a resource on it, otherwise, the contents of the mount point will hide. As well, the mount point must not be in use or the mount attempt will fail.

Common options that can be used when mounting a resource are described in Table 26-6.

Option	Description
async / sync (default=async)	Changes are written to disk after / before a command is complete.
fg / bg (default=fg)	Use "fg" (foreground) for resources that must be available to a client to boot successfully or operate properly. If a foreground mount fails, it is retried for "retry" minutes in the foreground until it either succeeds or is interrupted if "intr" option is also used. With "bg" (background), mount attempts are tried and retried for "retry" minutes in the background without hampering the system boot process or hanging the client.

Option	Description
hard / soft (default=hard)	With "hard" option, the client tries and retries to mount a resource until either it succeeds or is interrupted if "intr" option is also used. If the server goes down, processes using the mounted resource hang until the server comes back up. Use "soft" to avoid this situation. With this option, if a client attempts to mount a resource for "retrans" times unsuccessfully, an error message is displayed.
intr / nointr (default=nointr)	Use "intr" (interrupt) if you want to be able to manually interrupt a request. Use "nointr" for the opposite.
nfsvers=n (default=3)	NFS version to be used.
retrans=n (default=3)	This many times a client retransmits a read or write request after the first transmission times out. If the request does not succeed after n retransmissions, a "soft" mount displays an error message and a "hard" mount continues to retry.
retry=n (default=2 minutes and 10000 minutes)	For this duration (2 minutes with "fg" and 10,000 minutes with "bg") a client tries to mount a resource after the first try fails. With "intr", mount attempts can be interrupted before this many retries. If "nointr" is used, mount attempts must wait until this many retries have been made, mount succeeds or the client is rebooted.
rsize=n (default=32k)	Size of each read request from client to server.
rw / ro (default=rw)	"rw" (read/write) allows file modifications and "ro" (read-only) prevents from doing it.
suid / nosuid (default=suid)	"suid" enables users on a client to execute a setuid-enabled program located on the NFS mounted resource with the same privileges as the owner of the program has on it. If the program has *root* ownership, it is executed with *root* privileges regardless of who runs it. "nosuid" prevents users from running setuid programs.
timeo=n (default=7)	Sets timeout, in tenths of a second, for NFS read and write requests. If a request times out, this value is doubled and the request is attempted again for "retrans" times. When number of "retrans" attempts are made, a "soft" mount displays an error message while a "hard" mount continues to retry.
wsize=n (default=32k)	Size of each write request from client to server.

Table 26-6 mount Command Options for NFS

Managing NFS

Managing NFS involves exporting, mounting, viewing, unmounting and unexporting resources. Some of these tasks have been covered in the previous section; others are discussed below.

Viewing Exported and Mounted Resources

To verify the functionality of both the server and the client, *cd* into a resource mount point and run the *ll* command. If both commands run successfully, it means the resource is exported and mounted, and that there are no issues. Several commands such as *showmount*, *exportfs*, *df* and *mount* are available that allow you to view what resources are exported by the server, available to a particular client for mounting and mounted on a client. Let us look at some examples.

To view exported resources, execute any of the following on the NFS server:

```
# exportfs
# showmount −e
# cat /var/lib/nfs/etab
```

To view what resources are currently mounted by which NFS client, execute any of the following on the NFS server:

```
# showmount −a
All mount points on rhel02:
rhel03:/usr/share/man
rhel04:/usr/share/man
rhel01:/home
rhel04:/usr/local/bin
rhel01:/var/opt
# cat /var/lib/nfs/rmtab
```

To view mounted resources, execute any of the following on the NFS client:

```
# mount −v | grep nfs
# df −t nfs
```

File system	1K-blocks	Used	Available	Use%	Mounted on
rhel02:/usr/share/man	1257472	905600	349352	72%	/usr/share/man
rhel02:/home	20480	3112	17296	15%	/export/home
rhel02:/usr/local/bin	3006464	1665784	1330360	56%	/usr/local/bin
rhel02:/var/opt	1785856	1241872	539752	70%	/var/opt

```
# cat /etc/mtab | grep nfs
```

Unmounting a Resource

Follow the steps below to unmount a remote resource on an NFS client:

1. Make certain no users are accessing the resource (*/usr/share/man* for example). If a non-critical process is using the resource or a user is sitting in it, list their PIDs and usernames using the *fuser* command with −u option:

   ```
   # fuser −cu /usr/share/man
   /usr/share/man:    6797c(root)
   ```

2. Kill any processes using the resource or wait until the processes are terminated. To kill all processes holding up the resource, use −k option with the *fuser* command:

   ```
   # fuser −ck /usr/share/man
   /usr/share/man:    6797c
   ```

3. Run the following to unmount the resource:

   ```
   # umount /usr/share/man
   ```

4. Edit */etc/fstab* and remove the associated entry if you wish to delete it for good.

Unexporting a Resource

After ensuring with the *showmount* command that the resource to be unexported is not mounted by any clients, do the following on the NFS server to unexport it:

> # **exportfs –u /usr/share/man**

If you unexport a mounted resource, the next time a user on that client requests access to the resource, NFS will return "NFS stale file handle" error message.

To unexport all resources listed in */var/lib/nfs/etab* file, use the *exportfs* command with –au options:

> # **exportfs –au**

Monitoring NFS Activities

Monitoring NFS activities typically involves capturing and displaying NFS statistics between a client and server. A tool called *nfsstat* may be used for this purpose. This command supports options such as –c, –s and –r to capture client, server and RPC activities, respectively. With –m option, it displays all activities on mounted resources.

Here is a sample output of this command when run without any options:

> # **nfsstat**
> Server rpc stats:

calls	badcalls	badauth	badclnt	xdrcall
141	0	0	0	0

> Server nfs v3:

null	getattr	setattr	lookup	access	readlink
28 23%	37 31%	0 0%	2 1%	4 3%	0 0%
read	write	create	mkdir	symlink	mknod
0 0%	0 0%	0 0%	0 0%	0 0%	0 0%
remove	rmdir	rename	link	readdir	readdirplus
0 0%	0 0%	0 0%	0 0%	0 0%	1 0%

> . . . .

Understanding AutoFS

In previous sections, you learned about NFS and how to mount an NFS exported resource on a client. This is the standard mount method. In this section, you are going to look at the AutoFS (*Auto File System*) service that offers another method of mounting a resource.

AutoFS is the NFS client-side service, which automatically mounts an NFS resource on an as-needed basis. When an activity occurs in the mount point with a command such as *ls* or *cd*, the associated NFS resource gets mounted. When the resource is no longer accessed for a pre-defined period of time, it automatically gets unmounted.

Features and Benefits

There are several features and benefits associated with the AutoFS mount method as compared to the standard NFS mount method, and are described below:

- ✓ AutoFS requires that NFS resources be defined in text configuration files called *maps*, which are typically located in the */etc* directory. These maps may be managed centrally via NIS or LDAP. In contrast, the standard NFS mount information is defined in the */etc/fstab* file for each NFS resource that needs to be mounted automatically at system reboots. Additionally, the */etc/fstab* file must be maintained separately on each NFS client system.
- ✓ AutoFS does not require *root* privileges to mount available NFS resources. In comparison, with the standard NFS mount method, only *root* can mount them.
- ✓ With AutoFS, the NFS client boot process never hangs if the NFS server is down or inaccessible. With the standard NFS mount, when a client system boots up and an NFS server listed in the */etc/fstab* file is unavailable, the client may hang until either the mount request times out or the NFS server becomes available.
- ✓ With AutoFS, a resource is unmounted automatically if it is not accessed for ten minutes by default. With the standard NFS mount method, a resource stays mounted until it is manually unmounted or the client system shuts down.
- ✓ AutoFS supports wildcard characters and environment variables, whereas, the standard NFS mount method does not.
- ✓ A special map is available with AutoFS that mounts all available NFS resources from a reachable NFS server when a user requests access to a resource on that server without explicitly defining each one of them. The standard mount method does not have any such features available.

How AutoFS Works?

AutoFS service consists of a daemon called *automount* that mounts configured resources automatically when accessed. This daemon is invoked at system boot up. It reads the AutoFS master map and creates initial mount point entries in the */etc/mtab* file; however, the resources are not actually mounted at this time. When a user activity occurs under one of the initial mount points, the daemon contacts the *rpc.mountd* daemon on the NFS server and actually mounts the requested resource. If the resource remains idle for a certain time period, *automount* unmounts it by itself.

AutoFS uses RPC and its daemon is stateless and multi-threaded.

AutoFS Configuration File

The default configuration file for AutoFS is */etc/sysconfig/autofs*. This file is consulted when the AutoFS service is started or restarted. An excerpt from this file is shown below:

```
# cat /etc/sysconfig/autofs
MASTER_MAP_NAME="auto.master"
TIMEOUT=600
NEGATIVE_TIMEOUT=60
BROWSE_MODE="yes"
APPEND_OPTIONS="yes"
LOGGING="none"
OPTIONS=""
```

Several variables can be set in the file to modify the default behavior. Some of them are shown above and described in Table 26-7.

Option	Description
MASTER_MAP_NAME	Defines the master map name to be used. Default is /etc/auto.master.
TIMEOUT	Specifies, in seconds, the maximum idle time after which a resource is automatically unmounted. Default is 600.
NEGATIVE_TIMEOUT	Specifies, in seconds, a timeout value for failed mount attempts. Default is 60.
BROWSE_MODE	Defines if maps are to be made browseable or otherwise.
APPEND_OPTIONS	Defines additional options to OPTIONS.
LOGGING	Specifies a logging level. By default, it is turned off. Other options are verbose and debug.
OPTIONS	Defines any global options.

Table 26-7 AutoFS Options

Managing AutoFS Start and Stop

The *automount* daemon can be started, restarted, reloaded and stopped manually. It can also be configured to autostart at specific run levels.

To start AutoFS service:

service autofs start
Starting automount: [OK]

To restart AutoFS service:

service autofs restart
Stopping automount: [OK]
Starting automount: [OK]

To force AutoFS to re-read its configuration:

service autofs reload
Reloading maps

To stop AutoFS:

service autofs stop
Stopping automount: [OK]

To enable AutoFS to autostart at each system reboot:

chkconfig autofs on

To check the status of AutoFS:

```
# service autofs status
automount (pid 9050) is running...
```

The AutoFS Maps

As you know, AutoFS mounts NFS resources on-demand only. For this, it needs to know the resources to be mounted, source NFS server names and any mount options to be used. All this information is defined in AutoFS map files.

There are four types of AutoFS maps: *master*, *special*, *direct* and *indirect*. The following sub-sections examine each one of them.

Defining the Master Map

The */etc/auto.master* file is the default master map, which contains special, direct and indirect map information, and is defined in the */etc/sysconfig/autofs* file with the MASTER_MAP_NAME directive. A sample */etc/auto.master* file is shown below that displays how the three map entries look like:

```
# cat /etc/auto.master
/net        –hosts
/–          auto.direct
/misc       /etc/auto.misc
```

The first entry is for a special map directing AutoFS to use –hosts special map whenever a user attempts to access anything under */net*.

The second entry is for a direct map telling AutoFS to look for information in */etc/auto.direct* file.

The last entry is for an indirect map notifying AutoFS to refer to the */etc/auto.misc* file for further information. The umbrella mount point */misc* will precede all mount point entries listed in the */etc/auto.misc* file.

Defining the Special Map

The –hosts special map allows all resources exported by all accessible NFS servers to get mounted under the */net* directory without explicitly mounting each one of them. The */etc/auto.net* file is executed to obtain a list of accessible servers and available exported resources. Accessing */net/<NFS_server>* will cause AutoFS to automatically mount all resources available to the client from that NFS server. By default, an entry "/net –hosts" exists in the */etc/auto.master* file for this type of map, and is enabled. Do an *ll* on */net* to see which NFS servers are accessible:

```
# ll /net
dr-xr-xr-x  2  root  root  0  Jan 23  10:35  rhel02
```

The output indicates that NFS server *rhel02* is accessible and have resources available for mounting. *cd* into */net/rhel02* for further information.

The –hosts map is not recommended in an environment where there are many NFS servers exporting many resources as AutoFS mounts all available resources whether they are needed or not.

Defining a Direct Map

A direct map is used to mount resources automatically on any number of unrelated mount points. Some key points to note when working with direct maps are:

- ✓ Direct mounted resources are always visible to users.
- ✓ Local and direct mounted resources can co-exist under one parent directory.
- ✓ Each direct map entry adds an entry to the */etc/mtab* file.
- ✓ Accessing a directory containing many direct mount points mounts all resources.

Let us use a direct map on a client to mount the four resources from NFS server *rhel02*:

1. Edit */etc/auto.master* and add the following if it does not already exist:

       /–   /etc/auto.direct

   Each direct map entry consists of three fields: the first field is always /–, which identifies the entry as a direct map entry, the second field is optional and specifies any mount options (not shown) and the third field points to the direct map file where actual NFS server resource and mount point information is located.

2. Create */etc/auto.direct* file with the following entries:

/usr/share/man	–ro,sync	rhel02:/usr/share/man
/home	–rw,sync	rhel02:/home
/var/opt	–rw,sync	rhel02:/var/opt
/usr/local/bin	–rw,sync	rhel02:/usr/local/bin

3. Execute the following to force *automount* daemon to reload maps:

   # **service autofs reload**

4. Execute the *ll* command on each resource and then the *mount* command to verify that the resources are mounted and available for use:

   # **ll /usr/local/bin /usr/share/man /var/opt /home**
   # **mount –v | grep nfs**
   rhel02:/usr/local/bin on /usr/local/bin type nfs (rw,sync,addr=192.168.0.202)
   rhel02:/usr/share/man on /usr/share/man type nfs (ro,sync,addr=192.168.0.202)
   rhel02:/var/opt on /var/opt type nfs (rw,sync,addr=192.168.0.202)
   rhel02:/home on /home type nfs (rw,sync,addr=192.168.0.202)

Defining an Indirect Map

An indirect map is used to automatically mount resources under one common parent directory. Some key points to note when working with indirect maps are:

- ✓ Indirect mounted resources only become visible after being accessed.
- ✓ Local and indirect mounted resources cannot co-exist under the same parent directory.
- ✓ Each indirect map puts only one entry in the */etc/mtab* file.

✓ Accessing a directory containing many indirect mount points shows only the resources that are already mounted.

Let us use an indirect map to mount */usr/share/man* and */var/opt* resources from NFS server *rhel02*:

1. Edit */etc/auto.master* and ensure that the following default indirect map entry is defined:

   /misc   /etc/auto.misc

2. Edit */etc/auto.misc* file and add the following two entries to it. Each entry in this map has three fields: the first field identifies the relative pathname of a mount point directory, the second field is optional and specifies any mount options to be used and the third field identifies a resource to be mounted on the mount point identified in the first field.

   ```
   man          –ro,sync      rhel02:/usr/share/man
   opt          –rw,sync      rhel02:/var/opt
   bin          –rw,sync      rhel02:/usr/local
   ```

3. Execute the following to force *automount* daemon to reload maps:

   # **service autofs reload**

4. AutoFS creates *man*, *opt* and *bin* mount point sub-directories under */misc* as soon as it is forced to re-read and reload maps. Execute the *ll* command on each mount point and then run the *mount* command to verify that the resources are mounted and available for use:

   # **ll /misc/man /misc/opt /misc/bin**
   # **mount –v | grep rhel02**
   rhel02:/usr/share/man on /misc/man type nfs (ro,sync,addr=192.168.0.202)
   rhel02:/var/opt on /misc/opt type nfs (rw,sync,addr=192.168.0.202)
   rhel02:/usr/local on /misc/bin type nfs (rw,sync,addr=192.168.0.202)

There are several other entries pre-defined in the */etc/auto.misc* file for automounting CD, floppy and other removable media. Except for CD, which is configured to be automounted on */misc/cd* mount point, automounting other media is disabled by default. You need to uncomment the line entries for the media that you wish to be using and then force *automount* to reload the maps. An excerpt from the file is shown below:

cat /etc/auto.misc

```
. . . . . . . .
cd            -fstype=iso9660,ro,nosuid,nodev   :/dev/cdrom
# the following entries are samples to pique your imagination
#linux        -ro,soft,intr        ftp.example.org:/pub/linux
#boot         -fstype=ext2         :/dev/hda1
#floppy       -fstype=auto         :/dev/fd0
#floppy       -fstype=ext2         :/dev/fd0
#e2floppy     -fstype=ext2         :/dev/fd0
#jaz          -fstype=ext2         :/dev/sdc1
#removable    -fstype=ext2         :/dev/hdd
```

Mounting User Home Directories

AutoFS allows using two special characters in indirect maps. These special characters are & and *, and are used to replace references to NFS servers and mount points.

For example, with user home directories located under */home* and exported by more than one servers, the *automount* daemon will contact all available and reachable NFS servers concurrently when a user attempts to log in on an NFS client system. The daemon will mount only that user's home directory rather than the entire */home*. The indirect map entry for this type of substitution will look like:

```
*    –rw,soft,intr      &:/home/&
```

With this simple entry in place, there is no need to update any AutoFS configuration if NFS servers with */home* exported are added or removed. Similarly, if user home directories are added or deleted, there will be no impact on AutoFS.

The above entry can be placed in a separate map file such as */etc/auto.home*, in which case you will need to reflect the map name in the *auto.master* file as follows. The timeout value determines a period of inactivity in seconds for the resource to get unmounted automatically. If this value is not set, the default of 600 seconds takes effect as defined in the */etc/sysconfig/autofs* file.

```
/home       /etc/auto.home    --timeout=180
```

Reload the autofs maps after the changes have been completed.

Summary

This chapter introduced you to one of the most common system administration tasks, the Network File System. You learned and understood concepts, benefits, versions, security, daemons, commands, related files and startup scripts pertaining to Network File System. You studied how NFS server and client interact with each other, and looked at procedures for configuring them. You used commands that displayed exported and mounted NFS resources, unmounted and unexported resources, and captured and displayed NFS activity data.

You looked at Auto File System. You learned concepts, features and benefits associated with it. You were presented with information that helped you understand how it worked. You looked at associated daemon, command and configuration file.

You studied four types of AutoFS maps, their relationship and how to set them up. You looked at related advantages and disadvantages, and how only needed user home directories could be mounted from an available NFS server.

## 27

Samba

This chapter covers the following major topics:

✓ Describe Samba and and its features
✓ SELinux requirements for Samba
✓ Samba daemons, commands, configuration files and scripts
✓ Understand Samba software packages
✓ Configure a Samba server for file sharing using commands, Samba Server Configurator and SWAT
✓ Access a Samba share on RHEL and Windows
✓ Access a Windows share on RHEL

Common *Internet File System* (CIFS), originally called *Server Message Block* (SMB), is a networking protocol developed by Microsoft, IBM and Intel in late 1980s to enable Windows-based PCs to share file and print resources. This protocol has been in use in Windows operating systems as the primary native protocol for these purposes. On the other hand, software called *Samba* was developed in the Linux world to share the two types of resources with Microsoft systems using the SMB format. This allowed Linux systems to participate in Microsoft Windows workgroups and domains. As well, Samba allowed Linux systems to share file and print resources with other Linux systems, and UNIX.

Understanding Samba

In Samba terminology, the system that offers its file and print resources for sharing is referred to as *Samba server* and the system that accesses the resources is referred to as *Samba client*.

Features of Samba

Some common features of Samba are:

- ✓ Samba shares can be accessed on Windows systems as standard drive letters, and can be navigated via "Windows Explorer" or "Network Neighborhood".
- ✓ Windows shares can be mounted as Samba resources on RHEL.
- ✓ Samba server can be configured as a *Primary Domain Controller* (PDC) in Windows environment.
- ✓ Samba server can act as a *Windows Internet Name Service* (WINS) client or server.
- ✓ Samba server can be configured as an Active Directory member server on a Windows network.
- ✓ Samba server can act as a print server for Windows-based CIFS clients.
- ✓ RHEL and Windows domain usernames and passwords can be used on either platform for authentication.
- ✓ Samba shares can be accessed on other RHEL, Linux and UNIX systems, and vice versa.

SELinux Requirements for Samba

If SELinux is enforced, you need to disable its protection for Samba service to ensure smooth functionality. Use the *setsebool* command as demonstrated below, or the SELinux Configurator *system-config-selinux* as explained in Chapter 30 "System and Network Security". Specify only those Booleans that need to be disabled, leave others intact.

```
# setsebool –P samba_export_all_ro=1 samba_export_all_rw=1 samba_share_nfs=1 \
samba_enable_home_dirs=1 allow_smbd_anon_write=1 use_samba_home_dirs=1 \
nmbd_disable_trans=1 smbd_disable_trans=1 winbind_disable_trans=1
```

Use the *getsebool* command to verify:

```
# getsebool samba_export_all_ro samba_export_all_rw samba_share_nfs \
samba_enable_home_dirs allow_smbd_anon_write use_samba_home_dirs \
nmbd_disable_trans smbd_disable_trans winbind_disable_trans
samba_export_all_ro --> on
```

```
samba_export_all_rw --> on
samba_share_nfs --> on
samba_enable_home_dirs --> on
allow_smbd_anon_write --> on
use_samba_home_dirs --> on
nmbd_disable_trans --> on
smbd_disable_trans --> on
winbind_disable_trans --> on
```

Samba Daemons, Commands, Configuration Files and Scripts

When working with Samba, several daemons, commands, configuration files and scripts are involved. The tables given below list and explain them.

Table 27-1 describes Samba daemons.

Daemon	Description
smbd	Samba server daemon. Manages user authentication, resource locking, browser services and resource sharing.
nmbd	NetBIOS service daemon.

Table 27-1 Samba Daemons

Table 27-2 describes Samba commands.

Command	Description
mount	Client-side command to mount a Samba resource with *root* privileges.
mount.cifs	Client-side command to mount a Samba resource without *root* privileges.
nmblookup	Client-side command to query a WINS server.
smbclient	Client-side command to connect to Samba resources.
smbpasswd	Configures Samba users and passwords.
smbprint	Sends a print job to a Samba printer.
smbstatus	Displays the status of Samba connections.
testparm	Server-side command to test syntax of the */etc/samba/smb.conf* file.
umount	Client-side command to unmount a Samba resource with *root* privileges.
umount.cifs	Client-side command to unmount a Samba resource without *root* privileges.

Table 27-2 Samba Commands

Table 27-3 describes Samba configuration and functional files.

File	Description
/etc/samba/smb.conf	Samba server configuration file.
/etc/samba/smbusers	Maintains Samba and RHEL user mappings.
/etc/samba/smbpasswd	Maintains Samba user passwords. This file is used for authentication purposes.
/var/log/samba	Directory location for Samba log files.
/etc/sysconfig/samba	Contains default variables used when Samba is started.

Table 27-3 Samba Configuration and Functional Files

Table 27-4 describes Samba startup and shutdown script.

Scripts	Description
/etc/rc.d/init.d/smb	Starts and stops Samba daemons.

Table 27-4 Samba Startup and Shutdown Script

Understanding Samba Software Packages

There are several software packages that need to be installed on the system in order for it to be configured as a Samba server or client, or both. Samba support is added when Windows File Server software package group is chosen at install time. Table 27-5 describes the packages.

Package	Description
samba	Contains Samba server software.
samba-client	Contains Samba client software.
samba-common	Contains Samba man pages and general commands.
samba-swat	Contains Samba web administration tool.
system-config-samba	The Red Hat graphical Samba Server Configurator tool.

Table 27-5 Samba Software Packages

Configuring Samba for File Sharing

This section covers configuring a Samba server for sharing a resource and accessing it on another RHEL and a Windows system. It also describes how to mount a Windows share on RHEL.

Configuring a Samba Server Using Commands

Here are the steps to configure a Samba server to share /usr/share/man, /home and /var/spool/mail directories:

1. Check whether the required Samba software packages are installed:

   # **rpm –qa | grep samba**
   samba-swat-3.0.33-3.7.el5
   system-config-samba-1.2.41-3.el5
   samba-common-3.0.33-3.7.el5
   samba-client-3.0.33-3.7.el5
   samba-3.0.33-3.7.el5

   Install the packages if they are not already loaded using one of the software package installation methods described in Chapter 11 "Software Package Management".

2. Execute the following to make Samba autostart at system reboots:

   # **chkconfig smb on**

3. Allow traffic on port 445 to pass through the firewall, or simply stop and disable the firewall if it is not used. Consult Chapter 30 "System and Network Security" on how to perform these tasks.
4. Edit *smb.conf* file and specify names of resources to be shared, as well as other parameters. There are two major sections – Global Settings and Share Definitions – in the file. The former defines parameters that affect overall Samba behavior, and includes options for networking, logging, standalone server, domain members, domain controller, browser control, name resolution, printing and file systems. The latter defines share-specific attributes for home directories, printers and any other custom shares. Descriptions of some common attributes are given in Table 27-6. Note that # represents general comments and ; represents disabled Samba parameters in the file.

Parameter	Description
browseable	"yes" allows users on client systems to be able to browse files and directories.
authentication server	Used with domain and server authentication modes.
comment	Any description.
default case	Sets letter case.
dns proxy	"yes" to enable searches to use DNS.
encrypt passwords	"yes" to encrypt user passwords.
guest account	Specifies the name of a user account from */etc/passwd* that you wish to give guest access.
guest ok	"yes" enables guest account.
hosts allow	Allows specified network addresses to be able to access the shares.
interfaces	Specifies network and host IP addresses to be served in case there are more than one network interfaces.
invalid users	Disallows access to the specified users.
kerberos realm	Used with the active directory authentication mode.
log file	Defines a log file name in */var/log/samba* directory.
max log size	Specifies a size in KBs for the log file to grow before it is rotated.
netbios name	Name of the RHEL Samba server.
only guest	Allows access to only the guest user.
passdb backend	Used with security = user. Three options are supported: smbpasswd = uses */etc/samba/smbpasswd* file for authentication. tdbsam = uses trivial database. ldapsam = uses an LDAP database.
password server	Specifies the name of a server to be used for user authentication if security is set to domain or share.
path	Sets absolute path to the share.
printable	Section definition is for a printer.
printing	Defines "cups" as the default sub-system for printing.
public	"yes" creates public accessible resources.
read only	"yes" allows read-only access to resources.
realm	Specifies the name of an active directory realm if security is set to ads.
security	Defines one of the five supported security levels:

Parameter	Description
	ads = performs authentication from an active directory server.
	domain = performs authentication from a domain controller.
	server = performs authentication from a server.
	share = this system will be part of a peer to peer workgroup where the Samba users will be able to browse share contents without entering their login credentials.
	user = matches usernames/passwords with those on individual Windows systems. This is the default.
server string	Any description.
smb passwd file	Defines Samba user password file. Default is */etc/samba/smbpasswd*.
valid users	Allows full access to the specified users and groups only. Group names are prefixed with the @ sign.
wins proxy	"yes" enables non-WINS systems to use WINS proxy.
wins server	Sets IP address or hostname of a remote WINS server.
wins support	"yes" enables WINS server functionality on the local system.
workgroup	Name of Windows workgroup or domain.
writable	"yes" enables writing to the share.
write list	List of users and groups who can write to the share. Group names are prefixed with the @ sign.

Table 27-6 Samba Configuration Parameters

5. Append the following sections to the *smb.conf* file and comment out any duplicate entries conflicting with these:

```
[global]
        netbios name    = rhel01
        workgroup       = localwg
        server string   = Samba Server
        passdb backend  = smbpasswd
        hosts allow     = 192.168.0. 192.168.1. .getitcertify.com
        security        = user
        log file        = /var/log/samba/%m.log
        max log size    = 50
        load printers   = yes
        printcap name   = /etc/printcap

[project1]
        comment         = Project1 directory available to users aghori and bghori, and members of
                          project1 group
        browseable      = yes
        path            = /project1
        valid users     = aghori bghori @project1
        writable        = yes

[project2]
        comment         = Project2 directory with read/write permissions to users aghori and
                          bghori, and read permission to everyone else
```

browseable	= yes
path	= /project2
public	= no
writeable	= no
write list	= aghori bghori

6. Execute the *testparm* command to check for any syntax errors in the file. Use –v option to display all other default parameters that are not defined in the file.

 # testparm
Load smb config files from /etc/samba/smb.conf
Processing section "[project1]"
Processing section "[project2]"
Processing section "[printers]"
Loaded services file OK.
Server role: ROLE_STANDALONE
Press enter to see a dump of your service definitions

[global]
      workgroup = LOCALWG
      server string = Samba Server
      log file = /var/log/samba/%m.log
      max log size = 50
      printcap name = /etc/printcap
      hosts allow = 192.168.0., 192.168.1., .getitcertify.com

[project1]
      comment = Project1 directory available to users aghori and bghori, and members of project1 group
      path = /project1
      valid users = aghori, bghori, @project1
      read only = No

[project2]
      comment = Project2 directory with read/write permissions to users aghori and bghori, and read permission to everyone else
      path = /project2
      write list = aghori, bghori

[printers]
      comment = All Printers
      path = /var/spool/samba
      printable = Yes
      browseable = Yes

The [project1] section defines */project1* directory to be accessed by users *aghori* and *bghori*, as well as members of *project1* group with full permissions and the ability to browse the directory from systems on the 192.168.0 and 192.168.1 networks and *getitcertify.com* domain.

The [project2] section defines */project2* directory to be accessed by users *aghori* and *bghori* with read/write permissions and the ability to browse the directory from systems on the 192.168.0 and 192.168.1 networks and *getitcertify.com* domain. All other users will have read-only access to the share with browsing capability.

The [printers] section is uncommented in the file by default and it typically requires no modifications. By default, all printers configured on the system and defined in the */etc/cups/printers.conf* file are shared as Samba shares.

For additional information refer to Table 27-5.

7. Create users *aghori* and *bghori*, group *project1* and shares */project1* and */project2* if they do not already exist.
8. Add users *aghori* and *bghori* to Samba configuration and assign them a password such as *Welcome01*. This password can be different from their Linux passwords. The information is stored in */etc/samba/smbpasswd* file.

```
# smbpasswd –a aghori
New SMB password:
Retype new SMB password:
Added user aghori.
# smbpasswd –a bghori
New SMB password:
Retype new SMB password:
Added user bghori.
```

Besides –a, there are certain other options to the *smbpasswd* command. Table 27-7 lists and explains them.

Option	Description
–d	Disables the specified user.
–e	Enables the specified user.
–r	Changes a user password on the specified system.
–U	Changes the specified user's password on the system specified with –r option.
–x	Deletes the specified user.

Table 27-7 smbpasswd Command Options

Do a *cat* on the *smbpasswd* file to view what the previous command has added to it:

```
# cat /etc/samba/smbpasswd
aghori:503:C23413A8A1E7665F73251AA2B4314B90:1D863479E1AB3BD62A2BFAFA1ABAA
2DD:[U       ]:LCT-4A0B1C18:
bghori:504:C23413A8A1E7665F73251AA2B4314B90:1D863479E1AB3BD62A2BFAFA1ABAA
2DD:[U       ]:LCT-4A0B1C1C:
```

9. Start (or restart) Samba server daemons, or use the reload option if they are already running:

```
# service smb start
Starting SMB services:                    [ OK ]
Starting NMB services:                     [ OK ]
```

10. Execute the following to check the operational status of Samba:

```
# service smb status
smbd (pid 7505 7476 7418) is running...
nmbd (pid 7479) is running...
```

Configuring a Samba Server via Samba Server Configurator

To configure a Samba server using the Red Hat Samba Server Configurator, follow the steps below:

1. Execute *system-config-samba* in an X terminal window or choose (GNOME) System / (KDE) Main Menu → System → Samba. The Samba Server Configurator screen will open up as shown in Figure 27-1.

Figure 27-1 Samba Server Configurator

2. Click Add Share and a new dialog box "Create Samba Share" will appear. Specify a directory, share name and any optional description in the Basic tab. Also choose if you want the share to be writable and visible. Writable allows the share to be available as read-write; visible makes the share browseable.

Figure 27-2 Samba Server Configurator – Create Samba Share – Basic

3. Switch to the Access tab as shown in Figure 27-3 and select one of the two choices to provide selected or all users access to the share. If you choose the first option, you will be asked to enter usernames as defined in the */etc/passwd* file. These users will be added to the */etc/samba/smbpasswd* file. Click OK when done.

Figure 27-3 Samba Server Configurator – Create Samba Share - Access

4. Select Preferences → Server Settings on the main menu. Specify a workgroup and any optional description in the Basic tab as shown in Figure 27-4.

Figure 27-4 Samba Server Configurator – Server Settings – Basic

5. Click the Security tab and define security attributes. Consult Table 27-5.

Figure 27-5 Samba Server Configurator – Server Settings – Security

6. Click Preferences → Samba Users on the main menu once again. Choose a username from "Unix Username", specify a "Windows Username" and supply a password. The password will be saved in the */etc/samba/smbpasswd* file. One recommendation is to use the same username on both Windows and RHEL if possible to avoid confusion. Click OK when done.

Figure 27-6 Samba Server Configurator – Create New Samba User

All configuration information entered in the Samba Server Configurator is saved in the */etc/samba/smb.conf* file.

Configuring a Samba Server via Samba Web Administration Tool

To configure a Samba server using the *Samba Web Administration Tool* (SWAT), perform the following steps:

1. Execute the following to enable SWAT functionality to autostart at each system reboot:

   # **chkconfig swat on**

2. Open up a browser window on your RHEL system and type the following URL. By default, SWAT uses port 901. See Figure 27-7.

   http://localhost:901

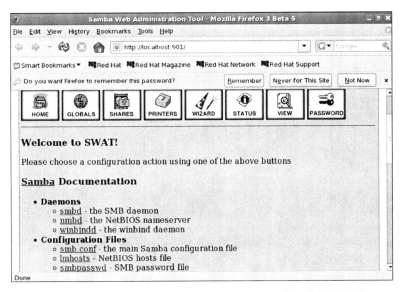

Figure 27-7 Samba Web Administration Tool (SWAT)

SWAT is more flexible, feature-rich and powerful than the Samba Server Configurator, and it provides a single interface for configuring and administering Samba shares along with offering a wealth of documentation on Samba. There are eight buttons across the top, of which GLOBALS

---

allows you to set and modify global parameters, SHARES and PRINTERS give you the ability to configure directory and print shares, WIZARD guides you through the configuration process, STATUS displays current status of the Samba server daemons, active connections and shares, VIEW displays current configuration and PASSWORD allows you to add, delete, enable or disable a Samba user account in addition to changing a user password.

Accessing a Samba Share on Another RHEL System

Here are the steps to access */project1* and */project2* shares on another RHEL system *rhel02*:

1. Log on to *rhel02* and ensure that the required Samba packages are installed as discussed earlier in this chapter.
2. Create mount points */project1* and */project2*:

   # **mkdir /project1 /project2**

3. Run the *smbclient* command to list available resources from *rhel01* using –L option and specify a username and associated password with –U option:

   # **smbclient –L rhel01 –U aghori%Welcome01**
   Domain=[RHEL01] OS=[Unix] Server=[Samba 3.0.33-3.7.el5]

   ```
           Sharename     Type     Comment
           ------------  ------   -----------
           IPC$          IPC      IPC Service (Samba Server)
           aghori        Disk     project1
           aghori        Disk     project2
   Domain=[RHEL01] OS=[Unix] Server=[Samba 3.0.33-3.7.el5]

           Server        Comment
           ---------     ------------


           Workgroup     Master
           -------------  ---------
           LOCALWG       RHEL01
           WORKGROUP     LOCALWG
   ```

4. Mount */project1* and */project2* using the *mount.cifs* command:

   # **mount.cifs //rhel01/project1 /project1 –o username=aghori –o **
   password=Welcome01
   # **mount.cifs //rhel01/project2 /project2 –o username=aghori –o **
   password=Welcome01

   The above can be executed as a regular user as well. As *root*, *mount* command with *–t cifs* may be used instead.

5. Execute the *smbstatus* command to verify the share:

```
# smbstatus
Samba version 3.0.33-3.7.el5
PID    Username    Group      Machine
-------------------------------------------------------------------
 5257  aghori      aghori     rhel01   (192.168.0.201)


Service   pid    machine         Connected at
-----------------------------------------------------
project1  3432   192.168.0.201   Sat Apr 18 00:37:41 2009
project2  3434   192.168.0.201   Sat Apr 18 00:37:43 2009

No locked files
```

Use the *df* or *mount* command to list the share and the *ll* command to list the contents.

6. If you wish the share to get automatically mounted each time *rhel02* is rebooted, edit */etc/fstab* file and add the following entries to it:

```
//rhel01/project1   /project1   cifs   credentials=/etc/samba/smbcred   0  0
//rhel01/project2   /project2   cifs   credentials=/etc/samba/smbcred   0  0
```

7. Create */etc/samba/smbcred* file and add the following to it:

```
# vi /etc/samba/smbcred
username=aghori
password=Welcome01
```

This setup ensures that the user credentials are obtained from the *smbcred* file when an attempt is made to mount the share.

With these entries placed in */etc/fstab* file, the shares can be manually mounted as:

```
# mount –at cifs
```

Another way of accessing the Samba share is to go to (GNOME) Places → Home Folder → File → Open Location. Enter smb:// and an icon associated with connected workgroups and/or domains will appear. Click the icon to view a list of all Windows and Samba systems with Samba shares available. Click *rhel01* and enter username and password when prompted to connect.

Accessing a Samba Share on Windows

The following procedure assumes that the Windows system has the hostname and IP address for *rhel01* defined in its *lmhosts* file. Verify that the Windows system is a member of the same workgroup or domain as the Samba server. To view this information, richt click My Computer, go to Properties and click Computer Name.

To access the shares, double click My Network Places and type the hostname of the Samba server as follows:

```
\\rhel01
```

Enter username and password as defined on the Samba server and a list of both shares will appear in the window that you can access as per the access rights defined. You may alternatively use Windows Explorer and type \\rhel01 to access the shares.

To map the shares as drives on the Windows system, right click My Computer and then click Map Network Drive. Enter the information for each share as per below:

        \\rhel01\project1
        \\rhel01\project2

This will connect to the Samba shares and display the contents.

Accessing a Windows Share on RHEL

The procedure to access a Windows-based share is exactly the same as discussed in sub-section "Accessing a Samba Share on Another RHEL System" with the exception that you will need to supply a correct hostname for the Windows server and a valid username and password for the share.

Unmounting a Share

Use the *umount* command and specify the Samba mount points to unmount the Samba shares:

 # umount /project1
 # umount /project2

Summary

This chapter discussed Samba. It provided an understanding of Samba features and listed SELinux requirements for it. The chapter described Samba daemons, commands, configurations files, scripts, and provided basic information on Samba software packages. It explained how to configure a Samba server for sharing files using commands, the Samba Server Configurator and Samba Web Administration Tool. The chapter further explained how a RHEL share could be accessed on another RHEL system and a Windows system, and how a Windows share could be accessed on a RHEL system.

28

Network Installation

This chapter covers the following major topics:

- ✓ Overview of network installation servers
- ✓ Configure NFS, FTP and HTTP installation servers
- ✓ Install RHEL using network installation servers
- ✓ Methods of booting a client system
- ✓ Prepare a bootable CD and a USB drive
- ✓ Boot and install RHEL via installation CD, bootable CD and USB drive
- ✓ Linux askmethod
- ✓ Benefits of using kickstart
- ✓ Create kickstart configuration file
- ✓ Install using kickstart
- ✓ Network boot

Installing RHEL on a computer from a network installation server is much faster than installing it via local CD/DVD media. What is required is a good working network link and approximately 4GB of disk space on the installation server to store the CD/DVD software image. RHEL supports three types of installation servers that are based on NFS, FTP and HTTP protocols. A client system where RHEL needs to be installed can be booted locally and then redirected to one of these network installation servers for loading the software. The client system can be configured during the installation or supplied with a file that contains all configuration information including disk partitioning. This way there is no need to go through the configuration process during installation, which makes the installation faster and fully automated. The most advanced form of installation can be invoked by booting the client system off a network boot server and then performing configuration and software loading using the same or another network installation server.

Configuring Network Installation Servers

The following sub-sections describe how to configure NFS, FTP and HTTP installation servers. On these servers, you can either copy the contents of installation CDs or the ISO images.

Configuring an NFS Installation Server

To configure an NFS installation server, follow the steps below:

1. Create a directory such as */rhel52/install_media* for storing RHEL installation software. Make sure that there is ~4GB free space available to hold the software. If not, create a separate partition or logical volume, format to ext3 file system type and mount it on */rhel52/install_media*. Follow the procedure in Chapter 13 "Disk Partitioning" and Chapter 14 "File Systems and Swap" on how to do it.
2. Perform a copy operation:

   For copying CD contents:

   a. Load installation CD 1 of 5 in the drive. The CD will automatically get mounted at */media/"RHEL-5.2 i386 Disc 1"* if you are using GUI. Otherwise, run the following to mount it on */mnt*:

      # **mount /dev/cdrom /mnt**

   b. Copy the entire directory structure to */rhel52/install_media*. The following assumes that the CD is mounted on */mnt*:

      # **cp –var /mnt/. /rhel52/install_media**

   c. Unmount and eject the CD after the *cp* command is finished:

      # **umount /mnt**
      # **eject**

   Repeat steps a through c for the rest of the CDs. Overwrite any files as prompted.

For copying ISO images, simply upload the images that were downloaded in Chapter 09 "Installation" into */rhel52/install_media*.

3. Disable SELinux protection for NFS. Consult Chapter 26 "NFS and AutoFS" on how to do it.
4. Allow NFS traffic to pass through the firewall, or simply stop and disable the firewall if it is not used. Consult Chapter 30 "System and Network Security" on how to perform these tasks.
5. Start (or restart) NFS service:

   # service nfs start

6. Append the following to */etc/exports* file using the vi editor or the NFS Configurator:

   /rhel52/install_media *(ro)

7. Export the directory:

   # exportfs –a

8. Run the following to check the status of the export:

   # exportfs

This completes the procedure for configuring an NFS installation server.

Configuring an FTP Installation Server

To configure an FTP installation server using very secure FTP, follow the steps below:

1. Perform steps 1 and 2 from the previous sub-section to copy installation software.
2. Disable SELinux protection for vsFTP. Consult Chapter 24 "Internet Services and Electronic Mail" on how to do it.
3. Perform step 4 from the previous sub-section to modify or disable the firewall.
4. Start (or restart) vsFTP service:

   # service vsftpd start

This completes the procedure for configuring an FTP installation server.

Configuring an HTTP Installation Server

To configure an HTTP installation server using the Apache web server, follow the steps below:

1. Perform steps 1 and 2 from "Configuring an NFS Installation Server" earlier in this chapter.
2. Disable SELinux protection for HTTP. Consult Chapter 29 "Web and Caching Proxy Servers" on how to do it.
3. Perform step 4 from "Configuring an NFS Installation Server" earlier in this chapter to modify or disable the firewall.
4. Start (or restart) HTTP service:

   # service httpd start

This completes the procedure for configuring an HTTP installation server.

Installing RHEL Using Network Installation Servers

There are several methods that you can employ the network installation servers discussed in the previous section to install RHEL on a client system. In this section you will perform a local boot via USB or CD/DVD and then install RHEL from the installation servers.

Methods of Booting a Client

There are four methods of booting a client and pointing it to a network source for RHEL installation. These methods are:

1. Booting locally with installation CD 1 or DVD
2. Booting locally with a bootable CD
3. Booting locally with a bootable USB drive
4. Booting remotely using PXE (*Pre-Execution Environment* or *Preboot Execution Environment*)

You can use any of these methods to begin a network installation. For #2 and #3 you will need to copy a boot file to a CD and USB to make them bootable. #4 is covered later in this chapter. The following sub-sections explain how to prepare a bootable CD and USB drive.

Preparing a Bootable CD

To prepare a bootable CD, copy *boot.iso* file from the first installation CD on to an empty CD. Run the following series of commands to copy the file from */mnt/images* to the */var/tmp* directory assuming the installation CD is mounted on */mnt*. Then eject the CD, insert an empty CD and run the *cdrecord* command. In the example below, */dev/hda* represents a PATA CD drive.

```
# cd /mnt/images && cp boot.iso /var/tmp
# eject
# cdrecord dev=/dev/hda –v /var/tmp/boot.iso
```

Preparing a Bootable USB Drive

To prepare a bootable USB drive, copy *diskboot.img* file from the first installation CD on to an empty USB drive. Run the following to copy the file from */mnt/images* to */dev/sdg* with an assumption that the installation CD is mounted on */mnt* and the device file for the USB drive is */dev/sdg*:

```
# cd /mnt/images && cat diskboot.img > /dev/sdg
```

Installing RHEL Using Installation CD, Bootable CD or USB Drive

Follow the steps below to begin installing RHEL:

1. Insert the first installation CD or the bootable CD in the drive, or insert the bootable USB drive in an available port.

Red Hat Certified Technician & Engineer

2. Boot the system and press Esc. A Boot Menu will appear as shown in Figure 28-1. Choose Removable Devices to boot off the USB drive or CD-ROM Drive for the CD medium. Press Enter to continue.

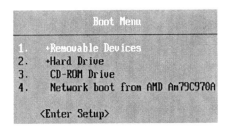

Figure 28-1 Boot Source Selection

3. The boot: prompt will appear if you have booted the system with the installation CD. Type "linux askmethod" at the prompt and press Enter. Go to step 6 if you have used the bootable CD or the USB drive to boot.

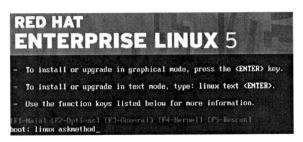

Figure 28-2 boot: Prompt

4. Choose a language to be used during the installation process. The default is English. Select a different language if you wish to. Press OK to continue.

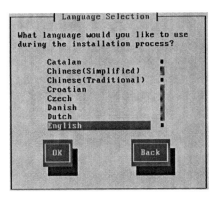

Figure 28-3 Language Selection

5. Choose a keyboard model attached to the computer. The default is the "US" keyboard. Select a different keyboard model if you wish to. Press OK to continue.

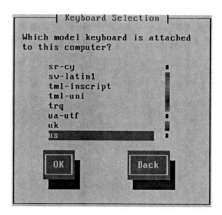

Figure 28-4 Keyboard Selection

6. The next screen will present a list of five installation methods – local CDROM, hard drive, NFS image, FTP and HTTP. Refer to Figure 28-5.

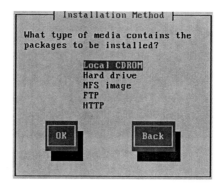

Figure 28-5 Installation Method Selection

Here is an explanation of the five methods:

Local CDROM – choose this method if you want to perform installation using RHEL installation CDs/DVD. Chapter 09 "Installation" covered this option at length.
Hard drive – choose this method if you have installation files or ISO images located on another up and running Linux or Windows partition on the same system.
NFS image – choose this method if you have installation files or ISO images located on a configured NFS server.
FTP – choose this method if you have installation files or ISO images located on a configured FTP server.
HTTP – choose this method if you have installation files or ISO images located on a configured HTTP server.

Choose NFS, FTP or HTTP as appropriate for this demonstration and press Enter.

7. Choose DHCP to get TCP/IP information for the new system or enter the information manually. Do not select "Enable IPv6 support".

Red Hat Certified Technician & Engineer

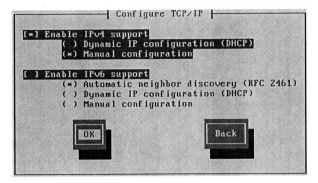

Figure 28-6 Configure TCP/IP

8. Enter IP address, netmask and gateway address to be assigned to this system as shown in Figure 28-7. Press OK to continue.

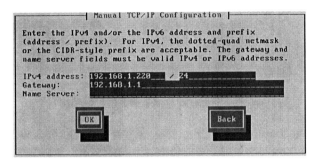

Figure 28-7 Manual TCP/IP Configuration

9. Supply the IP address for the NFS, FTP or HTTP server and the path where the installation files or ISO images are located. Figures 28-8, 28-9 and 28-10 display NFS, FTP and HTTP setup screens.

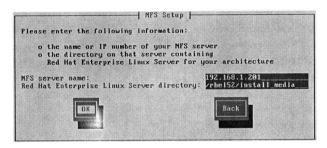

Figure 28-8 NFS Setup

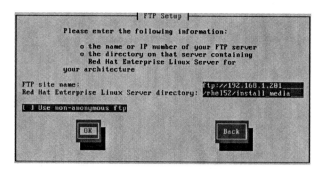

Figure 28-9 FTP Setup

Figure 28-10 HTTP Setup

10. If the information supplied in the previous step is correct, the installation of RHEL will begin and you will see graphical installation screens appearing one after the other showing progress as you saw them during the local CD installation method covered in Chapter 09 "Installation".

Installing RHEL via Kickstart

Kickstart allows you to perform a hands-off, fully-customized and faster installation of RHEL. What you need to do is to create a single configuration file and supply its name to the installation program, which will use the configuration information defined in the file to install and configure RHEL on the system. This eliminates the lengthy question / answer session that you would otherwise have to go through. The following are major advantages associated with using this method of installation:

✓ Fully automated, unattended installation.
✓ No configuration questions asked.
✓ Simultaneous installation on a number of systems.
✓ Identical configuration on a number of systems.
✓ Rapid deployment of any number of servers.

There are four major steps that need to be done in order to perform a successful kickstart installation. These steps are:

1. Making installation files/images available.
2. Creating kickstart configuration file.
3. Copying the kickstart configuration file to a USB, CD or network drive.

4. Beginning the installation process.

The following sub-sections explain each step.

Making Installation Files / Images Available

This step is to copy the installation files or ISO images to a directory and make that directory available over the network via NFS, FTP or HTTP protocol. See section "Configuring Network Installation Servers" earlier in this chapter for details.

Creating Kickstart Configuration File

Before you begin an automated kickstart installation, you will need to create a file and capture all required configuration information in it. This information will be used by kickstart to install and configure the system accordingly. You can create this file by either customizing */root/anaconda-ks.cfg* file or running the Red Hat Kickstart Configurator *system-config-kickstart* (or *ksconfig*). Both methods are explained below.

Using the /root/anaconda-ks.cfg File

During performing RHEL installation in Chapter 09 "Installation" and earlier in this chapter, you entered several pieces of configuration information. The installation program stored that information in the */root/anaconda-ks.cfg* file. You can customize this file as per requirements and use it for other client deployments.

The following displays contents of the *anaconda-ks.cfg* file, which was generated from the installation performed in Chapter 09 "Installation". Make a copy of this file such as */root/ks.cfg* and modify it for an install on a new system to be called *rhel10* with IP 192.168.0.210.

```
# cp /root/anaconda-ks.cfg /root/ks.cfg
# nl /root/ks.cfg
     1  # Kickstart file automatically generated by anaconda.
     2  install
     3  cdrom
     4  key --skip
     5  lang en_US.UTF-8
     6  keyboard us
     7  xconfig --defaultdesktop=GNOME --startxonboot
     8  network --device eth0 --bootproto static --ip 192.168.0.210 --netmask 255.255.255.0 --gateway
192.168.0.1 --nameserver 192.168.0.1 --hostname rhel10 --noipv6
     9  rootpw --iscrypted $1$J.Mh0drs$McLlyW1/JIzUg8zzI44mP1
    10  firewall --enabled --port=22:tcp
    11  authconfig --enableshadow --enablemd5
    12  selinux --enforcing
    13  timezone --utc America/New_York
    14  reboot
    15  firstboot --disable
    16  zerombr
    17  bootloader --location=mbr --driveorder=sda,sdb --append="rhgb quiet"
    18  # The following is the partition information you requested
```

```
19  # Note that any partitions you deleted are not expressed
20  # here so unless you clear all partitions first, this is
21  # not guaranteed to work
22  #clearpart --linux
23  #part /boot --fstype ext3 --size=1000 --ondisk=sda --asprimary
24  #part pv.4 --size=0 --grow --ondisk=sda
25  #volgroup vg00 --pesize=32768 pv.4
26  #logvol / --fstype ext3 --name=lvol1 --vgname=vg00 --size=1984
27  #logvol /home --fstype ext3 --name=lvol2 --vgname=vg00 --size=992
28  #logvol /tmp --fstype ext3 --name=lvol3 --vgname=vg00 --size=1984
29  #logvol /usr --fstype ext3 --name=lvol4 --vgname=vg00 --size=4992
30  #logvol /var --fstype ext3 --name=lvol5 --vgname=vg00 --size=4992
31  #logvol /opt --fstype ext3 --name=lvol6 --vgname=vg00 --size=4992
32  #logvol swap --fstype swap --name=lvol7 --vgname=vg00 --size=8000
33  %packages
34  @editors
35  @system-tools
36  @text-internet
37  @legacy-network-server
38  @dns-server
39  @gnome-desktop
40  @core
41  @base
42  @ftp-server
43  @network-server
44  @java
45  @legacy-software-support
46  @smb-server
47  @base-x
48  @graphics
49  @web-server
50  @printing
51  @kde-desktop
52  @mail-server
53  @server-cfg
54  @sound-and-video
55  @admin-tools
56  @development-tools
57  @graphical-internet
58  emacs
59  festival
60  audit
61  tftp-server
62  kexec-tools
63  device-mapper-multipath
64  vnc-server
65  xorg-x11-utils
66  xorg-x11-server-Xnest
67  xorg-x11-server-Xvfb
```

68 libsane-hpaio
69 imake
70 %post
71 chkconfig sendmail off

Let us analyze the file contents line by line so that you have a good understanding of it. The comments and empty lines will be ignored.

Line #2: Tells Anaconda to begin a fresh installation process. The other option is "upgrade", which upgrades an existing version of RHEL.

Line #3: Tells Anaconda to use this source for installation. Options are:

a. cdrom
b. harddrive --partition=/dev/sda3 --dir=/rhel52/install_media
c. nfs --server=192.168.0.201 --dir=/rhel52/install_media
d. url --url ftp://192.168.0.201/pub/rhel52/install_media
e. url --url http://192.168.0.201/rhel52/install_media

"cdrom" tells Anaconda to install RHEL using installation CDs. The second option will use the installation software or ISO images located on the same computer but in a different partition, and the remaining three options will use a configured NFS, FTP or HTTP server at 192.168.0.201 address.

Line #4: Tells Anaconda to skip installation number.

Line #5: Tells Anaconda to use US English during installation.

Line #6: Tells Anaconda to use the US keyboard type.

Line #7: Tells Anaconda to set GNOME as the default desktop, and start X Window and GNOME desktop after each system reboot.

Line #8: Tells Anaconda to configure the first network card *eth0* and assign it the specified IP address, netmask, gateway, name server IP and hostname with IPv6 support disabled. If you wish to obtain networking information from a configured DHCP server, use "network --device eth0 --bootproto dhcp" instead.

Line #9: Tells Anaconda to assign the specified password to the *root* user. You can copy and paste a *root* password from */etc/shadow* file from some other RHEL system.

Line #10: Tells Anaconda to enable the firewall and allow SSH traffic pass through TCP port 22. The other option available is to disable it.

Line #11: Tells Anaconda to enable password shadowing and encrypt all user passwords using md5.

Line #12: Tells Anaconda to enforce (enable) SELinux. Other options are "disabled" and "permissive".

Line #13: Tells Anaconda to set the hardware clock to America/New_York (*Eastern Time Zone*) timezone using offset from *Universal Time Coordinated* (UTC) (previously called *Greenwich Mean Time* – GMT).

Line #14: Tells Anaconda to reboot the system after installation is complete.

Line #15: Tells Anaconda to not run the firstboot program after installation is complete and the system is rebooted.

Line #16: Tells Anaconda to clear the *Master Boot Record* (MBR).

Line #17: Tells Anaconda to install the GRUB boot loader program on the MBR on hard disk drive *sda* (or *sdb* if *sda* is unavailable) and specify the string "rhgb quiet" with it.

Line #22: Tells Anaconda to clear all partition table information left from a previous RHEL installation on drive *sda*. Alternatively, if you wish to remove from *sda* all partitioning information including that from a previous RHEL installation or Windows, use the following:

```
clearpart --all --drives=sda
```

Line #23: Tells Anaconda to create a partition of size 1000MB on disk *sda* as the primary partition, create ext3 type file system structures in it and mount it on the */boot* mount point. Uncomment this line.

Line #24: Tells Anaconda to create LVM physical volume on the remaining *sda* disk space. Uncomment this line.

Line #25: Tells Anaconda to create *vg00* volume group with PE size 32MB on the physical volume created in the previous step. Uncomment this line.

Line #26: Tells Anaconda to create *lvol1* logical volume of size 1984MB in *vg00* volume group, create ext3 file system structures in it and mount it on the / mount point. Uncomment this line.

Lines #27 to #31: Tells Anaconda to create *lvol2* to *lvol6* logical volumes of the specified sizes in *vg00* volume group. Anaconda will initialize the logical volumes, create file system structures in them and mount them on the specified mount points. Uncomment these lines.

Line #32: Tells Anaconda to create *lvol7* logical volume of size 8000MB in *vg00* volume group to be used for swap purposes. Uncomment this line.

Lines #33 to #57: Tells Anaconda to install all the listed software package groups as part of the install process. Consult */Server/repodata/comps-rhel5-server-core.xml* or */Client/repodata/comps-rhel5-client-core.xml* on the first installation CD for a list of available package groups.

Lines #58 to #69: Tells Anaconda to install all the listed individual packages as part of the install process. Replace lines from 33 to 69 with an asterisk character if you wish to install each and every available package group and package.

Lines #70 and #71: Tells Anaconda to run the specified command *chkconfig sendmail off* after the installation is complete. You can specify additional post-installation commands in this section. Also available is the %pre section which is not defined in the file here. Commands listed under the %pre section are executed before the *ks.cfg* file is parsed.

There are several other keywords and options available that you may want to define in the kickstart configuration file, but not all of them are mandatory. If you leave an option out, Anaconda will prompt you to enter that missing piece of information during installation, which will make the installation not fully automated. Also make certain that the sequence of the sections in the file remains unchanged.

You can optionally specify any pre-installation and/or post-installation commands or scripts that you wish Anaconda to perform.

When you are done with the file, execute the *ksvalidator* command to check for any syntax errors and typos, and display them on the screen. You will then need to fix the issues and re-run the command.

 # ksvalidator /root/ks.cfg

If *ksvalidator* is unavailable, use one of the software package installation methods outlined in Chapter 11 "Software Package Management" to install it.

Using Kickstart Configurator

Execute *system-config-kickstart* to start the Kickstart Configurator program. If this tool is unavailable, install it with one of the software package installation methods outlined in Chapter 11 "Software Package Management".

There are eleven options available on the main screen, each of which is briefly explained below:

Basic Configuration (Figure 28-11): allows you to enter basic information such as language, keyboard type, mouse, timezone, root password and support for any other language plus three additional buttons at the bottom to enable or disable certain options.

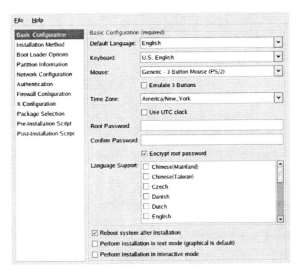

Figure 28-11 Kickstart Configurator – Basic Configuration

Installation Method (Figure 28-12): allows you to choose an installation type and method.

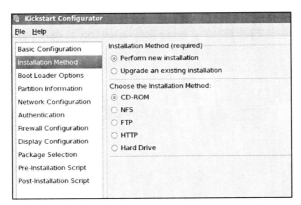

Figure 28-12 Kickstart Configurator – Installation Method

Boot Loader Options (Figure 28-13): allows you to choose boot loader-related settings. The "Use GRUB for the boot loader" is the default option in RHEL 5 and has advantages over LILO. If you

---

wish to specify a password for GRUB, you can do so here. Choose a location to place the boot loader, choices are MBR (preferred) and the /boot partition.

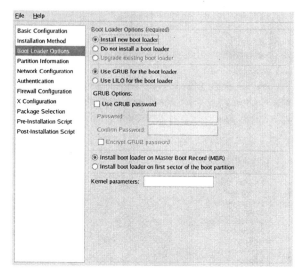

Figure 28-13 Kickstart Configurator – Boot Loader Options

Partition Information (Figure 28-14): allows you to enter partition-related configuration information. "Clear Master Boot Record" removes all existing GRUB/boot information from the MBR. The next set of three options enables you to remove all existing partitions including non-Linux partitions if there are any, remove all existing linux partitions only and preserve existing partitions. "Initialize the disk label" removes existing disk partitioning label and updates it with new partitioning scheme that you will choose here. Click Add button at the bottom to define partition information such as partition type and file system type, size and mount point. Click RAID to create RAID partitions as required. Refer to Chapter 09 "Installation" for details.

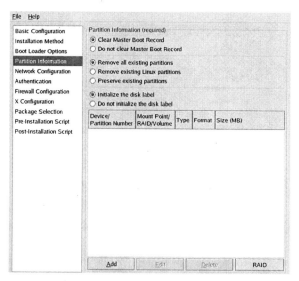

Figure 28-14 Kickstart Configurator – Partition Information

Network Configuration (Figure 28-15): allows you to configure one or more network interfaces. You can specify static configuration such as IP address, subnet mask, gateway address and DNS information or let a DHCP server supply that information. If you are going to be performing a network boot / network install, you will need to enable BOOTP here.

Figure 28-15 Kickstart Configurator – Network Configuration

Authentication (Figure 28-16): allows you to choose a type of user password security. Two choices "Use Shadow Passwords" and "Use MD5" are available. The former encrypts user passwords and stores them in the */etc/shadow* file and the latter performs MD5 encryption on them. In addition, you can enable NIS, LDAP, Kerberos 5, Hesiod, Samba and Name Service Cache, and supply information as required.

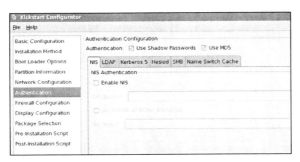

Figure 28-16 Kickstart Configurator – Authentication

Firewall Configuration (Figure 28-17): allows you to configure the firewall. For Internet-facing systems, you should have the firewall enabled. Specify one or more trusted network interface devices for which you need to activate the firewall services. Select network services and specify any ports that you need to enable to work through an enabled firewall. This screen also allows you to activate SELinux.

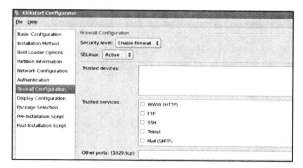

Figure 28-17 Kickstart Configurator – Firewall Configuration

Display Configuration (Figure 28-18): allows you to configure the X Window System. There are three tabs – General, Video Card and Monitor. The General tab is where you can choose the color depth and resolution, default desktop, whether to start X Window System on boot, and whether you want the Setup Agent to start at the first system reboot after the installation has been completed. Probe or choose a video card and monitor under the Video Card and Monitor tabs.

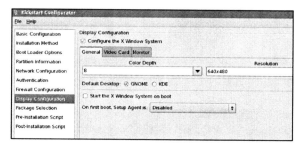

Figure 28-18 Kickstart Configurator – Display Configuration

Package Selection (Figure 28-19): allows you to select the packages to be installed.

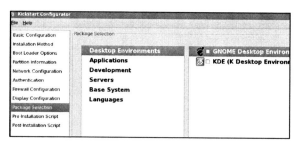

Figure 28-19 Kickstart Configurator – Package Selection

Pre-Installation and Post-Installation Scripts: allows you to add pre- and/or post-installation scripts.

When you are done with configuration settings, go to File → Save File and specify a name such as *ks.cfg* and location such as */root* to save it.

Copying Kickstart Configuration to a CD, USB or Network Drive

Now that you have the kickstart configuration file */root/ks.cfg* ready, burn it to a CD along with the */images/boot.iso* file, copy it to a USB drive along with the */images/diskboot.img* file or put it on a network directory such as */rhel52/kickstart*. For CD/USB copy, refer to sub-sections "Preparing a Bootable CD" and "Preparing a Bootable USB Drive" earlier in this chapter.

Beginning the Installation Process

Let us see how a client system can be booted with the kickstart configuration file located on a bootable CD, USB drive or network directory, and installed.

To boot the system via the bootable CD, insert the CD in the drive, start or restart the system and specify the following at the boot: prompt:

> boot: **linux ks=cdrom:/ks.cfg**

To boot the system via the bootable USB drive, insert the drive in a USB port, start or restart the system and specify the following at the boot: prompt:

> boot: **linux ks=hd:sdg:/ks.cfg**

To boot the system via the first RHEL installation CD, insert the CD in the drive, start or restart the system and specify the following at the boot: prompt to use the configuration file located on the USB drive:

> boot: **linux ks=hd:sdg:/ks.cfg**

To boot the system via the network, start or restart the system and specify the following at the boot: prompt to point it to the configuration file located on a configured NFS, FTP or HTTP server:

> boot: **linux ks=nfs:192.168.0.201/rhel52/kickstart/ks.cfg**
> boot: **linux ks=ftp:192.168.0.201/rhel52/kickstart/ks.cfg**
> boot: **linux ks=http://192.168.0.201/rhel52/kickstart/ks.cfg**

Although you have defined IP address information in the *ks.cfg* file, Anaconda will still look for a configured DHCP server to obtain this information. If it is unable to find one, it will begin a standard installation of RHEL rather than an automated, unattended install.

You may configure DHCP to send the kickstart configuration file to clients automatically. The following will need to be added to the */etc/dhcpd.conf* file. Restart DHCP services on the server after doing this modification.

> allow booting;
> allow bootp;
> next-server 192.168.0.201;
> filename "/rhel52/kickstart/ks.cfg"

The IP address specified is of the NFS server that has the *ks.cfg* file available at the specified location.

Network (PXE) Boot / Network Install

This is a fully automated installation and you do not have to do anything except pressing a key on the client system to search for a configured BootP server on the network to boot off (configuring a BootP server is beyond the scope of this book). The kickstart configuration file will sit on a network drive. You will need to configure a DHCP server by editing */etc/dhcpd.conf* and adding the name and location of *ks.cfg*. See Chapter 22 "DNS and DHCP" on how to configure a DHCP server. The entry in the file will look similar to the following:

```
allow booting;
allow bootp;
filename "/rhel52/kickstart/ks.cfg"
```

If the kickstart file is stored on a different server such as *rhel03*, add the following to the *dhcpd.conf* file to point the installation program to that server:

```
next-server rhel03
```

In order for network boot to function, you need to make certain that the network interface being used for booting has the capability to PXE boot.

Summary

In this chapter, you learned how to perform a network RHEL installation using various methods. You prepared an installation server that could be accessed by a client via NFS, FTP or HTTP protocol. You looked at various methods of booting a client and how to prepare a bootable CD and USB drive. You used the installation CD, bootable CD and bootable USB drive to initiate a local client boot, pull the OS image located on an NFS, FTP and HTTP server, and install it. The next major section in the chapter discussed hands-off installation, which included creating a kickstart configuration file by editing an existing file or using the Kickstart Configurator, and performing an install with it. At the end of the chapter, a topic on network boot and network install was touched upon.

## 29

Web and Caching Proxy Servers

This chapter covers the following major topics:

- ✓ Apache web server and its features
- ✓ Apache configuration and log files
- ✓ Analysis of httpd.conf file
- ✓ Apache security at firewall, SELinux and security context levels
- ✓ Understand general, and host and user level security directives
- ✓ Configure and test an Apache web server
- ✓ Overview of Apache virtual host
- ✓ Configure a virtual and a secure virtual host, and test them
- ✓ Overview of HTTP Configurator
- ✓ Basics of Squid web caching proxy server
- ✓ Squid daemon and associated files
- ✓ Understand Squid startup and configuration files
- ✓ SELinux requirements for Squid
- ✓ Configure and test a Squid server

Web

Web server software allows you to publish websites on the Internet or corporate intranets. The software runs on a system referred to as a *web server* and provides access to the hosted websites to users on the Internet or the corporate network. There are millions of web servers being used, running several kinds of web server software of which Apache is the most popular. This chapter presents detailed information on Apache web server as well as the Squid proxy server, which is used for caching frequently accessed web pages locally.

The Apache Web Server

Apache is undoubtedly the most popular, stable and secure web server software currently being used on the Internet and corporate networks. The latest version is 2.2.11, but this chapter is going to cover version 2.2.3, which supports features such as virtual hosts, access control, dynamic module loading and secure HTTP. Apache uses the *httpd* (hyper text transfer protocol) daemon to provide client access to web pages using the HTTP and HTTPS protocols.

Apache Features

Some of the key features associated with the Apache web server are:

- ✓ Supports files of sizes larger than 2GB.
- ✓ Supports encrypted authentication methods.
- ✓ Supports LDAP for authentication.
- ✓ Supports virtual hosts to host several websites on a single server with all websites sharing one IP address.
- ✓ Separate configuration files for separate services may be defined and stored at different directory locations.

Key Apache Files

Apache configuration files are located in the */etc/httpd* directory. The key configuration and other files are listed and explained in Table 29-1.

File	Description
/etc/httpd/conf/httpd.conf	Main Apache web server configuration file.
/etc/httpd/conf.d/ssl.conf	Secure web server configuration file.
/etc/httpd/conf.d/*.conf	Configuration files for supporting services.
.htaccess	Allows users to manage entire DocumentRoot contents or a specific directory within DocumentRoot depending on where it is placed.
/usr/lib/httpd/modules	Directory location for *httpd* specific modules.
/var/run/httpd.pid	File containing the PID of the *httpd* daemon.

Table 29-1 Key Apache Files

The primary configuration file for the web server is *httpd.conf* located in the */etc/httpd/conf* directory. This file requires another file */etc/httpd/conf.d/ssl.conf* for setting up a secure web server. There are many other configuration files located in */etc/httpd/conf.d* directory with *.conf* extension and are referenced when Apache server is started. An *ll* on the directory produces the following output:

ll /etc/httpd/conf.d

```
total 88
-rw-r–r--    1    root    root  295    Aug  6 07:23    manual.conf
-rw-r–r--    1    root    root 1796    Apr 22  2005     perl.conf
-rw-r–r--    1    root    root  560    Sep 12 11:12    php.conf
-rw-r–r--    1    root    root  566    Aug  6 07:23    proxy_ajp.conf
-rw-r–r--    1    root    root 1671    Jul 12  2006     python.conf
-rw-r–r--    1    root    root  392    Aug  6 07:23    README
-rw-r–r--    1    root    root  332    Mar 23 2007     squid.conf
-rw-r–r--    1    root    root 9677    Aug  6 07:23    ssl.conf
-rw-r–r--    1    root    root  352    Jul 12  2006     webalizer.conf
-rw-r–r--    1    root    root  299    Aug  6 07:23    welcome.conf
```

These files can be customized according to requirements. Moreover, you can create as many additional configuration files in this directory for your web pages as you wish. The syntax of all these files is almost identical to that of the *httpd.conf* file. The following sub-section explains the *httpd.conf* file and general directives used in it.

The httpd.conf File

The contents in the *httpd.conf* file are divided into three sections: global environment, main server configuration and virtual hosts, and are explained below:

Section 1: Global Environment – Directives defined in this section affect overall operation of the Apache web server. Some of the key directives are listed and described in Table 29-2.

Directive	Description
ServerTokens	Default is OS. Restricts as to what information is to be displayed in a user browser when the user hits a web page that does not exist on the website. This directive has six levels of restriction – Prod, Major, Minor, Min, OS and Full, with Prod limits the information to the web server software name only and Full displays the web server software name and version, operating system name as well as any optional modules being used. The rest are in between.
ServerRoot	Default is */etc/httpd*. Directory location for storing configuration files.
PidFile	Default is *run/httpd.pid* with respect to ServerRoot. Stores the PID of the *httpd* process.
Timeout	Default is 120 seconds. Specifies the time before receive and send requests time out.
KeepAlive	Default is off. Enables or disables more than one requests per connection (a.k.a. a *persistent connection*).
MaxKeepAliveRequests	Default is 100. Specifies maximum number of allowable requests during a persistent connection. A value of 0 allows an unlimited number.
KeepAliveTimeout	Default is 15 seconds. Specifies time to wait for the next request from the same client on the same connection.
StartServers	Specifies number of server processes to start.

Directive	Description
MinSpareServers	Specifies minimum number of spare server processes.
MaxSpareServers	Specifies maximum number of spare server processes.
ServerLimit	Specifies maximum number of allowable server processes.
MaxClients	Restricts number of concurrent requests.
MaxRequestsPerChild	Restricts requests per child server process.
MinSpareThreads	Specifies minimum number of spare threads.
MaxSpareThreads	Specifies maximum number of spare threads.
ThreadsPerChild	Specifies number of threads per child server process.
Listen	Default is 80. Specifies a port number to listen for client requests. Specify an IP address and a port if you wish to limit the web server to a specific address.
LoadModule	Specifies a module to be loaded when the web server starts.
Include	Default is *conf.d/*.conf* with respect to ServerRoot. Specifies the location of additional configuration files to be loaded.
ExtendedStatus	Default is off. Controls whether to generate a full (on) or partial (on) status information.
User	Default is *apache*. Specifies an owner name for the *httpd* daemon.
Group	Default is *apache*. Specifies a group name for the *httpd* daemon.

Table 29-2 Directives in Section 1 – Global Environment

Section 2: 'Main' server configuration – Directives defined in this section relate to the main server and also set default values for any virtual host containers that may be defined in section 3 of this file. Some of the key directives are listed and explained in Table 29-3.

Directive	Description
ServerAdmin	Default is root@localhost. Specifies an administrative e-mail address.
ServerName	Specifies a server name (or IP address) and port number.
UseCanonicalName	Default is off. Uses the hostname and port supplied by the client. If "on", it will use ServerName as the official name.
DocumentRoot	Default is */var/www/html*. Specifies a directory location for website files.
Options	Sets features such as Indexes, FileInfo, AuthConfig, Limit and FollowSymLinks associated with web directories.
AllowOverride	Default is none. Enables or disables overriding of directives defined in *.htaccess* files.
Order	Defines the order for evaluating allow and deny directives.
Allow	Allows access to specified hosts.
Deny	Denies access to specified hosts.
UserDir	Default is disabled. Specifies a directory location for user web pages. If enabled, contents located in the *~/public_html* directory become visible to web users.
DirectoryIndex	Default is */usr/share/doc/HTML/ndex.html*. Specifies a web page to be served when a user requests an index of a directory.
AccessFileName	Default is *.htaccess*. Specifies a file name in each directory which the server will use for access control information.
TypesConfig	Default is */etc/mime.types*. Sets a file name containing default file type mappings.

Directive	Description
DefaultType	Default is text/plain. Sets the default content type to use for a document if its MIME type is not found in */etc/mime.types*.
MIMEMagicFile	Default is *conf/magic* file with respect to ServerRoot. Tells the mod_mime_magic module where to look for hint definitions.
HostNameLookups	Default is off. Sets whether to resolve URLs for IP addresses.
EnableMMAP	Default is off. Defines whether to use memory mapping for file delivery.
EnableSendfile	Default is off. Defines whether to enable kernel support for file delivery.
ErrorLog	Default is *logs/error_log* with respect to ServerRoot. Specifies a location for the error log file.
LogLevel	Default is warn. Specifies a level of verbosity at which messages are to be logged.
LogFormat	Sets a format for log file contents.
CustomLog	Default is combined and stored in *logs/httpd/access_log* with respect to ServerRoot. Specifies a custom log file and identifies its format.
ServerSignature	Default is on. Adds a line that includes Apache server version, the ServerName directive and (optionally) the ServerAdmin directive (email address) to any server-generated documents such as error messages.
Alias	Defines a directory location outside of the DocumentRoot directory.
ScriptAlias	Specifies a directory location where CGI (*Common Gateway Interface*) scripts are stored.
IndexOptions	Controls how directory listings should appear.
AddIconByEncoding	Specifies an icon to be displayed for a file with encoding.
AddIconByType	Specifies an icon to be displayed for a file with type.
AddIcon	Specifies an icon to be displayed for a file with extension.
DefaultIcon	Specifies an icon to be displayed for files with no icons explicitly defined.
AddDescription	Defines a short description for a file in server-generated indexes.
ReadmeName	Default is *README.html*. Defines a README file name to be appended to the end of directory listings.
HeaderName	Default is *HEADER.html*. Defines a HEADER file name to be prepended to the start of directory listings.
IndexIgnore	Lists file extensions, partial and full file names, and wildcard expressions that are not to be included in directory listings.
DefaultLanguage	Specifies a default language for files with unspecified language tags.
AddLanguage	Assigns filename extensions to specific languages. Useful for multi-language sites.
LanguagePriority	Sets a language preference if not configured in client browsers.
ForceLanguagePriority	Specifies an action to be taken if a web page is not found in the preferred language.
AddDefaultCharset	Default is UTF-8. Sets a default character set for all web contents served.
AddType	Maps a file extension to a specified MIME type.
AddEncoding	Allows certain browsers to uncompress information online.
AddHandler	Maps a file extension to a specified handler.
AddOutputFilter	Maps a file extension to a specified filter.
BrowserMatch	Allows the server to send custom replies to different types of browsers.

Table 29-3 Directives in Section 2 – Main server configuration

Section 3: Virtual Hosts – Directives defined in this section are used if you wish to run multiple websites on the same server. Some of the key directives are listed and explained in Table 29-4.

Directive	Description
NameVirtualHost	Specifies a hostname or IP address for the virtual host.
ServerAdmin	Specifies an e-mail address for the webmaster.
DocumentRoot	Specifies the root directory where virtual host files are located.
ServerName	Specifies a URL for the virtual host.
ErrorLog	Specifies the location for an error log file with respect to ServerRoot.
CustomLog	Specifies the location for a custom log file with respect to ServerRoot.

Table 29-4 Directives in Section 3 – Virtual Hosts

A lot of information is defined within containers in the *httpd.conf* file. Three types of containers – module, file and directory – are commonly used, each of which begins and ends in a way listed in Table 29-5.

Container Begins	Container Ends
<VirtualHost .... >	</VirtualHost>
<IfModule .... >	</IfModule>
<Files .... >	</Files>
<Directory .... >	</Directory>

Table 29-5 Container Begin and End Syntax

Apache Log Files

Apache log files are located in the */var/log/httpd* directory, which is symbolically linked from the */etc/httpd/logs* directory. An *ll* on the directory is shown below. The *access_log* and *error_log* files log access to web server and error messages respectively. The ssl* files are only used if SSL certificates are employed.

```
# ll /var/log/httpd/*_log
-rw-r--r--  1 root root  5985 Feb 28  18:01  access_log
-rw-r--r--  1 root root  8469 Feb 28  18:01  error_log
-rw-r--r--  1 root root     0 Jan  3  14:14  ssl_access_log
-rw-r--r--  1 root root   126 Feb 24  04:02  ssl_error_log
-rw-r--r--  1 root root     0 Jan  3  14:14  ssl_request_log
```

The LogFormat directive as defined in the *httpd.conf* file is the standard log file format for Apache logs. Log related directives defined in the file are grepped and displayed below:

```
# cat /etc/httpd/conf/httpd.conf | grep Log | grep –v ^#
ErrorLog     logs/error_log
LogLevel     warn
LogFormat    "%h %l %u %t \"%r\" %>s %b \"%{Referer}i\" \"%{User-Agent}i\""  combined
LogFormat    "%h %l %u %t \"%r\" %>s %b"  common
LogFormat    "%{User-agent}i"  agent
CustomLog    logs/access_log  combined
```

The ErrorLog directive sets the log file name for Apache errors. The LogLevel is set to "warn", which instructs to log warning and higher level messages. The LogFormat directive supports four formats – combined, common, referrer and agent. "combined" combines what the other three formats log; "common" logs the name of the requesting host, the username and user ID of the client, the date and time of the request, the response returned and the number of bytes returned; "referrer" specifies the referrer system from where the client was redirected here and "agent" specifies the client software. Finally, set the CustomLog directive to where you wish the log information to go. It is recommended that you choose separate log files for each website configured on the server.

Apache Web Server Security Overview

Securing an Apache web server can be done at four levels: firewall, SELinux, file security context and *httpd.conf* file. These levels of security are described in the following sub-sections.

Security at the Firewall Level

If the firewall is enabled, run the Security Level Configurator *system-config-securitylevel* to open port 80 for the standard HTTP protocol, port 443 for the secure version of it and any other ports that you wish to be using.

Figure 29-1 Security Level Configurator – Graphical

A text version of the Security Level Configurator called *lokkit* can be used instead. See Figure 29-2. Select Customize and press Enter.

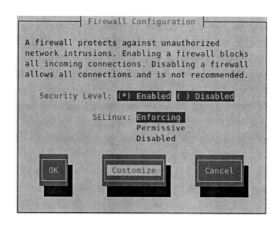

Figure 29-2 Security Level Configurator – Text Based

Other methods of performing the above are to run the *iptables* command or edit the */etc/sysconfig/iptables* file directly. You will need to restart the firewall as follows:

    # **service iptables restart**

Consult Chapter 30 "System and Network Security" for more information.

Security at the SELinux Level

If SELinux is enforced, you need to disable its protection for Apache server to ensure smooth functionality. Use the *setsebool* command as demonstrated below, or the SELinux Configurator *system-config-selinux* as explained in Chapter 30 "System and Network Security". Specify only those Booleans that need to be disabled, leave others intact.

    # **setsebool –P httpd_enable_cgi=1 allow_httpd_anon_write=1 **
    **httpd_can_network_connect=1 httpd_can_network_connect_db=1 **
    **allow_httpd_sys_script_anon_write=1 httpd_enable_homedirs=1 **
    **httpd_enable_ftp_server=1 httpd_builtin_scripting=1 httpd_disable_trans=1 **
    httpd_suexec_disable_trans=1 httpd_unified=1 httpd_tty_comm=1

Use the *getsebool* command to verify:

    # **getsebool httpd_enable_cgi allow_httpd_anon_write httpd_can_network_connect **
    **httpd_can_network_connect_db allow_httpd_sys_script_anon_write **
    **httpd_enable_homedirs httpd_enable_ftp_server httpd_builtin_scripting **
    httpd_disable_trans httpd_suexec_disable_trans httpd_unified httpd_tty_comm
    allow_httpd_anon_write --> on
    httpd_builtin_scripting --> on
    httpd_can_network_connect --> on
    httpd_can_network_connect_db --> on
    httpd_can_network_relay --> on
    httpd_disable_trans --> on
    httpd_enable_cgi --> on
    httpd_enable_ftp_server --> on

httpd_enable_homedirs --> on
httpd_suexec_disable_trans --> on
httpd_tty_comm --> on
httpd_unified --> on

SELinux File Security Context

Set appropriate security contexts on the directories with the *chcon* command where you have stored the web pages. This should be done only if SELinux is enabled. For example, if you have web contents in the */var/getitcertify/www/webcontents* directory, run the command as demonstrated below:

> # **chcon –Rvu system_u /var/getitcertify/www/webcontents**
> context of /var/getitcertify/www/webcontents changed to system_u:object_r:var_t
> # **chcon –Rvt httpd_sys_content_t /var/getitcertify/www/webcontents**
> context of /var/getitcertify/www/webcontents changed to system_u:object_r:httpd_sys_content_t

The –R option sets security contexts recursively, –v is used for verbosity, –u sets the context at user-level and –t sets the type on the specified directory.

Run the *ll* command with –Z option to confirm the settings:

> # **ll –Z /var/getitcertify/www**
> drwxr-xr-x   root   root   **system_u:object_r:httpd_sys_content_t** webcontents

Security in the httpd.conf File

There are several directives in the *httpd.conf* file that can be set appropriately to enhance the level of security. Some of the directives such as ServerTokens and UserDir work at the global level as explained in Table 29-2 earlier in this chapter. Other directives are set at the directory container level and are explained below.

General Security Directives

Within a directory container, you can configure several general security directives such as Options and AllowOverride that will enable you to limit the use of the directory container and hence the use of the website and web pages defined therein. Table 29-6 lists and explains the two directives.

Directive	Description
Options	ExecCGI: Allows web pages to execute CGI scripts.
	FollowSymLinks: Allows directories external to DocumentRoot to have symlinks.
	Indexes: Allows indexing of directories.
	Includes: Allows server-side includes.
	All: Allows all options besides MultiViews.
	None: Denies unauthorized users from executing CGI scripts located in DocumentRoot.

Directive	Description
AllowOverride	None: Denies normal users from modifying permissions on files in DocumentRoot. All: Allows all options except MultiViews. AuthConfig: Allows a directory to use the *.htaccess* file for overriding default values of authorization directives. FileInfo: Allows a directory to use the *.htaccess* file for overriding default values controlling document types.

Table 29-6 General Security Directives

A sample directory container is shown below with some selected directives from Table 29-6:

```
<Directory /var/getitcertify/www>
    Options ExecCGI FollowSymLinks Includes
    AllowOverride AuthConfig FileInfo
</Directory>
```

Security at the Host Level

This level of security enables you to allow or deny access requests to your web server from specific hosts, networks or domains based on the settings of the allow and deny directives. Table 29-7 provides examples to explain the usage of the two directives.

Allow / Deny	Effect
Allow from all	Allows access from all hosts.
Allow from rhel04	Allows access from *rhel04* system only.
Allow from 192.168.0	Allows access to systems on the 192.168.0 network only.
Allow from .getitcertify.com	Allows access to systems on the *getitcertify.com* domain only.
Deny from all	Denies access from all hosts.
Deny from rhel04	Denies access from *rhel04* system only.
Deny from 192.168.1	Denies access to systems on the 192.168.1 network only.
Deny from .getitcertify.com	Denies access to systems on the *getitcertify.com* domain only.

Table 29-7 Host Level Allow/Deny Directives

Table 29-8 describes a couple of combinations of the allow and deny directives in which they are evaluated by the Order directive, and explains the impact of the settings.

Order Directive	Effect
Order allow,deny	Allows access to hosts defined with the allow directive and denies all other hosts.
Order deny,allow	Denies access to hosts defined with the deny directive and allows all other hosts.

Table 29-8 Host Level Order Directive

The example directory container from above is shown below with added host level access control directives:

```
<Directory /var/getitcertify/www>
      Options ExecCGI FollowSymLinks Includes
      AllowOverride AuthConfig FileInfo
      Order allow,deny
      Allow from getitcertify.com
</Directory>
```

Security at the User Level

Securing an Apache server at the user level sets controls so only authorized users are able to access the website. These users will be assigned passwords that may or may not be different from their RHEL passwords. Several directives are available for controlling access at this level and are described in Table 29-9.

User Level Security Directives	Explanation
AuthType	Sets basic authentication.
AuthName	Adds general comments.
AuthUserFile	Defines the file that contains authorized user passwords.
AuthGroupFile	Defines the file that contains authorized group passwords.
Require	Specifies users or groups that are allowed. For example: Require user aghori → limits access to user *aghori* only. Require group dba → limits access to members of group *dba* only.

Table 29-9 User Level Security Directives

Configuring an Apache Web Server

The following is a series of steps that demonstrates configuring an Apache web server for *www.example.com* website with DocumentRoot directory */var/example/www*, web contents located in */var/example/www/webcontents* directory, accessible to users *aghori*, *bghori* and members of *webgrp* group from systems on the 192.168.1 and 192.168.2 networks on port 5001 on *eth0* interface, name of the index file *index.html* and log files located in DocumentRoot. Make sure that users on the 192.168.3 network do not have access to the web server.

1. Check whether Apache software packages are installed:

    # rpm –qa | grep httpd
    httpd-2.2.3-22.el5
    system-config-httpd-1.3.3.3-1.el5
    httpd-manual-2.2.3-11.el5_1.3

    Check which Apache modules are installed:

    # rpm –qa | grep ^mod
    mod_perl-2.0.2-6.3.el5
    mod_python-3.2.8-3.1
    mod_ssl-2.2.3-22.el5

Check whether graphical web browser *firefox* and textual web browser *elinks* are installed:

rpm –qa | egrep 'firefox|elinks'
firefox-3.0-0.beta5.6.el5
elinks-0.11.1-5.1.0.1.el5

Install the packages if they are not already installed using one of the software package installation methods described in Chapter 11 "Software Package Management".

2. Execute the following to make *httpd* autostart at system reboots:

   # **chkconfig httpd on**

3. Modify the following directives in the *httpd.conf* file as per supplied information. Leave other settings intact.

   DocumentRoot /var/example/www
   Listen 5001
   <Directory "/var/example/www">
      Options Indexes FollowSymLinks
      AllowOverride authconfig
      Order allow, deny
      Allow from 192.168.1 192.168.2
      Deny from 192.168.3
   </Directory>
   DirectoryIndex index.html
   AccessFileName .htaccess
   ErrorLog logs/error_log
   CustomLog logs/access_log combined

4. Execute the following to check the syntax of *httpd.conf*:

   # **httpd –t**
   Syntax OK

   For more detailed output, run any of the following:

   # **service httpd configtest**
   # **apachectl configtest**

5. Create DocumentRoot directory and a sub-directory *webcontents* for storing website contents:

   # **mkdir –p /var/example/www/webcontents**

6. Create *.htaccess* file in DocumentRoot and add appropriate directives:

   # **cd /var/example/www && vi .htaccess**
   AuthType Basic
   AuthName "This site is for example.com"

AuthUserFile "/etc/httpd/conf/.userdb"
Require user aghori bghori
AuthGroupFile "/etc/httpd/conf/.groupdb"
Require group webgrp

7. Set password for user *aghori* and *bghori* using the *htpasswd* command. With –c option, this command creates the specified file and save the information in it, and without this option, it only adds new entries to the file. The –m option tells the command to use MD5 encryption for passwords. Enter the password as prompted.

    # htpasswd –cm /etc/httpd/conf/.userdb aghori
    New password:
    Re-type new password:
    Adding password for user aghori
    # htpasswd –m /etc/httpd/conf/.userdb bghori
    New password:
    Re-type new password:
    Adding password for user bghori

8. Create */etc/httpd/conf/.groupdb* group file and add the following line to it:

    # vi /etc/httpd/conf/.groupdb
    webgrp: aghori

9. Change group membership on *.userdb* and *.groupdb* files to *apache*:

    # cd /etc/httpd/conf && chgrp apache .userdb .groupdb

10. Create *index.html* file in */var/example/www/webcontents* and some text to it:

    # vi /var/example/www/webcontents/index.html
    This web page is to test Apache web server.

11. Modify firewall settings to open port 5001 as described in sub-section "Security at the Firewall Level".
12. Modify SELinux settings as described in sub-section "Security at the SELinux Level".
13. Modify SELinux security contexts recursively on */var/example/www* and */etc/httpd/conf* directories as described in sub-section "SELinux File Security Context" so that *httpd* can read them.
14. Start (or restart) *httpd* daemon using any of the following:

    # apachectl start
    # service httpd start

15. Test the configuration by loading the *www.example.com/index* in both text and graphical browsers first on the local system and then on a system on the 192.168.1 or 192.168.2 network. You should be prompted for username and password. Enter *aghori* or *bghori* and the associated password to get in.

Run *elinks* at the command line and type the following URL to load *index.html*:

```
# elinks 127.0.0.1:5001/webcontents          # on the local system
# elinks 192.168.1.201:5001/webcontents      # on another system
```

Start the firefox browser and enter the URL *http://localhost:5001/webcontents* to bring up the the graphical version of *index.html*. To access the web page from another system, type *http://192.168.1.201:5001/webcontents* in a browser window.

Skip steps 6 to 9 if you do not wish to restrict access to the web server to users *aghori* and *bghori*, and group *webgrp*. Without these four steps performed, the access will be open to all users on the specified networks. As well, remove the AllowOverride and AccessFileName directives from the code added to the *httpd.conf* file in step 3. These directives will not be required.

Also, if you do not wish to restrict access to the web server to the 192.168.1 and 192.168.2 network users, you can simply take the Order and Allow directives out of the code.

The Apache Virtual Host

Apache allows you to create multiple virtual hosts with the ability to run multiple websites with different names on a single computer. These websites can either share a common IP address or have their own unique addresses. Virtual hosts sharing a common IP address are called *name-based* and those with dedicated IP addresses are referred to as *IP-based*. The primary configuration file for defining virtual hosts is */etc/httpd/conf/httpd.conf* (section 3) and that for secure virtual hosts is */etc/httpd/conf.d/ssl.conf*.

Configuring a Non-Secure Virtual Host

To configure a name-based virtual web server for domains *www.example.com* and *www.example.net* on *rhel09* to share 192.168.1.209 IP address on port 80, follow the steps below:

1. Perform steps 1 and 2 from section "Configuring an Apache Web Server".
2. Edit *httpd.conf* file and append the directives as follows. Refer to Table 29-4 and 29-6 for an explanation.

```
NameVirtualHost 192.168.1.209
<VirtualHost www.example.com>
    ServerName www.example.com
    ServerAdmin aghori@example.com
    DocumentRoot /var/example.com/www
    DirectoryIndex index.html
    ErrorLog logs/example-error_log
    CustomLog logs/example-access_log combined
    <Directory /var/example.com/www>
        Options Indexes FollowSymLinks ExecCGI Includes
    </Directory>
</VirtualHost>
<VirtualHost www.example.net>
    ServerName www.example.net
```

```
ServerAdmin aghori@example.net
DocumentRoot /var/example.net/www
DirectoryIndex index.html
ErrorLog logs/example-error_log
CustomLog logs/example-access_log combined
<Directory /var/example.net/www>
        Options Indexes FollowSymLinks ExecCGI Includes
</Directory>
</VirtualHost>
```

3. Execute the following to check the syntax of *httpd.conf*:

   # httpd –t
   Syntax OK

   For more detailed output, run any of the following:

   # httpd –S
   # service httpd configtest
   # apachectl configtest

4. Create the DocumentRoot directory if it does not already exist:

   # mkdir –p /var/example.com/www
   # mkdir –p /var/example.net/www

5. Create *index.html* files in both DocumentRoot directories and add some text to them:

   # vi /var/example.com/www/index.html
   This is a test website for example.com.
   # vi /var/example.net/www/index.html
   This is a test website for example.net.

6. Modify firewall settings to open port 80 as described in sub-section "Security at the Firewall Level".
7. Modify SELinux settings as described in sub-section "Security at the SELinux Level".
8. Modify SELinux security contexts recursively on both DocumentRoot directories as described in sub-section "SELinux File Security Context".
9. Edit */etc/hosts* file and add the following:

   192.168.1.209   rhel09   localhost   www.example.com   www.example.net

10. Start (or restart) the Apache server daemon:

    # service httpd restart
    Stopping httpd: [OK]
    Starting httpd: [OK]

11. Test the configuration by loading *www.example.com/index* and *www.example.net/index* on port 80 in both text and graphical browsers from the local and a remote system as explained in section "Configuring an Apache Web Server".

While visiting the websites, run the *tail* command with –f (follow) option on the *example-access_log* files in both DocumentRoot directories to view what is going on. For example:

 # tail –f /var/example.com/www/example-access_log
192.168.1.209 - - [28/Feb/2008:13:12:44 -0500] "GET / HTTP/1.1" 304 – "-" "Mozilla/5.0 (X11; U; Linux i686; en-US; rv:1.8.0.12) Gecko/20070718 Red Hat/1.5.0.12-3.el5 Firefox/1.5.0.12"

Configuring a Secure Virtual Host

Follow the steps below if you wish to configure secure websites for *www.example.com* and *www.example.net* instead to allow HTTPS connections only:

1. Perform steps 1 and 2 from section "Configuring an Apache Web Server".
2. Run the *rpm* command to check whether mod_ssl package is also installed:

   # rpm –qa | grep mod_ssl
   mod_ssl-2.2.3-11.el5

3. Edit */etc/httpd/conf.d/ssl.conf* file and append the directives as follows. Refer to Table 29-4 and 29-6 for an explanation.

   NameVirtualHost 192.168.1.209
   Listen 443
   <VirtualHost www.example.com>
       ServerName www.example.com
       ServerAdmin aghori@example.com
       DocumentRoot /var/example.com/www
       DirectoryIndex index.html
       ErrorLog logs/example_ssl-error_log
       CustomLog logs/example_ssl-access_log combined
       <Directory /var/example.com/www>
           Options Indexes FollowSymLinks ExecCGI Includes
       </Directory>
   </VirtualHost>
   <VirtualHost www.example.net>
       ServerName www.example.net
       ServerAdmin aghori@example.net
       DocumentRoot /var/example.net/www
       DirectoryIndex index.html
       ErrorLog logs/example_ssl-error_log
       CustomLog logs/example_ssl-access_log combined
       <Directory /var/example.net/www>
           Options Indexes FollowSymLinks ExecCGI Includes
       </Directory>
   </VirtualHost>

4. Execute the following to check the syntax of *ssl.conf*:

    # httpd –t
    Syntax OK

    For more detailed output, run any of the following:

    # httpd –S
    # service httpd configtest
    # apachectl configtest

5. Create *index.html* files in both DocumentRoot directories, and add some text to them:

    # vi /var/example.com/www/index.html
    This is a test secure website for www.example.com.
    # vi /var/example.net/www/index.html
    This is a test secure website for www.example.net.

6. Modify firewall settings to open port 443 as described in sub-section "Security at the Firewall Level".
7. Modify SELinux settings as described in sub-section "Security at the SELinux Level".
8. Modify SELinux security contexts recursively on both DocumentRoot directories as described in sub-section "SELinux File Security Context".
9. Perform steps 9 and 10 from sub-section "Configuring a Non-Secure Virtual Host".
10. Test the configuration by loading *https://www.example.com/index* and *https://www.example.net/index* on port 443 in both text and graphical browsers from the local and a remote system as explained in section "Configuring an Apache Web Server".

While visiting the websites, run the *tail* command with –f (follow) option on the *example_ssl-access_log* files in both DocumentRoot directories to view what is going on. For example:

 # tail –f /var/example.com/www/example_ssl-access_log

Overview of the HTTP Configurator

The Red Hat HTTP Configurator is the graphical interface for configuring virtual hosts and modifying several other directives. Input provided overwrites directive settings in the *httpd.conf* file. To start the tool, issue the *system-config-httpd* command in an X terminal window or choose (GNOME) System → Administration → Server Settings → HTTP or (KDE) Main Menu → System Tools → HTTP. Figure 29-3 displays the interface. Refer to Tables earlier in this chapter for details on directives.

Figure 29-3 HTTP Configurator – Main Tab

The Figure shows that there are four configuration tabs – Main, Virtual Hosts, Server and Performance Tuning. The Main tab, as displayed in Figure 29-3, is where you can enter basic configuration information such as server name, webmaster's email address, IP address and port number for listening to incoming requests.

The Virtual Hosts tab, Figure 29-4, allows you to add one or more new virtual hosts, and modify or delete an existing one. Some of the configurable items are virtual host name, DocumentRoot directory, webmaster's email address, type of virtual host, IP address or server name, SSL information for secure HTTP, error and access log file names and locations, log level, DNS lookup settings, settings for Options directive, CGI scripts and so on.

Figure 29-4 HTTP Configurator – Virtual Hosts Tab

The Server tab is where you can define the name and location for lock and PID files, the location for a core dump directory, and user and group names for the *httpd* daemon.

Figure 29-5 HTTP Configurator – Server Tab

The Performance Tuning tab allows you to define the maximum number of connections per server, maximum number of requests per connection, connection timeout value and settings for requests per connection.

Figure 29-6 HTTP Configurator – Performance Tuning Tab

Squid Web Caching Proxy Server

Squid is a caching server that caches frequently accessed information locally on disk resulting in faster overall Internet access. Squid also acts as a proxy server for protocols such as HTTP and FTP, and requests web pages on behalf of clients. In short, Squid offers both caching and proxy services with the ability of tracking websites being visited and limiting access to specific sites.

Squid may be configured on a group of systems on the network in a parent/sibling configuration, which allows each system within the group to consult its own cache first and then the cache on the other systems to get requested information before going to the Internet. Squid uses *Inter-Cache Protocol* (ICP) for data transfer among systems within the group.

Squid does not depend on TCP Wrappers for access control, rather, it has its own built-in mechanism for this purpose.

Squid Daemon, and Startup and Configuration Files

The Squid daemon is called *squid* and it is located in the */usr/sbin* directory. Squid startup and configuration files are listed and explained in Table 29-10.

File	Description
/etc/sysconfig/squid	Startup configuration file.
/etc/rc.d/init.d/squid	Startup and shutdown script.
/etc/squid	Directory location for configuration files.
/etc/squid/squid.conf	Main configuration file.
/var/log/squid	Directory location for log files. The access.log (logs requesting client information), cache.log (logs startup/shutdown, etc. information) and store.log (logs addition and deletion of information to/from cache) files are typically located here.
/var/spool/squid	Directory location for caching.

Table 29-10 Squid Startup and Configuration Files

The startup configuration file for Squid is */etc/sysconfig/squid* and it contains just a few directives:

```
# cat /etc/sysconfig/squid
# default squid options
# -D disables initial dns checks. If you most likely will not to have an
#   internet connection when you start squid, uncomment this
SQUID_OPTS="-D"
# Time to wait for Squid to shut down when asked. Should not be necessary most of the time.
SQUID_SHUTDOWN_TIMEOUT=100
```

There are only two directives in the default file and are explained in Table 29-11.

Directive	Description
SQUID_OPTS	Default is –D. Disables DNS checking at Squid startup.
SQUID_SHUTDOWN_TIMEOUT	Default is 100. Specifies the time in seconds to delay the beginning of Squid shutdown.

Table 29-11 Directives in Squid Startup File

The primary configuration file for Squid is */etc/squid/squid.conf*. Key directives defined in this file are listed and described in Table 29-12.

Directive	Description
http_port	Default is 3128. Specifies the port number to be used.
hierarchy_stoplist	Default is "cgi-bin ?". A list of words which, if found in a URL, causes the object to be handled directly by this Squid server.
access_log	Default is */var/log/squid/access.log*. Keeps track of pages as they are downloaded.
acl	*Access Control List*. Some options are: SSL_ports / Safe_ports: Specifies ports for caching traffic. localhost src 127.0.0.1/255.255.255.255: Allows access to the local host. src_net src 192.168.1.0/24: Allows access to the specified network. dst_net dst 192.168.2.0/24: Allows access to the destination network. Refer to Chapter 22 "DNS and DHCP" for additional acl directive usage information.

Directive	Description
cache_dir	Default is /var/spool/squid of size 100MB. Defines the caching directory and maximum size for caching contents.
cache_mem	Default is 8MB. Defines the amount of memory to be used for holding in-transit objects.
cache_peer	Allows you to connect the caches from multiple Squid servers in parent/sibling caching model.
http_access	allow – Allows queries from the specified system, domain or network. deny – Denies queries from the specified system, domain or network.
http_reply_access	allow – Responds to queries from the specified system, domain or network. deny – Does not respond to queries from the specified system, domain or network.
icp_access allow all	Allows all queries that use Inter-Cache Protocol (ICP).
refresh_pattern	Sets cached data refresh pattern based on when the data was last refreshed. Minimum and maximum values are supplied in minutes.
visible_hostname	Specifies the name of the Squid server.

Table 29-12 Directives in Squid Configuration File

SELinux Requirements for Squid

If SELinux is enforced, you need to disable its protection for Squid service to ensure smooth functionality. Use the *setsebool* command as demonstrated below, or the SELinux Configurator *system-config-selinux* as explained in Chapter 30 "System and Network Security". Specify only those Booleans that need to be disabled, leave others intact.

> # **setsebool –P squid_connect_any=1 squid_disable_trans=1**

Use the *getsebool* command to verify:

> # **getsebool –a | grep ^squid**
> squid_connect_any --> on
> squid_disable_trans --> on

Configuring a Squid Server for Proxy Services

To configure a system such as *rhel04* to function as a proxy server for all the systems on the local network on port 8080, be able to disallow access to the systems on the 192.168.5.0/24 network, and block access to *getitcertify.com* site, follow the steps below:

1. Check whether Squid software package is installed:

   > # **rpm –qa | grep squid**
   > squid-2.6.STABLE6-5.el5_1.3

   Install the package if it is not already loaded using one of the software package installation methods described in Chapter 11 "Software Package Management".

2. Execute the following to make Squid autostart at each system reboot:

chkconfig squid on

3. Modify firewall settings to open port 8080 as described in sub-section "Security at the Firewall Level".
4. Edit the */etc/squid/squid.conf* file and set the following directives:

   http_port 8080
   visible_hostname rhel04
   acl allow_net src 192.168.0.0/24
   acl deny_net src 192.168.5.0/24
   acl deny_dom dstdomain .getitcertify.com
   http_access allow allow_net
   http_access deny deny_net deny_dom

   The first line entry defines the port for Squid to listen on, the second one specifies the name of the Squid server, the next two set access control lists for the source networks, and the last pair configures them appropriately with the http_access directive.

5. Start Squid using any of the following. This will read the */etc/squid/squid.conf* file and start the *squid* daemon, which will begin listening on port 8080. It will create squid swap directories under the */var/spool/squid* directory as specified with the init_cache_dir directive in the */etc/rc.d/init.d/squid* startup file by running the *squid* command with –z option.

   # **service squid start**
   init_cache_dir /var/spool/squid... Starting squid: .   [OK]

6. Verify the operational status of Squid:

   # **service squid status**
   squid (pid 3337) is running...

7. Start *elinks* or firefox web browser on a system on the local network and configure it to use the IP address of the Squid server on port 8080 by setting manual proxy. Do a *tail* –f on Squid's log file */var/log/squid/access.log* on *rhel04* while browsing a site such as *www.redhat.com* or downloading a file from *ftp.redhat.com* to view what is going on in realtime.

This completes the procedure to configure a basic Squid proxy server.

Summary

In this chapter, you learned about Apache web server and Squid caching proxy server. You looked at associated startup and configuration files to understand directives used in them. You studied firewall and SELinux requirements for them, and saw procedures on how to configure an Apache web server, a virtual host, a secure virtual host and a Squid server. You looked at the HTTP graphical utility in addition to using command line tools. Finally, you tested web and proxy servers from browsers to ensure they were configured correctly.

30

System and Network Security

This chapter covers the following major topics:

- ✓ Ways to secure a system
- ✓ Secure shell benefits and how ssh encryption takes place
- ✓ Understand ssh configuration file
- ✓ Configure an ssh server and single sign-on user access
- ✓ Access RHEL from a Windows system via ssh
- ✓ Transfer files using scp and sftp
- ✓ Pluggable Authentication Module (PAM) and its use
- ✓ Introduction to TCP Wrappers
- ✓ Understand IPTables firewall
- ✓ Modify firewall rules at the command prompt and via Security Level Configurator
- ✓ Describe Network Address Translation
- ✓ Configure IP masquerading
- ✓ Describe Security Enhanced Linux
- ✓ Understand SELinux configuration file and security contexts
- ✓ Manage SELinux via commands and SELinux Configurator
- ✓ View SELinux-related alerts
- ✓ Common system hardening tasks

Running a system in a networked or an Internet-facing environment requires that some

measures be taken to make access to the system more secure by identifying the type and level of security needed, and implementing it. Security features such as file and directory permissions, user and group level permissions, and shadow password and password aging mechanisms have been discussed in previous chapters. Moreover, firewall and SELinux related security measures have also been discussed. This chapter covers additional features such as OpenSSH, PAM, TCP Wrappers and Network Address Translation, in addition to providing more details on firewall and SELinux. The chapter also covers system hardening in brief and lists a few recommendations that you might wish to consider to apply on your systems for security improvement.

The OpenSSH Service

Secure Shell (SSH) was created in 1995 to provide a secure mechanism for data transmission between source and destination systems over IP networks. SSH includes a set of utilities providing remote users the ability to log in, transfer files and execute commands securely using strong, hidden encryption and authentication. Due to their built-in powerful security features, SSH utilities have widely replaced the conventional, unsecured *telnet, rlogin, rsh, rcp* and *ftp* services in computing environments.

OpenSSH is a free, open source implementation of SSH. Once applied successfully on a system, the *telnetd, rlogind, rshd* and *ftpd* services can be disabled in the */etc/xinetd.d* directory, provided no user or application functionality is impacted. The secure command that replaces *rlogin, rsh* and *telnet* is called *ssh* and those that replace *rcp* and *ftp* are referred to as *scp* and *sftp*, respectively.

Secure shell uses TCP Wrappers for access control.

Private and Public Encryption Keys

Encryption is a way of transforming information into a scribbled form to hide the information from unauthorized users. Encryption is done at the sending end and the reverse process called *de-encryption* happens on the receiving side. The sending system transforms information using a *private* key and the receiving system reads it by using a *public* key. A private key is like a lock that requires a public key to open it. When a client sends information to a server where the keys were generated, the server decrypts the incoming public key and see if it matches with the private key. If the two matches, the server allows the request in and served, otherwise, it simply rejects the connection. Both private and public keys are randomly-generated long strings of alphanumeric characters attached to messages during ssh communication.

A private key must be kept secure since it is private to that one system only. The public key is distributed to clients. A system serves incoming ssh requests and based on the private/public key combination, it allows or denies them.

DSA and RSA are widely used encryption methods used with OpenSSH. DSA stands for *Digital Signature Algorithm* and RSA for *Rivest, Shamir, Adleman*.

How SSH Encryption Takes Place Without Private/Public Keys

SSH is based on the client/server model where a client piece (*ssh, scp* and *sftp*) makes a connection request and the server process *sshd* responds to it. Here is how an ssh communication channel is established:

- ✓ A user sends a connection request to the specified server using one of the ssh utilities.
- ✓ TCP Wrappers on the server evaluates the request for access control.
- ✓ The *sshd* daemon shares ssh protocol versions with the client and switches to a packet-based protocol for communication.
- ✓ The server prompts the user for password.
- ✓ The user responds by entering a password.
- ✓ The server process invokes a PAM's authentication module and matches the password entered against the encrypted password defined in the */etc/shadow* file. Upon validation, an encrypted communication channel is established for the user.

How SSH Authentication Takes Place With Private/Public Keys

Here is how SSH performs authentication using private/public keys:

- ✓ A user sends a connection request to the specified server using one of the ssh utilities.
- ✓ TCP Wrappers on the server evaluates the request for access control.
- ✓ The *sshd* daemon shares ssh protocol versions with the client and switches to a packet-based protocol for communication.
- ✓ The server prompts the user for public key (a.k.a. *passphrase*).
- ✓ The user responds by entering a public key.
- ✓ The server process decrypts the public key and matches it with the private key stored in that user's home directory. Upon validation, the user is allowed to get in and an encrypted communication session is established for the user.

Commands and Daemon, Configuration and Log Files

Several commands, daemon, configuration and log files are involved in the entire ssh communication setup process. Table 30-1 lists and explains them.

	Description
Command	
ssh-agent	Authentication Agent. Holds private keys used for DSA/RSA authentication.
ssh-add	Adds DSA/RSA characteristics to ssh-agent.
ssh-copy-id	Copies DSA/RSA keys to other systems.
ssh-keygen	Generates private and public keys.
ssh	Equivalent command to *telnet* and *rlogin*.
Daemon	
sshd	Server daemon to serve ssh client requests. Default port it listens on is 22.
sftp-server	Autostarted by *sshd* to serve incoming *sftp* requests.
Configuration and Log Files	
/etc/ssh/sshd_config	Defines *sshd* configuration.
/etc/ssh/ssh_config	Defines system-wide ssh client configuration defaults.
/etc/sysconfig/sshd	Startup configuration file for *sshd*.
/etc/rc.d/init.d/sshd	Startup script for *sshd*.
/var/log/secure	Logs all authentication information.

Table 30-1 OpenSSH Commands and Daemon, Configuration and Log Files

An excerpt from the configuration file */etc/ssh/sshd_config* showing only key directives is displayed below:

cat /etc/ssh/sshd_config

```
. . . . . . . .
#Port 22
Protocol 2
ListenAddress 192.168.0.201

. . . . . . . .
SyslogFacility AUTHPRIV
PermitRootLogin yes

. . . . . . . .
PasswordAuthentication yes
ChallengeResponseAuthentication no

. . . . . . . .
GSSAPIAuthentication yes
GSSAPICleanupCredentials yes
UsePAM yes
#AllowTcpForwarding yes
#GatewayPorts no
X11Forwarding yes

. . . . . . . .
PidFile /var/run/sshd.pid
. . . . . . .
Subsystem      sftp    /usr/libexec/openssh/sftp-server
```

Some of the key directives are explained in Table 30-2.

Directive	Description
Port	Default is 22. Specifies the port for ssh communication.
Protocol 2	Default is 2. Specifies the ssh protocol version to be used.
ListenAddress	Specifies the IP address to be used for incoming ssh requests.
SyslogFacility	Default is AUTHPRIV. Defines the facility code to be used when logging messages in */var/log/secure*.
PermitRootLogin	Default is no. Denies direct *root* login. "yes" allows *root* to log in and "without-password" allows it to log in without entering its password.
PasswordAuthentication	Default is yes. Enables local password authentication.
ChallengeResponseAuthentication	Default is no. Disables user authentication via PAM.
UsePAM	Default is yes. Enables or disables user authentication via PAM. If enabled, only *root* will be able to run the daemon.
GSSAPIAuthentication	Default is yes. Supports authentication via *Generic Security Services Application Programming Interface* (GSSAPI).
AcceptEnv	Allows a client to set global variables.
X11Forwarding	Default is yes. Allows remote access to GUI applications.
PidFile	Default is */var/run/sshd.pid*. Specifies the PID file for *sshd*.
Subsystem sftp	Enables encryption for sFTP file transfers.

Directive	Description
AllowUsers	Allows specific users to gain ssh access into the system. For example: AllowUsers aghori bghori AllowUsers aghori@rhel01 bghori@rhel02

Table 30-2 OpenSSH Server Configuration File

Configuring an OpenSSH Server

Follow the procedure below to configure the OpenSSH service on a system:

1. Check whether the required OpenSSH software packages are installed:

   # **rpm –qa | grep openssh**
   openssh-4.3p2-24.el5
   openssh-server-4.3p2-24.el5
   openssh-clients-4.3p2-24.el5
   openssh-askpass-4.3p2-24.el5

   Install the packages if they are not already loaded using one of the software package installation methods described in Chapter 11 "Software Package Management".

2. Execute the following to make *sshd* autostart at each system reboot:

   # **chkconfig sshd on**

3. Configure TCP Wrappers files */etc/hosts.allow* or */etc/hosts.deny* appropriately for *sshd* access control. Consult section "TCP Wrappers" later in this chapter for details.
4. Allow ssh traffic on port 22 to pass through the firewall, or simply stop and disable the firewall if it is not used. Consult "Netfilter, Firewall and IPTables" later in this chapter on how to perform these tasks.
5. Start (or restart) the *sshd* daemon:

   # **service sshd start**
   RHEL Secure Shell started

Accessing an OpenSSH Server Using User Password

This method works with *ssh*, *scp* and *sftp* commands.

To access an OpenSSH server such as *rhel01* from another RHEL system such as *rhel02*, run the *ssh* command on *rhel02*:

ssh rhel01
The authenticity of host 'rhel01 (192.168.0.201)' can't be established.
RSA key fingerprint is 2e:04:12:a2:8b:00:5a:6e:7f:0c:0f:8d:16:ad:41:1d.
Are you sure you want to continue connecting (yes/no)? **yes**
Warning: Permanently added 'rhel01,192.168.0.201' (RSA) to the list of known hosts.
root@rhel01's password:

Last login: Mon Mar 9 11:35:01 2009 from 192.168.0.202

Value of TERM has been set to "xterm".
WARNING: YOU ARE SUPERUSER !!\n

As displayed, you will need to enter yes when prompted and then the user's password on *rhel01* to log in. If you wish to log on as a different user such as *aghori*, specify the user's name with –l option as demonstrated below. An alternative way is to specify the username and then the hostname with the @ sign in between.

ssh rhel01 –l aghori
ssh aghori@rhel01
The authenticity of host 'rhel01 (192.168.0.201)' can't be established.
RSA key fingerprint is 2e:04:12:a2:8b:00:5a:6e:7f:0c:0f:8d:16:ad:41:1d.
Are you sure you want to continue connecting (yes/no)? **yes**
Warning: Permanently added 'rhel01,192.168.0.201' (RSA) to the list of known hosts.
aghori@rhel01's password:
Last login: Mon Mar 9 11:38:21 2009 from 192.168.0.202

On each subsequent login attempts from *rhel01* to *rhel02*, *aghori* will only have to enter his password to access *rhel02*.

Configuring Key-Based and Passwordless Authentication

Instead of entering a user password for authentication, you can generate encryption keys and use them. This method works with *ssh*, *scp* and *sftp* commands. The following outlines a step-by-step procedure on how to set this up for *user1* from *rhel01* to *rhel02*:

1. Log in to *rhel01* as *user1*.
2. Run the following to create ~/.ssh sub-directory along with two files – *id_dsa* (stores the private key) and *id_dsa.pub* (stores the public key) – underneath it. Enter a name and location of the file in which to save the key or press Enter to accept the default. Enter a passphrase for key-based authentication or simply press Enter for passwordless access.

    $ **ssh–keygen –t dsa**
    Generating public/private dsa key pair.
    Enter file in which to save the key (/home/user1/.ssh/id_dsa):
    Created directory '/home/user1/.ssh'.
    Enter passphrase (empty for no passphrase):
    Enter same passphrase again:
    Your identification has been saved in /home/user1/.ssh/id_dsa.
    Your public key has been saved in /home/user1/.ssh/id_dsa.pub.
    The key fingerprint is:
    9d:3f:cc:ea:71:67:fc:a9:96:b1:46:96:8d:fb:52:8a user1@rhel01

    The contents of *id_dsa* and *id_dsa.pub* files are shown below:

    $ **cat ~/.ssh/id_dsa**
    -----BEGIN DSA PRIVATE KEY-----

```
MIIBvQIBAAKBgQD2uxRLEL6lyKq2YKPQXnomxRVcdsb/hpRc5doA5/6csL6gfDRg
dxSTciL8lAsGNLz1jtAc5jbmLAY+n25M3YAEo3QVR70hMmG8IS2EJnbIZufSJFlO
/dP0HKAqnt7BFdOjo8RYTyOZghtt3kkVPBMxcXL9rn7Ct1vqA4R68LAmSwIVAKLY
ckV1rbCLWyj74PNLPah43Yd3AoGBANhKi+Z8Wfhv/pHgPBeDo25dhge7cQ/P1Dc3
h6lAZ8UMh5dIuUn/+0YzBJskeXVvN/8M4SVNwLFE1xJxxt+JDffle1zdV95xVE3q
wdeGGjXy1QAg+6S0G+Y2vIWj0gn0Xk2toCL70kFUIxvCtvmGJ5A7/bC3H10UnR0O
Nnvq+HCTAoGBAJayNvUTAwQ+eeW1WP3eadHhGxI92A8KW18R3aLllG/0gQpucy79
1VEqbIHxXmonwrZ9e+PO/B897FTvhktnG9GryERUoR8JLHahN3eNhFfMe7M8+/6s
jzb4bJixJpZcx2qdp+x+cz0v69fd/H15kzK1JgcxEnyAGmiyuxjD9uV6AhUAjot1
v09S2NR+TMAe/uhXF5ymg0s=
-----END DSA PRIVATE KEY-----
$ cat ~/.ssh/id_dsa.pub
ssh-dss
AAAAB3NzaC1kc3MAAACBALLWeYXY3b6stDt7usNtc7SWao59lQcCJlxbL0TPYTVMxsV5C
GVjzdJKCr7FO3Xt9rEPs3pzi6cUWhHGRvcvlcB/gANuxIlOz0+ZdgukwSJU3zkA2iak7feGkzODl
geYTU8RKWWpN5W3yMzp9hu7rzjKSsje1N2ajuIpDc6VsYxxAAAAFQDTv6TwXsto6Falj8nYJ
0+G8QqPhQAAAIBcCnx2U440hmu9ixffjFhU0WnA82qgB/7Vre1CvVb0/J1OFZsI683OfOIRzem
I/RNt9NA5gvG0AtGVuTEL2e51xpnBYkKdBhYVgL9cVifHVohCA1tWpF8msQCUiRtBBpvRD
yiw6JAM/pQXOmzuFtkRbw0jvreYffSkHmt6nsfEqAAAAIEAqFwDubwJhXY5BUaDKuPJ5Ojw
0rcwu0dDMpLKYtudci7Rn7Zf3i+coVGCUygg6+UuoBaC8bRRL290iqyBGpVuqEC+xTbvFeLhl
7lz4iE7N82M8pi8Tmvo/ZjWAvhBEhVhhPMmclhRvwhhxu4KQKYjfyqTpHw3Drb7CEAUFh/T5
Os= user1@rhel01
```

3. Copy *id_dsa.pub* file to *rhel02* using the *ssh-copy-id* command. This command creates *.ssh* directory on *rhel02* if it is not already there, and copies the file as *authorized_keys*.

```
$ ssh-copy-id –i ~/.ssh/id_dsa.pub rhel02
27
Enter passphrase for key '/home/user1/.ssh/id_dsa':
Now try logging into the machine, with "ssh 'rhel01'", and check in:

  .ssh/authorized_keys

to make sure we haven't added extra keys that you weren't expecting.
```

At the same time it also creates a file called *known_hosts* on *rhel01* and stores *rhel02*'s hostname, IP address and a unique key for identifying *rhel02*:

```
$ cat ~/.ssh/known_hosts
rhel01,192.168.0.201 ssh-rsa
AAAAB3NzaC1yc2EAAAABIwAAAQEAyi314JDAf6FWMYlOpj9QZwOKwf2cb6OdA25SMQ
PofLG4lMRQQYnlDg3PJpOHYf2rn5xKEVHkDVu+70a7TBO/99bciakCKJx6ih294wj2Kdpmyar
QBqXfeMXBIpOuvOQRYe9N6+J7sU/tZFhF83ON0/TltkLKrSTsuB/Iygn4auy76g1MbIFg20dync
cS8Re6hbuS9GwillnMORfSzS+PpfZH/JWuxStevY/rHSsCstWFSkfa86B/K1AqxRkvi+b1JB2nyJD
aOjoHzjGQHXsc21VJlCXoJPFpTyeDkdDqiC0VDAvcqmYLKbBqdAjYUAhmmduYJ3Zr29cV2I
MznOn5vQ==
```

4. Log in as *user1* on *rhel02* from *rhel01* using the *ssh* command. Answer "yes" if prompted and supply *user1*'s password:

```
$ ssh rhel02
The authenticity of host 'rhel01 (192.168.0.201)' can't be established.
RSA key fingerprint is be:d8:c9:79:19:45:f1:ae:78:98:8e:15:51:96:31:a2.
Are you sure you want to continue connecting (yes/no)? yes
Warning: Permanently added 'rhel01,192.168.0.201' (RSA) to the list of known hosts.
user1@rhel02's password:
Last login: Fri Jan 30 02:15:46 2009 from 192.168.0.201
```

On each subsequent login attempts, *user1* will be allowed passwordless access into *rhel02* provided a passphrase was not entered in step 2. If a passphrase was supplied, then each time *user1* tries to access *rhel02*, he will have to enter the passphrase to be allowed in.

Executing a Command Remotely Using ssh

Depending on keyless/password-based, keyless/passwordless or key-based/passwordless access setup, you may or may not be prompted for password or passphrase.

To execute a command on *rhel02* from *rhel01* using *ssh*:

```
# ssh rhel02 /bin/ls –l /etc/sysconfig
total 424
-rw-r----- 1 root root  514 Apr 20  2008 auditd
-rw-r--r-- 1 root root  286 Oct 15 08:43 authconfig
. . . . . . . .
```

Transferring Files Using scp

Depending on keyless/password-based, keyless/passwordless or key-based/passwordless access setup, you may or may not be prompted for password or passphrase.

To use *scp* to copy *install.log* from *root*'s home directory to */usr/local/etc* directory:

```
# scp ~/install.log /usr/local/etc
```

To use *scp* to copy *install.log* from *root*'s home directory on *rhel02* to its home directory on *rhel03*, run the following on *rhel02*:

```
# scp ~/install.log rhel03:~
```

To use *scp* to copy *install.log* from *root*'s home directory on *rhel02* to its home directory on *rhel03*, run the following on *rhel03*:

```
# scp rhel02:~/install.log ~
```

To use *scp* to copy */usr/local* on *rhel02* into */tmp* on *rhel03*, run the following on *rhel02* with –r and –p options. The two options will force *scp* to also copy sub-directories under */usr/local* and preserve timestamp and permissions, respectively.

```
# scp –rp /usr/local rhel03:/tmp
```

To repeat the above as user *aghori*:

scp –rp /usr/local aghori@rhel03:/tmp

Transferring Files Using sftp

Depending on keyless/password-based, keyless/passwordless or key-based/passwordless access setup, you may or may not be prompted for password or passphrase.

The interfaces for *sftp* and *ftp* are similar; *sftp* offers more file operation options than does *ftp*. Here is an example of how to get on to *rhel02* from *rhel01*:

sftp rhel02
Connecting to rhel02...
sftp>

Type ? at the prompt to list available commands. A short description of what each command does is also displayed.

sftp> ?
Available commands:

cd path	Change remote directory to 'path'
lcd path	Change local directory to 'path'
chgrp grp path	Change group of file 'path' to 'grp'
chmod mode path	Change permissions of file 'path' to 'mode'
chown own path	Change owner of file 'path' to 'own'
help	Display this help text
get remote-path [local-path]	Download file
lls [ls-options [path]]	Display local directory listing
ln oldpath newpath	Symlink remote file
lmkdir path	Create local directory
lpwd	Print local working directory
ls [path]	Display remote directory listing
lumask umask	Set local umask to 'umask'
mkdir path	Create remote directory
progress	Toggle display of progress meter
put local-path [remote-path]	Upload file
pwd	Display remote working directory
exit	Quit sftp
quit	Quit sftp
rename oldpath newpath	Rename remote file
rmdir path	Remove remote directory
rm path	Delete remote file
symlink oldpath newpath	Symlink remote file
version	Show SFTP version
!command	Execute 'command' in local shell
!	Escape to local shell
?	Synonym for help

Some of the common commands are *cd/lcd*, *get/put*, *ls/lls*, *pwd/lpwd*, *mkdir/rmdir*, *quit/exit*, *rename* and *rm*.

Accessing an OpenSSH Server from a Windows System

On the Windows side, several ssh client programs such as PuTTY, are available. PuTTY can be downloaded free of charge from the Internet. Figure 30-1 shows the PuTTY interface.

You will need to supply a hostname or an IP address of the system to log in to and check "SSH" under "Protocol". The ssh protocol uses port 22. Assign a name to this session and click Save to save it to avoid retyping this information in future.

The first time you try to ssh into a RHEL system such as *rhel02*, information similar to the following will be displayed:

```
The authenticity of host 'rhel02 (192.168.0.202)' can't be established.
RSA key fingerprint is be:d8:c9:79:19:45:f1:ae:78:98:8e:15:51:96:31:a2.
Are you sure you want to continue connecting (yes/no)? yes
Warning: Permanently added 'rhel02,192.168.0.202' (RSA) to the list of known hosts.
user1@rhel02's password:
Last login: Fri Jan 30 02:15:46 2009 from 192.168.0.203
```

Supply "yes" to the question and press Enter. This sets up encryption keys for the client system, and the message will not appear on subsequent login attempts.

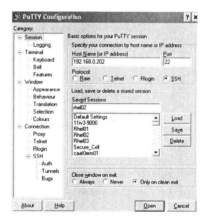

Figure 30-1 PuTTY Interface

Pluggable Authentication Modules (PAM)

The *Pluggable Authentication Modules* (PAM) is a standard set of dynamically loadable library routines (modules) stored in the */lib/security* (32-bit) or */lib64/security* (64-bit) directory. PAM is enabled by default in RHEL 5 and it employs an available authentication service on the system as required. For example, when user authentication is required, the request first goes to PAM which determines a correct verification method – */etc/passwd* file, */etc/shadow* file, NIS or LDAP – to be used. Users and programs that require authentication are unaware of what method is being used; PAM takes care of that on their behalf by referencing the "passwd:" line entry in the */etc/nsswitch.conf* file (See Chapter 22 "DNS and DHCP" and Chapter 23 "NIS and LDAP" on this file's details). Once an authentication method is identified, PAM gets that method and one or more modules from the */lib/security* or */lib64/security* directory engaged, which perform several tests and based on the outcome PAM allows or denies the user or program. The PAM framework provides an easy integration of additional security technologies into RHEL system entry commands.

PAM is also engaged when a user attempts to run a privileged tool such as a *system-config-** utility, the *reboot* command, the *su* command or the like. It references and runs appropriate files and modules to test whether the user trying to execute the command is authorized to do so.

The PAM configuration for each installed PAM-aware service and command is stored in the */etc/pam.d* directory. Each service and command has a file in here that corresponds to its name, and is customizable. Authentication, authorization and other checks for each service and command are performed via these files. These checks are grouped into four security mechanisms referred to as auth, account, password and session.

An *ll* on the directory is shown below:

ll /etc/pam.d

```
. . . . . . . .
-rw-r—r—    1  root  root     97 Dec 13  2006  authconfig
-rw-r—r—    1  root  root     97 Dec 13  2006  authconfig-gtk
-rw-r—r—    1  root  root     97 Dec 13  2006  authconfig-tui
-rw-r—r—    1  root  root    192 Jun 25  2007  chfn
-rw-r—r—    1  root  root    192 Jun 25  2007  chsh
-rw-r—r—    1  root  root    232 Jul 23  09:37  config-util
-rw-r—r—    1  root  root    125 Dec 15  2006  cpufreq-selector
-rw-------   1  root  root    297 Jun 22  2007  crond
-rw-r—r—    1  root  root     65 Aug  6 11:08  cups
-rw-r—r—    1  root  root     97 Jan 16  2007  dateconfig
-rw-r—r—    1  root  root    157 Dec 22  2006  dovecot
. . . . . . . .
```

The contents of one of the files */etc/pam.d/sshd* are displayed below:

cat /etc/pam.d/sshd

```
. . . . . . . .
auth      include    system-auth
account   required   pam_nologin.so
account   include    system-auth
password  include    system-auth
session   optional   pam_keyinit.so  force  revoke
session   include    system-auth
session   required   pam_loginuid.so
```

Each line in the file contains four columns. The first column holds a "module type", the second consists of a "control flag", the third column lists a "module name" and the last column contains any associated options.

The first column "module type" categorizes the modules into one of four security mechanisms for authentication and authorization reasons: *authentication management* (auth), *account management* (account), *password management* (password) and *session management* (session).

Authentication management authenticates or authorizes a user, account management determines if a user's account is valid by checking password, password aging attributes, login restrictions, etc., password management manages a user's password including any limitations set on it and session management establishes and terminates user login sessions.

The second column "control flag" determines an action to be taken based on the success or failure of the associated "module name". Five flags – required, requisite, sufficient, optional and include – are supported. A "required" flag calls the specified module and executes it. The result must be positive in order for an overall success of the authentication/authorization test. If a module failure occurs, PAM continues to execute the remaining modules listed in the file to determine a potential cause of the failure. The outcome of a "requisite" flag must also be successful, otherwise it will force PAM to stop checking the remaining modules, and quit. A "sufficient" flag performs user authentication/authorization if "required" modules are successful. The result of this flag is neglected if it fails. The "optional" flag does not impact the outcome of a module whether or not the module is successful. The "include" flag instructs PAM to include all the specified modules in the user authentication/authorization validation assessment.

The third column "module name" lists the name of a file to be invoked, followed by any optional arguments.

From the file contents displayed above for /etc/pam.d/sshd, the first line entry "auth include system-auth" means that all modules as defined in the system-auth file will be executed. The second line entry "account required pam_nologin.so" implies that the pam_nologin.so module will be executed and its success is critical to the success of the authentication/authorization process. A failure of the module will prevent the user from logging in.

As an example, add the following line to a PAM configuration file such as /etc/pam.d/vsftpd to limit access to specific users listed in a file such as /var/sp-users to be able to execute the pam_listfile.so module. The onerr=succeed (onerr=fail) specifies to return success, the item=user (tty, group, etc.) limits access to users listed in /var/sp-users and the sense=allow (sense=deny) allows only those users to be able to run the module.

        auth required pam_listfile.so onerr=succeed item=user sense=allow file=/var/sp-users

Some key PAM modules located in the /lib/security directory with their associated configuration files in /etc/security directory are listed and described in Table 30-3.

Module	Description
pam_access.so	Controls access to the system at the user, group and system (host, network, domain) levels.
pam_time.so	Controls login and command execution access based on time.
pam_limits.so	Limits user and process access to system resources.
pam_selinux.so	Defines default security context.
pam_securetty.so	Restricts direct root login to devices listed in /etc/securetty file.
pam_userdb.so	Controls user access.
pam_group.so	Limits group access to services.
pam_umask.so	Sets file creation mode.

Table 30-3 Key PAM Modules

All PAM-related messages are logged to the *var/log/secure* file. An excerpt from the file is shown below:

cat /var/log/secure
Apr 21 08:38:53 rhel01 sshd[5654]: pam_unix(sshd:session): session closed for user root
Apr 21 15:00:00 rhel01 sshd[4294]: pam_unix(sshd:auth): authentication failure; logname= uid=0 euid=0
tty=ssh ruser= rhost=aghori user=root
Apr 21 15:00:03 rhel01 sshd[4294]: Failed password for root from 192.168.0.219 port 1457 ssh2
Apr 21 15:00:04 rhel01 sshd[4294]: Accepted password for root from 192.168.0.219 port 1457 ssh2
Apr 21 15:00:04 rhel01 sshd[4294]: pam_unix(sshd:session): session opened for user root by (uid=0)
Apr 21 15:00:36 rhel01 gdm[5005]: pam_unix(gdm:session): session opened for user root by (uid=0)
Apr 21 15:23:18 rhel01 sshd[4294]: pam_unix(sshd:session): session closed for user root
Apr 21 19:45:37 rhel01 sshd[6926]: Accepted password for root from 192.168.0.219 port 2735 ssh2
Apr 21 19:45:37 rhel01 sshd[6926]: pam_unix(sshd:session): session opened for user root by (uid=0)

TCP Wrappers

TCP Wrappers is a host-based service that allows you to control access into a system from remote hosts sending service requests via *xinetd* daemon. The access can be controlled at the user or host level by specifying which users from which hosts, networks or domains are allowed or denied. The software package associated with TCP Wrappers is installed by default, as demonsrated by the *rpm* command output below, as part of RHEL 5 installation:

rpm –qa | grep wrappers
tcp_wrappers-7.6-40.4.el5

Two files – *hosts.allow* and *hosts.deny* – located in the */etc* directory are critical to the functionality. The default files contain no restrictions. The *.allow* file is referenced before the *.deny* file. If the files do not contain an entry for the requesting user or the hostname, network or domain, TCP Wrappers grants the incoming request access into the system.

The way it works is that when an *xinetd*-controlled client request comes in, *xinetd* consults the TCP Wrappers library */usr/lib/libwrap.so*, which scans the *.allow* file and instructs *xinetd* to start the server daemon for the client request if it finds a match in the file. If *.allow* does not contain an entry, TCP Wrappers consults *.deny*. If a match is found, *xinetd* denies access to the client, otherwise, it starts the server daemon and allows the request in. TCP Wrappers entertains only the first match as it scans the files. Any changes made to either file take effect right away.

The format of both files is identical and is based on "what:who" as shown below:

        <name of service daemon>:<list of clients>

The first column lists the name of a service daemon such as *telnetd*, *sshd* and *ftpd*, and the second column specifies a user name, hostname, network address or a domain name. Keywords ALL and EXCEPT may be used in either field to represent "all" or "open to all", and an "exception". The keyword LOCAL matches any hostnames or IP addresses that do not contain a leading dot, KNOWN matches any hostnames that can be resolved and UNKNOWN is the opposite of KNOWN.

Several combinations with an explanation are provided in Table 30-4 for a better understanding.

Entry	/etc/hosts.allow	/etc/hosts.deny
ALL:ALL	All users from all hosts are allowed.	All users from all hosts are denied.
ALL:aghori	User *aghori* is allowed from all hosts.	User *aghori* is denied from all hosts.
ALL:aghori@rhel01	User *aghori* is allowed only from *rhel01* host.	User *aghori* is denied only from *rhel01* host.
ALL:.getitcertify.com	All users on *getitcertify.com* domain are allowed.	All users on *getitcertify.com* domain are denied.
ALL:192.168.2.	All users on 192.168.2 network are allowed.	All users on 192.168.2 network are denied.
sshd:ALL	All users from all systems are allowed *ssh* access.	All users from all systems are denied *ssh* access.
sshd:LOCAL	All users on the local network are allowed *ssh* access.	All users on the local network are denied *ssh* access.
telnetd:192.168.2.	All users on 192.168.2 network are allowed *telnet* access.	All users on 192.168.2 network are denied *telnet* access.
telnetd:192.168.2.0/16	All users on 192.168.2 network with netmask 255.255.0.0 are allowed *telnet* access.	All users on 192.168.2 network with netmask 255.255.0.0 are denied *telnet* access.
telnetd:192.168.2. EXCEPT 192.168.2.25	All users on 192.168.2 network, except from host 192.168.2.25, are allowed *telnet* access.	All users on 192.168.2 network, except from host 192.168.2.25, are denied *telnet* access.
telnetd:192.168.2. EXCEPT 192.168.2.25, 192.168.2.26	All users on 192.168.2 network, except from hosts 192.168.2.25 and .26, are allowed *telnet* access.	All users on 192.168.2 network, except from hosts 192.168.2.25 and .26, are denied *telnet* access.
telnetd,sshd:192.168.2.	All users on 192.168.2 network are allowed *telnet* and *ssh* access.	All users on 192.168.2 network are denied *telnet* and *ssh* access.
telnetd,sshd@192.168.0.201: 192.168.2.	All users on 192.168.2 network are allowed *telnet* and *ssh* access via the interface configured with IP address 192.168.0.201.	All users on 192.168.2 network are denied *telnet* and *ssh* access via the interface configured with IP address 192.168.0.201.
ALL EXCEPT sshd:192.168.2.	All users on 192.168.2 network are allowed access to all but *ssh* service.	All users on 192.168.2 network are denied access to all but *ssh* service.
ALL:.getitcertify.com EXCEPT 192.168.2.0/24	All users on *getitcertify.com* domain except those on 192.168.2.0/24 network are allowed access to all services.	All users on 192.168.2.0/24 network except those on *getitcertify.com* domain are allowed access to all services.

Table 30-4 TCP Wrappers hosts.allow and hosts.deny Files

TCP Wrappers logs information to the */var/log/secure* file.

Netfilter, Firewall and IPTables

Netfilter is a framework that provides a set of hooks within the Linux kernel to enable it to intercept and manipulate data packets. A *firewall* is a protective layer configured between a private and a public network to segregate traffic. There are several types of firewalls one of which performs data packet filtering. As explained in Chapter 20 "Basic Networking", a data packet is formed as a result of a process called encapsulation where header information is attached to a message during the formation of a packet. The header includes information such as source and destination IP addresses, port and type of data. Based on pre-defined *rules*, a firewall intercepts each inbound and outbound data packet, inspects header information associated with it and decides whether to allow the packet to pass through.

RHEL comes standard with a host-based packet-filtering firewall software package called *IPTables* that can be used to control the flow of data packets. Run the *rpm* command to check the presence of the software:

> # **rpm –qa | grep iptables**
> iptables-1.3.5-4.el5

The primary configuration and startup file for the iptables firewall is */etc/sysconfig/iptables*. The */etc/rc.d/init.d/iptables* is the startup script, which reads the file and loads the rules defined in it. This file may be customized using a text editor, the *iptables* command, the *lokkit* command or the Security Level Configurator (*system-config-securitylevel* or *system-config-securitylevel-tui*).

Understanding IPTables Configuration File

An excerpt from the */etc/sysconfig/iptables* file is shown below:

> # **cat /etc/sysconfig/iptables**
> . . . .
> *filter
> :INPUT ACCEPT [0:0]
> :FORWARD ACCEPT [0:0]
> :OUTPUT ACCEPT [0:0]
> :RH-Firewall-1-INPUT – [0:0]
> -A INPUT –j RH-Firewall-1-INPUT
> -A FORWARD –j RH-Firewall-1-INPUT
> -A RH-Firewall-1-INPUT –i lo –j ACCEPT
> -A RH-Firewall-1-INPUT –p icmp –icmp-type any –j ACCEPT
> -A RH-Firewall-1-INPUT –p udp –m udp –dport 631 –j ACCEPT
> -A RH-Firewall-1-INPUT –p tcp –m tcp –dport 631 –j ACCEPT
> -A RH-Firewall-1-INPUT –p tcp –m tcp –dport 21 –j ACCEPT
> -A RH-Firewall-1-INPUT –m state –state NEW –m tcp –p tcp –dport 22 –j ACCEPT
> -A RH-Firewall-1-INPUT –j REJECT –reject-with icmp-host-prohibited
> COMMIT

IPTables allows you to define tables containing *chains* of rules with each table related to a different type of packet processing. In the output above, one default table called *filter* is defined, which includes three pre-defined chains (INPUT, FORWARD and OUTPUT) with the INPUT chain

---

containing several rules. Each inbound or outbound packet goes through at least one of the configured chains. Packets destined for the local system use the INPUT chain, packets originated from the local system use the OUTPUT chain and packets that need to be routed to a different network use the FORWARD chain. Chains have a policy called *target*, which can have a value such as ACCEPT, REJECT, DROP or LOG. The ACCEPT policy lets a packet pass through, the REJECT policy throws a packet away and sends a notification back, the DROP policy simply throws a packet away without sending a notification and the LOG policy sends packet information to the *syslogd* daemon for logging. Two additional pre-defined chains called PREROUTING and POSTROUTING may be used that deal with data packets immediately at their arrival in the system and departure from the system, respectively.

Also notice a "state" in the file contents above. Some of the common states are NEW, ESTABLISHED, RELATED and INVALID. The NEW state identifies packets that are not part of an existing communication, the ESTABLISHED state indicates that the packets are part of an existing communication, the RELATED state signifies packets that are generated in relation with some other existing communication and the INVALID state identifies packets that do not match other states.

It is imperative that you modify the default iptables rules to match the requirements of packet filtering associated with application accessibility.

Modifying IPTables Rules at the Command Prompt

The *iptables* command is used to modify iptables rules at the command prompt. This command supports several options, some of which are listed and described in Table 30-5.

Option	Description
–A	Appends a rule to a chain.
–D	Deletes a rule from a chain.
–F	Flushes a chain or a table.
–I	Inserts a rule in a chain.
–L	Displays currently loaded rules.
–N	Adds a new chain.
–X	Deletes a chain.
–d	Specifies a destintion address.
–i	Specifies a network interface to be used for inbound packets.
–j	Specifies where a packet will jump if it matches a rule.
–n	Specifies not to resolve IP to hostname and port number to service name.
–o	Specifies a network interface to be used for outbound packets.
–p	Defines a protocol as listed in the */etc/protocols* file.
–s	Specifies a source address.
–t	Specifies a type of table. Default is filter, which contains rulesets used for packet filtering.
–v	Prints verbose output.
--sport	Specifies one or a range of source ports.
--dport	Specifies one or a range of destination ports.

Table 30-5 iptables Command Options

Let us take a look at a few examples to understand how the *iptables* command works and what can be performed with it.

To display iptables rules currently in place, use –L option with the command:

```
# iptables –L
Chain INPUT (policy ACCEPT)
target                  prot    opt     source          destination
RH-Firewall-1-INPUT     all     --      anywhere        anywhere

Chain FORWARD (policy ACCEPT)
target                  prot    opt     source          destination
RH-Firewall-1-INPUT     all     --      anywhere        anywhere

Chain OUTPUT (policy ACCEPT)
target                  prot    opt     source          destination

Chain RH-Firewall-1-INPUT (2 references)
target      prot    opt     source          destination
ACCEPT      all     --      anywhere        anywhere
ACCEPT      icmp    --      anywhere        anywhere        icmp any
ACCEPT      esp     --      anywhere        anywhere
ACCEPT      ah      --      anywhere        anywhere
ACCEPT      udp     --      anywhere        anywhere        udp dpt:ipp
ACCEPT      tcp     --      anywhere        anywhere        tcp dpt:ipp
ACCEPT      all     --      anywhere        anywhere        state RELATED,ESTABLISHED
ACCEPT      tcp     --      anywhere        anywhere        state NEW tcp dpt:ssh
REJECT      all     --      anywhere        anywhere        reject-with icmp-host-prohibited
```

To append a rule to the filter table (–t, no need to specify this table name since it is the default) to allow inbound HTTP traffic on port 80 from 192.168.1 network with the default class C netmask:

 # iptables –t filter –A INPUT –s 192.168.1.0/24 –p tcp --dport 80 –j ACCEPT

To insert a rule in the filter table to reject all inbound traffic from 192.168.3 network with the default class C netmask on *eth1* interface and send a notification back:

 # iptables –I INPUT –s 192.168.3.0/24 –i eth1 –j REJECT

To append a rule to the filter table to reject outbound ICMP traffic to all systems on 192.168.3 network except 192.168.3.3 without sending a notification back:

 # iptables –A OUTPUT –d ! 192.168.3.3 –p icmp –j DROP

To delete the above rule:

 # iptables –D OUTPUT –d ! 192.168.3.3 –p icmp –j DROP

To append a rule to forward all inbound traffic from 192.168.1.0 network to 192.168.2.0 network:

 # iptables –A FORWARD –s 192.168.1.0 –d 192.168.2.0 –j ACCEPT

To insert a rule to allow only the first incoming FTP connection request on port 21:

 # iptables –I INPUT –m state --state NEW –p tcp --dport 21 –j ACCEPT

To append a rule to disallow all outgoing connection requests on port 25:

 # iptables –A OUTPUT –m state --state NEW –p tcp --dport 25 –j DROP

To save all the rules defined above in the *etc/sysconfig/iptables* file:

 # service iptables save
Saving firewall rules to /etc/sysconfig/iptables: [OK]

This is how the new rules will be stored in the *iptables* file:

 # cat /etc/sysconfig/iptables

```
. . . . . . . .
-A INPUT -p tcp -m state --state NEW -m tcp --dport 21 -j ACCEPT
-A INPUT -s 192.168.3.0/255.255.255.0 -i eth1 -j REJECT --reject-with icmp-port-unreachable
-A INPUT -s 192.168.1.0/255.255.255.0 -p tcp -m tcp --dport 80 -j ACCEPT
-A FORWARD -s 192.168.1.0 -d 192.168.2.0 -j ACCEPT
-A OUTPUT -p tcp -m state --state NEW -m tcp --dport 25 -j DROP
. . . . . . . .
```

Alternatively, you can edit the *etc/sysconfig/iptables* file and manually add the rules as shown above so they are available across system reboots.

To add a custom chain called NEW_CHAIN:

 # iptables –N NEW_CHAIN

To flush (or delete) all rules in the OUTPUT chain:

 # iptables –F OUTPUT

To flush (or delete) all rules from all chains:

 # iptables –F

Managing IPTables Start and Stop

IPTables can be started, restarted and stopped manually. It can also be configured to start automatically at specific run levels.

To start the iptables service:

 # service iptables start
Applying iptables firewall rules: [OK]

To restart the iptables service:

 # service iptables restart

Flushing firewall rules:	[OK]
Setting chains to policy ACCEPT: filter	[OK]
Unloading iptables modules:	[OK]
Applying iptables firewall rules:	[OK]

To stop the iptables service:

 # service iptables stop

Flushing firewall rules:	[OK]
Setting chains to policy ACCEPT: filter	[OK]
Unloading iptables modules:	[OK]

To enable the iptables service to autostart at each system reboot:

 # chkconfig iptables on

To check the status of the iptables service:

 # service iptables status
Table: filter
Chain INPUT (policy ACCEPT)

num	target	prot	opt	source	destination	
1	ACCEPT	tcp	--	0.0.0.0/0	0.0.0.0/0	state NEW tcp dpt:21
2	REJECT	all	--	192.168.3.0/24	0.0.0.0/0	reject-with icmp-port-unreachable
3	RH-Firewall-1-INPUT	all	--	0.0.0.0/0	0.0.0.0/0	
4	ACCEPT	tcp	--	192.168.1.0/24	0.0.0.0/0	tcp dpt:80

Chain FORWARD (policy ACCEPT)

num	target	prot	opt	source	destination
1	RH-Firewall-1-INPUT	all	--	0.0.0.0/0	0.0.0.0/0
2	ACCEPT	all	--	192.168.1.0	192.168.2.0

Chain OUTPUT (policy ACCEPT)

num	target	prot	opt	source	destination	
1	DROP	tcp	--	0.0.0.0/0	0.0.0.0/0	state NEW tcp dpt:25

Chain RH-Firewall-1-INPUT (2 references)

num	target	prot	opt	source	destination	
1	ACCEPT	all	--	0.0.0.0/0	0.0.0.0/0	
2	ACCEPT	icmp	--	0.0.0.0/0	0.0.0.0/0	icmp type 255
3	ACCEPT	esp	--	0.0.0.0/0	0.0.0.0/0	
4	ACCEPT	udp	--	0.0.0.0/0	0.0.0.0/0	udp dpt:631
5	ACCEPT	tcp	--	0.0.0.0/0	0.0.0.0/0	tcp dpt:631
6	ACCEPT	all	--	0.0.0.0/0	0.0.0.0/0	state RELATED,ESTABLISHED
7	ACCEPT	tcp	--	0.0.0.0/0	0.0.0.0/0	state NEW tcp dpt:22
8	REJECT	all	--	0.0.0.0/0	0.0.0.0/0	reject-with icmp-host-prohibited

Modifying IPTables Rules Using Security Level Configurator

To configure iptables rules using the Security Level Configurator, follow the steps below:

1. Execute *system-config-securitylevel* in an X terminal window or choose (GNOME) System / (KDE) Main Menu → Administration → Security Level and Firewall. The Security Level and Firewall Configurator screen will open up as shown in Figure 30-2.

Figure 30-2 Security Level and Firewall Administration Tool

2. Choose Enabled/Disabled to enable or disable the iptables service, a service such as FTP, Mail, NFS4, SSH, Samba and HTTPS to enable or disable it or click Add to open or close a specific network port.

Alternatively, you can use the *lokkit* or the *system-config-securitylevel* command at the prompt to perform these activities. All settings made using any of these tools are saved in the */etc/sysconfig/iptables* file.

Network Address Translation

Network Address Translation (NAT) is a netfilter function whereby a system on an internal network such as a home or corporate network, can access external networks such as the Internet using a single, registered IP address configured on an intermediary device such as a router, a firewall, a combination of both, or a computer running RHEL or other operating system. *IP masquerading* is a kind of NAT, which allows several systems on an internal network to be able to access external networks using an intermediary device. With masquerading, requests originated from any of the internal systems appear to the outside world as being originated from the intermediary device. The intermediary device stores IP addresses of source systems, along with randomly-generated port numbers assigned to them, in its cache to keep traffic segregated for each system.

In addition to IP masquerading, which works with configured and active network interfaces, there are two other NAT techniques called DNAT (*Destination NAT*) and SNAT (*Source NAT*). DNAT is typically defined in the PREROUTING chain and it translates the destination IP address of an outbound packet and performs the opposite function for any replies. In contrast, SNAT, similar to

IP masquerading, is usually defined in the POSTROUTING chain and it translates the source IP address of an outbound packet to the IP address of an intermediary device.

The key benefits associated with using NATting are:

✓ Hides one or more internal IP addresses from the outside world.
✓ Only one registered (or official) IP address is required.

Configuring IP Masquerading

Follow the steps below to enable IP masquerading on *rhel01* with internal address 192.168.0.201 configured on *eth0* and an official address 198.202.11.15 on *eth1* for an Internet connectivity. Assume default network parameters for both. Refer to Chapter 21 "Network Interface Administration and Routing" on how to configure network interfaces.

1. Ensure *eth0* is configured correctly with 192.168.0.201 address.
2. Ensure *eth1* is configured correctly with 198.202.11.15 address.
3. Configure IP masquerading using one of the iptables firewall configuration tools explained in the previous section. The following demonstrates using the *iptables* command:

   # **iptables –t nat –I POSTROUTING –o eth1 –s 192.168.0.0/24 –j MASQUERADE**

4. Run the following to save the rule in the */etc/sysconfig/iptables* file:

   # **service iptables save**

5. Start (or restart) the iptables firewall service as explained in the previous section.
6. Configure IP forwarding on *rhel01* so the inbound traffic from internal systems is forwarded to the registered address for an Internet access. Edit the */etc/sysctl.conf* file and set the following directive to 1 so the value gets set at every system reboot:

   net.ipv4.ip_forward = 1

7. Execute the *sysctl* command with –p option, or the following for this change to take effect immediately:

   # **echo 1 > /proc/sys/net/ipv4/ip_forward**

8. Configure 198.202.11.15 as the default gateway address on systems on the internal network.

Now you should be able to access the Internet from any system on the internal network.

Security Enhanced Linux

Security Enhanced Linux (SELinux) is an implementation of a powerful, yet flexible *Mandatory Access Control* (MAC) architecture developed by the *National Security Agency* (NSA) with the assistance of Linux community for enhanced, granular security control in Linux. Compared with the standard Unix/Linux *Discretionary Access Control* (DAC) security architecture, MAC provides an added layer of protection for objects such as file, directory, application, process, etc.

SELinux allows you to set security policies using *type enforcement* and *role-based access control*. These elements identify an extensible set of domains/types and roles, respectively. Each process has an associated domain and each object within the domain has an associated type. Likewise, each process has an associated role to ensure that system and user processes are separated. By default, any process or service that is not explicitly permitted, is denied.

SELinux can be enabled with full restrictions in place (called *enforcing*) or enabled with no restrictions (called *permissive*). The permissive mode can be used for troubleshooting purposes as it only logs security violations but does not actually restrict any programs. The third option is to completely disable it. When activated in enforcing mode, SELinux supports two policies – *targeted* and *strict*. Under the targeted policy, there are no limitations set on any service daemons except for the ones on which you set it exclusively. The strict policy, on the other hand, is the opposite of the targeted policy. Under this policy, all services are protected by default except for the ones that you unrestrict explicitly. RHEL 5 supports only the targeted policy.

SELinux Configuration File

The key configuration file for SELinux is */etc/selinux/config* and the default contents of it are displayed below:

```
# cat /etc/selinux/config
# This file controls the state of SELinux on the system.
# SELINUX= can take one of these three values:
#     enforcing - SELinux security policy is enforced.
#     permissive - SELinux prints warnings instead of enforcing.
#     disabled - SELinux is fully disabled.
SELINUX=enforcing
# SELINUXTYPE= type of policy in use. Possible values are:
#     targeted - Only targeted network daemons are protected.
#     strict - Full SELinux protection.
SELINUXTYPE=targeted
```

The SELINUX directive in the file defines the activation mode for SELinux. "Enforcing" activates it and allows or denies actions based on configured settings. "Permissive" activates SELinux, but allows all actions. It records all security violations; however, it does not hinder actions being taken. This mode is useful from a troubleshooting perspective and developing or tuning SELinux security policy. The SELINUXTYPE directive sets the type of policy to be enforced. In "targeted" mode, which is also the default mode, SELinux enables you to set allow/deny controls on individual services. The "strict" mode denies access to all services.

SELinux Security Contexts

SELinux security contexts define security attributes set on individual files and processes. There are three types of attributes associated with security contexts and are referred to as *subject*, *object* and *action*. The subject attribute represents a user type, user or process, the object attribute identifies a role associated with the subject and the action attribute determines what to do.

To display current security contexts on files and directories, do an *ll* with –Z option on */root* directory for instance. The highlighted column indicates subject, object and action in that order.

ll –Z /root

```
-rw-------       root root   system_u:object_r:user_home_t   anaconda-ks.cfg
drwxr-xr-x       root root   root:object_r:user_home_t        Desktop
-rw-r--r--       root root   root:object_r:user_home_t        install.log
-rw-r--r--       root root   root:object_r:user_home_t        install.log.syslog
-rw-r--r--       root root   root:object_r:user_home_t        ks.cfg
```

The subject field in the output contains system_u for system files and root for the *root* user; it may also contain user_u to indicate normal users. The object field contains object_r for files and may contain system_r to symbolize files and users. The action field contains user_home_t and may include one of several actions.

File context for all files in the system are stored in */etc/selinux/targeted/contexts/files/file_contexts* file as shown below:

cat /etc/selinux/targeted/contexts/files/file_contexts

```
/.*      system_u:object_r:default_t:s0
/xen(/.*)?     system_u:object_r:xen_image_t:s0
/mnt(/[^/]*)   -l    system_u:object_r:mnt_t:s0
/mnt(/[^/]*)?  -d    system_u:object_r:mnt_t:s0
/lib(64)?/dbus-1/dbus-daemon-launch-helper    --    system_u:object_r:bin_t:s0
/bin/.* system_u:object_r:bin_t:s0
/dev/.* system_u:object_r:device_t:s0
/lib/.*  system_u:object_r:lib_t:s0
/var/.*  system_u:object_r:var_t:s0
/etc/.*  system_u:object_r:etc_t:s0
/srv/.*  system_u:object_r:var_t:s0
/sys/.*  <<none>>
/usr/.*  system_u:object_r:usr_t:s0
/tmp/.*  <<none>>
/opt/.*  system_u:object_r:usr_t:s0

. . . . . . . .
```

By default, files created in a directory inherit the security contexts set on the directory. If a file is moved to another directory, it takes its security contexts with it, which may not be the same as the destination directory's. In this situation, you might want to correct the file contexts in that directory using the *restorecon* command as explained later in this chapter.

To display current security contexts on running processes, run the *ps* command with –Z option:

ps –efZ

LABEL	UID	PID	PPID	C	STIME	TTY	TIME	CMD
system_u:system_r:init_t	root	1	0	0	Feb26	?	00:00:02	init [5]
system_u:system_r:kernel_t	root	2	1	0	Feb26	?	00:00:00	[migration/0]
system_u:system_r:udev_t:SystemLow-SystemHigh	root	418	1	0	Feb26	?	00:00:01	/sbin/udevd -d
system_u:system_r:auditd_t	root	1837	1	0	Feb26	?	00:00:00	auditd
system_u:system_r:audisp_t	root	1839	1837	0	Feb26	?	00:00:00	/sbin/audispd
system_u:system_r:restorecond_t	root	1858	1	0	Feb26	?	00:00:00	/usr/sbin/restorecond
system_u:system_r:syslogd_t	root	1869	1	0	Feb26	?	00:00:00	syslogd -m 0

. . . .

The action field determines what sort of protection is applied to the process. Any process that is unprotected would have an action set to "unconfined_t".

Checking Current Activation Mode

You can check the SELinux activation mode by running the *getenforce* command:

```
# getenforce
Enforcing
```

Modifying the Activation Mode

You can modify the activation mode from enforcing to permissive using the *setenforce* command, toggling the switch in the */selinux/enforce* file or modifying the SELINUX directive in the */etc/selinux/config* file. You will need to reboot the system for the changes to take effect.

```
# setenforce permissve
# setenforce 0
# echo 0 > /selinux/enforce
# vi /etc/selinux/config
SELINUX=permissive
```

SELinux cannot be disabled with the methods indicated above. You have to modify the SELINUX directive in the */etc/selinux/config* file or set the selinux directive in the */boot/grub/grub.conf* file as shown below, and reboot the system:

```
# vi /etc/selinux/config
SELINUX=disabled
# vi /boot/grub/grub.conf
selinux=0
```

Activation mode for SELinux may be altered using the Security Level Configurator *system-config-securitylevel* or the SELinux Configurator *system-config-selinux*.

Checking the Status of SELinux

Run the *sestatus* command to check the status of SELinux:

```
# sestatus
SELinux status:              enabled
SELinuxfs mount:             /selinux
Current mode:                enforcing
Mode from config file:       enforcing
Policy version:              21
Policy from config file:     targeted
```

With –v option, the *sestatus* command also reports on security contexts set on files and processes by consulting the */etc/sestatus.conf* file. The default *sestatus.conf* file is shown below:

```
# cat /etc/sestatus.conf
[files]
/etc/passwd
/etc/shadow
/bin/bash
/bin/login
/bin/sh
/sbin/agetty
/sbin/init
/sbin/mingetty
/usr/sbin/sshd
/lib/libc.so.6
/lib/ld-linux.so.2
/lib/ld.so.1
[process]
/sbin/mingetty
/sbin/agetty
/usr/sbin/sshd
```

Modifying Security Contexts

The *chcon* command is used for modifying SELinux security contexts on a file or directory. This command can alter the settings at user (–u option), type (–t option) and role (–r option) levels.

To modify SELinux settings on */root/anaconda-ks.cfg* file and */root* directory, run the command as demonstrated below:

```
# chcon –vt staff_home_t /root/anaconda-ks.cfg
context of /root/anaconda-ks.cfg changed to system_u:object_r:staff_home_t
# chcon –vu user_u –t public_content_t /root
context of /root changed to user_u:object_r:public_content_t
```

If you wish to perform the above operation recursively on the */root* directory, use –R option with the command. The –v option is used for verbosity.

Run the *ll* command with –Z option to verify the change:

```
# ll –dZ /root
drwxr-x---    root  root   user_u:object_r:public_content_t  /root
```

To copy security contexts of */etc/passwd* to */etc/group*, use --reference option:

```
# chcon –v --reference /etc/passwd /etc/group
context of /etc/group changed to system_u:object_r:etc_t
```

The directory */etc/selinux/targeted/contexts/files* contains default contexts set on files and directories.

To revert the security contexts to the default settings on the */root* directory, use the *restorecon* command with –F option:

```
# restorecon –F /root
# ll –dZ /root
drwxr-x---   root  root  root:object_r:user_home_dir_t      /root
```

Configuring SELinux via SELinux Configurator

SELinux Configurator is a graphical tool that allows you to perform a number of configuration and management tasks for SELinux including setting SELinux activation mode (enforcing or permissive), disabling it (disabled) and setting default policy type (targeted or strict) from the main menu interface, shown in Figure 30-3, which comes up when you start the SELinux Configurator using the *system-config-selinux* command or choosing (GNOME) System / (KDE) Main Menu → Administration → SELinux Management.

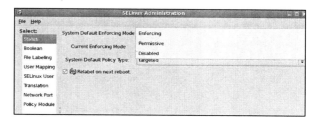

Figure 30-3 SELinux Configurator – Main Menu

There are eight categories as displayed in the left pane. Each category can be selected to modify several settings available within it. The first category is Status, which is already covered. The other seven categories are explained below.

Booleans

Under this category there are several classes defined with each class containing choices pertaining to the class. See Figure 30-4.

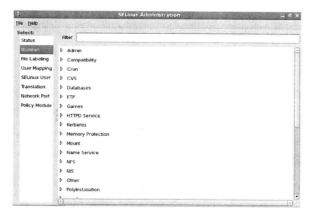

Figure 30-4 SELinux Configurator – Booleans

Any of these settings can be toggled between enable and disable, and hence are referred to as *booleans*. Any modifications done are stored in the corresponding directive file located in the */selinux/booleans* directory. The directory listing for */selinux/booleans* is displayed below:

```
# ll /selinux/booleans
total 0
-rw-r--r--    1  root  root  0  Jan 30 11:34      allow_console_login
-rw-r--r--    1  root  root  0  Jan 30 11:34      allow_cvs_read_shadow
-rw-r--r--    1  root  root  0  Jan 30 11:34      allow_daemons_dump_core
-rw-r--r--    1  root  root  0  Jan 30 11:34      allow_daemons_use_tty
. . . . . . . .
```

Any of these booleans may be altered using either the *setsebool* or the *togglesebool* command. For example, to toggle the value of allow_console_login directive, use any of the following:

```
# setsebool allow_console_login 1
# togglesebool allow_console_login
allow_console_login: inactive
# togglesebool allow_console_login
allow_console_login: active
```

These commands make the change take effect right away without rebooting the system, and store a 0 (disable) or 1 (enable) in the */selinux/syslogd/allow_console_login* file.

Use the *getsebool* command to verify:

```
# getsebool allow_console_login
allow_console_login --> on
```

Some key directive settings from various classes as displayed in Figure 30-4 are highlighted below:

Admin – Allows you to permit/prohibit daemons to be able to use unallocated tty terminals and write corefiles to the root directory, programs to read files from non-standard locations and processes from loading kernel modules and modifying kernel SELinux policy.

Compatibility – Allows you to permit/prohibit sysadm_t to debug or ptrace applications.

Cron – Allows you to permit/prohibit system cron jobs to be able to relabel file system for restoring file contexts, and enable/disable SELinux protection for *crond* and extra rules in the cron domain to support fcron.

CVS – Allows you to permit/prohibit CVS daemon to be able to read shadow passwords, and enable/disable SELinux protection for cvs daemon.

Databases – Allows you to permit/prohibit users to connect to mysql socket, and enable/disable SELinux protection for *mysqld* and *postgresql* daemons.

FTP – Allows you to permit/prohibit *ftpd* full access to the system, to run directly without *inetd*, to upload files to directories labeled public_content_rw_t, to use CIFS or NFS for public file transfer, to read/write files in the user home directories, and enable/disable SELinux protection for *ftpd*.

HTTPD Service – Allows you to permit/prohibit Apache to use mod_auth_pam, support cgi scripts, connect to the network and databases, write files to public directories labeled public_content_rw_t, act as a relay, read home directories, run as an FTP server, run SSI executables in the same domain as system CGI scripts, support built-in scripting, write files to public directories labeled public_content_rw_t, and enable/disable SELinux protection for *httpd* and http suexec. Also allows you to unify Apache handling of all content files and to communicate with the terminal.

Kerberos – Allows you to permit/prohibit daemons to be able to use kerberos files, and enable/disable SELinux protection for *kadmind* (kerberos administrative daemon) and *krb5kdc* (kerberos 5 key control daemon).

Memory Protection – Allows you to set several directives related to memory protection. The default settings typically work well unless you have a specific need to modify them.

Mount [related to automount] – Allows you to permit/prohibit *automount* daemon to mount any directories or files, and enable/disable SELinux protection for *automount* daemon.

Name Service – Allows you to permit/prohibit *named* to overwrite master zone files and enable/disable SELinux protection for *named* and *nscd*.

NFS – Allows you to permit/prohibit *gssd* (general security services daemon) to read temp directory, NFS servers to modify public files used for public file transfer services, NFS to share any file/directory read-only or read/write, and enable/disable SELinux protection for *gssd* and *nfsd*, and support for NFS home directories.

NIS – Allows you to permit/prohibit daemons to run with NIS, and enable/disable SELinux protection for *yppasswdd*, *ypxfrd* and *ypbind*.

Other – Allows you to enable/disable support for miscellaneous directives.

Polyinstatiation – Allows you to enable/disable support for polyinstatiation directory.

pppd [point to point protocol daemon] – Allows you to permit/prohibit *pppd* to insert modules into the kernel and be run by regular users, and enable/disable SELinux protection for the mozilla *pppd*.

Printing – Allows you to enable/disable SELinux protection for *cupsd* backend server, *cupsd*, *cupsd_lpd* and cups *hplip* daemons, and enable/disable the use of *lpd* instead of *cupsd*.

rsync – Allows you to permit/prohibit *rsync* to write files to public directories labeled public_content_rw_t, and enable/disable SELinux protection for *rsync* daemon.

Samba – Allows you to permit/prohibit Samba to act as a domain controller, be able to add users, groups and change passwords, share any files/directories read-only and read/write, share user home directories, write files to public directories labeled public_content_rw_t, allow users to log in with CIFS home directories, and enable/disable SELinux protection for *nmbd*, *smbd* and *winbind*.

SASL Authentication Server – Allows you to permit/prohibit sasl (simple authentication and security layer) authentication server to read */etc/shadow* file, and enable/disable SELinux protection for *saslauthd* daemon.

SELinux Service Protection – Allows you to enable/disable SELinux protection for a number of services such as *dhcp, dovecot, fetchmail, fingerd, hotplug, inetd, klogd, lpd, ntpd, portmap, postfix, rlogind, rshd, setroubleshoot, syslogd, tcpd, telnetd* and *ypserv*.

Spam Assassin – Allows you to permit/prohibit spam assassin daemon network access.

Spam Protection – Allows you to permit/prohibit *spamd* to access home directories, and enable/disable SELinux protection for *spamd*.

Squid – Allows you to permit/prohibit *squid* daemon to connect to the network, and enable/disable SELinux protection for *squid* daemon.

SSH – Allows you to permit/prohibit ssh logins as sysadm_r:sysadm_t, and ssh to run as an *xinetd* service and be able to run *ssh-keygen* command.

Universal SSL Tunnel – Allows you to permit/prohibit *stunnel* daemon to be able to run outside of *xinetd*, and enable/disable SELinux protection for *stunnel*.

User Privs – Allows you to permit/prohibit *cdrecord* to be able to read nfs, samba, removable devices, user temp and untrusted content files, normal users to execute *ping*, direct mouse access, control network interfaces, run TCP servers, run *dmesg* command, stat tty files and so on.

Web Applications – Allows you to permit/prohibit evolution, thunderbird and mozilla browser to be able to read user files, programs to read untrusted content without relabel, web applications to write untrusted contents to disk, and enable/disable SELinux protection for evolution, web browsers and thunderbird.

Xserver – Allows you to permit/prohibit clients to write to X shared memory, and xdm logins as sysadm_r:sysadm_t.

Zebra – Allows you to permit/prohibit zebra daemon to be able to write to its configuration files.

File Labeling

Allows you to modify SELinux security contexts on files.

Figure 30-5 SELinux File Labeling

User Mapping

Allows you to modify extended attributes for regular and administrative users.

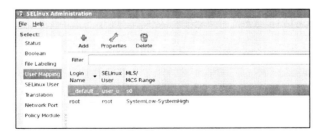

Figure 30-6 SELinux User Mapping

SELinux User

Allows you to set default roles for regular users, system users and the *root* user.

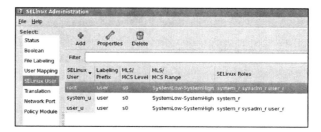

Figure 30-7 SELinux User

Translation

Allows you to set sensitivity levels.

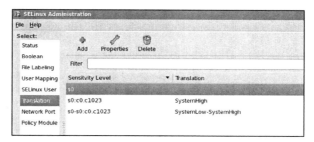

Figure 30-8 SELinux Translation

Network Port

Allows you to set services with ports, and choose protocol.

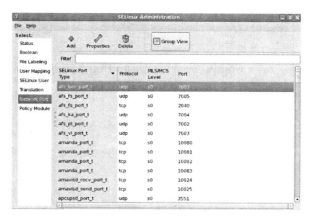

Figure 30-9 SELinux Network Port

Policy Module

Displays versions associated with modules.

Figure 30-10 SELinux Policy Module

Viewing Alerts with SELinux Troubleshooter Browser

The SELinux troubleshooter browser is a tool that lets you view SELinux related issues conveniently in a graphical setting. It identifies issues, describes causes and offers suggestions on fixing among providing other associated assistance. This tool is invoked with the *sealert* command with –b option or by choosing (GNOME) Applications → System Tools → SELinux Troubleshooter or (KDE) Main Menu → System → SELinux Troubleshooter.

sealert –b

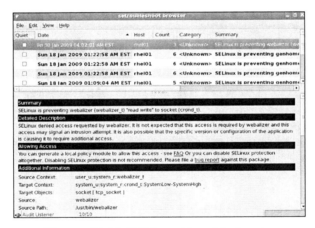

Figure 30-11 SELinux Troubleshooter

In order for this tool to work, you must have the *setroubleshootd* daemon running. This daemon is invokved when the system enters run level 3 and runs the */etc/rc.d/init.d/setroubleshoot* script. SELinux messages are logged to the */var/log/messages* file with an "avc" label and can be viewed with this tool easily.

Common System Hardening Tasks

Some RHEL system hardening best practices are listed below. Many of them have been covered earlier in the book. Not all of these need to be configured on every system, but implementing the ones that suit requirements ensure a safer and more protected system against unknown and outside threats. Before applying any of these, make certain that it does not disrupt any application functionality.

1. Install the latest security updates periodically from RHN using the *yum* command.
2. Activate SELinux in enforcing mode and enable desired services/directives only.
3. Implement iptables firewall to limit the use of ports and services.
4. Implement TCP Wrappers for access control.
5. Use the secure cousins of POP3 and IMAP.
6. Disable instant messengers.
7. Disable or remove dormant user accounts.
8. Disable the use of the *write* command by setting "mesg –n" in system-wide user profiles.
9. Create a hidden home directory such as */.root* for *root* user with 700 permissions.
10. Set the umask value to 077 for the *root* user.
11. Check the contents of *passwd*, *shadow*, *group* and *gshadow* files periodically for any discrepancies.
12. Check log files on a regular basis for any security issues.
13. Disable unused *xinetd*-controlled services.
14. Disable *telnet, rlogin, rsh, rcp* and *ftp,* and use *ssh, scp* and *sftp* instead.
15. Disable system users such as *root* from using *ftp.*
16. Disable direct *root* login except at the system console.
17. Control the use of setuid and setgid programs.
18. Set 777 permissions and sticky bit on world-writeable directories.
19. Disable the use of NFS client, NFS server and AutoFS provided they are not in use. If NFS server must be used, make certain that the resources are exported to specific systems only.
20. Disable the use of NIS and LDAP unless they are needed.
21. Limit the use of *cron* and *at* via user entries in appropriate files. If *at* is not used, remove the */etc/at.* * files. Remove *cron.deny* and update *cron.allow* file with entries for only those users that must require *cron* scheduling ability.
22. Implement the use of *sudo.* Force system administrators to log in with their user IDs and use *sudo* to run privileged commands. Allow application and database administrators limited *sudo* access to privileged commands.
23. Use */etc/issue* or */etc/motd* file to display system usage security policy messages at login.

Summary

This chapter discussed ways of securing a system. You looked at benefits associated with using secure shell and how ssh encrypts information. You understood the contents of the ssh configuration file and configured an ssh server and single sign-on user access. You saw how to access a remote system via ssh and from a Windows system. You transferred files using scp and sftp tools.

Next, you looked at Pluggable Authentication Module and associated benefits. You studied TCP Wrappers and IPTables firewall, and modified firewall rules at the command prompt and using a graphical tool. You learned Network Address Translation and how to configure IP masquerading.

Finally, you studied SELinux at length. At the end of the chapter, a list of common system security recommendations was provided that you should be looking at implementing as appropriate to elevate system security level.

## 31

System, Network and Security Troubleshooting

This chapter covers the following major topics:

- ✓ Introduction to troubleshooting
- ✓ Linux rescue mode and how to use it
- ✓ Install a lost or corrupted bootloader and file
- ✓ Troubleshoot and resolve boot problems
- ✓ Troubleshoot and resolve networking and name resolution issues
- ✓ Troubleshoot and resolve issues with file transfer, resource sharing, time synchronization, mail, web and caching services
- ✓ Troubleshoot and resolve issues with X Window system and display/desktop managers
- ✓ Troubleshoot and resolve miscellaneous issues such as those related to disk quota

In a corporate server environment problems occur all the time and it is one of the responsibilities of the system administrator to troubleshoot and resolve them. Problems generally occur due to a misconfiguration, an incomplete configuration or a malfunctioning component, and need to be addressed to bring the system or the affected service back to its expected state of operation. Various troubleshooting approaches may be employed depending on an individual's knowledge and experience; one of the approaches that I normally follow is *Gather-Analyze-Identify-Solve-Validate* (GAISV) whereby you *gather* required data (error messages, log files, configuration files, etc.), *analyze* the data, *identify* a potential root cause of the problem, *solve* the issue and *validate* the fix. A problem may occur due to more than one causes and in such a situation all the causes need to be determined and fixed. Causes of some problems may be identified easily and resolved quickly, many problems take a long time and require a lot of data and a deep analysis before an exact root cause is identified and a fix is implemented.

In this chapter, troubleshooting and associated resolution is covered from system, network and security administration perspectives.

System administration: configuration issues associated with X Window, display and desktop managers, software packages, users and groups, disk partitioning, file systems, swap spaces, system boot, kernel, print services and job scheduling, and include service not coming up after a system reboot, file system corruption, system become unbootable, kernel corrupted or missing, kernel parameters not accepting new values, printer not printing, print requests not going to an intended printer, graphical desktop not coming up and configured file systems not getting mounted after a system reboot.

Network administration: configuration issues related to network interfaces, routing, DNS, DHCP, NIS, LDAP, Internet services, mail system, NTP, NFS, AutoFS, Samba and web servers, and include network card software driver not installed, duplicate IP addresses on the network, wrong IP address assignments, incorrect subnet mask, incorrect routing table entries, IP address and other network parameters lost at system reboot, network interface not in UP state, name resolution not functioning as desired, system time not synchronizing with an external clock and remote file systems inaccessible.

Security administration: configuration issues associated with secure shell utilities, PAM, TCP Wrappers, firewall, NATting and SELinux, and include systems not talking to one another, logging and connection issues, and services not working as desired.

Knowledge obtained from reading the book and experience gained by performing exercises thus far will aid in identifying and resolving configuration issues presented in this chapter.

From RHCT and RHCE troubleshooting and system maintenance exams viewpoint, only limited troubleshooting scenarios are presented here having relevance with system boot failures arising from bootloader, module and file system errors; network issues resulting from misconfigured networking and hostname resolution; and other problems with services such as file transfer, resource sharing, time synchronization, mail, web, caching and secure shell. These issues may or may not involve SELinux security contexts. Although not part of the exams, but troubleshooting scenarios linked with X Window and GUI are also included.

Before jumping into troubleshooting scenarios for boot failure, it is imperative to understand how a RHEL system can be booted into a special system recovery mode called *Linux rescue mode* and how to use and interact with it to resolve boot issues.

Linux Rescue Mode and How to Use It

The linux rescue environment allows you to fix boot issues such as reinstalling a corrupted stage 1 boot loader or accessing a problematic */boot* file system, that have rendered the system unbootable. A minimal set of key commands are available in the rescue mode to help troubleshoot and resolve problems. These commands include the *vi* and *nano* editors as well as tools to manage file and directory operations, software packages, LVM, RAID and standard partitioning, file systems and swap, processes and kernel, archiving and compression, and network interfaces and connectivity. All rescue mode boot messages are logged to the */tmp/anaconda.log* file and system logging activities to the */tmp/syslog* file.

Booting the System into Linux Rescue Mode

Follow the procedure below to boot the system into the rescue mode:

1. Boot the system with the first installation CD/DVD or the bootable CD / USB created in Chapter 28 "Network Installation".
2. Type "linux rescue" at the boot: or isolinux prompt as appropriate.

Figure 31-1 Booting into Linux Rescue Mode

3. Select language and keyboard on subsequent screens.
4. Select whether you want network interfaces to start. If you choose yes, you will be asked if you want to configure *eth0*. Choosing yes will let you to enter IP information that you wish to assign to this interface and choosing no will let you define gateway and primary/secondary DNS servers. If you do not wish to enter this information at this time, simply press OK and then the Continue button twice to go to the next screen. If you chose no at the initial question that asked whether you wanted network interfaces started, you would be taken directly to the next screen.
5. Three options – Continue, Read-Only and Skip – appear as shown in Figure 31-2.

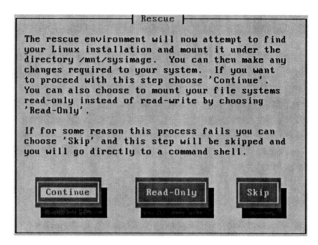

Figure 31-2 Linux Rescue Mode Options

"Continue" mounts local file systems as defined in */etc/fstab* file in read/write mode, "Read-Only" mounts them in read-only mode and "Skip" does not mount any file systems. Whichever option you choose, the system will take you to the command prompt to run administrative commands for solving a boot issue.

The "Continue" and "Read-Only" Options

Choosing either one searches for a RHEL installation and, if found, mounts the / file system on */mnt/sysimage* in read/write (Continue) or read-only (Read-Only) mode.

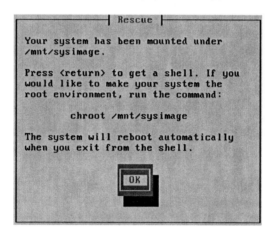

Figure 31-3 Linux Rescue Mode – Continue and Read-Only Options

Press the OK button to go to the command prompt.

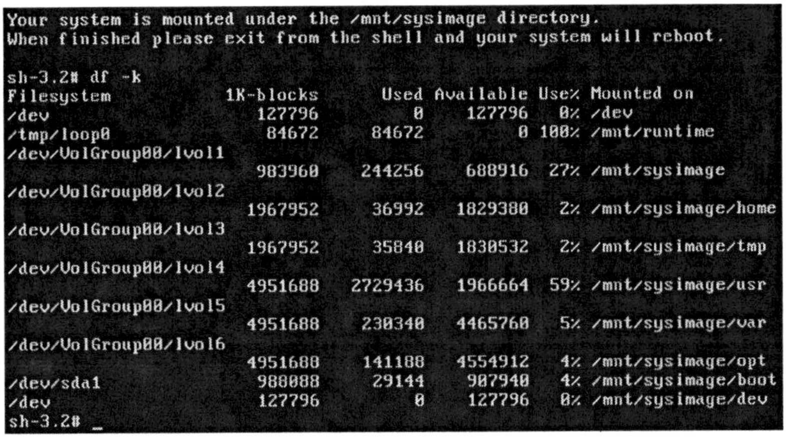

```
Your system is mounted under the /mnt/sysimage directory.
When finished please exit from the shell and your system will reboot.

sh-3.2# df -k
Filesystem            1K-blocks      Used Available Use% Mounted on
/dev                     127796         0    127796   0% /dev
/tmp/loop0                84672     84672         0 100% /mnt/runtime
/dev/VolGroup00/lvol1
                         983960    244256    688916  27% /mnt/sysimage
/dev/VolGroup00/lvol2
                        1967952     36992   1829380   2% /mnt/sysimage/home
/dev/VolGroup00/lvol3
                        1967952     35840   1830532   2% /mnt/sysimage/tmp
/dev/VolGroup00/lvol4
                        4951688   2729436   1966664  59% /mnt/sysimage/usr
/dev/VolGroup00/lvol5
                        4951688    230340   4465760   5% /mnt/sysimage/var
/dev/VolGroup00/lvol6
                        4951688    141188   4554912   4% /mnt/sysimage/opt
/dev/sda1                988088     29144    907940   4% /mnt/sysimage/boot
/dev                     127796         0    127796   0% /mnt/sysimage/dev
sh-3.2# _
```

Figure 31-4 Linux Rescue Mode – File Systems Mounted on /mnt/sysimage

Other file systems such as */boot* as shown in Figure 31-4 will be mounted on */mnt/sysimage/boot*, */usr* on */mnt/sysimage/usr* and so on. In case a file system listed in */etc/fstab* cannot be mounted, the following error message will be displayed:

An error occurred trying to mount some or all of your file system

At this point, you can run the following command to make all file systems appear as if they are mounted directly under */*:

chroot /mnt/sysimage

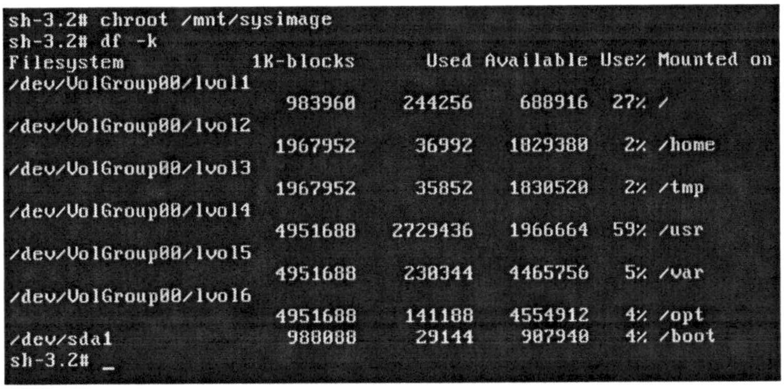

```
sh-3.2# chroot /mnt/sysimage
sh-3.2# df -k
Filesystem            1K-blocks      Used Available Use% Mounted on
/dev/VolGroup00/lvol1
                         983960    244256    688916  27% /
/dev/VolGroup00/lvol2
                        1967952     36992   1829380   2% /home
/dev/VolGroup00/lvol3
                        1967952     35852   1830520   2% /tmp
/dev/VolGroup00/lvol4
                        4951688   2729436   1966664  59% /usr
/dev/VolGroup00/lvol5
                        4951688    230344   4465756   5% /var
/dev/VolGroup00/lvol6
                        4951688    141188   4554912   4% /opt
/dev/sda1                988088     29144    907940   4% /boot
sh-3.2# _
```

Figure 31-5 Linux Rescue Mode – File Systems Mounted Normally

The Skip Option

This option forces the rescue environment to load a minimal root image into RAM disk created by the kernel. It then takes you to the command prompt where you can run basic commands.

```
When finished please exit from the shell and your system will reboot.

sh-3.2# df -k
Filesystem          1K-blocks     Used Available Use% Mounted on
/dev                   127796        0    127796   0% /dev
/tmp/loop0              84672    84672         0 100% /mnt/runtime
sh-3.2# _
```

Figure 31-6 Linux Rescue Mode – Skip Option

This option should be chosen if you need to run *fsck* on a raw device before mounting a file system in it.

Reinstalling a Corrupted Bootloader

Once in the rescue mode, you can reinstall a corrupted GRUB bootloader. As you already know, GRUB stage 1 can be installed on the MBR or a disk partition such as /. Here is how you would reinstall GRUB on MBR located on */dev/sda* disk using the *grub-install* command:

> # **grub-install --root-directory=/mnt/sysimage /dev/sda**
> Probing devices to guess BIOS drives. This may take a long time.
> Installation finished. No error reported.
> This is the contents of the device map /mnt/sysimage/boot/grub/device.map.
> Check if this is correct or not. If any of the lines is incorrect, fix it and re-run the script `grub-install'.
>
> (hd0)   /dev/sda

Replace */dev/sda* with */dev/sda1* if the location of the bootloader program is on that file system. Execute the *exit* command to reboot the system.

If the above does not work, exit out of the chroot environment, run the *grub* command to get to the grub prompt and then the commands as shown below to fix the bootloader and reboot the system:

> # **grub**
> grub> **root (hd0,0)**
> grub> **setup (hd0)**
> grub> **quit**
> # **exit**

Installing a Lost File in Linux Rescue Mode

A key system file or command can get corrupted or lost and prevent a successful system boot up. Some of the necessary files and commands that must be available in order for the system to boot normally are */boot/grub/grub.conf*, */etc/passwd*, */etc/inittab*, */etc/fstab*, */sbin/init*, */bin/mount* and */bin/bash*. If any of these is deleted, it will need to be reinstalled, created, or restored from backup. For example, if */sbin/init* command is corrupted or erased, you can load the SysVinit package. Likewise, the */bin/mount* command is part of util-linux package, which has to be installed to get the command back. Here is how you would reinstall */sbin/init*:

1. Boot the system into linux rescue mode. Enable networking to be able to connect to a network installation source. Choose Continue so the file systems are mounted read/write.
2. Run the *chroot* command to make file systems appear under /:

chroot /mnt/sysimage

3. Mount the NFS file system that contains the required package. For example, if the NFS server is 192.168.0.202 with */rhel02/packages* directory exported and holding installable packages, run the following to mount it on */dvdrom* (assuming */dvdrom* exists):

   # mount –t nfs 192.168.0.202:/rhel02/packages /dvdrom

4. Execute the *rpm* command with --force option to install the package and overwrite any existing installed files that belong to the package:

   # rpm –ivh --force --root /mnt/sysimage /dvdrom/Server/SysVinit-2.86-14*.rpm

5. Confirm the file installation:

   # ls –l /sbin/init

6. Execute the *exit* command twice to quit the chroot environment and reboot the system.

Troubleshooting and Resolving System Boot Issues

Boot problems generally occur due to misconfiguration in */boot/grub/grub.conf* boot configuration file, */etc/inittab* initialization file, */etc/fstab* file system table or a missing file in the */boot* file system. The boot file is updated during kernel upgrade and the system might become unbootable if something is not right in this file. An unbootable system can be booted into the rescue mode to fix the problem. There are situations where interacting with GRUB gives you the ability to fix an incorrect directive in *grub.conf*. Ensure that you read messages displayed when the system boots up to get an idea as to where the root cause of the issue might be. The following sub-sections present several troubleshooting scenarios and possible solutions that require booting the system into the rescue mode, and other boot modes explained in Chapter 15 "Shutdown and Boot". For each issue, a short description is provided and the resolution follows the GAISV model.

Issue: "root user password is lost, forgotten or has expired"

Gather: *root* user password is lost, forgotten or has expired.
Analyze: No administrators recall the password nor have they stored it at a safe place. No *root* session is running and no other users have *sudo* access to change *root*'s password or activate the account.
Identify: The system has to be rebooted into single user mode to change the password or activate the account.
Solve: Boot the system into single user mode and type *passwd root* at the prompt to change the password or *chage –E –1 root* to reactivate the account. Type *exit* to go to the default run level.
Validate: Validate the fix by logging in with *root* after the system has been up.

Issue: "passwd: Authentication token manipulation error"

Gather: *root* user password cannot be changed in single user mode. No regular users have *sudo* access to modify it. The system has already been rebooted and no *root* login session is available.

Analyze: The error message indicates that there is something wrong with either */etc/passwd* or */etc/shadow* file. Boot into single user mode and check whether the files exist. Also check permissions on the files with the *ll* command, and attributes with the *lsattr* command to verify the file is not immutable.

Identify: The */etc/shadow* file does not exist.

Solve: Boot the system into single user mode and execute the *pwconv* command to recreate the *shadow* file. Execute the *passwd* command and change the *root*'s password. Type *exit* to boot to the default run level.

Validate: Validate the fix by logging in with *root* after the system has been up.

Issue: "Operating system not found"

Gather: The very first sector of the boot disk that stores MBR, appears to be corrupted or deleted.

Analyze: It appears that MBR is deleted or corrupted.

Identify: MBR may have been corrupted or overwritten unintentionally with a command such as *dd if=/dev/zero of=/dev/sda bs=384 count=1*.

Solve: Boot the system into the rescue mode (networking off, Continue). Run *chroot /mnt/sysimage* and then *grub-install --root-directory=/mnt/sysimage /dev/sda* to install grub bootloader in MBR. Execute the *exit* command twice to quit and reboot the system. Alternatively, type *grub* at the shell prompt to go to the grub> prompt and execute *root (hd0,0)*, *setup (hd0)*, *quit* and then the *exit* command to fix the bootloader and reboot the system.

Validate: Validate the fix when the system attempts to reboot.

Issue: "The system stops at the grub> prompt"

Gather: System is unable to boot and no data is available.

Analyze: It appears that the system is unable to read or find the *grub.conf* file.

Identify: The *grub.conf* file is missing, deleted or renamed, or titles in the file are either commented or not listed.

Solve: Boot the system into the rescue mode (networking on, Continue). Run *chroot /mnt/sysimage* and change directory into */boot/grub*. Restore, rename, create or fix the *grub.conf* file. Execute the *exit* command twice to quit and reboot the system.

Validate: Validate the fix when the system attempts to reboot.

Issue: "Error 1: Filename must be either an absolute pathname or blocklist"

Gather: System attempts to boot but is unable to find the name or location of a key file.

Analyze: The *grub.conf* file appears to have an invalid file pathname.

Identify: The *grub.conf* file has an invalid kernel or initrd file pathname defined in it.

Solve: Boot the system and interact with the GRUB menu by pressing any key within the number of seconds defined in *grub.conf* with the timeout directive. Press e for edit and review the root, kernel and initrd directives for any typos. Highlight the problem entry and press e to edit it. Fix the directive and press b to boot. After the system is back up, change directory into */boot/grub* and edit the *grub.conf* file to fix the typo for good.

Validate: Validate the fix as the system boots up. You may want to reboot the system again to validate the permanent fix.

Issue: "Error 11: Unrecognized device string"

Gather: System attempts to boot but is unable to find a correct boot device.
Analyze: The *grub.conf* file appears to have an invalid directive.
Identify: The *grub.conf* file has an invalid root directive.
Solve: Boot the system and interact with the GRUB menu by pressing any key within the number of seconds defined in *grub.conf* with the timeout directive. Press e for edit and then again to edit the root directive. Fix the directive and press b to boot. After the system is back up, change directory into */boot/grub* and edit the *grub.conf* file to fix the typo permanently.
Validate: Validate the fix while the system boots up. You may want to reboot the system again to validate the permanent fix.

Issue: "Error 15: File not found"

Gather: System attempts to boot but is unable to find a key file.
Analyze: The *grub.conf* file appears to have an invalid name for the kernel or the initrd file, or one of these files is missing from the */boot* file system.
Identify: Fix the kernel or the initrd file in the */boot* file system or the associated filename in *grub.conf*.
Solve: Boot the system into the rescue mode (networking on, Continue). Run *chroot /mnt/sysimage* and change directory into */boot/grub*. Edit the *grub.conf* file and fix the filename if the problem is there, otherwise, *cd* into */boot* and ensure that the kernel and initrd files exist and their names correspond to the names specified in *grub.conf*. If one or both files are missing, restore them from backup. Execute the *exit* command twice to quit and reboot the system.
Validate: Validate the fix while the system boots up.

Issue: "Error 17: Cannot mount selected partition"

Gather: System attempts to boot but is unable to mount the root file system.
Analyze: It appears that the root directive that defines the primary disk and the root file system in the *grub.conf* file is invalid.
Identify: Fix the root directive in *grub.conf*.
Solve: Boot the system and interact with the GRUB menu by pressing any key within the number of seconds defined in *grub.conf* with the timeout directive. Press e for edit and then again to edit the root directive. Fix the directive and press b to boot. After the system is back up, change directory into */boot/grub* and edit *grub.conf* to fix the typo permanently.
Validate: Validate the fix while the system boots up. You may want to reboot the system again to validate the permanent fix.

Issue: "Error 19: Linux kernel must be loaded before initrd"

Gather: System attempts to boot but is unable to find a kernel file.
Analyze: It appears that the kernel directive in *grub.conf* is invalid or commented, or the kernel file is missing from */boot*.
Identify: Fix the kernel directive in *grub.conf*. Restore */boot/kernel** from backup.
Solve: Boot the system and interact with the GRUB menu by pressing any key within the number of seconds defined in *grub.conf* with the timeout directive. Press e for edit and highlight the kernel directive. Fix the directive and press b to boot. After the system is back up, change directory into */boot/grub* and edit *grub.conf* to fix the directive permanently. If this is not the issue and the kernel file itself is missing, corrupted or lost, reboot the system into the rescue mode and try to locate a

backup kernel file. If found, edit the *grub.conf* file and modify the kernel directive to point to that file.

Validate: Validate the fix while the system boots up. You may want to reboot the system again to validate the permanent fix.

Issue: "Error 21: Selected disk does not exist"

Gather: System attempts to boot but is unable to locate the boot disk that contains the root file system.

Analyze: It appears that the root directive that defines the primary disk and the root file system in the *grub.conf* file is invalid.

Identify: Fix the root directive in *grub.conf*.

Solve: Boot the system and interact with the GRUB menu by pressing any key within the number of seconds defined in *grub.conf* with the timeout directive. Press e for edit and then again to edit the root directive. Fix the directive and press b to boot. After the system is back up, change directory into */boot/grub* and edit *grub.conf* to fix the typo permanently.

Validate: Validate the fix while the system boots up. You may want to reboot the system again to validate the permanent fix.

Issue: "Error 22: No such partition"

Gather: System attempts to boot but is unable to locate the root file system.

Analyze: It appears that the root directive that defines the primary disk and the root partition in the *grub.conf* file is invalid, or the kernel file is not on the selected disk/partition.

Identify: The *grub.conf* file has an invalid partition entry in the root directive, or the kernel file is not on the selected disk/partition.

Solve: Boot the system and interact with the GRUB menu by pressing any key within the number of seconds defined in *grub.conf* with the timeout directive. Press e for edit and review the root and kernel directives for any typos. Highlight the problem entry and press e to edit it. Fix the directive and press b to boot. After the system is back up, change directory into */boot/grub* and edit the *grub.conf* file to fix the root directive permanently.

Validate: Validate the fix while the system boots up. You may want to reboot the system again to validate the permanent fix.

Issue: "Error 23: Error while parsing number"

Gather: System attempts to boot but is unable to find the disk or partition that contains the operating system.

Analyze: The disk and/or partition number is incorrect in the root directive.

Identify: The *grub.conf* file has an invalid disk and/or partition entry in the root directive.

Solve: Boot the system and interact with the GRUB menu by pressing any key within the number of seconds defined in *grub.conf* with the timeout directive. Press e for edit and then again to edit the root directive. Fix the directive and press b to boot. After the system is back up, change directory into */boot/grub* and edit the *grub.conf* file to fix the root directive permanently.

Validate: Validate the fix while the system boots up. You may want to reboot the system again to validate the permanent fix.

Issue: "Error 27: Unrecognized command"

Gather: System attempts to boot but encounters an invalid command.

Analyze: It appears that an invalid command is defined in the *grub.conf* file.
Identify: Fix or remove the invalid command from the *grub.conf* file.
Solve: Boot the system into the rescue mode (networking off, Continue). Run *chroot /mnt/sysimage* and change directory into */boot/grub*. Edit the *grub.conf* file and fix or remove the invalid command entry. Execute the *exit* command twice to quit and reboot the system.
Validate: Validate the fix while the system boots up.

Issue: "Error 30: Invalid argument"

Gather: System attempts to boot but encounters an invalid argument supplied with a command.
Analyze: It appears that an argument supplied with a command in the *grub.conf* file is invalid.
Identify: Fix or remove the invalid argument supplied with a command in the *grub.conf* file.
Solve: Boot the system and interact with the GRUB menu by pressing any key within the number of seconds defined in *grub.conf* with the timeout directive. Press e for edit and review the root, kernel and initrd directives for any typos. Highlight the problem entry and press e to edit it. Fix the directive and press b to boot. After the system is back up, change directory into */boot/grub* and edit the *grub.conf* file to fix the directive permanently.
Validate: Validate the fix while the system boots up. You may want to reboot the system again to validate the permanent fix.

Issue: "Kernel panic – not syncing: VFS: Unable to mount root fs on unknown-block(0,0)"

Gather: System attempts to boot and encounters an error while loading the kernel.
Analyze: It appears that the initrd directive in the *grub.conf* file is invalid or commented.
Identify: Fix the initrd directive in the *grub.conf* file.
Solve: Boot the system and interact with the GRUB menu by pressing any key within the number of seconds defined in *grub.conf* with the timeout directive. Press e for edit, highlight the initrd directive and press e again. Fix the directive and press b to boot. After the system is back up, change directory into */boot/grub* and edit the *grub.conf* file to fix the initrd directive permanently.
Validate: Validate the fix while the system boots up. You may want to reboot the system to validate the permanent fix.

Issues: "VFS: Can't find ext3 filesystem on dev dm-1", "mount: error mounting /dev/root on /sysroot as ext3: Invalid argument", "setuproot: moving /dev failed: No such file or directory", "setuproot: error mounting /proc: No such file or directory" and a few other errors

Gather: System attempts to boot and loads the kernel but encounters a problem while accessing the root file system and generates several messages. The system is using LVM for disk management.
Analyze: It appears that the location of the root volume group as specified with the kernel directive in the *grub.conf* file is incorrect.
Identify: Fix the kernel directive in the *grub.conf* file.
Solve: Boot the system and interact with the GRUB menu by pressing any key within the number of seconds defined in *grub.conf* with the timeout directive. Press e for edit, highlight the kernel directive and press e again. Fix the logical volume name and press b to boot. After the system is back up, change directory into */boot/grub* and edit the *grub.conf* file to fix the initrd directive permanently.

Validate: Validate the fix while the system boots up. You may want to reboot the system again to validate the permanent fix.

Issue: "/sbin/init: ro: No such file or directory"

Gather: System attempts to boot, loads the kernel, remounts the root file system and tries to run the */sbin/init* command for system initialization but is unable to find the command.
Analyze: The *init* command appears to be lost, renamed or corrupted.
Identify: */sbin/init* is lost, renamed or corrupted.
Solve: Boot the system into the rescue mode (networking on, Continue). Run *chroot /mnt/sysimage* and change directory into */sbin*. Check if a backup of the *init* file is present. If yes, copy it as *init*, otherwise, reinstall the SysVinit package as explained earlier in this chapter or use the *rpm2cpio* command as explained in Chapter 11 "Software Package Management" to retrieve the package contents at a temporary location and copy the *init* file from there to */sbin*. Execute the *exit* command twice to quit and reboot the system.
Validate: Validate the fix while the system boots up.

Issue: "exec of init (/sbin/init) failed!!!: Exec format error"

Gather: System attempts to boot, loads the kernel, remounts the root file system and tries to run the */sbin/init* command for system initialization.
Analyze: The *init* command appears to be corrupted.
Identify: */sbin/init* is corrupted.
Solve: Boot the system into the rescue mode (networking on, Continue). Run *chroot /mnt/sysimage* and change directory into */sbin*. Check if a backup of the *init* file is present. If yes, copy it as *init*, otherwise, reinstall the SysVinit package as explained earlier in this chapter or use the *rpm2cpio* command as explained in Chapter 11 "Software Package Management" to retrieve the package contents at a temporary location and copy the *init* file from there to */sbin*. Execute the *exit* command twice to quit and reboot the system.
Validate: Validate the fix while the system boots up.

Issue: "INIT: No inittab file found"

Gather: System attempts to boot, loads the kernel, remounts the root file system and runs the */sbin/init* command for system initialization. The */sbin/init* command tries to source the */etc/inittab* file but is unable to find it.
Analyze: The *inittab* file is renamed or lost.
Identify: The */etc/inittab* is lost.
Solve: Boot the system into the rescue mode (networking on, Continue). Run *chroot /mnt/sysimage* and change directory into */etc*. Check if a backup of the *inittab* file is present. If yes, copy it as *inittab*, otherwise, reinstall the SysVinit package as explained earlier in this chapter or use the *rpm2cpio* command as explained in Chapter 11 "Software Package Management" to retrieve the package contents at a temporary location and copy the *inittab* file from there to */etc*. Execute the *exit* command to quit and reboot the system.
Validate: Validate the fix as the system boots up.

Issue: "/etc/rc.d/rc.sysinit: line 28: mount: command not found"

Gather: During the boot process, the system displays the message and continues to boot. It stalls later when attempting to mount local file systems from the */etc/fstab* file.

Analyze: Analyze the messages displayed during the system boot. Some key file systems such as */var* do not appear to be mounted. Also, the */bin/mount* command appears to be lost.

Identify: The *mount* command may be lost, renamed or corrupted.

Solve: Boot the system into the rescue mode (networking on, Continue). Run *chroot /mnt/sysimage* and change directory into */bin*. Check if a backup of the *mount* file is present. If yes, copy it as *mount*, otherwise, reinstall the SysVinit package as explained earlier in this chapter or use the *rpm2cpio* command as explained in Chapter 11 "Software Package Management" to retrieve the package contents at a temporary location and copy the *mount* file from there to */bin*. Execute the *exit* command twice to quit and reboot the system.

Validate: Validate the fix while the system boots up.

Issue: "fsck.ext3: Unable to resolve 'LABEL=boot'"

Gather: During the boot process, the system attempts to mount or remount all local file systems. The label associated with the */boot* file system appears to be incorrect.

Analyze: The label for */boot* file system appears to be incorrect in the *fstab* file.

Identify: The label for */boot* file system is incorrect in the *fstab* file.

Solve: Boot the system into single user mode as explained in Chapter 15 "Shutdown and Boot" and run the *e2label* command on */dev/sda1* to determine the correct label. Edit the *fstab* file and change the label to what was returned by *e2label*. Execute the *reboot* command.

Validate: Watch the console messages as the system boots up to ensure that the problem does not reappear.

Issue: "The system reboots each time it tries to boot up"

Gather: System starts up fine but then it switches into run level 6.

Analyze: It appears that the system is attempting to switch into run level 6 each time it boots up. The initdefault directive in the *inittab* file may be set to run level 6 or the "l5:5:wait:/etc/rc.d/rc 5" directive may be set to "l5:5:wait:/etc/rc.d/rc 6".

Identify: The initdefault directive is set to 6 in the *inittab* file.

Solve: Boot the system into single user mode as explained in Chapter 15 "Shutdown and Boot", open up the *inittab* file and change the initdefault directive to run level 5. Execute the *exit* command to let the system boot into run level 5.

Validate: Watch if the system still shows the same behavior.

Issue: "Remounting root file system in read-write mode ...... [FAILED]"

Gather: System starts up fine but is unable to mount the root file system in read-write mode. The system takes a long time at "Starting system logger" during the boot process and then displays a number of error messages before displaying a login prompt.

Analyze: It appears that somehow the system is unable to mount the root file system in read-write mode. The file system appears to have an invalid mount option in */etc/fstab*.

Identify: The mount option is invalid in */etc/fstab* for the file system.

Solve: Boot the system into the rescue mode (networking off, Continue). Run *chroot /mnt/sysimage* and edit */etc/fstab* to fix the option. Execute the *exit* command twice to quit and reboot the system.

Validate: Watch the boot process messages to see if the problem reappears.

Troubleshooting and Resolving Networking & Name Resolution Issues

Problems associated with networking generally occur due to misconfiguration in interface scripts located in the */etc/sysconfig/network-scripts* directory, and */etc/sysconfig/network* and */etc/hosts* files. Each time configuration for an interface is modified, files in the *network-scripts* directory are updated. The *network* file stores key information such as the system's hostname and the *hosts* file defines hostname to IP address mappings. Several commands such as *ping, ifconfig, ip, hostname, ifup, ifdown, ethtool, arp, netstat, route, traceroute, tracepath* and *mtr* are available in addition to the Network Configurator to assist you with troubleshooting and resolving networking issues. The configuration files and the commands are explained at length in Chapter 20 "Basic Networking" and Chapter 21 "Network Interface Administration and Routing".

Problems pertaining to hostname resolution generally occur due to misconfiguration in */etc/hosts, /etc/resolv.conf, /etc/nsswitch.conf* and */etc/host.conf* files. The *hosts* file defines hostname to IP address mappings; the *resolv.conf* file defines the default DNS domain, name servers and domains to be searched for name queries; the *nsswitch.conf* file lists the sequence in which name resolution sources are referenced for queries; and the *host.conf* file is used if *nsswitch.conf* does not exist. Several commands such as *ping, dig, host* and *nslookup* are available for assistance. If DHCP is employed, two directives PEERDNS=yes and BOOTPROTO=dhcp are set in the associated network interface configuration file located in the */etc/sysconfig/network-scripts* directory. With these settings in place, DHCP pulls DNS configuration and populates *resolv.conf*. BIND and DHCP configuration files and commands are explained at length in Chapter 22 "DNS and DHCP".

The following provides certain example scenarios and their fixes.

Issue: "Users do not get login prompt when attempting to connect"

Gather: System boots up fine but it does not display a login prompt to users when they attempt to connect using either the IP address or the hostname.
Analyze: It appears that the IP address or the hostname has been changed. It is also possible that networking is set to off in the *network* file. Check the IP address and hostname with the *ifconfig* and *hostname* commands. Check interface configuration in *ifcfg-eth** files.
Identify: It is identified that NETWORKING directive in the *network* file is set to no.
Solve: Log on to the console screen and open up the file in a text editor. Change the directive's value to yes. Execute *service network start* to bring up all configured interfaces.
Validate: Validate the fix with the *ifconfig* command. Ask users to retry to connect.

Issue: "System is accessible with IP address but not with hostname"

Gather: System boots up fine and users are able to connect to it using the IP address but they do not see a login prompt when they try to connect using the hostname.
Analyze: It appears that the hostname has been changed. Check the hostname with the *hostname* command. Check the HOSTNAME directive in the *network* file and the host's entry in the *hosts* file.
Identify: It is found that the HOSTNAME directive in the *network* file is set incorrectly.
Solve: Exit the file and change the directive's value to the actual hostname of the system by consulting the *hosts* file. Reboot the system when done.
Validate: Validate the fix after the system is back up by asking users to retry to connect using hostname.

Issue: "System is inaccessible on a specific network interface"

Gather: System boots up fine. It has dual configured network interfaces. Users have been able to connect to the system using either interface. Now, they can connect via one interface only.
Analyze: It appears that the IP address or the hostname has been changed on that interface. It is also possible that the interface configuration is changed. Check the IP address and hostname with the *ifconfig* and *hostname* commands. Check the value of the ONBOOT directive as well as other directives in the affected interface's *ifcfg-eth** file.
Identify: It is concluded that the ONBOOT directive in the affected interface's *ifcfg-eth** file is set to no.
Solve: Edit the file and change the directive's value to yes. Execute *service network reload* to bring up all configured interfaces.
Validate: Validate the fix with the *ifconfig* command. Ask users to retry.

Issue: "/etc/resolv.conf gets overwritten at every system reboot"

Gather: System boots up fine. All network interfaces get configured and are operational.
Analyze: It appears that DHCP is enabled and the PEERDNS directive is set to yes in the affected network interface's configuration file *ifcfg-eth**.
Identify: PEERDNS directive needs to be set to no so *resolv.conf* file does not get overwritten.
Solve: Edit the appropriate *ifcfg-eth** file and change the PEERDNS directive to no. Execute *service network restart* to stop and restart all configured interfaces.
Validate: Validate the fix by checking if the contents of *resolv.conf* are overwritten after the interface is restarted.

Troubleshooting and Resolving FTP Issues

Problems pertaining to FTP generally occur due to misconfiguration in the */etc/vsftpd/vsftpd.conf* file. There are several other files such as */etc/services*, */etc/hosts.allow* and */etc/hosts.deny* that also get involved during the process of FTP communication session setup. FTP's file transfer activities are logged to the */var/log/xferlog* file and the */var/log/messages* file stores all other FTP activities. These log files provide a wealth of information that may help you in troubleshooting. FTP uses the *vsftpd* daemon to establish server and client communication. Commands such as *ping*, *telnet* and *lftp* are available to aid in testing and troubleshooting. Refer to Chapter 24 "Internet Services and Electronic Mail" for details.

Since FTP is a network service, a stable network infrastructure is necessary for its proper operation.

The following provides a few FTP-specific problems and their fixes.

Issue: "Unable to log into a configured FTP server anonymously"

Gather: Users are unable to log into a configured vsFTP server anonymously.
Analyze: Ensure anonymous access is enabled in *vsftpd.conf* file. There are certain associated directives. Check to ensure they are correrctly set.
Identify: The anonymous_enable directive is set to NO.
Solve: Edit *vsftpd.conf* and change the directive's value to YES. Run *service vsftpd reload*.
Validate: Ask users to try again to connect.

Issue: "Unable to upload files to a configured FTP server anonymously"

Gather: Users are unable to upload files to a configured vsFTP server anonymously.
Analyze: Ensure access to upload files anonymously is enabled in *vsftpd.conf* file. There are certain directives related to anonymous access. Check to ensure they are correrctly set.
Identify: The anon_upload_enable directive is set to NO.
Solve: Edit *vsftpd.conf* and change the directive's value to YES. Run *service vsftpd reload*.
Validate: Ask users to try again to upload.

Issue: "No users from a specific network are able to access a configured FTP server"

Gather: Users from systems on a specific network are unable to connect to a configured vsFTP server.
Analyze: Check TCP Wrappers files */etc/hosts.allow* and */etc/hosts.deny* whether the network is allowed access.
Identify: The network address is restricted in the *hosts.deny* file.
Solve: Edit *hosts.deny* and modify access to allow the network.
Validate: Ask users on the network to retry to connect.

Issue: "Certain users are unable to log into a configured FTP server"

Gather: Some (not all) users are unable to log into a configured vsFTP server.
Analyze: Check the value of userlist_enable directive in */etc/vsftpd/vsftpd.conf* file. Check *ftpusers* and *user_list* files in */etc/vsftpd* directory to ensure the users are not denied access.
Identify: The users are listed in the *ftpusers* file.
Solve: Edit *ftpusers* file and remove the usernames.
Validate: Ask users to try to connect again.

Troubleshooting and Resolving NFS Issues

Problems pertaining to NFS server and client generally occur due to misconfiguration in files such as */etc/exports*, */etc/sysconfig/nfs* and */etc/fstab*. There are several other files such as */etc/rpc*, */var/lib/nfs/etab*, */var/lib/nfs/rmtab* and */etc/mtab* that also get involved during NFS communication. Likewise, there are many server- and client-side daemons that run to ensure server and client talk to each other properly. These daemons include *portmap*, *rpc.mountd*, *rpc.nfsd*, *rpc.lockd* and *rpc.statd*. Several commands such as *ping*, *exportfs*, *mount*, *umount*, *showmount*, *rpcinfo* and *nfsstat* are available for a troubleshooting assistance standpoint.

Since NFS is a network service, a stable network infrastructure is necessary for its proper operation.

The following provides a few NFS-specific problems and their fixes.

Issue: "NFS Server Not Responding"

Gather: NFS client displays this message when it attempts to mount an NFS resource.
Analyze: This message usually appears when an NFS server is down, too busy or there is something not right with the network. Use the *ping* command to test the connectivity between the NFS server and client. Run the *dig*, *nslookup* or *host* command on both server and client to check that they "see" each other correctly.

Identify: It is determined that there is some network connectivity issue between the server and the client.
Solve: Use *ifconfig* command or edit the affected network interface's configuration file in the */etc/sysconfig/network-scripts* directory to fix any configuration issues. Restart network services with *service network restart*.
Validate: Validate the fix by retrying to mount the resource on the client.

Issue: "mount clntudp_create: RPC: Program not registered"

Gather: NFS client or server displays this message when a command such as *showmount* is executed to check available NFS resources.
Analyze: This message usually appears when the *rpc.mountd* daemon is stopped on the NFS server. Run *service nfs status* to check the status of the daemon.
Identify: It is identified that the *rpc.mountd* daemon is not running on the server.
Solve: Run *service nfs restart* to restart NFS processes.
Validate: Validate the fix by running the *showmount* command again.

Issue: "mount: mount to NFS server failed: System Error: Connection refused"

Gather: NFS client displays this message when it tries to mount a remote resource.
Analyze: This message usually appears when the *portmap* daemon is stopped on the NFS server. Run *service portmap status* to check the status of the daemon.
Identify: It is found that the *portmap* daemon is not running on the server.
Solve: Run *service portmap start* to start the *portmap* process.
Validate: Validate the fix by attempting to remount the resource.

Issue: "Permission Denied"

Gather: NFS client displays this message when it tries to mount a remote resource.
Analyze: This message occurs when a client tries to mount a resource which is not exported to it.
Identify: It is found that the resource is not exported to the client.
Solve: Export the resource to the client using the *exportfs* command or edit */etc/exports* file and add an entry for it.
Validate: Validate the fix by attempting to remount the resource.

Issue: "Mount Request from unknown host"

Gather: NFS server logs the error to */var/log/messages* when a system not on its exports list attempts to mount an exported resource.
Analyze: This message occurs on the NFS server when a resource is attempted to be mounted on a system that is not on the server's exports list.
Identify: The client name needs to be added to the server's exports list for the resource.
Solve: Edit */etc/exports* file on the server and ensure that the resource is exported to the client.
Validate: Validate the fix by reattempting to mount the resource.

Troubleshooting and Resolving Samba Issues

Problems pertaining to Samba server and client generally occur due to misconfiguration in the */etc/samba/smb.conf* file. Samba has its own set of log files located in the */var/log/samba* directory. These log files provide a wealth of information that may help you in your troubleshooting efforts. Samba uses two daemons – *smbd* and *nmbd* – that respond to client requests. Several commands such as *ping, testparm, mount, mount.cifs, smbclient, smbpasswd, smbstatus, umount, umount.cifs* and *smbprint* are available to aid in troubleshooting, in addition to the Samba Server Configurator and Samba Web Administration Tool. Refer to Chapter 27 "Samba" for details.

Since Samba is a network service, a stable network infrastructure is necessary for its proper operation.

The following provides a few Samba-specific problems and their fixes.

Issue: "Unable to access a Samba share"

Gather: A configured Samba share is inaccessible on client systems.
Analyze: Check *smb.conf*. Run *testparm* to validate the syntax of the file. Check if the Samba daemons are running.
Identify: It appears that the section for the share is commented out in the file.
Solve: Edit *smb.conf* and uncomment the entry. Run *testparm* to test the configuration.
Validate: Try again to access the share on the clients.

Issue: "Users on 192.168.3 network are unable to access Samba shares"

Gather: A configured Samba share is inaccessible on client systems on the 192.168.3 network.
Analyze: Check *smb.conf* for "hosts allow" setting. Check if the Samba daemons are running.
Identify: It appears that "hosts allow" does not list 192.168.3 network specifically.
Solve: Edit *smb.conf* and add 192.168.3 network IP. Run *testparm* to test the configuration.
Validate: Try again to access the share on systems on the 192.168.3 network.

Issue: "Samba shared printers are invisible on clients"

Gather: Configured printers are shared but are not visible on client systems.
Analyze: Check printers section in *smb.conf* for yes/no value of the browseable directive.
Identify: The printers are set to non-browseable in *smb.conf* file.
Solve: Edit *smb.conf* and change the directive's value to yes. Run *testparm* to test the configuration.
Validate: Try again and you should be able to browse the printers.

Issue: "Samba shares are world accessible"

Gather: All Samba shares are visible and accessible on all systems.
Analyze: Check "hosts allow" setting in *smb.conf* file.
Identify: The directive is not defined.
Solve: Edit *smb.conf* and add the directive to limit share's access to specific systems, networks or domains. Run *testparm* to test the configuration.
Validate: Try accessing the shares on a system or network that is not specifically allowed in the *smb.conf* file.

Troubleshooting and Resolving NTP Issues

Problems pertaining to NTP generally occur due to misconfiguration in the */etc/ntp.conf* file. This file contains all configuration information for NTP. Commands such as *ntpdate* and *ntpq* are available in addition to the Date/Time Configurator to assist you with troubleshooting and resolving NTP related issues. The configuration files, commands and the Configurator are explained at length in Chapter 25 "Network Time Protocol".

Since NTP is a network service, a stable network infrastructure is necessary for its proper operation.

The following provides some example scenarios and their fixes.

Issue: "No suitable server for synchronization found"

Gather: This message indicates that the NTP server is not responding for some reason. Packets are sent to it with no replies returning.
Analyze: It appears that the NTP server is down, unreachable, over busy or the *ntpd* daemon is stopped. It normally takes a while for *ntpd* to be ready after it is started to respond to NTP client requests.
Identify: Check to ensure that the *ntpd* daemon on the server is running.
Solve: Run *service ntpd restart* on the time server to restart NTP service.
Validate: Wait for a few minutes and then check the synchronization status on the client.

Issue: "Startup delay"

Gather: This message indicates that there is a delay in the response from the server.
Analyze: It appears that *ntpd* is just started on the client. It usually takes a few minutes before an NTP client/server binding is established.
Identify: It takes an NTP client five poll cycles to bind itself with a server or peer. During this time *ntpd* does not respond to client time requests. A server must itself be bound to a higher stratum time server before it is able to provide time to clients.
Solve: Do nothing and wait for sometime. Run *ntpq –p* after 10 minutes.
Validate: *ntpq –p* should show you that a communication channel between the client and server has established and the time difference is being reduced.

Issue: "Synchronization lost"

Gather: This message indicates that the client has lost synchronization with the NTP server.
Analyze: It appears that NTP client has lost synchronization with the time server it was bound to and now it is in the process of choosing another to make time adjustments with. If a system makes such adjustments frequently, there is a potential of network congestion.
Identify: Restart the daemon on the server and fix any network issues.
Solve: Use *ntpq –p* to examine dispersion statistics. Fix any network issues in order for NTP to function smoothly. You may need to stop the *ntpd* daemon and run *ntpdate* to check communication with the time server.
Validate: Check the output of *ntpq –p* to see if it still shows anything unusual.

Troubleshooting and Resolving Mail System Issues

Problems related to sendmail, postfix and dovecot mail systems generally occur due to malfunctioning name resolution or a misconfiguration. There are several files associated with these services. See Chapter 24 "Internet Services and Electronic Mail" for details.

Since mail is a network service, a stable network infrastructure is necessary for its proper operation.

The following provides a few mail system related problems and their fixes.

Issue: "The following addresses had transient non-fatal errors .. reason: 550 Host unknown"

Gather: This error message appears when a configured mail system attempts to send a message.
Analyze: It appears that name resolution is not working, or one or more destination addresses are invalid. Check if DNS is working properly. Check for any access restrictions.
Identify: A destination address cannot be resolved.
Solve: Check *resolv.conf*, *host.conf* and *nsswitch.conf* files, and fix any configuration issues.
Validate: Resend the message to validate the fix.

Issue: "Unable to receive emails from 192.168.3 network"

Gather: No users on 192.168.3 network are able to receive emails.
Analyze: It appears that the name resolution is not working, one or more destination addresses are invalid, or the network is denied access. Check if DNS is working properly. Check for any access restrictions. Check if the network is allowed.
Identify: The network is restricted in the */etc/mail/access* file with "@192.168.3 REJECT" entry.
Solve: Edit *access* file and remove the entry.
Validate: Ask users on the 192.168.3 network to retry.

Issue: "Masquerading not working"

Gather: sendmail is configured to send all outbound messages as being originated from *getitcertify.com* domain, but this is not working.
Analyze: It appears that MASQUERADE_AS directive in *sendmail.mc* file is not set.
Identify: The directive is not defined.
Solve: Edit *sendmail.mc* and add "MASQUERADE_AS(`geticertify.com`)dnl" line entry to it. Run *m4 /etc/mail/sendmail.mc > /etc/mail/sendmail.cf* to rebuild *sendmail.cf*.
Validate: Try again and see if you get the correct name associated with outbound messages.

Troubleshooting and Resolving Apache Issues

Problems pertaining to Apache generally occur due to misconfiguration in the *httpd.conf* or *ssl.conf* file, or one of the files in the */etc/httpd/conf.d* directory. Apache has its own set of log files located in the */var/log/httpd* directory. These log files provide a wealth of information that may help you in troubleshooting. Apache's daemon is *httpd*, which enables client and server communication. Several commands such as *httpd* and *htpasswd* in addition to HTTP Configurator are available to aid in troubleshooting. Refer to Chapter 29 "Web and Caching Proxy Servers" for details.

Since Apache is a network service, a stable network infrastructure is necessary for its proper operation.

The following provides a few Apache-specific problems and their fixes.

Issue: "404 file not found"

Gather: This message appears in a browser when users attempt to access a website.
Analyze: This message appears on the local host as well as on remote systems. Check if *index.html* file exists in DocumentRoot directory with proper SELinux file context. Run the *ls* command on the file with –Z option to validate.
Identify: It appears that the *index.html* file was deleted.
Solve: Restore the file from backup or create a new file. Make sure that it has the correct SELinux file context.
Validate: Ask users to access the website again.

Issue: "Cannot bind to an address"

Gather: Apache attempts to start but displays a message similar to this.
Analyze: Another *httpd* daemon might be running. The configured port might already be in use by some other network service.
Identify: The *httpd* daemon is running but is not owned by user *apache*.
Solve: Stop the daemon, log in as user *apache* and start the daemon.
Validate: Check the log file with *tail –f* to ensure the fix is working.

Troubleshooting and Resolving Squid Issues

Problems pertaining to Squid server generally occur due to misconfiguration in the */etc/squid/squid.conf* file. All Squid activities are logged to the */var/log/squid* file. Squid daemon is called *master*. Refer to Chapter 29 "Web and Caching Proxy Servers" for details.

Since Squid is a network service, a stable network infrastructure is necessary for its proper operation.

The following provides a few Samba-specific problems and their fixes.

Issue: "Squid is unable to cache web pages"

Gather: Squid does not seem to be able to cache any web pages.
Analyze: Scan *squid.conf* file for any missing or misconfigured directives.
Identify: The http_port directive in the file is set to 8080, but firewall indicates that 3128 is open for Squid.
Solve: Edit *squid.conf* and set the directive http_port to 3128. Restart Squid with *service squid restart*.
Validate: Check if web pages are now being cached.

Issue: "Cannot connect through the web proxy server"

Gather: This message usually appears if there are any access restrictions set.
Analyze: Scan *squid.conf* file for access settings.
Identify: It is determined that the network where the users are trying to connect from is denied access.
Solve: Edit *squid.conf* and enable access for the network. Restart Squid with *service squid restart*.
Validate: Validate the fix by reconnecting.

Troubleshooting and Resolving X Window and GUI Issues

If you encounter issues with the X server, you need to check and validate the */etc/X11/xorg.conf* file, the operational status of the X font server and the setting of the initdefault directive in the */etc/inittab* file.

For the */etc/X11/xorg.conf* file, execute *X –probeonly* at the command prompt to simulate the start of X and watch the output for any errors, use any text editor or the Display Configurator *system-config-display* to view or modify the configuration information or run *Xorg –configure* to regenerate the file. Refer to Chapter 10 "X Window System and Desktop Managers" for details.

Let us take a look at a few troubleshooting scenarios to enhance understanding.

Issue: "X Window system does not autostart"

Gather: X Window does not start automatically at system reboot.
Analyze: Check the setting of initdefault and "x:5:respawn:/etc/X11/prefdm –nodaemon" directives in the *inittab* file. Try starting X in run level 3 with the *startx* command. Run *strace –o /tmp/x.out X* and analyze the output in the */tmp/x.out* file. Run *tail –f* on */var/log/messages* for any clues. Edit */etc/syslog.conf* file and add "*.debug /var/log/debug" and restart *syslogd* using *service syslog reload*.
Identify: If X Window starts up fine in run level 3, either the initdefault directive is not set to run level 5 or the "x:5:respawn:/etc/X11/prefdm –nodaemon" directive is commented out in *initab* file.
Solve: Edit */etc/inittab* and fix the misconfigured directive. Run *init 3* at the command prompt to transition to run level 3, and then bring the system back to run level 5 with *init 5*.
Validate: Check to ensure that X starts up fine.

Issue: "Failed to start the X server"

Gather: X Window attempts to start but some misconfiguration prevents it from coming up.
Analyze: The system displays a potential reason and starts the Display Configurator if you select yes when prompted to fix the issue.
Identify: The Section "Screen" in the */etc/X11/xorg.conf* file has an issue. It may be commented out or has a typo.
Solve: Press OK when the Display Configurator is invoked, which will automatically fix the Section "Screen" in the file. Alternatively, choose not to fix it when prompted and the system will display a text login prompt. Log in as *root* and edit */etc/X11/xorg.conf* to fix the identified section. Run *init 3* at the command prompt to transition to run level 3 and then bring the system back to run level 5 with *init 5*.
Validate: Check to ensure that X starts up fine.

Issue: "Error loading the X server"

Gather: X Window attempts to start but something prevents it from loading.
Analyze: A file system such as */tmp* or */home* is full, user quota on */home* might be an issue, X font server may not be running or the video hardware may be configured incorrectly. Run the *df* command to check if */tmp* or */home* are full. Run *quota* commands to check settings on */home*. Run *service xfs status* to check the operational status of X font server. Execute the Display Configurator to check video hardware settings.

Identify: The */tmp* file system is full.

Solve: Make some room in */tmp* by either extending the size of it using appropriate LVM/partitioning commands or removing unnecessary files. Run *init 3* at the command prompt to transition to run level 3 and then bring the system back to run level 5 with *init 5*.

Validate: Check to ensure that X server starts up.

Issue: "Server Authorization directory (daemon/ServAuthDir) is set to /var/gdm but this does not exist. Please correct GDM configuration and restart GDM"

Gather: During the boot process, the system displays several error messages and takes much longer than usual to start the system logger service.

Analyze: Analyze the messages displayed during the system boot. */var* appears to be unmounted.

Identify: */var* appears to be commented out in */etc/fstab*, or is corrupted.

Solve: Edit */etc/fstab* and uncomment the */var* file system entry. Execute *fsck* if required.

Validate: Reboot the system and validate the fix.

Issue: "Configured XDM Display Manager does not come up"

Gather: System boots up normally and starts the GNOME display manager instead of XDM.

Analyze: Check the value of the prefdm directive in the */etc/X11/prefdm* file.

Identify: The value is set incorrectly.

Solve: Edit */etc/X11/prefdm* file and fix any typos in the prefdm directive. Alternatively, define DISPLAYMANAGER=XDM in the */etc/sysconfig/desktop* file. Run *init 3* at the command prompt to transition to run level 3 and then bring the system back to run level 5 with *init 5*.

Validate: Check to ensure that the correct display manager starts when the system boots into run level 5.

Troubleshooting and Resolving Miscellaneous Issues

Miscellaneous issues may be related to quota management and other system and network topics. The following provides a quota-related issue and its fix.

Issue: "User cannot create a file in his home directory"

Gather: There is a large amount of free file system space in */home* but still the user is unable to create a file in his home directory that is located in */home*.

Analyze: It appears that disk quota has been exhausted for the user.

Identify: Check whether quota is set on the file system and what limits are defined for the user. Use the *quota* command.

Solve: Increase the quota limit for the user or have him remove unnecessary files to make room.

Validate: Ask the user to validate the fix by creating a file in his home directory.

Summary

This chapter shed light on system, network and security troubleshooting topics from RHCT and RHCE exam perspectives. At the beginning, an introduction to troubleshooting and GAISV model was presented. You looked at the Linux rescue mode that provides an interface allowing you to fix problems related to system boot including restoring/recovering any lost or damaged command or crucial configuration file and fixing a ruined bootloader. You were explained how to boot a system successfully into linux rescue mode by selecting appropriate choices.

The remainder of the chapter covered a number of troubleshooting scenarios covering issues related to system boot, networking, name resolution, file transfer, resource sharing, time synchronization, mail systems, web servers, caching servers, X Window system, display/desktop managers and user disk quota.

Appendix A: RHCT Exam Practice Exercises

Time Duration: 2 hours
Passing Score: 70%

Instruction 01: Exercises provided in this and the next appendix are in addition to troubleshooting scenarios presented in Chapter 31 "System, Network and Security Troubleshooting" from an RHCT/RHCE exam perspective. No solutions are provided for the exercises as it is assumed that installation and configuration tasks provided in this book have been performed successfully.

Instruction 02: It is assumed that there are three networks 192.168.0, 192.168.1 and 192.168.2 for domains *www.example.com*, *www.example.net* and *www.example.org*, respectively. The *example.com* domain includes trusted systems, *example.net* contains untrusted systems and *example.org* includes all other systems. All exercises are assumed to be performed on the 192.168.0 network unless otherwise noted.

Instruction 03: For each of these exercises, ensure that the settings and modifications made are available across system reboots. Also ensure that configured services work properly with SELinux mode set to enforcing and iptables firewall enabled.

Instruction 04: It is assumed that a pre-configured server called *server1* is available with RHEL 5 loaded, two network interfaces with 192.168.0.201/24 (gateway 192.168.0.1) on *eth0* and 192.168.1.201/24 (gateway 192.168.1.1) on *eth1*, default run level 5, RHEL software packages available for installation at pub/Server yum repository, SELinux enabled in enforcing mode, iptables firewall enabled, NIS server configured with domain *testdom*, master DNS server configured, DHCP server configured, NTP server configured, and exporting */testdir* via NFS.

Instruction 05: It is assumed that you have access to a virtual machine or a standalone system to be called *client1* loaded with base RHEL 5 operating system, two unconfigured network interfaces connected to 192.168.0 and 192.168.1 networks, has TCP/IP networking disabled, default run level 3, default display manager GNOME, default desktop GNOME, SELinux enabled in permissive mode, iptables firewall disabled, *root* password lost, NIS/DNS/LDAP/DHCP/NTP client and server capabilities disabled, about 10GB of free disk space available on the lone */dev/sda* disk, and with the following disk partitioning configuration:

Mount Point	FS Type	Size (MB)	Volume Group	Logical Volume	Partition
/	ext3	1000	N/A	N/A	Standard
/boot	ext3	500	N/A	N/A	N/A
/home	ext3	500	vg01	homevol	N/A
/tmp	ext3	1000	N/A	N/A	Standard
/usr	ext3	3000	vg01	usrvol	N/A
/var	ext3	1000	N/A	N/A	RAID 1
/opt	ext3	500	N/A	N/A	RAID 1
N/A	swap	1000	N/A	N/A	RAID 1

This is the system where you will be performing all the exercises provided in this and the next appendix.

Exercise 01: The *root* user password is lost and you are unable to log on. Change the *root* password to Welcome01.

Exercise 02: Configure *eth0* network interface to have hostname *client1*, static IP address 192.168.0.202/24, gateway 192.168.0.1 and broadcast address 192.168.0.255.

Exercise 03: Configure *eth1* network interface with IP address 192.168.1.202/24, gateway 192.168.1.1 and broadcast address 192.168.1.255.

Exercise 04: Modify the configuration so the default run level for the system is set to 5.

Exercise 05: Set the default desktop environment for new users to KDE.

Exercise 06: Configure a private yum repository to install packages from.

Exercise 07: Modify SELinux mode to enforcing.

Exercise 08: Configure slave DNS service for the local network.

Exercise 09: Configure DNS client to get queries resolved from *server1*.

Exercise 10: Configure DHCP service for the local network to assign IP addresses between the range 192.168.0.2 and 192.168.0.100 with two IPs 192.168.0.101 and 192.168.0.102 reserved for systems with MAC addresses XXXXXX and YYYYYY.

Exercise 11: Create *user1*, *user2*, *user3* and *user4* accounts with home directories in */home*. Set their passwords to Temp123$ and make *user2* and *user3* accounts to expire on December 31, 2010.

Exercise 12: Configure quota for *user1* and *user2* so that they cannot store any data in their home directories beyond 70MB. The lower limit should be 50MB.

Exercise 13: Create a file called *testfile* in *user2*'s home directory and configure ACLs on it to allow *user3* and *user4* to be able to read, write and execute it.

Exercise 14: Create a RAID 1 partition of size 500MB with label PART01, mount point */mntpart01* and ext3 type file system structures.

Exercise 15: Create a RAID 1 swap partition of size 500MB with label SWAP01.

Exercise 16: Create a logical volume *linuxadm* of size 500MB in *vg01* volume group with label LINUXADM, mount point */linuxadm* and ext3 type file system structures. Define a group called *linuxadm* and change group membership on */linuxadm* to *linuxadm*. Set read/write/execute permissions on */linuxadm* for the owner and group members, and no permissions for others.

Exercise 17: Create a logical volume *lvol1* of size 500MB in *vg02* volume group with label LVOL1, mount point */mntlvol1* and ext3 type file system structures. Also create a swap logical volume called *swaplvol1* of size 300MB in *vg02* volume group with label SWAPLVOL1.

Exercise 18: Add *linuxadm* to *users1* and *user4* as secondary group. Give both users full access to */linuxadm* to read, write and execute each other's files without modifying any permissions or ownership/group membership.

Exercise 19: Configure *eth1:1* logical interface with IP address 192.168.2.202/24 and gateway 192.168.2.255.

Exercise 20: Install vsftp, httpd, squid, bind and system-config-* packages.

Exercise 21: Extend *homevol* in *vg01* by 300MB online and without losing any data.

Exercise 22: Configure a cron job to search for core files in */usr* and delete them the first day of each week at 11:49pm.

Exercise 23: Add a local print queue called *lplocal* using raw printer model/driver and make it system default. Create a print class called *prn_class* and add *lplocal* to it.

Exercise 24: Set permissions on */linuxadm* so that all files created underneath get the parent group membership.

Exercise 25: Configure */mntlvol1* so that users can delete their own files only and not other users'.

Exercise 26: Install a new kernel and make it default. Do not overwrite the existing kernel.

Exercise 27: Configure the system to act as an IP forwarder.

Exercise 28: Configure the system to be able to receive syslog messages from other systems on the network, and record them locally.

Exercise 29: Enable cron access for *root* and *user3* users only and deny to everyone else.

Exercise 30: Perform a full dump of */home* in */tmp*.

Exercise 31: Set the default system-wide display environment to KDE.

Exercise 32: Set the primary command prompt for user root to display hostname, username and current working directory information.

Exercise 33: Write an interactive shell script in */home/user2* that displays directory contents and prompts to enter a file name for deletion.

Exercise 34: Change the default base home directory for new users to */usr*.

Appendix B: RHCE Exam Practice Exercises

Time Duration: 3.5 hours (this includes 2 hours of RHCT)
Passing Score: 70%

Instructions: See instructions provided in Appendix A.

Exercise 01: Configure DNS client.

Exercise 02: Configure NIS client and ensure that home directory for *nisuser1* located under */home/server1* on the NIS server gets automatically mounted under */home* when *nisuser1* logs in on *client1*.

Exercise 03: Configure LDAP client with search base dc=getitcertify and dc=com with locally signed TLS SSL encryption enabled.

Exercise 04: Activate SELinux in enforcing mode.

Exercise 05: Enable ssh and allow access from the local network and deny from *example.net* and *example.org*.

Exercise 06: Disable direct *root* user logins via ssh.

Exercise 07: Allow telnet access into the system from local and trusted networks only.

Exercise 08: Configure anonymous FTP access and allow systems in the local and trusted networks, and disallow from everywhere else.

Exercise 09: Configure FTP service with no access from *example.org* and *example.net* networks. Allow *user1* and *user2* access and deny *user3* and *user4*.

Exercise 10: Configure Samba to share */linuxadm* accessible to *user1* and *user3* from the local network only with write and browse capabilities.

Exercise 11: Configure NFS to share */mntlvol1* in read-only and */mntpart01* in read/write mode to users on the local network only. Use AutoFS to make them automounted on *client1* itself.

Exercise 12: Configure a basic web server for *www.example.com* with access wide open to everyone to display the contents of *index.html* file.

Exercise 13: Configure a web server for *www.example.com* to listen on port 3000 with DocumentRoot */var/example/www*, web contents in */var/example/www/webcontents*, index file *index.html* and accessible to *user1* and *user2* from local network only. Make sure that users on *example.net* and *example.org* do not have access to the web server.

Exercise 14: Configure a non-secure name-based virtual web server for *www.example.com* and *www.example.net* to share 192.168.0.202 IP address on port 8000.

Exercise 15: Configure a secure name-based virtual web server for *www.example.com* and *www.example.net* on port 3020.

Exercise 16: Configure sendmail service for the local network only and have mail for user *user2* go to *user4*, domain *example.net* to *user3* and any mail for user *admin* go to *user1*.

Exercise 17: Block all mail from *example.net*.

Exercise 18: Configure Squid on port 8090 accessible to local network users only.

Exercise 19: Enable pop3s and imaps protocols and allow access to local network users with all mail blocked from *example.net* and *example.org*.

Exercise 20: Configure so *user2* is able to access mail using imaps.

Exercise 21: Configure sendmail so all mail go out via *smtp.example.com* and appear to be originating from *example.com*. Have all mail for *info@example.com* received by *admin@example.com*.

Exercise 22: Configure a caching nameserver.

Exercise 23: Configure iptables firewall to allow incoming ftp and ssh traffic on *example.com*, drop traffic on *example.net* and reject from *example.org*.

Exercise 24: Add a new chain called new_chain to iptables to allow ftp and ssh traffic on *eth0* and *eth1* interfaces respectively.

Exercise 25: Configure NTP client to get time updates from *server1*.

Exercise 26: Configure AutoFS to mount *server1:/testdir* to *client1:/testdir* with timeout set to 8 minutes.

Appendix C: Summary of Commands

This table provides a list of significant RHEL commands and their short description. Although there are hundreds of commands available in the operating system software, only those that are used more oftenly are covered.

File and Directory

cat	Creates a small file, joins two files and displays contents of a file.
cd	Changes directory.
chattr	Changes attributes on files/directories in ext2/ext3 file system.
cp	Copies files/directories.
diff	Compares files/directories for differences.
file	Displays file type.
find	Searches for files using various criteria.
getfacl	Displays ACL settings on a file/directory.
grep/egrep/fgrep	Matches text within text files.
head/tail	Displays beginning/ending of a text file.
ln	Links files/directories.
locate	Finds files by name.
ls/ll	Lists files/directories in different formats.
lsattr	Lists file/directory attributes.
mkdir	Creates a directory.
more/less	Displays text file contents one screenful at a time.
mv	Moves and renames files/directories.
nano	A text editor.
nautilus	Graphical file manager.
pwd	Displays full path to the current working directory.
rcp	Copies files/directories from one system to another.
rm	Removes files/directories.
rmdir	Removes an empty directory.
setfacl	Sets ACL attributes on a file/directory.
sort	Sorts text files or given input.
stat	Displays files or file system statistical information.
strings	Extracts and displays legible information out of a non-text file.
touch	Creates an empty file. Updates time stamp on an existing file.
vi	A text editor.
view	Displays a text file.
vim	The enhanced version of vi editor.
wc	Displays number of lines, characters, words and bytes.
whereis	Displays full pathname to a program or command, and its manual pages.
which	Displays full pathname to a program or command.

Shells, Scripting and Variables

alias/unalias	Sets/unsets shortcuts.
awk	A programming language.
cut	Extracts selected columns.
echo	Displays variable values and echos arguments.
env	Displays or modifies current environment variables.
exit	Terminates a process or shell script.
export	Makes a variable a global variable.
history	Displays previously executed commands.
pr	Prints a file on the display terminal.
read	Prompts for user input.
sed	Stream editor for filtering and transforming text.
set	Displays set variables.
tee	Sends output to two locations.
tr	Translates characters.

Process and Process Monitoring

gnome-system-monitor	Graphical tool for viewing and monitoring system processes and processor/memory/swap usage.
kill	Sends a signal to one or more processes.
killall	Kills all active processes.
lsof	Lists open files.
nice	Executes a command at a non-default priority.
nohup	Runs a command immune to hangup signals.
pidof	Displays the PID of a running process.
pgreg	Displays processes.
pkill	Sends a signal to one or more processes.
ps	Displays running processes.
renice	Changes priority of a running process.
top	Displays real-time information on running processes.
uptime	Displays how long a system has been up for.

Hardware and Devices

dmesg	Gathers and displays system diagnostics messages.
hal-device	Manages devices that conform to the Hardware Abstraction Layer standard.
hal-device-manager	Graphical equivalent of hal-device command.
hwclock	Displays and sets the hardware clock.
kudzu	Detects and configures new or modified hardware.
lshal	Lists all devices Hardware Abstraction Layer knows about.
lspci	Lists PCI devices.
lsusb	Lists USB devices.
pccardctl	Controls PCMCIA cards.
udevcontrol	Manages hardware device events.
udevinfo	Displays hardware device information.
udevmonitor	Displays hardware device events.
udevtest	Simulates a udev execution.
tty	Displays full device path to the terminal session.

Installation

cdrecord	Burns CDs/DVDs.
eject	Ejects removable media.
ksvalidator	Validates the syntax of a Kickstart configuration file.
mkbootdisk	Creates a standalone boot media.
rhn_check	Checks for and executes queued tasks on Ret Hat Network.
rhn_register	Registers a system on Red Hat Network.
system-config-kickstart	Graphical tool for build and modifying a Kickstart configuration file.

X Window and Desktop Managers

X	Starts the X server.
startx	Starts an X window session.
switchdesk	Switches into another desktop environment.
system-config-display	Graphical tool for configuring video hardware.
xterm	Terminal emulator for X.

Software Packages

rpm	Performs rpm package management tasks.
rpm2cpio	Extracts cpio archive from an rpm package.
rpmbuild	Builds an rpm package.
rpmquery	Queries rpm packages.
rpmverify	Verifies rpm packages.
pirut	Graphical tool for installing and removing rpm packages.
pup	Graphical tool for updating rpm packages.
system-config-packages	Graphical tool for listing, searching, installing and removing rpm packages.
yum	Performs rpm package management tasks flexibly.

Users and Groups

chage	Changes expiry information on a user password.
chfn	Changes user information used by the finger command.
chgrp	Changes group membership on a file/directory.
chmod	Changes permissions on a file/directory.
chown	Changes ownership (and group membership) on a file/directory.
chsh	Changes a user's login shell permanently.
faillog	Displays faillog records and sets login failure limits.
gpasswd	Administers /etc/group file.
groupadd	Creates a group account.
groupdel	Deletes a group account.
groupmod	Modifies a group account.
groups	Displays secondary group membership for a user.
grpck	Checks /etc/group for consistency.
grpconv	Converts to shadow groups mechanism.
grpunconv	Unconverts from shadow groups mechanism.
id	Displays a user's identity information.
last	Displays history of successful user login/logout attempts.
lastb	Displays history of unsuccessful user login attempts.
lastlog	Displays the most recent login attempts.
logname	Displays a user's login name.
newgrp	Switches to a new group temporarily.
passwd	Changes user password.

pwck	Checks /etc/passwd for consistency.
pwconv	Converts to shadow passwd mechanism.
pwunconv	Unconverts from shadow password mechanism.
su	Switches to a different user.
umask	Displays or sets file mode creation mask.
useradd	Creates a new user account.
userdel	Deletes a user account.
usermod	Modifies a user account.
users	Displays a list of currently logged in users.
sudo	Executes a command as another user.
utmpdump	Displays the contents of utmp, btmp and wtmp files.
vigr	Opens /etc/shadow file in vi and locks it.
vipw	Opens /etc/passwd file in vi and locks it.
w	Displays who is currently logged in, what he is doing and how long the system has been up for.
wall	Broadcasts a system wide message.
who	Displays a list of currently logged in users.
whoami	Displays effective user name.
system-config-users	Graphical tool for managing user and group accounts.

Disk Partitioning

fdisk	Disk partition management tool.
lvcreate/lvremove	Creates/removes a logical volume.
lvdisplay	Displays information about a logical volume.
lvextend/lvreduce	Extends/reduces the size of a logical volume.
lvrename	Renames a logical volume.
lvresize	Resizes a logical volume.
lvs	Displays basic logical volume information.
mdadm	Manages software RAID devices.
mknod	Creates a device file.
parted	Another disk partition management tool.
partprobe	Informs RHEL of partition table changes.
pvcreate	Creates a physical volume by initializing a disk or partition.
pvdisplay	Displays information about a physical volume.
pvmove	Moves allocated physical extents from one physical volume to another.
pvremove	Removes LVM metadata information from a physical volume.
pvs/pvscan	Displays basic physical volume information.
system-config-lvm	Graphical tool for managing LVM.
vgcreate/vgremove	Creates/removes a volume group.
vgdisplay	Displays information about a volume group.
vgextend/vgreduce	Adds/removes a physical volume to a volume group.
vgs	Displays basic volume group information.

File System, Quota and Swap

baobab	Graphical tool for analyzing disk space utilization.
blkid	Displays block device attributes.
df	Displays disk utilization.
du	Displays directory or file system utilization.
dumpe2fs	Displays ext2/ext3 file system information.

e2fsck	Checks and repairs an ext2/ext3 file system.
e2label	Displays or changes the label on an ext2/ext3 file system.
edquota	Edits/sets/copies user quota settings.
findfs	Searches for a file system by label or UUID.
free	Displays amount of free and used physical memory and swap.
fsck	Checks and repairs a file system.
fuser	Lists/kills processes using a file system.
mke2fs / mkfs.ext2	Creates an ext2/ext3 file system.
mkfs	Creates a file system.
mklost+found	Creates a lost+found directory.
mkswap	Creates device or file system swap.
mount/umount	Connects/disconnects a file system to/from directory tree.
quota	Displays quota settings and usage status.
quotacheck	Checks quota usage.
quotaoff	Disables quota on a file system.
quotaon	Enables quota on a file system.
repquota	Reports quota usage.
resize2fs	Resizes an ext2/ext3 file system.
swapon	Activates a swap space.
swapoff	Deactivates a swap space.
tune2fs	Modifies tunable parameters on an ext2/ext3 file system.
vmstat	Displays virtual memory statistics.

Shutdown and Boot

chkconfig	Sets/queries run level information for services.
grub-install	Installs GRUB.
halt	Shuts a system down.
init	Changes run levels and spawns new processes.
ntsysv	Configures the start and stop of services.
poweroff	Shuts a system down and turns its power off.
reboot	Shuts a system down and reboots it.
runlevel	Displays the current and previous system run levels.
service	Manages the start and stop of a service.
serviceconf	Graphical tool for managing service start and stop.
shutdown	Shuts a system down.
system-config-services	Same as serviceconf.
grub> cat	Displays the contents of grub.conf.
grub> find	Locates disk and partition that contains grub.conf.
grub> root	Displays/loads a root partition.
grub> setup	Checks/installs GRUB in MBR or partition.

Kernel

depmod	Scans the system, finds modules and updates modules.dep file.
lsmod	Displays a list of currently loaded modules.
make	Recompiles a program.
mkinitrd	Creates initial ramdisk images.
modinfo	Displays information about modules.
modprobe	Adds/removes modules from kernel.
patch	Applies a diff file to an original, used for patching kernel.

| rmmod | Removes a module from kernel. |
| sysctl | Configures kernel parameters at runtime. |

Backup, Restore and Compression

bzip2/bunzip2	Compresses/uncompresses files.
cpio	Creates file archives.
dd	Performs bit by bit copy.
dump/restore	Performs ext2/ext3 file system backups/restores.
file-roller	Graphical tool for archiving files.
gzip/gunzip	Compresses/uncompresses files.
mkisofs	Creates an ISO image of data.
rsync	Copies files faster and more efficiently than rcp.
tar	Archives files.
zip/unzip	Compresses/uncompresses files.

Print Services

accept/reject	Allows/disallows users to submit print requests.
cupsenable/cupsdisable	Activates/deactivates printers and printer classes.
lp/lpr	Sends a print request to a printer or printer class.
lpadmin	Configures CUPS printers and classes.
lpc	Privides limited control over CUPS printers and printer classes.
lpq	Displays printer queue status.
lpmove	Moves print jobs from one print destination to another.
lprm	Cancels submitted print requests.
lpstat	Displays printer status information.
system-config-printer	Graphical tool for managing printers and printer classes.

Job Scheduling and System Logging

anacron	Executes commands periodically.
at	Submits/lists/deletes at jobs.
atq	Lists pending at jobs.
atrm	Deletes pending at jobs.
crontab	Schedules cron jobs.

Networking, Interface Administration and Routing

arp	Displays/modifies MAC-IP address translation.
ethtool	Displays/modifies Ethernet interface settings.
hostname	Displays/sets system name.
ifconfig	Displays/configures a network interface.
ifup / ifdown	Brings up/down an interface.
ip	Displays/manipulates interfaces and routing.
mtr	Investigates network connectivity between two hosts.
netstat	Displays network interface and routing information.
ping	Tests connectivity between two interfaces or systems.
route	Displays/manages routing table.
system-config-network	Graphical tool for managing network interfaces and routing.
tcpdump	Dumps traffic on a network interface for diagnostic purposes.
tracepath	Traces path to a network system.
traceroute	Traces packets to determine route to a network system.
uname	Displays summary information about a system.

DNS and DHCP

dhclient	Obtains IP address and other network information from a DHCP server.
dig	DNS lookup and troubleshooting utility.
dns-keygen	Generates a secret key to be shared between rndc and named.
host	DNS lookup utility.
named-checkconf	Checks and validates DNS configuration file.
named-checkzone	Checks and validates a DNS zone file.
nslookup	Queries DNS for name resolution.
rndc	Controls the behavior of DNS.

NIS and LDAP

authconfig	Configures system authentication resources.
getent	Gets entries from administrative database.
ldapsearch	Queries an LDAP server.
openssl	Allows using various cryptography functions.
system-config-authentication	Graphical tool for configuring and managing NIS and LDAP.
ypcat	Displays contents of an NIS map.
ypmatch	Greps for a pattern in an NIS map.
yppasswd	Changes a user password in NIS maps.
yppoll	Queries NIS server for NIS maps.
ypset	Binds to an NIS server.
ypwhich	Displays NIS server name the client is bound to.

Internet Services and Electronic Mail

alternatives	Creates, removes, maintains and displays information about the symlinks comprising the alternatives system.
finger	Displays user information.
ftp	Uploads and downloads files.
lftp	Uploads and downloads files.
mail/mailx	Sends and reads mail.
mailstats	Displays mail statistics.
mutt	An MUA.
newaliases	Rebuilds mail aliases database.
postconf	Configures Postfix.
rcp	Transfers files between two UNIX systems.
rlogin	Logs a user in to a remote UNIX system.
telnet	Displays a login prompt for supplying user information.
wget	Downloads files from the Internet.

Network Time Protocol (NTP)

ntpdate	Sets date/time via NTP.
ntpq	Queries NTP daemon.
ntptrace	Displays NTP server hierarchy.
system-config-date / system-config-time	Graphical tool for configuring and managing NTP.

NFS, AutoFS and Samba

exportfs	NFS exports and unexports resources.
mount.cifs / umount.cifs	Mounts/unmounts Samba resources.

---

nfsstat	Displays NFS usage statistics.
rpcinfo	Displays RPC information.
nmblookup	Netbios name lookup utility.
showmount	Displays remote NFS mounts.
smbclient	Accesses Samba resources.
smbpasswd	Sets password for Samba users.
smbstatus	Displays the status of Samba shares.
system-config-nfs	Graphical tool for configuring NFS.
system-config-samba	Graphical tool for configuring Samba.
testparm	Checks for syntax errors in Samba configuration file.

Apache and Squid

apachectl	Controls the behavior of httpd daemon.
elinks	A textual Internet browser.
firefox	A graphical Internet browser.
htpasswd	Manages user files for basic authentication.
system-config-httpd	Graphical tool for configuring Apache server.

System and Network Security

chcon	Changes SELinux security context.
chroot	Changes root directory for the specified command.
getenforce	Displays the current operational mode of SELinux.
getsebool	Displays the current value of an SELinux Boolean.
iptables	Configures and manages packet filtering and natting.
restorecon	Restores default SELinux security contexts on files.
scp	Transfers files securely.
sealert	Client interface for SELinux troubleshooting.
semanage	Manages certain elements of SELinux policy.
setenforce	Sets the default operational mode for SELinux.
setsebool	Sets a new value of an SELinux Boolean.
sftp	Transfers files securely.
ssh	Opens up a secure login session on a remote system.
ssh-add	Adds DSA/RSA keys to the authentication agent.
ssh-agent	Authentication agent that holds private keys for authentication.
ssh-copy-id	Installs public key to a remote system's authorized_keys file.
ssh-keygen	Generates, manages and converts public/private keys for ssh.
system-config-securitylevel	Graphical tool for enabling/disabling iptables firewall, allowing/denying services and setting SELinux operational mode.
system-config-selinux	Graphical tool for managing SELinux.

Miscellaneous

apropos	Searches whatis database for keyword.
cal	Displays calendar.
clear	Clears a terminal screen.
date	Displays/sets system date/time.
man	Displays manual pages.
system-config-soundcard	Graphical tool for configuring sound hardware.
whatis	Searches whatis database for short description of matched words.

Appendix D: Summary of Files

This table contains a list of a variety of configuration, startup, log and other important RHEL files along with their short description.

Hardware and Devices

/etc/modprobe.conf	Defines optional modules loaded at system boot.
/etc/rc.d/init.d/haldaemon	HAL start/stop script.
/etc/udev/	Stores udev files.
/etc/udev/rules.d	Stores rules applied to devices being added or removed.
/etc/udev/udev.conf	udev configuration file.
/proc/cpuinfo	Maintains runtime CPU information.
/proc/filesystems	Maintains runtime list of supported file systems.
/proc/ide	Maintains runtime information on IDE devices.
/proc/interrupts	Maintains runtime information about IRQs.
/proc/iomem	Maintains runtime information on I/O memory mapping.
/proc/ioports	Maintains runtime list of I/O port regions in use.
/proc/mdstat	Maintains runtime information on software RAID devices.
/proc/meminfo	Maintains runtime information on used and free physical memory and swap, as well as information about shared memory and buffers used by the kernel.
/proc/modules	Maintains runtime list of loaded modules.
/proc/mounts	Maintains runtime list of mounted file systems.
/proc/partitions	Maintains runtime major and minor number information on partitions with associated partition names and size.
/proc/scsi/	Maintains runtime information on SCSI devices.
/proc/stat	Maintains runtime kernel and system statistics.
/proc/swaps	Maintains runtime information about swap areas.
/proc/sys/	Maintains runtime information on kernel parameters.
/proc/uptime	Maintains runtime information on system uptime and idle processes.
/proc/vmstat	Maintains runtime virtual memory information.
/var/log/dmesg	Logs diagnostic messages.
/var/run/haldaemon.pid	Contains the PID for hald.

X Window and Desktop Managers

/etc/sysconfig/desktop	Defines system-wide default display and desktop managers.
/etc/X11/	Stores X-related files.
/etc/X11/prefdm	Defines preferred display manager.
/etc/X11/xinit/	Stores X startup and configuration files.
/etc/X11/xorg.conf	Primary X configuration file for the X server.
/var/run/xfs.pid	Contains the PID for X font server.

Software Packages

| /etc/yum.conf | Default configuration file for yum. |
| /etc/yum.repos.d/ | Defines software repository configuration information. |

Users and Groups

~/.bash_logout	Per-user file to define commands to be executed prior to user logging out.
~/.bash_profile	Per-user initialization file to set environment variables.
~/.bashrc	Per-user initialization file to define functions and aliases.
/etc/bashrc	System-wide initialization file to define functions and aliases.
/etc/group	Maintains a database of defined groups.
/etc/gshadow	Contains group password information.
/etc/login.defs	Contains defaults in addition to the ones defined in /etc/default/useradd file used at user creation.
/etc/passwd	Maintains a database of defined users.
/etc/profile	System-wide initialization file to set environment variables.
/etc/profile.d/	Stores scripts called by /etc/profile.
/etc/shadow	Stores user passwords and password aging information.
/etc/skel/	Stores templates copied to user home directories at user creation.
/var/log/btmp	Maintains a history of failed user login attempts.
/var/log/faillog	Maintains a more detailed history of failed user login attempts.
/var/log/wtmp	Maintains a history of successful user login attempts.

Disk Partitioning

| /etc/lvm/backup | Stores volume group information. |

File Systems, Quota and Swap

/*/lost+found/	Exists in every file system to hold orphan files.
/etc/fstab	Contains file system and swap entries to be mounted automatically at each system boot.
/etc/mtab	Lists currently-mounted file systems.

Shutdown and Boot

/boot/grub/grub.conf	Contains boot information.
/etc/inittab	Initialization table used by the init command.
/etc/issue	Contents of this file are printed as login banner.
/etc/motd	Contents of this file are displayed when a user logs in.
/etc/rc.d/init.d/	Stores startup & shutdown scripts.
/etc/sysconfig/	Stores base initialization configuration for services.
/mnt/sysimage	Virtual file system created in rescue mode to mount file systems.

Kernel

/etc/sysctl.conf	Stores user-defined kernel parameters.
/lib/modules	Stores kernel modules.
/usr/src/	Used for building new kernel based on source code.

Backup, Restore and Compression

| /etc/dumpdates | Updated by the dump command with backup time stamps. |

Print Services

/etc/cups/	Contains CUPS configuration and other data.
/etc/cups/classes.conf	Contains information about printer classes.
/etc/cups/client.conf	Defines CUPS client configuration.
/etc/cups/cupsd.conf	Main CUPS configuration file.
/etc/cups/interfaces/	Contains one file per configured printer that includes interface program to be used for the printer.
/etc/cups/mime.convs	Contains file format filters.
/etc/cups/mime.types	Defines file types.
/etc/cups/pdftops.conf	Defines language-specific PDF fonts.
/etc/cups/ppd/	Contains custom printer settings.
/etc/cups/printers.conf	Stores CUPS configuration.
/etc/cups/pstoraster.convs	Contains a conversion filter for PostScript printers.
/etc/cups/snmp.conf	Defines parameters for discovery of network printers.
/etc/cups/ssl/	Contains SSL certificates.
/etc/printcap	Defines SAMBA-shared printers.
/etc/rc.d/init.d/cups	CUPS start/stop script.
/var/log/cups/	Contains CUPS log files.
/var/spool/cups/	Holds CUPS requests temporarily.
/var/run/cupsd.pid	Contains the PID for cupsd.

Job Scheduling and System Logging

/etc/anacrontab	Defines jobs managed by anacron.
/etc/at.allow	Determines who can submit at jobs.
/etc/at.deny	Determines who cannot submit at jobs.
/etc/cron.allow	Determines who can submit cron jobs.
/etc/cron.d/	Another location for storing cron files.
/etc/cron.daily/	Contains scripts to be run daily via cron.
/etc/cron.deny	Determines who cannot submit cron jobs.
/etc/cron.hourly/	Contains scripts to be run hourly via cron.
/etc/cron.monthly/	Contrains scripts to be run monthly via cron.
/etc/crontab	Master crontab file that contains scripts to be run via cron.
/etc/cron.weekly/	Contains scripts to be run weekly via cron.
/etc/rc.d/init.d/anacron	anacron start/stop script.
/etc/rc.d/init.d/atd	at start/stop script.
/etc/rc.d/init.d/crond	cron start/stop script.
/etc/rc.d/init.d/syslogd	syslogd start/stop script.
/etc/syslog.conf	Configuration file for syslogd service.
/var/log/cron	Logs executed at and cron jobs.
/var/log/messages	Logs all system activities.
/var/spool/at	Spools scheduled at jobs.
/var/spool/cron	Spools scheduled cron jobs.
/var/run/atd.pid	Contains the PID for atd.
/var/run/crond.pid	Contains the PID for crond.

Networking, Interface Administration and Routing

| /etc/ | Holds DNS configuration in a chrooted setup. |

/etc/hosts	Contains hostnames (and optionally aliases) with corresponding IP addresses.
/etc/rc.d/init.d/network	Networking start/stop script.
/etc/sysconfig/network	Contains base network configuration.
/etc/sysconfig/networking/	Contains base networking configuration.
/etc/sysconfig/network-scripts/	Contains network interface configuration.

DNS ($ROOTDIR is either / or /var/named/chroot) and DHCP

/etc/dhcpd.conf	Contains DHCP configuration information.
/etc/host.conf	Determines the lookup order for hostname resolution.
/etc/nsswitch.conf	Determines the lookup order for hostname resolution. Used if /etc/host.conf is unavailable.
/etc/resolv.conf	Defines DNS client configuration.
/etc/rc.d/init.d/dhcpd	DHCP server start/stop script.
/etc/rc.d/init.d/named	DNS start/stop script.
/etc/sysconfig/dhcpd	Contains base DHCP configuration.
/etc/sysconfig/named	Contains base DNS configuration.
$ROOTDIR/etc/named.conf	Contains boot information for DNS servers.
$ROOTDIR/etc/named.ca	Contains root server entries.
$ROOTDIR/etc/\named.caching_nameserver.conf	Contains default settings for caching DNS server.
$ROOTDIR/etc/named.rfc1912.conf	Contains default zones.
$ROOTDIR/etc/rndc.conf	Defines settings for rndc.
$ROOTDIR/etc/rndc.key	Defines security key used by rndc.
$ROOTDIR/var/named	Holds DNS zone files in a chrooted setup.
/usr/share/doc/bind*/sample/	Contains default configuration and zone files.
/var/run/named.pid	Contains the PID for named.

NIS and LDAP

/etc/ldap.conf	Contains default LDAP configuration.
/etc/openldap/ldap.conf	Contains PAM and NSS LDAP module data.
/etc/pam.d/system-auth-ac	Generated when system-config-authconfig is executed to modify NIS/LDAP settings.
/etc/rc.d/init.d/portmap	Portmap service start/stop script.
/etc/rc.d/init.d/ypbind	NIS client start/stop script.
/etc/sysconfig/authconfig	Contains base NIS and LDAP configuration.
/etc/yp.conf	Contains NIS binding configuration settings.
/var/yp/	Contains NIS maps and other related data.
/var/yp/binding/	Holds NIS binding information.

Internet Services and Electronic Mail

/etc/aliases	Defines user aliases for sendmail and postfix.
/etc/aliases.db	This file is generated from the contents of /etc/aliases.
/etc/alternatives/mta	Symlink to the default MTA.
/etc/dovecot.conf	Dovecot configuration file.
/etc/mail/access	Contains access control information to reject, discard and relay mail.
/etc/mail/access.db	Generated from the contents of /etc/mail/access.
/etc/mail/domaintable	Contains domain mappings to forward mail to.
/etc/mail/domaintable.db	Generated from the contents of /etc/mail/domaintable.

/etc/mail/local-host-names	Contains hostnames or domain names for which the local system acts as an outgoing mail server.
/etc/mail/mailertable	Defines routing information to a specific domain.
/etc/mail/mailertable.db	Generated from the contents of /etc/mail/mailertable.
/etc/mail/Makefile	Compiles the sendmail.mc macro file.
/etc/mail/sendmail.cf	Defines configuration rules for incoming mail.
/etc/mail/sendmail.mc	Contains macros. Contents of this file are used to regenerate the sendmail.cf file when sendmail service is started or restarted.
/etc/mail/spamassasin/	Stores spam control configuration.
/etc/mail/submit.cf	Defines configuration rules for outgoing mail.
/etc/mail/submit.mc	Contains macros. Contents of this file are used to regenerate the submit.cf file when sendmail service is started or restarted.
/etc/mail/trusted-users	Contains usernames who could send mail without generating any warning messages.
/etc/mail/virtusertable	Virtual user table. Defines mail forwarding for external users.
/etc/mail/virtusertable.db	Generated from the contents of /etc/mail/virtusertable.
/etc/networks	Contains information about known networks.
/etc/pki/dovecot/certs/dovecot.pem	Contains default SSL certificate.
/etc/pki/dovecot/dovecot-openssl.cnf	Defines configuration used to regenerate default SSL certificate and private key.
/etc/pki/dovecot/private/dovecot.pem	Contains default private key.
/etc/postfix/master.cf	List services to be used by Postfix and starts them when the Postfix daemon is started.
/etc/postfix/main.cf	Defines global Postfix configuration.
/etc/protocols	Lists available protocols.
/etc/rc.d/init.d/dovecot	Dovecot start/stop script.
/etc/rc.d/init.d/postfix	Postfix start/stop script.
/etc/rc.d/init.d/sendmail	sendmail start/stop script.
/etc/rc.d/init.d/vsftpd	vsFTP service start/stop script.
/etc/rpc	Contains a list of RPC services along with port numbers.
/etc/services	Contains services with corresponding port numbers.
/etc/securetty	Disables direct telnet access into the system.
/etc/sysconfig/sendmail	Contains base sendmail configuration.
/etc/vsftpd/ftpusers	Contains a list of users that are denied vsftp access.
/etc/vsftpd/user_list	Contains a list of users that are allowed or denied vsftp access based on the value of the userlist_deny directive.
/etc/vsftpd/vsftpd.conf	vsftp service configuration file.
/etc/xinetd.conf	Internet service daemon's configuration file.
/etc/xinetd.d/	Contains xinetd-controlled services.
/usr/share/doc/dovecot*/\ examples/mkcert.sh	Script to regenerate SSL certificate and private key.
/var/log/maillog	Logs mail transfer information.
/var/spool/mail/	Stores incoming user mail.
/var/spool/mqueue/	Stores submitted mail until it is sent out.
/var/run/sendmail.pid	Contains the PID for sendmail service.
/var/run/sm-client.pid	Contains the PID for sendmail client service.

| /var/run/xinetd.pid | Contains the PID for xinetd. |

Network Time Protocol (NTP)

/etc/ntp.conf	Contains NTP service configuration.
/etc/ntp/ntp.key	Defines encryption for NTP.
/etc/rc.d/init.d/ntpd	NTP start/stop script.
/var/lib/ntp/drift	Maintains information to help ntpd keep track of local system clock accuracy.
/var/run/ntpd.pid	Contains the PID for ntpd.

NFS, AutoFS and Samba

/etc/auto.master	Defines direct, indirect and special AutoFS maps.
/etc/auto.misc	Defines entries for automounting removable devices.
/etc/exports	Contains entries to be NFS exported.
/etc/fstab	Contains entries for file systems and swap spaces that are automatically mounted when system boots up.
/etc/rc.d/init.d/autofs	AutoFS start/stop script.
/etc/rc.d/init.d/nfs	NFS start/stop script.
/etc/rc.d/init.d/smb	Samba start/stop script.
/etc/samba/smb.conf	Samba server configuration file.
/etc/samba/smbpasswd	Maintains Samba user passwords.
/etc/samba/smbusers	Maintains Samba and system user mappings.
/etc/sysconfig/nfs	Contains base NFS configuration.
/etc/sysconfig/samba	Contains base Samba configuration.
/var/lib/nfs/etab	Maintains a list of remotely mounted NFS resources.
/var/log/samba/	Holds Samba logs.
/var/run/	Contains PIDs for NFS and Samba.

Apache and Squid

.htaccess	Based on the location of this file, Apache allows users to manage entire DocumentRoot or a specific directory under DocumentRoot.
/etc/httpd/conf/httpd.conf	Contains Apache server configuration.
/etc/httpd/conf.d/*.conf	Additional configuration files for Apache.
/etc/httpd/conf.d/ssl.conf	Contains Apache secure server configuration.
/etc/rc.d/init.d/httpd	Apache start/stop script.
/etc/rc.d/init.d/squid	Squid start/stop script.
/etc/squid/	Holds Squid-related information.
/etc/squid/squid.conf	Contains Squid configuration.
/etc/sysconfig/squid	Contains base Squid configuration.
/usr/lib/httpd/modules/	Stores Apache modules.
/var/log/httpd/*log	Holds Apache log files for both secure and non-secure servers.
/var/log/squid/	Holds Squid logs.
/var/run/httpd.pid	Contains Apache server PID.
/var/run/squid.pid	Contains Squid service PID.
/var/spool/squid/	Default directory used by Squid for caching.
/var/run/	Contains PIDs for Apache and Squid.

System and Network Security

~/.ssh/	Stores user authentication/authorization information.
/etc/hosts.allow	TCP Wrappers file that contains entries for hosts, networks and domains that are allowed access.
/etc/hosts.deny	TCP Wrappers file that contains entries for hosts, networks and domains that are denied access.
/etc/pam.d/	Stores information for each PAM-aware service.
/etc/rc.d/init.d/iptables	IPTables start/stop script.
/etc/rc.d/init.d/sshd	Secure shell start/stop script.
/etc/selinux/config	SELinux configuration file.
/etc/selinux/targeted/context/files/	Stores SELinux security contexts for files and directories.
/etc/selinux/targeted/context/users/	Stores SELinux security contexts for users.
/etc/sestatus.conf	Lists files and processes whose security contexts are displayed with the sestatus command.
/etc/ssh/	Stores ssh configuration information.
/etc/ssh/ssh_config	Holds system-wide ssh client configuration.
/etc/ssh/sshd_config	Holds system-wide ssh server configuration.
/etc/sysconfig/iptables	Contains base IPTables firewall configuration.
/selinux/	Stores current SELinux configuration.
/var/log/secure	Captures security-related information.
/var/run/sshd	Contains the PID for sshd.

Miscellaneous

/etc/rc.d/init.d/rhnsd	RHN start/stop script.
/etc/sysconfig/rhnsd	Contains base RHN configuration.

Appendix E: Summary of System Daemons

This table lists several key daemon programs and their short description. These daemons are critical to proper service operation.

Hardware and Devices
hald	Keeps track of connected devices.
udevd	Receives device add and delete information from kernel and passes it onto udev for processing.

File systems, Quota and Swap
kswapd	Handles kernel paging services.

Shutdown and Boot
init	Primary Initialization daemon.

Print Services
cupsd	Print scheduler daemon.

Job Scheduling and System Logging
atd	Executes queued at jobs.
crond	Executes scheduled cron jobs.
klogd	Logs kernel messages.
syslogd	Logs system messages.

DNS and DHCP
dhcpd	DHCP server daemon.
named	DNS server daemon.

NIS and LDAP
rpc.yppasswdd	Manages NIS user password change requests.
slapd	Serves LDAP client requests.
ypbind	Runs on all NIS servers and clients to bind with an NIS server.

Internet Services and Electronic Mail
ftpd	FTP server daemon.
fingerd	Provides user information to clients.
master	Postfix master server process.
nqmgr	Responsible for mail transmission, relay and local delivery.
pickup	Postfix local mail retrieval daemon.
rlogind	Remote login daemon to serve rlogin client requests.
sendmail	Sends and receives mail.
smtpd	Mail transfer server daemon.
telnetd	Remote login daemon to serve telnet client requests.

| vsftpd | FTP server daemon for secure file transfers. |
| xinetd | Master internet services daemon. |

Network Time Protocol (NTP)
| ntpd | Provides time to clients and peers. |

NFS, AutoFS and Samba
automount	Manages AutoFS mounts.
nmbd	Provides NetBIOS over IP naming services to client systems.
portmap	Forwards incoming RPC requests to appropriate RPC daemons.
rpc.idmapd	Controls UID/GID mappings with usernames/groupnames.
rpc.lockd	Provides NFS file locking services.
rpc.mountd	Responds to NFS client mount requests, and provides status of exported and mounted resources.
rpc.nfsd	Handles NFS client requests.
rpc.rquotad	Provides statistics on disk quota.
rpc.statd	Works with rpc.lockd to provide crash and recovery services.
smbd	Samba server daemon.

Apache and Squid
| httpd | Provides HTTP access to clients. |
| squid | Provides proxy and caching service to client requests. |

System and Network Security
| sshd | Provides secure encrypted communication channel between systems over an insecure network. |

Miscellaneous
| rhnsd | Queries Red Hat Network for updates and other information. |
| setroubleshootd | Checks and alerts for new SELinux AVC messages. |

Bibliography

The following websites, forums and guides were referenced in writing this book:

1. www.redhat.com
2. www.centos.org
3. www.hp.com
4. www.ibm.com
5. www.unix.org
6. www.linux.org
7. www.linuxhq.com
8. www.isc.org
9. www.itrc.hp.com
10. www.wikipedia.org
11. www.gnome.org
12. www.kde.org
13. www.pathname.com/fhs
14. www.cups.org
15. www.linuxprinting.org
16. www.ntp.org
17. www.samba.org
18. www.sendmail.org
19. www.postfix.org
20. www.dovecot.org
21. www.apache.org
22. www.squid-cache.org
23. www.openssh.org
24. www.netfilter.org
25. www.nsa.gov/selinux
26. www.opensource.org
27. RedHat installation guide
28. RedHat deployment guide
29. HP-UX 11i v3 book by Asghar Ghori (ISBN: 978-1-606-436547)

Glossary

. (single dot)	Represents current directory.
.. (double dots)	Represents parent directory of the current directory.
Absolute mode	A method of giving permissions to a file or directory.
Absolute path	A pathname that begins with a /.
Access Control List	A method of allocating file permissions to a specific user or group.
Access mode	See file permissions.
ACL	See Access Control List.
Address Resolution Protocol	A protocol used to determine a system's Ethernet address when its IP address is known.
Address space	Memory location that a process can refer.
Anaconda	RHEL's installation program.
Apache	A famous HTTP web server software.
Archive	A file that contains one or more compressed files.
Argument	A value passed to a command or program.
ARP	See Address Resolution Protocol.
ASCII	An acronym for American Standard Code for Information Interchange.
Auditing	System and user activity record and analysis.
Authentication	The process of identifying a user to a system.
AutoFS	The NFS client-side service that automatically mounts and unmounts an NFS resource on an as-needed basis.
Automounter	See AutoFS.
Background process	A process that runs in the background.
Backup	Process of saving data on an alternative media such as a tape or another disk.
Berkeley Internet Name Domain	A UC Berkeley implementation of DNS. See also DNS.
BIND	See Berkeley Internet Name Domain.
BIOS	Basic I/O System. Software code that sits in the computer's non-volatile memory and is executed when the system is booted.
Block	A collection of bytes of data transmitted as a single unit.
Block device file	A device file associated with devices that transfer data in blocks. For example, disk, CD and DVD devices.
Boot	The process of starting up a system.
Bridge	A network device that connects two LANs together provided they use the same data-link layer protocol.
Broadcast client	An NTP client that listens to time broadcasts over the network.
Broadcast server	An NTP server that broadcasts time over the network.
Bus	Data communication path among devices in a computer system.
Bus topology	A connectivity technique with computers and other devices networked via a single backbone cable.
Cache	A temporary storage area on the system where frequently accessed information is duplicated for quick future access.

Caching DNS	A system that obtains zone information from a primary or slave DNS server and caches in its memory to respond quickly to client queries.
Caching proxy	A type of proxy server that caches frequently accessed web pages locally for faster access.
Character special file	A device file associated with devices that transfer data serially. For example, disk, tape, serial and other such devices.
Child process	A sub-process started by a process.
CIFS	Common Internet File System. Allows resources to be shared among Linux, UNIX and non-UNIX systems. Also may be referred to as Samba.
Command	An instruction given to the system to perform a task.
Command aliasing	Allows creating command shortcuts.
Command history	A feature that maintains a log of all commands executed at the command line.
Command interpreter	See Shell.
Command line editing	Allows editing at the command line.
Command prompt	The OS prompt where you type commands.
Compression	The process of compressing information.
Concatenation	A technique whereby two or more disks or partitions are added to form a larger storage container.
Core	A core is a processor that shares the chip with another core. Dual-core and quad-core processor chips are common.
Crash	An abnormal system shutdown caused by electrical outage or kernel malfunction, etc.
CUPS	Common Unix Printing System. The default printing system in RHEL.
Current directory	The present working directory.
Daemon	A server process that runs in the background and responds to client requests.
De-encapsulation	The reverse of encapsulation. See Encapsulation.
Default	Pre-defined values or settings that are automatically accepted by commands or programs.
Defunct process	See Zombie process.
Desktop manager	Software such as KDE or GNOME that provides graphical environment for users to interact with the system.
Device	A peripheral such as a printer, disk drive or a CD/DVD device.
Device driver	The software that controls a device.
Device file	See Special file.
Differential backup	Copies the data that has been modified since it was last backed up as part of a full backup.
Direct Memory Access	Allows hardware devices to access system memory without processor intervention.
Directory structure	Inverted tree-like Linux/UNIX directory structure.
Disk partitioning	Creating multiple partitions on a given hard drive so as to access them as separate logical containers for data storage.
Display manager	Presents users with graphical login screen. Examples are KDE and GNOME.
Distinguished name	A fully qualified object path in LDAP DIT.
DIT	Directory Information Tree. An LDAP directory hierarchy.
DMA	See Direct Memory Access.
DNS	Domain Name System. A widely used name resolution method on the Internet.
Domain	A group of computers configured to use a service such as DNS or NIS.

Driver	See Device driver.
EIDE	Enhanced IDE. An enhanced version of IDE drives. See IDE.
Encapsulation	The process of forming a packet through the seven OSI layers.
EOF	Marks the End OF File.
EOL	Marks the End Of Line.
Ethernet	A family of networking technologies designed for LANs.
Export	Making a file, directory or a file system available over the network as a share.
Extent	The smallest unit of space allocation in LVM. It is always contiguous. See Logical extent and Physical extent.
Fibre channel	A family of networking technologies designed for storage networking.
File descriptor	A unique, per-process integer value used to refer to an open file.
File permissions	Read, write, execute or no permission assigned to a file or directory at the user, group or public level.
File system	A grouping of files stored in special data structures.
Filter	A command that performs data transformation on the given input.
Firewall	A software or a dedicated hardware device used for blocking unauthorized access into a computer or network.
FireWire	A bus interface standard designed for very fast communication.
Firstboot process	Program that starts at first system reboot after a system has been installed to customize authentication, firewall, network, timezone and other services.
Forwarding DNS	A system that forwards client requests to other DNS servers.
Full backup	A self-contained copy of selected data.
Full path	See Absolute path.
Gateway	A device that links two networks that run completely different protocols.
GID	See Group ID.
Globbing	See Regular expression.
GNOME	GNU Object Model Environment. An intuitive graphical user environment.
GNU	GNU Not Unix. A project initiated to develop a completely free Unix-like operating system.
GPL	General Public License that allows the use of software developed under GNU project to be available for free to the general public.
Group	A collection of users that requires same permissions on a set of files.
Group ID	A unique identification number assigned to a group.
GRUB	GRand Unified Bootloader is a GNU bootloader program that supports multiboot functionality.
GUI	Graphical User Interface.
HAL	See Hardware Abstraction Layer.
Hardening	See Security hardening.
Hardware Abstraction Layer	A piece of software implemented in between the kernel and the underlying system hardware to hide differences in hardware from the kernel to enable it to run on a variety of hardware platforms.
Home directory	A directory where a user lands when he logs into the system.
Hostname	A unique name assigned to a node on a network.
Hub	A network device that receives data from one or more directions and forwards it to one or more directions.
Hybrid topology	A mix of star and bus topologies.
IDE	Integrated Drive Electronics. A hard disk technology.
Incremental backup	Copies only the data that has been modified since its last full, incremental or differential backup was performed.

Inode	An index node number holds a file's properties including permissions, size and creation/modification time as well as contains a pointer to the data blocks that actually store the file data.
Interface card	A card that allows a system to communicate to external devices.
Internet	A complex network of computers and routers.
Interrupt request	A signal sent by a device to the processor to request processing time.
I/O redirection	A shell feature that gets input from a non-default location and sends output and error messages to non-default locations.
IP address	A unique 32- or 128-bit software address assigned to a node on a network.
IPTables	A host-based packet-filtering firewall software to control the flow of data packets.
IRQ	See Interrupt request.
Job control	A shell feature that allows a process to be taken to background, brought to foreground, and to suspend its execution.
Job scheduling	Execution of commands, programs or scripts at a later time in future.
KDE	K Desktop Environment is an intuitive graphical user environment.
Kernel	Software piece that controls an entire system including all hardware and software.
Kickstart	A technique to perform a hands-off, fully-customized and automated installation of RHEL.
LAN	See Local Area Network.
LDAP	Lightweight Directory Access Protocol.
LDIF	LDAP Data Interchange Format. A special format used by LDAP for importing and exporting LDAP data among LDAP servers.
Link	An object that associates a file name to any type of file.
Link count	Number of links that refers to a file.
Linux	An open source version of the UNIX operating system.
Load balancing	A technique whereby more than one servers serve client requests to share the load.
Local Area Network	A campus-wide network of computing devices.
Local printer	A printer connected directly to a computer.
Logical extent	A unit of space allocation for logical volumes in LVM.
Logical volume	A logical container that holds a file system or swap.
Login	A process that begins when a user enters a username and password at the login prompt.
Login directory	See Home directory.
LVM	Logical Volume Manager. A disk partitioning solution.
MAC address	A unique 48-bit hardware address of a network interface. Also called physical address, ethernet address and hardware address.
Machine	A computer, system, RHEL workstation, RHEL desktop or a RHEL server.
Mail Delivery Agent	Software that delivers mail to recipient inboxes.
Mail Transfer Agent	Software that transfers mail from one system to another.
Mail User Agent	Mail client application that a user interacts with.
Major number	Points to a device driver.
Masquerading	A technique whereby systems on an internal network access external networks or the Internet using an intermediary device (router, firewall or RHEL system) so that requests originated from any of the internal systems appear to the outside world as being originated from the intermediary device.
MDA	See Mail Delivery Agent.

Metacharacters	Characters that have special meaning to the shell.
Minor number	Points to an individual device controlled by a specific device driver.
MIO card	See Multi I/O card.
Mirror	An exact copy of original data.
Mirroring	The process of creating mirrors.
Module	Modules are device drivers that are used to control hardware devices and software components.
Mounting	Attaching a device (a file system, a CD/DVD) to the directory structure.
MTA	See Mail Transfer Agent.
MUA	See Mail User Agent.
Multifunction card	An interface card that provides two or more different types of I/O connections.
Multi I/O card	See Multifunction card.
Named pipe	Allows two unrelated processes to talk to each other and exchange data.
Name resolution	A technique to determine IP address by providing hostname.
Name space	A hierarchical organization of all DNS domains on the Internet.
NAT	See Network Address Translation.
Netfilter	A framework that provides a set of hooks within the kernel to enable it to intercept and manipulate data packets.
Netmask	See Subnet mask.
Network	Two or more computers joined together to share resources.
Network Address Translation	Allows a system on an internal network to access external networks or the Internet using a single, registered IP address configured on an intermediary device (router, firewall or RHEL system).
Network printer	A printer connected to a network port and has an IP address and hostname.
Network Time Protocol	A protocol used to synchronize system clock.
NFS	Network File System. Allows Linux and UNIX systems to share files, directories and file systems.
NFS client	A system that mounts an exported Linux or UNIX resource.
NFS server	A system that exports a resource for mounting by an NFS client.
NIS	Network Information Service. Allows Linux and UNIX systems to manage administrative data centrally.
NIS client	Linux or UNIX system that binds itself with an NIS server for accessing administrative data.
NIS server	Maintains and makes available shared administrative data.
Node	A device connected directly to a network port and has a hostname and an IP address associated with it. A node could be a computer, an X terminal, a printer, a router, a hub, a switch, and so on.
Node name	A unique name assigned to a node.
NTP	See Network Time Protocol.
Octal mode	A method for setting permissions on a file or directory using octal numbering system.
Octal numbering system	A 3 digit numbering system that represents values from 0 to 7.
Open source	Any software whose source code is published and is accessible at no cost to the general public under GNU GPL for copy, modification and redistribution.
OpenSSH	Free implementation of secure shell services and utilities.
Open Systems Interconnection	A layered networking model that provides guidelines to networking equipment manufacturers to develop their products for multi-vendor interoperability.

Orphan process	An alive child process of a terminated parent process.
OSI	See Open Systems Interconnection.
Owner	A user who creates a file or starts a process.
PAM	See Pluggable Authentication Module.
Parent directory	A directory one level above the current directory in the file system hierarchy.
Parent process ID	The ID of a process that starts a child process.
PATA	Parallel Advanced Technology Attachment. A hard disk technology that is widely known as IDE and EIDE. See IDE.
Password aging	A mechanism that provides enhanced control on user passwords.
Pattern matching	See Regular expression.
PCI	Peripheral Component Interconnect. A local bus that connects various peripheral devices to the system.
PCIe	See PCI Express.
PCI Express	A superior PCI technology intended to replace PCI and PCI-X.
Performance monitoring	The process of acquiring data from system components for analysis and decision-making purposes.
Permission	Right to read, write or execute.
Physical extent	A unit of space allocation on physical volumes in LVM.
Physical volume	A hard drive or a partition logically brought under LVM control.
PID	See Process ID.
Pipe	Sends output from one command as input to the second command.
Plug and play	Ability of the operating system to add a removable device to the system without user intervention.
Pluggable Authentication Module	A set of library routines that allows using any authentication service available on a system for user authentication, password modification and user account validation purposes.
Port	A number appended to an IP address. This number could be associated with a well-known service or is randomly generated.
POST	Power On Self Test runs at system boot to test hardware.
PPID	See Parent process ID.
Primary DNS	A system that acts as the primary provider of DNS zones.
Primary prompt	The symbol where commands and programs are typed for execution.
Process	Any command, program or daemon that runs on a system.
Process ID	An identification number assigned by kernel to each process spawned.
Processor	A CPU. It may contain more than one cores.
Prompt	See Primary prompt and Secondary prompt.
Protocol	A common language that two nodes understand to communicate.
Proxy	A system that acts on behalf of other systems to access network services.
PXE	Pre-Execution Environment or Preboot Execution Environment enables a system to boot off a network boot server.
Quota	A mechanism to limit user access to file system space.
RAID	Redundant Array of Independent Disks. A disk arrangement technique that allows for enhanced performance and fault tolerance.
RAID array	A disk storage subsystem that uses hardware RAID.
Recovery	A function that recovers a crashed system to its previous normal state. It may require restoring lost data files.
Redirection	Getting input from and sending output to non-default destinations.
Referral	An entity defined on an LDAP server to forward a client request to some other LDAP server that contains the client requested information.

Regular expression	A string of characters commonly used for pattern matching and globbing.
Relative path	A path to a file relative to the current user location in the file system hierarchy.
Remote printer	A printer accessed by users on remote systems.
Repeater	A network device that removes unwanted noise from incoming signals, and amplifies and regenerates the signals to cover longer distances.
Replica	A slave LDAP server that shares master LDAP server's load and provides high availability.
Repository	A directory location to store software packages for downloading and installing.
Rescue mode	A special boot mode for fixing and recovering an unbootable system.
Resolver	The client-side of DNS.
Restore	The process of retrieving data from an offline media.
RHEL	Red Hat Enterprise Linux.
Ring topology	A wiring scheme in which nodes are connected in a ring or closed loop so that information is passed from one node to another in a circular fashion.
Root	See Superuser.
Router	A device that routes data packets from one network to another.
Routing	The process of choosing a path over which to send a data packet.
RPM	Red Hat Package Manager. A file format used for software packaging.
Run control levels	Different levels of RHEL operation.
Samba client	A system that accesses a Samba-shared resource.
Samba server	A system that shares a resource for Samba clients.
SAS	Serial Attached SCSI. A faster bus than SCSI intended to replace SCSI devices.
SATA	Serial Advanced Technology Attachment. This disk technology is a successor to the PATA drives.
Schema	A set of attributes and object classes.
Script	A text program written to perform a series of tasks.
SCSI	Small Computer System Interface. A parallel interface used to connect peripheral devices to the system.
Search path	A list of directories where the system looks for the specified command.
Secondary prompt	A prompt indicating that the entered command needs more input.
Secure shell	A set of tools that gives secure access to a system.
Security Enhanced Linux	An implementation of Mandatory Access Control architecture for enhanced and granular control.
Security hardening	Implementation of security measures to enhance system security.
SELinux	See Security Enhanced Linux.
Server (hardware)	Typically a larger and more powerful system that offers services to network users.
Server (software)	A process or daemon that runs on the system to serve client requests.
Set Group ID	Sets real and effective group IDs.
Set User ID	Sets real and effective user IDs.
Setgid	See Set group ID.
Setuid	See Set user ID.
Shadow password	A mechanism to store passwords and password aging data in a secure file.
Shared memory	A portion in physical memory created by a process to share it with other processes that communicate with that process.
Shell	The Linux/UNIX command interpreter that sits between a user and kernel.
Shell program	See Script.
Shell script	See Script.

Shell scripting	Programming in a Linux/UNIX shell to automate a given task.
Signal	A software interrupt sent to a process.
Single user mode	An operating system state in which the system cannot be accessed over the network.
Slave DNS	A system that acts as an alternate provider of DNS zones.
Slot	A receptacle for an I/O card in a computer system.
Socket	A bi-directional named pipe used for interprocess communication.
Software RAID	A disk partitioning scheme that provides better performance or fault tolerance, or a combination.
Special characters	See Metacharacters.
Special file	A file that points to a specific device.
Squid	A server software that provides proxy and caching capabilities.
Standard error	A location to send error messages generated by a command.
Standard input	A location to obtain input from. The default is the keyboard.
Standard output	A location to send output, other than error messages, generated by a command.
Star topology	A wiring scheme in which each node is connected to an interconnect device such as a hub or switch so as to form a star.
Stderr	See Standard error.
Stdin	See Standard input.
Stdout	See Standard output.
Sticky bit	Disallows non-onwers to delete files located in a directory.
Stratum level	The categorization of NTP time sources based on reliability and accuracy.
String	A series of characters.
Striping	A software RAID technique that provides improved performance and increased availability.
Subnet	One of the smaller networks formed by dividing an IP address.
Subnet mask	Segregates the network bits from the node bits.
Subnetting	The process of dividing an IP address into several smaller subnetworks.
Superblock	A small portion in a file system that holds the file system's critical information.
Superuser	A user with unlimited powers on a RHEL system.
Swap	Alternative disk or file system location for demand paging.
Switch	A network device that looks at the MAC address and switches the packet to the correct destination port based on the MAC address.
Symbolic link	A shortcut created to point to a file located somewhere in the file system tree.
Symbolic mode	A method of setting permissions on a file using non-decimal values.
Symlink	See Symbolic link.
System	A computer or partition in a computer that runs RHEL.
System Administrator	Person responsible for installing, configuring and managing a RHEL system.
System call	A mechanism that applications use to request service from the kernel.
System console	A display terminal that acts as the system console.
System recovery	The process of recovering an unbootable system.
Tab completion	Allows completing a file or command name by typing a partial name at the command line and then hitting the Tab key twice.
TCP/IP	Transmission Control Protocol / Internet Protocol. A stacked, standard suite of protocols for computer communication.
TCP Wrappers	A security software for limiting access into a system at user and host levels.
Terminal	A window where commands are executed.
Tilde substitution	Using tilde character as a shortcut to move around in the directory tree.

Red Hat Certified Technician & Engineer

Topology	Ways of connecting network nodes together.
Tty	Refers to a terminal.
Udev	Device manager that dynamically provides nodes for the devices physically available on the system.
UID	See User ID.
Unmounting	Detaching a mounted file system or a CD/DVD from the directory structure.
USB	Universal Serial Bus. A bus standard to connect peripheral devices.
User ID	A unique identification number assigned to a user.
Variable	A temporary storage of data in memory.
Virtual console	One of several console screens available for system access.
Virtual file system	A file system that is created in memory at system boot and gets destroyed when the system is shut down.
Virtual host	An approach to host more than one websites on a single system using unique or shared IP addresses.
Virtual machine	A technology to create several logical computers out of a single physical computer.
Volume group	A logical container that holds physical volumes, logical volumes, file systems and swap.
WAN	See Wide Area Network.
Web	A system of interlinked hypertext documents accessed over a network or the Internet via a web browser.
Web server	A system or service that provides web clients access to website pages.
Wide Area Network	A network with systems located geographically apart.
Wildcard characters	See Metacharacters.
X font server	A service that supplies fonts for accessed and used by an X server.
X Window System	A protocol that provides users with a graphical interface for system interaction.
Zombie process	A child process that terminated abnormally and whose parent process still waits for it.
Zone	A delegated portion of a DNS name space.

Index

Breinigsville, PA USA
13 October 2009
225746BV00002B/25/P